CL5

THE POLITICS OF THE PRESIDENCY

THE POLITICS OF THE PRESIDENCY

REVISED THIRD EDITION

NORMAN C. THOMAS
University of Cincinnati

JOSEPH A. PIKA
University of Delaware

RICHARD A. WATSON
University of Missouri-Columbia

CQ PRESS A DIVISION OF CONGRESSIONAL QUARTERLY INC.
WASHINGTON, D.C.

CONTENTS

TABLES AND FIGURES

TABLES

FIGURES

PREFACE

AFTER MORE THAN TWO CENTURIES of change and development, the presidency stands not only as the nation's preeminent public office but also its most problematic. Because presidents today are far more important for peace and prosperity than were their nineteenth century counterparts, ensuring the selection of qualified candidates and enhancing the winner's effectiveness in office are major concerns of specialists and citizens alike. In the post–World War II period, however, few presidents have left office with a record of unqualified success. In fact, academic and media observers have labeled each presidency since Lyndon Johnson's as "failures."

Johnson enjoyed unparalleled success in getting his Great Society legislative program through Congress, but he could not extricate himself or the country from the Vietnam War. Nixon managed to bring the war to an end, but Watergate cost him the confidence of the country. Ford and Carter failed to convince voters that they could exercise effective leadership. Like Johnson, Reagan succeeded in getting Congress to approve his program of economic reforms, but the budgetary consequences of those policies and his mishandling of the Iran-contra affair tarnished his reputation. George Bush was threatened by the same difficulties that beset Ford and Carter—a perception of ineffectiveness. But given the inflated expectations of performance held by the public and political elites, it is reasonable to wonder if any president can be considered a success.

Our focus in *The Politics of the Presidency* is on how presidents govern—in the country and in Washington. The book views the presidency as essentially a political office; that is, the chief executive must govern more through skilled political leadership than through the assertion of constitutional prerogatives. We also examine how effectiveness in office varies with the character, personality, and political style of the incumbent. Major political developments in society, the U.S. political system, and the international arena also affect how well or poorly a president does in office. By examining this full range of influences, *The Politics of the Presidency* provides a comprehensive treatment of the nation's most important political office.

xiii

Part I begins with an analysis of the origins and development of the presidency as well as changing conceptions of the office. It then explores the president's relationships with the public in electoral politics and in the process of governing. Next, it examines the kinds of people who have become president and the interactions between them and the office. Part II analyzes the president's relations with other government elites—members of Congress, the bureaucracy, and the judiciary. In Part III the focus shifts to how presidents formulate and implement domestic, economic, and national security policies. The book concludes with an assessment of the condition of the presidency as the twentieth century comes to a close.

With the third edition of *The Politics of the Presidency*, Joseph Pika joins Norman Thomas and Richard Watson, who has retired, as coauthor. Pika has revised and rewritten Chapters 1–4 and is primarily responsible for them. Thomas has extensively revised and accepts major responsibility for Chapters 5–10. The concluding chapter is a joint effort. The imprint of Professor Watson, who originally conceived of the book, is present throughout.

In preparing this revision, we have drawn on scholarly and journalistic analyses, historical and legal materials, and, where appropriate, behavioral and quantitative research. We have incorporated findings from many of the extensive studies of the presidency that have appeared since publication of the second edition. We have updated the book to include the final years of the Reagan presidency, the results of the 1988 nomination and election contests, and major developments during the first three and a half years of the Bush presidency—the 1990 budget deal between the administration and Congress, the Persian Gulf War, and the changes on the Supreme Court. Other innovations, such as adding an opening chapter on institutional developments and combining the two chapters on elections into a single new chapter, resulted from our experiences with the text in the classroom.

We have further revised the third edition to take account of the 1992 presidential election, which was surely one of the most interesting and unusual in recent decades. The Democrats recaptured the White House and ended twelve years of divided party control of the national government. However, the highly successful independent candidacy of H. Ross Perot and Republican gains in elections to the House of Representatives left President Bill Clinton with an ambiguous mandate to implement the sweeping policy changes he promised in his campaign. We have incorporated the returns and an analysis of the 1992 presidential election in Chapter 2, "Election Politics," and added an epilogue describing the transition to the Clinton presidency. The changes in the elections chapter give it currency until late 1996. The epilogue refers back to many points made earlier in the book, thus providing a basis for following developments during the Clinton presidency.

A note on the language: in writing about the people who have served as president we have followed the convention of using male pronouns. There are several reasons. So far only men have held the office, use of the plural is not always accurate, and "he or she" is cumbersome when repeated many times. We are confident that in the not too distant future the nation will elect a woman president or vice president, and we hope that when the time comes we will be skillful enough to make the appropriate linguistic adjustments.

We have benefited from manuscript reviews by Professors Michael Nelson of Rhodes College, Morris Ogul of the University of Pittsburgh, and Steven Shull of the University of New Orleans, as well as suggestions made by Roger T. Johnson, two anonymous reviewers, and other colleagues who have used the previous edition.

We are grateful to Brenda Carter and Carolyn Goldinger of CQ Press for their contributions to the third edition and the revision.

PART I
THE PRESIDENT AND THE PUBLIC

1 THE CHANGING PRESIDENCY

The nation has long revered its first president, shown in this portrait as a contemplative father of his country.

FOR MOST AMERICANS THE president is the focal point of public life. Almost every night they see the president on television newscasts interpreting the day's events, meeting with foreign dignitaries, or grappling with national problems. This person appears to be in charge, and such recurrent images of an engaged leader are reassuring. But the reality of the presidency rests on a very different truth: presidents are seldom in command and usually must negotiate with others to achieve their goals. In short, politics is inescapable, and it is only by exercising adroit political skill in winning public support and knowing how to use it that a president can succeed in office. For more than three decades, this lesson has dominated scholarly accounts of the presidency, but it has not always been fully appreciated either by the public or the presidents themselves, as reflected in changing conceptions of the office.

3

Conceptions of the Presidency

When Harry S. Truman and Lyndon Baines Johnson assumed office from the vice presidency, the public rallied to support them. But both left office repudiated by their own parties after they involved the country in controversial military conflicts abroad. Richard Nixon, reelected by a landslide in 1972, resigned two years later after congressional investigations revealed his abuse of power. Neither president who followed Nixon, Gerald R. Ford and Jimmy Carter, was reelected, and the reputation of Ronald Reagan's presidency was damaged by the Iran-contra controversy. Almost every modern president experienced such a decline in public approval.

Dramatic changes in presidential fortunes are not new to American politics, nor are the alternative interpretations offered to explain their meaning. Scholars' conceptions of the presidency have varied substantially over the past fifty years and are likely to be recast as the office continues to change in the future. Students of the modern presidency have identified three conceptions of the office: the heroic, the imperial, and the post-imperial.

The Heroic Presidency

The 1950s and 1960s were the era of what has been termed the *heroic* presidency. Writing about the office in 1960, at the end of Dwight D. Eisenhower's second term, Clinton Rossiter expressed his belief that the American presidency is "one of the few truly successful institutions created by men in their endless quest for the blessings of free government."[1] His book analyzing the power and limitations of the presidency clearly glorifies the office and the "great" presidents who have shaped it—George Washington, Thomas Jefferson, Andrew Jackson, Abraham Lincoln, Theodore Roosevelt, Woodrow Wilson, Franklin D. Roosevelt, and Harry Truman. Predicting "a long and exciting future for the American Presidency,"[2] Rossiter concluded his analysis with a poetic celebration of the institution:

It is, finally, an office of freedom. The Presidency is a standing reproach to those petty doctrinaires who insist that executive power is inherently undemocratic; for, to the exact contrary, it has been more responsive to the needs and dreams of giant democracy than any other office or institution in the whole mosaic of American life. It is no less a reproach to those easy generalizers who think that Lord Acton had the very last word on the corrupting effects of power, for, again, to the contrary, his doctrine finds small confirmation in the history of the Presidency. The vast power of this office has not been "poison," as Henry Adams wrote in scorn; rather, it has elevated often and corrupted never, chiefly because those who held it recognized the true source of the power and were ennobled by the knowledge.[3]

Also appearing in 1960 was the first edition of Richard E. Neustadt's *Presidential Power: The Politics of Leadership,* considered by many to be the most perceptive analysis of the office ever written. Like Rossiter, Neustadt is a great admirer of the American presidency. He expressed concern, however, that the limitations of the office, especially those stemming from a "government of separated institutions *sharing* power," threaten to make the president a clerk rather than a leader.[4] To rectify this situation, Neustadt proposed that chief executives seek their political power by bargaining with other political actors—members of Congress, bureaucrats, and party leaders, for example—persuading them that "what he wants of them is what their own appraisal of their own responsibilities requires them to do in their interest, not his."[5] Neustadt's analysis of three modern presidents—Franklin Roosevelt, Truman, and Eisenhower—convinced him that FDR's temperament and understanding of political power made him by far the most successful: "No modern President has been more nearly master in the White House."[6] Toward the end of the book Neustadt made a sweeping statement that epitomizes his glorification of the office:

The contributions that a President can make to government are indispensable. Assuming that he knows what power is and wants it, those contributions cannot help but be forthcoming in some measure as by-products of his search for personal influence. In a relative but real sense one can say of a President what Eisenhower's first Secretary of Defense once said of General Motors: what is good for the country is good for the President and vice versa.[7]

In 1965, during the Johnson administration, yet another study appeared celebrating the heroic American presidency—James MacGregor Burns's *Presidential Government: The Crucible of Leadership.* Analyzing the performance of the presidency in history, Burns chose as his model a man who never served as president. Alexander Hamilton was an influential member of the Washington administration who "succeeded in 'turning government high,' so high that Washington's administration stands as one of the truly creative presidencies in American history."[8] Burns's analysis of the characteristics of a Hamiltonian president (he includes Washington, Lincoln, and the two Roosevelts) parallels that espoused by Neustadt: they are heroic leaders who build a loyal personal political organization and expediently use their reputations, prestige, patronage, power, and political friendships, as well as tactics of co-opting and disorganizing the opposition party leadership, to achieve the results they want.[9] Unlike Neustadt, however, who made no mention of the ends for which presidential power is to be used, Burns examined the performance of the presidency to determine whether it has served the basic values of American society. His conclusion affirms the concept of the heroic president:

For in presidential government Americans have established one of the most powerful political institutions in the free world. They have fashioned, sometimes unwittingly, a weapon that has served them well in the long struggle for freedom and equality at home and in the search for stable and democratic politics abroad. They have grasped the uses of power, and as Harold Laski said, great power makes great leadership possible.[10]

Although these three important presidential scholars of the 1950s and 1960s differed in some respects, for the most part they agreed on the existence and value of a heroic institution. Writing in 1970, Thomas E. Cronin labeled this perspective the "textbook presidency" because it was adopted not only by presidential scholars but also by writers of general American government textbooks of the era, who described the presidency in glowing terms. Underlying their view of the office was a common assumption: the national government should be the leader in solving the problems of an increasingly interdependent world and of U.S. domestic society as well. The authors of these books on the presidency were political liberals who saw the office as the only institution in the political system that can understand the needs of all Americans, including the disadvantaged, and that has a nationwide constituency providing the political support to meet those needs.

Cronin went on to note that conditions in the late 1960s, in particular the inability of President Johnson to end the Vietnam War, were beginning to tarnish the heroic image of the presidency.[11] As the following section indicates, the 1970s did indeed usher in a radically different version of the nation's highest office.

The Imperial Presidency

Studies appearing between 1970 and 1973 characterized the office as the "imperial presidency," a term coined by Arthur Schlesinger, Jr., who served in John F. Kennedy's White House, in his 1973 book by that name. Before Schlesinger, however, in 1970 George Reedy, a White House aide under President Johnson, described the office as "the American monarchy." The thesis of Reedy's book, *The Twilight of the Presidency*, is that, far from ennobling its occupants, the office creates "an environment in which men cannot function in any kind of decent and human relationship to the people whom they are supposed to lead."[12] At fault are presidential "courts" composed of sycophants who tell presidents what they want to hear and who thereby isolate them from the harsh facts of political life. Denied the presence of peer pressure and of people who tell them when they are wrong, presidents exaggerate their own importance and competence.

Schlesinger's study benefited not only from the insights gained from the Vietnam War but also from the Watergate scandal. He found the origins of the imperial presidency in foreign policy, "from the capture by the Presidency of the most vital of national decisions, the decision to go to war."[13] Tracing presidential arrogation of the war power from Congress, with which the Founders intended it be shared, Schlesinger noted that the trend became more pronounced after World War II, especially under Johnson and Nixon. Presidential imperialism spread into the domestic sphere as Nixon employed a number of measures to deal with those who opposed him: he impounded funds appropriated by Congress, dismantled the Office of Economic Opportunity without congressional authorization, made excessive claims of executive privilege to withhold vital information from Congress, and used a special investigative unit to conduct illegal surveillance of U.S. citizens. In fact, Schlesinger described the Nixon presidency not only as "imperial" but also as "plebiscitary," a concept borrowed from Napoleon and, more recently, from former French president Charles de Gaulle. When a plebiscitary leader is elected, "he personifies the majority and all resistance to his will is undemocratic," at least until the next election.[14] Nixon's presidency renewed traditional American concerns about the threat of tyranny associated with a powerful executive.

In 1975, the year after Nixon was forced to resign, Sen. Walter F.

Mondale, D-Minn., analyzed the contemporary presidency in his book, *The Accountability of Power: Toward a Responsible Presidency*. He stated that Vietnam burst "the bubble of Presidential ascendancy and omniscience" and that Watergate initiated a "wholesale decline in Americans' belief in the viability and honesty of their governmental institutions."[15] Mondale blamed the imperial presidency not only on the occupants of that office but also on Congress, which regularly voted appropriations for U.S. military involvement in Vietnam, and the American people, who knew what their tax money was buying.

The message of presidency analysts writing in the first half of the 1970s was, therefore, precisely the opposite of those who wrote about the office in the 1950s and 1960s. As William Andrews describes the transformation, "Hallowed Be the Presidency" became "Deliver Us from Presidents."[16] The radical change in viewpoint cannot be attributed to a different type of analyst. Reedy, Schlesinger, and Mondale shared the same political philosophy as those who examined the presidency in the earlier period: all were liberals. Over time, these writers came to appreciate that the vast powers of the presidency, which could be used for purposes such as ameliorating domestic social and economic problems and winning World War II, also could be used to wage a futile, costly conflict in Southeast Asia and launch an all-out attack on political "enemies," which led to the abuses of Watergate. Just when it seemed, however, that presidential scholars agreed upon the true nature of the presidency, a new conception of the office began to develop.

The Post–Imperial Presidency

In 1978, three years after Senator Mondale's book was published, Fred Greenstein noted another change in the contemporary American presidency. Observing the rapid turnover in presidents—from 1961 to 1978, five chief executives had served, three of them since 1974—Greenstein suggested that such a short tenure in office had required the chief executive

to have a hurried approach to the making of policy . . . to engage in activities that are politically risky: simply to win office he needs to raise aspirations about what he will be able to contribute to the nation; once in office, the difficulty of meeting those aspirations opens up the temptation to cut corners—for example, to rush legislation through Congress and leave considerations of political implementation for later on.[17]

Greenstein went on to outline "the intractable political environment of the post-imperial presidency," which includes a Congress whose leaders cannot serve as "effective intermediaries between their Congress and the president"; a weakened party system over which the president is no longer chief; aggressive media that initially idealize new presidents and then "quickly search out their warts"; and a presidential bureaucracy that "has expanded to the point where the president is victimized rather than helped by members of a staff whom he cannot begin to supervise."[18] He also noted the "presidency-curbing legislation" passed by Congress in the 1970s. New laws required the president to consult Congress "in every possible instance" before committing troops to combat and to report to Congress all executive agreements made with foreign powers; limited the power of the president to reorganize executive departments and to impound funds appropriated by Congress; and made the appointment of the director and deputy directors of the Office of Management and Budget subject to Senate confirmation. Greenstein's analysis demonstrates that the presidency of the late 1970s was anything but imperial.

In 1980 British journalist Godfrey Hodgson presented similar conclusions about the office in *All Things to All Men: The False Promise of the American Presidency*. In Hodgson's view, presidents are isolated from other elements of the U.S. political system through which they could make the system work: the bureaucracy, Congress, their own political party, the media, and even the American people. Presidents also face social and economic problems so difficult and complex that they "have little chance of making any real progress in the direction of solving them within their first term of office. Moreover, they have virtually no hope of making *visible* progress toward solving them in time to have a positive effect on their own prospects of being reelected."[19] As Hodgson summarized the situation, "Never has so powerful a leader been so impotent to do what he wants to do, what he is pledged to do, what he is expected to do, and what he knows he must do."[20]

The presidency of the last half of the 1970s bore little resemblance to the imperial presidency of the first half. Some observers, like Hodgson, thought the office was "impotent." Others, like Cronin, asked whether it was "imperiled."[21] Cronin maintained that the experiences of the post-imperial presidency led many political liberals, who had feared the office in the mid-1970s, to conclude that Congress was incapable of leading the nation's affairs and to call for a resurgent and vigorous presidency. Indeed, part of Ronald Reagan's appeal to the voters in the 1980 election was a pledge to restore the strength of the office.

The Reagan presidency was characterized several different ways. In 1983 Richard Nathan noted approvingly the successful establishment under Reagan of the "administrative presidency strategy," first attempted by Nixon.[22] This strategy uses administrative rather than legislative means to accomplish presidential policy objectives whenever it is possible to do so. Others pointed out, however, that such maneuvers politicized the federal bureaucracy and weakened the civil service by increasing the number of policy-sensitive positions filled by political appointees instead of career civil servants.[23] In 1984 Bert Rockman suggested in his thought-provoking book, *The Leadership Question*, that answers lay not in more "presidentialism"—efforts to strengthen presidential leadership—but in "making the whole of government more effective."[24] A year later Theodore Lowi argued that a plebiscitary presidency, entailing a direct relationship between the president and the American people, had been developing since 1933 and had come to maturity under Reagan. The result, Lowi asserted, is the pathological growth of big government and the eclipse of Congress and the party system.[25] In contrast, in a 1986 study, Rockman described the plebiscitary presidency in favorable terms: along with institutional restraints, it is the answer to the problem of presidential accountability.[26]

Two other books published in the late 1980s expressed further concerns regarding the institutional development of the presidency. Lester Seligman and Cary Covington argued that the success of presidents in governing the nation depends on their ability to translate their winning electoral coalition into a "core governing coalition [that] constitutes a working majority in each relevant policymaking and implementing arena."[27] They maintain that presidents have been unable to connect the voters and interests that they mobilized to win the presidency with Congress, the federal bureaucracy, and major national interest groups. This failure requires presidents to govern on the basis of ad hoc coalitions fashioned to deal with specific issues and problems. Consequently, presidential leadership is increasingly problematic: some presidents may not be effective at organizing issue-specific coalitions. Even those who do so successfully in one policy arena may fail in others.

In contrast to Seligman and Covington, who see domestic politics as the source of the major challenges facing the presidency, Richard Rose locates them in foreign affairs.[28] He argues that the end of the hegemonic position the United States enjoyed in international relations from 1945 to 1968 and the growth of worldwide economic interdependence have transformed the presidency. Although the international responsibilities of the United States remain substantial, the president's resources for meeting them have diminished. The president can no longer dominate foreign governments and their leaders, but must bargain with them and win their support through persuasion, as George Bush did in 1991 during the Persian Gulf War. To a considerable extent, the president's success depends, in Rose's view, on the ability to "cooperate and compete" in the international system.[29]

Finally, in a new edition of his earlier work, Schlesinger surveys developments since 1973. In his view, the Reagan administration passed two of the three essential tests that determine the existence of an imperial presidency.[30] Much like Nixon, Reagan defended "'almost royal' prerogatives" in exercising presidential war-making power.[31] He also reasserted the need for government secrecy through aggressive use of the document classification system and by exercising an unconditional claim of executive privilege, the president's supposed right to deny information to Congress. The combination of secrecy and expansive interpretation of presidential war powers led Reagan, like many of his predecessors in the post–World War II period, to rely heavily on covert action to project American influence in the world. The Iran-contra affair revealed an administration operating on the basis of "secret laws," "secret decrees," and "White House indifference to legal and constitutional standards."[32]

But Schlesinger finds an important difference between Nixon and Reagan. "Unlike Nixon . . . Reagan did not bring the imperial Presidency into its final stage—the policy of stigmatizing opponents of the president as traitors to the republic."[33] Therefore, while it might be tempting to describe the Reagan experience as "the imperial presidency revitalized," Schlesinger seems to suggest that another description is more appropriate: "the indestructible presidency."[34] Placing the post–Nixon era in perspective, one can see that those who feared the presidency would be brought to its knees by an assertive Congress and an aggressive media failed to recognize the fundamental strength of the institution both under the Constitution and in the minds of the public. What had been lacking were presidents who could provide the nation with a sense of direction and the ability to persuade the nation to follow their vision.[35]

Schlesinger returns, in short, to emphasizing the need for heroic leadership.

The Presidency: Changeable and Political

In our view, it is inaccurate to describe the presidency as heroic, imperial, post-imperial, imperiled, or indestructible. Such characterizations fall short because they treat temporary conditions as though they were permanent—they mistake a snapshot for a portrait. The rapidity with which conceptions of the office and the office itself have changed over the past thirty years testifies to the error of this approach.

The presidency is variable for several reasons. First, in no other public office do the personality, character, and political style of the incumbent make as much difference as in the presidency. As an institution, the presidency exhibits important continuities across administrations, but the entry of each new occupant has an undeniably pervasive effect on the position's operation. The presidency also is heavily influenced by changes outside the office and throughout the U.S. political system—whether in the formal political structure (Congress, the executive branch, the courts), in the informal political institutions (political parties and interest groups), in society at large, in the mass media, or in conditions surrounding substantive issues, particularly national security and the economy. Because of their extensive responsibilities, presidents must contend with all of these influences. Furthermore, although the Constitution and historical precedents give structure to the office, the powers of the presidency are so vast and vague that incumbents have tremendous latitude in shaping the office to their particular desires.

The presidency is not only highly *changeable* but also essentially *political*. Although on occasion, especially in times of crisis, presidents rule by asserting their constitutional prerogatives, they usually are forced to govern by political maneuvering, by trying to convince and persuade the many participants in the political process. While Americans were held hostage in Iran, for example, President Carter invoked a number of constitutional prerogatives, but they did not help him handle the problems of the domestic economy or alter the perceived decline of U.S. power and prestige in the world—conditions that contributed substantially to his defeat in the 1980 election. Moreover, the changes that occurred in the first year of the Reagan administration resulted not from the president's exercising constitutional prerogatives but from his successful maneuvering with executive officials, members of Congress, political party and interest group leaders, representatives of the media, and the American public. Since then, these same political actors have effectively limited the changes in domestic and economic policy that Presidents Reagan and Bush wanted to make. On the eve of ordering American forces into combat, a power that administration spokespersons had steadfastly asserted was the president's to exercise, Bush sought congressional authorization. He recognized that the political costs of using force unilaterally can be devastating.

Our perception of the presidency as a changeable and political office explains its appearance over time as heroic, imperial, post-imperial, imperiled, and indestructible. It has assumed all these forms, and it is likely to assume still others as the office and the concerns of scholars develop. This book does not claim, however, to provide a comprehensive theory of the American presidency or of presidential behavior. Rather, it maintains that greater understanding of the presidency and the actions of presidents can be gained by keeping in mind the true character of the office.

Those who invented the presidency in 1787 did not expect the office to become the nation's central political institution. In fact, Article II of the Constitution, which deals with the executive branch, is known for its brevity and lack of clarity, particularly in comparison with the carefully detailed description of the legislative branch found in Article I. But within the presidency's vague constitutional description lay the seeds of a far more powerful position, one that has grown through elaboration of its explicit, *enumerated* powers as well as interpretation of its implied, *inherent* powers. Moreover, over the years Congress and the public have caused the range of responsibilities associated with the presidency to expand, particularly in response to changes in society and America's position in the world. What has developed over two centuries is the office that now stands at the center of American government and American politics.

It is ironic that the presidency has come to play such a central and complex role in national life. Invented at the Constitutional Convention by delegates unsure of what they wanted, the position gained stature and a set of precedents from its initial occupant, George Washington. During the nineteenth century, however, the office languished, so much so, in fact, that Lord Bryce, the British chronicler of American government, felt compelled to explain in 1890 that great men do not become president because of the institution's weaknesses. Government during this period centered on Congress and political parties, an American invention that the Founders did not anticipate. A few presidents—most notably Jefferson, Jackson, and Lincoln—seemed to suggest the future, but most receded as quickly from history as they did from the political scene.

How, then, did the presidency come to assume its present exalted position? The answer is complex and involves a variety of factors. At one level, the original design of the office—its structure, mode of selection, and powers—continues to exercise important influence on its operation today. The office has changed over time, however, partly in response to the influence of its occupants, partly in response to changing expectations in Congress and the public, and partly in response to internal dynamics of institutional development. A comprehensive view of the office and its occupants requires that we address all of these influences while recognizing their interrelatedness.

Constitutional Design

When they convened in Philadelphia, delegates to the Constitutional Convention had little sense of what the executive in the new or revised scheme of government would look like. Nor did they devise solutions to the major design issues, leaving several of the most critical questions to be dealt with by the Committee on Postponed Matters just before adjourning in September 1787. If James Madison, commonly credited as the chief architect of the Constitution, had prevailed, today's president would be a ceremonial head of state, doing the bidding of Congress. The Virginia Plan, offered by Madison on the convention's first working day, provided for an executive of unspecified size and tenure, selected by the legislature, and with unclear powers.[36] What emerged was an office quite different from Madison's design and with far greater potential in the scheme of government.

Throughout its deliberations, the convention vacillated between two disparate concepts of a national executive.[37] The weak model foresaw an executive whose primary function would be to carry out the will of the legislature. This task was to be accomplished through a plural executive or, if only one man headed the branch, a strong council that would share his powers and hold him in check. Congress would choose the chief executive for a limited term; moreover, he could not be reappointed immediately and would even be subject to removal by the legislative body during his term of office. The executive's powers would be limited and delegated to him by Congress, which would also make appointments to the executive branch and hold the authority to make treaties and declare war. There would be no executive veto of laws passed by Congress.

At the other extreme was the idea of a strong executive, independent of Congress and responsible for important functions in the new government. Under this concept, a single chief executive, chosen by some means other than legislative appointment, would have no limit placed on tenure. If the president was removable at all, it would be only for definite, enumerated reasons, and then only after impeachment and conviction by a judicial body or the legislature. Presidential powers would be derived from the Constitution and not be subject to legislative interference. He would appoint judicial and diplomatic officials and participate in the execution of foreign affairs, including the making of treaties. He would have a veto (preferably absolute) over legislation passed by Congress, a power that he would exercise either alone or in conjunction with the judiciary. There would be no executive council at all, or, if one did exist, it would be a purely advisory body whose actions would not bind the chief executive.

Credit usually goes to a small group of delegates who used their strategic positions within the convention's working committees to fashion an office that more closely corresponds to the strong model. James Wilson, delegate from Pennsylvania, was probably the most persistent exponent of a strong national executive and deserves to be called the father of the presidency. Wilson fought hard for a unitary rather than a plural executive. (One proposal would have had an executive committee of three people, one from each geographic region.) Wilson also argued against creating a council of revision to be entrusted with power to veto legislation. He preferred giving the president an absolute veto, a battle he lost when the decision was for a veto that the legislature could override. In the same way, after a losing effort to establish direct popular election of the president, Wilson proposed a selection procedure much like the one eventually adopted, the electoral college, which introduced the possibility of popular participation. Wilson was able to exact several of these concessions while serving on the Committee of Detail, which also pushed for a constitutional grant of powers rather than relying on the legislature to establish responsibilities for the executive.[38]

In addition to Wilson, several other delegates influenced the design of the presidency. Gouverneur Morris, also from Pennsylvania, used his position on two working committees—Style and Unfinished Business—to strengthen the executive. The Style Committee provided the president with the basis for broadly construed discretionary powers with the ambiguous wording that begins Article II: "The executive Power shall be vested in a President of the United States of America." The Unfinished Business Committee proposed selection through an electoral college, an explicit rejection of selection by the legislature, a position that had earlier been adopted by votes of the convention on several occasions.[39] Alexander Hamilton of New York advocated the need for executive authority, although he did so by endorsing the British model; that is, he advocated an elected American king. Washington, the leading candidate for president, calmed delegates' concerns about creating an office with powers that might be abused, providing behind-the-scenes rather than vocal support. Finally, Madison was persuaded to accept an executive stronger than he had originally envisioned in his draft plan.[40]

Tyranny Versus Effectiveness

These five delegates and their fifty colleagues brought two conflicting attitudes to the task of designing an executive office: a healthy skepticism for executive power and a new appreciation of its necessity. Most commentators stress the distrust of executive authority derived from the pre-revolutionary period when colonial governors implemented edicts from London that colonists regarded as violations of their fundamental rights. After many decades of relative neglect by the mother country, the colonists were outraged at being forced to pay new taxes designed to support British troops sent to America for the French and Indian Wars. The resulting rebellion was justified in the Declaration of Independence as a fitting response to the arbitrary actions of King George III. (Although Parliament was the real source of the pressure, the king was an easier target.) This bout with tyranny produced a healthy distrust of executives that was mirrored in the state governments created during the Revolutionary War and under the Articles of Confederation. State constitutions during this period typically had weak governors chosen by the legislature for a single brief term, usually one year. Governors often shared powers with a council.

The Articles of Confederation, a compact among the thirteen colonies adopted in 1781, had provided for a national legislative body with a single house in which each state had an equal vote. There was no provision at all for independent executive and judicial branches. In time, however, a reaction set in against this type of legislative democracy. Attempts to administer laws through ad hoc committees, councils, or conventions proved unsuccessful; and it was ultimately necessary for Congress to create permanent departments of diplomacy, war, and finance and to appoint eminent men, such as Robert Livingston, John Jay, and Robert Morris, to head their activities.[41] Calling the constitutional convention signaled a desire for more effective central government, and there was growing awareness of how executives could contribute to improved efficiency. New York's constitution, a striking exception to general practice, provided for a governor chosen by direct election to a three-year term with unlimited reeligibility. Massachusetts voters adopted a constitution that included a popularly elected governor (who could be reelected) with substantial powers, including that of vetoing legislative acts.

The ambivalence over executive power exhibited by the convention has become a permanent feature of American political culture. Like the delegates in 1787, Americans have had to confront the tradeoff between tyranny and effectiveness, the one to be feared and the other to be prized. The antifederalists, who opposed ratification of the Constitution, frequently pointed to the risks inherent in a national executive, a post some considered even more threatening than its British counterpart. George Mason argued, "We are not constituting a British monarchy, but a more dangerous monarchy, an elective one."[42] But others saw the newly created presidency as essential to effective government, the source of energy, dispatch, and responsibility in the conduct of domestic and foreign affairs. These differing views are found in the three conceptions of the office already reviewed.

The presidency created by the convention most closely resembles the strong executive model (see Table 1-1). The president is chosen by the electoral college, which will be discussed in Chapter 2. The process is national in scope, providing for a unique perspective on problems. Originally, no limit was placed on a president's eligibility to run for another term, and the removal process was made difficult: presidents may be removed only for specific causes (treason, bribery, high crimes, and misdemeanors), and then only by an impeachment charge brought by the House of Representatives and conviction by vote of two-thirds of the members of the Senate. Specific powers are granted by the Constitution,

Table 1-1 Models of Executive Considered by the Constitutional Convention

Elements of executive	Weak-executive model	Strong-executive model	Decision by convention
Relation to Congress	To put into effect will of Congress	Powers independent of Congress	Powers independent of Congress but with checks and balances
Number of executive	Plural or single individual checked by council	Single individual with no council or only advisory one	Single individual with Senate advisory on some matters
Method of choosing	By Congress	By means other than congressional selection	Electoral college
Tenure	Limited term; not immediately renewable	No limitation	Unlimited
Method of removal	By Congress during term of office	Only for definite, enumerated reasons after impeachment and conviction by judicial body or Congress	For treason, bribery, high crimes and misdemeanors, by impeachment by majority of House and conviction by two-thirds of Senate
Scope and source of powers	Limited powers delegated by Congress	Broad powers from Constitution, not subject to congressional interference	Broad powers delegated by Constitution
Appointment and foreign policy and war-making powers	None—province of Congress	Would appoint judicial and diplomatic officials and participate in foreign policy and war-making powers, including making of treaties	Appoints executive and judicial officials with consent of Senate; shares foreign policy and war-making powers with Congress; Senate must approve treaties negotiated by president
Veto	None	Veto over legislation passed by Congress, exercised alone or with judiciary	Qualified veto, may be overridden by two-thirds vote of House and Senate

Source: Joseph E. Kallenbach, *The American Chief Executive* (New York: Harper & Row, 1966), chap. 2.

and, thanks to the efforts of Gouverneur Morris, the president is given a basis for claiming broad, undefined authority.

At the same time, the president does not enjoy all the prerogatives of the strong executive model. The veto power is not absolute: a veto can be overridden by a two-thirds vote in each of the two houses of Congress. Moreover, the appointment power is subject to the advice and consent of the Senate, as is the authority to negotiate treaties. Thus, although the Founders did not create a council that shares all the chief executive's powers, they did grant the upper chamber a check on specified presidential actions.

Several amendments to the Constitution changed aspects of the original design: the Twelfth provided an important clarification in the selection of the president and vice president; the Twentieth moved the beginning of their term to January from March; and the Twenty-second limited the tenure of the chief executive to no more than two terms—probably the most significant change from the original design.[43] The Twenty-fifth Amendment dealt with one of the problems left unresolved by the convention, presidential disability and succession. Nevertheless, the essential constitutional framework of the presidential office remains just as it was created two centuries ago.

But what did the Founders intend for the president to do? George Mason was not the only observer struck by the near-monarchical nature of the office designed in Philadelphia. Henry Jones Ford, reflecting on the office's evolution on the eve of the twentieth century, described it in similar terms. "The truth is that in the presidential office, as it has been constituted since Jackson's time, American democracy has revived the oldest political institution of the race, the elective kingship."[44] What Ford stressed was the president's special relationship with the people, which carries with it the ability to mobilize public support behind their government. Only the barest outlines of this powerful position are visible in the enumerated powers of the chief executive.

Constitutional Roles: Complexity and Ambiguity

A time-honored way for political scientists to think about the president's powers and responsibilities is to concentrate on the multiple roles discernible in the constitutional design.[45] Most frequently, observers identify five roles found in Article II, Sections 2 and 3, that comprise the central elements of a presidential job description *(see Appendix C).*

Commander in Chief. Article II, Section 2, set forth the first enumerated executive power, but did it merely confer a title on the president or imply wide-ranging powers in times of emergency? From this germ of constitutional power has grown the enormous control that modern presidents exercise over a permanent military establishment and its deployment. The Constitution stipulates that the legislative and executive branches share the war power, but the pressure of events and the presidency's institutional advantages in taking decisive action have led Congress to give greater discretion to the executive. Nor was this delegation of power completely unexpected. Recognizing the need to repel attacks when Congress was not in session, the convention altered language describing the role of Congress in armed hostilities from "make" war to "declare" war, thereby expanding the president's realm of discretionary action. Over time, presidents have invoked the commander in chief clause to justify military expenditures without congressional authorization, emergency powers to suppress rebellion, the internment of American citizens of Japanese descent during World War II, and the seizure of domestic steel mills during the undeclared armed conflict in Korea.[46] Moreover, presidents have initiated the use of force far more frequently than they have awaited congressional authorization.

Chief Administrator. This role for the president is more implicit than explicit as set forth in the Constitution. It rests on the executive power clause as well as passages dealing with the right to require opinions from the heads of government departments and the power to make personnel appointments subject to whatever approval Congress may require. As the national government has grown, so too has the significance of these powers, but Congress has jealously guarded its own appointment and oversight powers, thereby denying the president anything approximating a monopoly of administrative power.

Chief Diplomat. When combined with the president's expanded war power, constitutional primacy in the conduct of foreign affairs establishes the office's claim to being the government's principal agent in the world if not its "sole organ." Presidents are not only authorized to make treaties "by and with the Advice and Consent of the Senate," but also they are empowered to nominate ambassadors, subject to Senate approval, and to receive diplomatic emissaries from abroad. Presidents have varied in how closely they collaborated with the Senate in making treaties, most waiting until after negotiations have been concluded before allowing any Senate participation. More significant, the conduct of foreign affairs has come to rely on executive agreements between heads of state in place of treaties. These agreements are not subject to Senate approval.[47]

Chief Legislator. A nascent constitutional role that stressed negative (the veto) rather than positive leadership, this feature of the job did not fully develop until the twentieth century. Today, the president's power to provide leadership for Congress rests primarily on the ability to shape the legislative agenda. Now considered a task for all presidents to fulfill, it stems from language in Article II, Section 3, that obliges the president to give "the Congress Information of the State of the Union," and to recommend such other measures for its consideration as deemed "necessary and expedient." Presidents now routinely develop extensive legislative agendas and present them to Congress and the nation at the beginning of each year. Moreover, the development of an activist national government has led presidents, their aides, and cabinet secretaries to submit detailed proposals for legislative consideration rather than await congressional reaction to their ideas. During an era of divided government—when one party controls the presidency and the other party controls Congress—the veto power has once again come to the fore.

Chief Magistrate. Perhaps the least clearly recognized area of presidential activity, but one that was important to the Founders' conception of executive power, was the general charge that "he shall take Care that the Laws be faithfully executed." Eighteenth century conceptions of executive power did not draw sharp distinctions with judicial power: each type of official interpreted and applied the laws in the process of enforcing them. In addition, relations between these two branches of the new government were less distant during the 1790s than is the case today.[48] Presidents, in short, play a complementary role to that of the courts in the enforcement of federal laws; the executive branch helps by apprehending criminals and exercising responsibility for prosecution.

Despite being enumerated in the Constitution, what is most striking about these presidential responsibilities is their ambiguity. As a consequence, their effect on behavior—*what* presidents should do and *how* presidents should behave—is limited. Multiplicity provides presidents with the opportunity to select among a range of activities, and ambiguity gives them maximum flexibility in deciding how to go about the job. The constitutional job description is permissive rather than confining, providing presidents with great freedom in deciding how to invest energy but leaving them open to criticism for failing to fulfill tasks of lesser interest.

Functional Roles and Inherent Powers

Political scientists have described a set of functional roles that may be thought of as bundles of activities associated with a formal position. Fred Greenstein has argued that one distinguishing feature of the American executive is the combination of two functional roles that are separated in many other political systems. Presidents serve as both head of state and prime minister, positions that are separate and occupied by different people in most other western political systems. Obvious examples are the British system with its monarch and prime minister and the German system with an elected president and chancellor. Typically, heads of state perform ceremonial tasks in their capacity of symbolizing the entire nation. Prime ministers are charged with partisan political leadership— proposing agendas, formulating policies, addressing potentially divisive national issues.[49] Greenstein suggests that several consequences flow from this "condensation" of roles, the most significant of which is "role strain." "As head of state the president needs to be a national unifier, much like a constitutional monarch; yet as politician he must also be responsive to the intrinsically divisive demands made of prime ministers in other democracies. This conjunction can enhance the president's influence by reinforcing policy appeals with patriotic emotions, but it can also have the reverse effect of holding presidents to unrealistically idealized standards of comportment and performance."[50]

Finally, the convention accepted John Locke's idea that executive power provided for a largely undefined grant of *inherent* power derived from the nature of government itself. As Locke wrote, "prerogative" authorized executives "to act according to discretion for the public good, without prescription of the law and sometimes even against it."[51] Since Washington's first term in office, generations of American political elites have struggled over the claims made by presidents and their supporters based on the indefinite grant of executive power found in the opening phrases of Article II. Although such claims may be based on very different justifications, their effects are the same if resolved in the president's favor—expansion of the office, which has happened steadily throughout our history.[52]

Expansion of the Presidency

A number of influences have reshaped the American presidency since its constitutional beginnings, perhaps none more than the occupants of the office. Some had relatively coherent conceptions of the office and its powers, and others had an impact while being responsive to the needs of the moment. Not surprisingly, several of these momentous presidencies coincided with crises facing the nation arising from either domestic or foreign sources. Rather than being inhibited by the ambiguities of power, these presidents shaped the office in which they served by adopting broad interpretations of their responsibilities. In addition, changes in the presidency have been established by Congress through statute, as a result of presidential actions that later became customary practices, and through institutional development.

Expansion by Individual President

In a number of cases, presidents have significantly expanded the office and its powers, but there is no guarantee that every incumbent will have such an enduring effect. Constitutional scholar Edward S. Corwin wrote in 1957, "Taken by and large, the history of the presidency is a history of aggrandizement, but the story is a highly discontinuous one."[53] At the time of his landmark study, Corwin estimated that one of every three presidents "has contributed to the development of its powers; under other incumbents things have either stood still or gone backward."[54]

Many of the expansions have occurred when presidents claimed "the silences of the Constitution"; that is, they sought to exploit the ambiguity or absence of constitutional clarification in their own favor.[55] It is customary for political histories of the presidency to examine precedents established by a small group of notable officeholders who provided their successors with an institutional legacy that left the office more powerful than before. As Corwin explained, "Precedents established by a forceful or politically successful personality in the office are available to less gifted successors, and permanently so because of the difficulty with which the Constitution is amended."[56] Which presidents qualify for such select company? Corwin's classic analysis focused on seven: Washington,

Jefferson, Jackson, Lincoln, Wilson, and the two Roosevelts.[57] Other scholars and historians have selected the same group.[58]

George Washington. Because he was the first person to occupy the presidency, Washington was conscious that his actions could establish precedents for his successors. Soon after his inauguration he expressed the opinion that "many things which appear of little importance in themselves . . . may have great and durable consequences from their having been established at the commencement of a new general government."[59] Consequently, Washington often turned to his group of department heads for advice on political matters. In doing so, he went beyond the constitutional provision to gather their written opinions on subjects relating to the duties of their offices and solicited their oral judgments as a group on any matter he put before them. Washington established the precedent that department heads should support the president's policies; he forced Secretary of State Edmund Randolph to resign because of his failure to back the administration's foreign policy. With the president's blessing, Secretary of the Treasury Hamilton created and steered through Congress a broad economic program, setting the stage for later liaison between the executive and legislative branches.

In foreign policy Washington quickly established the prerogatives of the president by receiving an emissary from the new French government, making it clear that presidents have the right to receive ambassadors and to grant diplomatic recognition to foreign countries. When he sought the Senate's advice on treaty negotiations with certain Indian tribes, and the Senate delayed by referring the matter to committee, Washington stalked out of the chamber in anger, vowing never again to bring such a matter to the Senate. Since then, no president has sought that body's counsel on the negotiation of a treaty, despite the constitutional instruction that presidents "shall make such treaties with its advice."[60] When the House of Representatives demanded that he present papers pertaining to the negotiation of the Jay Treaty, Washington refused to do so on the grounds that the Constitution granted the lower chamber of Congress no authority in such matters.

Thomas Jefferson. Jefferson epitomized the president who could stretch the powers of the office when the occasion demanded it. When Napoleon unexpectedly offered French lands (the Louisiana Purchase) at a favorable price, Jefferson reconsidered his narrow interpretation of the national government's powers and chose direct action, becoming the first of many presidents who decided to respond to political rather than legal considerations. Jefferson also was the first president to govern through personal leadership of a political party. Using members of the Democratic-Republican party in Congress as his medium, he dominated the political affairs of the legislature. His control extended to decisions of the party caucus (which, unlike today's counterpart, exercised significant powers over legislation) and to the appointment and removal of standing committee members, as well as party officials in Congress. So strong was his leadership that he pushed the drastic Embargo Act of 1807 through both houses in one day. But his control was not restricted to crises. It is a testament to Jefferson's domination that he did not veto a single piece of legislation: no law he seriously opposed was reported out of the Congress during his eight years in office.

Andrew Jackson. In contrast to Jefferson, Jackson became a strong president by asserting his independence of the legislative branch as well as virtually all other centers of government authority. His administration was characterized by conflicts with Congress over issues large and small including appointments to diplomatic and judicial posts and creation of a national bank, which was supported by the legislature but opposed and undermined by Jackson. The full range of Jackson's disputes with Congress is reflected in his use of the veto; with twelve, he was the first president to use this power to any significant degree. Jackson asserted that the president's right to judge the constitutionality of legislation was no less than that of the Supreme Court, and on one occasion he dared Chief Justice John Marshall to enforce a ruling that went against the president's view. He acted decisively to protect the rights of the national government against the states when South Carolina threatened to secede from the Union. Jackson declared the action treasonous and pushed a bill through Congress giving him the power to use force to prevent it.

Jackson succeeded in these defiant actions because he was the first president whose authority rested on a popular constituency. Chosen not by a congressional caucus but by a national convention reflecting grassroots party support *(see Chapter 2),* Jackson considered himself the "tribune of the people." When he had disagreements with members of Congress, he went over their heads and appealed to the population for support of his policies; to keep control of his administration, he instituted the spoils system (so named for the idea that "to the victor belong the spoils") to reward his political friends and punish his enemies. Jackson transformed the presidency from an elitist to a popular office.

Abraham Lincoln. The nineteenth century presidency reached the zenith of its powers during the Civil War administration of Abraham Lincoln. He stretched the executive's emergency powers further than ever before during the eleven weeks from the outbreak of hostilities at Fort Sumter, South Carolina, on April 12, 1861, until he called Congress into special session July 4. This period has been described as a time of "quasi-presidential dictatorship."[61] Lincoln unilaterally authorized a series of drastic actions: he called up the militia and volunteers, blockaded Southern ports, expanded the army and navy beyond the limits set by statute, pledged the credit of the United States without congressional authority to do so, closed the mails to "treasonous" correspondence, arrested persons suspected of disloyalty, and suspended the writ of habeas corpus in areas around the nation's capital. Admitting that most of these matters lay within the jurisdiction of Congress rather than the president, Lincoln asserted that they were done because of popular demand and public necessity, and with the trust "that Congress would readily ratify them." But he deliberately chose not to call the national legislature into special session until he was ready to do so, and then he presented it with *faits accomplis.*

Although Lincoln's presidency was most dramatic in those early days of hostilities, he continued to exercise firm control over the war during the entire time he was in the White House. He controlled the mails and newspapers, confiscated property of people suspected of impeding the conduct of the war, and even tried civilians in military courts in areas where the regular courts were operating. To justify such actions, he appealed to military necessity, asserting that the commander in chief clause and the take care (that the laws be faithfully executed) clause combined to create a "war power" for the president that was virtually unlimited. Lincoln's success in defending that position is demonstrated by the fact that neither Congress nor the courts placed any significant limits on his actions.

Theodore Roosevelt. In contrast to the domestic crisis that shaped Lincoln's presidency, Roosevelt's took its impetus from the emergence of the United States as a world power at the beginning of the twentieth century. Concerned over the rise of Japan as a threat to American interests in the Pacific, Roosevelt sought and obtained a major role in negotiating the Portsmouth Treaty, which terminated the Russo–Japanese War of 1905. Closer to home he intervened in the affairs of neighbors to the south when he considered it vital to the national interests of the United States, sending troops to the Dominican Republic and Cuba. Even more blatant was Roosevelt's role in fomenting the rebellion of Panama against Colombia so that the United States could acquire rights to build a canal. An avowed nationalist with the desire to expand U.S. influence in international affairs, Roosevelt ordered the navy to sail around the world as a demonstration of American military might. When Congress balked at the expense, he countered that there were sufficient funds to get the navy halfway there; if the lawmakers wanted the fleet back home, they would have to provide the money for the return trip.

Roosevelt also responded vigorously to the rapid industrialization of American life. He had charges pressed against corporations that violated antitrust laws, and he pushed legislation through Congress that gave the Interstate Commerce Commission power to reduce railroad rates. When coal mine operators in Colorado refused to agree to arbitration of a dispute with their workers, Roosevelt threatened to have troops seize the mines and administer them as a receiver for the government. He was the first American chief executive to intervene in a labor dispute who did *not* take management's side. Roosevelt also championed major reclamation and conservation projects, as well as meat inspection and pure food and drug laws.

Perhaps most important, Roosevelt did much to popularize the presidency after three decades of lackluster leaders. (Of the eight men who served from Lincoln through William McKinley, only Grover Cleveland is considered at all significant.) A dynamic personality, an attractive family, and love of the public spotlight enabled Roosevelt "to put the presidency on the front page of every newspaper in America."[62] Considering himself (as did Jackson) the "tribune of the people" and seeing the office as a "bully pulpit" from which the incumbent should set the tone of American life, Roosevelt was the first president to provide meeting rooms for the members of the press and to hold informal news conferences to link the presidency with the people.

Roosevelt was the first president to rely on broad discretionary authority in peacetime as well as in crisis.[63] His style of leadership depended upon extensive use of popular rhetoric, a distinctive reinterpretation of statesmanship that ushered in the era of the "rhetorical presidency."[64] Roosevelt explained after leaving office that his concept of the president as "steward of the people" held that "it was not only his right but his duty to do anything that the needs of the nation demanded unless such action was forbidden by the Constitution or by the laws." He continued, "Under this interpretation of executive power I did and caused to be done many things not previously done by the president and the heads of the departments. I did not usurp power, but I did greatly broaden the use of executive power."[65]

Woodrow Wilson. While Theodore Roosevelt laid the groundwork for use of popular appeals, Wilson linked inspirational rhetoric to a broad program of action in an effort to address domestic and foreign affairs in much the same way as a British prime minister. Jeffrey Tulis has argued that this effort rested on a systematic, ambitious reinterpretation of the president's role in the constitutional order.[66] A skilled public speaker, Wilson was the first president since John Adams to go before Congress in person to give his State of the Union message, a practice we now take for granted.[67] Like Jefferson, he was a powerful party chief who worked through congressional leaders and the Democratic caucus to influence legislation. Nor did he hesitate to take his case to the people, casting himself as the interpreter as well as the representative of their interests.

During his first term in office Wilson pushed through a vast program of economic reform that lowered tariffs, raised taxes on the wealthy, created a central banking system, regulated unfair trade practices, provided low-interest loans to farmers, and established an eight-hour day for railroad employees. When the United States became involved in World War I during his second term, rather than prosecute it through unilateral executive action, Wilson went to Congress and obtained authority to control the economic as well as the military aspects of the war. This grant gave him the power to allocate food and fuel, to license trade with the enemy, to censor the mail, to regulate the foreign language press of the country, and to operate railroads, water transportation systems, and telegraph and telephone facilities. At the end of the war he made a triumphant trip to Europe, where he assumed the leading role in the writing of the Versailles peace treaty.

Wilson also provided a lesson in how *not* to work with Congress: his adamant refusal to accept any reservations proposed by the Senate for the League of Nations Covenant of the Treaty of Versailles ensured that the United States would not participate. Wilson's archenemy, Sen. Henry Cabot Lodge, R-Mass., calculated that the president's intransigence and personal hatred of him would be so intense that he would reject all compromises proposed to the treaty. Lodge was right: Wilson, spurning the advice of his wife and of close friends such as Col. Edward House, avowed it "better a thousand times to go down fighting than to dip your colors to dishonorable compromise." A trip to win popular support for the league ended in failure and a personal breakdown; as a result, the country whose leader proposed the League of Nations ended up not belonging to the organization at all.

Franklin D. Roosevelt. Confronted by enormous domestic and international crises, Franklin Roosevelt began a program of action and innovation unmatched by any chief executive in our history. In most respects, his service is now used as a yardstick against which the performance of his successors is measured.[68] When he came into office in March 1933, business failures were legion, 12 million people were unemployed, banks all over the country were closed or doing business under restrictions, and Americans had lost confidence in their leaders as well as in themselves. Counseling the nation in his inaugural address—the first of four—that "the only thing we have to fear is fear itself," the new chief executive swung into action: a four-day bank holiday was declared, and an emergency banking bill was prepared within a day's time. During Roosevelt's first 100 days in office, the nation witnessed a social and economic revolution in the form of his New Deal. Congress adopted a series of far-reaching government programs insuring bank deposits, providing crop payments for farmers, establishing codes of fair competition for industry, granting labor the right to organize, providing relief and jobs for the unemployed, and creating the Tennessee Valley Authority, a government corporation, to develop that region. With these measures and others such as Social Security, public housing, unemployment compensation, and the like, Roosevelt established the concept of the "positive state" in America—a government that had the obligation to take the lead in providing for the welfare of all the people.

Internationally, Roosevelt extended diplomatic recognition to the Soviet Union, embarked on the Good Neighbor policy toward South

America, and pushed through the Reciprocal Trade Program, which lowered tariffs with other nations. In his second term, FDR began the slow and difficult task of preparing the nation for its eventual entry into World War II: he funneled aid to the Allies; traded fifty "over-age" destroyers to Britain for naval and air bases in the British West Indies, Argentia (Newfoundland), and Bermuda; and obtained the passage of the nation's first peacetime draft. After Pearl Harbor, in his own words, "Dr. New Deal" became "Dr. Win-the-War." He took over the economic control of the war effort granted him by Congress and established the victorious strategy of concentrating on defeating Germany before Japan. While hostilities were still going on, he took the lead in setting up the United Nations. Unfortunately, he died before he could see the organization established in 1945.

Roosevelt was an innovator whose actions reshaped the presidential office. He was not only an effective legislative leader but also a skilled administrator responsible for a thorough reorganization of the executive branch, including the creation of the Executive Office of the President (see Chapter 6). Even more important, FDR was probably the most effective molder of public opinion the nation has ever known. He pioneered the use of "fireside chats" over radio to explain his actions to the people. In addition, he raised the presidential press conference to new heights as a tool of public persuasion. As a man who could take idealistic goals, reduce them to manageable and practical programs, and then sell them to Congress and the American people, Roosevelt has no peer.

Expansion Through Statute

Congress is another major source of change in the presidency. Legislators have mandated activities that earlier presidents exercised on a discretionary basis or have formally delegated responsibility for activities that traditionally resided with Congress. One of the contemporary presidency's major responsibilities—serving as the nation's economic manager—is nowhere suggested in the Constitution.[69] Most observers trace this added presidential duty to passage of the Employment Act of 1946. As James Sundquist explains, the act "compels the president to maintain a continuous surveillance of the nation's economy, to report on the state of its health at least annually, and if there are signs of pathology—inflation, recession, stagnation—to recommend corrective action."[70] To assist with this task, the president was given a staff of professional economists, the

Council of Economic Advisers, to prepare the Economic Report, one of the three formal communications submitted annually by the president to Congress (the State of the Union and Budget messages are the other two).

This statutory expansion of presidential responsibilities formalized activities that had gravitated to the White House under FDR, with the significant difference that government intervention in the economy was to precede (and prevent) depressions rather than come after the fact. The principle of presidential leadership, however, had been established with Roosevelt's activism of 1933, which stood in such sharp contrast to the inaction of his predecessor, Herbert Hoover. Although it gave the president new tasks to fulfill, Congress did not surrender its traditional right to alter presidential proposals, thereby ensuring that tax rates and spending proposals would remain a mainstay of partisan politics as well as legislative-executive relations. (The politics of economic policy making are examined in detail in Chapter 9.)

Congress has taken comparable action in other areas as well. During the same period, following World War II, the president was charged with the task of coordinating national security policy—foreign policy, intelligence collection and evaluation, and defense policy—through the mechanism of the National Security Council (NSC). Harry Truman resisted the newly created NSC as an intrusion on his powers and was slow to use it. In fact, no president can be *required* to use such a structure, but the more conflictive setting of the cold war saw one president after another establish administrative machinery designed to achieve the same goal, coordination of American foreign policy *(see Chapter 10)*. Thus, we find that Congress may encourage presidents to provide leadership in areas that are either wholly absent from the original constitutional design, or encourage executives to devise new ways to exercise their traditional responsibilities.

Expansion Through Custom and Practice

Across a wide range of presidential activities, "action based on usage may acquire legitimacy."[71] Nowhere in the Constitution did it say that presidents would serve as leaders of their party, but that task has been associated with the office since Thomas Jefferson first established his dominance of the Democratic-Republicans' congressional caucus. Enormous variation may be found in how presidents pursue such activities and in how successful they are. At times, they have been virtually abandoned by their partisan allies (Rutherford B. Hayes) and at other times seemed to derive greater influence by appearing to serve "above" party (Eisenhower). If the political parties continue to weaken or have difficulty reasserting themselves as structures vital to the operation of democracy, we might expect this informal part of the president's job description to disappear.

A second example of precedent and custom can be found in Theodore Roosevelt's attempt to mediate a labor-management dispute. Earlier presidents had intervened on the side of company owners, but Roosevelt put his prestige on the line when he sought to resolve the anthracite coal strike of 1902, a struggle that had paralyzed a vital industry. Other presidents followed suit with Wilson intervening in eight major disputes, Harding in two, FDR in eleven, and Truman in three.[72] The response of one president to emergency conditions had become an accepted precedent for his successors, if they wished to pursue it.

Institutional Sources of Change

Finally, it needs to be recognized that the modern presidency is no longer a one-person job, a reality that may have significant consequences for the office's evolution. Although designed to be unitary rather than plural, the modern presidency has become a working collectivity in order to dispatch the many responsibilities placed at the president's door. This new, complex institution employs nearly 1,500 full-time assistants in the White House and in the specialized units of the Executive Office of the President, an administrative structure created in 1939 to accommodate Franklin Roosevelt's many aides. Bradley Patterson points out that within the White House one can identify twenty policy and political staff specializations, supplemented by another seven professional staff units. Another six to eight staff units operate outside the White House proper as part of the Executive Office of the President.[73]

Given this bureaucratic structure, it is reasonable to expect the presidency to be susceptible to some of the same developmental dynamics as other organizations, including tendencies toward highly refined divisions of labor and staff specialization. One notable change in the modern presidency is the emergence of a highly professional team of public relations experts charged with portraying presidents in the most favorable light and projecting their influence on public life.[74] Other changes in the presidency's environment, such as inflated public expectations and expanded media coverage, help account for much of this development, but so does a staff system designed to help presidents reach new parts of the public in ever more effective ways. By the late 1970s, more than 30 percent of the White House staff was specifically assigned to deal with media relations or policy, but a more realistic estimate would find somewhere between 60 percent and 85 percent of the president's aides engaged in promotional operations.[75] With such a mammoth effort afoot, it is hardly surprising to find commentators expressing concern about the concentration on image and style rather than reality and substance.

Students of the presidency commonly divide the institution's development into two major periods: traditional and modern. In this view, the presidency of Franklin Roosevelt was the turning point. FDR's long tenure in the office, combined with his dramatically activist style, placed a distinctive imprint on the position with which his successors have had to contend. Fred Greenstein argues that the modern presidency, as shaped by FDR, is distinguished by four features: (1) the president is expected to develop a legislative program and to persuade Congress to enact it; (2) presidents regularly engage in direct policy making through actions not requiring congressional approval; (3) the presidential office has become an extensive bureaucracy designed to enable presidents to undertake points 1 and 2; and (4) presidents have come to symbolize the nation and to personify its government to such an extent that the public holds them primarily responsible for its condition and closely monitors their performance through intensive coverage carried in the media.[76]

A number of scholars recently have sought to resuscitate our appreciation of presidents from the traditional period and to erase the impression that they were highly forgettable.[77] Their efforts have reawakened interest in the historic dimensions of the office and its development, a sensitivity reflected throughout this book. But like most other political scientists, we will concentrate our discussion on the modern period while recognizing that important precedents were established much earlier.

Understanding the presidency's institutional development provides an important perspective on roles played by the office, but one also needs to address a less concrete question: What does the presidency *mean* to Americans? The final section of this chapter focuses on the office's emotional and psychological significance.

Presidential Culture

The presidency has always been important in American civic life, but it may have assumed even greater proportions in the modern era, assisted by new technologies and resting on new conceptions of the office. The office acquired mythic dimensions when it was filled by the country's first true hero. George Washington, argues Seymour Martin Lipset, supplied the virtues of a charismatic leader who serves as "symbol of the new nation, its hero who embodies in his person its values and aspirations. But more than merely symbolizing the new nation, he legitimizes the state, the new secular government, by endowing it with his 'gift of grace,'" the near magical qualities such leaders supposedly possess.[78] A cult of personality grew up around Washington so that well into the nineteenth century citizens displayed his likeness in their homes, named their children after him, and paid him endless tributes.

In the process of contributing stability and identity to the new nation, Washington also endowed the presidential office with a special meaning that has become part of our collective heritage. Bruce Buchanan refers to this as *presidential culture,* "widely held meanings of the presidency, derived from selected episodes in the history of the institution and transmitted from one generation to the next by political socialization."[79] Buchanan explains that families, teachers, and the media sustain this view of the presidency as an office with the ability to deliver the nation from danger as a result of its occupants' greatness. Somehow, it is widely believed, the institution "has the potential to make extraordinary events happen" and the incumbent "should be able to realize that potential."[80] Occupants of the position, then, are expected to live up to these levels of performance and are roundly criticized when they fall short.

Why have such unrealistic expectations taken hold? One reason is that we have glorified the memories of past presidents. The "great" presidents, particularly those who took decisive action and bold initiatives, and even some of the "not so great" are treated as folk heroes and enshrined in a national mythology—figures whose births we celebrate, whose virtues we are urged to emulate, whose achievements we memorialize, and whose sex lives continue to interest us long after their deaths. School children throughout America are regaled with stories of Washington and Lincoln every February while looking at bulletin boards featuring their silhouettes. Every summer, thousands of vacationers make the pilgrimage to visit shrines located along the Potomac in Washington, D.C., or scattered throughout the nation in presidential libraries and museums. But historical and popular glorification do not constitute the full story.

A number of political scientists have pointed to the importance of the presidency in meeting the emotional and psychological needs of the populace. In particular, it is argued that citizens have expressive needs for confidence, security, reassurance, and pride in citizenship.[81] In the view of Murray Edelman, citizens suffer from a "general sense of anxiety about the comprehensive function played in human affairs by chance, ignorance, and inability to comprehend, plan, and take responsibility for remote and complicated contingencies." The natural response is to seek emotional comfort through attachment to reassuring symbols, "and what symbol can be more reassuring than the incumbent of a high position who knows what to do and is willing to act, especially when others are bewildered and alone?"[82] We know that American children develop a highly idealized image of presidents that emphasizes both their power and benevolence, a source of reassurance that may be transferred from childhood to adulthood.

Fred Greenstein suggests additional psychological needs that are met through the presidency. Citizens seeking to sort through the complexity of political life turn to presidents for cognitive assistance. Presidents personify the government and make it possible to become engaged by what would otherwise be an impersonal abstraction. By following the president's activities, citizens may also experience a sort of vicarious participation in public affairs, giving them a sense of power and control that ordinarily would be unavailable. As a symbol of stability, predictability, and national unity, the president soothes fears and enables us to proceed with our daily lives.[83]

Symbols, in fact, are central to the character of the presidential office, which has become particularly "potent as a symbol of the public welfare, built-in benevolence, and competence to lead."[84] Barbara Hinckley points out that "symbols evoke ideas the society wants to believe are true . . . [they] can substitute for something that does not exist otherwise."[85] In fact, Hinckley argues, because the Constitution failed to clarify the presidency's nature and responsibilities, symbols have become enormously significant: "The office is undefined; thus presidents become what people want them to be."[86] And the people want them to be many things. The list of desirable personal attributes is impressive, as Ray Price, an aide to Richard Nixon during the 1968 campaign, pointed out in a memo to the staff:

> People identify with a President in a way they do with no other public figure. Potential presidents are measured against an ideal that's a combination of leading

man, God, father, hero, pope, king, with maybe just a touch of the avenging Furies thrown in. They want him to be larger than life, a living legend, and yet quintessentially human; someone to be held up to their children as a model; someone to be cherished by themselves as a revered member of the family, in somewhat the same way in which peasant families pray to the icon in the corner. Reverence goes where power is.[87]

The problem for candidate Nixon was how to project an image that would match these public expectations.

Hinckley's research reveals that incumbents as well as candidates seek to project desirable images and that the terms used by presidents to depict themselves and their office have been remarkably consistent. Over a forty-year period, presidents from Truman to Reagan have portrayed themselves in speeches as "alone in the government, equivalent to the nation, religious and cultural leaders who shun politics and elections."[88] In other words, the self-image presidents project to the nation reinforces the mystique and majesty that are integral features of the modern presidency and confirms the confidence that citizens have placed in the leader on whom they depend to contend with distant sources of pain and uncertainty. The underlying message in these accounts is clear: *presidents tell the public what it wants to hear.*

Many unsettling implications flow from this line of analysis. What if presidents compensate for their failure to achieve real success in managing the economy or in conducting foreign policy by projecting the *appearance* of policy success? Would the press or the public be capable of seeing through such deception? Probably not, suggests Theodore Lowi. Instead, modern presidents must function in the face of a dangerous imbalance: "the expectations of the masses have grown faster than the capacity of presidential government to meet them."[89] Modern presidents, argues Lowi, resort to illusions to cover failures and seek quick fixes for their flagging public support in foreign adventures. Such pathological behavior—portrayed by Lowi as rooted in the presidential institution, not in individual presidents' personalities—is ultimately self-defeating because it does nothing more than further inflate expectations and ensure public disappointment.

Part of this dynamic can be traced to advances in the means of communication. Television, argues Bruce Miroff, gives the president an unequalled vehicle "to display his leadership qualities" through presidential spectacles.[90] As Miroff explains, a spectacle is the utilization of modern media, especially television, to present the president in visible and highly dramatic actions designed to establish a favorable public identity. It is the presentation of the president in actions that minimize the potential for public interruption and treat citizens as passive spectators. Most important, it is the presentation of actions which are meaningful less for what they accomplish, in the sense of substantive outcome, than for what they signify. Actions in a presidential spectacle serve as gestures rather than as means.[91]

Military intervention in Grenada, he suggests, was a prime example of such a spectacle the effectiveness of which was enhanced by the high level of secrecy maintained about the military operation. Vivid images of Ronald Reagan as a decisive and determined opponent of communist expansion were etched in the minds of Americans while the reality was considerably less impressive. An appreciation of the emotional and psychological roles the president assumes makes us realize that this kind of spectacle may meet not only the president's needs but also the public's.

Conclusion

There can be little doubt that today's presidency is a far cry from the office designed by the Constitutional Convention. Responsibilities have grown enormously as have means to fulfill them, although probably not at the same pace. Unlike the office that was launched in 1789, today's presidency is firmly rooted in the national consciousness as the consequence of childhood socialization and a secular mythology whose idealized images are magnified with the passage of time. There is no way to determine whether today's office means more to Americans than it did two centuries ago in terms of the emotional and psychological needs it meets, but certainly it occupies a more central—some would argue excessive—place in the public consciousness.

The presidency is not a static construct, however. As this overview of institutional development demonstrates, how Americans see the office and what they want from it can and will change over time. In this continuing process, features of the past will be carried forward and continue to shape the institution and its occupants, while more immediate forces provide new twists to the definition, sometimes through law, constitutional amendments, and other formal means, but more often through informal means. At the formal level, individual presidents enjoy considerable freedom in determining what they will do and how they will do it, but they also must respond to informal expectations if they hope to be successful.

Even with powers grounded in the Constitution, expanded through practice, and enhanced by powerful public expectations, presidents remain preeminently political beings. Moreover, their political tasks are unusually complex; not only must they perform on the public stage of mass politics, but also they must master the intricacies of elite politics, a game played among skilled insiders. In the following chapters, we first examine "public politics" (Chapters 2, 3, and 4) and then turn to the skills that presidents bring to relations with other public elites (Chapters 5, 6, and 7). These separate dimensions are linked in discussions of major policy areas (Chapters 8, 9, and 10).

NOTES

1. Clinton Rossiter, *The American Presidency*, rev. ed. (New York: Harcourt, Brace, 1960), 15.

2. Ibid., 237.

3. Ibid., 260–261.

4. Richard E. Neustadt, *Presidential Power: The Politics of Leadership* (New York: Wiley, 1960), 33.

5. Ibid., 46.

6. Ibid., 161.

7. Ibid., 195.

8. James MacGregor Burns, *Presidential Government: The Crucible of Leadership* (Boston: Houghton Mifflin, 1965), 28.

9. Ibid., 113–114.

10. Ibid., 351.

11. Thomas E. Cronin, "The Textbook Presidency" (Paper delivered at the annual meeting of the American Political Science Association, Los Angeles, Calif., Sept. 8–12, 1970). Reprinted in *Perspectives on the Presidency: A Collection*, ed. Stanley Bach and George T. Sulzner (Lexington, Mass.: D. C. Heath, 1974), 54–74.

12. George Reedy, *The Twilight of the Presidency* (New York: New American Library, 1970), x.

13. Arthur M. Schlesinger, Jr., *The Imperial Presidency* (Boston: Houghton Mifflin, 1983), ix.

14. Ibid., 254.

15. Walter F. Mondale, *The Accountability of Power: Toward a Responsible Presidency* (New York: David McKay, 1975), 4.

16. William G. Andrews, "The Presidency, Congress, and Constitutional Theory," in *The Presidency in Contemporary Context*, ed. Norman C. Thomas (New York: Dodd, Mead, 1973), 13, 17.

17. Fred I. Greenstein, "Change and Continuity in the Modern Presidency," in *The New American Political System*, ed. Anthony King (Washington, D.C.: American Enterprise Institute, 1978), 65.

18. Ibid., 70–75.

19. Godfrey Hodgson, *All Things to All Men: The False Promise of the American Presidency* (New York: Simon & Schuster, 1980), 225.

20. Ibid., 13.

21. Thomas E. Cronin, "An Imperiled Presidency?" in *The Post–Imperial Presidency*, ed. Vincent Davis (New Brunswick, N.J.: Transaction Books, 1980).

22. Richard P. Nathan, *The Administrative Presidency* (New York: Wiley, 1983).

23. Chester A. Newland, "A Mid-Term Appraisal—The Reagan Presidency, Limited Government and Political Administration," *Public Administration Review* 43 (January/ February 1983): 1–21; and Edie N. Goldenberg, "The Permanent Government in an Era of Retrenchment and Redirection," in *The Reagan Presidency and the Governing of America*, ed. Lester M. Salamon and Michael S. Lund (Washington, D.C.: Urban Institute Press, 1984), 381–404.

24. Bert A. Rockman, *The Leadership Question: The Presidency and the American Political System* (New York: Praeger, 1984), 236.

25. Theodore J. Lowi, *The Personal Presidency: Power Invested, Promise Unfulfilled* (Ithaca, N.Y.: Cornell University Press, 1985).

26. Bert A. Rockman, "The Modern Presidency and Theories of Accountability: Old Wine and Old Bottles," *Congress and the Presidency* 13 (Autumn 1986): 135–156.

27. Lester G. Seligman and Cary R. Covington, *The Coalitional Presidency* (Chicago: Dorsey, 1989), 12.

28. Richard Rose, *The Postmodern President: The White House Meets the World* (Chatham, N.J.: Chatham House, 1988).

29. Ibid., 28.

30. Arthur M. Schlesinger, Jr., *The Imperial Presidency* (Boston: Houghton Mifflin, 1989) 441.

31. Ibid., 443.

32. Ibid., 453.

33. Ibid., 457.

34. Ibid., 431, 436.

35. Ibid., 438.

36. Sidney M. Milkis and Michael Nelson, *The American Presidency: Origins and Development, 1776–1990* (Washington, D.C.: CQ Press, 1990), 13–14, chap. 2. Also see chap. 1, note 19, where it is suggested that the Pinckney Plan may actually have provided considerable guidance for designing the presidency.

37. Joseph E. Kallenbach, *The American Chief Executive: The Presidency and the Governorship* (New York: Harper & Row, 1966), chap. 2.

38. Edward S. Corwin, *The President: Office and Powers, 1787–1984*, 5th ed. (New York: New York University Press, 1984), 11.

39. Ibid., 11–13.

40. Michael Nelson, "Constitutional Beginnings," in *Guide to the Presidency*, ed. Michael Nelson (Washington, D.C.: Congressional Quarterly, 1989), 3–22. Much of the same material also can be found in Milkis and Nelson, *The American Presidency*, chap. 1.

41. C. C. Thach, Jr., *The Creation of the Presidency, 1775–1789: A Study in Constitutional History* (Baltimore: The Johns Hopkins University Press, 1922), chap. 3.

42. Nelson, *Guide to the Presidency*, 29.

43. Although presidents are limited to two elected terms, it is possible to serve for as many as ten years. A vice president who became president because of death, impeachment, or resignation and served no more than two years could be elected to two terms.

44. As cited in Corwin, *The President*, 28. Original from Henry Jones Ford, *The Rise and Growth of American Politics* (New York: Macmillan, 1898).

45. The term *role* often has been criticized by social scientists for lacking analytic rigor; nonetheless, *role* remains a powerful metaphor for understanding human behavior. During the 1960s analysts seemed almost to compete in developing an ever-lengthening list of roles filled by the president. See David L. Paletz, "Perspectives on the Presidency," in *The Institutionalized Presidency*, ed. Norman Thomas and Hans Baade (Dobbs Ferry, N.Y.: Oceana, 1972), 8–18.

46. Louis Fisher, *Constitutional Conflicts Between Congress and the President*, 3d ed. rev. (Lawrence: University Press of Kansas, 1991), chap. 9.

47. Ibid., chap. 8.

48. Robert Scigliano, "The Presidency and the Judiciary," in *The Presidency and the Political System*, 3d ed., ed. Michael Nelson (Washington, D.C.: CQ Press, 1990), 473–476.

49. Fred I. Greenstein, "In Search of a Modern Presidency," in *Leadership in the Modern Presidency*, ed. Fred I. Greenstein (Cambridge, Mass.: Harvard University Press, 1989), 3, 346. Also see Greenstein, *The Hidden-Hand Presidency* (New York: Basic Books, 1982), 4–5. In the latter, Greenstein (note 4, 252) attributes the initial functional role treatment to Clinton Rossiter in his classic text, *The American Presidency*.

50. Greenstein, "In Search of a Modern Presidency," 3.

51. John Locke, *Two Treatises of Civil Government* (New York: Dutton, 1924), 199.

52. For a thoughtful discussion of many of these incidents see Christopher H. Pyle and Richard M. Pious, *The President, Congress and the Constitution: Power and Legitimacy in American Politics* (New York: Free Press, 1984). The varying grounds for claiming inherent power are reviewed on pages 76–78.

53. Corwin, *The President*, 30.

54. Ibid.

55. Richard M. Pious, *The American Presidency* (New York: Basic Books, 1979), 333. Also cited in Milkis and Nelson, *The American Presidency*, 69.

56. Corwin, *The President*, 30.

57. Ibid., chap. 1.

58. Clinton Rossiter selected the same seven and added Harry Truman. See Rossiter, *The American Presidency*, rev. ed. (New York: Harcourt Brace, 1960), chaps. 3, 5. Finally, four separate polls of historians, evaluating the leadership skills of all the presidents, rate highest Corwin's original seven chief executives. See chap. 4 for further discussion.

59. Leonard White, *The Federalists: A Study in Administrative History* (New York: Macmillan, 1967), 99.

60. As a matter of political strategy presidents now often seek the advice of influential individual senators. Woodrow Wilson's failure to consult with prominent Republican senators about the Treaty of Versailles probably contributed to his failure to get it approved, a lesson for his successors.

61. Alfred Kelly and Winfred Harbison, *The American Constitution: Its Origins and Development*, 4th ed. (New York: Norton, 1970), 424.

62. Rossiter, *The American Presidency*, rev. ed., 102.

63. Milkis and Nelson, *The American Presidency*, 193.

64. Jeffrey K. Tulis, *The Rhetorical Presidency* (Princeton, N.J.: Princeton University Press, 1987), chap. 4.

65. From *The Autobiography of Theodore Roosevelt*, excerpted in *Classics of the American Presidency*, ed. Harry Bailey (Oak Park, Ill.: Moore Publishing, 1980), 35.

66. Tulis, *The Rhetorical Presidency*, chap. 5. Also see Jeffrey K. Tulis, "The Two Constitutional Presidencies," in *The Presidency and the Political System*, 3d ed., ed. Michael Nelson (Washington, D.C.: CQ Press, 1990).

67. Thomas Jefferson had discontinued the practice as an undesirable indication of monarchist tendencies.

68. William E. Leuchtenberg, *In the Shadow of FDR: From Harry Truman to Ronald Reagan,* rev. ed. (Ithaca, N.Y.: Cornell University Press, 1985).

69. James L. Sundquist uses the term "economic stabilizer" and earlier, Clinton Rossiter had used the term "Manager of Prosperity." See Sundquist, *The Decline and Resurgence of Congress* (Washington, D.C.: Brookings, 1981), chap. 4.

70. Ibid., 66–67.

71. Fisher, *Constitutional Conflicts,* 24.

72. Corwin, *The President,* 175–177.

73. On White House staffing, see Bradley H. Patterson, Jr., *The Ring of Power: The White House Staff and Its Expanding Role in Government* (New York: Basic Books, 1988). On the larger development of presidential staffing, see John Hart, *The Presidential Branch* (New York: Pergamon Press, 1987).

74. For an essay that challenges the desirability of such a manifest presence, see Bruce Miroff, "Monopolizing the Public Space: The President as a Problem for Democratic Politics," in *Rethinking the Presidency,* ed. Thomas E. Cronin (Boston: Little, Brown, 1982).

75. Michael B. Grossman and Martha J. Kumar, *Portraying the President: The White House and the News Media* (Baltimore, Md.: The Johns Hopkins University Press, 1981), 83–84.

76. Fred I. Greenstein, "Change and Continuity in the Modern Presidency," in *The New American Political System,* ed. Anthony King (Washington, D.C.: American Enterprise Institute, 1979), 45–46.

77. See especially Milkis and Nelson, *The American Presidency,* chapters 4–7; Tulis, *The Rhetorical Presidency;* and Stephen Skowronek, "Presidential Leadership in Political Time," in *The Presidency and the Political System,* 3d ed.

78. Seymour Martin Lipset, *The First New Nation: The United States in Historical and Comparative Perspective,* (New York: Norton, 1979 ed.), 18.

79. Bruce Buchanan, *The Citizen's Presidency: Standards of Choice and Judgment* (Washington, D.C.: CQ Press, 1987), 25.

80. Ibid., 28.

81. See especially Murray Edelman, *The Symbolic Uses of Politics* (Urbana: University of Illinois Press, 1964); and Fred I. Greenstein, "What the President Means to Americans: Presidential 'Choice' Between Elections," in *Choosing the President,* ed. James David Barber (Englewood Cliffs, N.J.: Prentice-Hall, 1974).

82. Edelman, *The Symbolic Uses of Politics,* 76–77.

83. Greenstein, "What the President Means to Americans," 144–147. It should be noted that in this later essay Greenstein deemphasized the likelihood that children socialized to a positive feeling about the president as an authority figure would extend this reliance on an "unconscious symbolic surrogate of childhood authority figures" into adulthood (page 142).

84. Murray Edelman, "The Politics of Persuasion," in *Choosing the President,* 172.

85. Barbara Hinckley, *The Symbolic Presidency: How Presidents Portray Themselves* (New York: Routledge, 1990), 5.

86. Ibid., 8.

87. As cited in Michael Novak, *Choosing Our King: Powerful Symbols in Presidential Politics* (New York: Macmillan, 1974), 44.

88. Hinckley, *The Symbolic Presidency,* 133.

89. Theodore J. Lowi, *The Personal President* (Ithaca, N.Y.: Cornell University Press, 1985), xii.

90. Bruce Miroff, "The Presidency and the Public: Leadership as Spectacle," in *The Presidency and the Political System*, 2d ed., esp. 271–277.

91. Bruce Miroff, "Secrecy and Spectacle: Reflections on the Dangers of the Presidency," in *The Presidency in American Politics*, ed. Paul Brace, Christine B. Harrington, and Gary King (New York: New York University Press, 1989), 157. Also see Miroff, "Monopolizing the Public Space," in *Rethinking the Presidency*.

READINGS

Burns, James MacGregor. *Presidential Government: The Crucible of Leadership*. Boston: Houghton Mifflin, 1965.

Corwin, Edward S. *The President: Office and Powers*. New York: New York University Press, 1984.

Heclo, Hugh, and Lester M. Salamon, eds. *The Illusion of Presidential Government*. Boulder, Colo.: Westview, 1981.

Kallenbach, Joseph E. *The American Chief Executive*. New York: Harper & Row, 1966.

Lowi, Theodore J. *The Personal President: Power Invested, Promise Unfulfilled*. Ithaca, N.Y.: Cornell University Press, 1985.

Nelson, Michael, ed. *The Presidency and the Political System*, 3d ed. Washington, D.C.: CQ Press, 1990.

Neustadt, Richard E. *Presidential Power and the Modern Presidents: The Politics of Leadership from Roosevelt to Reagan*. New York: Free Press, 1990.

Rockman, Bert A. *The Leadership Question: The Presidency and the American Political System*. New York: Praeger, 1984.

Rose, Richard. *The Postmodern President: George Bush Meets the World*, 2d ed. Chatham, N.J.: Chatham House, 1991.

Rossiter, Clinton. *The American Presidency*, rev. ed. New York: Harcourt, Brace, 1960.

Seligman, Lester G., and Cary R. Covington. *The Coalitional Presidency*. Chicago: Dorsey, 1989.

2 ELECTION POLITICS

For almost a century Americans have delighted in expressing their preferences in primary campaigns, symbolized by this collage of historical buttons.

THE FOCAL POINT OF AMERI-can political life is the presidential election. More citizens participate in this process than in any other aspect of civic life, and their choice has enormous significance for the nation and, indeed, for the world. Historians use presidential terms to break history into four-year blocks of time, and policy making at the federal level follows the same rhythm. The election also serves as a unifying event, a collective celebration of democracy coming at the conclusion of an elaborate pageant replete with familiar rituals, colorful characters, and plot lines that remain dramatic despite their repetition every four years.

Today's selection process bears little resemblance to what the Founders outlined in the original Constitution. Most of the changes have been extra-constitutional; that is, they result from the evolution of political parties, the media, and citizen expectations rather

than constitutional amendments. There has been almost constant tinker-
ing with the rules governing this aspect of American politics, with the
movement consistently toward greater democratization. Most dissatisfaction with the process centers on the remnants of indirect democracy that
persist, particularly the national party conventions and the electoral college, but some argue that democratization may have gone too far. The
most important question that can be asked about U.S. presidential elections is whether they produce winners with the requisite abilities and
skills.

At the conclusion of this chapter, we review recommendations for
reform intended to improve system performance and provide for a greater
degree of direct democracy. To appreciate the current selection process
and suggestions for reform, it is useful to gain an understanding of the
major transformations the system has undergone.

Evolution of the Selection Process

In 1789 and 1792 electing a president was simple. Each member of the
electoral college cast two votes, one of which had to be for a person
outside of his state. Both times George Washington was elected by unanimous votes.[1] And both times John Adams received the second highest
number of votes to become the vice president. In 1789 the process took
four months to complete: electors were chosen on the first Wednesday of
January, met in their respective states to vote on the first Wednesday in
February, and the votes were counted on April 6. In 1792 the procedure
took even less time. The contrast with today's process could not be
sharper: candidates now launch nomination campaigns up to two years
before the general election, spending millions of dollars in pursuit of the
office.

Consensus support for Washington ensured smooth operation of the
selection procedure during the first two elections: there was widespread
confidence that the nation's wartime hero would govern in the interest of
all the people. The erosion of that consensus triggered the development of
a separate nomination procedure. Policy differences in Congress created
the basis for an important institution not mentioned in the Constitution—
the political party. By the early 1790s the Federalist party had formed
around the economic policies of Secretary of the Treasury Alexander
Hamilton, and his supporters in Congress backed his programs.[2] Resign-

ing as secretary of state in 1793, Thomas Jefferson joined James Madison, then serving in the House of Representatives, as a critic of Hamilton's policies, and they formed the rival Republican party.[3] By the mid-1790s cohesive pro- and anti-administration blocs had formed in Congress, and congressional candidates were labeled Democratic-Republicans or Federalists.[4] Washington's retirement at the end of his second term opened the presidential election to party politics.

The rise of parties fundamentally altered presidential selection by creating a separate nomination stage: the parties had to devise a method for choosing their nominees. Influence over presidential selection shifted from the local notables who had served as electors to party elites whose character has evolved over time. In 1796 the Federalists' leaders chose their candidate, John Adams, and the Democratic-Republicans relied on their party members in Congress to nominate Jefferson as their standard-bearer. Four years later the Federalists adopted their opponents' idea, and the congressional caucus became the nominating mechanism for both parties, a practice that continued until 1824.

Political parties also had an almost immediate impact on the electoral college. Electors became party loyalists whose discipline was apparent in 1800 when Jefferson, the Democratic-Republicans' candidate for president, and Aaron Burr, the party's candidate for vice president, tied in the electoral college voting. Loyal to their party, the electors had cast their ballots for both candidates, but the Constitution had no provision for counting the ballots separately for president and vice president. Jefferson and Burr each received seventy-three votes to President Adams's sixty-five. The election was decided in the House of Representatives where Jefferson won, but only after thirty-six ballots. Hamilton broke the tie by throwing his support behind Jefferson, his longtime rival. Party loyalty, with infrequent exceptions, has prevailed in electoral college balloting ever since. The Twelfth Amendment to the Constitution, ratified in 1804, provided for separate presidential and vice presidential balloting in the electoral college to prevent a similar deadlock.[5]

The congressional caucus allowed members of Congress, already assembled in the nation's capital and facing minimal transportation problems, to select a nominee. Because legislators were familiar with potential presidential candidates from all parts of the new country, they were the logical agents for choosing candidates for an office with a nationwide constituency. Caucuses provided a peer review of candidates' credentials, with one group of politicians assessing another's skills, abilities, and political appeal. But the congressional caucus had serious flaws. It violated the separation of powers principle of the Constitution by giving members of the legislative body a routine role in choosing the president rather than only in the event of an electoral college deadlock. The caucus could not represent areas in which the party had lost the previous congressional election, a problem quickly encountered by the Federalists. Moreover, interested and informed citizens who participated in grass-roots party activities, especially campaigns, had no means to participate in congressional caucus deliberations.

The 1824 election brought an end to nomination by congressional caucus. First, the Democratic-Republicans in Congress insisted on nominating Secretary of the Treasury William Crawford, who had suffered a debilitating stroke. Then, in the general election Andrew Jackson, proposed by the Tennessee legislature, won more popular votes and more electoral votes than any other candidate, but failed to achieve a majority in the electoral college. The election had to be decided by the House where John Quincy Adams emerged victorious after he agreed to make Henry Clay, another of the five contestants, secretary of state in return for his support. These shenanigans permanently discredited King Caucus, as its critics called it. "Favorite sons" nominated by state legislatures and conventions dominated the 1828 campaign, but this method proved too decentralized to select a national official. A device was needed that would represent party elements throughout the country and at the same time facilitate the nomination of a candidate.

National Party Conventions

What developed was the party convention, an assembly made truly national by including delegates from all the states. Rail transportation made such meetings feasible, and the expanding citizen participation in presidential elections made the change necessary. Influence over selection of the party nominee therefore shifted to state and local party leaders, particularly those able to commit large blocs of delegate votes to a candidate.

Two minor parties with no appreciable representation in Congress, the Anti-Masons and National Republicans, led the way with conventions in 1831.[6] The Democrats, under President Andrew Jackson (elected in 1828), also held a convention in 1832 to rally support. Major political parties have nominated their presidential and vice presidential candidates by holding national conventions ever since. National committees composed of state party leaders call the presidential nominating conventions into session to choose nominees and to adopt a platform of common policy positions.[7] Delegates are selected by states and allocated primarily on the basis of population.

Although today's conventions in some ways resemble those of 150 years ago, the nomination process has undergone drastic revision, especially since 1968. Just as influence over selection of the party nominee shifted from Congress to party leaders, it has moved within the party from a small group of organization professionals to a broad base of activists and voters. This shift, the origins of which can be traced to the development of presidential primary elections early in the twentieth century (Florida passed the first primary election law in 1901), accelerated rapidly after 1968. Modern conventions serve as ratifying assemblies rather than deliberative bodies, and candidates with popular appeal have the advantage over those whose appeal is primarily with party leaders.

Under the system that operated from roughly 1850 to 1950, party leaders from the largest states could bargain over presidential nominations. Most influential were those who controlled large blocs of delegates and would throw their support behind a candidate for the right price. These power brokers—hence the term *brokered conventions*—might seek a program commitment in the platform, a place in the president's cabinet, or other forms of federal patronage in return for support. To be successful, candidates had to curry favor with party and elected officials before and during the national convention. An effective campaign manager might tour the country selling the candidate's virtues and securing delegate commitments prior to the convention, but about half the conventions began with no sense of the likely outcome. Protracted bargaining and negotiation among powerful state and local party leaders was often the result; the Democrats needed 103 ballots cast over seventeen days to nominate John W. Davis in 1924, an effort that must have seemed pointless when he attracted only 29 percent of the popular vote. Nevertheless, the convention was a deliberative body that reached decisions on common policy positions as well as on nominees. Providing a way to accommodate the demands of major elements within the party established the base for a nationwide campaign.

In this respect, modern conventions are quite different. Not since 1952, when the Democrats needed three ballots to nominate Gov. Adlai Stevenson of Illinois for president, has it taken more than one ballot to determine either party's nominee.[8] Raucous floor battles over procedures and delegate credentials have given way to a stream of symbols and speakers whose selection is carefully choreographed to appeal to a prime-time television audience. Although much of the convention's business is still conducted in backroom meetings, the most important business—determining who the presidential nominee will be—already has been decided through the grueling primary and caucus process used to select convention delegates. Compared to their forerunners, modern conventions conduct their business in a routinized fashion, adhere to a set of enforceable national party standards for delegate selection and demographic representation, and are more heavily influenced by rank-and-file party supporters than by the party's organization leaders.[9] Adoption of these changes, however, appeared gradually through a process often fraught with conflict that centered on the rules governing delegate selection.

The Contemporary Selection Process

The pace of change accelerated when the Democratic party adopted a set of internal reforms following their loss in 1968. In addition to the actions already noted, rules adopted by a variety of actors—100 state political parties and fifty legislatures, the national political parties, and Congress—reformed the process. Sometimes individuals even turn to the courts to interpret provisions of these regulations and reconcile conflicts among them. In addition, the rules have been adjusted so drastically and so often, particularly in the Democratic party, that candidates and their supporters find it difficult to keep up with them.

Reform has been especially pervasive in the nomination process. Following their tumultuous convention in 1968, when Vietnam War protesters clashed with police in the streets of Chicago, the Democrats adopted a set of guidelines that reduced the influence of party leaders, encouraged participation by rank-and-file Democrats, and expanded convention representation of previously underrepresented groups, particularly women and African Americans. The result was a pronounced shift of influence within the party from *party professionals* toward *amateurs*, a term encompassing citizens who become engaged in the presidential contest because of a short-term concern such as an attractive candidate (candidate enthusiasts) or an especially important issue (issue enthusiasts).

States, seeking to conform to the party's new guidelines on participation, adopted the primary as the preferred means to select delegates to the national convention. In 1968 only seventeen states chose delegates through primaries; in 1992, thirty-seven states and the District of Columbia did so.[10] Because of these changes, nominations are more apt to reflect the voters' concerns. Conventions changed accordingly: nominations are now determined by the party supporters who selected delegates during the preceding primaries and caucuses.

But abandoning the convention's traditional deliberative role, some argue, has come at a heavy cost. By sacrificing the peer review exercised by fellow professionals, the Democratic party, in particular, may have chosen less capable nominees. Moreover, the changes have enhanced the importance of the media. By operating as the principal source of information about the candidates and by emphasizing the "horse race"—who is ahead—the media have become enormously influential during the delegate selection process. So not everyone is satisfied with the general movement toward a more democratized selection process, and several counter-reforms appeared during the 1980s.

Now that the historical context has been set and some of the current concerns about the nomination process have been previewed, the discussion focuses on how the contemporary selection process operates. Despite the seemingly perpetual flux that characterizes presidential elections, it is possible to identify four stages in the process: (1) the pool of eligible candidates is defined; (2) following the primaries and caucuses, the parties nominate their candidates at the national conventions; (3) the general election campaign is waged, culminating in election day; and (4) the electoral college validates the results.

No two presidential election cycles are identical, but the customary time line is relatively predictable *(Figure 2-1)*. Potential candidates maneuver for position during the one or two years preceding the election year. Selection of convention delegates begins in February of the election year, with conventions typically scheduled in mid-July for the out-party and mid-August for the party that controls the presidency. In 1992 the Democrats met in New York for four days starting July 13, and the Republicans met in Houston August 17 through August 20. Traditionally, the general election campaign begins on Labor Day and runs to election day, the first Tuesday following the first Monday in November, but the planning for modern campaigns begins once the identity of major party nomi-

Figure 2.1 The 1992 Presidential Contest Time Line

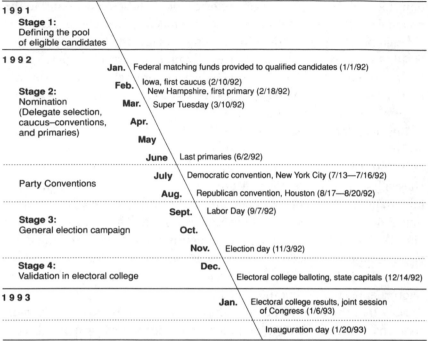

nees becomes clear. Electors cast ballots in their state capitols in mid-December. Finally, those ballots are officially tabulated during the first week in January during a joint session of the U.S. Congress, which is presided over by the incumbent vice president. The duly elected president is inaugurated on January 20, a date set in the Twentieth Amendment to the Constitution.

Defining the Pool of Eligibles

Who is eligible to serve as president? The formal rules relating to the candidates' qualifications are minimal and have been remarkably stable over time. Individuals need to meet only three requirements, which are set forth in Article II, Section 1, of the Constitution. One must be a "natural born" citizen, at least thirty-five years of age, and a resident of the United States for fourteen years or longer.[11] Approximately 90 million Americans meet these constitutional requirements, but the pool of plausible candidates is far smaller than that of possible candidates.

The informal requirements for the presidency are less easy to satisfy than the formal. People who entertain presidential ambitions must have what is generally called "political availability"; that is, they must have the political experiences and personal characteristics that make them attractive to political activists and to the general voting public. Potential candidates accumulate these credentials through personal and career decisions made long before the presidential election year.

There is no explicit checklist of job qualifications for the presidency. The closest that one can come to determining what particular political experiences and personal characteristics put an individual in line for a presidential nomination is to look at past candidates. Even this approach poses some difficulties because the attitudes of political leaders and the American public change over time.

Political Experience of Candidates

Who is nominated to run for president? Overwhelmingly, the answer is people with experience in one of a few civilian, elective, political offices. Since 1932 nominees, with only two exceptions, have been drawn from one of four positions: the presidency, the vice presidency, a state governorship, or a U.S. Senate seat.[12] (See Appendix A.) Candidates with other backgrounds try for the nomination but are seldom successful. For example, in 1988 three aspirants who lacked experience in elected office sought the nomination, but the nominees, George Bush and Michael Dukakis, boasted backgrounds consistent with the general pattern. Jesse Jackson, a minister and civil rights organizer, Marion G. "Pat" Robertson, a television evangelist and businessman, and Alexander Haig, a retired military officer, ran unsuccessful campaigns. In 1992 H. Ross Perot, a billionaire businessman, sought election without a party nomination.

Nominees' backgrounds have changed very little since the last half of the nineteenth century.[13] Moreover, since 1932 the party controlling the presidency has turned to the presidency or vice presidency for candidates, while the out-party has turned first to governors and then to the Senate for its candidates.

Presidents and Vice Presidents. In only one of the last sixteen elections from 1932 to 1992 has the name of an incumbent president or vice president not been on the ballot. Twelve times, the incumbent president was renominated, and in three of the four instances when the incumbent

president was either prohibited by the Twenty-second Amendment from running again (Eisenhower in 1960 and Reagan in 1988) or declined to do so (Truman in 1952 and Johnson in 1968), the incumbent vice president won his party's nomination. The exception occurred in 1952 when President Harry Truman chose not to run for reelection and the vice president, seventy-five-year-old Alben Barkley, ranked only sixth of the fourteen candidates nominated on the first ballot at the Democratic convention. Stevenson became the nominee. One can argue that the presidency itself has been the major source of candidates for the office, and the principal variation in recruitment has occurred in the out-party.

There are no guarantees that an incumbent president or vice president will win the party's nomination, but it is enormously difficult for the party in power to remove these figures from the national ticket. Incumbents have considerable advantages when it comes to winning renomination, as demonstrated by Gerald Ford in 1976 and Jimmy Carter in 1980. Both faced stiff challenges within their own parties, but overcame them for several reasons: party leaders are reluctant to admit to the voters that they made a mistake four years earlier; incumbents can exercise considerable discretion in directing federal programs toward politically important areas or in making executive branch appointments; and presidents enjoy far greater media exposure than others seeking the nomination. As a result, even unpopular presidents tend to be renominated. The Republicans chose Herbert Hoover again in 1932 in the midst of the Great Depression, and the Democrats renominated Carter when both inflation and unemployment were high, Americans were being held hostage in Iran, and Soviet troops occupied Afghanistan.

Incumbent vice presidents are more likely to win their party's nomination today than in the past.[14] Recent presidential candidates have chosen running mates who are arguably more capable than their predecessors, which makes these individuals more viable prospects for the presidency, although Bush's selection of Sen. Dan Quayle of Indiana raised questions concerning his experience and maturity. Moreover, presidents now assign their vice presidents meaningful responsibilities, including political party activities (especially campaigning in off-year elections), liaison assignments with social groups, and diplomatic missions to foreign countries. As the position's visibility and significance has increased, so have the political chances of its occupants improved.[15]

If it was an asset in securing the party's nomination, the vice presidency seemed to be a liability in winning the general election until Bush broke a 152–year-old tradition of losing campaigns. Richard Nixon and Hubert Humphrey lost as incumbents in 1960 and 1968, as did Walter Mondale in 1984 after four years in the private sector.

Senators and Governors. Since 1932 the party out of power has nominated nine governors, three senators, two former vice presidents, one general (Dwight Eisenhower), and one businessman (Wendell Willkie). (See Table 2-1.) Both major parties have looked to governors as promising candidates except for the period from 1960 to 1972 when Sens. John Kennedy (D–1960), Barry Goldwater (R–1964), and George McGovern (D–1972), as well as former vice president Nixon (R–1968) won the nomination. Governorships later regained prominence with the nomination of former governors Carter (D–1976) and Ronald Reagan (R–1980) as well as sitting governors Michael Dukakis (D–1988) and Bill Clinton (D–1992). Only once did the party out of power not turn to a governor during this most recent period when former vice president Mondale was the Democratic nominee in 1984. Mondale, however, shared a significant characteristic with Carter and Reagan: all were out of office when they sought the nomination, which gave them the freedom to run a full-time campaign.

It is possible to argue that these patterns understate the importance of

Table 2-1 Principal Experience of In- and Out-Party Candidates Before Gaining Nomination, 1932–1992

Election Year	In Party	Out Party
1932	President (R)	Governor (D)
1936	President (D)	Governor (R)
1940	President (D)	Businessman (R)
1944	President (D)	Governor (R)
1948	President (D)	Governor (R)
1952	Governor (D)	General/educator (R)
1956	President (R)	Governor (former) (D)
1960	Vice president (R)	Senator (D)
1964	President (D)	Senator (R)
1968	Vice president (D)	Vice president (former) (R)
1972	President (R)	Senator (D)
1976	President (R)	Governor (former) (D)
1980	President (D)	Governor (former) (R)
1984	President (R)	Vice president (former) (D)
1988	Vice president (R)	Governor (D)
1992	President (R)	Governor (D)

the Senate as a recruiting ground for president. Certainly, many senators have sought their parties' presidential nomination since the early 1950s. Senators share the political and media spotlight focused on the capital, enjoy the opportunity to address major public problems and develop a record in foreign affairs, and usually can pursue the presidency without giving up their legislative seat. Nonetheless, only twice in American history have senators been elected directly to the White House (Harding in 1920 and Kennedy in 1960).[16]

Instead, the Senate has served as an important stepping stone to the *vice presidency*, which then gave its occupants the inside track either to assume the presidency through succession or to win nomination on their own. This role of the Senate can be seen in the careers of Vice Presidents Truman, Nixon, Johnson, Humphrey, and Mondale, who served as senators immediately before assuming their executive posts. Gerald Ford, who succeeded to the presidency when Nixon resigned in 1974, had moved into the vice presidency from the House of Representatives, also the principal elective experience of George Bush (although a decade earlier) before he joined Ronald Reagan on the national ticket in 1980. Service in the Senate, therefore, *has* been an important source of experience for presidents since 1932, but almost all have needed seasoning in the vice presidency.

Although the office regained prominence during the 1970s and 1980s, the competitive position of governors seeking the presidency may be weaker today than in the past. Governors today have less potential for winning the presidential nomination than they did prior to 1968. It is difficult for them to gain national publicity unless they serve in states with large cities that function as national media centers. Governor Clinton of Arkansas was an exception to this rule. Nor do governors have responsibilities of consequence in foreign affairs; instead, they are more closely tied to their home states, particularly when the state legislature is in session, than are senators. They may serve only short stints in office either because of legal limitations on their tenure or because of public disappointment at their failure to solve major domestic problems without increasing taxes. Becoming sufficiently well known to be a viable presidential candidate is a major task.

Carter's election in 1976 and Reagan's bid for the nomination that year and election in 1980 indicate, however, that governors may enjoy some advantages as candidates, particularly if they are *not* in office when they seek the presidency, a point driven home by Dukakis's defeat in 1988. Unlike Dukakis, Carter and Reagan were free to devote themselves full time to the demanding task of winning the nomination, an opportunity not available to the senators who sought the presidency in both of those years. Clinton, however, secured the nomination and the presidency in 1992 while serving as governor. Governors can claim valuable executive experience in managing large-scale public enterprises and thousands of state government employees in contrast to a senator's essentially legislative duties and direction of a small personal staff. A governor's on-the-job training is likely to be attractive to citizens concerned with the burgeoning costs of government and the problems of controlling the federal bureaucracy. Moreover, the public's concern with foreign affairs has declined since 1976 and been replaced by anxiety over the domestic economy, a shift that may counteract some of the advantages senators held over governors as presidential candidates during the 1960s and 1970s. This shift in public attitudes was evident in 1992 when Clinton benefited from the cold war's reduced prominence.

Personal Characteristics of Candidates

Although millions meet the formal requirements for president, far fewer meet the informal criteria that have guided choices in the past. Most constraining have been the limits imposed by social conventions on gender and race. So far only males of European heritage have been nominated for president by either of the two major parties, although several women and African Americans have waged national campaigns over the past twenty years, and former representative Geraldine Ferraro of New York was the Democrats' 1984 nominee for vice president. Presidential aspirants also have had to pass other "tests" based on personal characteristics, although these informal requirements have undergone change over the past three decades.[17]

Until 1960 it seemed that candidates had to meet unspoken demographic and religious requirements—that they hail from English ethnic stock and practice a Protestant religion. These tests have weakened in the intervening years. John Kennedy's successful candidacy in 1960 challenged the traditional preference for Protestants; Alfred Smith, also a Catholic, was nominated by the Democrats in 1928 but lost the general election. Today, little is made of the fact when Catholics pursue the nomination. Republican senator Barry Goldwater was the first nominee from a partly Jewish background. Other recent candidates have come from Irish, Norwegian, and Greek heritage, suggesting that the traditional preference for English stock has weakened.

Representing an idealized version of home and family life also seemed to be essential to winning a party's nomination. These criteria have undergone modest change, but other considerations may have taken their place. Nelson Rockefeller's 1963 divorce from his wife of more than thirty years and his rapid remarriage virtually ensured the failure of his efforts to win the Republican nomination in 1964 and 1968. The marital status of several later candidates was an issue, but in 1980 Ronald Reagan became the country's first president to have divorced and remarried.

Changes in public expectations of candidates coincided with more general changes in public attitudes and behavior regarding divorce. However, other moral and ethical tests may have become more important. Gary Hart's widely reported extramarital affair ended his presidential hopes for 1988, even though he began the campaign as the clear front-runner. Bill Clinton's alleged extramarital relationships also became an issue in 1992. Sen. Joseph Biden's campaign foundered on charges that he had plagiarized campaign speeches and misrepresented his record in 1987. Although traditional moral and ethical tests regarding divorce may have changed, it is not clear which standards will continue to receive media attention and elicit public response, particularly in an era when religion and political activism seem to mix more readily than in the past.

Thus, several of the informal qualifications applied to the presidency have altered with the passage of time, probably in response to changes in the nomination process itself as well as broader currents in U.S. society. One observer suggests that the proliferation of presidential primaries "provides a forum in which prejudices can be addressed openly."[18] The vice presidential nomination offers a way to confront traditional social views indirectly, as was the case with Ferraro. We might expect something similar to happen with an African American candidate in the near future.

The development of a more common culture and the nationalization of American life in general, brought about by modern communication and transportation, have reduced the importance of parochial concerns—the candidates' religious, ethnic, or geographical background—and increased the emphasis on their experience in the national political arena and their association with national issues. Moreover, as other groups that are still socially or politically disadvantaged—African Americans, women, and immigrants from Asia, Mexico, and eastern and southern Europe—begin to occupy governorships and seats in the U.S. Senate, they will enhance their chances of becoming serious candidates for the presidency.[19]

Competing for the Nomination

Once the pool of eligible candidates is established, the selection process begins. This phase has two major components: choosing delegates to the two parties' national conventions and selecting the nominees at the conventions. By far the more complicated of these steps, the selection of delegates has been the principal focus of party reform efforts since 1968. As already mentioned, these reforms have fundamentally altered the convention's role: once a deliberative assembly, it now anoints the winner of the primary and caucus contests as the party's standard bearer and serves as a backdrop for launching the ticket's general election campaign. Should the convention begin without a distinct front-runner, deliberation would once again be possible, a situation made more likely if many candidates pursue the nomination.

Prior to the conventions, candidates crisscross the country in pursuit of delegates, who then attend the convention to select the party's nominee. Delegates are chosen by three methods: they can be named by party leaders such as members of the party's state committee; be elected by a state convention attended by delegates themselves selected at caucuses (party meetings) held in precincts, wards, counties, or congressional districts; or chosen by direct election in presidential primaries. In 1992 delegate selection began February 10 when nearly 30,000 Iowans began a four-tiered process to select national convention delegates. In the weeks following these local precinct caucuses, county and congressional district conventions were held prior to the June 20 Iowa state conventions where fifty-seven Democratic and twenty-three Republican delegates were selected.

The first presidential primary of 1992 was held in New Hampshire February 18. Delegate selection extended into June when four states held primaries, the last of thirty-seven Republican and thirty-six Democratic primary contests, including those in the District of Columbia. Through this complex structure, the Republicans chose 2,210 delegates to attend their national convention, and the Democrats selected 4,288 for theirs.

Table 2-2 Delegates to 1992 Presidential Conventions by Selection Procedure

Selection Method	Delegates (N)	Percentage of Convention
Democrats		
Primaries	2,868	66.9%
Caucuses	648	15.1
Superdelegates	772	18.0
Total	4,288	
Republicans		
Primaries	1,855	83.9
Caucuses	355	16.1
Total	2,210	

Sources: Democratic National Committee; Republican National Committee.

Consistent with post–1968 reforms, most of these delegates were chosen through primaries—two-thirds of the Democratic delegates and more than three-fourths of the Republican delegates *(see Table 2-2)*. Millions of Americans participate in the process: in 1988, for example, 23.23 million voted in Democratic primary elections, and another 12.17 million in Republican primaries.[20] Caucus participation is less easily calculated, but in 1988 an estimated 855,000 attended twenty-two Democratic caucuses, and 236,000 attended nine of the eighteen Republican caucuses for which figures are available.[21]

In truth, the nomination contest begins much earlier than January of the election year. For example, in pursuing the 1988 nomination, former Delaware governor Pierre "Pete" DuPont officially declared his candidacy in September 1986; thirteen others followed suit in 1987, nine before the Fourth of July. By starting their campaigns early, candidates hope to amass the financial backing, attract the media attention, and generate the popular support necessary to ensure eventual victory. This trend toward early announcements slowed in 1992 when only one candidate, Paul Tsongas, declared for the nomination before June 30, 1991. Potential candidates were deterred by the strong public approval still expressed for President Bush.

The Nomination Campaign

The nomination campaign is a winnowing process in which each of the two major parties eliminates from the pool of potential candidates all but the one who will represent the party in the general election. As political scientist Austin Ranney points out, the nomination phase of the campaign is more important than the election stage, because "the parties' nominating processes eliminate far more presidential possibilities than do the voters' electing processes."[22] A nomination campaign is long, arduous, and relatively unstructured: aspirants typically do not know how many opponents they will face or who they will be; candidates start up to two years early and drop out along the way; and, instead of a simultaneous nationwide campaign, the competition takes place in stages with candidates hopscotching the nation in pursuit of votes. Planning and conducting such a campaign are enormously difficult. Most first-time candidates must organize a nationwide political effort, a task that dwarfs the campaign required to win a Senate seat or governorship in even the largest states.

Preliminary planning is essential, and presidential hopefuls spend considerable time before January of the election year laying the groundwork for their effort. Journalist Arthur Hadley calls this period the "invisible primary," a testing ground for the would-be president waged behind the scenes to determine whether his or her candidacy is viable.[23] Candidates must assemble a staff to develop campaign strategy and identify a larger group of people willing to do the advance work necessary to organize states for the upcoming primaries and caucuses. Visits are made to party organizations throughout the country, but especially in pivotal states such as Iowa and New Hampshire, to curry favor with activists. Competition often takes on the trappings of a full-fledged campaign with candidates broadcasting television ads, engaging in debates, and seeking to finish well in prenomination popularity contests or "straw polls."

Because their coverage provides name recognition and potentially positive publicity, developing a favorable relationship with the media is crucial during this phase of the contest. Those who are ignored because reporters and commentators do not regard them as serious contenders find it almost impossible to become candidates. Adverse publicity can seriously damage a candidacy: Hart's and Biden's 1988 campaigns were scuttled during the "invisible primary" stage.

Financing Nomination Campaigns

It is now more important than ever that candidates for the nomination begin raising funds early. Candidates can qualify to receive federal funds that match individual contributions of $250 or less if they can raise

$100,000 in individual contributions, with at least $5,000 collected in twenty different states. By checking a box on their federal income tax forms, taxpayers authorize the government to set aside $1.00 of their tax payments for public financing of campaigns, but with recent expenditures exceeding revenues, the voluntary financing arrangement may be endangered. Candidates who accept public financing—and since 1976 only Republican John Connally has chosen not to do so—must also accept limitations on total expenditures and a cap on spending in individual states that is based on population. For 1992 the national expenditure ceiling for the prenomination campaign was $33.1 million.

By providing partial funding of nomination campaigns, reformers sought to replace the financial support of a small number of "fat cats" who previously bankrolled candidates, with a system based on citizen contributions.[24] In 1992, eleven candidates qualified for $41.8 million in matching funds, down from $67.5 million in 1988. The federal government also provided $10.6 million to the Democratic and Republican parties to finance their nominating conventions. The Federal Election Commission, a bipartisan body of six members nominated by the president and confirmed by the Senate, oversees the administration of these provisions.

Despite the establishment of a new public financing system, loopholes remain. One of the largest in 1988 was the precandidacy PAC (political action committee). Candidates for the nomination remain undeclared for as long as possible and establish a PAC to finance their pre-announcement activities. Nine of the major party candidates in 1988 established such PACs, which collectively spent $25.2 million. Vice President Bush led the way with $10.8 million, followed by Sen. Robert Dole, R-Kan., ($6.54 million) and Rep. Jack Kemp, R-N.Y., ($4.16 million).[25] Once candidacy is officially announced, the statutory restrictions apply.

Although loopholes persist, campaign finance legislation has had a significant effect on presidential nominations. The sources and techniques for raising money have changed radically. Candidates now get funding from a large number of individual contributors, often through direct mail solicitation.[26] Public funds also open the door for people who formerly could not afford to mount a nomination campaign because large contributors would not support them. Even third party candidates, such as Lenora Fulani of the New Alliance party, qualified for federal funds at the nominating stage in 1988 and 1992. Financial disparities among candidates may not be as great as once was the case, but candidate resources are still unequal. In 1988 and 1992 George Bush easily outdistanced the financing of his competition. Michael Dukakis and Bill Clinton led the Democratic fields in fund raising in the same years.[27] Superior financial resources enable candidates to compete in more of the early nomination contests, help them expand their fund-raising lead, enable them to survive poor results, and make them stronger in later primaries. Failing to do well in early caucus and primary contests means more than losing delegates to opponents; it also means that contributions stop. Moreover, under the campaign finance law, federal matching funds must be cut off within thirty days if a candidate receives less than 10 percent of the votes in two consecutive primaries.

Candidates must decide not only how to raise funds but also how to spend them. In the face of overall campaign spending limits as well as expenditure limits in each state, money must be carefully allocated. Because they want to win the first primaries and caucuses, candidates are inclined to spend heavily in the very early stage of the campaign, which can create problems in later competition.

Dynamics of the Contest

Candidates who begin the election year as leaders in the public opinion polls frequently go on to win nomination. This pattern prevailed from 1936 through 1968. In four more recent contests, however, the front-runner among Democrats ultimately was replaced by a dark horse. George McGovern trailed Edmund Muskie in January 1972 with only 3 percent support; Jimmy Carter was the choice of only 4 percent in January 1976, with Hubert Humphrey leading; Gary Hart led Michael Dukakis 23 percent to 16 percent in January 1988, with Dukakis's support rising from only 3 percent a year earlier. Bill Clinton, with 17 percent, trailed Jerry Brown's 21 percent in January 1992 and stood in fifth place among Democratic contenders with just 9 percent support two months earlier. Leaders in the polls, therefore, cannot afford to relax after achieving early popularity: the final choice of the nominee depends on presidential primaries and caucus-convention contests.

When deciding which contests they should emphasize in their nomination campaigns, candidates take into account the premium placed on competing in as many locations as funds will allow. This is especially true for Democrats whose rules call for proportional allocation of delegates: so long as candidates achieve the minimum of at least 15 percent of the vote, they are awarded a share of delegates proportional to the vote share.[28] A critical consideration, however, is the date of the primary. The earliest contest, traditionally New Hampshire, usually attracts most of the major contenders because it is the first test of rank-and-file voter sentiment. Although the number of New Hampshire delegates is small—in 1992, only 24 of 4,288 Democratic delegates, and 23 of 2,210 Republican delegates—victory ensures immediate attention, as it did with Kennedy in 1960 and Carter in 1976. Paul Tsongas was the unexpected victor in 1992 after Bill Clinton was damaged by revelations about his personal life, but the publicity greatly increased Clinton's name recognition. If a candidate loses, but draws a greater percentage of the vote than expected, the media may interpret the results as a "moral" victory. Eugene McCarthy in 1968, George McGovern in 1972, and Patrick Buchanan in 1992 benefited from such results. The relatively small New Hampshire electorate also enables candidates with modest financial resources to conduct labor-intensive campaigns.[29]

A new twist in the 1988 campaign was the round of primaries held on Tuesday, March 8—Super Tuesday. Twenty states selected delegates, sixteen through primaries and four through caucuses. In 1992 only eleven states participated in Super Tuesday, but the impact was more consistent with the Democratic designers' intent to boost the chances of a moderate to conservative candidate. Clinton won all six of the southern primaries and two caucuses, while Tsongas, his principal rival, claimed victories in just two primaries and one caucus. Texas and Florida, with the largest delegate totals, went to Clinton; in 1988 they had gone to the nonsoutherner Dukakis. Bush, who swept all sixteen of the 1988 Super Tuesday primaries, repeated this success in 1992 by winning all of the March 10 contests against Patrick Buchanan and David Duke.

Although smaller in 1992, Super Tuesday contests selected 783 Democratic delegates and 403 Republican delegates, roughly 18 percent of their respective convention totals. Because of these large stakes, observers have termed the process *front-loaded*, meaning that a significant number of delegates is chosen early. In all, twenty-three states selected delegates between March 3 and March 10, and nearly one-half of all Democratic convention delegates were named by March 18.

If early contests provide no definite leader, later primaries may reveal shifts in voter preference or become the important contests. The California primary, for example, traditionally has occurred near the end of the primary season. In this position, Golden State voters might determine a party's nominee. Both Goldwater in 1964 and McGovern in 1972 owed their ultimate selection to primary victories in California, which delivered the largest bloc of convention delegates in a winner-take-all contest, a rule that still holds for Republicans.

State caucuses operate in the shadow of the primaries, although they remain important for candidates able to mobilize an intensely motivated group of supporters. But the Iowa caucuses diminished in importance as a launching pad for presidential contenders in 1988 and 1992. For example, in 1988 Richard Gephardt and Robert Dole came in first in Iowa, but dropped out of the nomination contest by the end of March; in 1992 contenders for the Democratic nomination recognized the dominant position of Tom Harkin, the home-state senator, and chose not to compete in Iowa. When primaries do not produce a clear victor, candidates devote more attention to delegates chosen in caucus-convention states. In 1976 both Gerald Ford and Ronald Reagan diligently pursued delegates chosen in Republican party caucuses and conventions, especially in the period immediately preceding the Republican convention. In the end, Ford owed his nomination to the previously uncommitted delegations, such as Mississippi, that cast their ballots at the national convention in his favor. Similarly, Mondale was forty votes short of a first-ballot nomination in 1984 and aggressively pursued support among uncommitted delegates from caucus states to achieve his success.

Media Influence and Campaign Consultants

The media play an enormous role in the nomination campaign. They interpret results and serve as the principal vehicle for candidates to make appeals, both paid and unpaid. As the nomination process has grown in complexity, the influence of the media also has grown. Candidates who must campaign in more than a score of states within ten days, as they did in 1992, necessarily rely on the media to communicate with large numbers of potential voters. Televised advertisements, network- and station-sponsored debates, and prime-time news coverage are critical to candidates' efforts. Talk-show appearances became an important avenue in 1992.

The media tend to focus attention on the game aspects of the early contests, particularly those in Iowa and New Hampshire. Typically, they use a winner-take-all principle that, regardless of how narrow the victory or the number of popular votes involved, gives virtually all the publicity to the victorious candidate. In the 1976 Iowa caucuses, for example, Carter was declared the "clear winner" and described as leading the pack of contenders even though he received only about 14,000 votes, 28 percent of the 50,000 cast; he actually trailed the "uncommitted" group.[30] A surprise showing by a runner-up may garner most attention: after winning a mere 16 percent of the votes to finish an unexpected second in the Iowa caucuses in 1984, Hart got as much publicity as Mondale, who captured three times as many votes.[31]

As the elements of campaigning discussed in the preceding sections suggest, presidential nominating campaigns are highly complex operations that call for a variety of specialists. Pollsters help candidates assess their nomination prospects and provide vital feedback on voters' reactions to the candidates and their campaigns, on the issues that concern people, and on the attitudes of social and economic groups about such issues. Media consultants help candidates develop a favorable image, write their speeches, and plan their television appearances, and direct mail specialists raise money and get out the vote. Beginning with the 1952 presidential election, candidates have turned to political consultants, rather than party officials, to organize these diverse operations, develop strategy, and manage the overall campaign.

As the fate of presidential candidates passed from a small group of party professionals to rank-and-file voters, media-based appeals grew in importance. Voter attitudes evolve during the course of the nomination contest, in large part because of the media's influence. In the early stages of the contest the media help determine who the viable candidates are; then, once the state primaries and caucuses begin, they label the "winners" and "losers," often influencing the results of future state contests, as voters as well as contributors gravitate toward the winners and desert the losers. Public opinion polls reflecting voters' presidential preferences are a fixture of media coverage.

Moreover, all these elements—the attitudes of voters, the media, the polls, and the state contest results—influence one another. Candidates who receive favorable treatment from the media tend to do well in the primaries, and their showing there, in turn, raises their standings in the polls. Favorable polls impress media representatives as well as political activists and many rank-and-file voters, leading to more victories for the poll leaders in both nonprimary and primary contests. The result of this reinforcement process is that by the time the delegates gather for their party's national convention, one candidate usually has enough delegates to receive the nomination.[32] The last remaining hurdle for the front-runner to navigate is for the most part automatic—the party's national convention.

The National Convention

No part of the selection process has undergone more dramatic change than the presidential nominating conventions. Long the province of king-makers, today's conventions are largely media extravaganzas carefully choreographed to project images designed to reawaken party loyalty, appeal to contemporary public concerns, and project the most desirable aspects of the newly anointed presidential ticket. In short, the national convention is important to presidential candidates for two reasons. First, whatever may have happened during the long search for delegates, the actual nomination occurs at the convention. Second, the convention provides opportunities for candidates to strengthen their chances to win the general election.

Nominating the Ticket

Since the early 1950s conventions have offered little drama about the choice of the presidential nominee. In the twenty-four conventions held by the two major parties since World War II, only two nominees—Thomas Dewey in 1948 and Adlai Stevenson in 1952—failed to win a majority of the convention votes on the first ballot. In all other cases, victory has gone to the candidate who arrived at the convention with the largest number of pledged delegates.

Selecting the vice presidential nominee is the convention's final chore and the only chance to create any suspense. Although in theory the delegates make the choice, it has been a matter of political custom since 1940 to allow presidential nominees to pick their own running mates. Typically, the nominees confer with leaders whose judgment they trust, and, when they make their decisions, the word is passed to the delegates. Parties traditionally attempt to balance the ticket—that is, broaden its appeal by selecting a person who differs in certain ways from the presidential nominee. Bush's links to the Eastern establishment and moderate wings of the Republican party complemented the conservative, western

Reagan in 1980. Ferraro balanced the 1984 Democratic ticket geographically and other ways: the first woman to serve as a major party candidate in a presidential contest, she was also the first Italian-American.

In 1988 the media reaction to Bush's selection of Dan Quayle nearly overshadowed the Republican convention. Quayle brought generational balance, a new criterion, to the ticket, and he was enthusiastically supported by the party's conservative wing. His major disadvantage was the attention he drew. The media raised questions about Quayle's ability to perform as president should the need arise, his service in the National Guard during the Vietnam War, and his modest academic performance. The Democrats sought to resurrect the Boston-Austin axis forged by the Kennedy-Johnson ticket in 1960, but the choice of Lloyd Bentsen also produced problems. Republicans jumped on the policy differences between the Democratic candidates, and Jesse Jackson's supporters were upset when he was not given the ticket's second position. In 1992 Quayle remained on the Republican ticket despite speculation about his replacement. Clinton violated political tradition by selecting Al Gore, a fellow southerner and baby boomer, rather than balancing the ticket, but the choice was well received by the party faithful and probably helped Clinton erode Republican support in this crucial region.

The final night of the convention is devoted to acceptance speeches. The presidential nominee tries to make peace with former competitors and to reunite various party factions that have confronted one another during the long campaign and the hectic days of the convention. Major party figures usually come to the stage and pledge their support for the winner in the upcoming campaign.

Conducting Party Business

Several decisions that precede the nomination balloting can significantly affect both the choice of nominee and the outcome of the general election. The convention's location may boost the chances of a favorite son candidate—for example, Chicago for Adlai Stevenson in 1952—or prove an insurmountable disadvantage, such as the Democrats' 1968 debacle in the same city. At times credentials committees have had to resolve disputes between contending delegations; their decisions on who would be considered the official delegates could influence the outcome. George McGovern's selection by the Democrats in 1972 rested on the refusal to seat delegates chosen through means inconsistent with party guidelines adopted since the previous convention. Candidates trailing the front-runner sometimes use a rules question as their last-ditch effort to derail the nomination, a ploy attempted by Reagan in 1976 and Sen. Edward Kennedy in 1980. Defeated candidates also may lay the groundwork for the next competition and seek new rules more favorable to their next candidacy. Jackson forces used this strategy at the 1988 Democratic convention, but Jackson then declined to run in 1992.

Parties continue the writing and adopting of a convention platform, although participants acknowledge that winning presidential candidates may disavow planks with which they disagree. Because delegates, party leaders, and major groups affiliated with the party have strong feelings about some issues, the platform provides an opportunity to resolve differences and find a politically palatable position.[33] Civil rights and the Vietnam War once prompted major disagreements within the Democratic party; civil rights, foreign policy, and abortion have been major bones of contention among Republicans.

Despite intraparty differences, conventions provide strong incentives for compromise, to bring back to the fold a disgruntled segment of the party that might otherwise offer only lukewarm support during the fall election or launch a third party effort. To avoid such damage, almost every presidential candidate decides to provide major rivals and their supporters with concessions in the platform. President Ford in 1976 allowed Ronald Reagan's views to prevail on several major platform provisions, including criticism of détente, the administration's strategy for dealing with the Soviet Union. In 1988 Dukakis accepted modified versions of nine Jesse Jackson platform positions in exchange for Jackson's acceptance of a shorter, less-detailed party statement.

The General Election

With nominees selected, the nation moves into the general election period. Candidates must develop new political appeals for this stage of the process, which is a one-on-one contest that pits the nominees of the two major parties against each other (although a strong independent candidate like Ross Perot may also run). The campaign's audience increases greatly—more than twice as many people vote in the general election as participate in the nomination process. Candidates and staff members therefore must decide how they can win the support of these new voters as well as appeal to people who identify with the other party and partisans who backed losing candidates for the nomination. A further complication is time: this nationwide phase of the presidential contest is compressed into a mere ten weeks, traditionally running from Labor Day to election day.

The general election phase differs from the nomination phase for two reasons: the way the electoral college works and the distinctive provisions of the campaign finance laws. Compared to changes effected in the nomination stage, the constitutional requirements surrounding the president's election have been remarkably stable over time, but campaign finance laws have undergone significant change since 1972. Both are critical considerations in how the campaign is waged.

The Electoral College

To understand how candidates plan and carry out their general election strategies, it is necessary to keep in mind the ultimate goal, which is to win a majority of electoral college votes. Two hundred years ago delegates to the constitutional convention rejected the two most popular plans for choosing the president. They felt that selection by Congress violated the separation of powers principle, but they did not have enough confidence in the people's wisdom to approve direct popular election.[34] The newly devised plan was complicated: each state legislature would choose electors, by whatever means it desired, equal to its total number of senators and representatives in Congress (but none of the electors could be members of Congress or hold other national office); the individual electors would assemble at a fixed time in their respective state capitals and cast two votes each for president; the votes would be transmitted to the seat of government and opened and counted during a joint session of Congress. Whoever received the largest number of electoral votes, provided a majority—one more than half—had been obtained, would be declared the winner. If no candidate received a majority, the House of Representatives, voting by states (one state delegation, one vote), would choose the president from among the five candidates receiving the highest number of electoral votes. After the president was chosen, the person with the next highest number of electoral votes became the vice president. If two or more of these contenders received an equal number of electoral votes, the Senate would choose the vice president from among them. As noted, these procedures were modified in 1804 by the Twelfth Amendment, which established separate balloting for president and vice president and reduced the field to three candidates if the House and Senate had to vote.

This method of selection resolved the struggle between large and small states, upheld states' rights by allowing the state legislatures to decide how the electors should be chosen, and left open the possibility that electors could reflect the popular vote for president in their state. With the rapid expansion of popular participation, state legislators began giving the right to choose electors to the general electorate; by 1836 all states except South Carolina had adopted such rules, and the latter did so in 1860.

At first, electoral votes were determined by congressional districts—the winner of a popular vote plurality in each district would receive the associated electoral vote, with the statewide popular vote winner getting the two electoral votes representing senators. Legislatures soon, however, began to adopt the "unit" or "general-ticket" rule, whereby all the state's electoral votes went to the candidate who received the plurality of the statewide popular vote. This rule benefited the state's majority party and maximized the state's influence in the election by permitting it to throw all its electoral votes to one candidate. By 1836 the district plan had vanished and the unit system had taken its place. Since then two states have returned to the old plan: Maine has followed the district plan since 1969, and Nebraska adopted it for 1992.

The final product is a strange method for choosing a chief executive. Although most Americans view the system as a popular election, it is not. When voters mark their ballots, the vote actually determines which slate of electors pledged to support the party's presidential candidate will have the opportunity to vote. In a few states, electors' names appear on the ballot either with or without the presidential candidate's name. The electors are party loyalists, chosen in primaries, at conventions, or by state committees. In mid-December the electors associated with the winning candidate meet in their state capitals to cast ballots. (About one-third of the states attempt by law to bind the electors to vote for the popular-vote winner, but there is some question whether such laws are constitutional.) The electoral votes are transmitted to Washington, D.C., and counted early in January of the following year. Next, the presiding officer of the Senate, who is the incumbent vice president, announces the outcome before a joint session of Congress. If, as usually happens, one candidate receives an absolute majority of the electoral votes, currently 270, the vice president officially declares that candidate to be president. Because the popular vote winner usually wins in the electoral college as well, we call this final stage of the selection process the "validation" of the popular vote outcome.

Financing the General Election

The financial resources needed to mount a nationwide campaign are significantly greater than those required to win the nomination. For the general election, complete public financing is provided to nominees of the major parties, and any party that won 25 percent or more of the popular vote in the last presidential election is considered a major party. In the 1992 presidential election, the federal government gave each major party candidate $55.24 million, up from $46.1 million in 1988. Ross Perot sought no federal funds. To qualify, nominees must not accept other direct contributions to their campaign. Candidates of minor parties, those that won between 5 percent and 25 percent of the vote in the previous election, receive partial public financing. Candidates of parties ineligible for public financing (those that won less than 5 percent of the vote in the previous election) can be partially reimbursed after the current election if they receive at least 5 percent of that vote.

Campaign expenditures other than those from public funding may be made from two sources. There is no limit on *independent campaign expenditures*, which are made by individuals or political committees that advocate the defeat or election of a presidential candidate but are not made in conjunction with a candidate's campaign. In addition, a 1979 amendment to the campaign finance law permits state and local party organizations to spend money for any purpose except campaign advertising and the hiring of outside personnel. These funds, commonly called *soft money*, are used for grass-roots activities such as distributing campaign buttons, stickers, and yard signs, registering voters, and transporting them to the polls. Spending from both these sources has grown considerably: in 1988 there were independent expenditures of $10.1 million, and soft money totaled $43 million.[35]

Since public financing was introduced in the 1976 election, major party candidates need no longer depend on wealthy contributors and other private sources to finance their campaigns. The law also has the effect of limiting and equalizing the expenditures made by the two major party candidates, which is a distinct advantage for the Democrats because Republican presidential candidates historically have had more money to spend than their opponents.[36] Finally, the law benefits the candidates of the two major parties, who receive full public financing of their general election campaigns, in contrast to minor party candidates, who are entitled to only partial financing, if any at all. The funds available to cover the 1996 election may not be sufficient: the FEC projects a balance of $124 million, which would eliminate all funding for primary campaigns and fall short of general election needs.

Targeting the Campaign

As in the nomination process, presidential candidates must decide which states will be the focus of their efforts in the fall campaign. By far the most important consideration is the electoral college. The candidate's task is clear: to win the presidency, he or she must win a majority—270—of the 538 electoral votes.[37] This fact places a premium on carrying the states with the largest number of electoral votes (see Figure 2–2). In 1992, by winning the eleven largest states—California, New York, Texas, Florida, Pennsylvania, Illinois, Ohio, Michigan, New Jersey, North Carolina, and Georgia—a candidate could win the presidency while losing the other thirty-nine states. Naturally, candidates from both major political parties concentrate their personal visits on the most populous states.[38]

Another element that affects candidates' decisions on where to campaign is the political situation in a particular state—that is, whether the state generally goes to one party's candidate or whether it swings back and forth from one election to the next. Distinctly one-party states are likely to be slighted by both of the major party candidates—both will think it a waste of time although for different reasons. Swing states with large populations naturally draw a good deal of attention from presidential candidates of both parties.

In formulating campaign strategy, therefore, candidates and their advisers start with the electoral map as modified by calculations of probable success. The electoral college creates fifty-one separate presidential contests—fifty states plus the District of Columbia—based on the winner-take-all principle, the goal of which is a popular vote victory in each, no matter how small the margin of victory may be. The winner in a large state benefits from the unit or general-ticket system by getting all of the state's electoral votes. In 1988 George Bush, the popular vote winner in California, received all forty-seven electoral votes, almost 18 percent of the total required for election, although he defeated Michael Dukakis by just

Figure 2.2 State Size by Number of Electoral Votes, 1992

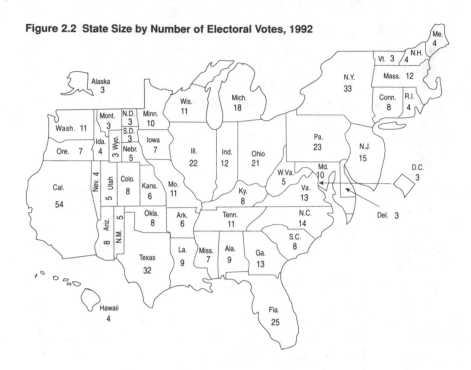

352,684 votes out of the 9.757 million cast, a mere 3.6 percent margin of victory. In 1992 Bill Clinton won California, now an even larger electoral prize with fifty-four votes, 20 percent of the total needed for election.

Electoral votes were reapportioned for the 1992 presidential election, reflecting the results of the 1990 census. Eight states gained seats in the House of Representatives, and thirteen lost seats; the states' electoral vote totals were adjusted accordingly, with political influence moving (along with the population) from the Northeast/Midwest to the South/ Southwest. The biggest gains were recorded in California—its delegation increased by seven seats—Florida (four seats), and Texas (three seats). On the other end, New York lost three seats, while Illinois, Michigan, Ohio, and Pennsylvania lost two seats each, and several other states lost one seat.[39]

The regions that have been important in recent presidential contests are the Middle Atlantic states (New York, Pennsylvania, and New Jersey) and the Midwest states of Ohio, Michigan, Illinois, and Missouri. Together these seven highly industrial states controlled 155 electoral votes in the

1984 and 1988 elections. These states also tend to be highly competitive, which means that campaign efforts there can be very important in deciding which candidate prevails. Despite their collective loss of twelve electoral votes for the 1992 election due to reapportionment, these states once again proved to be a major election battleground.

Before 1992 the Democrats had confronted a particularly difficult strategic situation: in looking at presidential balloting between 1968 and 1984, some commentators described the Republicans as having constructed an "electoral lock" on the presidency because twenty-three states with 202 electoral votes had gone for the Republican candidate in each of the five elections. Bush carried all but two of these states in 1988. Democratic candidates had won only the District of Columbia with the same level of consistency.[40] Several West Coast, Rocky Mountain, and Midwest states comprised this staunchly Republican cohort along with a few surprises such as Illinois, New Jersey, and Virginia.

A good part of the Democrats' problem can be traced to the historic realignment of the South in presidential politics. Long a bastion of solid Democratic support and critical to their candidates' success—no Democrat had ever won the White House without carrying a majority of southern states—southern voters have not supported the party's nominee since 1976 when they helped to elect Jimmy Carter, the first southern presidential nominee other than Lyndon Baines Johnson, who had succeeded to the office, since before the Civil War. Even that support evaporated in 1980 when only Georgia supported its favorite son. No southern state voted for the Democratic ticket in 1984 or 1988. The Solid South was a Republican stronghold until Clinton cut into Bush's support in 1992. Democrats have been strongest in the Northeast and mid-Atlantic states, but Clinton added support from the West, Midwest, and the Mountain States. In 1992 the Democrats won each state that had voted for Dukakis and added all but one of the twelve where he had won at least 45 percent of the vote in 1988. This provided the base needed for victory.[41]

Electoral college considerations remain crucial throughout the campaign. Bush's strategy in 1988 was to solidify expected support in the South and Rocky Mountain states and then confront Dukakis in potential swing states that would be essential for his victory, particularly Ohio and New Jersey. Dukakis, still trailing Bush after the second debate in 1988, focused his efforts on eighteen states with just enough electoral votes to win. The tables were turned in 1992. Entering the campaign's final week,

Bush was behind, but the polls showed a narrowing of Clinton's lead. Ohio, Kentucky, Michigan, Missouri, and Wisconsin became the focus of Bush's efforts, which were complicated by Perot's strong appeal. With such a narrow margin for error, it is not surprising to find that both Bush and Dukakis went down to defeat. Although Ross Perot won 19 percent of the popular vote in 1992, he won no electoral votes, the usual fate of third party and independent candidates.[42]

Appealing for Public Support

Presidential campaigns spend millions of dollars and untold hours of effort pursuing two goals: to motivate people to vote on election day and to win their support for a particular candidate. Several factors other than campaign appeals determine who votes and how. Voters' choices depend on their long-term political predispositions, such as political party loyalties and social group affiliations, and their reactions to short-term forces, such as the particular candidates and issues involved in specific elections. Candidates and their team of campaign professionals try to design appeals that activate these influences, attract support, and counter perceived weaknesses.

Because the general election audience is larger and the time shorter, presidential candidates use their resources primarily for mass media appeals. Advertising expenditures have risen accordingly; in 1988, for example, the Bush/Quayle and Dukakis/Bentsen campaigns each spent more than half of the $46.1 million they received in public funding on television and radio advertising, with the lion's share devoted to television. In fact, these Bush/Quayle expenditures constituted a whopping 68 percent of their public subsidy, while the Democrats spent 51 percent of theirs.[43] Since 1952 television has been the chief source of campaign information for most Americans. In addition, polls indicate that people are more inclined to believe what they see on television than what they read in the newspapers or hear on the radio.

Long-Term Influences. Students of elections have categorized influences on voter decisions as either long-term or short-term. Long-term influences include partisanship and group membership, while the short-term include issues, candidate image, and campaign incidents.

Partisan loyalty, although still important for a large part of the public, has become less significant as a determinant of election outcomes. Conditions have changed considerably since a group of researchers studying presidential elections in the 1950s concluded that the single most important determinant of voting at that time was the *party identification* of the voter.[44] This general psychological attachment, shaped by family and social groups, tended to intensify with age. For the average person looking for guidance on how to vote amid the complexities of personalities, issues, and events of the 1950s, the party label of the candidates was the most important reference point. At that time partisanship was also fairly constant—about 45 percent of Americans in 1952 and 1956 said they thought of themselves as Democrats, and about 28 percent viewed themselves as Republicans, for a combined total of nearly three-fourths of the electorate. When asked to classify themselves further as "strong" or "weak" partisans, both Republicans and Democrats tended to divide equally between those two categories. Independents in 1952 and 1956 averaged about 23 percent of the electorate.

In the mid- to late-1960s, however, partisan affiliation in the United States began to change *(see Table 2-3)*. Beginning with the 1968 election, the number of independents started to increase, primarily at the expense of the Democrats, until they constituted one-third of the electorate in 1972. Even those voters who stayed with the Democrats were more inclined than formerly to say they were weak rather than strong party members. Since 1968 more people also identify themselves as independents than as Republicans. This trend progressed one step further in 1988 with some polls even finding that independents outnumbered Democrats for the first time. The rise in independents has occurred primarily among young people, particularly those who entered the electorate in 1964 or later. Voters who came of age since that time are much more likely to be

Table 2-3 Party Identification, 1952–1988 (Percent)

Party	1952	1956	1960	1964	1968	1972	1976	1980	1984	1988
Strong Democrat	22	21	20	27	20	15	15	18	17	18
Weak Democrat	25	23	25	25	25	26	25	23	20	18
Total	47	44	45	52	45	41	40	41	37	36
Strong Republican	14	14	16	11	10	10	9	9	10	14
Weak Republican	13	15	14	14	15	13	14	14	15	14
Total	27	29	30	25	25	23	23	23	25	28
Independent	22	24	23	23	30	35	37	34	34	36

Source: *Statistical Abstract of the United States,* 1990, table 442 (Washington, D.C.: Government Printing Office, 1990).

political independents than are voters of earlier political generations, a development that has been linked to the influence of Vietnam and Watergate.

The decline in partisanship reached its peak between 1972 and 1976. The proportion of independents has not changed significantly in the presidential elections since then. Although the trend away from party affiliation appears to have stopped, the parties have been unable to lure the public back. Since 1980 modest Republican gains of roughly 5 percent to 10 percent have been offset by Democratic losses of the same size. The picture has remained remarkably stable since 1972, with just under two-thirds of citizens expressing a party identification. Considered in light of their enormous success in winning presidential elections, Republican gains have been limited, although they may still have had an impact on election results.

Given the patterns of party identification, it is not surprising to find that Democrats have designed appeals to reinforce traditional party loyalties, while Republicans, as the minority party, have urged voters to ignore party labels. Moreover, Republicans have associated themselves with the memories of former Democratic leaders; Ronald Reagan, who before his political conversion in the 1960s had been a lifelong Democrat, used this technique effectively.

Social group membership is another potentially important influence on voting that candidates try to tap. Patterns of group support established during the New Deal have persisted during succeeding decades although with decreasing vibrancy. In the 1940s Democrats received most of their support from southerners, blacks, Catholics, and people with limited education, lower incomes, and a working-class background. Republican candidates were supported by northerners, whites, Protestants, and people with more education, higher incomes, and a professional or business background. Table 2-4 shows how various groups voted in selected presidential elections from 1952 through 1992. The support of many groups for their traditional party's candidates declined over the forty-year period. The most significant drop for the Democrats came in the southern white vote: by 1988 only one in three white votes in the South went to Dukakis, and only 26 percent of white males supported the Democrat.[45] The only group that significantly increased its support for its traditional party candidate over this period was nonwhites, whose support for Democrats was stronger between 1964 and 1988 than in 1952.[46]

Table 2-4 also shows that group preferences can vary greatly from election to election. In 1964, when the very conservative Barry Goldwater was the Republican standard-bearer, all the groups, including those that typically support the GOP, supported the Democratic candidate, Lyndon Johnson. In 1972 the opposite occurred; when the very liberal George McGovern ran on the Democratic ticket, all the groups that usually sympathize with that party, except for nonwhites, voted for Richard Nixon, the Republican candidate. In 1992 Bush's support declined from 1988 levels in virtually every category, but the decline was especially marked among men, the college educated, and baby boomers, the voters between thirty and forty-nine.

The weakening of party loyalties means that candidates must target many groups. Organized labor, far from a monolithic entity, has been seriously divided in recent elections, and ethnic groups have been openly courted by both camps. Moreover, new groups have emerged as critical factors: women, fundamentalist Christians, and young voters have attracted particular attention. But because many American voters have lost their partisan anchor, short-term influences, such as candidates, issues, events, and presidential performance are now more important to them.

Short-Term Influences. What are voters looking for in a president? Pollsters working with presidential campaigns try to project their candidate's most attractive features and direct voter attention to the opponent's least attractive features. During the 1984 campaign, for example, the Michigan Center for Political Studies asked citizens to evaluate Reagan and Mondale on twelve specific personal traits, combined into four summary measures: (1) leadership (commands respect, is inspiring, provides strong leadership); (2) competence (is hard-working, intelligent, and knowledgeable); (3) integrity (is decent, is moral, sets a good example); and (4) empathy (is compassionate, is kind, "really cares about people like you"). In contrast to some expectations, Reagan was favored over Mondale on only two of those four measures, leadership and integrity. Mondale prevailed on competence and empathy, and only on leadership was Reagan's margin substantial.[47]

In a 1988 election day poll, voters concerned with experience and competence overwhelmingly supported Bush, while those who wanted a more caring president and one more likely to introduce change disproportionately supported Dukakis. Those who saw Dukakis as too liberal pre-

Table 2-4 Group Voting Patterns in Presidential Elections, Selected Years (Percent)

| | 1952 | | 1960 | | 1964 | | 1968 | | | 1972 | |
| | | (R) | | (R) | | (R) | | (R) | | | (R) |
	Stevenson	Eisenhower	Kennedy	Nixon	Johnson	Goldwater	Humphrey	Nixon	Wallace	McGovern	Nixon
Group											
Sex											
male	47	53	52	48	60	40	41	43	16	37	63
female	42	58	49	51	62	38	45	43	12	38	62
Race											
white	43	57	49	51	59	41	38	47	15	32	68
nonwhite	79	21	68	32	94	6	35	12	3	87	13
Education											
college	34	66	39	61	52	48	37	54	9	37	63
high school	45	55	52	48	62	38	42	43	15	34	66
grade school	52	48	55	45	66	34	52	33	15	49	51
Occupation											
professional,											
business	36	64	42	58	54	46	34	56	10	31	69
white collar	40	60	48	52	57	43	41	47	12	36	64
manual	55	45	60	40	71	29	50	35	15	43	57
Age											
under 30	51	49	54	45	64	36	47	38	15	48	52
30–49	47	53	54	46	63	37	44	41	15	33	67
50 and											
older	39	61	46	54	59	41	41	47	12	36	64
Religion											
Protestant	37	63	38	62	55	45	35	49	16	30	70
Catholic	56	44	78	22	76	24	59	33	8	48	52
Region											
East	45	55	53	47	68	32	50	43	7	42	58
Midwest	42	58	48	52	61	39	44	47	9	40	60
South	51	49	51	49	52	48	31	36	33	29	71
West	42	58	49	51	60	40	44	49	7	41	59
Members of											
labor union											
families	61	39	65	35	73	27	56	29	15	46	54
National	45	55	50	50	61	39	43	43	14	38	62

Source: Excerped from *Gallup Report,* November 1988, 6, 7; *The Gallup Poll Monthly,* November 1992, 9.

Table 2-4 (Continued)

1976 (R)		1980 (R)			1988 (R)		1992 (R)		
Carter	Ford	Carter	Reagan	Anderson	Dukakis	Bush	Bush	Clinton	Perot
53	45	38	53	7	44	56	37	39	19
48	51	44	49	6	48	52	36	48	10
46	52	36	56	7	41	59	40	40	15
85	15	86	10	2	82	18	12	76	4
42	55	35	53	10	42	58	39	43	14
54	46	43	51	5	46	54	37	45	12
58	41	54	42	3	55	45	35	43	15
42	56	33	55	10	NA	NA	NA	NA	NA
50	48	40	51	9	NA	NA	NA	NA	NA
58	41	48	46	5	NA	NA	NA	NA	NA
53	45	47	41	11	37	63	44	38	14
48	49	38	52	8	45	55	35	43	17
52	48	41	54	4	49	51	37	46	11
46	53	39	54	6	42	58	NA	NA	NA
57	42	46	47	6	51	49	NA	NA	NA
51	47	43	47	9	51	49	33	47	15
48	50	41	51	7	47	53	35	45	13
54	45	44	52	3	40	60	42	40	13
46	51	35	54	9	46	54	36	43	15
63	36	50	43	5	63	37	NA	NA	NA
50	48	41	51	7	46	54	37	44	14

dictably supported Bush, but those worried about dirty campaigns leaned toward Dukakis.[48] In a 1992 exit poll that asked voters what qualities mattered most in deciding how they voted, 36 percent cited a candidate's ability to bring about change. Clinton won 67 percent of those votes, and Bush only 5 percent. Clinton also led among voters concerned about which candidate had the best plan for the nation, cared about people, and had the best vice presidential candidate. Bush led among voters concerned with experience, trustworthiness, and good judgment in a crisis.[49] Bush seemed to derive greater benefit from candidate characteristics in 1988, but Clinton had the advantage in 1992.

Because the public focuses so much attention in a presidential campaign on the candidates themselves, the personality and character the aspirants project are particularly important. Each campaign organization strives to create a composite image of its candidate's most attractive features. To do this sometimes means transforming liabilities into assets: age becomes mature judgment (Dwight Eisenhower); youth and inexperience becomes vigor (John Kennedy). Alternatively, a candidate can direct attention to the opponent's personal liabilities, a move that has proved beneficial even though some voters see such an effort as dirty campaigning and beneath the dignity of the office.

The 1988 and 1992 campaigns provide good examples of how candidates try to shape each other's image. Bush succeeded in creating a negative portrait of Dukakis in 1988, but the tactic proved less successful against Clinton. Dukakis enjoyed a largely favorable image before the summer conventions, but Bush's pollsters discovered it was based on very little information.[50] Small groups of Democrats who had supported Reagan in 1980 and 1984 were interviewed to determine which features of Dukakis's record they found most upsetting. The campaign then portrayed the Democrat as sympathetic to criminals, weak on defense, opposed to saying the pledge of allegiance in school, and a liberal who favored high taxes and big government. In turn, Dukakis tried to link Bush to the Iran-contra incident, the illicit international drug activities of Panamanian leader Manuel Noriega, and ethics violations committed throughout the Reagan years, but the effort was far less successful.[51] Bush's strategy in 1992 was less focused until the campaign's final weeks, when trust and taxes emerged as the central issues. Earlier, Bush pursued several of the themes that had worked in 1988: Clinton was described as the failed governor of a small state with crime and environmental problems. Bush also questioned Clinton's antiwar activities when he was a student overseas and suggested something sinister about his trip to Moscow while a student. Unlike 1988, however, observers demanded more supporting evidence, and Clinton met all negative charges with broadcast rebuttals and attacks of his own that focused on Bush's role in the Iran-contra incident, pro-Iraq actions of his administration prior to the Persian Gulf war, and Bush's violation of 1988 campaign promises. By leaving no charge unanswered, Clinton succeeded where Dukakis faltered.

Issues are the other major short-term influence on voting behavior. University of Michigan researchers in the 1950s suggested that issues influence a voter's choice only if three conditions are present: the voter is aware that an issue or a number of issues exist; issues are of some personal concern to the voter; and the voter perceives that one party better represents his or her position than the other party does.[52] When the three conditions were applied to U.S. voters in the 1952 and 1956 presidential elections, researchers found that these criteria existed for relatively few voters. About one-third of the respondents were unaware of *any* of the sixteen principal issues about which they were questioned. Even the two-thirds who were aware of one or more issues frequently had no personal concern about them. Finally, a number of those who were aware and concerned about issues were unable to perceive differences between the two parties' positions. The analysts concluded that issues *potentially* determined the choice of, at the most, only one-third of the electorate. (The proportion who *actually* voted as they did because of issues could have been, and probably was, even less.)

Studies of political attitudes in the 1960s and 1970s demonstrate a change: the number and types of issues of which voters were aware increased.[53] Voters during the Eisenhower years had exhibited some interest in traditional domestic matters, such as welfare and labor-management relationships, and in a few foreign policy issues, like the threat of communism and the danger of the atomic bomb. Beginning with the 1964 election, however, voters' interests broadened to include concerns such as civil rights and the Vietnam War. The war in particular remained an important consideration in the 1968 and 1972 contests and was joined by new matters such as crime, disorder, and juvenile delinquency—sometimes referred to collectively along with race problems as "social issues." Naturally, the issues that are salient vary from election to election.

Incumbency. Incumbency may be viewed as a candidate characteristic that also involves issues. Service in the job provides experience that no one else can claim. Incumbency also provides concrete advantages in conducting a campaign: one already has national campaign experience (true for all incumbents in U.S. history except Gerald Ford), media coverage is easier to obtain, and there is considerable discretion in allocating benefits selectively. As noted earlier, incumbency has been especially important since World War II because of the pattern of recruitment. Until 1988 incumbency seemed to provide advantages solely to presidents and not to incumbent vice presidents, but Bush's victory may have altered that.

Of the four incumbent presidents who ran for reelection between 1976 and 1992, only Reagan succeeded, and of the last three incumbent vice presidents who sought the presidency, only Bush was elected. The defeats of Ford, Carter, and Bush demonstrate the disadvantages of incumbency, particularly if service in the presidency coincides with negative economic developments such as recession and high inflation or an unresolved foreign crisis for which a president is blamed, even if erroneously. Experience in the job, then, is not a political plus if a sitting president's record is considered weak or national conditions seem to have deteriorated under the incumbent's stewardship. The president may be held accountable by voters who cast their ballots *retrospectively* rather than *prospectively;* in other words, voters evaluate past performance rather than predict future performance.

Retrospective voting has been suggested as the major explanation of Carter's defeat in 1980. To illustrate the problem, one can contrast what many perceived as Carter's failure to resolve the hostage crisis in Iran with the respect that many believed the nation enjoyed after Reagan's first term. It must also be remembered, however, that both the 1976 and 1980 elections were extremely close: in 1976 an incumbent who had never run for national office almost surged to victory in the final weeks of the campaign, and in 1980 polls indicated that Carter and Reagan were virtually neck-and-neck going into the final weekend of the campaign. Even in these instances, one can argue that incumbency proved more beneficial than detrimental to the campaign efforts.

Presidential Debates. Voters have the opportunity to assess the issue positions and personal characteristics of presidential and vice presidential contenders during nationally televised debates. Debates were staged first in 1960 and then each year since 1976, and they quickly became the most important and most widely watched campaign events. Candidates recognize the danger of making a mistake or an embarrassing gaffe on live television, a particular danger for incumbents. Ford misspoke in 1976 when he suggested that countries of Eastern Europe were not under Soviet domination; Reagan appeared to be confused and out of touch during his first debate with Mondale in 1984, but rallied in the second encounter. Challengers try to demonstrate their knowledge of issues and their presidential bearing to a nationwide audience. Kennedy in 1960 and Reagan in 1980 seem to have benefited the most from debating a more experienced opponent in part because they exceeded performance expectations and dispelled negative impressions. Most candidates prepare carefully prior to the meeting and follow a conservative game plan of reemphasizing themes already made prominent during the campaign. As a result, the exchanges often seem wooden rather than extemporaneous, an impression heightened by the cautious rules approved by the respective camps.

Trailing badly in the 1988 polls, Dukakis had his best chance to close the gap in the debates. Although he demonstrated mastery of substance, he failed to project warmth. This coldness was most apparent during the second debate when he was asked a blunt question: "Governor, if Kitty Dukakis were raped and murdered, would you favor the irrevocable death penalty for the killer?" Dukakis patiently repeated his lifelong opposition to the death penalty. As he was in need of a major victory, this performance was viewed as a disappointment. In 1992 the first three-way presidential debates in history included Perot whose performance in the first of three meetings excited public interest. He was funny, irreverent, and obviously at ease. However, Perot seemed to fade in the later debates, while Clinton performed consistently. Bush was oddly passive until the final debate. The encounters probably made the public more comfortable with both Clinton and Perot while confirming unease with Bush.

Single vice presidential debates were held in 1988 and 1992. Dan Quayle's performance was the focus of both encounters. Much younger than Lloyd Bentsen, his 1988 opponent, Quayle was repeatedly asked what he would do if forced to assume the duties of president. When Quayle compared himself to former president John F. Kennedy, Bentsen pounced with withering directness: "Senator, I served with Jack Kennedy. I knew Jack Kennedy. Jack Kennedy was a friend of mine. Senator, you're no Jack Kennedy." Quayle never recovered. In 1992 Quayle debated Al Gore, the Democrat, and James Stockdale, Perot's running mate. Stockdale watched as his younger opponents struggled to dominate one another. At one point the retired admiral even turned off his hearing aid. Few commentators were pleased with the vice presidential debate, which resembled a mud-wrestling contest more than a way to determine who was best qualified to succeed to the presidency.

Televised debates enable even the least engaged citizen to develop an impression of the major party contenders. It remains unclear, however, whether those impressions truly reflect the candidates' credentials or are an artifact of staging.

Election Day

One of the ironies of U.S. presidential elections since 1960 is that, although more citizens have acquired the right to vote, a smaller proportion of them have exercised that right. As Table 2-5 indicates, the estimated number of people of voting age has more than doubled since Franklin Roosevelt was first elected in 1932. After reaching a peak in 1960, however, the percentage of people who voted declined in the next five presidential elections and resumed its decline in 1988 after a modest increase in 1984. In 1988 only 50.1 percent of the eligible voting age population went to the polls, the second lowest turnout recorded for a presidential election in the twentieth century. This pattern was reversed dramatically in 1992 when an estimated 55.9 percent of the eligible voters went to the polls.[54]

The decline in voter participation ran counter to some of the traditional theories of why people do not vote. Restrictive laws, particularly those pertaining to registration and voting, are said to prevent citizens from going to the polls. Yet many states had eased such restrictions, and Congress has facilitated voting in presidential elections for new residents, so that it was easier for a person to register and to vote for president in 1988 than it was in 1960. A person's lack of education is often put forward as a reason for not voting, but the level of education of U.S. citizens has risen as participation declined. Lack of political information is yet another frequently cited explanation; however, because of increased use of the mass media, and particularly because of televised presidential debates, more Americans than ever are made aware of the candidates and their views on public issues. Finally, close political races are supposed to stimulate peo-

Table 2-5 Participation of General Public in Presidential Elections, 1932–1992

Year	Estimated population of voting age (in millions)	Number of votes cast (in millions)	Number of votes as percentage of population of voting age
1932	75.8	39.7	52.4
1936	80.2	45.6	56.0
1940	84.7	49.9	58.9
1944	85.7	48.0	56.0
1948	95.6	48.8	51.1
1952	99.9	61.6	61.6
1956	104.5	62.0	59.3
1960	109.7	68.8	62.8
1964	114.1	70.6	61.9
1968	120.3	73.2	60.9
1972[a]	140.8	77.6	55.1
1976[a]	152.3	81.6	53.6
1980[a]	164.6	86.5	52.6
1984[a]	174.5	92.7	53.1
1988[a]	182.8	91.6	50.1
1992[a]	187.0 (est.)	104.6	55.9

Source: "Projections of the Voting-Age Population, for States: November 1990," *Current Population Reports*, Series P-25, No. 1059, table no. 5 (Washington, D.C.: U.S. Government Printing Office, 1990). Federal Election Commission Record, February 1993, 4.

[a] Elections in which persons eighteen to twenty years old were eligible to vote in all states.

ple to get out and vote because they think their ballot will make a difference in the outcome. Pollsters predicted that the 1964 and 1972 elections would be landslides and that the 1968, 1976, and 1980 elections would be close contests, but a smaller percentage of people voted in 1968 than in 1964, and participation also declined in 1976 and 1980 despite close contests. In 1984 there was a slight (.5 percent) increase in participation, even though the outcome was hardly in doubt, while participation declined in 1988, a closer contest.

Why did voting decline in recent years or surge in 1992? Paul Abramson, John Aldrich, and David Rohde link the decline to the erosion in political party identification, and lower political efficacy, the belief that citizens can influence what government does.[55] The public's disaffection with government policies, particularly the failure to solve economic and social problems, also may have discouraged voters. Future studies will compare the 1992 contest with its predecessors to determine whether Perot's presence, widespread concern about the future, renewed confidence in the political process, or a shift in partisan loyalties helped produce the highest percentage turnout since 1968.

Validation

Translating the popular vote into the official outcome is the final stage of the selection process, in which the electoral college produces the true winner. It has been more than a century since the constitutionally prescribed process failed to do so or produced a winner who was not also the "people's choice," but we have been dangerously close to electoral college *misfires* on a number of occasions.

Three possible problems remained even after presidential and vice presidential balloting were separated. The electoral college does not ensure that the candidate who receives the most popular votes wins the presidency: John Quincy Adams in 1824, Rutherford B. Hayes in 1876, and Benjamin Harrison in 1888 became president even though they finished second in total popular vote to their respective political opponents, Andrew Jackson, Samuel Tilden, and Grover Cleveland. The same thing would have happened in 1976 if some 9,000 voters in Hawaii and Ohio had shifted their ballots to President Ford, giving him a victory even though Carter had won the popular vote.

Candidates also may fail to win an electoral college majority, thereby throwing selection into the House of Representatives. This situation occurred in the elections of 1800, 1824, and 1876. In 1948 Harry S. Truman defeated Thomas Dewey by more than 2 million popular votes, but if some 12,000 people in California and Ohio had voted for Dewey rather than the president, the election would have been thrown into the House of Representatives. The same thing could have happened in 1960 and 1968 with the shift of a few thousand votes in close states.

The 1968 election illustrates another danger of the electoral college system: an elector need not cast his or her ballot for the candidate who wins the plurality of votes in the elector's state. This problem of the *faithless elector* has occurred seven times in the twentieth century, most recently in 1988 when an elector from West Virginia cast her vote for Bentsen as president rather than Dukakis. It is not particularly dangerous when isolated electors refuse to follow the result of their state's popular vote, but the possibility of widespread desertion from the popular choice is another matter. If the popular vote outcome had made it clear in 1968 that

Nixon was unlikely to win a majority of the electoral votes in 1968, third party candidate George Wallace would have been in a position to trade his forty-five electors for policy commitments from Nixon. Had Nixon agreed, the deal would have given him enough electoral votes to gain victory and prevent the selection from being made in the House.[56]

The electoral college as it operates today violates some of the major tenets of political equality that are central to our contemporary understanding of democracy. Each person's vote does not count equally: one's influence on the outcome depends on the political situation in one's state. For the many Americans who support a losing candidate, it is as though they had not voted at all, because under the general-ticket system all the electoral votes of a state go to the candidate who wins a plurality of its popular votes. Citizens who live in populous, politically competitive states have a premium placed on their vote because they are in a position to affect how large blocs of electoral votes are cast. Similarly, permitting the House of Representatives, voting by states, to select the president of the United States is not consistent with the "one person, one vote" principle that has become a central tenet of modern American democracy.

Proposals to reform the electoral college system promise to remove the possibility of system failures and uphold a more modern understanding of democracy. They range from the rather modest suggestion to prohibit faithless electors—votes would be cast automatically—to scrapping the present system altogether and moving to direct popular election. Intermediate suggestions would nationalize the district plan used in Maine and Nebraska, divide electoral votes proportionally between (or among) the contenders, or provide the popular vote winner with 100 bonus votes, enough to ensure his or her victory in the electoral college. No proposal is foolproof; most have to develop means to guard against new problems. Moreover, any change requires passage of a constitutional amendment by Congress, which is problematic because national legislators will calculate how the new system would affect their state's influence on the outcome (or affect their own chances to pursue the office) and vote accordingly. Therefore, prospects for change are not especially good until the system actually misfires or comes so close that the public demands action.

Is the electoral college a constitutional anachronism that should no longer be preserved? Why not move to direct popular election? Defenders of the current system note that the most serious misfires occurred during periods of intense political divisiveness (for example, 1824 and 1876) when alternative selection systems would have been just as severely tested. Several of the twentieth century "close-calls," such as 1948 and 1968, occurred when political parties were suffering serious internal divisions. An examination of the historical conditions surrounding the misfires shows that only 1888 offers a clear example of a popular vote winner who lost, but even in this case the loser, Cleveland, had failed to meet one of the other requirements for success in the electoral college: broad distribution of support. Cleveland won fewer states than Harrison, receiving huge majorities in several while losing by slim majorities in even more. With this pattern of support, it is an open question which candidate was truly the people's choice.[57]

Defenders of the present system argue that far from having performed badly, the system has been remarkably successful in producing peaceful resolutions even in years of unusual turmoil. The system's virtues include the requirement that candidates not only receive sufficient popular support but also that support is sufficiently distributed geographically to enable the winner to govern. Ethnic minority groups, it is argued, receive special leverage under the present system because they are concentrated in states with large electoral vote totals and receive attention because their support might make the difference between a candidate winning *all* of the electoral votes or *none* of them. Finally, there is concern that a system of direct election would encourage the development of minor parties based on regional or ideological interests who might organize in hopes of denying any candidate a majority or winning plurality and thereby force a runoff. Two-party stability, it is suggested, would be threatened.[58]

Thus, analysts of the American political system differ over the wisdom of retaining the present electoral system, a difference of opinion echoed by the authors of this book. Each of us is concerned with legitimacy, but views the dangers differently. One of us believes that the present system, flawed as it may be, offers the advantage of continuity, something that yet another electoral reform following those initiated after 1968 is likely to endanger. The others fear that a misfire would dangerously imperil system legitimacy and, therefore, endorse reforms more consistent with direct popular election. As this brief review indicates, the debate is likely to continue.

Transitions to Governing

For the individual and election team that prevail in this long, grueling process, victory requires a change in focus. Successful candidates suddenly realize that winning the election is the means to an end, not an end in itself. Making that transition is sometimes difficult, as we review in the Epilogue. It involves putting together a team of political executives to staff the new administration as well as establishing a list of program and policy priorities. Much of this is accomplished during the *transition*, the period between election and inauguration. Many other tasks are tackled during the first six months of the new administration. Governing, however, offers a new set of problems. Frequently, the techniques that proved successful during the election are simply transferred over to help meet the new challenges, but such methods are seldom sufficient to ensure success. In the modern presidency, governing involves some of the same activities as getting elected, but the two are far from identical, a lesson that some incumbents are slow to learn.

The burning question for everyone is how effective will the president be in leading the nation. Presidents vary along a wide range of dimensions—abilities, interests, personality—even as the office exhibits certain commonalities over time. In Chapter 4, we turn to the problem of understanding the ways that a president's personal characteristics influence performance in office, and subsequent chapters focus on the presidents' political success. First, however, we examine the president's relationship with the public *between* elections, a relationship that has grown increasingly important in modern times.

NOTES

1. James Monroe is the only other candidate to approach this distinction; he won all but one electoral college vote in 1820. *Guide to the Presidency*, ed. Michael Nelson (Washington, D.C.: Congressional Quarterly, 1990), 1406.
2. William Chambers, *Political Parties in a New Nation: The American Experience, 1776–1809* (New York: Oxford University Press, 1963), chap. 2.
3. In the early 1820s the Republican party became known as the Democratic-Republicans and in 1840 was officially designated as the Democratic party. Paul David, Ralph Goldman, and Richard Bain, *The Politics of National Party Conventions* (New York: Vintage, 1964), chap. 3.
4. Joseph Charles, *The Origins of the American Party System* (New York: Harper Torch, 1956), 83–94.
5. Other constitutional amendments dealing with presidential selection have ex-

panded participation (Amendments 15, 19, 24, 26), set the term of office (20, 22), or sought to cope with death or disability (20, 25).

6. David, Goldman, and Bain, *National Party Conventions*, 50. The National Republican party was soon to give way to the Whigs, with many Whig supporters joining the Republican party when it was formed in the 1850s (pages 57–59).

7. Ibid., 61.

8. First-ballot convention decisions have been surprisingly prevalent. Through 1992, the two major parties selected their candidates on the first ballot at fifty-one of seventy-seven conventions. Many of the multiballot conventions were held from 1840 to 1888, when sixteen of the twenty-two went past the first ballot. What distinguishes the post–1952 era is that *none* of the twenty conventions has gone past one ballot.

9. Richard C. Bain and Judith H. Parris, *Convention Decisions and Voting Records*, 2d ed. (Washington: Brookings, 1973), 1–6.

10. In three states, one party chose delegates through the primary method, and the other used a caucus. The Republicans used primaries in Idaho and North Dakota, and the Democrats did so in South Carolina.

11. Naturalized citizens (such as former secretary of state Henry Kissinger, who was born in Germany) do not meet this requirement. There is some question whether persons born abroad of American citizens (one such is George Romney, former governor of Michigan and 1968 presidential contender, who was born of American parents in France) are also legally barred from the presidency by this stipulation.

12. The two exceptions were Wendell Willkie, the president of a public utility company, who was nominated by the Republicans in 1940, and Dwight D. Eisenhower, a career military man and World War II hero, who became the successful GOP candidate in 1952.

13. John Aldrich, "Methods and Actors: The Relationship of Processes to Candidates," in *Presidential Selection*, ed. Alexander Heard and Michael Nelson (Durham, N.C.: Duke University Press, 1987).

14. Before Richard Nixon's selection in 1960, the last incumbent vice president to be nominated was Martin Van Buren in 1836.

15. Joseph A. Pika, "Bush, Quayle, and the New Vice Presidency," in *The Presidency and the Political System*, 3d ed., ed. Michael Nelson (Washington, D.C.: CQ Press, 1990).

16. Ronald Elving, "The Senators' Lane to the Presidency," *Congressional Quarterly Weekly Report*, May 20, 1989, 1218.

17. For a statement of informal expectations from three decades ago see Sidney Hyman, "Nine Tests for the Presidential Hopeful," *New York Times*, Jan. 4, 1959, sec. 5, 1–11.

18. Michael Nelson, "Who Vies for President?" in *Presidential Selection*, 144.

19. For example, Jesse Jackson finished third behind Walter Mondale and Gary Hart for the 1984 Democratic nomination and second for the 1988 nomination.

20. Harold W. Stanley and Richard G. Niemi, *Vital Statistics on American Politics*, 2d ed. (Washington, D.C.: CQ Press, 1990), tables 3–3, 3–4.

21. Ibid., tables 3–5, 3–6.

22. Austin Ranney, "Changing the Rules of the Nominating Game," in *Choosing the President*, ed. James David Barber (Englewood Cliffs, N.J.: Prentice-Hall, 1974), 71.

23. Arthur Hadley, *The Invisible Primary* (Englewood Cliffs, N.J.: Prentice-Hall, 1976).

24. Individuals are limited to contributions of $1,000 to a presidential candidate for each election (the nomination and general election are considered separate contests), $5,000 to a political action committee (one that contributes to more than one candi-

date), $20,000 to the national committee of a political party, and a total contribution of no more than $25,000 a year. Presidential candidates are free to spend an unlimited amount of their own and their immediate family's money on their campaigns, but if they accept public financing, their contributions to their own campaign are limited to $50,000 per election.

25. Herbert E. Alexander and Monica Bauer, *Financing the 1988 Election* (Boulder, Colo.: Westview, 1991), table 2.5, 16.

26. Not all individual contributions are small, and it is legal for political action committees to help finance nomination campaigns, but their contributions are not matched by federal funds as in the case of individuals. Vice President Bush, for example, received $1,000 contributions (the maximum) from 16,500 individuals in 1988 for a total of $16.5 million. Cumulatively, PACs contributed $3.114 million during the 1988 prenomination campaign, but that sum represented only 1.4 percent of total funding. Alexander and Bauer, *Financing the 1988 Election*, 23, 25.

27. At the time of writing, only the 1988 figures are complete. Bush raised $18.7 million in 1988 to Dole's $14.0 million and Pat Robertson's $14.0 million. Dukakis raised $10.6 million, with Richard Gephardt ($4.4 million), Al Gore ($3.8 million), and Paul Simon ($3.8 million) trailing badly. Alexander and Bauer, *Financing the 1988 Election*, 20.

28. In 1984 the minimum was 20 percent, a rule that favored front-runner Walter Mondale. Complaints from defeated candidates Jesse Jackson and Gary Hart resulted in lowering the qualifying level to 15 percent for the 1988 contest and continued in 1992. Most Republican contests have been conducted under "winner-take-all" rules, although some states used proportional rules for both parties.

29. Only about 120,000 Democrats were registered in New Hampshire in 1976, and the Carter organization stated that it contacted about 95 percent of them. The state was therefore ideal for the former governor in the early stages of the nomination contest: he had not yet acquired substantial financial resources for media expenditures, and his contingent of Georgia volunteers could conduct an effective door-to-door campaign.

30. C. Anthony Broh, *A Horse of a Different Color: Television's Treatment of Jesse Jackson's 1984 Presidential Campaign* (Washington, D.C.: Joint Center for Political Studies, 1987), 4.

31. Ibid., 11.

32. Exceptions to this pattern can be found when two candidates ended the preconvention period fairly even, which occurred between Ford and Reagan (1976), McGovern and Humphrey (1972), and Mondale and Hart (1984), but in each case the preconvention leader took the nomination.

33. Judith Parris, *The Convention Problem: Issues in Reform of Presidential Nominating Procedures* (Washington, D.C.: Brookings, 1972), 110.

34. Max Farrand, *The Framing of the Constitution of the United States* (New Haven, Conn.: Yale University Press, 1913), 160. There is some question whether it was doubt in the public's ability or concern about the natural tendency to support a "favorite son" that motivated delegates to reject direct election. See William C. Kimberling, "Electing the President: The Genius of the Electoral College," *FEC Journal* (Fall 1988): 12.

35. Alexander and Bauer, *Financing the 1988 Election*, table 2.1, 12.

36. Although presidential candidates are free to refuse public funds, no major paraty nominee has done so in the general election, perhaps because raising money from individuals and groups is now more difficult with the maximum contribution limitations in place. Candidates may also think the public favors the use of public rather than private funds.

37. The Twenty-third Amendment, ratified in 1961, gave the District of Columbia the right to participate in presidential elections. Previously, District residents were excluded. Their inclusion accounts for having three more electoral votes (538) than the total number of senators and representatives—535.

38. In 1992 Bill Clinton won eight of the eleven most populous states. In contrast, George Bush won ten of these states in 1988.

39. Reapportionment was complex following the 1990 census. Because of widespread criticism, the Census Bureau agreed to conduct a postcensus survey to determine the extent to which some population groups had been undercounted. The results of that study would have called for further changes in congressional representation. However, the secretary of commerce recommended following the initial census findings rather than the adjusted figures. The electoral vote totals presented in this paragraph are based on the initial findings.

40. For a general discussion of this pattern, see Michael Nelson, "Constitutional Aspects of the Elections," in *The Elections of 1988* (Washington, D.C.: CQ Press, 1990), 192–195. Also see Everett Carll Ladd, "On Mandates, Realignments, and the 1984 Presidential Election," *Political Science Quarterly* 100:1 (Spring 1985): 17ff.

41. Dukakis won electoral votes from the District of Columbia and ten states in 1988: Hawaii, Iowa, Massachusetts, Minnesota, New York, Oregon, Rhode Island, Washington, West Virginia, and Wisconsin. He won 45 percent or more of the vote in California, Colorado, Connecticut, Illinois, Maryland, Michigan, Missouri, Montana, New Mexico, Pennsylvania, South Dakota, and Vermont. Of these states, only South Dakota did not support Clinton in 1992. Clinton won five southern states and trailed Bush in the region's popular vote, as well.

42. Perot's share of the popular vote was the second best by an independent or third-party candidate in the twentieth century, surpassed only by Theodore Roosevelt's 27 percent in 1912. In comparison, George Wallace received nearly 14 percent of the popular vote in 1968, and John Anderson received 6 percent in 1980. Wallace's support was concentrated in the South, and he won forty-six electoral votes. Like Perot's support, Anderson's was scattered nationwide, and he also won no electoral votes.

43. Calculated by the authors based on data found in Alexander and Bauer, *Financing the 1988 Election*, 36. Bush/Quayle spent $31.458 million on broadcast media during the general election, and Dukakis/Bentsen spent $23.350 million on media.

44. Angus Campbell, Philip Converse, Warren Miller, and Donald Stokes, *The American Voter*, abr. ed. (New York: Wiley, 1964).

45. Gerald M. Pomper, "The Presidential Election," in *The Election of 1988: Reports and Interpretations*, ed Gerald Pomper (Chatham, N.J: Chatham House, 1989), 136.

46. Offsetting gains in nonwhite voting, white fundamentalist or evangelical Christians have gained significance in national politics. This group has become solidly Republican and in 1988 comprised nearly as large a proportion of the voting population as blacks (9 percent versus 10 percent). See poll results reported in Pomper, "The Presidential Election," 134.

47. J. Merrill Shanks and Warren Miller, "Policy Direction and Performance Evaluation: Complementary Explanations of the Reagan Elections" (Paper delivered at the annual meeting of the American Political Science Association, New Orleans, Aug. 29–Sept. 1, 1985), 60, 69.

48. Pomper, "Presidential Contest," 143. The results of this CNN/*Los Angeles Times* poll also can be found in *National Journal*, Nov. 12, 1988, 2854.

49. Voter Research and Surveys exit polls as reported in Paul J. Quirk and Jon K. Dallager, "The Election: A 'New Democrat' and a New Kind of Presidential Campaign," in *The Elections of 1992*, Michael Nelson, ed. (Washington: CQ Press, 1993) 81.

50. Marjorie Randon Hershey, "The Campaign and the Media" in *The Elections of 1988*, 78.
51. Ibid., 80–83; Paul J. Quirk, "The Election," in *The Elections of 1988*, 76.
52. Campbell et al., *The American Voter*, chap. 7.
53. For 1960s data, see Gerald Pomper, *Voters' Choice: Varieties of American Electoral Behavior* (New York: Dodd Mead, 1975), chap. 8. For 1970s data see Norman Nie, Sidney Verba, John Petrocik, *The Changing American Voter* (Cambridge, Mass.: Harvard University Press, 1979), chap. 7.
54. The Federal Election Commission estimated that 187,033,000 Americans were of voting age and that 104,552,736 voted in 1992, an increase of about 13 million voters over the 1988 total. Twenty-three candidates shared the votes, although only four, Bush, Clinton, Perot, and Libertarian party candidate Andre Marrou, were on ballots in all fifty states. Federal Election Commission, press release, Jan. 14, 1993.
55. Paul R. Abramson, John H. Aldrich, and David W. Rohde, *Change and Continuity in the 1980 Elections* (Washington, D.C.: CQ Press, 1982), chap. 4.
56. Wallace actually earned forty-five electoral votes but received forty-six because one elector in North Carolina (won by Nixon) cast his vote for the Alabama governor. In 1960, 1972, 1976, and 1988 single electors in Oklahoma, Virginia, Washington, and West Virginia also failed to cast their ballots for the candidate receiving the popular vote plurality in their state. For complete results of electoral college voting, see *Guide to the Presidency*, 1403–28; see note b on 1427 for a list of "faithless electors."
57. Kimberling, "Electing the President," 16.
58. Ibid., 19–20.

READINGS

Abramson, Paul R., John H. Aldrich, and David W. Rohde. *Change and Continuity in the 1980 Elections*. Washington, D.C.: CQ Press, 1982.
———. *Change and Continuity in the 1984 Elections*. Washington, D.C.: CQ Press, 1986.
———. *Change and Continuity in the 1988 Elections*. Washington, D.C.: CQ Press, 1990.
Alexander, Herbert E., and Monica Bauer. *Financing the 1988 Election*. Boulder, Colo.: Westview, 1991.
Bartels, Larry M. *Presidential Primaries and the Dynamics of Public Choice*. Princeton, N.J.: Princeton University Press, 1988.
Campbell, Angus, Philip Converse, Warren Miller, and Donald Stokes. *The American Voter*. abr. ed. New York: Wiley, 1964.
Heard, Alexander, and Michael Nelson, eds. *Presidential Selection*. Durham. N.C.: Duke University Press, 1987.
Nie, Norman, Sidney Verba, and John Petrocik. *The Changing American Voter*. Cambridge, Mass.: Harvard University Press, 1979.
Shafer, Byron E. *Quiet Revolution: The Struggle for the Democratic Party and the Shaping of Post Reform Politics*. New York: Russell Sage Foundation, 1983.

3 PUBLIC POLITICS

FOR NEARLY A CENTURY, students of the presidency have argued that the chief executive's continuing relationship with the American public is a major factor in governing the nation. Writing in 1900 Henry Jones Ford concluded that only presidents can "define issues in such a way that public opinion can pass upon them decisively."[1] Woodrow Wilson, anticipating his own approach to the office, echoed that sentiment: "His [the president's] is the only national voice in affairs. Let him once win the admiration and confidence of the country; and no other single force can withstand him; no combination of forces will easily overpower him."[2]

If anything, the president's position has been strengthened during the last half of this century. In 1960 Richard Neustadt explained how the president's "public prestige," in other words, the president's "standing with the public outside Washington," influ-

Ever since President William Howard Taft threw out the first baseball of the 1910 major league season in Washington, most presidents have observed the tradition.

ences the decisions of other government officials and nongovernmental elites—members of Congress, the bureaucracy, state governors, military commanders, party politicians, journalists, and foreign diplomats.[3] By the mid-1980s Samuel Kernell argued that "going public," issuing campaignlike appeals for citizen support, had become the key to presidential success in the modern era, rather than the traditional strategy of bargaining with other elites.[4] In short, presidents cannot afford to stop courting voters after the returns are in on election day; modern chief executives must woo the American public between elections just as they do during elections.

In courting this support, presidents must take into account existing public attitudes, especially citizens' attitudes toward the institution of the presidency and the incumbent. Presidents hope to secure the public support they need for governing the nation by triggering favorable predispositions and building their own attractiveness as leaders.

This chapter begins with an analysis of enduring public attitudes toward the presidency and then considers the ways chief executives try to hold the support of the American people. The third principal section examines an important element in the between-elections campaign, the relationship between the president and the media. The fourth section analyzes the president's relationship with one particular segment of the broader American public—members of his own political party.

Public Attitudes Toward the Presidency

Citizens relate to the presidency on both conscious and subconscious levels. At the conscious level, people develop attitudes toward three major components of a political system: the political community of which they are a part; the regime, or formal and informal "rules of the game" followed in the constitutional system; and the authorities, or public officials who hold positions in the government structure.[5] If these attitudes are sufficiently strong and positive, the public may follow its leaders even if it does not like the particular incumbent or the policies that leader advocates.

The president, it can be argued, is the focus of public attitudes in each of these three areas. Like the British monarch, the U.S. chief executive is the symbol of the nation, a personification of government capable of inspiring feelings of loyalty and patriotism, particularly in times of crisis when the leader becomes the rallying point for national efforts. For example, Franklin D. Roosevelt's political friends and foes alike turned to him for leadership when the Japanese attacked Pearl Harbor in December 1941. And even when American forces initiate military action—when Ronald Reagan decided to invade the Caribbean island of Grenada in 1983—calls to support the president quickly drown out critical voices.

Because presidents are central figures in the constitutional system, they can benefit from upholding the accepted rules of the game or suffer from violating them. Many Americans felt that Richard Nixon violated his constitutional obligations as well as basic democratic values by placing himself above the law during the Watergate incident; evidence indicated that he participated in a cover-up designed to hide the truth about an illegal break-in directed by White House aides. Finally, presidents are major actors in the policy-making process; the positions they adopt elicit support or opposition, and their overall performance in office becomes the object of citizen evaluations.

Fred Greenstein has suggested that presidents, in serving as objects of these political attitudes, meet a variety of psychological needs held by the citizenry. As a *cognitive aid*, the president can make government and politics comprehensible; by focusing on the president's activities, citizens simplify a distant and complex world. In other words, the president comes to personify politics. The president also provides an *outlet for feelings* experienced by supporters and opponents, giving citizens the opportunity to develop and express emotions about politics. On the subconscious level, some citizens may seek *vicarious participation*, a desire to identify with a powerful political figure much as people do with fictional figures and entertainment personalities. Presidents symbolize *national unity* as well as *stability* and *predictability*, providing citizens with psychologically satisfying feelings that may meet fundamental needs for membership and reassurance. Finally, presidents serve as a *lightning rod* within the political system, a figure to blame for bad times and to credit for good times.[6] Because presidents play a central role in the nightly dramas communicated on television news, their importance as objects of psychological feelings may be greater today than ever before.

Beyond basic beliefs and psychological needs, the public also has views about the day-to-day operation of the political system—in particular, the major issues of the day and the policies the government should follow in dealing with them. These views, which are generally assumed to be less stable and enduring than beliefs about the political culture, are often described as matters of "public opinion." A citizen's attitudes on policy issues and presidential performance depend on his or her identity with a particular group, such as a political party, and his or her social, economic, and geographical background. As the nation's leading political figure, the president is expected to develop and help put into effect controversial policies that are binding on the entire populace. People respond favorably or unfavorably to the president's particular personality and political style and to the events that occur while he is in office. They also assess the president by the way he relates to particular groups—their political party or the opposition, as well as social (religious, ethnic, racial), economic (business, labor), and geographical divisions of the population.

Thus, many diverse attitudes affect public opinion toward the president. At times, people see him as the embodiment of the nation; on other occasions people link him with a particular issue or policy they favor or oppose. After examining the symbolic importance accorded the presidency, we analyze the ways children and adults view presidents and the factors that affect their thinking about chief executives.

Symbolic Dimensions of the Presidency

The Ronald Reagan Presidential Library opened on November 4, 1991, a day marked by speeches from five presidents (Nixon, Ford, Carter, Reagan, and Bush—the largest number of former and current chief executives alive at the same time since 1861) and appearances by six first ladies (including Lady Bird Johnson) as well as offspring from two other presidents. It was perhaps the largest assemblage of presidents and presidential families in history.[7] The newest presidential library cost $60 million to construct and devotes 22,000 of its 153,000 square feet to exhibits commemorating the Reagan years. Each of the last ten presidents—Hoover through Reagan—has had a library erected in his name to house the papers of his administration and his prepresidential career, explain his record to the public, and define his legacy to the nation. Like all the others, the Reagan structure combines commemoration with facilities for research. Most visitors choose only to view relics from a president's life, items drawn from childhood through retirement, and to reexperience personal memories and moments of drama through museumlike displays, many of which are interactive.

The presidential libraries, therefore, have a significance that extends beyond their ostensible purposes. In many respects, they can be viewed as ten shrines constructed to commemorate the lives and achievements of the most recent heroes in the nation's collective memory, a veritable presidential pantheon whose most sacred shrines, the Washington Monument and Lincoln Memorial, are located in Washington, D.C. Presidents stand at the center of what might be termed an "American mythology," a collection of stories and interpretations loosely linked to historical events, but that serve larger purposes in our collective experience—to celebrate basic values held in common, extol national virtues, and maintain unity in the face of enormous national diversity. In addition to the commemorative sites, Americans have created national holidays, public rituals, and icons, as well as a collection of stories, some of them apocryphal, that are passed on to our children. All attest to the presidency's symbolic importance.

Ceremony and pomp surround the presidency, another indication of the importance of the office in national life. A presidential inauguration resembles the coronation of a king, complete with the taking of an oath in the presence of notables and "the hailing by the multitudes."[8] Public appearances are accompanied by a display of the special presidential seal and the playing of "Hail to the Chief" as the president arrives. News conferences are conducted under a set of rules designed to communicate deference and respect as much as elicit hard news.

Particular occasions have been elevated to ritualistic status. The State of the Union message, for example, allows the president to outline an agenda for Congress and the nation. This ceremony was resurrected by Woodrow Wilson after a century of disuse; today it is an annual occasion for high drama and solemn pronouncements aimed as much at the prime time television audience as the political elites in attendance. Members of Congress, the cabinet, and the diplomatic corps as well as distinguished visitors gather in the House chamber and chatter expectantly until the sergeant-at-arms solemnly announces the president's arrival, at which point the audience respectfully rises to its feet and applauds. Following a formal introduction from the Speaker of the House, there is another standing ovation. After the speech, a phalanx of congressional leaders accompanies the president who leaves the hall with members reaching out along the way to shake hands or just to touch the presidential person.

These outward manifestations of respect, made part of recurrent governing rituals, indicate the near-reverence accorded the position of president. Respect for the *presidency* as distinct from the *president*, the current officeholder, is deeply ingrained in American political culture. George Washington and his advisers gave the office dignity by enhancing its ceremonial functions and designing a set of "republican rituals" for which no direct precedents existed, based on their exclusive experience with monarchy.[9] But Washington's major contribution to the presidency was to imbue the office with nearly mythical stature. The hero worship lavished on Washington during his lifetime and the subsequent cult that developed in commemorating his service to the nation ensured that the presidency will always be associated with the nation's own sense of moral virtue and collective destiny.[10]

Washington's birthday became a day of national celebration second only to the Fourth of July. Abraham Lincoln's birthday also was celebrated as a holiday until the two were combined into Presidents' Day. Every February American school children are taught stories about these presidents whose youthful endeavors illustrate the fundamental virtues of truthfulness ("Father, I cannot tell a lie"), honesty in business (walking miles to return change), and hard work (wilderness surveyor and railsplitter). At one time, Washington's likeness was so widely displayed that it became a virtual icon, the picture of a venerated saint displayed by fervent believers in hopes of deriving blessings.[11] In like ways, we celebrate the lives of Washington's successors, but we also expect them to live up to the heroic qualities of their predecessors during service in this most sacred of America's political positions.

Consistent with this symbolic role, the nation routinely turns to the president to perform a variety of ceremonial chores, many of which are minor, such as lighting the national Christmas tree and issuing proclamations on the observance of special days. But Americans also call upon presidents to perform more important symbolic tasks such as helping citizens deal with their collective grief in the face of disaster. For example, President Reagan expressed the feelings of millions when he publicly mourned the crew lost in the explosion of the space shuttle *Challenger* in 1986.

The presidency, more than any other aspect of political life, links Americans with both the past and the future. In focusing on the current White House occupant, citizens simultaneously derive a sense of fulfillment from past accomplishments and reassurance about the future. But presidential symbolism is not necessarily static; that is, its content may reflect contemporary changes in those qualities Americans expect from the chief executive and may be altered in the future as the public sees fit. Barbara Hinckley argues that presidents and their speechwriters are highly attuned to the public's expectations of a president. In turn, the White House projects "a symbolic presentation of the presidential office" expressed through the chief executive's public actions and statements.[12] With remarkable consistency, the picture portrayed to the public from Truman through Reagan (and we can safely assume through Bush) has emphasized several common themes: the president, the American people, and the nation are indistinguishable from each other and together carry out most of the work of "government"; Congress, when mentioned, usually is dismissed rather than recognized as an equal branch of government; identifiable population groups share in the larger purposes that unite the nation; political and electoral activity is far less prominent in presidential discourse than references to religious objects like God and the Bible; presidents are without peers and enjoy a unique relationship with the public.[13]

As Hinckley suggests, the public might be able to reshape the presidency and its position in the constitutional order by altering expectations of the office and its occupants. But this possibility may be more theoretical than real. As we have seen, enormous pressures for continuity have developed around the presidential office; expectations of heroic performance and belief in the identity between presidents and the nation are attitudes that are deeply embedded in the political culture. Collectively, these beliefs about the presidency provide the incumbent with a remarkably durable base of popular support. Moreover, through their actions and speeches, presidents may directly and indirectly play on these symbolic meanings and benefit from an additional upsurge in public support. Some of these efforts are strained, as when presidents associate themselves with other popular heroes by phoning the locker room of the winning team in the World Series or the Super Bowl. Other efforts may be dangerous. Would a president, for example, intentionally feign a national security alert to benefit from the symbolic unity the nation feels in such crises? Some speculate that President Nixon did so in October 1973 when he placed American military forces on worldwide alert as the Watergate investigation was advancing.

Symbolism is not the only factor shaping public attitudes toward the presidency, but it would be wrong to ignore its impact. Symbols are likely to be no less important in American culture than in the foreign cultures where we are more accustomed to recognize their significance.

Developing Children's Attitudes Toward the Presidency

Cultural attitudes like those discussed in the preceding section are transmitted to new generations through a process social scientists call "political socialization." Considerable attention has been devoted to the attitudes that children develop toward the presidency. During the Eisenhower and Kennedy administrations, three major studies of the political attitudes of white, urban, middle-class children, ages seven through thirteen, showed the importance of the president in a child's world.[14] For younger children, presidents share the spotlight with the local mayor and police officers as visible political officials, but as children grow older the president becomes more prominent, and children place more emphasis on his power. Not until they are teenagers are children aware that the president shares the running of the government with Congress and the Supreme Court. In the *cognitive* (knowing) world of the young child, therefore, the president personifies the government. These early studies also underscored the *affective* (emotional) dimension of children's attitudes toward the president. Not only are they aware of the president's importance, but also they think of him as a "good" person who cares about people, wants to help them, and wants to "get things done." For the young child the president is both powerful and benevolent; only when the child grows older does he or she view the president less favorably.

Researchers have offered several explanations for the favorable attitudes of young children. Parents who view the president favorably pass on these views to their children; those who do not, often tend to suppress their unfavorable views for fear of undermining the child's respect for authority. Children's favorable attitudes toward other authority figures, particularly their fathers, might carry over into their respect for the president, who becomes a kind of family figure "writ large." A third explanation for children's favorable views emphasizes their sense of vulnerability—they want to believe the president is a good person who will protect rather than threaten them. But it was discovered that children are able to distinguish between the person temporarily occupying the office and the presidency itself. They therefore can respect the institution without respecting the incumbent, an attitude that could carry over into

their adult years and provide a solid basis of support for the U.S. political
system.

Subsequent research has found that not everyone experiences the same
socialization. Poor children in Kentucky were found to be much less
favorably disposed toward the president, regarding him as less honest, less
hard working, less caring, and less knowledgeable than had the urban
middle-class children of previous studies.[15] Nearly a quarter of these children viewed the president as a malevolent rather than a benevolent
leader. After revelations of the Watergate scandal, a group of middle-class
children were less likely to idealize the chief executive than their earlier
counterparts, nor did they assign the president as important a role in
running the country or in making its laws.[16] Children interviewed at the
time of the Watergate hearings, which were televised, had a much less
idealized view of the president than another group studied in 1969 and
1970, at the height of the Vietnam War. Fred Greenstein concluded that
children had been more insulated from the political turmoil of the 1960s
and its subsequent effects than they were from the Watergate scandal of
the 1970s.[17]

Can we expect socialization experiences during the 1960s and 1970s to
have lingering effects? Most findings suggest not. Studies have found a
less benevolent image of the president among both middle-class and Appalachian students, but there is evidence that by early 1975, some of the
extremely negative feelings revealed in 1973 had moderated.[18]

Thus, children's attitudes may be shaped by their social and economic
backgrounds, norms from the geographic area in which they live, and by
salient political events, such as Watergate. Children may have different
affective and cognitive views of the president: they may dislike a president
but still think he is an important and powerful political leader. They also
can distinguish between the personal qualities of a president and his
performance in office. Moreover, within a relatively brief time, the images
that children have of the president began to return to the pre–Watergate
pattern. Finally, because children as a group do not necessarily regard all
presidents favorably, this research casts doubt on the view that a base of
presidential support *automatically* carries over into the adult years. Rather,
as following sections will indicate, presidents must exert considerable
effort to win support from American citizens.

Attitudes of Adults

Although the president does not dominate the political world of adults the way he does that of young children, he is still by far the most visible person in the American political system. Not surprisingly, the president is the public official most likely to be correctly identified in surveys. He also enjoys general respect and admiration; in Gallup polls asking Americans to name the man, living anywhere in the world, whom they most admire, the president of the United States is almost always the first choice.[19] The first lady usually heads the list of most admired women.

Favorable attitudes are expressed toward the "generalized abstract" president rather than toward any specific incumbent.[20] In one survey, most persons agreed that the president "stands for our country" and that they sleep better when a president they trust is watching over the country. They also tended to believe that the president should be given a chance to work out his policies before he is criticized and that, even if the president is wrong, once he has committed the nation to action, people should be supportive. Most respondents also believed that in time of crisis in domestic or foreign affairs, all citizens should rally to support the president. Citizens more likely to be supportive were those who are older, who belong to a more conservative religious denomination, who have little formal education, who identify with the lower or working class, who have a low-prestige occupation, and who are black and female. Specific psychological traits were associated with people providing high presidential support—in particular, personal inflexibility and authoritarianism. Individuals who favorably evaluated the entire American political system also were likely to be highly supportive of the president.

The public also develops attitudes toward particular occupants of the office. Since the end of World War II, the Gallup organization periodically has polled a cross-section of Americans on whether they approve or disapprove of the way the president is handling the job. The emphasis of the question is on performance in office rather than personal qualities.

A study by John Mueller, based on his analysis of the answers to that Gallup question from 1946 to 1970, shows that all the presidents of that period, except for Dwight Eisenhower, declined in popularity over the course of their term in office.[21] They typically start with a high level of support, as the public accords them a measure of trust that they will do well in the job. As presidents undertake various actions, however, they antagonize more and more groups. Mueller explains that a "coalition of minorities" forms as different groups respond unfavorably to presidential decisions, as businesses did when President Kennedy forced them to roll back a steel price rise in 1962, and as southerners did when he sent federal officials to the South to enforce integration. Although the various groups become unhappy with the president for different reasons, the result is a progressive decline in the president's popularity.[22] In addition to this overall downward trend, public opinion on the presidency is affected by certain kinds of events. A downturn in the economy, particularly if it increases the rate of unemployment, harms presidential popularity. (A decrease in unemployment, however, does not improve the president's popularity.) International events can affect public opinion either way. A dramatic event, involving national and presidential prestige, may inspire Americans to "rally 'round the flag" and support their chief executive. They do so even if things turn out badly, as they did at the Bay of Pigs in 1961 when the U.S. effort to help ex-Cuban forces invade the island and overthrow Fidel Castro ended in a fiasco. But wars that drag on and involve significant casualties, such as those in Korea and Vietnam, ultimately harm the president's popularity. Jimmy Carter's inability to solve the 1979–1980 hostage crisis in Iran had a similar effect.

Finally, the party affiliation of adults in the United States affects their opinion of the president's performance. Those who identify with the party out of power start with much less support for the president than members of the president's party. In addition, those in the out-party are more easily alienated by the president's policies or by unfavorable events; they also tend to resume criticism sooner after the temporary favorable effect of an international crisis. As a result, presidents enjoy far less support at the end of their term from out-party identifiers than from in-party identifiers.

Subsequent studies confirm some of Mueller's major findings. The chief executive's prestige is generally high at the beginning of a term as the public grants him the opportunity to establish successful relationships with other public officials.[23] One study found that wars and military crises affect public support for an average duration of five months.[24] Another found that some events during the years from 1953 to 1980 substantially increased the president's approval rate—for example, U.S. action against the Soviet Union during the 1962 missile crisis in Cuba and the ending of the Vietnam War—while others, such as the Bay of Pigs and the ending of the Korean War, did not.[25] George Edwards concludes that events that

generate sudden increases in presidential popularity are "highly idiosyn-
cratic and do not seem to significantly differ from other events that were
not followed by significant surges in presidential approval."[26]

Economic factors affect presidential popularity. In addition to the rate
of unemployment, the rate of inflation also influences the public attitude
toward the president.[27] Edwards found that in assessing President Carter,
Democrats were strongly affected by unemployment statistics, while Republicans were more concerned with inflation.[28] Another analyst has
determined that increases in both unemployment and inflation convince
the public that things are getting worse economically and therefore de-
press the president's popularity.[29]

Scholars have challenged Mueller's theory that the coalition of minorities causes a steady, long-term decline in presidents' popularity. James
Stimson suggests instead that the decline is cyclical, reaching a low point
the third year of a president's term and then rising again in the fourth year
as the president who is seeking reelection manipulates events to his advantage.[30] The president who does not stand for reelection also benefits in
the fourth year in office because, as he is retiring, his motives are less open
to cynical interpretation. Stimson attributes the decline in popularity not
to the president's alienating various groups but to the public's becoming
disillusioned with presidential performance, as the unrealistic expectations about what the chief executive can accomplish are not fulfilled.
Stimson suggests that the less well informed segments of the American
public are most likely to harbor such expectations.

Kernell, too, maintains that events rather than time in office affect a
president's prestige.[31] Moreover, it is not presidents' decisions that determine their popularity, as the coalition-of-minorities factor suggests;
rather, presidents are judged by real conditions and events that occur on
their watch. They also are held accountable by the American public for
what they *do not* do: if a president does not attempt to deal with a major
problem, such as the energy crisis, and it persists, his popularity declines.

Figure 3-1 shows results of the Gallup poll on presidential performance
during the Carter, Reagan, and Bush administrations. Reagan and Bush
began with initial approval rates of only 51 percent, low compared to
Jimmy Carter's 66 percent rating. Carter's approval ratings suffered steady
erosion except for a rally in public support after the Soviet Union invaded
Afghanistan and Iran seized U.S. hostages in fall 1979. Carter's rating
declined as the hostage crisis remained unresolved and took a dramatic

Figure 3.1 Presidential Approval, 1977–1992

Percent

Note: Question: "Do you approve or disapprove of the way _____ (last name of president) is handling his job as president?"

Source: The Gallup Opinion Index as analyzed by Harold W. Stanley and Richard G. Niemi, *Vital Statistics on American Politics*, 3d ed. (Washington, D.C.: CQ Press, 1992), Figure 8-2.

nose dive following the unsuccessful hostage rescue attempt in 1980. He left office with barely a third of the citizenry approving his performance.

Both Reagan and Bush enjoyed significant improvements from their initial low ratings. Reagan's rating rose to 68 percent following the unsuccessful attempt on his life by John Hinckley, Jr., in late March 1981. His popularity began to decline in mid-1981 and continued to do so as the economy worsened, reaching its lowest point in early 1983. When the economy began to improve, so did Reagan's approval rate, which increased steadily in 1983 and ended on a high note late that year following the invasion of Grenada. His approval rate remained constant during the first half of 1984 and then rose at the time of the summer Olympics and the fall election campaign. President Reagan's ratings remained high throughout most of 1986, the second year of his second term, before plummeting by sixteen percentage points after the revelation of the Iran-contra affair, the largest single monthly decline in the history of Gallup surveys on presidential approval ratings. Nonetheless, Reagan's low point never rivaled Carter's. Reagan's ratings gradually recovered and by the end of 1988 had returned to a healthy level.

Bush's approval ratings also went through dramatic changes. From the initial low, they rose to 70 percent by June 1989, hit 80 percent in January 1990, increased to nearly 90 percent following the Persian Gulf War, and plunged to less than 50 percent at the beginning of 1992. During his first year in office Bush was the beneficiary of favorable foreign policy developments: the disintegration of communism in Eastern Europe and the highly popular U.S. invasion of Panama to seize Manuel Noriega. His ratings declined in the early fall of 1990 because of conflict with Congress over the budget and concerns about the American military response to Iraq's invasion of Kuwait. Bush's approval ratings went into the stratosphere, however, following the successful war in the gulf, hitting 89 percent during the week of February 28–March 3, 1991, the highest Gallup poll rating in history. Declines from that level were inevitable but began to accelerate late in 1991 as the recession lingered and questions were raised about the president's lack of a game plan. Going into the 1992 election year, momentum was decidedly against Bush.

Edwards emphasizes that the public judges presidents by their *policies*. As he put it, "Evidently the public evaluates the president more on the basis of how it thinks the government is performing on economic policy than how it thinks the economy itself is performing."[32] Moreover, people assess economic policy by how it affects the entire nation, not just their personal situation. He finds a similar pattern in public judgments of presidents' handling of war, with the nation's welfare rather than an individual's own experience considered most important.

It is not just events that determine how a president is regarded but how the public *perceives* those events. The perception, in turn, depends on how the mass media report the news. If there is a discrepancy between the balance of good and bad news and the way the president was regarded before the reporting of that news, his popularity moves in the direction of the discrepancy.[33] It has also been determined that a relationship exists between the amount of television news time accorded the president, as well as the proportion of positive coverage, and how the public views him.[34] Negative coverage also affects the president's opinion ratings.[35] A similar connection exists between the number of nationwide radio or television broadcasts a president makes and the amount of support received from the American public.[36]

Public views toward presidents, therefore, reflect long-term attitudes on the office as an institution as well as short-term responses to a particular incumbent based on international and domestic events, the state of the economy, policies of the president, news reports on events, and the president's use of the media. The next section analyzes how chief executives use such influences to enhance their popularity with the American public.

Projecting A Favorable Image

Presidents are not passive objects of public attitudes. Rather, presidents and their aides take the initiative in shaping public perceptions. In doing this, they fashion appeals for different kinds of audiences, including the general public and particular segments of that public, represented primarily by interest groups.

Appealing to the Public

Consistent with the positive attitudes that Americans hold toward the presidency's symbolic roles, chief executives seek to present themselves in those terms, that is, to personalize the American political system and to embody American ideals. They do this through conscious choices about what they do, where they travel, and what they say.

There are ample opportunities for presidents to emphasize the ceremonial aspects of the office. Each year the president receives innumerable invitations to appear at national conventions, public gatherings, and celebrations, as well as requests to endorse various worthwhile causes. Responses vary widely. Important groups may garner a visit and speech. If deemed worthy, the president may make an appearance to dedicate a new hospital, dam, or library. At times, he may even make a televised appeal or merely lend his name in behalf of a cause. Dwight Eisenhower, for example, began the practice of proclaiming a "national day of prayer" in coordination with Catholics, Jews, and major Protestant denominations.

Major holidays offer the opportunity to stir the public's patriotic sentiments. For example, on his first Fourth of July in the White House,

Ronald Reagan held a picnic complete with a gigantic fireworks display. Five years later, he helped commemorate the restoration of the Statue of Liberty, again on the Fourth of July, in a televised celebration with appearances by big name entertainers.

Trips emphasize the president's role as head of state, particularly trips abroad because the chief executive becomes the representative of the United States and the American people. Eisenhower visited eleven foreign countries, Kennedy toured Europe with his wife, and Nixon made historic visits to mainland China and the Soviet Union. Nixon's visits coincided with his reelection campaign and provided him an added benefit. Early in his term, Carter went to Great Britain to meet with leaders of the major Western industrial nations. Reagan attended a similar conference in Canada during his first year in office and later in his first term visited China, the Normandy beaches of France (which became the backdrop for dramatic reelection ads), and his family's ancestral home in Ireland.[37]

To a lesser extent, domestic trips also enhance the image of the president as a national leader. As Louis Koenig points out, George Washington initiated a "grand tour" of two-months' duration by visiting the South in 1791, a region where suspicions of central authority had run strong during the constitutional ratification campaign.[38] Modern presidents have continued Washington's tradition, often dispensing patronage to states and localities along the way. Travel to special locations frequently is used to highlight particular themes. In 1985, for example, Reagan kicked off his tax reform proposal in Williamsburg, Virginia, calling it the "new American Revolution."[39] Bush traveled to Arizona in 1991 to use the Grand Canyon as a spectacular prop for a message on the environment.

Not all presidential trips turn out well, however. Woodrow Wilson's ill-fated attempt to take his case for the Versailles peace treaty to the American people ended in failure. He collapsed near the end of his tour and was disabled for a long period. Moreover, the citizens failed to respond to his pleas, and some historians have concluded that not a single senator's vote was changed by this difficult journey. Reagan's trip to Europe in 1985 included a visit to a cemetery at Bitburg, West Germany, to symbolize reconciliation between the United States and its former enemy. When it was discovered that officers of the Waffen S.S., the military arm of Hitler's elite corps, were buried there, many people criticized Reagan for appearing to honor an organization responsible for the mass killings of the Holocaust. Finally, the difficulty experienced by George

Bush during his trip to the Far East in late 1991 seemed to symbolize his declining political fortunes. Corporate executives accompanying the president argued publicly with their hosts, and the president was personally embarrassed when a stomach virus attacked at the worst possible time— during a state dinner with the Japanese prime minister, which was captured on videotape.

Although their occurrence cannot be planned, crises and a president's responses to them may also improve his standing when opinion rallies 'round the flag. What is most important is that the president appear to be decisive, as Kennedy did in the Cuban missile crisis, and Ford did in the *Mayaguez* incident with Cambodia after the Vietnam War, and that Americans perceive the president as defending the interests of the nation from foreign or domestic threats. To the extent possible, therefore, the White House works to project the right kind of image. Bruce Miroff suggests that during the Grenada invasion of 1983, effective management of stories and pictures about the president's handling of a sudden crisis and a news blackout of the invasion enabled Reagan to reap substantial rewards in public support.[40] The president portrayed the Grenada invasion as an end to "our days of weakness," a successful rescue of endangered American students, and the liberation of peaceful islanders from a communist plot. Miroff calls the deliberate projection of images "to shape public understanding and gain popular support" a "spectacle."[41] And although he traces the roots of such White House efforts to the Kennedy administration, Miroff suggests that they are becoming more frequent.

Unlike basic attitudes of political culture, which link the chief executive with the country, the constitutional system, and the presidential office, attitudes relating the president to less stable matters of public opinion are much more likely to be unfavorable. People may respect the presidency as an institution but may not like the personality or political style of the incumbent. They may agree with the broad, general rules of the game and the basic values that the president embodies but disagree with his positions on controversial issues of public policy. They may also feel that the president is unsympathetic with certain economic, social, or political groups with which they identify or that he is partial to groups they oppose. Presidents must take these factors into account when they attempt to shape public attitudes that link them with the day-to-day operation of the American political system.

One tactic presidents use is to try to create a favorable impression of themselves as individuals. This approach may take the form of emphasizing their "down-to-earth" qualities, the traits that make them "ordinary" people. When Gerald Ford first succeeded to the presidency, much was made of the fact that he toasted his own English muffins for breakfast. At his swearing-in ceremony, Carter wore a dark business suit rather than the traditional morning coat, and then he walked up Pennsylvania Avenue to the White House rather than riding at the head of the inaugural parade as his predecessors had done. He also participated in a call-in radio show and visited a New England community for a mock town meeting, staying overnight with a family who had supported his presidential campaign. Reagan saw to it that he was frequently photographed in informal Western attire, often astride his favorite horse or chopping wood on his ranch. Bush made it known that he loves country music and pork rinds, hates broccoli, plays baseball, enjoys fishing, and drives his cigarette boat as fast as possible. Presidents also like to be pictured as family men, surrounded by an adoring wife and respectful children. These images are stressed during election campaigns and continue to be seen throughout the White House years.

Perhaps the president's most difficult task in fostering favorable public attitudes is assuaging opposition to his stands on public policy issues, some of which may be controversial. One way chief executives deal with this difficult problem is to sensitize themselves to public views by paying close attention to the results of public opinion polls conducted by organizations such as Gallup, Harris, and television network-press alliances such as CBS and the *New York Times.* Starting with Franklin Roosevelt, presidents have hired their own pollsters—for example, Patrick Caddell worked for Carter and Richard Wirthlin for Reagan—to probe public attitudes more deeply on the issues in which the chief executives are particularly interested. Although presidents may not choose to follow the sentiments of a majority of Americans, a knowledge of public attitudes is helpful: Carter used polls to measure how effectively he was getting his message across to the public; Reagan used them to determine when the mood of the country was amenable to his proposals.[42]

Targeted Communications: Presidents and Interest Groups

Just as scholars discovered that political socialization may vary by subgroups, we also know that opinions vary by group. People who organize to advocate a particular interest are highly attentive to public issues that affect their members. These groups also have ongoing links with Congress and the bureaucracy that provide them with policy-making influence. The president, therefore, must also communicate with these specific populations. For example, presidents give major public addresses on business to conventions of the National Association of Manufacturers or the Chamber of Commerce of the United States, and on labor relations to meetings of the AFL-CIO. Chief executives also dispatch surrogates, such as cabinet officers, to speak on their behalf and in support of the administration's programs. Moreover, White House aides serve as a channel for private communications with group representatives and will sometimes arrange meetings with the president.

Interest groups want to hear about current matters of public policy, but they also want to be reassured that the president is sympathetic to the problems group members face. Not surprisingly, chief executives pay particular attention to the groups that helped them get elected. In this way, they hope to convert their electoral coalition into one that helps them govern, as well. Democratic presidents typically have focused on labor unions and civil rights organizations; Republicans have concentrated on business and professional organizations. At the same time, presidents know that as the leader of the nation, they are supposed to represent *all* the people, not just those who supported their election. Chief executives cannot afford to ignore prominent interest groups, even those that are politically opposed to them. Nixon addressed the annual convention of the AFL-CIO, and Reagan went before an assembly of the National Association for the Advancement of Colored People even though these organizations had not endorsed them.

Presidents also have established channels for routine communication with particular groups through systematic White House liaison. Truman used David Niles, formerly on FDR's staff, as a liaison with several minority groups, including blacks and Jews.[43] Eisenhower, who cultivated an image of being above politics, deemphasized, but did not completely ignore, group relations, and the Kennedy and Johnson administrations designated White House staff members to work with Jews, Catholics, and other groups. Gradually, however, the range of group ties became more predictable so that the Nixon, Ford, Carter, Reagan, and Bush administrations assigned aides to work full-time with eight population groups: business, labor, Jews, consumers, blacks, women, Hispanics, and the elderly.[44] Most of these ties are pursued through the Office of Public

Liaison, a White House staff unit first conceived in the Nixon administration and consolidated in one unit under Ford. The office has continued to be a part of each subsequent administration and has sometimes played an important role in promoting administration policies. Staff members develop mailing lists of groups within their "portfolio" so that newsletters and explanations of administration policy can be mailed to the most interested people.

Thus, the official representation of interest groups in the White House has become institutionalized in the administrations of both political parties. People who serve in the liaison office play two roles in the political process. One is to articulate the demands of interest groups inside White House circles; this role was emphasized by Margaret "Midge" Costanza, Carter's first public liaison chief. A feminist, Costanza supported the use of federal funds for abortion even though the president disagreed with that position. The other role is to rally the support of interest groups behind the president's programs, a task assumed by Ann Wexler, who followed Costanza as head of the office in the Carter administration. Despite this dual purpose, there is little doubt that the office exists primarily to further the president's wishes rather than those of interest groups, and, as Costanza learned by being dismissed, aides who reverse these priorities encounter difficulties.[45]

Presidents, then, attempt to shape the attitudes of both the general public and specific publics as a way to garner favor and support.[46] Their success in that endeavor depends to a considerable extent upon the ability to communicate their appeals through the media, the subject of the following section.

The President and the Media

Historically, the most important link between the president and the American public has been the press. In the early years of the Republic the press was as partisan as it is in many European countries today. The partisan press reached its peak during the presidency of Andrew Jackson when federal officeholders were expected to subscribe to the administration organ, the *Washington Globe,* which was financed primarily by revenues derived from the printing of official government notices.[47]

The partisan press began to decline during the presidency of Abraham Lincoln. The establishment of the Government Printing Office in 1860 destroyed the printing-contract patronage that had supported former administration organs; in addition, Lincoln felt that tying himself to one newspaper would limit his relationships with others.[48] Other factors also contributed to the demise of the partisan press. The invention of the telegraph led to the formation of wire services. Information distributed by wire to all parts of the country tended to be standardized and politically neutral to avoid antagonizing the diverse readerships of the various subscribing newspapers. Increased use of the press for advertising provided newspapers with a secure financial base independent of the support of presidential administrations. By the end of the nineteenth century "news about the White House was transmitted to the public by independent, nonpartisan news organizations," a factor that continues to affect relationships between the president and the press today.[49]

In this century, two new media, radio in the 1920s and television in the 1950s, took their place beside newspapers as channels between the chief executive and citizens, and those media continue to undergo evolution, for example, the development of cable television.[50] Electronic media made it possible for presidents to establish direct contact with people rather than having their message relayed (and interpreted) by journalists.

The Presidential Media

Today, the words and actions of the U.S. president are covered by an enormous variety of media. These media differ not only in the way they deal with executive branch developments but also in their target audience. In addition, they vary greatly in importance to chief executives and their programs. Over the last four decades the way Americans get information has undergone a fundamental change. In 1959, 57 percent of the public claimed to get most of their news from newspapers and 51 percent from television (more than one response was allowed in the survey); but by 1988 only 42 percent cited newspapers as a principal source and 65 percent said television.[51] This pattern developed with the spread of television ownership: only 9 percent of households had television sets in 1950, a figure that grew to 87 percent by 1960 and 98 percent by 1980.[52] As one would expect, White House attention to television coverage rose over the same period.

In addition, the White House must be attentive to the most influential media figures—a select group of columnists, elite reporters, anchors of the broadcast news, and executives of the media organizations. Columnists deal in matters of opinion rather than just factual developments affecting the presidency. "They are guaranteed space, they have no assigned topics, they are freed from the pressure of breaking news stories at deadline, and they have the opportunity to introduce their own perspectives into their stories."[53] George Will epitomizes this sort of columnist, and he appears regularly on television. Elite reporters cover current developments affecting the presidency, explain why certain events have occurred, and examine the effect they are likely to have on the president's program and the governing of the country. David Broder, another member of the elite corps, is both chief political reporter and a columnist for the *Washington Post*.

Syndicated columnists and elite reporters earn White House attention because they reach powerful audiences outside government, including business and labor leaders, lobbyists, and academics, as well as top officials in government—members of Congress, members of the bureaucracy, judges, governors, and mayors. These reporters and columnists influence views on the political feasibility of a president's proposed programs and on their likely effects on various segments of the population.

Television anchors, such as Dan Rather, Peter Jennings, and Tom Brokaw, are important to the president because of the size of the audience they reach, a total of nearly 30 million people each weekday night.[54] Because far more people watch television than read newspapers, the information the ordinary citizen receives about the presidency depends on what is included in the nightly broadcasts. Bureau chiefs and other media executives determine which stories are covered, how they are handled, which reporters are assigned to cover the White House, and who should be represented in "pools" that travel with the chief executive to cover significant events.

The basic task of the presidential press corps is to wait around the White House to see if any of the daily events merit coverage. Their importance to the president and their prestige with fellow reporters depend on the organization to which they belong. Reporters with the *New York Times* and *Washington Post* are considered the most influential by virtue of their readership—beside public officials and important people in the private sector, their readers are the other Washington reporters.[55] These publications (particularly the *Times*) influence decisions on which news stories will be carried on network television broadcasts.[56]

Reporters for the three major television networks loom large in the presidential media because most viewers tend to believe what they see on television; that is, it helps to determine reality for them. At the same time, television coverage of the presidency has serious limitations: very little time is devoted to the most important stories (about seventy-five seconds on the average); emphasis is placed on events that are visually exciting; a focus on the president personalizes complex developments; and broadcasts usually lack in-depth reporting and analysis.[57]

The nation's three major news magazines, *Time, Newsweek,* and *U.S. News and World Report,* bring national news to a broad readership throughout the country; their reporters benefit from having weekly rather than daily deadlines and from combining their efforts into a single, in-depth account. Also significant are the reporters for the wire services—Associated Press (AP) and United Press International (UPI)—because they provide coverage of the president for newspapers across the country that subscribe to their services. Wire service reporters cover "hard news" rather than analysis and focus on the official and personal activities of the president—what Michael Grossman and Martha Kumar refer to as "body-watching."[58] Because they often prepare several stories a day for client newspapers with different deadlines and must cater to the diverse interests of this broad clientele, they have little opportunity for in-depth or interpretative reporting.

Beyond this inner circle of Washington reporters are the many other national journalists who work for a wide variety of news organizations.[59] In addition are the reporters who provide coverage for radio stations around the country (including those that belong to commercial networks as well as those affiliated with the National Public Radio system) and photographers who provide a pictorial record of the presidency.

Channels of Presidential Communication

Because the media interested in the presidency differ in prestige and influence, the chief executive and members of the administration use different techniques and channels of communication to manage the flow of information about the president. Formal communications are provided to all members of the presidential media, but there are also special arrangements through which information is given to select segments. The rules of communications also vary. Some statements may be quoted verbatim and attributed to the president or to one of the top officials in the administration. Other statements are "not for direct quotation," which means that the source may be named but the remarks must be paraphrased. Still others are for "background only"; that is, the information may be reported but not attributed to a source. Finally, "off-the-record" information is provided only for the reporter's general knowledge and understanding and is not to be reported in any form. Moreover, different individuals and units within the executive branch serve as channels to members of the presidential media.

The Press Secretary. The most important person in the executive branch for day-to-day contact with the presidential media is the White House press secretary. Holding two daily briefings, the press secretary provides routine information on executive branch appointments and resignations, on presidential actions and policies, and on the president's schedule—who is visiting that day, meetings, and travel plans. By the end of an administration there may have been more than 2,000 such encounters. In addition, the press secretary holds private meetings with select reporters to provide background information to explain the president's actions on a particular problem or program.

The press secretary's job includes several sometimes contradictory roles: as a conduit, the secretary communicates messages in both directions between the administration and the media; as an agent, the secretary tries to balance serving the interests of the president, members of the White House staff, and members of the media.[60] Although the press secretary serves these three constituencies, the most important constituent is always the president. The secretary can perform well only if granted continuous access to and the confidence of the president so that journalists may assume that the news comes from the chief executive. If a president tries to be his own press secretary, as may have been true of Lyndon Johnson, even a capable and influential person like Bill Moyers will not succeed in managing the message.[61] When secretaries are excluded from White House decisions, their credibility suffers.

Press secretaries of the modern era have varied in effectiveness. Among those considered successful are Stephen Early from Franklin Roosevelt's staff, James Hagerty from Eisenhower's, and Jody Powell, who served under Carter. Hagerty and Powell benefited from the fact that their presidents kept them informed on virtually everything that was going on in the White House. Not all press secretaries have garnered praise. Some have been unpopular with their White House colleagues, and others were openly disdained by reporters. Larry Speakes, press spokesman for Ronald Reagan, provoked cries of outrage when he admitted in his memoirs that he had manufactured quotes during the president's Iceland summit meeting with Soviet General Secretary Gorbachev in November 1985. Fearing that Reagan was being upstaged, Speakes created a public relations solution to the problem, and the fabricated quotes were given prominent attention back home.[62]

The Presidential Press Conference. Beginning with the administration of Woodrow Wilson, presidents have held press conferences to try to influence public opinion and to gauge what is on people's minds as revealed by the questions put to them. Over the years, however, each president has used the institution in his own way. Warren G. Harding, Calvin Coolidge, and Herbert Hoover required that questions be submitted in advance. This practice began when Harding, unprepared for a question about a treaty, gave an erroneous and damaging interpretation of it. Beginning with FDR, presidents have permitted spontaneous questioning, but followed careful rules concerning attribution. With the advent of press conferences that were televised live under Kennedy (Eisenhower had allowed taping, but the White House controlled which clips could be broadcast), presidents turned to other ways to minimize risks. Members of the president's staff draw up a list of questions likely to be asked by reporters, together with suggested answers and supporting information. Presidents have held full-scale mock news conferences for practice. Reagan, for example, liked two-hour practices, dividing the time between foreign policy and domestic policy. Errors would be pointed out, and the president's performance critiqued by staff. On the day of the news conference, photos of the reporters expected to attend were fixed to their likely places on a seating chart, and difficult questions were reviewed.[63]

Reporters sometimes ask "planted" questions, which are suggested by members of the president's staff; these questions naturally receive carefully prepared answers. Moreover, presidents control the interchange. At times, the White House limits questions to domestic policy or foreign policy, and presidents can always refuse to answer certain questions on the grounds that the subject matter is too sensitive for public discussion, a frequent response to foreign and military questions.

The success of a press conference depends on the skills of the president. Harry Truman, who enjoyed the give and take of exchanges with reporters, performed poorly in formal encounters: he tended to answer questions quickly rather than thoughtfully, and he was unable to envision just how his words would look in print or how they might be interpreted. Dwight Eisenhower also came across badly. He appeared to have trouble expressing himself clearly and grammatically and displayed meager knowledge about many vital issues of the day. It has since been revealed that he may have used this as a tactic to avoid sensitive issues.[64]

Franklin Roosevelt and John Kennedy were masters of the press conference. FDR had a keen sense of what was newsworthy and even suggested reporters' lead stories to them. He also prepared members of the press for actions he took on controversial problems by educating them initially with confidential background information; consequently, reporters tended to support his decisions because they understood his reasoning. Kennedy, who had served a brief stint as a newspaperman and enjoyed the company of reporters, used his press conferences to great advantage; his ability to field difficult questions impressed not only the members of the press but also the public. Although Jimmy Carter was not as effective as either Roosevelt or Kennedy, his overall performance in press conferences is considered successful; he came across as calm, well prepared, frank, and articulate.

Despite differences among presidents on how well they handle the press conference, there are some similarities in its use by all chief executives, such as scheduling frequency. Since the advent of television, press conferences have been held less often.[65] Presidents also are less likely to schedule press conferences during periods of international crisis, especially when major policy options are being weighed. After an important decision has been made (such as entering the Korean War or invading Cambodia), a president may schedule a conference to present the nation with a *fait accompli*. Also, news conferences are more likely to be held when the president's standing in the polls is declining rather than rising; perhaps they are considered a way to improve the president's public image, but no one wants to rock the boat when things are going well.[66]

Most people who have studied or been involved in the press conference have concluded that it serves primarily the interests of the president rather than the media. As George Reedy, press secretary to Lyndon Johnson, has pointed out, a president rarely receives an unexpected question on an important issue in a press conference, and, should that happen, the president could respond with a witty or a noncommittal remark.[67] Grossman

Table 3-1 Presidential News Conferences with White House Correspondents, 1929–1991

President	Average number of press conferences per month	Total number of press conferences
Hoover (1929–1933)	5.6	268
Roosevelt (1933–1945)	6.9	998
Truman (1945–1953)	3.6	334
Eisenhower (1953–1961)	2.0	193
Kennedy (1961–1963)	1.9	65
Johnson (1963–1969)	2.2	135
Nixon (1969–1974)	0.6	39
Ford (1974–1977)	1.3	39
Carter (1977–1981)	1.2	59
Reagan (1981–1989)	0.6	53
Bush (1989–1991)[a]	1.5	45

Source: Harold W. Stanley and Richard G. Niemi, *Vital Statistics on American Politics*, 3d ed. (Washington, D.C.: CQ Press, 1992), Table 2-4, 59.

[a] As of June 15, 1991.

and Kumar summarize the president's advantage as follows: "The President decides when to hold a conference, how much notice reporters will be given, who will ask the questions, and what the answers will be."[68]

Despite these advantages, the frequency of press conferences has declined *(see Table 3-1)*. George Bush has averaged the most press conferences per month since Lyndon Johnson (in eighteen months Bush exceeded Reagan's eight-year total) but he is still far below the pretelevision presidents.[69] The decline in frequency parallels the rise in televised coverage; each press conference may now be regarded as a more newsworthy event and therefore discourage the more informal exchanges that occurred earlier.

George Bush has altered the format for most of his conferences by returning to a more informal exchange with the media, achieved by holding most of his sessions during mid-day rather than prime-time evening hours. As a result, the press conferences are less widely viewed (CNN is the principal source of coverage), but the president earns points with the press for his accessibility. As one observer noted, Bush "does not use the press corps as a prop to speak to the American people, as other presidents have."[70]

Other Presidential Channels of Communication. In some instances presidents may want to communicate directly with the American people without having their remarks filtered by reporters or columnists. Although he held relatively few press conferences, Richard Nixon appeared more often on prime-time television during his first eighteen months in office than did presidents Eisenhower, Kennedy, and Johnson combined, during their first eighteen months. In this way, a president can avoid searching questions from the press, a strategy Nixon adopted in the 1968 presidential campaign. The television networks responded by having reporters and columnists analyze Nixon's remarks immediately after a speech; the administration complained that some of these comments—dubbed "instant analysis"—were excessively critical, and the practice was discontinued for a time, a sign that intimidation can sometimes work as a White House strategy for dealing with the press.

Even presidents who enjoy and do well in regular press conferences turn to other means of communicating directly with citizens. FDR made effective use of radio for his famous "fireside chats," a technique that enabled him to create the feeling that he was coming directly into American homes and speaking personally to each of his millions of listeners. Carter used the same approach in his first television address to the nation: seated before an open hearth and wearing a cardigan sweater, the new president sought to project an image of informality and to underscore his concern with the nation's energy crisis.

In managing their relationships with the media, presidents must take into account their particular strengths and weaknesses. Nicknamed the Great Communicator, Reagan benefited enormously from his previous professional experience in radio, films, and television. To take advantage of those skills, the president frequently addressed the nation on prime-time television and used a series of Saturday radio broadcasts to explain and justify his administration's policies. The administration also avoided or restricted its use of other media formats that President Reagan did not handle as well as prepared speeches, specifically those that required him to give spontaneous answers to questions. He did not participate in call-in shows and seldom invited reporters to the White House for informal, on-the-record question and answer sessions. Reagan seldom would answer impromptu questions from reporters at photo sessions, and he held fewer press conferences in eight years than President Carter did in four.

Reagan's reluctance to hold press conferences was a reversal of his practice as governor of California. Lou Cannon, probably the closest observer of Reagan's political career, argues that regular press conferences had provided policy discipline for Governor Reagan—he had to become familiar with government programs to conduct the sessions. This discipline was lost in the White House after aides became concerned about his poor performances at several of the first-year press conferences and discouraged meeting with reporters.[71] As a result, nationally televised speeches became "the basic mode of public communication during his presidency."[72] It was not that Reagan gave substantially more major addresses than his predecessors,[73] but he seemed to use the occasions to greater effect as befits someone with "a sense of theater that propels him to tell stories in their most theatrically imposing manner," the evaluation offered by Ken Kachigian, one of Reagan's speechwriters.[74] Reagan thus used the natural drama of appearances before joint sessions of Congress to launch his economic plan in 1981 and the Strategic Defense Initiative, which became known as Star Wars, in 1983.

Bush offered a marked contrast with Reagan. He held more press conferences and made fewer televised speeches to the nation. Bush's first televised Oval Office speech was not made until September 6, 1989, and was marked by a major distraction. The speech was designed to focus on illicit drugs and the administration's antidrug program. Like Reagan often did, Bush used a prop, in this case, a bag of crack cocaine bought virtually on the White House doorstep, across the street in Lafayette Park. It was later revealed that the drug dealer had been lured to the location so that federal officials could make the buy and the president could make the claim more dramatic. The contrived nature of the incident undermined the message.[75]

Director of Communications. Since the administration of Lyndon Johnson, the White House has assigned someone to oversee the general message and symbolism projected to the public, a position known as director of communications. At times, more than one person takes on this job. For example, in his first term, President Reagan benefited greatly not only from the skill and experience of Director of Communications David Gergen, but also from that of James A. Baker III and Michael Deaver, other members of the White House staff who carefully managed his media and public image.

This team was especially adept at selecting the "line of the day," based around a story or "photo-opportunity" featuring the president that would dominate the evening news, as well as a "theme for the week," selected to coordinate communication throughout the entire administration. Managing these undertakings required sensitivity to media rhythms, an eye for the dramatic, and a sense of politics. The absence of this team was keenly felt in Reagan's second term when the images were not nearly so favorable. Similarly, one explanation for the slump in Bush's popularity in mid-1990 and mid-1991 was the absence of a senior White House official with extensive political experience to manage the communication message.[76]

Regardless of how carefully the White House plans, the nature and timing of events also influence how the media and the American people view the president. The potentially damaging effects of the bombing of the Marine barracks in Lebanon in late 1983 were mitigated by stories, shortly following, on the successful invasion of Grenada. In contrast, there was no mitigating development in late 1986: the story on the Iran arms shipment was followed immediately by another on the alleged diversion of profits from the arms sale to assist the contras in Central America. Moreover, the complexity and long-term nature of the Iran-contra affair meant that media and public attention focused on the matter for a protracted time as one revelation after another was released.

Relations Between the President and the Media: Conflict or Collusion?

It is common for presidents to view the press unfavorably. George Washington, whom journalists treated rather well, was inclined not to run for a second term because of what he considered a critical press.[77] From that beginning, virtually all presidents have expressed outrage, indignation, resentment, or consternation over their treatment in the media.

In turn, members of the press have criticized the way presidents handle media relations. Typically, chief executives are accused of "managing" the news and, as their terms in office progress, of becoming increasingly "isolated" from the media and the American people. Some, such as Lyndon Johnson and Richard Nixon, also were charged with deliberately lying to the media and the public.

There is little question that a built-in conflict exists between the president and the media. Chief executives want to suppress information they feel will endanger the nation's security or put their administrations in a bad light. Members of the media are eager for news, however sensitive it may be, and they have an interest in criticizing the president and his associates as a means of getting the public's attention and thereby creating a demand for their services.

Despite the potential for conflict, there is a basis for cooperation between presidents and the press that ultimately produces a collusive relationship.[78] Quite simply, the two are mutually dependent: neither presidents nor the press can perform their jobs without the assistance of the other, and cooperation is, therefore, mutually beneficial. The president must be able to communicate with the public through the media, and the media must have the administration's cooperation if they are to cover the most important official in the national government and give the public an accurate assessment of presidential activities. Moreover, the White House offers a range of media services designed to seduce reporters into favorable coverage. The product is an *exchange relationship,* a set of negotiated terms for the interaction between media and the president that favors the White House and disadvantages the public.[79] As David Broder has argued, "We have been drawn into a circle of working relationships and even friendships with the people we are supposed to cover. The distinction between press and government has tended to become erased."[80]

Grossman and Kumar's analysis of media coverage is devoted to six presidents over a twenty-five year period; it shows that, for the most part, coverage has been favorable.[81] From 1953 to 1978 positive stories on the president outnumbered negative stories in *Time* magazine and the *New York Times,* and the same finding held for the "CBS Evening News" from 1968 to 1978. Pictures, particularly those appearing in newspapers, tended to be favorable even when they accompanied a negative story. The number of unfavorable stories rose during the Vietnam War and Watergate scandal, but after 1974 the treatment of the president became more favorable again.[82]

Grossman and Kumar argue that the general relationship between the president and the media goes through certain predictable phases.[83] During the initial period of "alliance," both parties agree that the focus should be on the new administration's appointees and its proposed goals and policies—the presidency is "open"; reporters are likely "to have their phone calls answered, to be granted interviews, and to get information that has not been specifically restricted."[84] During the second phase, "competition," the president wants to concentrate on portraying members of his administration as part of a happy team, committed to common goals and policies, while the media focus on conflicts among personalities in the administration and controversies over policies.[85] Presidents restrict access to themselves and others in the administration and may even go on the attack against especially critical reporters or organizations. The final phase of presidential-media relationships is "detachment." Surrogates manage the news, and presidents appear only in favorable settings scheduled to coincide with major events. The media, in turn, engage in more investigative reporting and seek information from sources other than the White House.

Many people in the executive branch help presidents deal with the media, but the media also have their share of resources. A large number of reporters cover the White House, many of whom have expertise in substantive areas such as law, science, welfare, and defense policy.[86] Nonetheless, members of the media may not use their skills to full advantage. James Fallows argues that journalists covering the presidency generally lack confidence in dealing with the substance of policies and consequently focus their coverage on four areas where they feel most comfortable: administration scandals, internal dissension, a public gaffe or tactical blunder, and the ebb and flow of electoral contests and public opinion polls.[87] The result, according to Fallows, is unintended collusion between the presidency and the media that keeps the public less rather than more informed about American government. This line of criticism goes beyond those who believe that particular presidents received less vigorous scrutiny than they deserved. For example, some have suggested that Reagan's vaunted "Teflon coating" was the product of poor journalism.[88] But the limitations noted by Fallows arise from deep-seated journalistic norms and practices, not their flawed application.

As we have seen, presidents are not powerless to influence the impressions that the public develops of them and their programs. One segment of the public is most likely to to be supportive— members of the president's political party, the subject of the final section of this chapter.

Presidents and Parties

Parties have been important to presidents since 1796, but this relationship has undergone dramatic change throughout American history, particularly over the past fifty years. As reviewed in Chapter 2, political parties emerged early in American history despite concern that they represented a potentially divisive influence. Since the election of 1796, when

Washington retired from office, parties have been central structures in the presidential selection process, nominating candidates, helping diverse social and economic interests to coalesce under a common banner, mobilizing voters, organizing campaigns, raising funds, recruiting personnel for the winning administration, mediating relations with interest groups, and helping to develop programmatic appeals. In modern times, however, responsibility for most of these activities has been transferred elsewhere. With the advent of "personalized politics"—electoral competition that concentrates on candidates more than traditional party loyalties—the link between presidents and their political parties has changed. Campaign staffs are personal constructs almost wholly independent of party structures, and televised ads are the principal means of mobilizing voters. Once in office, presidents use White House aides to recruit personnel, maintain liaison with interest groups, and develop program ideas. In short, presidents are now less dependent on their parties both for winning elections and for governing. Modern presidents largely preempt the services traditionally performed by party leaders.[89]

Thus, the relationship between presidents and their parties has undergone significant change. On the one hand, today's presidents are less constrained by party leaders and structures than in the past. After thirty years of decline, American parties are less powerful organizations run by leaders who are considerably less independent than in earlier days. On the other hand, presidents no longer rely exclusively on these broad-based public structures to muster support behind presidential initiatives.

Altering the Traditional President-Party Relationship

Thomas Jefferson, once a staunch critic of political parties, became the most powerful party leader to occupy the presidency. By exercising control over fellow partisans in Congress, he used the party as a means to govern the nation.[90] Throughout the nineteenth century, parties were the means to effectively link political elites with the public and then bridge the institutional distances so carefully created under the Constitution.[91] The relationship between presidents and party became even more critical with the emergence of an activist conception of the presidency, a change usually associated with Theodore Roosevelt and Woodrow Wilson. When harnessed by a program-minded executive, parties could serve as agents of change and progress, an instrument to facilitate presidential leadership much as Jefferson had demonstrated. But the central concerns of American parties were customarily focused on far more mundane and parochial pursuits—patronage jobs, public contracts, and subsidies—that made them close allies of Congress and resistant to presidential control. As decentralized structures reflecting local conditions and concerns, parties acted far more often as impediments to change and enemies of central leadership than they did as instruments of such efforts. This posed minimal difficulty to most nineteenth century presidents, but became a serious hindrance to the kind of heroic leadership routinely expected in the twentieth century.

Sidney Milkis argues that Franklin Roosevelt's actions ultimately altered the nature of American political parties. Roosevelt abandoned the usual practices of filling administration vacancies with party loyalists, turning instead to committed New Dealers. He attempted to unseat uncooperative members of his own party by supporting challengers to conservative Democrats in primary elections in twelve states during 1938. Party rules governing the presidential nomination were changed to weaken the influence of southern leaders. Roosevelt forged a direct, personal relationship with citizens through the radio to replace the mediated relationship via political parties. And, by creating administrative machinery subject to presidential control, it was made feasible for "the president [to] govern in the absence of party government."[92]

In Milkis's view, subsequent presidents, particularly Johnson and Nixon introduced changes that were consistent with the path of development set in motion by Roosevelt.[93] Johnson ran party affairs from the White House, weakening national and local party organizations. Nixon created the wholly autonomous Committee for the Reelection of the President (CREEP), which hastened the decline of not only Republican party organizations, but also his own presidency. Republican fortunes hit their low point after Nixon resigned from the presidency in disgrace on August 9, 1974; many Republican members of Congress suffered defeat in the November 1974 elections, and Republican identification dropped precipitously. By the mid-1970s, these developments had combined with other trends in American politics (post-1968 reforms in the nomination process, the development of single-issue interest groups, the rise of the professional campaign consultant) to leave the party system largely irrelevant. Presidents Ford and Carter had the misfortune of serving when party fortunes were at their nadir.

Today, the situation may have changed once again. Presidents Reagan and Bush took actions that may not only have revitalized but also reconstructed the Republican party. Both raised large sums of money in behalf of party candidates, an activity other presidents have undertaken but which Reagan and Bush pursued with special vigor. Bush, in particular, brought an extensive history of party service to the White House having served as a county chairman in Texas during the 1960s and as chairman of the Republican National Committee during the Watergate crisis. The result has been a renewal of national party organizations, which have become more important than ever before in American history by raising funds, providing important services to local and national candidates, and serving as a stimulus for policy debate. Republican revitalization occurred first, with the Democrats following suit.

It is possible that a strengthened national party will prove to be more consistent with the president's need to take action at the center of government. Public officials, party leaders, and party activists still look to the president to serve as chief of the party that helped to put him in the White House. However, revitalizing party structures also means that presidents are creating rivals for influence, a development that could prove to be inconsistent with their short-term needs. So long as parties are useful as a vehicle to organize and manage the government, we might expect presidents to continue supporting such revitalization efforts, but once their helpfulness comes into question, presidents might begin to question the value of party building.

Presidents, Party, and Elections

Presidents also try to boost their party by influencing the outcome of elections. As the head of the national ticket, most presidential candidates work to get their party's candidates elected to Congress. Such support is especially valued if it comes from a popular incumbent who is expected to win in November. But it is possible for a chief executive to have little to do with the party's congressional candidates, a strategy Nixon followed in 1972 in his quest to win support from traditionally Democratic voters.

Most presidents also try to influence the outcome of midterm congressional elections, those held between presidential elections, in hopes of minimizing the loss of seats that the president's party customarily experiences in these contests.[94] Assistance in the form of joint campaign appearances, fund raising, and televised speeches cannot be provided to everyone, and the decisions about where to concentrate efforts are often difficult. Should help be channeled to candidates in crucial competitive contests, to close political friends, or important party figures? What about legislators who have voted against the administration's proposals? Of the presidents who have served since Eisenhower, only Johnson chose not to campaign actively in 1966 in the midst of the Vietnam War. Given his background in party affairs, it is not surprising to discover that Bush pursued an aggressive strategy of presidential support during the 1990 midterm election. He helped to recruit some candidates, committed at least one day a week to campaign-related visits after Labor Day, increased his time commitment to three or four days a week as election day approached, and was credited with having raised $80 million in behalf of candidates.[95]

But it is surprising how seldom presidents attempt to pick their party's nominees for Senate and House seats. A study by William Riker and William Bast of approximately 1,200 congressional nomination campaigns from 1943 to 1960 indicated that presidents endorsed only thirty-seven candidates, only seventeen of whom won both the nomination and the general election.[96] Even a popular president such as Franklin Roosevelt had only partial success in his 1938 foray into congressional nominations: of his twelve endorsees that year, only six got to Congress, but, by violating traditional norms, the president suffered a more serious setback. Riker and Bast attribute this limited presidential involvement in congressional nomination contests to the long tradition of such contests being exclusively state or district business. Presidents also are reluctant to make an enemy in Congress by endorsing the wrong candidate.

If the battle lines in a congressional nomination have not been drawn, however, a president can influence the selection of congressional candidates by taking early action in support of prospective contenders. Chief executives attempt to build a base of support in Congress by recruiting candidates who share their views on public policy. Presidents also work discreetly behind the scenes through sympathetic state and local political leaders to interest people in running and may use their influence to funnel needed funds to candidates they favor.

There are limits to what a president can accomplish, however, especially in elections for the House of Representatives. For one thing, the sheer number of contests (435 every two years) precludes participation in many of them. For another, there is good evidence that the off-year House elections are primarily local, not national, events. Scholars who have examined off-year congressional elections report the same basic finding: how people vote has more to do with their evaluations of the congressional candidates than with their assessment of the president.[97] Moreover, incumbency is a valuable asset for congressional candidates; they benefit from previous campaign experience, close relationships with voters, greater knowledge of issues, and superior financial resources, which give them a considerable advantage over their opponents.[98] Presidents who attempt to campaign against sitting members of Congress therefore face almost insurmountable odds.

Midterm election outcomes depend on the condition of the national economy and the president's standing in public opinion polls at the time of the elections.[99] Voting in these contests tends to be *negative;* that is, those who disapproved of the president's performance in office are more likely to cast their ballot in such elections than those who approve of his performance.[100] Gary Jacobson contends that the president's role in congressional elections is essentially indirect: the state of the economy and the president's ratings in the public opinion polls influence the caliber of candidates who run in congressional elections. If, for example, these are not favorable, the opposition party will be able to field an unusually large proportion of formidable challengers with well-financed campaigns, and the president's party in Congress may lose a considerable number of seats.[101]

Senatorial midterm elections offer a somewhat more encouraging opportunity for presidents who wish to influence results. Approximately one-third of the Senate's 100 seats are at stake every two years, so the chief executive can concentrate on these contests in a way that is not possible for House races. Although sitting senators are in the same position as House members in being able to bring their name to the attention of constituents, incumbency is not as advantageous for a senator as it is for a House member, because most Senate races are hard fought. Challengers are much more visible to the electorate than are those who run against House incumbents. Popular presidents, therefore, are better able to help candidates who challenge incumbent senators of the opposite party by increasing the challengers' visibility through public association.

Senate elections since the early 1960s demonstrate the combined effect of these factors. In 1962, when John Kennedy was president, his party lost five seats in the House but picked up two in the Senate; in 1974, when Gerald Ford succeeded to the presidency after Nixon's forced resignation, Republicans lost forty-eight House seats but only five Senate seats. Republicans lost eight House seats in 1990 but gained one seat in the Senate *(see Table 3-2).*

Table 3-2 Gains and Losses of President's Party in House and Senate Off-Year Elections, 1942–1990

Year	President	President's party	Change in House seats	Change in Senate seats
1942	Roosevelt	Democratic	− 50	− 8
1946	Truman	Democratic	− 54	− 11
1950	Truman	Democratic	− 29	− 5
1954	Eisenhower	Republican	− 18	− 1
1958	Eisenhower	Republican	− 47	− 12
1962	Kennedy	Democratic	− 5	+ 2
1966	Johnson	Democratic	− 48	− 4
1970	Nixon	Republican	− 12	+ 1
1974	Ford	Republican	− 48	− 5
1978	Carter	Democratic	− 16	− 3
1982	Reagan	Republican	− 27	+ 1
1986	Reagan	Republican	− 5	− 8
1990	Bush	Republican	− 8	+ 1

Source: *Statistical Abstract of the United States* (Washington, D.C.: Government Printing Office, 1986), 247. Data for 1986 and 1990 are from *Congressional Quarterly Weekly Report*, November 8, 1986, 2803; and November 10, 1990, 3796.

Note: Data represent the difference between the number of seats held by the president's party in present and preceding Congress.

At times the president avoids playing party leader. Because voting in the U.S. Congress does not follow strict party lines, presidents often need support from members of the other party. (Chapter 6 examines this matter further.) Eisenhower depended on votes from Democratic members of Congress for many of his programs, particularly in foreign policy; Kennedy and Johnson received crucial Republican support on civil rights legislation as a result of the efforts of Everett Dirksen, the Republican floor leader in the Senate; Carter won passage of the Panama Canal Treaty only because of Republican support; and Reagan's budget victories in 1981 rested on a coalition of Republicans and Southern Democrats in the House. In such circumstances, it is not surprising to find presidents reluctant to engage in aggressive partisan conflict. Campaign rhetoric can be taken personally by members of the opposition party, making it more difficult for the president to win their future support on legislation.

The President and Party Programs

One area of partisan activity the president clearly dominates is the preparation of party programs for dealing with major national problems. A president seeking reelection has the greatest influence in the writing of the party platform at the national convention. The incumbent also has the opportunity to identify party issues and programs during the course of the presidential campaign and may choose to emphasize certain parts of the platform, ignore others, or even take stands at variance with those contained in the document.

Traditionally, students of American politics have concluded that party platforms and presidential campaign speeches are not to be taken seriously. (The platform planks are for candidates to "run" on, not to "stand" on; campaign promises are merely rhetoric and do not constitute commitments on the candidate's part.) Other studies have called into question these somewhat cynical views. As noted in Chapter 2, Gerald Pomper's analysis of the platforms of the Republican and Democratic parties from 1944 through 1978 revealed that presidents took the pledges seriously, and that they worked with Congress or issued executive orders to enact most of their campaign commitments.[102] Fred Grogan found that both Johnson and Nixon acted on more than half of the promises they made in campaign speeches in 1964 and 1968, respectively.[103] Arnold Muller's analysis of Eisenhower's and Kennedy's campaign pledges determined that each of them took action on about three-fourths of his promises.[104] Jeff Fishel's study of the pledges and actions of Kennedy, Johnson, Nixon, Carter, and Reagan concluded that these five presidents acted on some two-thirds of their campaign promises.[105]

Although George Bush has been one of the most party-oriented presidents in the modern era, he has encountered surprising criticism from Republican members of Congress. The most serious breach occurred in October 1990 after Bush entered into an agreement with congressional Democrats on a package of spending cuts and revenue increases for the 1991 fiscal year budget. In brief, the negotiations conducted throughout the summer and fall were based on the president's willingness to forgo his principal policy commitment from the 1988 election—the promise to oppose new taxes. As part of the agreement, Bush accepted increased excise taxes on gasoline, cigarettes, and alcoholic beverages, as well as sales taxes on luxury purchases. In addition, Bush gave up his fight for a cut in the capital gains tax. When the budget agreement was announced just a month before the mid-term election, House Republicans, led by the Minority Whip Newt Gingrich, abandoned the president and voted against the plan. Their action set off a chain reaction among Democrats that defeated the proposal. The package that eventually passed later in the month was even less favorable to the Republican position.

This episode is instructive. Not only did the president lose the immediate battle, but for a time he also lost the leadership on progams within his party.[106] Although presidents do not automatically exercise this type of leadership in their parties, there is a strong expectation that they will do so. When leaders get too far out in front of their followers and violate this expectation, it can exact a heavy price.

The extent to which presidential programs become reality depends to a considerable degree on the president's influence over the party within the government, the officials in the legislative and executive branches who are either elected under a partisan label or appointed primarily because of their party activities or because it is expected that they will implement party views on public policy matters. A president usually has little control over party activities in Congress. Most senators and representatives are elected independently of the president. Moreover, the president has comparatively little influence over the organization of his party in Congress. Although Thomas Jefferson determined who his party's leaders would be, for the most part American chief executives have been chary of interfering with the right of Congress to choose its own people. Dwight Eisenhower was forced to work with Senate Republican leader William Knowland, whose views on foreign policy were quite different from his own. During part of John Kennedy's administration, the Democratic Speaker of the House was John McCormack, a political rival from Kennedy's home state.

The president has more influence over the party in the executive branch. (Chapter 6 examines the president's relations with the executive branch.) The chief executive can make appointments to policy-making posts that both reward individuals for their service to the party and permit them to influence the administration of government programs. In particular, his closest political advisers on the White House staff constitute what is, in effect, the president's personal party: individuals who have labored in the presidential campaign want to protect their chief's interests and promote the administration's policies after they assume their new posts.[107] Ronald Reagan demonstrated the potential influence that a president can exercise over the bureaucracy by carefully selecting political appointees in accordance with ideology as well as shared party affiliation.

The Rhetorical Presidency

The president's relationship with the American people between elections has undergone significant changes. Kernell contends that presidents used to promote their programs primarily by negotiating with other political elites in Congress and the executive branch, but today they more often choose to "go public"; that is, a president resorts to "promoting himself and his policies in Washington by appealing to the American public for support."[108] He does this by means of public addresses, public appearances, and political travel. James Ceaser and his associates make the same point. Referring to this development as "the rise of the rhetorical presidency," they argue that "presidential speech and action increasingly reflect the opinion that speaking is governing. Speeches are written to become the events to which people react no less than the 'real' events themselves."[109]

There are several reasons for this development. The mass media—first radio, and then television—enabled the president to communicate directly with the American people and to reach the public instantaneously. In addition, the tactics of the campaign are now carried into the governing process: Washington "outsiders"—Carter and Reagan are examples— used the same approaches in governing as they used in winning the nomination and the election. As Ceaser and his associates explain, "So formative has the campaign become of our tastes for oratory and of our conception of leadership that presidential speech and governing have come more and more to imitate the model of the campaign."[110] They also contend that beginning with Woodrow Wilson, presidents changed their view of leadership: a president now employs "oratory to create an active public opinion that, if necessary, will pressure the Congress into accepting his program."[111] Kernell sees this development as a somewhat more recent one, a practice presidents use because the elites with whom they must bargain are more numerous, fragmented, and politically independent than before.[112]

Although these new developments undoubtedly have affected the presidency, the fact remains that public opinion cannot be transformed directly into public policy. If the president wants to see his programs adopted and implemented, he must use the powers and institutional arrangements of his office, and he must work with Congress, the executive branch, and the courts to accomplish his purpose. In Chapter 4 we examine the personality traits and skills that presidents bring to this task.

NOTES

1. Henry Jones Ford, *The Rise and Growth of American Politics: A Sketch of Constitutional Development* (New York: Macmillan, 1900), 283.
2. Woodrow Wilson, *Constitutional Government in the United States* (New York: Columbia University Press, 1908, 1961), 68.
3. Richard Neustadt, *Presidential Power: The Politics of Leadership* (New York: Wiley, 1960), 86–107.
4. Samuel Kernell, *Going Public: New Strategies of Presidential Leadership* (Washington, D.C.: CQ Press, 1986).
5. David Easton, *A Systems Analysis of Political Life* (New York: Wiley, 1965), chaps. 10–13.
6. Fred I. Greenstein, "What the President Means to Americans: Presidential Choice Between Elections," in *Choosing the President*, ed. James David Barber (Englewood Cliffs, N.J.: Prentice-Hall, 1974), 144–146.
7. *New York Times*, Nov. 5, 1991.
8. Joseph E. Kallenbach, *The American Chief Executive: The Presidency and the Governorship* (New York: Harper & Row, 1966), 275.
9. Barry Schwartz, *George Washington: The Making of an American Symbol* (Ithaca, N.Y.: Cornell University Press, 1987), 58–63.
10. Ibid., esp. part 2.
11. Schwartz's discussion of public portrayals of Washington and their iconography is especially valuable. Students might want to note whose portraits appear on the most widely circulated coins and currency.
12. Barbara Hinckley, *The Symbolic Presidency: How Presidents Portray Themselves* (New York: Routledge, 1990), 130.
13. Ibid., 131 133.
14. Fred Greenstein, *Children and Politics* (New Haven, Conn.: Yale University Press, 1965); Robert Hess and Judith Torney, *The Development of Political Attitudes in Children* (Chicago: Aldine, 1967); David Easton and Jack Dennis, *Children in the Political System: Origins of Political Legitimacy* (New York: McGraw-Hill, 1969).
15. Dean Jaros, Herbert Hirsch, and Frederick J. Fleron, Jr., "The Malevolent Leader: Political Socialization in an American Subculture," *American Political Science Review* (June 1968): 564–575.
16. Jack Dennis and Carol Webster, "Children's Images of the President and Government in 1962 and 1974," *American Politics Quarterly* (October 1975): 398.
17. Greenstein, "What the President Means to Americans."
18. Christopher Arterton, "The Impact of Watergate on Children's Attitudes towards Political Authority," *Political Science Quarterly* (June 1974): 269–288; Christopher Arterton, "Watergate and Children's Attitudes towards Political Authority Revisited," *Political Science Quarterly* (Fall 1975): 477–496; Dean Jaros and John Shoemaker, "The Malevolent Unindicted Co-conspirator: Watergate and Appalachian Youth," *American Politics Quarterly* (October 1976): 483–505.
19. Findings of the Survey Research Center at the University of Michigan in the

mid-1960s indicated that of all the occupations in the United States, including "famous doctor," "president of a large corporation like General Motors," "bishop or other church official," "Supreme Court justice," and "senator," more than half the adults named the president as the most respected.

20. Samuel Kernell, Peter Sperlich, and Aaron Wildavsky, "Public Support for Presidents," in *Perspectives on the Presidency*, ed. Aaron Wildavsky (Boston: Little, Brown, 1975), 148–181.

21. John Mueller, *War, Presidents and Public Opinion* (New York: Wiley, 1973).

22. Ibid. Mueller attributes Eisenhower's continued high popularity ratings in office to a number of reasons, including his personal appeal, the credit he received for ending the Korean War, his "amateur" political status, which allowed him to appear "above the battle," and the fact that he made few changes in domestic policy and so did not antagonize groups as much as other presidents.

23. Samuel Kernell, "Explaining Presidential Popularity," *American Political Science Review* (June 1978): 506–522.

24. Jong Lee, "Rallying Around the Flag: Foreign Policy Events and Presidential Popularity," *Presidential Studies Quarterly* (Fall 1977): 252–256.

25. George C. Edwards III, *The Public Presidency: The Pursuit of Popular Support* (New York: St. Martin's Press, 1983), 239–247.

26. Ibid., 247.

27. Henry Kenski, "The Impact of Economic Conditions on Presidential Popularity," *Journal of Politics* (August 1977): 764–773; Kristen Monroe, "Economic Influences on Presidential Popularity," *Public Opinion Quarterly* (Fall 1978): 360–369.

28. Edwards, *The Public Presidency*, 235.

29. Robert Shapiro, "Politics and the Federal Reserve," *Public Interest* (Winter 1982): 119–139.

30. James Stimson, "Public Support for American Presidents: A Cyclical Model," *Public Opinion Quarterly* (Spring 1976): 1–21. Another possible reason the incumbent president's performance ratings tend to rise in the fourth year is that when potential political opponents begin to appear on the scene, citizens compare the president with these real people rather than with an abstract ideal of a chief executive.

31. Kernell, "Explaining Presidential Popularity."

32. Edwards, *The Public Presidency*, 233.

33. Richard Brody and Benjamin Page, "The Impact of Events on Presidential Popularity: The Johnson and Nixon Administrations," in *Perspectives on the Presidency*.

34. Donald Singleton, "The Role of Broadcasting in Presidential Popularity: An Exploration in Presidential Power" (Paper delivered at the 1976 annual meeting of the International Communication Association).

35. Fred Smoller, "The Six-O'Clock Presidency: Patterns of Network Coverage of the President," *Presidential Studies Quarterly* (Winter 1986): 42–43.

36. Timothy Haight and Richard Brody, "The Mass Media and Presidential Popularity: Presidential Broadcasting and News in the Nixon Administration," *Communications Research* (Spring 1977): 41–60.

37. Foreign trips have other benefits as well. Not only are they flattering to the people of the visited country, but they also appeal to ethnic groups at home with ties to those nations.

38. Louis Koenig, *The Chief Executive*, rev. ed. (New York: Harcourt, Brace and World, 1968), 188.

39. Kernell, *Going Public*, 93.

40. Bruce Miroff, "The Presidency and the Public: Leadership as Spectacle," in *The Presidency and the Political System*, 3d ed., ed. Michael Nelson (Washington, D.C.: CQ Press, 1991).

41. Ibid., 290.

42. Edwards, *The Public Presidency*, 16–17.

43. Joseph A. Pika, "Interest Groups and the White House under Roosevelt and Truman," *Political Science Quarterly* (Winter 1987–88): 647–668.

44. Joseph A. Pika, "Interest Groups and the Executive: Presidential Intervention," in *Interest Group Politics*, ed. Allan J. Cigler and Burdett A. Loomis (Washington, D.C.: CQ Press, 1983), 318. Also see Joseph A. Pika, "Opening Doors for Kindred Souls: The White House Office of Public Liaison," in *Interest Group Politics*, 3d ed., ed. Allan J. Cigler and Burdett A. Loomis (Washington, D.C.: CQ Press, 1991); and Martha Joynt Kumar and Michael Baruch Grossman, "Political Communications from the White House: The Interest Group Connection," *Presidential Studies Quarterly* (Winter 1986): 92–101.

45. Kumar and Grossman, "Political Communications," 98.

46. In some instances, however, presidents attack special interest groups. John Kennedy publicly castigated the steel companies when, contrary to what he understood to be an understanding with them, they raised steel prices in 1962. See Grant McConnell, *Steel and the Presidency* (New York: Norton, 1963). During his presidency Jimmy Carter publicly criticized oil companies, as well as doctors and lawyers, for being unduly concerned with their own financial interests rather than those of society in general. Such actions usually reflect a president's unhappiness with the attitudes of particular groups toward his policies but may also be calculated to curry the favor of members of the general public, who resent the attitudes of groups they feel are too rich and powerful.

47. James Pollard, *The Presidents and the Press* (New York: Macmillan, 1947), chap. 1.

48. William Rivers, *The Opinion-Makers* (Boston: Beacon Press, 1967), 7.

49. Michael Baruch Grossman and Martha Joynt Kumar, *Portraying the President: The White House and the News Media* (Baltimore: The Johns Hopkins University Press, 1981), 19.

50. Austin Ranney, "Broadcasting, Narrowcasting, and Politics," in *The New American Political System*, 2d ed., ed. Anthony King (Washington, D.C.: American Enterprise Institute Press, 1990).

51. Harold W. Stanley and Richard G. Niemi, *Vital Statistics on American Politics*, 3d ed. (Washington, D.C.: CQ Press, 1992), table 2-13, 74.

52. Ibid., table 2-1, 53.

53. Grossman and Kumar, *Portraying the President*, 209–210.

54. Stanley and Niemi, *Vital Statistics on American Politics*, 3d ed., table 2-2, 55.

55. Stephen Hess, *The Washington Reporters* (Washington, D.C.: Brookings, 1981), chap. 2; Leon Segal, *Reporters and Officials* (Lexington, Mass.: D.C. Heath, 1973), chap. 1.

56. Hess, *The Washington Reporters*, 31.

57. There are some notable exceptions to this rule. The "MacNeil-Lehrer Report," broadcast nightly by the Public Broadcasting Service (PBS), takes an hour to examine two or three topics in depth; ABC's "Nightline" looks at one topic for half an hour. PBS's "Washington Week in Review" uses major political reporters, such as Hedrick Smith, formerly with the *New York Times*, and Haynes Johnson of the *Washington Post*, to analyze the significant news developments of the previous week.

58. Grossman and Kumar, *Portraying the President*, 43.

59. Worthy of note are reporters who write high-quality, in-depth pieces for the *Wall Street Journal*—a weekday publication available throughout the United States, with a large daily circulation. Other skilled journalists work for elite publications with specialized readerships, such as *Business Week, Congressional Quarterly, National Jour-*

nal, and *New Republic;* for large, regional, daily newspapers, such as the *Los Angeles Times, Baltimore Sun,* and *Chicago Tribune;* and for the chains, such as Knight-Ridder or Scripps-Howard, that provide service to many newspapers.

60. Grossman and Kumar, *Portraying the President,* chap. 5.

61. M. L. Stein, *When Presidents Meet the Press* (New York: Julian Messner, 1969), 166.

62. Larry Speakes, *Speaking Out: Inside the Reagan White House* (New York: Scribners, 1988), 136.

63. Bradley H. Patterson, Jr., *The Ring of Power: The White House Staff and Its Expanding Role in Government* (New York: Basic Books, 1988), 174.

64. Fred Greenstein. *The Hidden-Hand Presidency: Eisenhower as Leader* (New York: Basic Books, 1982), 66–70.

65. William Lammers, "Presidential Press Conference Schedules: Who Hides and When?" *Political Science Quarterly* (Spring 1981): 261–278.

66. Jarol Manheim and William Lammers, "The News Conference and Presidential Leadership of Public Opinion: Does the Tail Wag the Dog?" *Presidential Studies Quarterly* (Spring 1981): 177–188.

67. George Reedy, *The Twilight of the Presidency* (New York: New American Library, 1970), 164.

68. Grossman and Kumar, *Portraying the President,* 244.

69. George C. Edwards, "The Politics of Inclusion," in *The Bush Presidency: First Appraisals,* eds. Colin Campbell, S.J., and Bert A. Rockman (Chatham, N.J.: Chatham House, 1991), 148.

70. Ibid.

71. Lou Cannon, *President Reagan: The Role of a Lifetime* (New York: Simon & Schuster, 1991), 158–160.

72. Ibid., 118.

73. Barbara Hinckley found that during his first four years in office, Reagan averaged 5.5 major addresses per year compared to a low of 4.0 for Truman, Johnson, and Carter; 5.0 for Eisenhower, Kennedy, and Ford; and 6.0 for Nixon. Only Eisenhower, Nixon, and Reagan had as many as 7 such addresses in a single year, and Reagan ranked second to Nixon in total addresses, 24 to 22. *The Symbolic Presidency: How Presidents Portray Themselves* (New York: Routledge, 1990), table 1.1, 19.

74. Quoted in Cannon, *President Reagan,* 99.

75. Edwards, "George Bush and The Public Presidency," 146; Miroff, "The Presidency and the Public," 309–310.

76. Colin Campbell, S.J., "The White House and Presidency Under the 'Let's Deal' President," in *The Bush Presidency,* 214.

77. Pollard, *The Presidents and the Press,* 14.

78. Grossman and Kumar, *Portraying the President,* chap. 1.

79. Michael Grossman and Francis Rourke, "The Media and the Presidency: An Exchange Analysis," *Political Science Quarterly* (Fall 1976): 455–470.

80. David Broder, as quoted by Bradley Patterson, Jr., in *The Ring of Power,* 170.

81. Grossman and Kumar, *Portraying the President,* chap. 10.

82. A more recent analysis of the "CBS Evening News" from 1968 to 1985 found that in eleven of the seventeen years studied, the president received more negative than positive coverage; in addition, negative stories became more numerous with each year of a president's term as well as from one administration to the next. See Smoller, "The Six O'Clock Presidency." It should be noted that Smoller's analysis is based on transcripts of the CBS broadcasts, while Grossman and Kumar used films of the broadcasts.

83. Grossman and Kumar, *Portraying the President,* chap. 11.

84. Ibid., 178.

85. This tendency first became apparent during the second year of the Reagan administration when reporters began to ask him more embarrassing questions (for instance, why he did not set an example by making more generous donations to private charities). They also appeared not to take seriously the president's statement that members of his administration were one big happy family.

86. Stephen Hess showed that in 1978, 73 percent were college graduates and 33 percent had graduate degrees (*The Washington Reporters*, 83); Leo Rosten reported that in 1936, 51 percent were college graduates, and 6 percent had an advanced academic degree. See *The Washington Correspondents* (New York: Harcourt, Brace, 1937, 159–160.

87. James Fallows, "The Presidency and the Press," in *The Presidency in the Political System*, 3d ed.

88. Mark Hertsgaard, *On Bended Knee* (New York: Farrar, Straus & Giroux, 1988).

89. See the discussion by Sidney M. Milkis, "The Presidency and Political Parties," in *The Presidency and the Political System*, 3d ed.

90. James MacGregor Burns, *The Deadlock of Democracy: Four-Party Politics in America* (Englewood Cliffs, N.J.: Prentice-Hall, 1963), 36.

91. Stephen Skowronek argues that along with the court system, political parties proved essential to the survival of the new political system by linking governments at center and periphery, reducing the effects of socio-economic divisions, and bridging constitutional separations. See *Building a New American State: The Expansion of National Administrative Capacities, 1877–1920* (Cambridge: Cambridge University Press, 1982), esp. 3–46.

92. Milkis, "The Presidency and Political Parties," 357.

93. Milkis devotes little attention to Eisenhower. It might be argued that Ike contributed to the pattern of change in numerous ways. By cultivating the image of being "above politics," Ike made parties seem less relevant to presidential leadership. This conduct was consistent with his appeal to ticket-splitters, those who crossed over from the Democratic party to vote for Eisenhower while still supporting other Democratic candidates. Finally, Eisenhower set up a number of campaign committees outside the Republican party at least partly to encourage Democratic support.

94. Losses by the president's party in midterm elections have been remarkably predictable. In the thirty-three midterm elections between 1862 and 1990, the president's party lost seats in the House of Representatives in thirty-one (1902 and 1934 are the exceptions) and in the Senate in nineteen of the elections. Stanley and Niemi, *Vital Statistics on American Politics*, 3d ed., table 7-4, 203.

95. Burt Solomon, "Bush Takes to the Campaign Trail . . . But Are Voters Paying Attention?" *National Journal* (Oct. 27, 1990), 2614–15.

96. William Riker and William Bast, "Presidential Action in Congressional Nominations," in *The Presidency*, ed. Aaron Wildavsky (Boston: Little, Brown, 1969).

97. Thomas Mann presents his findings on the 1974 elections in *Unsafe at Any Margin: Interpreting Congressional Elections* (Washington, D.C.: American Enterprise Institute, 1978), 92; Lyn Ragsdale presents her findings on the 1978 elections in "The Fiction of Congressional Elections as Presidential Events," *American Politics Quarterly* (October 1980): 375–398.

98. David Leuthold, *Electioneering in a Democracy: Campaigns for Congress* (New York: Wiley, 1968).

99. Edward Tufte, "Determinants of the Outcomes of Midterm Congressional Elections," *American Political Science Review* (September 1975): 812–826.

100. Samuel Kernell, "Presidential Popularity and Negative Voting: An Alternative Explanation of the Midterm Decline of the Presidential Party," *American Political Science Review* (March 1977): 44–66.

101. Gary Jacobson, *The Politics of Congressional Elections* (Boston: Little, Brown, 1983), 138ff.

102. Gerald Pomper with Susan Lederman, *Elections in America: Control and Influence in Democratic Politics,* 2d ed. (New York: Longman, 1980), chap. 8.

103. Fred Grogan, "Candidate Promises and Presidential Performance" (Paper delivered at the annual meeting of the Midwest Political Science Association, Chicago, April 21–23, 1977).

104. Arnold Muller, "Public Policy and the Presidential Election Process: A Study of Promise and Performance" (Ph.D. diss., University of Missouri-Columbia, 1986), 351.

105. Jeff Fishel, *Presidents and Promises: From Campaign Pledge to Presidential Performance* (Washington, D.C.: CQ Press, 1985), 38.

106. For discussions of these events see portions of the following essays included in *The Bush Presidency:* Paul J. Quirk, "Domestic Policy: Divided Government and Cooperative Presidential Leadership"; Barbara Sinclair, "Governing Unheroically (and Sometimes Unappetizingly): Bush and the 101st Congress"; and Anthony King and Giles Alston, "Good Government and the Politics of High Exposure."

107. Lester Seligman, "The Presidential Office and the President as Party Leader," *Law and Contemporary Problems* (Autumn 1956): 724–734.

108. Kernell, *Going Public,* 1.

109. James Ceaser, Glen Thurow, Jeffrey Tulis, and Joseph Bessette, "The Rise of the Rhetorical Presidency," *Political Studies Quarterly* (Spring 1981): 159.

110. Ibid., 167.

111. Ibid., 163.

112. Kernell, *Going Public,* esp. chap. 2.

READINGS

Cornwell, Elmer. *Presidential Leadership of Public Opinion.* Bloomington: Indiana University Press, 1965.

Edwards, George C., III. *The Public Presidency: The Pursuit of Popular Support.* New York: St. Martin's Press, 1983.

Fishel, Jeff. *Presidents and Promises: From Campaign Pledge to Presidential Performance.* Washington, D.C.: CQ Press, 1985.

Grossman, Michael Baruch, and Martha Joynt Kumar. *Portraying the President: The White House and the News Media.* Baltimore: The Johns Hopkins University Press, 1981.

Harmel, Robert, ed. *Presidents and Their Parties: Leadership or Neglect?* New York: Praeger, 1984.

Hess, Stephen. *The Washington Reporters.* Washington, D.C.: Brookings, 1981.

Hinckley, Barbara. *The Symbolic Presidency: How Presidents Portray Themselves.* New York: Routledge, 1990.

Kernell, Samuel. *Going Public: New Strategies of Presidential Leadership.* Washington, D.C.: CQ Press, 1986.

Mueller, John. *War, Presidents and Public Opinion.* New York: Wiley, 1973.

Schwartz, Barry. *George Washington: The Making of an American Symbol.* Ithaca, N.Y.: Cornell University Press, 1987.

4 PRESIDENTIAL CHARACTER AND PERFORMANCE

Whether he was delivering a speech on the campaign trail or riding a horse at Camp David, Ronald Reagan's message to the American public conveyed optimism and confidence.

WHAT KIND OF PEOPLE HAVE served as president, and how have their personal qualities shaped their conduct? These are the broad questions addressed in this chapter. We are especially concerned with the backgrounds, skills, psychological traits, and management styles of presidents and how these factors influence their performance in office. We therefore examine the abilities and attitudes that presidents develop before entering office, ways in which their personalities affect how they do the job, and habitual ways of performing work. We also look at the way presidents interact with their staffs, those assistants whose positions were created as a way to extend presidents' personal capabilities. To conclude, we take a close look at Ronald Reagan in an effort to understand the factors that shaped a particular president's performance in office.

Determinants and Evaluation of Performance

For generations, historians and political scientists have argued among themselves about just how important a leader's characteristics are for understanding and explaining events. Does one, for example, place great significance on the intelligence, stature, and wisdom of Abraham Lincoln in explaining the Union's ultimate victory over the Confederacy? Or was victory the product of forces beyond Lincoln's control, such as the changing nature of modern warfare in an industrial age, which favored the North? Did America and the Soviet Union avert nuclear war during the Cuban missile crisis of 1962 because of the decision style adopted by John F. Kennedy? Or was the outcome the result of organizational routines for crisis management and other random occurrences perhaps not even intended by either side during the confrontation? The larger questions, then, are just what importance should one ascribe to the president's personal characteristics, and are these elements powerful predictors of performance in office?

Although specialists have not reached agreement on the importance of these factors, there is widespread belief that it does indeed matter—and probably a great deal—just who is president. Certainly the time, effort, and money devoted to selecting the president suggest that this is the case. This confidence in the difference that an individual can make is revealed when citizens proudly explain that they "voted for the person, not the party." Believing in the ultimate importance of individuals in shaping events is consistent with deeply held American attitudes. These cultural orientations have been underlined by the treatment accorded presidents in the mass media, particularly during the television era when political problems and their attempted solutions have become highly personalized. Public attention focuses on the president, and this individual has come to embody the larger political process. Moreover, presidents and their media advisers encourage personalization when it emphasizes traits that the public regards as highly desirable, such as decisiveness and strength of character.

There is broad consensus among students of the presidency that each chief executive brings to the job a combination of attitudes, skills, strengths, and shortcomings that will influence his or her performance in office and may at times have an enduring effect on the nation's history. There is less agreement, however, on the relative significance of these causal factors and exactly how they are related to job performance and policy outcomes. A number of analysts have suggested ways to conceptualize these issues; a modified, considerably simplified diagram based on two of the most prominent treatments is presented in Figure 4-1.

As well as enduring personality traits, all presidents develop attitudes toward the full array of political structures, institutions, and relationships. Their characteristics and attitudes take shape within a social context. In addition, their professional experiences prior to entering office, particularly as they relate to role demands of the presidency, produce a personal style that may be more or less congruent with the demands of serving as chief executive. This personal style, translated into a repertoire of skills and competencies, is brought to the presidency after first being filtered by the selection process. Ultimately, presidents may be more or less likely to produce successful outcomes as these individual traits interact with the situations they confront. In concentrating on the importance of leaders' individual characteristics, one recognizes that presidents are in the position to have potentially momentous impacts on political events. Even if the environment, forces beyond the control of the individual leader, has a determinative effect on events, "environments are always mediated by the individuals on whom they act."[1]

Just as analysts disagree over the determinants of presidential behavior, there is no consensus on how to evaluate a president's performance, although the general public and professional presidency watchers engage in evaluations all the time. Polls provide current, short-term assessments of public approval *(discussed in Chapter 3)*, and journalists are constantly assessing the administration's record in dealing with Congress or in ad-

Figure 4.1 Relationship of Background to Performance

Sources: Bert Rockman, *The Leadership Question* (New York: Praeger, 1984), 189; Fred Greenstein, *Personality and Politics* (New York: Norton, 1975), 27.

dressing particular areas of public policy. Certain evaluation points have become institutionalized: the end of an administration's first 100 days in office (a carry-over from FDR's first term) always produces a spate of articles. Other evaluation points are mid-term (the end of two years) and departure from office. In other words, the public, journalists, and academics are constantly engaged in *contemporary evaluation* of performance.

Scholars and others use a variety of criteria in reaching these evaluations. Bruce Buchanan has drawn broad distinctions between subjective and objective criteria. Judgments based on subjective grounds emphasize the "appearance and demeanor" of leadership, including success in projecting the image of integrity and charisma; the "moral desirability of a president's means or ends"; and the pragmatic test of self-interest—the extent to which the president contributed to an individual's well-being. Objective criteria, on which professionals make their evaluations, focus on presidential skill in making things happen, especially short-term successes, or on the lasting results produced for the nation.[2] For example, in reflecting on the record of achievements by the Reagan administration, a number of works adopted the long view in assessing the administration's legacy. As Bert Rockman put it, politicians can "leave greater or lesser footprints. Assessing the depth and durability of those marks is hazardous while the administration under evaluation is still in power. The real answers will come later—much later."[3]

Since 1948 various scholars, primarily historians, have been asked on several occasions to "rate" American presidents. In essence, they were to assess the "depth and durability" of presidential footprints and provide a *historical evaluation*. The results from five of these efforts are reported in Table 4-1. Each poll was structured a bit differently and surveyed a different panel of "experts."[4] Even so, one finds considerable consensus among participants on the top ten and the bottom ten, a result that led Robert Murray and Tim Blessing to conclude that historians "had in mind more than vague and uncritical generalities when they evaluated presidential performances."[5] Assessments of recent presidents are particularly susceptible to change with the passage of time. Note how Eisenhower moved up from twentieth place in 1962 to ninth in 1982. Truman's standing among professionals was already strong by 1962 and has remained so.

In addition to 846 completed surveys, Murray and Blessing conducted sixty in-depth interviews with historians to determine their evaluative criteria. The most important personal trait contributing to presidential

Table 4-1 Ratings of U.S. Presidents

Schlesinger poll (1948)	Schlesinger poll (1962)	Maranell-Dodder poll (1970)	Tribune poll (1982)	Murray-Blessing poll[a] (1982)
		Accomplishments of administration	Ten best presidents	
Great	Great			Great
1. Lincoln	1. Lincoln	1. Lincoln	1. Lincoln (best)	1. Lincoln
2. Washington	2. Washington	2. F. Roosevelt	2. Washington	2. F. Roosevelt
3. F. Roosevelt	3. F. Roosevelt	3. Washington	3. F. Roosevelt	3. Washington
4. Wilson	4. Wilson	4. Jefferson	4. T. Roosevelt	4. Jefferson
5. Jefferson	5. Jefferson	5. T. Roosevelt	5. Jefferson	
6. Jackson		6. Truman	6. Wilson	Near great
	Near great	7. Wilson	7. Jackson	5. T. Roosevelt
Near great	6. Jackson	8. Jackson	8. Truman	6. Wilson
7. T. Roosevelt	7. T. Roosevelt	9. L. Johnson	9. Eisenhower	7. Jackson
8. Cleveland	8. Polk	10. Polk	10. Polk (10th best)	8. Truman
9. J. Adams	Truman (tie)	11. J. Adams		
10. Polk	9. J. Adams	12. Kennedy	Ten worst	Above average
	10. Cleveland	13. Monroe	presidents	9. J. Adams
Average		14. Cleveland	1. Harding (worst)	10. L. Johnson
11. J. Q. Adams	Average	15. Madison	2. Nixon	11. Eisenhower
12. Monroe	11. Madison	16. Taft	3. Buchanan	12. Polk
13. Hayes	12. J. Q. Adams	17. McKinley	4. Pierce	13. Kennedy
14. Madison	13. Hayes	18. J. Q. Adams	5. Grant	14. Madison
15. Van Buren	14. McKinley	19. Hoover	6. Fillmore	15. Monroe
16. Taft	15. Taft	20. Eisenhower	7. A. Johnson	16. J. Q. Adams
17. Arthur	16. Van Buren	21. A. Johnson	8. Coolidge	17. Cleveland
18. McKinley	17. Monroe	22. Van Buren	9. Tyler	
19. A. Johnson	18. Hoover	23. Arthur	10. Carter (10th worst)	Average
20. Hoover	19. B. Harrison	24. Hayes		18. McKinley
21. B. Harrison	20. Arthur	25. Tyler		19. Taft
	Eisenhower (tie)	26. B. Harrison		20. Van Buren
Below average	21. A. Johnson	27. Taylor		21. Hoover
22. Tyler		28. Buchanan		22. Hayes
23. Coolidge	Below average	29. Fillmore		23. Arthur
24. Fillmore	22. Taylor	30. Coolidge		24. Ford
25. Taylor	23. Tyler	31. Pierce		25. Carter
26. Buchanan	24. Fillmore	32. Grant		26. B. Harrison
27. Pierce	25. Coolidge	33. Harding		
	26. Pierce			Below average
Failure	27. Buchanan			27. Taylor
28. Grant				28. Reagan
29. Harding	Failure			29. Tyler
	28. Grant			30. Fillmore
	29. Harding			31. Coolidge
				32. Pierce
				Failure
				33. A. Johnson
				34. Buchanan
				35. Nixon
				36. Grant
				37. Harding

Note: These ratings result from surveys of scholars and range in number from 49 to 846.

[a] The rating of President Reagan was obtained in a separate poll conducted in 1989.

Source: Harold W. Stanley and Richard G. Niemi, *Vital Statistics on American Politics*, 3d ed. (Washington, D.C.: CQ Press, 1992), Table 8-2, 258–259.

achievement, in the view of these historians, was decisiveness; intelligence, particularly the capacity for growth, and integrity were close behind.[6] Greatness, many seemed to feel, is achieved by those leaders able to exercise moral, inspirational leadership, who have "a capacity for creative innovation and an imagination that was fired by a clear vision of the future."[7] James MacGregor Burns's discussion of leadership emphasizes similar abilities as the source of "transformational" leadership where presidents appeal to the higher goals and motives of followers to achieve true change.[8]

In assessing performance, it is also necessary to factor in an additional consideration: modern presidents no longer govern alone. Since the 1930s they have been assisted by a large number of aides appointed to serve in the Executive Office of the President, who may prove a genuine asset in helping presidents exercise their responsibilities. A president's personal capabilities may be amplified by careful selection and use of these aides.

In examining the importance of individual characteristics, we turn first to a discussion of the backgrounds from which presidents have been drawn. As depicted in Figure 4-1, a president's life and occupational experiences are distant from the actual service in office and should therefore have only limited power to explain performance. Nonetheless, the patterns uncovered tell us something about leadership in America.

What Manner of Person?

Each president brings to the office a cumulation of experience derived from a position in American society and previous professional experience. The selection process, rather than producing a random sampling of Americans, favors some backgrounds over others. After reviewing the historical pattern for social background and education, it is not surprising to find that presidents have disproportionately been drawn from traditionally dominant groups in American society. It is less clear, however, just what this has meant for their performance in office.

Social Background

Although there is no single indicator of social status upon which all Americans would agree, occupation is probably the most important criterion for social ranking in the United States.[9] Moreover, the occupation of a person's father provides a reasonably accurate picture of his or her class origins. By analyzing such origins, one can determine the extent to which presidents have achieved their positions of power as a result of their own ability or thanks to the advantages of family background.[10] The presidency has long been cited as an example of how ability can enable individuals to overcome disadvantages and rise to positions of power. But the reality of presidents' personal histories, argues Edward Pessen, contradicts "the log cabin myth" and demonstrates that "the political race here as elsewhere has usually been won by those who had the advantage of starting from a favorable position."[11] Pessen uses a complex conceptualization of class in characterizing the family background of each president through Reagan in terms of six groupings: upper upper and lower upper, upper middle and lower middle, upper lower and lower lower.[12] In making his evaluations, Pessen compared the presidents' family backgrounds to the economic and social conditions that existed at the time.

Four distinguished American families alone produced eight American presidents, one-fifth of the total.[13] Included were John Adams and his son John Quincy Adams; James Madison and Zachary Taylor, who had grandparents in common; William Henry Harrison and his grandson Benjamin Harrison; and cousins Theodore and Franklin Roosevelt. All four families meet Pessen's criteria for upper-class status as depicted in Table 4-2. It is also not uncommon to find that presidents come from politically prominent families, a background that, more often than not, is also upper class. John Tyler was the son of a Virginia governor; William Howard Taft's father served as secretary of war, attorney general, and ambassador to Austria and Russia; and John Kennedy's father was the chairman of the Securities and Exchange Commission and ambassador to Great Britain. Franklin Pierce's father was governor of New Hampshire, but Pessen locates the family between the lower upper and upper middle classes. One would also expect to find George Bush (unranked by Pessen) among those with upper-class backgrounds; Bush's father accumulated a considerable fortune working on Wall Street before he was elected to the Senate from Connecticut.

Several chief executives had upper-class origins, but their fathers did not hold high political office. George Washington, Thomas Jefferson, and James Monroe were sons of wealthy farmers who were not in politics. Rounding out Pessen's upper-class group is James K. Polk, whose family was notably more prosperous than its neighbors, and Woodrow Wilson, whose father was a minister, a profession of considerable social prestige. The fathers of Chester Arthur and Grover Cleveland also were ministers,

Table 4-2 Pessen's Analysis of Presidential Social Class

Social Class	President
Upper-Upper	G. Washington, T. Jefferson, J. Madison, J. Q. Adams, W. H. Harrison, J. Tyler, Z. Taylor, B. Harrison, T. Roosevelt, W. H. Taft, F. D. Roosevelt
Middle-Upper	J. Polk, J. Kennedy
Lower-Upper	J. Adams, J. Monroe, W. Wilson
Lower-Upper/ Upper-Middle	F. Pierce, R. Hayes, G. Cleveland, W. Harding, C. Coolidge, H. Truman
Upper-Middle	A. Jackson, M. Van Buren, J. Buchanan, U. S. Grant, C. Arthur, W. McKinley, H. Hoover, L. Johnson, G. Ford, J. Carter
Middle	A. Lincoln, D. Eisenhower, R. Reagan
Lower-Middle	M. Fillmore, J. Garfield, R. Nixon
Upper-Lower	A. Johnson
Lower-Lower	None

Source: Edward Pessen, *The Log Cabin Myth: The Social Backgrounds of the Presidents* (New Haven, Conn.: Yale University Press, 1984), 68.

but Pessen ranks them as upper middle and lower upper, respectively. Pessen locates a number of presidents, including Pierce, Hayes, Harding, Coolidge, and Truman, in a special bridge category between upper-class and middle-class origins. Altogether, Pessen considers sixteen presidents to be drawn from upper-class roots and six more as bordering on this exclusive group—a total of twenty-two (Bush would make twenty-three), more than half of those who have served in the White House.

Another ten presidents fall within Pessen's upper-middle category, leaving only seven who can be regarded as drawn from middle- or lower-class roots. The presidents who were most socially disadvantaged include Andrew Johnson, whose father held a variety of jobs including janitor and porter at an inn; Millard Fillmore, who was probably the only president truly born in a log cabin as the son of a dirt farmer; and James Garfield, whose father pulled the family into prosperity through manual labor as a midwest canal worker. Despite the many schoolbook stories about Lincoln's modest background, his father owned more property and livestock at the time of Abraham's birth than the majority of his neighbors, and his prominence in the community continued to grow. Three more recent presidents—Eisenhower, Nixon, and Reagan—were the sons of poor men who tried numerous jobs without much success. Eisenhower's father was a mechanic in a creamery for a time after an investment failed; Nixon's father was a streetcar conductor in Columbus, Ohio, before trying his luck as a painter, carpenter, glass worker, and sheep rancher; and Reagan's father worked on and off as an itinerant shoe salesman.

Three chief executives—Jackson, Hayes, and Hoover—were born after their fathers died; they were raised by relatives who were better off than their own parents. Jackson's condition was sufficiently comfortable to afford him an education at a private school. Hoover's uncle, who raised him, headed a private academy that later became Pacific University. An upper-middle-class background was economically secure and sometimes prosperous: Van Buren's father kept a tavern; Buchanan's was a successful merchant; and Grant's did well as a tanner. McKinley's father manufactured pig iron and invested in mining. The fathers of three recent presidents—Johnson, Ford, and Carter—met mixed success in business; Johnson's father traded in commodities and livestock; Ford's stepfather (the president was born Leslie King and adopted as Gerald R. Ford, Jr.) operated a paint and lumber business; Carter's father founded a successful peanut warehouse.

Although presidents have come from diverse backgrounds, those with upper-class origins have been the most prevalent, while most others were drawn from prosperous and socially respected backgrounds. Even so, one can discern some changes over time. The first six chief executives came from socially, and in many cases politically, prominent families. Not wholly by coincidence, they served during the period when presidential candidates were nominated by congressional caucus. After both political parties adopted the national nominating convention in the early 1830s, the picture changed, with some presidents continuing to come from prominent families (John Tyler and Zachary Taylor, for example), while others from less-privileged backgrounds also began to make it to the White House. Fillmore, Lincoln, A. Johnson, and Garfield—four presidents with the humblest origins—are concentrated in the period 1850–1880. Few generalizations can be made, however, about twentieth century presidents, who come from distinctly upper-class families (the two Roosevelts, Taft, Wilson, Kennedy, and Bush) as well as more modest circumstances (Eisenhower, Nixon, and Reagan).

Education

Education is often closely correlated with social class, a pattern that holds true for the presidency. Most U.S. presidents have been well educated. Only nine of the forty did not have any formal instruction at a college or university. Moreover, the trend has been toward chief executives with greater college training. Of the seventeen who have occupied the presidency in this century, only one, Harry Truman, did not attend an institution of higher learning.[14] The universities and colleges that presidents attended are among the most highly regarded in the nation. Harvard University leads the list with five chief executives as alumni—the two Adamses, the two Roosevelts, and Kennedy. Alma maters of other presidents include major private universities such as Princeton (Madison and Wilson), Yale (Taft and Bush), Stanford (Hoover), and a wide variety of prestigious, smaller private colleges, such as Allegheny (McKinley), Amherst (Coolidge), Bowdoin (Pierce), Dickinson (Buchanan), Hampden-Sidney (W. H. Harrison), Kenyon (Hayes), Union College (Arthur), and Williams (Garfield). Although less prevalent than private institutions, well-known public universities also figure among the alma maters of the presidents: Miami of Ohio (B. Harrison), the University of Michigan (Ford), the University of North Carolina (Polk), William and Mary (Jefferson, Monroe, and Tyler), and two service academies, Annapolis (Carter) and West Point (Grant and Eisenhower). Twentieth century presidents hailing from families with more modest social standing attended less prestigious institutions: Johnson attended Southwest Texas State Teachers College; Nixon graduated from Whittier College in California before attending Duke University law school; Reagan majored in economics and sociology at Eureka College in Illinois.

The fact that so many presidents attended prestigious institutions of higher learning probably has less to do with their innate abilities or career aspirations than with family status or their desire to improve their economic and social positions through education. A classic example is James Garfield, the son of a canal construction worker, who died when Garfield was two. Garfield managed, after a long struggle for education, to graduate from Williams College and then become principal of a church school before being admitted to the bar and eventually going into politics. More presidents attended private rather than public schools because private schools were established earlier, particularly in the northeastern states, such as New York and Massachusetts, which have produced ten presidents, and the midwestern states, such as Ohio, which has produced six presidents. Several postwar presidents, including Eisenhower, Johnson, Ford, and Carter, attended public institutions, a trend that may become more pronounced in the future. The selection of more presidents from states in which there are more public than private universities (such as the western states) would contribute to this trend. Although most citizens today would probably agree that a college education is essential if presidents are to understand the many complex problems confronting the nation, there is no direct correlation between quality of institution or years of training and performance.

Career Experience

Although the family occupational backgrounds of the presidents are fairly broad, their own careers prior to and outside politics have been much less diverse. Twenty-four of the forty chief executives practiced law at some time in their lives. Other occupations include the military (W. H. Harrison, Taylor, Grant, and Eisenhower), education (Wilson and Lyndon Johnson), journalism (Harding and Kennedy), engineering (Hoover), and entertainment (Reagan). Two presidents, Washington and Madison, were gentleman farmers. Carter combined farming with his family peanut business after he gave up his career as a Navy engineer to return home to Georgia when his father died. Two presidents who pursued less prestigious careers before entering public life were Truman, who, in addition to trying his hand at farming, was a haberdasher and a railroad timekeeper, and Andrew Johnson, who was a tailor. It is not surprising that so many presidents were lawyers because that profession is closely linked with a political career. Law is a prestigious occupation, rewards skill in interpersonal negotiation and conciliation as well as verbal and argumentative facility, and enables its practitioners to return to private life more readily than is true of medicine or engineering, for example.[15] Although the law is a natural profession for presidents, in recent years fewer chief executives have come from that occupation. Of the nine presidents since World War II, only two, Nixon and Ford, were lawyers. As increasing numbers of people from nonlegal backgrounds—business and teaching, in particular—become senators and governors, the positions from which today's presidents often are recruited, still more presidents without legal training may occupy the White House.

As noted in the discussion of presidential selection, most candidates have little difficulty meeting the formal requirements of office, but informal requirements, although changing in content, are far more restrictive. The most pervasive of these informal requirements is previous experience in elective or appointive public office. The only exceptions to this rule are three career military officers, Zachary Taylor, Ulysses S. Grant, and Dwight D. Eisenhower, whose heroic exploits in the Mexican War, Civil War, and World War II, respectively, thrust them suddenly into the vortex of presidential politics. Not only did these three presidents lack experience in civilian office, but as professional military men they had not even been involved in partisan activities. Taylor, elected as the Whig candidate in 1848, had never voted before in a presidential election and had no party affiliation.[16] Grant, the Republican party candidate elected in 1868, had voted for James Buchanan, the Democratic standard-bearer in 1856, and had political views that have been described as "obscure."[17] Even more perplexing for party leaders was Eisenhower, the Republican party candidate in 1952 and 1956, whom a number of liberal Democratic leaders had tried to draft for their party's nomination in 1948.[18]

For most U.S. chief executives, the road to the presidency involved a long apprenticeship in public office with careers usually beginning at lower levels of the political system when they were in their twenties or thirties. Andrew Johnson and Calvin Coolidge began their public careers as city aldermen or councilmen. Others were first elected to county offices: John Adams was a highway surveyor, Truman a member of the county court, holding an administrative, not a judicial, position. Some presidents, including Andrew Jackson, James Buchanan, Grover Cleveland, William McKinley, and William Howard Taft, entered the public service as prosecuting or district attorney; others, such as Rutherford B. Hayes and Benjamin Harrison, served as city solicitor or attorney. Several chief executives, Jefferson, Lincoln, and the two Roosevelts among them, began their public careers as state legislators.

The typical career pattern for these presidents was to move up the political ladder by winning offices representing progressively larger constituencies. Approximately two-thirds of the presidents served in either the House of Representatives or the Senate or both. There are, of course, exceptions. Woodrow Wilson spent most of his adult life as a professor of government and later as president of Princeton University; in 1910, at age fifty-four, he was elected governor of New Jersey, just two years before he won the presidency. Ronald Reagan was primarily a radio, movie, and television performer until his fifties, when he became active in national politics in the 1964 presidential campaign on behalf of Barry Goldwater. In 1966 he was elected to the first of two terms as governor of California; in 1980 he was elected president. Neither William Howard Taft nor Herbert Hoover held any elective office before being chosen as president. Taft served as a judge at the county, state, and federal level, and later became governor general of the Philippines and secretary of war. Hoover chaired the Commission for Relief in Belgium, oversaw prices, production, and distribution of food during World War I as U.S. food administrator, and later served as secretary of commerce in the Harding and Coolidge administrations.

Most presidents come to the White House directly from another high public office. (See the discussion in Chapter 2.) Typical positions include the vice presidency, appointive executive office, state governorships, and Senate seats. From one era to the next in U.S. political history, these offices have varied in the extent to which their occupants have been favored or disfavored in their pursuit of the presidency.

How is experience related to performance? Most observers assume that experience can make a president more or less familiar with the problems confronting the nation as well as with the institutions and people who must collectively address these problems. Moreover, an earlier career in elective office may enable individuals to develop the skills necessary for exercising leadership—bargaining skills, facility in public speaking, and the capacity to inspire others. Candidates, therefore, usually argue that their particular blend of experience—whether in state, national, or nonpublic sectors—has made them best qualified for the position.

Background–Performance Links

How have scholars linked these biographical characteristics to presidential performance? Are there systematic patterns that would enable the public to predict which candidates will enjoy greatest success in office? Unfortunately, there are no simple answers.

As noted, most presidents achieved political success with a substantial boost from their family circumstances, advantages that included political and social standing as well as educational and professional opportunities unavailable to most of their fellow citizens. Edward Pessen finds that this pattern of recruitment has had important implications for the attitudes brought into the Oval Office. Political parties consistently have sought candidates with a "reliable social philosophy," which is likely to be found among those "who have thrived under American society's prevailing arrangements."[19] Pessen concludes that "the common characteristic [of presidents] . . . for all their dissimilarities in other respects, has been the essential conservatism of their social, economic, and political beliefs . . . all of them were champions of the prevailing order."[20] It seems likely that most presidential aspirants will sustain the status quo. The selection process is not neutral in relation to social class.

Two sociologists, E. Digby Baltzell and Howard G. Schneiderman, have more specifically sought to link class origin with performance in office. They correlate Pessen's analysis of class origins with a ranking of presidential performance based on the Murray-Blessing survey of American historians.[21] Their conclusion challenges some of the myths surrounding the presidency. "There has been . . . not only a high correlation between high social origins and getting to the presidency, as Pessen clearly has shown, [but] once elected to office, men of privileged origins have performed far better than those of lower social status."[22] Of the eight presidents ranked by historians as great or near great, five were from upper-class families (Washington, Jefferson, T. Roosevelt, Wilson, and F. Roosevelt), two from the upper-middle class (Jackson and Truman), and only one from the middle and lower classes (Lincoln, who is generally ranked number one). In contrast, no presidents drawn from the upper class are found among those regarded by historians as failures (A. Johnson, Buchanan, Nixon, Grant, and Harding). Overall, Baltzell and Schneiderman find that eleven of the fifteen upper-class presidents (73 percent) were judged to have performed above average in office, while only six of the twenty-one presidents drawn from below the upper class (29 percent) were comparably rated.[23] Although they do not provide a clear explanation for how background is translated into success, these analysts suggest that an upper-class background does make a difference: "Our best aristocratic traditions have stressed *doing* a better job rather than the prevalent, middle-class ideology which has always stressed *getting* a better job."[24]

Richard Neustadt is probably the foremost advocate of electing an experienced politician to the presidency. As he has argued since the first edition of his influential book, *Presidential Power*, appeared in 1960, "The Presidency is no place for amateurs."[25] This seemed an apt aphorism to capture the difficulties experienced by Dwight Eisenhower in the presidency, although evaluations of his performance as president have risen with the passage of time. As articulated in some of Neustadt's later editions, experience enhances presidents' self-confidence, which in turn makes it easier for them to make the choices about power that are critical to success. Yet, "the quality of experience" may count "more than the quantity," an admission that Neustadt had to make after two highly experienced presidents, Lyndon Johnson and Richard Nixon, seemed to fail in office. He ultimately concludes that "the variety of experience is such that none of it can be applied predictively with confidence."[26] Bert Rockman reaches a similar conclusion after looking at the length and types of government experience in relation to performance. In comparing the government experience of the top ten and bottom ten presidents as ranked by an expert panel, the bottom ten actually had modestly *greater* government experience than the top ten (16.9 mean years versus 15.1) and more than twice as many years of congressional experience (7.6 mean years versus 3.7).[27] Experience, it appears, offers no guarantee of success.

We are left with fundamental uncertainties about how life experience may have a bearing on performance. In addition to social class and career experience, however, there has also been considerable interest in the psychological traits that presidents bring to the office, the subject of the next section.

Psychological Characteristics of U.S. Presidents

In October 1972, just before voters were to choose between Richard Nixon and George McGovern, political scientist James David Barber drew attention to the inherent shortcomings of focusing on life experience when deciding how to vote. Barber made a prediction. The person who would win had grown up as part of a Republican family in a small town. He had excelled in school, studied piano, had a younger brother rowdier than himself, and had been elected president of his college class. Following military service during World War II, he had attended graduate school and followed an uncertain career path until gaining election to Congress in a contest marked by anticommunist appeals. After two terms in the House and service in the Senate, he was considered a member of his party's liberal wing and respected for hard work and independent thinking. Although the election outcome was virtually certain, Barber had no need to predict a winner because the description fit both Nixon *and* McGovern. Despite the similarities in life experiences, few doubted that the two would make very different presidents.[28]

The degree of similarity between the major party candidates in 1972 was uncanny even in light of the broadly similar backgrounds from which presidents are drawn. Yet, no two people, regardless of how similar their life circumstances, will bring identical personalities to the office. They inevitably bring a set of distinctive psychological characteristics, features that may loom large under the intense pressures that concentrate on the presidency. In terms of Figure 4-1, psychological traits are more proximate to presidential behavior than life experiences, but that does not make them easier to study or evaluate. Fred Greenstein points out that psychologists view personality as a complex phenomenon, involving diverse factors such as how people adapt to the world around them by screening reality (cognition), how they express their feelings (affect), and how they relate to others (identification).[29] These structures are likely to be deeply rooted, making it even more necessary to "infer" their existence rather than to observe them directly. Personality, in short, is a construct introduced by the analyst to account for the regularities in a person's behavior. For these reasons, examinations of psychological characteristics are more uncertain and subjective than are examinations of professional experience and social backgrounds.

Despite these problems, political scientists and historians have used psychological concepts to help explain why political figures behave as they do, a field of study that has come to be known as *psychobiography*. Several presidents, including Wilson, LBJ, Nixon, and Carter, have been the subjects of such biographies.[30] These studies tend to concentrate on the childhood experiences of the subjects, particularly their relationships with their parents, and how such experiences shaped their perceptions of themselves, their self-confidence or lack of it, and their psychological needs.

Even with the upsurge in interest, analysts remain divided on precisely how to conduct these studies and the theoretical framework within which they should be conducted. Two broad approaches can be adopted: single-subject case studies seek to develop a comprehensive analysis of the full array of behaviors manifested by one person with particular attention to explaining the origins of recurrent patterns; multicase studies also rely on close examination of biographical materials but seek to draw conclusions from similarities found among several actors' behavior.[31] An example of a single-subject case study is Alexander George and Juliette George's highly acclaimed, comprehensive work on Woodrow Wilson, which attempts to explain his strikingly complex and contradictory behavior. James David Barber's study, *The Presidential Character*, has identified similarities between Wilson's conduct and that of three other presidents, Hoover, LBJ, and Nixon, so that they may be treated as examples of a similar personality type.

Practitioners of these two styles of inquiry disagree, sometimes quite strongly, on how analysis should proceed.[32] There are multiple, competing theories of personality and a lack of established rules on how such research should be conducted. Although the research remains controversial, it would be unrealistic to overlook the importance of personality in trying to understand the presidency because this office imposes fewer constraints on the occupant's behavior than any other in American government. In other words, there is enormous opportunity for presidents to be themselves in performing their day-to-day responsibilities.

Barber's Approach to Studying Personality

In addition to the prediction concerning the 1972 election already noted, Barber made a more famous forecast that brought considerable attention to himself and to the study of presidential personality. Barber predicted that Nixon would be susceptible to the same "danger" as Wilson, Hoover, and LBJ, namely "rigid adherence to a failing line of policy."[33] Given the right set of circumstances, Nixon was likely to pursue a self-defeating plan of action even in the face of mounting evidence of its likely failure. The causes were rooted in his personality—his emotional needs—no less than they had been for the other three presidents Barber cited. Nixon's conduct during Watergate, the extended investigations conducted by Congress during 1973 and 1974 into questionable campaign practices of the 1972 election, seemed to validate the prediction and the method on which it was based.

How did Barber arrive at such a conclusion? Was his prediction lucky, or had he uncovered the secret of how to predict presidential performance in office based on systematic personality analysis? If so, the next step would be to produce more informed decisions by making such insights available to voters before an election.

Barber attempts to identify broad character patterns that will predict broad patterns of presidential conduct in office. Central to his analysis are three personal characteristics—*character, world view,* and *style*—and two environmental conditions—*power situation* and *climate of expectations.* Together, these elements determine the likelihood of presidential success. Character, the most important of Barber's analytic constructs, develops during childhood and is expressed in two analytic dimensions: energy and affect. Presidents may be active or passive in terms of the effort invested in their job; they also may be positive or negative about their position. Both dimensions influence performance.

The resulting four-cell typology is presented in Figure 4-2, with the principal personality trait identified by Barber for each type. *Active-positives* evidence personal growth and adaptability; they enjoy their work and find it a challenge to use power productively as a means to pursue goals beneficial to others. Their success rests on a fundamental sense of self-confidence expressed in goal-oriented behavior. Nonetheless, they are flexible in their pursuit of goals and willing to change or abandon them altogether rather than suffer a costly political defeat. In short, they are pragmatic politicians. Barber's active-positives include FDR, Truman, Kennedy, Ford, Carter, and, most recently, George Bush.

Active-negative presidents also invest a great deal of energy in being president, but unlike their active-positive counterparts, they do not appear to derive enjoyment from serving in the office. Rather than exercising political power for the benefit of the citizenry, active-negative chief executives seem to seek power for its own sake, exhibiting a compulsiveness as if they are driven to pursue a political career rather than doing it because

Figure 4.2 Barber's Typology of Character

		Affect	
		Positive	Negative
Activity Level	Active	**Adaptive,** self-confident, power used as means to achieve beneficial results	**Compulsive,** power as a means to self-realization; "driven"; problem managing aggression
	Passive	**Compliant,** seek to be loved; easily manipulated; low self-esteem	**Withdrawn,** respond to sense of duty; avoid power; low self-esteem

Source: James David Barber, *The Presidential Character: Predicting Performance in the White House,* 3d ed. (Englewood Cliffs, N.J.: Prentice-Hall, 1992).

the career gives them pleasure. This behavior arises from a poor self-image and lack of self-confidence, traits caused by painful childhood experiences; they seek power and domination over others as compensation for their own lack of self-esteem. In this pursuit, active-negatives may come to believe that the policies they favor are morally right, vital to the nation's interest, and impossible to compromise. A course of action may be pursued even if it obviously is not working, a pattern of "rigidification" that can ultimately cause their own political failure. Thus, they constitute a great danger to the nation. Barber classifies four twentieth century presidents as active-negatives: Wilson, Hoover, Johnson, and Nixon.

Passive-positive presidents are not in politics to seek power either for the betterment of the American people or to compensate for their own sense of inadequacy. Rather, they choose politics because they are, in Barber's terms, "political lovers." They genuinely enjoy people and want to help them by doing small favors; in return, they get the feeling that they are wanted and loved. Barber suggests that passive-positive presidents have low self-esteem combined with a superficial optimism about life; they tend to let others set goals for them and find it difficult to make decisions. The danger they pose is one of drift, leaving the affairs of state undirected. Barber uses three presidents to illustrate passive-positive chief executives: Taft, Harding, and Reagan.

Passive-negative presidents combine two characteristics one would *not* expect to find in the person who attains the nation's highest office: an unwillingness to invest much energy in that office and a lack of pleasure in serving. Such persons pursue public service because they believe it is something they *ought to do*. Passive-negative presidents have a fundamental sense of uselessness and compensate for that feeling by dutifully agreeing to work on behalf of their fellow citizens. Two presidents who exemplify passive-negative chief executives are Coolidge and Eisenhower.

Barber also examines two other personal factors that influence presidential behavior, but play a smaller role in his analysis than does character. *World view* consists of a president's "politically relevant beliefs, particularly his conceptions of social causality, human nature, and the central moral conflicts of the time."[34] Rather than dealing with specific policy issues, these attitudes are general in nature and are therefore more likely to have wide applicability. Barber sees them as developed primarily during adolescence.

Figure 4.3 Barber's Characterization of Modern Presidents

		Affect	
		Positive	Negative
Activity Level	Active	Franklin Roosevelt Harry Truman John F. Kennedy Gerald R. Ford George Bush	Woodrow Wilson Herbert Hoover Lyndon Johnson Richard Nixon
	Passive	William H. Taft Warren Harding Ronald Reagan	Calvin Coolidge Dwight Eisenhower

Source: James David Barber, *The Presidential Character: Predicting Performance in the White House*, 3d ed. (Englewood Cliffs, N.J.: Prentice-Hall, 1992).

Style is the president's "habitual way of performing three political roles: rhetoric, personal relations, and homework."[35] In other words, style focuses on how presidents typically work with words, people, and substantive problems. These patterns are developed largely during early adulthood, particularly in conjunction with the president's "first independent political success," which usually occurs in college or in a first elective or appointive office. Character "colors" both world view and style but does not determine them in any direct way.

Barber has analyzed the life histories of all presidents since Taft, thereby covering all but two of the twentieth century presidents. These analyses are summarized in Figure 4-3. Some of his classifications have been highly controversial, but since 1972 his views of each candidate have been sought out by journalists during presidential elections, and he offers a prediction of how the new president will perform in office on the eve of inauguration day.

Barber's View of George Bush

True to form, Barber published a prediction for George Bush on January 19, 1989, in the *New York Times*. The central concern that Americans should have with the soon-to-be-inaugurated president, according to Barber, was his perpetual search for a mission. As Barber observed, "The ultimate danger is war. That was Mr. Bush's first big mission."[36] In the expanded version of this analysis found in the 1992 edition of *Presidential Character*, Barber argues that all evidence points to an active-positive character, but that Bush's uncertain world view remains an ongoing problem in understanding his behavior.

Barber's account is brief and straightforward. Bush hails from a privileged background that amply met his childhood and adolescent needs (a sheltered family life, prep school, summers in Kennebunkport), with the great exception of providing a close relationship with his father. Nonetheless, Bush has struggled throughout his life to establish independence from his parents while living up to the standards they set. Evidence for this assertion can be found in instances where Bush went against parental advice and expectations: he enlisted in the Navy at age eighteen against their advice, turned down a job on Wall Street arranged by his father for a career in the Texas oil business, and resisted pressures to become politically active; but he emulated his father by seeking success in business and then entering politics at the very time of his father's retirement. Bush's unpredictable behavior later in life, argues Barber, can be traced "to the continuing ambivalence between pro-parent and anti-parent beliefs, so that what he did was to go with them for a while and then against them for a while, registering in the reality of his life a need to do a pair of opposites rather than the need to concord them into a guiding unity." Bush expresses his ambivalence in a pattern of making unexpected career decisions reflecting a "need to surprise others."[37]

Barber's primary evidence of these tendencies during Bush's service as president is drawn from the Persian Gulf conflict. The administration reversed its pre-August 1990 position of support for the Iraqi regime of Saddam Hussein to undertake an enormous military action (see Chapter 10). The initial defensive deployment of American forces (Desert Shield) was replaced with a massive use of offensive fire power (Desert Storm). During the crisis, Bush seemed to undergo major mood swings, and his justification for American policy seemed to shift weekly from ensuring "jobs, jobs, jobs," to protecting Saudi Arabia, to liberating Kuwait, to defending the rule of law among nations. In short, Barber argues that Bush has lacked vision and a sense of direction throughout his life, a pattern he brought with him into the White House.

Reactions to Barber

Because Barber's work has been widely popularized in the press, it is important to assess its analytic quality. Academics have been especially critical. For some observers, it suffers from the fundamental problem com-

mon to all studies in the field—reductionism, paying "insufficient attention to the full range of possible psychological and non-psychological
determinants of behavior."[38] Students of psychology, it is argued, give
insufficient attention to the structures within which presidents serve (the
so-called institutional presidency) and the impact of the environment,
including the nature of the problems they confront, the political support
they enjoy, and the constraints within which they operate. Although
Barber identifies and discusses three aspects of presidential personality as
well as two features of the situation within which presidents serve, his
analysis clearly emphasizes character.

Barber's classification of presidents also has been questioned. The behavior patterns associated with his character types fit some presidents
grouped into the same cell better than others. For example, evidence on
Eisenhower published after Barber completed his analysis suggests that
Ike was really a more active president than was generally recognized
when he was in office.[39] In the case of Hoover, it has been suggested that
his continuation of a non-interventionist policy in the face of continued
failure as the Great Depression deepened did not arise from the same roots
as the "rigidification" found in Barber's other active-negative cases.
Hoover's reluctance to employ extensive federal aid to restore the economy might better be understood as arising from his world view rather
than from his unresolved emotional needs.[40] Another study, using markedly different methods, finds Ronald Reagan's personality to be most
similar to those of FDR and Kennedy, although Barber considered Reagan
a passive-positive and the other two active-positives.[41] In fact, Barber
acknowledges that no president fits any of the types perfectly and that
each is a mixture of all four types.[42] Nonetheless, he argues that it is
possible to identify a dominant pattern.

Is Barber guilty of positing an ideal personality type that may also
conceal a partisan bias? When Barber's study first appeared, all the active-
positives were liberal Democrats. With the publication of three later editions, activism, optimism, and flexibility have been found to characterize
Republicans Ford and Bush, as well. If the approach is biased, therefore, it
seems to be in favor of the heroic model of presidential leadership that
assigns principal responsibility for solving national problems to the White
House. Barber recognizes that not all active-positives will be successful in
office. For example, Carter may have brought a healthy outlook to the
position, but in Barber's view public expectations were especially impor-

tant in limiting his success. Active-positives also may pose risks for the political system; their "hunger for and attention to results" may lead them to challenge structures and norms that the public believes are better preserved than overturned.[43] Franklin Roosevelt's effort in 1937 to alter the structure of the Supreme Court by increasing its membership to as many as fifteen posed a challenge to the tradition of checks and balances and illustrates this possible danger.[44]

Does Barber allow for the possibility that types other than active-positives can achieve substantial success in office? Jeffrey Tulis argues that in Barber's terms Abraham Lincoln should be considered an active-negative, but few would argue that Lincoln's stewardship of the nation during the Civil War was not successful.[45] Michael Nelson points out that presidents ranked by historians among the top ten in recent performance surveys reveal a mixture of Barber's personality types: three were active-positives (Jefferson, FDR, and Truman); four were active-negatives (Adams, Wilson, LBJ, and Lincoln); and two were passive-negatives (Washington and Eisenhower).[46] It is important, however, to distinguish between "probable success" and "risk." As Nelson's discussion demonstrates, no personality type ensures success or failure, but Barber would argue that the risk of undesirable conduct is greater with some types than with others. In particular, active-negatives present the risk of pursuing self-defeating policies when the situation they confront triggers the rigidification response.

Barber's work does not represent a panacea to a nation searching for effective leaders. Like most of social science, Barber's work is best thought of in terms of probabilities rather than certainties. In the long run, Barber aspires to present voters with the kind of information on candidate backgrounds and records that would improve the likelihood of informed electoral choices, but the kind of research necessary for personality analysis is difficult to undertake at any time and perhaps most difficult in the heat of an electoral contest. Journalists may be able to improve their coverage of candidates' records and identify behavior patterns of concern, but the chance of conducting a complete study of candidates' personalities in the midst of a campaign is negligible. Nor is it clear who in our society should be given such inordinate influence as to declare some personalities "fit" and others as "unfit" for office. Therefore, the practical value of Barber's work remains a controversial and open question.

Management Styles of Modern Presidents

Presidents do not govern alone. Traditional presidents—those serving prior to Franklin Roosevelt—drew heavily on the assistance of cabinet secretaries and the bureaucracies they headed. Since the Roosevelt administration, another source of advice and assistance has emerged to supplement more traditional sources of help. The modern presidency has become a collectivity of political and policy specialists whose expertise is placed at the president's disposal. To what extent do presidents avail themselves of these institutional sources of assistance? How do they structure their advisory systems and make decisions? This section is a brief discussion of the development of presidential staffing and the management styles presidents use with these assistants.

Just as important as attitudes drawn from life experiences, and skills developed in earlier careers, is a president's aptitude for management. Aides have the potential to magnify whatever skills presidents bring to the office and to compensate for their shortcomings. Moreover, it is possible that having a layer of advisers between the president and his performance may reduce the impact of undesirable personality traits on the operation of the office.

The Development of Presidential Staffing

The presidential staff has grown substantially since its modern structure was authorized by Congress in 1939. Today, the Executive Office of the President houses a wide range of expert staff units including the well-known Office of Management and Budget, Council of Economic Advisers, and National Security Council (all discussed more fully in later chapters), as well as the lesser-known Office of U.S. Trade Representative and Office of Science and Technology Policy. Perhaps best known, and certainly most notorious in Washington circles, is the White House Office, a unit that has traditionally emphasized the president's personal and political concerns.

Like other presidents before him, FDR had a limited number of aides working in his behalf, many in clerical positions who were borrowed from other parts of the federal bureaucracy. Looking for a justification to expand these resources, in 1936 Roosevelt appointed a blue-ribbon group of public administration professors, headed by Louis Brownlow, to study the management needs of the modern president. The resulting structure, based on recommendations from that group but reorganized many times since, has always been viewed as a response to the Brownlow Commission's opening sentence: "The President needs help." As Roosevelt and others recognized, the president required additional "eyes and ears" as well as brains to help him discharge the ever-growing list of responsibilities placed at the White House door. Presidential staffing, therefore, is an attempt to help presidents avoid the danger of "overload," the possibility that demands of the job will exceed the capacity of any individual whose time and ability are finite. While the staff is a way to *amplify* the capabilities brought by one person to the presidency, it also may be seen as a structure that can *buffer* the direct impact of a president's personality on performance. Presidents have been given great latitude in their use of staff resources, a flexibility that ensures responsiveness to new problems and perceived needs.

Staff size, although a recurrent political issue, is difficult to monitor with precision. Best estimates place the size of today's Executive Office in excess of 1,700 employees.[47] Moreover, the percentage of positions at higher levels of policy-making responsibility appears to have increased substantially over the years.[48] Staff growth has been accompanied by a shift in influence, as well, with one analyst going so far as to suggest that the new structure constitutes a "presidential branch" of government distinct from the larger executive branch.[49] Clearly, presidents can draw upon a wide range of assistance located both outside and within the presidency.

Presidential Management Styles

Style is no doubt an overused term in describing characteristic patterns of presidential behavior, but a number of analysts have focused more narrowly on how presidents structure and use their advisory systems in making decisions. We term this a president's *management style*. Alexander George identifies three personality factors that determine a president's management style: the executive's habitual ways of dealing with information (acquiring, storing, retrieving, evaluating, and using it); the president's sense of competence in dealing personally with problems, which in turn determines the tasks delegated to others; and the president's orientation toward conflict, particularly the tolerance for competition and dissent among advisers.[50]

Because it is based on personality characteristics, each president's management style is unique. However, most analysts agree that recent presidents have chosen to operate within one of three advisory structures consistent with their management style.[51] The *formalistic* pattern emphasizes clear division of labor among staff assistants, well-defined procedures, and a carefully controlled flow of information to the president, usually through a chief of staff, who tries to deflect problems not worthy of presidential attention. Truman, Eisenhower, and Nixon constructed and operated such systems, although differences in operation reflected the unique combination of needs and contributions each of these men brought to the presidency. The *competitive* pattern, typified by FDR, encouraged conflict among advisers and thrived on diversity of opinion with the president reserving ultimate judgment to himself. Conflict is endemic to decision making within the American government, but FDR encouraged even more of it. Under a *collegial* system, emphasis is on group problem-solving, teamwork, and shared responsibility for outcomes, with the president participating in the process and choosing among identified options. Kennedy, particularly in his decision making during the Cuban missile crisis, typified this style.

Presidents may follow more than one pattern or construct a hybrid. Ford followed a collegial pattern in domestic policy, but was more formalistic in foreign policy.[52] Carter's system has been described as a mixture of collegial and formalistic elements.[53] Reagan, whose management style is examined more closely below, constructed a variant of the formalistic and collegial models during his first term that drew considerable praise from many observers, particularly when its successor in the second term proved notably less successful.[54]

In general, formalistic structures seem to place more modest demands on presidential time and knowledge. Time is conserved by delegating a larger range of tasks to others, which also may increase the probability that experts will deal with the problem. Because much of the work in a formal system is processed in written form, it is less appropriate for presidents who prefer to rely upon group interaction, discussion, and even argument as part of the decision-making process. Competitive and collegial structures both place heavier demands on the president who not only must rely more heavily on his own substantive knowledge in making choices among competing alternatives, but also be able to monitor a policy-making process that is inherently political in nature. Advisers and the policy areas they represent push hard for the president to adopt their solution to a problem, and the maneuvers used to gain an advantage during such policy struggles are believed to be the keys to success. Unfortunately, winning such battles may come at the expense of good decisions.

In the modern era, Democratic presidents, using Franklin Roosevelt as a model, often have adopted a more interactive advisory system, sometimes described as a "spokes-in-a-wheel" system with the president at the center of several principal aides in and out of the White House. Such a system encourages dispute and argumentation. Republican presidents, with some exceptions, generally have operated within a more highly structured system where the chief executive interacts with a narrower range of advisers and relies more heavily on systematic review processes. This approach is thought to be less susceptible to political maneuvering.

Is one pattern more conducive to success than the others? Each has strengths and weaknesses, but unfortunately analysts disagree on the criteria to be used in evaluating the styles, and they even disagree on how the systems perform. There are no reliable measures of which systems produce decisions of higher quality or greater political responsiveness, within reasonable spans of time.[55] Moreover, if the advisory systems ultimately reflect the kind of personality variables identified by Alexander George, it would be impossible to identify one as preferable because it might be inappropriate for the particular president asked to use it.

Multiple Advocacy: Learning A Management Style

The best-known effort to prescribe a specific decision process for presidents to follow is Alexander George's system of *multiple advocacy*.[56] In essence, George has suggested that presidents should be able to learn a set of techniques to follow in managing advisers and making decisions. Although recognizing that a given president may find this style "uncongenial to his cognitive style and work habits," George nonetheless believes that the advantages would make it worthwhile for a president to consider.[57] For example, Richard Nixon found it painful to be the object of direct, face-to-face argument among his advisers, but he might have modified the system to derive its benefits.[58]

George defines multiple advocacy as a *mixed* system that tries to ensure that presidents benefit from a wide review of policy options and hear a variety of viewpoints before making a final policy decision. It tries to build upon the inevitable conflict that arises among individual advisers and bureaucratic agencies by channeling that conflict in productive ways. The overall process must be structured so that every relevant viewpoint receives a fair hearing. One of the major tasks, then, in operating such a system is to monitor the breadth of options being considered and the opportunities that advocates of such views have to be heard. To operate such a system, the president requires a full-time assistant, a "custodian-manager" who acts as an "honest broker" among the advisers pushing their positions on the president.

George's hope is that systematic review of options, one of the claimed benefits of a formalistic system, also can be achieved under multiple advocacy, with the added benefit of the open debate and discussion that are encouraged by competitive and collegial systems. The president should act as a magistrate—"one who listens to the arguments made, evaluates them, poses issues and asks questions, and finally judges which action to take either from among those articulated by advocates or as formulated independently by himself after hearing them."[59] Consistent with this role, presidents need to suppress the urge to announce their own preferences early in the process and ensure that they remain faithful to the premise on which the system rests, the guarantee of giving an equal hearing to all views.

Such a process can be time-consuming, and George recognizes that presidents would have to decide when it should be used. There may be times when presidents feel that they already know the policy they wish to pursue. Nothing will prohibit them from exercising such discretion. As George recognizes, even though advisers may have become indispensable to modern presidents, constitutional responsibility in the American executive remains unitary, not collective. Only two names appear on the election ballot—the president's and the vice president's—and because vice presidents have virtually no independent powers, presidents are singularly responsible for the discharge of executive responsibilities.

Even George does not believe that use of a multiple advocacy system and the magistrate presidential style that accompanies it can ensure good decisions. Rather, he urges its adoption as a way to prevent the bad decisions that result from faulty procedures and to improve the quality of information made available to presidents.[60] There are no guarantees of success.

Understanding Ronald Reagan

Explaining presidential behavior and linking its determinants to performance is much like putting together the pieces of a puzzle, but a puzzle whose final shape is uncertain. One way to illustrate how background, experience, personality, and management style shape behavior and performance is to take an in-depth look at an individual case. Even though he has moved off center stage, Ronald Reagan's life offers an excellent opportunity to examine the interaction of these factors. Because many regard Reagan as a figure of historic proportions comparable to FDR, he has attracted far more scholarly attention than his successor, George Bush. Reagan advanced programs that were highly controversial and did so in a style that was hardly less so. It is natural, then, for his personality, beliefs, and governing to be the subject of intense interest.

Reagan's life presents an intriguing set of contradictions. He was elected to office as a Republican who approvingly quoted Democrats and benefited from emphasizing his own conversion from rabid New Dealer to conservative; he was a former union official who fashioned a new career by defending big business; he was a divorcé who lauded family values; he was a small-town hero (an Andy Hardy character) who made good first in Hollywood and then in Washington; he was a man seemingly without ambition who rose to success in the job coveted by some of the most ambitious people in American society. How does one make sense of the whole? The following sketch draws upon a partial list of the many works that focus on Reagan, including, but by no means limited to, Barber's analysis.[61]

Reagan's Family Background

Ronald Reagan's cultural roots can be traced to the Mississippi Valley of the last half of the nineteenth century. But, as Garry Wills points out, Reagan's family lacked real physical roots. His father was an itinerant salesman who moved his family with great frequency among a number of small Illinois communities, although Reagan thinks of Dixon as his home town. The moves had a lingering effect: Lou Cannon comments, "though Reagan left Dixon as soon as he could, the small town never left him."[62] One of the few constants in the young Reagan's life was his mother, whose commitment to the Disciples of Christ provided him with a model of sobriety, morality, and community service, as well as an opportunity to participate in church-centered theatrical productions. His involvement in church activities was so intense that Wills concludes "he was as close to being a 'minister's kid' as one can be without actually moving into the rectory."[63] Overall, Reagan's "was not a youth that stimulated much independence of thought or action":[64] his schooling was disrupted by the frequent moves, and his church activities emphasized faithful observance of strict teachings.

There was tension between Reagan's temperance-advocating Disciple mother and his Catholic father, who was a heavy drinker. Ronald most resembled his mother: it was her religion he followed, and he valued the same associations with a more acceptable social circle. His brother Neil returned to his father's church, was more outgoing, and gravitated toward a working-class social set. But from his father the younger Reagan absorbed the gift for telling a good story and his strong views against racial or religious prejudice.

Adolescence was particularly important for Reagan. He revealed remarkable discipline and responsibility during six summers as a lifeguard at a beach on the Rock River for twelve hours a day, seven days a week, a substantial feat for someone between the age of sixteen and twenty-two. "Dutch" Reagan was credited with seventy-seven rescues, many reported on the front page of the local paper. Wills suggests that his church activities and lifeguarding largely met the same needs: they provided "stability, discipline, an authority recognized and not resented."[65] And Cannon adds that "being a lifeguard [was] a job perfectly suited to his personality. Lifeguards are solitary objects of adoration who intervene in moments of crisis and perform heroic acts without becoming involved in the lives of those they rescue."[66]

During a nostalgic return to the Eureka College campus in the midst of the 1980 presidential campaign, Reagan stated that "everything good that has happened to me—everything—started here on this campus in those four years that still are such a part of my life."[67] There is little indication that he was recalling intellectual stimulation. What all biographers have emphasized was the continuing effect that Reagan's participation in a campuswide strike had on his style and his later political career. Reagan remembers playing the central role in this campus drama by proposing to a mass meeting of students and faculty that they join in a common protest; what stands out in his memory is the emotional response that his words elicited and the rightness of their cause. But as Garry Wills has shown,

Reagan's recollection of events is severely flawed, casting himself in a far more central role than was really the case and ignoring many of the details that complicate the issues in question.[68] Nonetheless, it is reasonable to conclude, as Barber does, that this experience (what Barber considers Reagan's "first independent political success") firmly established a political style based on rhetoric that became Reagan's central approach to political life.

What keys to Reagan's personality can be found in his youth? Nancy Reagan has attributed her husband's inner-directedness and the distance he maintains from most people around him to his frequent relocations as a child that produced a sense of "never feeling any roots anywhere and never having an old friend for a long, long time."[69] Others have suggested that the key to understanding Reagan's personality lies in his attitude toward his father's drinking. Reagan has recounted the trauma of once discovering his father passed out on the porch; later, he feared that his father's drinking would embarrass him in front of actor friends. Some have even suggested that these experiences produced a personal insecurity that leads Reagan to fear dependence on outside influences.[70] But Cannon suggests another interpretation: Reagan is the "resilient child of an alcoholic," someone who did not suffer adversely from the effects of having an alcoholic parent, primarily because of the efforts of an adoring mother.[71] After all, Reagan never rejected his father. He invited his parents to move to California once he had established his acting career. Barber suggests a much less favorable interpretation: Reagan's youth began a lifetime of "pretending: that he really could see the blackboard [he is severely nearsighted], that his father was not really a drunk, that he really could play football, that he really did belong in the rich kids' crowd."[72]

Reagan's Career

Reagan's path to the White House was atypical. He did not enter public office until relatively late in life when he became governor of California in 1966 at age fifty-five. But political activities were not new to him, and Cannon describes Reagan as having been "a political person all his life."[73] This description was true of Reagan in high school and college, but even more so in Hollywood. He served multiple terms as president of the Screen Actors Guild, a post that engaged him in battles with organized crime and communist influences, about which he testified before Congress, as well as internecine feuds among contending unions. As a lifelong Democrat and rabid supporter of the New Deal, he campaigned actively for a variety of candidates including Harry Truman and Hubert Humphrey in 1948 and the liberal Helen Gahagan Douglas, who lost a California Senate race to Richard Nixon in 1950. In 1952 and 1956, however, Reagan supported the Eisenhower-Nixon ticket; by 1960 he had moved 180 degrees from his position a decade earlier by campaigning on Richard Nixon's behalf for president.

Reagan changed his party registration to Republican in 1962 and rose to prominence in 1964 during a nationally televised speech in support of Barry Goldwater; he delivered a message no less radical in content than the candidate's but did so in a far more reassuring manner. This appearance proved to be the launching pad for his subsequent rise to power when a group of wealthy California Republicans decided that he had a promising political future. After two terms in Sacramento, he finished a close second to Gerald Ford for the Republican presidential nomination in 1976, thereby becoming the front-runner and eventual nominee in 1980. He was the oldest president ever elected to the office, turning seventy shortly after his inauguration in January 1981.

Reagan's political career followed more than thirty years in the radio, motion picture, and television industries. After graduating from college, he became a midwestern radio celebrity, relying on a warm, persuasive voice and a carefully honed skill of delivering advertising copy with a note of spontaneity. After moving to Hollywood, he made fifty-two films, most with Warner Brothers as a leading man in B-movies, the second tier of feature films. He never quite broke into the circle of top marquee attractions. World War II disrupted his career just when it seemed poised to take off; throughout the war, Reagan remained in the continental United States making training films. He married two actresses: his marriage to Jane Wyman ended in divorce in 1947, and in 1952 he married starlet Nancy Davis. Nancy Reagan and her conservative stepfather are credited with reshaping his political views, and she proved to be his most enthusiastic supporter and trusted adviser in fashioning a new political career. From 1954 to 1962 Reagan served as corporate spokesperson for General Electric, hosting a television series for the sponsor and traveling across the country to deliver a message that became increasingly critical of government growth, wasteful programs, and encroachment on corporate America. By helping Reagan develop the skills of a political candidate, this job served as the functional equivalent of electoral politics: "he learned how to conserve his voice and how to fill his martini glass with water until the last reception of the day . . . he learned how to listen to a live audience."[74] Reagan estimated that he "gave as many as fourteen speeches a day and spent a total of two years of the eight he was under contract to General Electric on the road."[75]

By the time he sought public office, Reagan was certainly no amateur as a campaigner. The Speech, as it came to be known, had been honed to a basic message with a number of variations. Along the way, however, he developed a number of habits that posed serious problems for campaign advisers in each of his subsequent races—principally, the use of stories for the effect they had on an audience even if they strayed from the truth.

How was Reagan influenced by this pre-presidential career experience? As Cannon observes, "Even when he was gone from Hollywood, Hollywood was never gone from him," just as the small-town influence of Dixon, Illinois, continued throughout his life.[76] The lingering effects manifested themselves in several ways. Reagan adopted an "actor's approach to the presidency," relying heavily on staff to help him meet the needs of a performance; in communicating with the public, the president and his aides judged "stories by their impact rather than their accuracy," producing a constant temptation to tell the public what it wanted to hear; in dealing with heads of state and congressional leaders, the president tried to get by with "charm and cue cards" rather than by mastering the substance of public problems; Reagan was most concerned and engaged by discussions of the "scripts and scenes of the presidency," what might be termed the theatrical features of leadership.[77] Barber's analysis is even harsher; Reagan was "a President continually in search of directors to tell him what to do," the product of a lifetime of success based on following scripts prepared by others.[78] Moreover, in the view of one of his former aides, Reagan was "'not really looking to make a decision. He is looking for lines to repeat when the time comes to sell. He thinks of himself not so much as the person who decides but rather as the person who markets.'"[79]

Reagan's Ideology

To what extent was Reagan a driving force within his own administration? Did he have strong views that shaped the direction of policy and programs? Some of the more positive accounts of his administration emphasize that Reagan's beliefs served as a beacon to guide the actions of political allies as well as those subject to his direction, such as career members of the bureaucracy. But there is little evidence that Reagan is a deep or particularly analytic thinker. Moreover, the radical transformation of his personal beliefs that occurred with the changes in his life circumstances suggests that his views were the product of something other than careful reflection. Reagan's world view is significant for understanding his behavior as president, and the range of interpretations is quite wide. Barber has suggested that Reagan's "conservatism has been circumstantial, not visceral"; he became a conservative by convenience since his views resulted from "a desire to please the very rich mentors who picked him up and brought him to where he is today."[80] Such a pattern, argues Barber, can be seen throughout Reagan's life from the desire to associate with the high society crowd in high school to the willingness to modify his speeches so they would conform to the best interests of General Electric. This interpretation is consistent with Barber's classification of Reagan as a passive-positive, who typically lack goals of their own.

Fred Greenstein, on the other hand, attributes far greater significance to Reagan's beliefs, even if they did migrate from "keen Roosevelt liberalism to enthusiastically strong conservatism." This change, he argues, was "in close synchronization with the changes in his own life circumstances from Depression child to big business spokesman."[81] Moreover, Greenstein credits Reagan with being sufficiently secure emotionally to avoid being a rigid ideologue, allowing him "to adapt the positions he derives from doctrine if circumstances force him to recognize that they cannot be altered or will not work"; in other words, he is a pragmatic ideologue.[82] Even so, Reagan could prove highly "resistant to reconsidering policies in the areas closest to his central beliefs," especially reducing tax rates and shrinking the federal government.[83]

One of the most favorable interpretations of Reagan's beliefs and his efforts to effect a moral revolution is offered by William K. Muir, Jr., who finds three central themes in Reagan's presidential rhetoric.[84] Partnership replaced the footrace as the dominant metaphor for society, providing a new basis for voluntary cooperation through association rather than relying on government efforts to constrain rampant individualism. Human imperfection and evil became a central theme of Reagan's rhetoric to restore a sense that individuals were responsible for their own behavior. Finally, Muir credits Reagan with stressing spiritual dignity as a measure of personal achievement rather than material accumulation. These themes, argues Muir, were self-consciously woven into the president's public addresses by his speechwriters, repeated frequently to religious audiences, and broadcast even more broadly by his cabinet members. At the heart of this effort lay a dedication to freedom rather than equality, a commitment most clearly articulated in Reagan's nationally televised speech of 1964, "A Time for Choosing." This speech, which decried the demoralizing effect of government on individual liberty, became "the conscience of the Reagan presidency."[85] Muir, therefore, believes that Reagan's world view was not only coherent, but that it also had a galvanizing effect on his administration and the nation.

Finally, Hugh Heclo argues that it is far too simple to view Reaganism—the distinctive combination of pre-existing ideas that characterized the Reagan era—in terms of one politician's thinking. In his view, Reagan headed a political movement; assembling this coalition of forces "had the effect of putting together a distinctive collection of ideas capable of making a strong claim on American public thought."[86] Like the contradictions that characterized Reagan himself, Heclo finds that Reaganism defies consistency: "antigovernment nationalism" stressed the unproductive intrusion of central government that was preventing the full development of the nation's potential; "communitarian individualism" held that voluntary efforts and community activity should meet the needs of the less fortunate just as neighbors have always done; "free-market radicalism" combined with "nostalgic futurism" to reassure Americans that progress could once again be achieved by allowing markets and technological development to proceed unimpeded. At the heart of this public philosophy, argues Heclo, was the faith that salvation lies "in returning to the bedrock consensus of American politics—the traditional values of family, work, private enterprise, and nation—that have been forgotten."[87] The attractiveness of this creed was enhanced by its appeal to patriotism, the confidence displayed by its exponents, and the optimism of its message.

One should not dismiss the significance of Reagan's world views as an influence on his own conduct in office as well as that of his associates. Fred Greenstein considers him "unique among the modern presidents in his depth—and one might add duration—of ideological commitment."[88] His beliefs were so general, however, that departures could be readily rationalized. They posed fewer limits on Reagan's tactical decisions than is usually the case with strong ideologues. But given the way Reagan's views reflected his own life changes, it is difficult to regard them as only of secondary importance or as insignificant.

Reagan's Management Style

After eight years in the California governorship, Reagan entered the presidency with an established set of practices and preferences about how to manage an executive position. Moreover, he brought with him a number of aides who had served him in Sacramento and who knew his personal proclivities as well as his strengths and weaknesses. Edwin Meese, William P. Clark, and Michael Deaver worked closely with Reagan throughout much of the first term and facilitated the transfer of Reagan's management style to Washington.[89]

Reagan followed a management style variously described as "hands-off," "clean desk," and "chairman of the board."[90] What all these terms have in common is distance and detachment—Reagan distanced himself from most details of policy substance and from most day-to-day operations of his staff and the government. The president preferred one-page summaries of policy problems (known as "mini memos"), disliked briefings, and was known to fall asleep during cabinet meetings. The problems that most engaged his interest involved image projection and bargaining, particularly when negotiations were with Congress and when he needed to personally win legislators' voting support.

Paul Quirk has described Reagan's overall approach to the job as the "minimalist" presidency, a distinct departure from Jimmy Carter's pursuit of the "self-reliant" model of presidential leadership based on being "thoroughly involved, completely informed, and prompt."[91] Reagan believed his role was to "personally establish the general policies and goals of his administration, select cabinet and other key personnel who shared his commitments, then delegate broad authority to them so that they could work out the particulars."[92] But for all his detachment, Reagan could be intensely committed to achieving his goals. As Bert Rockman points out, the result was a strange combination. The architects who devised the administrative system within which Reagan operated had to take into account two features of the president's style: his deep commitment to a few strongly held goals and a remarkable detachment from details.[93]

Even Lou Cannon, Reagan's generally understanding if not always sympathetic biographer, seems to question whether this minimalist approach was enough for a president to adopt. Cannon offers a damning description of Reagan's conduct of the office: Reagan was "uncurious about most aspects of public policy," substituted "anecdotes for analysis," "didn't know enough about public policy to participate fully in his presidency—and often didn't realize how much he didn't know," "spent more time at the movies during his presidency than at anything else," including 183 weekend trips to Camp David where he could be certain to take in a double feature.[94]

Throughout the first term, aides defended Reagan's management style as making the presidency possible to accomplish, something that over-achieving predecessors (the Carter experience was still fresh in people's minds) had been unable to do. There was far less enthusiasm during the second term when the president's inattentiveness was identified as con-tributing to some of the administration's worst performances, as outlined in the next section. It is not coincidental that the aides with greatest experience in meeting Reagan's needs departed from the White House at the beginning of the second term. Reagan, like any minimalist president, was heavily dependent on the success of those to whom tasks were dele-gated. The new cast of White House aides was far less familiar with ways to compensate for the president's own lack of effort and information.

Conclusions About Ronald Reagan

With the passage of time, historians and political scientists may evalu-ate presidents differently. It is possible that new evidence will also pro-duce a new understanding of a president's behavior. As noted earlier, there is widespread appreciation today of Dwight Eisenhower's under-stated style of leadership, which was unrecognized while he was in office. Are professionals likely to change their evaluations of Ronald Reagan? The parallels between Reagan and Eisenhower are striking: they are the only two presidents to have served two full terms in the post–World War II era; both left office with relatively high public approval ratings; both were Republicans; both were evaluated by Barber as "passive," the only two passive presidents in the postwar period. Fred Greenstein, the fore-most revisionist interpreter of Ike's style has asked, "If an Eisenhower's reputation can be reversed in a few decades, what are we to expect of Ronald Reagan?"[95]

Barber has not been convinced that he was wrong about Eisenhower, and his initial evaluation provides a basis for interpreting much of Reagan's performance in office. On the eve of Reagan's inauguration, Barber wrote, "As president, he will be dangerous."[96] This prediction arose from Barber's belief that Reagan, as a passive-positive seeking affection, would be susceptible to "drift" and "have disaster thrust upon him."[97] It is tempting to read some of the low moments of the Reagan presidency in light of this interpretation: the burgeoning budget deficits that reached historical dimensions; the clumsy involvement in Lebanon that seemed to lack a clear purpose; the Iran-contra affair, which revealed that presidential aides working in the National Security Council had sold arms to the government of Iran in expectation that American hostages held in Lebanon would be released, and then funneled profits from the sales to the anti–Sandinista rebels in Nicaragua as a way to bypass congressional limitations on U.S. support *(see Chapter 10)*. Reagan seemed out of touch in each of these episodes. He did not seem to appreciate the link between his cherished economic program and the long-term consequences of persistent deficits. Administration policy in Lebanon received a jolting reality check with the bombing of the Marine barracks in Beirut, which precipitated the withdrawal of American forces. And investigations into the Iran-contra affair revealed an uninformed, inattentive president unaware of the day-to-day operations of his own staff. Drift seems apparent in each instance.

Greenstein surveys what we now know of Reagan based on accounts from investigative journalists, memoirs already published by his White House associates, and public inquiries. He concludes that Reagan also was more active than was generally appreciated, but in a very different way from Eisenhower. Reagan was very much engaged as a public communicator and a private persuader. As the administration's principal spokesperson, he was unsurpassed by any president since the rise of the rhetorical presidency at the turn of the century; he was also active in numerous efforts of face-to-face persuasion. But there is little to indicate that Reagan was engaged by analyzing and evaluating policy options. Unlike other passive-positives, Reagan had little difficulty making decisions based on the options offered to him by advisers, but unlike Eisenhower he had little interest in delving into the underpinnings of those options. Reagan's strongest views on policy established the context for administration policy—the defense build-up, lowered tax rates, reduced government spending, consistent anticommunism—but the details were always left for others to determine. There was a fundamental passivity on some dimensions, but active engagement on others. Far from being another "hidden-hand" president like Eisenhower, Greenstein concludes that Reagan will be seen as a "no-hands" president.[98]

Again, Lou Cannon provides a sympathetic interpretation for this perplexing portrait by suggesting that Reagan ranked high on some forms of intelligence but low on others. This view rests on a theory of "multiple intelligences" with Reagan doing well on interpersonal and language intelligence but poorly on "logical mathematical intelligence," which includes the kind of analytic and reasoning skills in which lawyers and successful politicians normally excel.[99] Overall, Cannon's portrait of the Reagan experience is highly critical of the president's performance.

As this sketch demonstrates, there is no definitive answer to the riddle of Ronald Reagan, and the debate among interpreters can be expected to continue. Like every other president before him, Reagan brought a mix of orientations and experiences to the presidency that were sometimes detrimental and sometimes beneficial to his performance in office. The final balance will differ from analyst to analyst and probably change with the passage of time.

Seeking Presidential Success

Paul Quirk has posed a deceptively simple question: "What does a president need to know?" Quirk identifies a list of presidential competencies that could serve as the basis for making decisions about how best to allocate the president's time, energy, and talent as well as that of the White House staff, the innermost group of presidential advisers.[100] In Quirk's view, presidents require a minimal level of *substantive familiarity* so that intelligent choices can be made among policy options. Moreover, presidents need to have a degree of *process sensibility* that reflects familiarity with how government decisions are made and carried out as well as how such systems might best be designed. Finally, presidents need the capacity for *policy promotion*, the means that make it possible to achieve their goals through bargaining with other Washington elites and through appeals for broad public support. Every president brings a different mix of personal competencies to the job and needs to compensate for personal weaknesses or to complement strengths with the help of others. In Quirk's view, it is critical that each president have a well-designed strategy for how to succeed, what he terms *strategic competence*. This strategy will involve decisions on how to allocate time, energy, and talent in relation to mastering substantive issues, delegating tasks, and establishing the prerequisites for successful delegation, for example, selecting personnel.[101]

How are these competencies developed? Implicitly, Quirk seems to suggest that experience in government at the federal level is a critical qualification for presidents to bring to the position. Without it, adequate levels of process and substantive familiarity would be difficult to develop. But Quirk's advice is directed more to presidents than voters. Above all else, Quirk urges presidents to approach the office self-consciously with an eye to developing a management strategy—know yourself and take the steps necessary for effectiveness. Only in this way can presidents hope to achieve some measure of success. It is not clear how readily presidents will accept such advice. Are they likely to be sufficiently self-critical to recognize their own shortcomings? One might expect that anyone imbued with ambition and flush with success will proceed to the task of governing filled with self-confidence. Moreover, one might expect that those presidents whose personalities drive them to pursue achievement will be least likely to undertake self-analysis.

In many respects, this chapter has explored a question similar to the one posed by Quirk. *What personal qualities make a successful president?* As we have seen, there are no simple answers to that question. Competencies may be part of the solution, but so are temperament and attitudes. As this chapter demonstrates, we have little sense of how the qualities necessary for success are derived from family background, career experience, personality, and beliefs. This is true in no small measure because success is the product of these personal qualities interacting with the constraints and opportunities of situations. Despite this fundamental uncertainty, there remains a pervasive confidence that the president's personal qualities have the utmost effect on performance in office, and, therefore, the American people are likely to continue their search for men and, perhaps one day, women with heroic qualities.

NOTES

1. Fred I. Greenstein, "Can Personality and Politics Be Studied Systematically?" *Political Psychology* 13, No. 1 (1992): 109. For a general discussion of studying personality and politics with special attention to the presidency, see Fred I. Greenstein, *Personality and Politics: Problems of Evidence, Inference and Conceptualization* (New York: Norton, 1975); and Bert Rockman, *The Leadership Question: The Presidency and the American System* (New York: Praeger, 1984).

2. Bruce Buchanan, *The Citizen's Presidency* (Washington, D.C.: CQ Press, 1987), 102–104. Buchanan proposes a set of "competent process standards" that are more susceptible to empirical verification. See *The Citizen's Presidency*, 108–134.

3. Bert Rockman, "Conclusions: An Imprint but Not a Revolution," in *The Reagan Revolution?* ed. B. B. Kymlicka and Jean V. Matthews (Chicago: Dorsey, 1988), 205. Other works in this vein include the following: Larry Berman, ed., *Looking Back on the Reagan Presidency* (Baltimore: The Johns Hopkins University Press, 1990); Sidney Blumenthal and Thomas Byrne Edsall, eds., *The Reagan Legacy* (New York: Pantheon Books, 1988); Charles O. Jones, ed., *The Reagan Legacy: Promise and Performance* (Chatham, N.J.: Chatham House, 1988); and John L. Palmer, ed., *Perspectives on the Reagan Years* (Washington, D.C.: Urban Institute, 1986).

4. Schlesinger's initial effort polled fifty-five scholars, and his second included seventy-five, with historians comprising the greater part of each group. Maranell and Dodder included results from 571 historians, and the *Chicago Tribune* poll focused on forty-nine scholars who had studied individual presidents. Finally, the Murray-Blessing poll was based on 846 responses to a nineteen-page, 180-question survey that was sent to 1,997 Ph.D-holding American historians with assistant professor rank (an additional 107 responses were returned late). For information on poll samples, see Henry J. Abraham, *Justices and Presidents* (New York: Oxford University Press, 1985), appendix B. For discussion of these efforts as well as their own, see Robert K. Murray and Tim H. Blessing, *Greatness in the White House: Rating the Presidents, Washington Through Carter* (University Park: University of Pennsylvania Press, 1988), chaps. 1 and 2. The ranking of Ronald Reagan is found in *Vital Statistics on American Politics*, 3d ed., by Harold W. Stanley and Richard G. Niemi (Washington, D.C.: CQ Press, 1992), table 8-2, 258–259, as reported in an update of the Murray-Blessing study.

5. Murray and Blessing, *Greatness in the White House*, 24.

6. Ibid., 41–43, and appendix 8, 139. The personal traits conducive to success also were examined in terms of how they changed for different times. For the modern era, 1945 to the present, respondents ranked intelligence first and integrity second, with other qualities in declining order: sensitivity to popular demands, charisma, previous political experience, pleasing physical appearance, intense patriotism, and an aristocratic bearing.

7. Ibid., 63.

8. James MacGregor Burns, *Leadership* (New York: Harper & Row, 1977)

9. Donald Matthews, *The Social Background of Political Decision Makers* (New York: Random House, 1954), 23.

10. Edward Pessen, *The Log Cabin Myth: The Social Backgrounds of the Presidents* (New Haven, Conn.: Yale University Press, 1984), 56–57.

11. Ibid., 171.

12. Ibid., 56–63. Pessen views a family's class as a combination of wealth and possessions, income and occupational prestige, lifestyle, status, influence, and power. He recognizes, moreover, that analysts' characterizations are subjective.

13. Sidney Hyman, *The American President* (New York: Harper, 1954), 221.

14. Truman attended night classes at the Kansas City Law School, but it was a proprietary institution not then affiliated with a university. It is now part of the Law School of the University of Missouri-Kansas City.

15. Max Weber, "Politics as a Vocation," in *Max Weber: Essays in Sociology*, ed. H. H. Gerth and C. W. Mills (New York: Oxford University Press, 1946), 85.

16. Hugh Montgomery-Massingberd, ed., *Burke's Presidential Families of the U.S.A.* (London: Burke's Peerage, 1975), 250.

17. Ibid., 320.

18. Robert Donovan, *Conflict and Crisis: The Presidency of Harry S Truman, 1945–48* (New York: Praeger, 1977), chap. 40. It should also be noted that military officers have demonstrated leadership skills and may be called upon to develop substantial political skill while building careers or in dealing with foreign leaders. Eisenhower, for example, did both.

19. Pessen, *The Log Cabin Myth,* 172.

20. Ibid., 171.

21. E. Digby Baltzell and Howard G. Schneiderman, "Social Class in the Oval Office," *Society* 26, No. 6 (September/October 1988): 42–49. The ranking of presidential performance used in this study was conducted by Robert K. Murray and Tim H. Blessing and was first published in the *Journal of American History* 70, No. 3 (December 1983): 535–555.

22. Ibid., 47.

23. W. H. Harrison and Garfield were not rated because of the brief time they served in office.

24. Baltzell and Schneiderman, "Social Class in the Oval Office," 49.

25. Richard Neustadt, *Presidential Power and the Modern Presidents* (New York: Free Press, 1991), 151.

26. Ibid., 205.

27. Rockman, *Leadership Question,* 212. Rockman uses a performance ranking compiled by the *Chicago Tribune* in 1982.

28. We are indebted to Leonard P. Stark, a former student at the University of Delaware, for this account and continuing stimulation on the subject of presidential personality. See his senior honors thesis, "Personality and Presidential Selection: Evaluating Character and Experience in the 1988 Election," unpublished, June 1991, 47–48. Barber's article was "The Question of Presidential Character," *Saturday Review,* Sept. 23, 1972, 62–66.

29. Fred Greenstein, *Personality and Politics: Problems of Evidence, Inference and Conceptualization,* 2d ed. (New York: Norton, 1975), 3.

30. Alexander George and Juliette George, *Woodrow Wilson and Colonel House: A Personality Study* (New York: John Day, 1956); Bruce Mazlish, *In Search of Nixon: A Psychohistorical Inquiry* (Baltimore: Pelican, 1973); Doris Kearns, *Lyndon Johnson and the American Dream* (New York: Harper & Row, 1976); Betty Glad, *Jimmy Carter: In Search of the Great White House* (New York: Norton, 1980).

31. For an extended discussion, see Greenstein's treatment of these issues in *Personality and Politics,* chaps. 3 and 4, as well as the introduction to the 1975 edition.

32. See, for example, Alexander George's discussion of Barber's book, *The Presidential Character: Predicting Performance in the White House.* George, "Assessing Presidential Character," *World Politics* 26 (January 1974): 234–282.

33. James David Barber, *The Presidential Character: Predicting Performance in the White House,* 3d ed. (Englewood Cliffs, N.J.: Prentice-Hall, 1985), 347.

34. Ibid., 5.

35. Ibid.

36. This article, originally found on the *New York Times* op ed page, is reprinted in Barber, *Presidential Character,* 4th ed. (Englewood Cliffs, N.J.: Prentice-Hall, 1992), 458–460.

37. Barber, *Presidential Character,* 4th ed., 474, 475.

38. Greenstein, *Personality and Politics,* 19.

39. Fred Greenstein, *The Hidden-Hand Presidency* (New York: Basic Books, 1982). Barber, however, has responded that the new evidence confirms his original analysis even more fully. Barber, *Presidential Character,* 3d ed., 511–515.

40. See George, "Assessing Presidential Character"; and Michael Nelson, "The Psychological Presidency," in *The Presidency and the Political System*, 3d ed., ed. Michael Nelson (Washington, D.C.: CQ Press, 1990).

41. Dean Keith Simonton, *Why Presidents Succeed: A Political Psychology of Leadership* (New Haven, Conn.: Yale University Press, 1987), 151–152.

42. Barber, *Presidential Character*, 2d. ed., 449.

43. Ibid. 246.

44. Ibid., 243–246.

45. Jeffrey Tulis, "On Presidential Character," in *The Presidency in the Constitutional Order*, ed. Jeffrey Tulis and Joseph M. Bessette (Baton Rouge: Louisiana State University Press, 1981), 283–313.

46. Michael Nelson, "The Psychological Presidency," 201. Four presidents who finished in the top ten were not listed because Barber has not classified them: they are Jackson, Polk, T. Roosevelt, and McKinley.

47. Stanley and Niemi, *Vital Statistics on American Politics*, 3d ed., 265–267.

48. Joseph A. Pika, "Management Style and the Organizational Matrix: Studying White House Operations," *Administration and Society* 20, No. 1 (May 1988): 11.

49. John Hart, *The Presidential Branch* (New York: Pergamon Press, 1987).

50. Alexander George, *Presidential Decisionmaking in Foreign Policy* (Boulder, Colo.: Westview, 1980), 139–168.

51. The three basic structures were identified in the early 1970s by R. T. Johnson and have been the object of much discussion. Richard Tanner Johnson, *Managing the White House* (New York: Harper & Row, 1974). Also see Johnson, "Presidential Style," in *Perspectives on the Presidency*, Aaron Wildavsky, ed. (Boston: Little, Brown, 1975).

52. Roger Porter, "A Healing Presidency," in *Leadership in the Modern Presidency*, ed. Fred Greenstein (Cambridge, Mass.: Harvard University Press, 1988), 218.

53. George, *Presidential Decisionmaking*, 159.

54. Colin Campbell, *Managing the Presidency: Carter, Reagan, and the Search for Executive Harmony* (Pittsburgh: University of Pittsburgh Press, 1986), 93–111; James Pfiffner, *The Strategic Presidency: Hitting the Ground Running* (Chicago: Dorsey, 1988), 30–37; Bruce Buchanan, *The Citizen's Presidency* (Washington, D.C.: CQ Press, 1987), 124–133.

55. Pika, "Management Style and the Organizational Matrix," 9.

56. Alexander George, "The Case for Multiple Advocacy in Making Foreign Policy," *American Political Science Review* 66 (September 1972): 751–785. Also see George, *Presidential Decisionmaking*, chap. 11.

57. George, *Presidential Decisionmaking*, 203.

58. Ibid., 203–204.

59. Ibid., 201.

60. Ibid., 204.

61. Some may wonder why George Bush is not the topic of this sketch. Because Bush has attracted far less academic attention, the body of material on which such an effort would rest is much thinner than a focus on Reagan. The principal sources used in completing this sketch are the following: Barber, *Presidential Character*, 3d ed.; Fred I. Greenstein, "Reagan and the Lore of the Modern Presidency: What Have We Learned?" in *The Reagan Presidency: An Early Assessment*, ed. Fred I. Greenstein (Baltimore: The Johns Hopkins University Press, 1983); Garry Wills, *Reagan's America* (New York: Penguin Books, 1988); Lou Cannon, *Reagan* (New York: Perigee Books, 1982); Lou Cannon, *President Reagan: The Role of a Lifetime* (New York: Simon & Schuster, 1991); William K. Muir, Jr., "Ronald Reagan: The Primacy of Rhetoric," in *Leadership in the Modern Presidency*.

62. Cannon, *Reagan*, 24.

63. Wills, *Reagan's America*, 2.

64. Ibid., 43.

65. Ibid., 40.

66. Cannon, *The Role of a Lifetime*, 216.

67. Quoted in Cannon, *Reagan*, 34.

68. Wills, *Reagan's America*, 52–63.

69. As quoted in Cannon, *The Role of a Lifetime*, 213.

70. See Wills's discussion of this interpretation offered by Robert Dallek. Wills, *Reagan's America*, 41–43.

71. Cannon, *The Role of a Lifetime*, 210–211. To support this interpretation, Cannon cites research completed by Emmy E. Werner, "Resilient Offspring of Alcoholics: A Longitudinal Study from Birth to Age 18," *Journal of Studies on Alcohol* (January 1986).

72. Barber, *Presidential Character*, 3d ed., 487.

73. Cannon, *Reagan*, 71.

74. Ibid., 94.

75. Ibid., 93.

76. Cannon, *The Role of a Lifetime*, 64.

77. Ibid., 60, 57, 53.

78. Barber, *Presidential Character*, 3d ed., 498.

79. As quoted in ibid., 496.

80. Ibid., 472.

81. Greenstein, "Reagan and the Lore of the Modern Presidency," 165.

82. Ibid., 167.

83. Ibid., 171.

84. Muir, "Ronald Reagan: The Primacy of Rhetoric," 266–282.

85. Ibid., 288–289.

86. Hugh Heclo, "Reaganism and the Search for a Public Philosophy," in *Perspectives on the Reagan Years*, ed. John L. Palmer (Washington, D.C.: Urban Institute Press, 1986), 40.

87. Ibid., 47.

88. Greenstein, "Reagan and the Lore of the Modern Presidency," 171.

89. Meese was Reagan's White House counselor and later became the attorney general; Clark entered as deputy secretary of state and became the president's national security assistant in 1982; Deaver served as assistant White House chief of staff throughout the first term, was a confidant of Nancy Reagan, and oversaw the president's public relations.

90. Bert Rockman, "The Style and Organization of the Reagan Presidency," in *The Reagan Legacy: Promise and Performance*, ed. Charles O. Jones (Chatham, N.J.: Chatham House, 1988); Richard E. Neustadt, comments at University of California at Davis conference on "The Legacy of the Reagan Presidency," May 26, 1988; Paul J. Quirk, "Presidential Competence," in *The Presidency and the Political System*, 3d ed.

91. Quirk, "Presidential Competence," 165.

92. Ibid., 167.

93. Rockman, "The Style and Organization of the Reagan Presidency," 9–10.

94. Cannon, *The Role of a Lifetime*, 135, 132, 130, 56.

95. Fred I. Greenstein, "Ronald Reagan—Another Hidden-Hand Ike?" *PS* 23 (March 1990): 7–13.

96. Barber, *Presidential Character*, 3d ed., 462.

97. Ibid., 463.

98. Greenstein, "Ronald Reagan—Another Hidden-Hand Ike?" 12.

99. Cannon, *The Role of a Lifetime*, 137–138.

100. Quirk, "Presidential Competence"; and Paul Quirk, "What Must a President Know?" *Transaction/Society* 23 (January/February 1983).

101. Quirk, "Presidential Competence," 170.

READINGS

Barber, James David. *The Presidential Character*. 4th ed. Englewood Cliffs, N.J.: Prentice-Hall, 1992.

George, Alexander, and Juliette George. *Woodrow Wilson and Colonel House: A Personality Study*. New York: John Day, 1956.

Greenstein, Fred. *Personality and Politics: Problems of Evidence, Inference and Conceptualization*. New York: Norton, 1975.

Hargrove, Erwin. *Presidential Leadership: Personality and Political Style*. New York: Macmillan, 1966.

Kearns, Doris. *Lyndon Johnson and the American Dream*. New York: Harper & Row, 1976.

Mazlish, Bruce. *In Search of Nixon: A Psychohistorical Inquiry*. Baltimore: Pelican, 1973.

Pessen, Edward. *The Log Cabin Myth: The Social Backgrounds of the Presidents*. New Haven, Conn.: Yale University Press, 1984.

Rockman, Bert A. *The Leadership Question: The Presidency and the American System*. New York: Praeger, 1984.

Tugwell, Rexford. *How They Became President*. New York: Simon & Schuster, 1968.

PART II
THE PRESIDENT AND
THE GOVERNMENT

5　LEGISLATIVE POLITICS

By vetoing bills simply because he had policy disagreements with Congress, President Andrew Jackson set a precedent that strengthened the presidency. His opponents depicted him as a tyrant, trampling on the Constitution.

ON OCTOBER 5, 1990, THE House of Representatives rejected a budget agreement that had been reached after four months of difficult negotiations between congressional leaders and the Bush administration. To move the negotiations forward, President George Bush had repudiated his campaign pledge that there would be "no new taxes" and staked his reputation as a shrewd, pragmatic Washington insider on approval of the agreement. Not only did it fail, but also 60 percent of House Republicans, 105 of 176, voted against it. Although Congress and the president managed to conclude a budget deal before the November 6 midterm elections, Bush's approval ratings in the opinion polls fell by almost twenty points in three months, and questions arose about his ability to lead Congress. Nor were Bush's difficulties with Congress confined to the struggle over the 1991 budget. A Congressional Quarterly study reported that Bush's success rate on bills that his administration contested in Congress in 1991 was only 54.2 percent, the fifth weakest performance by a president since 1953 when CQ began keeping track of congressional actions on presidential positions. Only his own 46.8 percent success rate for 1990; Ronald Reagan's scores of 43.5 percent in 1987 and 47.4 percent in 1988, levels reflecting the effects of the Iran-contra affair; and Gerald Ford's 53.8 percent success rate in 1976 were lower.[1]

The pattern of Bush's relations with Congress is comparable with the experience of Presidents Nixon, Ford, and Carter, and of Reagan in his last two years. To understand how Bush became locked into no-win struggles just as his predecessors had, one must examine the politics of presidential-congressional relations and the ways modern presidents have managed them.

Presidents usually discover, upon taking office, that the skills and techniques of leadership that enabled them to capture their party's nomination and win the election are not identical with those needed to sustain their popularity. Nomination and electoral politics require the ability to raise money, to build an organization composed of election professionals, to project an attractive and engaging image, and to sense the concerns of the public, but the politics of governing—that is, legislating and administering—requires talents that can move a complex, cumbersome government to "get things done." These talents include persuasion, personal and organizational leadership, and managerial skill.

Americans tend to judge presidents primarily by their performance in office. A principal criterion of evaluation is the president's ability to persuade Congress to pass his legislative program. National political leaders expect the president to develop legislative proposals that will achieve the administration's goals; the public and members of the news media expect the president to steer those proposals through Congress. Unwillingness or inability to meet these expectations usually results in loss of presidential popularity and assessments of ineffectiveness or failure. Even presidents philosophically opposed to an active federal government, such as Dwight D. Eisenhower, find themselves unable to resist the pressures to provide legislative leadership. The public expects presidents to address and solve national problems, but most solutions require congressional approval, which is not always forthcoming. This chapter examines the president's relations with Congress. It begins by tracing the development of the chief executive's legislative role in the twentieth century and then presents an analysis of the constitutional relationship between the president and Congress. A discussion of the president's formal legislative powers and a description of presidential strategies follow. The chapter then analyzes the basis of the president's support in Congress. Finally, it explores how the president's influence on Congress can be evaluated.

Development of the President's Legislative Role

The Constitution, in Article I, Section 8, gives Congress "all the legislative powers herein granted." Quite clearly, the Framers expected that Congress would have primary responsibility for formulating national policy and that the president's legislative role would be minor. Until the twentieth century most presidents did limit their involvement in the congressional process. Even Thomas Jefferson and Abraham Lincoln, who were most inclined to try to lead Congress, encountered strong opposition, and their activism did not alter the pattern of congressional supremacy.[2]

Early in the twentieth century, under the leadership of Theodore Roosevelt and Woodrow Wilson, the presidency acquired a greatly expanded legislative role as the national government responded to the problems of industrialization and urbanization. Roosevelt worked closely with congressional leaders and sent several messages to Congress that defined a legislative program. He saw it as the duty of the president to "take a very active interest in getting the right kind of legislation."[3] Wilson, who, as a political science professor, had argued that strong presidential leadership of Congress was needed if the nation was to cope with its growing problems, actively participated in the legislative process.[4] He took the lead in defining the goals of his program, helped formulate bills, reinstated the practice abandoned since 1796 of personally delivering the State of the Union message to Congress, used members of his cabinet to build congressional support for bills, and personally lobbied for some of his most important measures, such as the Federal Reserve Act and the Clayton Antitrust Act.

The next major expansion of the president's legislative role occurred under Franklin D. Roosevelt. Taking office in 1933 when the economy was mired in the depths of the Great Depression, FDR called Congress into a special session that lasted for 100 days. During that period the new president proposed, and Congress passed, legislation designed to meet the economic crisis. Together they overhauled the banking system, authorized a program of industrial self-government under the National Recovery Administration, buttressed farm income through passage of the Agricultural Adjustment Act, regulated financial markets under the Truth in Securities Act, and created the Tennessee Valley Authority, a program of comprehensive development of one of the nation's most depressed areas.

During the remainder of his first term FDR continued to submit, and Congress to pass, a series of measures designed to help farmers, industrial workers, and individual citizens. The legislation promoted soil conservation and restricted excess agricultural production; it guaranteed labor the right to organize and bargain collectively; and it established a system of social insurance to protect people against the loss of work due to economic slowdowns, physical disability, or old age. Additional legislation established administrative agencies to implement the New Deal statutes.

FDR's principal mode of operation was to send to Congress messages that analyzed a problem and outlined his proposed solution. Often a draft bill accompanied or followed the messages. He then assigned aides to monitor the bills and lobby for their passage. Beginning in 1935 coordination of his legislative program was accomplished through a clearance process administered by the Bureau of the Budget.[5] FDR also made extensive use of the veto as a means of bending Congress to his will; he threatened to veto legislation that failed to meet his demands or that he regarded as unwise or contrary to his purposes. His major contribution was to establish the expectation that the president would be actively involved at all stages of the legislative process by submitting a legislative program to Congress, working for its passage, and coordinating its implementation.

FDR's two immediate successors, Harry S. Truman and Dwight Eisenhower, institutionalized the president's legislative role by creating structures and processes to assist in carrying it out on a regular, systematic basis.[6] The Bureau of the Budget and members of the White House staff acted for the president. By the mid-1960s it appeared to some observers that the presidency had come to dominate the legislative process. Writing in 1965, Samuel P. Huntington remarked that "the congressional role in legislation has largely been reduced to delay and amendment." Such tasks as initiative in formulating legislation, assignment of legislative priorities, generation of support for legislation, and determination of the final content of legislation had "shifted to the executive branch," which, in Huntington's view, had gained "at the expense of Congress."[7] Others have argued, however, that although congressional and presidential roles in the legislative process have changed substantially, Congress remains a vitally important participant. The president's program is critical in determining the congressional agenda, but Congress is constantly modifying and altering policy through appropriations, amendments, and renewals of statutory authorizations.[8]

Moreover, Congress and the president are not engaged in a zero-sum game in which the power of one necessarily decreases as the power of the other increases. In an absolute sense, since 1933 Congress has increased its power as an instrument of government by vastly expanding the subjects on which it has legislated. During that time, however, the power of Congress as an innovator of public policy has declined relative to that of the president. In three brief periods of legislative activity—1933–1937, 1964–1965, and 1981—activist presidents (FDR, Johnson, and Reagan) led responsive Congresses in the adoption of major changes in domestic policy. Congress also responded to presidential leadership in establishing the role of the United States in world affairs during and immediately following World War II.

Nevertheless, there have also been periods in which Congress substantially increased its authority vis-à-vis the president. During the 1970s, for example, Congress expanded its control over the executive branch through increased use of the legislative veto (see Chapter 6), curbed presidential use of military force abroad through passage of the War Powers Resolution of 1973 (see Chapter 10), and strengthened its ability to determine the amount of federal spending through revamping of the congressional budget process (see Chapter 9).

The always-present potential for presidential leadership of Congress became dramatically evident in 1981 when Ronald Reagan took office following his landslide victory. Reagan quickly took command of conservative congressional majorities, which passed his taxing and spending proposals and sharply altered the course that domestic social and economic policy had been following since the 1930s.[9] But Reagan's period of dominance was short-lived; congressional critics of his policies regrouped in 1982, support among Republican legislators sagged, and concerns shifted to deficits in the range of $100–200 billion in his 1983–1989 budgets. Reagan discovered, as had Roosevelt in 1937 and Lyndon Johnson in 1966, that congressional approval of a president's program is not automatic. Congressional support must be cultivated and maintained, and when the conditions that created it change, it can rapidly disappear. Without such support, presidents face frustration and ineffectuality. Rather than emulate his predecessor by presenting an aggressive legislative program, President Bush offered very modest initiatives. Even so, he was unable to develop sustained congressional support.

The Presidential–Congressional Relationship

There is inherent tension between Congress and the presidency, yet cooperation between the two institutions is necessary if the government is to act in a significant way. The Constitution creates institutional competition through the separation of powers, but it also mandates a sharing of powers among the branches of government. Joint action by the president and Congress is required to authorize programs, appropriate money to pay for them, and levy taxes to provide the funds. Neither branch can achieve its goals or operate the government without the participation of the other. However, since 1970 presidential-congressional relations have become competitive because of the distrust between the branches and intensified party differences between Republican presidents and congressional Democrats.[10]

The Separation of Powers

James Madison's *Federalist* No. 51 makes it clear that the Framers had contemplated presidential-congressional conflict:

To what expedient . . . shall we finally resort, for maintaining in practice the necessary partition of power among the several departments, as laid down in the constitution? The only answer that can be given is . . . by so contriving the interior structure of the government as its several constituent parts may, by their mutual relations, be the means of keeping each other in their proper places. . . .

In order to lay a due foundation for that separate and distinct exercise of the different powers of the government, which to a certain extent is admitted on all hands to be essential to the preservation of liberty, it is evident that each department should have a will of its own. . . .

But the great security against a gradual concentration of the several powers in the same department consists in giving to those who administer each department the necessary constitutional means and personal motives to resist the encroachments of the others. . . . Ambition must be made to counteract ambition. The interests of the man must be connected with the constitutional rights of the place.[11]

Since 1789 the task of governing the United States has been to overcome the constitutional dispersion, and simultaneous sharing, of power among competing institutions. The most important division of power, from the standpoint of making and implementing national policies, is that between the president and Congress. The pattern of the presidential-congressional relationship has not been static. According to Lawrence C. Dodd, a cyclical pattern of power aggrandizement by Congress or the presidency and resurgence by the other institution has operated from the beginning of government under the Constitution.[12] In the nineteenth century the institutional surges and declines oscillated evenly within well-defined boundaries and returned at the end of each cycle to the balance envisioned in the Constitution. However, the economic, social, and technological transformations and the emergence from political isolation that occurred during the twentieth century created problems and conditions that called increasingly for executive rather than legislative decision making. The presidency could act more quickly, more decisively, and more consistently than Congress, which has had difficulty ascertaining its institutional will and coherently pursuing its goals.

In consequence, presidential surges have resulted in permanent expansions of executive power and presidential aggrandizements, such as Johnson's use of the war powers to involve the United States in the Vietnam War *(see Chapter 10)* or Richard Nixon's sweeping claims of executive privilege and his extensive impoundments of appropriated funds *(see Chapter 6)*. Although Congress managed to reassert its constitutional authority during the 1970s,[13] the cycle turned again in the 1980s toward increased reliance on presidential power. The nation found that it needed presidential leadership to deal with difficult problems such as severe inflation, economic interdependence, and international terrorism.

Sources of Presidential–Congressional Conflict

Forces promoting conflict are always present in the presidential-congressional relationship. In addition to institutional competition born of the separation of powers, conflict stems from the difference in the constituencies of the members of Congress and the president and from the fragmentation of power within Congress. The 535 members of Congress represent constituencies that vary in geographical area, population, economic structure, and social composition. Each congressional constituency is but a part of the nation. Every member of Congress depends for reelection on constituency-based political forces. Therefore, different members speak for different economic, social, and geographical interests, and all members are necessarily somewhat parochial at times in their policy orientations. Consequently, claims by certain members to be acting in behalf of the national interest must be judged in the context of their constituency interests.

Because congressional parties lack the power to command the votes of their members, there is no institutional basis for any of the elected party leaders of either house to speak on its behalf. The only way the national interest emerges in Congress is through bargaining between members and blocs of members responsive to particular interests. This practice results in the formation of temporary majority coalitions to pass specific measures. Congressional policy making is thus deliberate, incremental or piecemeal, and reactive. Congress often is unable to maintain consistency in its actions in different policy areas or cohesiveness within areas. Speed, efficiency, consistency, and cohesiveness usually are lacking, except in a crisis.

In contrast, the president's constituency is the entire nation. Only the president can claim to speak authoritatively in behalf of the national interest or to act for various inarticulate and unorganized interests who are not adequately represented in Congress. He can resist the demands of well-organized particular interests by posing as the champion of the national interest (even though there may be times when *he* too responds to such pressures). The difficulty that Congress encounters in determining and speaking for the national interest, and the ease with which the president may do so, stem from their differing constituencies and are a continuing source of tension between them.

Changes in electoral politics also have widened the gap between presidents and Congress in the process of governing the nation. Members of Congress have become political entrepreneurs who routinely seek reelection on the basis of constituency-based electoral coalitions that are largely independent of party membership.[14] (Since 1946 more than 90 percent of House and 75 percent of Senate incumbents who have sought reelection have been successful.[15]) They are nominated in direct primaries, their campaigns are financed heavily from nonparty sources, and they sustain electoral support through activities unrelated to their party, such as providing service to constituents. Presidents can exert little leverage on them through appeals to party loyalty or the exercise of party discipline. Moreover, there has been a decline in the strength of presidential coattails and an increase in the number of constituencies supporting a presidential candidate of one party and electing members of Congress from the opposition.

This separation of presidential and congressional electoral coalitions has resulted in a divided government that has reduced pressures on members to support their party's president. It is clear that a president whose party controls both houses of Congress enjoys certain advantages by virtue of party loyalty that is not available to a president faced with a Congress controlled by the opposition party. Since 1932 Democratic presidents have had to deal with an opposition Congress only in 1947 and 1948, while Republican occupants of the White House have confronted full opposition control in all years except 1953–1954 and 1981–1986 *(see Table 5-1).*

Analysts are sharply divided in their assessments of the consequences of divided partisan control of the government. The critics of divided government argue that it renders unworkable the already cumbersome and inefficient separation of powers structure established in the Constitution.[16] The critics blame the large federal budget deficits of the 1980s and 1990s on divided government, arguing that under it major policy decisions have become "the result of an institutionally structured bargaining process, with each party possessing a veto," in which the parties engage in a game of fiscal "chicken" waiting to see who will be first to back down.[17] Each branch of government, it is argued, has a stake in the failure of the other. Finally, these critics charge that divided government undermines electoral accountability because it is impossible for voters to hold either party responsible for the policies adopted and the results achieved since the last election.

In contrast, David Mayhew concluded, after a systematic empirical analysis of legislation and congressional investigations since World War II, that it does not make "much difference whether party control of the American government happens to be unified or divided."[18] Morris Fiorina also challenges the conventional wisdom with respect to divided government. Although acknowledging that it results in more "conflictual" congressional-presidential relations, he points out that it is an option available to the electorate under the Constitution and asks whether its consequences are "necessarily bad."[19] He argues that although divided government may limit the potential for social gain through public policy,

Table 5-1 Partisan Control of the Presidency and Congress, 1933–1992

Dates	Presidency	Congress
1933–1946	Democratic	Democratic
1947–1948	Democratic	*Republican*
1947–1948	Democratic	Democratic
1949–1952	Democratic	Democratic
1953–1954	*Republican*	*Republican*
1955–1960	*Republican*	Democratic
1961–1968	Democratic	Democratic
1969–1976	*Republican*	Democratic
1977–1980	Democratic	Democratic
1981–1986	*Republican*	Senate-*Rep.* House-Dem.
1987–1992	*Republican*	Democratic

it also limits potential loss through government action.[20] Finally, Fiorina suggests that divided government is the American electorate's way of establishing the coalition governments that are common in multiparty systems.[21] Whether the effects of divided government are benign or not is, as the saying goes, in the eye of the beholder. Without question, it has dominated presidential-congressional relations for most of the past quarter century.

The inability of Congress to match the decisiveness, cohesion, and consistency of the presidency as a national policy-making institution is also a product of the fragmented structure of its internal authority. Widely recognized are the weakness of congressional parties, the limited power of party leaders, the absence of party discipline in congressional voting, the presence of strong committees and subcommittees, and the ambitions of individual members to enhance their reelection chances and to advance to higher office.[22]

Former presidential aide and secretary of the Department of Health, Education and Welfare Joseph Califano has charged that Congress is short on institutional will.[23] An internally fragmented Congress that lacks will is not without power, but it tends to be a negative and restraining force on the presidency. Also, Congress usually is more comfortable with distributive policies and programs, which provide benefits on a widespread basis, than with redistributive policies, which change the allocation of wealth and power in society.

According to Roger Davidson and Walter Oleszek, Congress, as presently constituted, values the function of "representation" over that of "lawmaking."[24] They mean that Congress is responsive primarily to constituency interests and to well-organized interest groups. Ironically, the presidency might be said to stress the law-making function whereby electoral mandates are translated into policies that are adopted by congressional coalitions.

Patterns of Presidential–Congressional Policy Making

The Constitution mandates cooperation between Congress and the president. Congress has the legislative powers of the government, and its approval is necessary for any kind of executive action. The president can veto measures passed by Congress. Within the boundaries set by the Constitution and by political conditions, most relationships between the presidency and Congress in making national policy involve potential conflict. The patterns in the relationship vary according to issues, presidential leadership styles, and political context. Presidential domination tends to prevail in foreign and military policy and those issues to which presidents attach high priority, such as Lyndon Johnson's Great Society program in 1964 and 1965.[25] Congressional domination was the prevailing pattern in the 1970s, when Congress passed major legislation on the environment, consumer protection, and occupational safety; and Congress always has prevailed on public works. Stalemate characterized much of the energy legislation proposed by presidents in the 1970s, as well as proposals for reducing the federal budget deficit in the 1980s and 1990s. Occasionally, a proposal may be stalemated for years and then move rapidly to passage as conditions change or a new president takes office. Medicare provides a good example. Proposals for national health insurance had languished in Congress since first advanced by President Truman in 1946. The political climate turned favorable for liberal social legislation in 1964 and 1965, following the assassination of John F. Kennedy. Responding to Johnson's forceful leadership, Congress enacted legislation authorizing national health insurance for the elderly (Medicare) in 1965.

Presidential leadership style is related to the pattern of congressional relations with the presidency. An activist president who is committed to an extensive legislative program, such as FDR or Johnson, normally tries to dominate Congress, whereas a president who is more restrained and less active, such as Dwight Eisenhower or Gerald R. Ford, may be more inclined toward cooperation or may accept considerable congressional initiative in program development. Ronald Reagan, an activist with a conservative agenda that did not require extensive new legislation, adopted various patterns in his relations with Congress. To achieve his primary goals of reducing the role of the federal government and strengthening the armed forces, he attempted to establish presidential domination. On issues of less importance to him, such as farm policy and Social Security financing, he was willing to share responsibility with Congress. When he disagreed with Congress, as he did over reducing the federal budget deficit, he was willing to settle for a stalemate, but on no matters of consequence did he accept congressional domination. George Bush, a conservative with a limited agenda, sought congenial relations with Congress, but many crucial issues—the deficit, taxes, and civil rights— remained stalemated because of irreconcilable differences on which neither was willing to compromise.

No president in the modern era, which began with FDR, has sought stalemate with Congress, although such a condition has developed on occasion. Stalemates occur more often during periods of divided government than when one party is in power in both branches. A necessary condition for stalemate is a sharp division of opinion between the president and the congressional majority. During the Nixon and Ford administrations presidential-congressional relations were stalemated over several major bills, as two conservative Republican presidents quarreled with liberal Democratic Congresses about presidential prerogatives and spending priorities. From 1982 through 1992, Presidents Reagan and Bush and Congress were stalemated for several months each year over proposed budgets for the ensuing fiscal year. Their disagreements focused on how to reduce projected deficits of $100 billion to $300 billion. Democratic congressional leaders were joined by some of their Republican counterparts in pressing the two presidents to ease their opposition to cuts in defense spending and to selective tax increases. The presidents insisted that the only means of reducing the deficits was through deep cuts in spending for domestic programs, which most members of Congress were reluctant to do. The results were generally unsatisfactory to both sides: large deficits with small reductions in spending and no major tax increases.

The President's Legislative Powers

The president has two sets of tools at his disposal for the accomplishment of his legislative goals: (1) the formal powers vested in him by the

Constitution and by statute and (2) the informal resources inherent in the office. The chief executive uses both sets of tools simultaneously and in conjunction with each other. In the interest of analytical clarity, however, this chapter will examine them separately.

The Constitution sets out the president's legislative role. Article II, Section 3, authorizes him to call Congress into special session and requires him "from time to time to give the Congress information on the state of the Union, and to recommend to their consideration such measures as he shall judge necessary and expedient." Article I, Section 7, makes the president a direct participant in the legislative process by providing for his approval or disapproval of "every bill" and "every order, resolution, or vote to which the concurrence of the Senate and House may be necessary." These formal legislative powers are augmented by statutory delegations of authority to the president and to administrative agencies and by implied powers derived from the general grant of executive power in Article II. These delegated and implied powers serve as the basis for presidential legislation through the issuance of executive orders *(see Chapter 6)*.

Special Sessions

The president's power to call Congress into special session is less important today than it was in the past, primarily because Congress, since the 1930s, remains in session for much of the year, taking periodic short recesses. The expansion in government activity, the complexity of the appropriations process, and the change from indefinite to specific term authorizations of federal programs have so increased the congressional workload that early adjournments have all but disappeared. When Congress was not in almost continuous session, the president could call it back to Washington to consider specific proposals. Calling a special session placed responsibility for action on Congress.

Perhaps the most effective modern use of this power was made by FDR in March 1933 shortly after his inauguration. The special session met for 100 days and enacted the first stage of the New Deal program of economic recovery and social reform statutes. A dramatic exercise of the special session power occurred in July 1948, when President Truman called the Republican-controlled Congress back to Washington from its summer recess to give it the opportunity to enact several major planks in the party's 1948 platform.[26] When Congress failed to act, as Truman had anticipated, he made that inaction the theme in his successful reelection campaign.

Messages

Although contemporary presidents have not gained much leverage over Congress by controlling its sessions, they derive substantial power by virtue of their constitutional duty to report to Congress on the state of the nation and to recommend legislation they deem necessary. Since the Budget and Accounting Act of 1921 and the Employment Act of 1946, Congress has required that the president annually submit messages to it that explain and justify his budget and that report on the condition of the economy. The State of the Union message, the budget message, and the economic report have enabled presidents since Truman to set the congressional agenda by laying before Congress a comprehensive legislative program. These mandatory messages announce the president's goals and priorities along with his assessment of the nation's problems, and they are also an attempt to bring the force of public opinion to bear upon Congress. Special messages emphasizing specific problems and proposing bills to deal with them complete the definition of the president's program. (Chapter 8 examines the development of that program.)

Although individual members of Congress introduce a multitude of bills independently of the president, the chief executive is in a position to dominate the congressional agenda. Congress, the public, and the federal bureaucracy expect the president to take the initiative in the legislative process. In the twentieth century, members of Congress have come "almost routinely to demand that the president—not their own leaders—develop new policies and programs" to deal with the complex problems the nation faces.[27] Naturally, when presidents do not propose legislation that addresses important issues and problems, members of Congress can be expected to take the initiative, which is what happened during the Bush administration with respect to civil rights, immigration, and health insurance.

The Veto Power

The Constitution establishes a major legislative role for the president by requiring his approval of measures passed by Congress (Article I, Section 7, paragraph 2). Within ten days (Sundays excepted) after a bill or joint resolution is presented to the president, he must either: (1) sign it into law; (2) disapprove or veto it and return it to the house of Congress in which it originated along with a message explaining his action; or (3) take no action on it, in which case it becomes law without his signature at the end of ten days. If Congress adjourns within that ten-day period and the president does not sign a measure awaiting his action, then it does not become law. In this instance the president exercises a "pocket veto." The president's action is final because adjournment prevents a measure from being returned to Congress for reconsideration and a possible override.

The veto is the president's ultimate legislative weapon; it carries the weight of two-thirds of the members of each house of Congress. In his classic treatise *Congressional Government*, Woodrow Wilson noted the importance of the veto even at a time when Congress dominated the national government: "For in the exercise of his power of veto, which is, of course, beyond all comparison, his most formidable prerogative, the President acts not as the executive but as a third branch of the legislature."[28] But Wilson did not foresee that modern presidents would employ the veto as a significant instrument of policy control over Congress. Charles L. Black, Jr., argues that the Framers of the Constitution intended that the veto be used sparingly and then only to protect the presidency from unconstitutional congressional encroachments. To support his interpretation, Black notes that the first six presidents employed the veto for that limited purpose.[29]

Louis Fisher rejects Black's narrow interpretation of the veto as not well founded and points out that both Washington and Madison vetoed bills on other than constitutional grounds.[30] In addition, Alexander Hamilton in *Federalist* No. 73 provides clear indication that the Framers contemplated broad, substantive use of the veto:

[The veto] not only serves as a shield to the Executive, but it furnishes an additional security against the enaction of improper laws. It establishes a salutary check upon the legislative body calculated to guard the community against the effects of faction, precipitancy, or any impulse unfriendly to the public good, which may happen to influence a majority of that body. . . . The primary inducement to conferring the power in question upon the Executive is to enable him to defend himself; the secondary one is to increase the chances of the community against the passing of bad laws through haste, inadvertence, or design.[31]

Fisher also has argued that the Framers did not anticipate such developments as the growth of government activity, the rise of political parties, and the attachment of "riders" (unrelated amendments) to appropriations bills; hence one should not give much weight to arguments that the veto is used excessively.[32]

Andrew Jackson adopted a broad interpretation of the veto power as giving him the right to reject legislation on the basis of its wisdom, merit, or equity as well as on constitutional grounds.[33] This "tribunative" view of the veto has been espoused by modern presidents (since 1933), some of whom have used it frequently.

The data in Table 5-2 demonstrate a much more extensive use of the veto by Presidents Roosevelt, Truman, and Eisenhower than by presidents who have served since 1960. It also shows that from 1961 through 1991, Democratic presidents, whose party controlled the Senate from 1961 to 1980 and 1987 to 1991 and the House during the entire period, vetoed fewer bills than the Republicans, who faced opposition majorities most of the time. President Reagan, operating with a Republican majority in the Senate, vetoed sixty-eight bills during his two terms in office.

Table 5-2 Presidential Vetoes of Bills, 1933–1991

President	Regular vetoes	Pocket vetoes	Total	Number of vetoes overridden	Percentage of vetoes overridden
FDR (1933–1945)	372	263	635	9	1.4
Truman (1945–1953)	191	67	258	12	4.7
Eisenhower (1953–1961)	79	109	188	2	1.1
Kennedy (1961–1963)	12	9	21	0	0
Johnson (1963–1969)	18	11	29	0	0
Nixon (1969–1974)	26	17	43	7	16.3
Ford (1974–1977)	49	19	68	12	17.6
Carter (1977–1981)	13	18	31	2	6.5
Reagan (1981–1989)	41	27	68	8	11.8
Bush (1989–1991)	20	4	24	0	0

Sources: *Guide to the Presidency*, ed. Michael Nelson (Washington, D.C.: Congressional Quarterly, 1989), 451; *Congressional Quarterly Weekly Report*, various issues.

The effect of the veto power on policy is both negative and positive. It is negative by nature; once used, it signifies an impasse between the president and Congress, and policy is unchanged. Sometimes a president finds that the veto is the most effective means of communicating his intentions to Congress. Ford's sixty-eight vetoes, for example, were his way of conveying his social and economic policy preferences to a liberal Democratic Congress. The positive aspect of the veto lies in its use as a bargaining tool to "shape, alter, or deter legislation."[34] By threatening to exercise the veto—a threat made credible only by actual use—the president can define the limits of his willingness to compromise with Congress. He can state in advance what he will and will not accept, thereby reducing the likelihood of a showdown over a bill. Selective and sensitive use of the threat to veto can be a means of avoiding or of reconciling conflict with Congress. For example, in his first two years President Bush frequently threatened to veto bills as a way to "stimulate serious bargaining."[35] By not making empty threats and picking them carefully, Bush managed to avoid over-rides.

When presidents veto bills they do so most often because they regard the legislation as unwise public policy. In a study of presidential veto messages of 169 public bills "of national consequence" from 1933 to 1981, Richard A. Watson found that presidents gave five general reasons for vetoing legislation: (1) unwise on policy grounds (111 bills); (2) lack of fiscal soundness (33 bills); (3) unconstitutionality (10 bills); (4) administrative unworkability (9 bills); and (5) to protect the executive against legislative encroachment (6 bills).[36] In a related study, Albert Ringlestein reported that "the categories of and reasons for presidential vetoes are remarkably similar from president to president," largely because they are protecting the prerogatives of their office from Congress.[37]

The strategic aspects of presidential vetoes have received attention in a systematic analysis of vetoes and congressional responses between 1945 and 1980 by David Rhode and Dennis Simon. They found that the decision to veto, the override attempt, and the success of those attempts depended on the "political environment (e.g., stage of the electoral cycle) and the political resources of the president."[38] They determined that public support was critical for the success of vetoes and for congressional overrides. However, dependence on public support places the president in a "catch 22" situation. As support declines, use of the veto increases, but so does the likelihood of an override.[39] The strategic incentive for the president is to act divisively so as to form partisan or ideological factions on initial passage of the legislation. Timing also enters strategic calculations—the use or threat of a veto is more effective early in the administration. Another strategic consideration is the choice of issues—a social welfare bill imposes more demands on resources than, say, a government management measure.[40] Presidents do not veto bills on the basis of purely subjective judgments or random advice. Rather, they rely on a systematic procedure, begun during Franklin Roosevelt's administration, for the analysis of enrolled bills (those that have passed both houses of

Congress) once they are "received" (that is, once they have arrived at the White House).[41]

The Legislative Reference Division of the Office of Management and Budget (OMB) immediately solicits reactions to a measure from the pertinent departments and agencies and from the budget examiners in the OMB program divisions that have jurisdiction over the bill. Recommendations and supportive rationales for presidential action on the legislation are due from the agencies and examiners within forty-eight hours. Legislative Reference collates the materials and prepares for the president a memorandum that summarizes the features of the legislation, reviews agency reactions, and states OMB's recommendations. One study of presidential disposition of enrolled bill recommendations during the Nixon-Ford administration found that a presumptive bias exists in favor of enrolled bills. A favorable OMB recommendation almost ensures that the president will sign a bill. A negative recommendation, however, is more of a danger signal, and the president and his staff will examine closely the recommendation of the "lead" agency in the federal bureaucracy. When OMB and the lead agency disagree, the president is likely to sign the bill. OMB disapproval carries more weight, however, than disapproval by the lead agency (see Table 5-3).

The White House staff does not act independently on enrolled bills; rather, it bases its advice on the positions of the Office of Management and Budget and the lead agency. The goals of Nixon and Ford, two Republican presidents facing an opposition Congress, were "to rule and win."[42] That they withstood more than three-fourths of the efforts of Congress to override their vetoes indicates that they were quite successful. The enrolled bill process was an important advisory mechanism in their exercise of the veto power.

Table 5-3 OMB and Lead Agency Recommendations and Presidential Action on Enrolled Bills, January 1969–June 1976

Pattern of advice	Approval by president (Percent)
OMB approval/lead agency approval	96%
OMB approval/lead agency disapproval	95
OMB disapproval/lead agency approval	65
OMB disapproval/lead agency disapproval	35

Source: Stephen J. Wayne, Richard L. Cole, and James F. C. Hyde, "Advising the President on Enrolled Legislation," *Political Science Quarterly* 94 (Summer 1979): 310.

The President's Legislative Influence

In 1960 Richard Neustadt startled students of the presidency when, in his now celebrated treatise *Presidential Power*, he asserted that the formal powers of the president amounted to little more than a clerkship. The Constitution, Neustadt argued, placed the president in a position of mostly providing services to other participants in national politics. "Presidential power," Neustadt declared, "is the power to persuade."[43] As the preceding examination of the president's formal legislative powers suggests, this is frequently the case in his relations with Congress. It is not enough for the president to present a legislative program to Congress; he also must persuade congressional majorities to enact each statutory component of that program. To do so, the president employs mostly informal rather than formal methods of influence. These informal legislative tools can be used to exert both indirect and direct pressure on Congress.

Indirect Influence

The principal way a president attempts to influence Congress indirectly is through appeals to the public and by enlisting the support of interest groups. Popular appeals are likely to be most effective when there is evidence of substantial public support for the president's position and when Congress is reluctant to follow his lead. In such circumstances, a careful presidential appeal can generate pressure that causes Congress to act. The tactic is less likely to succeed when public opinion is divided and when there is substantial opposition to the president's position. Presidents also are more likely to use popular appeals successfully in a crisis that appears to require congressional action.

There is at least one major limitation to presidential appeals for popular support. The president can antagonize Congress by too frequently "going over its head" to the people. In doing so he attacks, directly or by implication, the wisdom and the motives of Congress and its members. Presidents have found that selective use of popular appeals can be effective, but indiscriminate use of the device is likely to be counterproductive over time.

Obtaining and marshaling the support of interest groups has become increasingly important to presidents in their efforts to apply leverage on Congress. Since the mid-1960s interest groups have grown in number and in the scope of their efforts to shape national policy. The proliferation of interest groups and the intensification of their activities stem in part from the declining role of parties as mechanisms for linking public opinion with public policy and in part from the increased participation of citizens in national policy politics.

Interest groups, which have become the major vehicle for such participation, take an active part in policy making through informal alliances with congressional committees and administrative agencies.[44] Presidents find it helpful, if not necessary, to obtain the backing of interest groups before moving on major legislation, and the national officers and federal relations directors of important groups often are consulted in the process of formulating such legislation. Interest group representatives are regularly appointed to presidential advisory bodies such as commissions and task forces, and they serve on advisory councils to administrative agencies. (Presidential liaison with interest groups is examined in Chapter 8.)

Direct Influence

Presidents use two informal tools in their direct efforts to persuade members of Congress. They may grant or withhold services and amenities they have at their disposal as rewards for support or sanctions for lack of it; and they may involve themselves in the legislative process. Presidents vary greatly in their skills at exploiting these resources.

Favors. Presidents often gain leverage with members of Congress by bestowing or denying favors. Such favors may be given directly to an individual member or to important people in his or her constituency, or the favor may be of benefit to the constituency itself.[45] Favors given as rewards to individual members include: appointments with the president and other high-ranking officials; letters or telephone calls from the president expressing thanks for support on important bills; campaign assistance in the form of cash contributions from the party's national committee, a presidential visit to the constituency, or a presidential endorsement; the opportunity to announce the award of federal grants to recipients in the constituency; invitations to be present at bill-signing ceremonies, to attend White House social functions, and to accompany the president on trips; and White House memorabilia such as pens, cuff links, and photographs. Favors for influential congressional constituents include appointments, appearances by administration officials at organization meetings, invitations to social functions, mailings on important occasions such as anniversaries, memorabilia, and VIP treatment such as White House mess privileges. To some extent all members of Congress share in such benefits, but the president's supporters have more ready access to them and feel more comfortable asking for them.

The most important constituency-related rewards are jobs and projects. There are jobs at all levels of the federal government that are exempt from the Civil Service and are filled by appointment. Congressional recommendations by members of the president's party greatly influence the selection of U.S. district court judges, U.S. attorneys, U.S. marshals, customs collectors for ports of entry, and a variety of lesser positions. Patronage is not an unalloyed advantage to the president, however, because disappointed job-seekers inevitably are resentful. Projects include military installations; research and administrative facilities; public works such as buildings, dams, and navigational improvements to rivers and harbors; government contracts with local firms; grants to local governments and educational institutions; and the deposit of federal funds in banks. Presidential control over projects is exercised through the bureaucracy, and it is limited by previous decisions that have produced the current pattern of government activities. In other words, some benefits will necessarily go to constituencies of the president's congressional opponents.

In granting favors to build congressional support, a president confronts a dilemma: how to attract marginal members without alienating those in the core of his coalition.[46] Cary Covington, in a study of favors granted in the period 1961–1969, found that Presidents Kennedy and Johnson dealt with the problem by distributing favors according to principles that varied according to types of favors. He identified two broad types of favors: symbolic and substantive. The former have "essentially intrinsic value" to the recipients, while the value of the latter is "instrumental."[47] A factor analysis of fifteen specific favors yielded five categories: VIP Symbolic, which have intrinsic value and high visibility or connote a close relationship with the president; General Symbolic, which also are intrinsically valuable but neither visible nor intimate; General Substantive, which have clear instrumental value; Informational Substantive, which involve efforts to keep members informed on relevant issues; and Executive Briefing, which is a favor similar in character to Informational Substantive favors.[48]

Covington found that the presidents distributed VIP Symbolic favors so as "to give special attention" to congressional leaders and allocated General Symbolic favors to marginal supporters as a way of building "potential future support." They reserved General Substantive and Informational Substantive favors "for members who have established reputations or who have proven themselves to be reliable supporters." This pattern of distributing favors "enables presidents to retain the support of his core coalition and the sympathy of [congressional] leaders . . . while simultaneously . . . generating future support, or at least weakening future opposition."[49]

Involvement in the Legislative Process. The president can use his involvement in the legislative process, but to do so well requires knowledge and skill, which are the product of his political background, experience, and leadership style. To turn his participation in the legislative process to his advantage, the president should have knowledge of Congress and the Washington community, a sense of timing, a willingness to consult with congressional leaders and to give them notice in advance of major actions, sensitivity to the institutional prerogatives of Congress and to the personal and political needs of its members, and a balance between firmness and flexibility in resolving differences with Congress.

No president has ever possessed all of these skills, nor is one likely to do so. By most accounts, however, Lyndon Johnson exhibited more of them than any other modern president and made the most effective use of his involvement in the legislative process. Johnson believed that constant, intense attention by the president and his administration was necessary to move his legislative program through Congress.[50] His success in persuading Congress to enact the unfinished agenda of President Kennedy's New Frontier program and his own Great Society bills in 1964 and 1965 makes his approach to Congress a good example for study. To avoid misleading the reader, however, it should be noted that Johnson's legislative triumphs were aided in no small measure by contextual factors for which he could not claim full credit, including public support for the New Frontier measures in the aftermath of the Kennedy assassination, sizable partisan and ideological support in Congress, and popular support for him and his legislative program.

According to George C. Edwards, Johnson grounded his legislative strategy in intimate knowledge of Congress as an institution and of its most influential members.[51] He knew whom to approach on various issues and how to approach them. Johnson also placed considerable emphasis on proper timing. He waited to send bills to Congress until the moment seemed right for the maximum support and least opposition. He sent bills singly rather than in a package so that opposition would not develop automatically around several measures at once. In addition, Johnson took care to consult with important senators and representatives in formulating legislation. Just before sending a bill to Congress, Johnson and his top aides would hold a briefing for congressional leaders in which they explained its features. He also gave influential senators notice of major appointments that required confirmation. Another feature of Johnson's congressional strategy was to make cabinet members responsible for the success of legislation in their areas and to use the cabinet to help coordinate administration liaison with Congress. Finally, when crucial votes were approaching on Capitol Hill, Johnson made intense personal appeals to the members whose votes served as cues for others and to members who were identified as uncommitted or wavering.

Johnson was effective in building congressional coalitions in support of his program. Through an analysis of head counts, used by Johnson's congressional liaison office to track House members' positions on bills over time, Terry Sullivan found that the Johnson administration built coalitions by "converting hard core opponents."[52] Sullivan cautions, however, that the influence gained through conversions was not dramatic as it was obtained within the confines of "representative and institutional forces."[53]

Johnson's approach to congressional relations worked well until the political context changed as a consequence of the Vietnam War. The president lost much of his touch with Congress as he became increasingly involved in foreign policy matters and as the momentum of the Great Society gave way to the unpopularity of the war. The loss of forty-eight Democratic seats in the House of Representatives in the 1966 congressional elections also adversely affected Johnson's ability to push bills through Congress.

Like Johnson, President Ford had intimate knowledge of Congress, and he worked diligently to maintain good relations with its leaders, but his success was limited. In contrast, Richard Nixon disdained personal efforts to court Congress, yet he enjoyed modest legislative success early in his administration. His relations with Congress turned sour when he challenged the Democratic majority directly by impounding appropriated funds and by asserting a sweeping doctrine of executive privilege under which administration officials refused to provide information to congressional committees.

Still, it seems clear that the Johnson approach, entailing detailed knowledge of Congress, respect for its constitutional prerogatives, sensitivity to the personal and constituency needs of its members, and the organizational and political capacity to build coalitions, can only increase a president's influence. If the president is able to create a friendly climate on Capitol Hill, one that is not hostile to him personally and in which his proposals are received with an open mind, then his prospects for success are greatly enhanced. President Carter's inability to create such a climate is often cited as a reason for the limited success of some of his major legislative goals, such as welfare reform and a comprehensive energy conservation program. In contrast, President Reagan's congenial manner and relaxed style helped establish within Congress an attitude toward his legislative program that was generally positive and not openly hostile. Reagan's ability to create a friendly climate in his congressional relations appears to have been an important factor in the passage of tax reform legislation in 1986. At critical points during the 99th Congress the tax bill seemed doomed, only to be resurrected as members responded to presidential appeals for an equitable tax system.[54]

President Bush's relations with Congress demonstrate that a congenial climate may be unrelated to presidential success. A former member of the House, Bush knew many members of Congress well and maintained close contact with them. Through the end of his third year, however, Bush had prevailed on fewer congressional roll calls than his predecessors at similar points in their first terms.[55] His failure to define a domestic legislative agenda placed him in a position of reacting to the Democrats' agenda and having to rely on a veto strategy. He was, however, successful in having Congress sustain his vetoes.

Modes of Presidential-Congressional Relations

In their relations with Congress, presidents can follow several modes or patterns of behavior: bargaining, arm-twisting, confrontation, and detachment. As befits a relationship among professional politicians, bargaining is the predominant mode of presidential-congressional relations. Occasionally, the president bargains directly with members of Congress whose support is regarded as essential to the passage of a bill. In May 1981, for example, the Reagan administration agreed to revive a costly program to support the price of sugar in exchange for the votes of four Democratic representatives from Louisiana on a comprehensive budget reduction bill.[56]

Presidents usually try to avoid such explicit bargains because they have limited resources available to trade, and the desire among members for these resources is keen.[57] Moreover, Congress is so large and congressional power so decentralized that it is not possible for presidents to bargain extensively over most bills. In some instances the president may be unable or unwilling to bargain. Fortunately, much presidential-congressional bargaining is implicit. Rather than a quid pro quo exchange of favors for votes, implicit bargaining involves generalized trading in which tacit exchanges of support and favors occur.

If bargaining does not result in the approval of his legislative proposals, the president may resort to stronger methods such as arm-twisting, which involves intense, even extraordinary, pressure and threats. In one sense, arm-twisting is an intensified extension of bargaining, but it entails something more, a direct threat of punishment or retaliation if the member's opposition continues.

The most frequent practitioner of arm-twisting among modern presidents was Lyndon Johnson. When more gentle efforts at persuasion failed or when a previously supportive member opposed him on an important issue, Johnson resorted to tactics such as deliberate embarrassment, threats, and reprisals. On occasion, when President Carter was opposed by Democratic members, he threatened them with the loss of projects for their constituencies, but he was less consistent than Johnson in taking reprisals. In contrast, President Eisenhower was most reluctant to pressure Congress. Arm-twisting is understandably an unpopular presidential tactic and, if used frequently, creates resentment and hostility. Still, judicious demonstration that there are costs associated with sustained opposition or desertion by normal supporters strengthens a president's bargaining position.

Presidents who are unable to gain support for their proposals through bargaining and arm-twisting have two additional methods for dealing with Congress: confrontation and detachment. Confrontation might consist of appeals to the public, direct challenges to congressional authority, assertion of presidential prerogative, or similar tactics. President Nixon confronted Congress often and more sharply than any modern president. Disdaining the role of legislative coalition builder, Nixon saw himself instead as deserving of congressional support by virtue of his election mandate and his constitutional position as chief executive. Between 1971 and 1973, for example, he challenged congressional spending decisions that were at variance with his budget proposals by impounding, or refusing to spend, more than $30 billion that Congress had appropriated. Nixon also asserted a sweeping doctrine of executive privilege that denied Congress the authority to question thousands of executive branch officials and to obtain access to routine documentary information.

There are occasions when easing presidential pressures on Congress may be productive. President Carter's energy legislation, which passed in modified form as separate bills in 1978, 1979, and 1980, demonstrates that a willingness to compromise after an intense effort can result in partial success. Also, ending the attempt to pass legislation that has little or no chance, such as Carter's welfare reform proposals in 1977 and 1979, enables an administration to concentrate its energies on other bills with greater chance of success.

A strategy of confrontation is unlikely to result in sustained congressional responsiveness to presidential initiatives. Congress has constitutional prerogatives and constituency bases of support that enable it to resist presidential domination. The imperatives for cooperation between the two branches are so great that most presidents try to avoid confrontations with Congress and enter them only when the constitutional integrity of the presidency is at issue.

The need for cooperation also works against detachment as a presidential strategy for dealing with Congress. Detachment is feasible only if the president has little or no disposition toward positive government action. Given the scope and magnitude of that activity, it is highly unlikely that any president today could leave Congress to its own initiatives. Even President Eisenhower, perhaps the most passive of modern presidents and the one most deferential to Congress, recognized the importance of good relations with it by establishing an office of congressional relations in the White House.

Organizing Congressional Liaison

The Eisenhower administration formalized presidential relations with Congress. Under the direction of presidential assistant Bryce Harlow, the liaison office provided information to members of Congress, helped Republicans with constituency-related matters, and lobbied for presidential proposals through explanation and low-key persuasion. During the Kennedy and Johnson administrations, the congressional liaison staff, under presidential assistant Lawrence F. O'Brien, actively asserted itself on behalf of presidential proposals. The staff was deeply involved in the formulation of the president's legislative program, and it furnished a congressional perspective to the process. It also worked closely with department and agency legislative personnel in the preparation of legislative proposals, and it coordinated bureaucratic lobbying with its own efforts.

By the end of the Johnson administration the congressional liaison operation had expanded from the rudimentary efforts under Eisenhower to establish a friendly climate on Capitol Hill to a complex set of activities that now includes intensive lobbying, intelligence gathering, representation, and coordination of executive branch legislative activity. Lobbying involves efforts, through persuasion and use of formal powers, to form congressional coalitions to enact the president's program. Intelligence gathering is the acquisition and evaluation of information about Congress, especially the policy preferences and constituency concerns of individual members. It is of special importance in determining the prospects for passing specific bills. Centralized headcounts—the voting intentions of members on a particular bill—are another way presidents gather information. They use that information to enhance their bargaining position with members of Congress.[58] Representation entails acting as spokesperson for the president's position to members of Congress as well as presenting congressional views within the White House. Coordination of executive branch relations with Congress ranges from monitoring and tracking bills, to collaborating with departments' liaison offices, to controlling departments' staff appointments.

The basic structure of the congressional liaison staff has remained intact since the Kennedy administration. Operational staff, who maintain daily contact with members of Congress, are assigned to the House or the Senate. The Senate staff deals primarily with members whom they know personally or with whom they have some reason for developing a working relationship, such as ideological compatibility or regional background. House liaison staff are assigned to work with members on a geographical basis. Under Kennedy, for example, three staff members were assigned to work with urban and eastern Democrats, southern Democrats, and nonurban and western Democrats.[59] Presidents Nixon and Ford assigned a staff member to work with southern Democrats in addition to making geographical assignments among Republicans. Other ways also have been tried: Nixon, Ford, and Carter were unsuccessful in their attempts to organize liaison staff contacts according to substantive issues.[60] Issue-based assignments fail, apparently, because of the uneven flow of work related to issues and because there is too much opportunity for certain problems and members to be neglected. Although the Carter administration abandoned issue-based organization of congressional liaison, it did not return to the geographical system. Rather, it based staff assignments for both houses on prior personal knowledge or contact. Staff assignments in the Reagan and Bush liaison offices have followed the traditional pattern.

Presidential liaison with Congress is now thoroughly institutionalized. The organizational structure of the staff is fairly well fixed (assignments on the basis of the two houses of Congress with geographical subdivision within each house), its activities and tactics are accepted by Congress, and the services it provides to Congress and the president have become routine. The liaison operation is expected to dispense favors and conduct presidential bargaining with Congress. Congressional leaders expect to share in presidential legislative policy making, and members of Congress know that the president will use the liaison office to push his legislative program.

The President and Legislation

If all presidents approach Congress with the same formal powers and informal tools of influence and operate through well-established institutional arrangements, what accounts for the success or failure of their legislative efforts? Studies have identified at least six factors that affect the president's ability to achieve his legislative goals: his partisan and ideological support in Congress, his popular support, his style in dealing with Congress, the contexts in which the president must operate, cyclical trends in presidential-congressional relations, and the content of his program. It is not possible to assess the relative importance of each factor, but all of them have come into play since 1933, when FDR inaugurated the modern legislative presidency. The first five factors will be examined here; the sixth in Chapter 8.

Congressional Support

The president's support in Congress depends heavily on the size and cohesiveness of his party's strength there. George Edwards has shown that from 1961 to 1986, three Democratic and three Republican presidents consistently received strong support on roll call votes from the congressional members of their parties.[61] This was the case on four measures of presidential support among members of Congress.[62] Edwards and Jon Bond and Richard Fleisher have found, however, that Republican presidents receive stronger support on foreign policy legislation than on domestic policy issues, primarily because of increased backing from liberal Democrats.[63]

It is interesting to note that partisan support for presidents in Congress apparently owes little to the storied effect of presidential coattails. Jacobson has pointed out that the ability of presidents to transfer their electoral appeal to congressional candidates of their parties declined steadily from 1948 to 1988.[64] Even in 1984, when President Reagan won a landslide victory over Democrat Walter Mondale, the measurable coattail effect was weak, but stronger than in 1980 and 1988.[65] Edwards attributes the decline in the power of coattails to increased split-ticket voting, the reduced competitiveness of House seats, and the electoral success of incumbents since 1952. The consequences of the reduced coattail effect are the loss of presidential leverage with Congress and greater difficulty for presidents in winning congressional approval of their major legislative proposals.

Because the president cannot rely on full support from the members of his party, he must build coalitions by obtaining support from some members of the opposition.[66] Coalition building is especially important when the opposition controls one or both houses of Congress, a condition that has occurred in twenty of the last twenty-four years. Several factors other than party membership influence congressional voting decisions: these include constituency pressures, state and regional loyalty, ideological orientations, and the influence of interest groups.[67] On many occasions, presidents have received crucial support from the opposition. President Eisenhower, for example, successfully sought Democratic votes on foreign policy matters; Republicans contributed sizable pluralities to the enactment of civil rights legislation in the 1960s; conservative Democrats mainly from the South often supported the domestic policy proposals of

Presidents Nixon and Ford; and conservative Democrats in the House were essential to President Reagan's 1981 legislative victories. Since then, however, the conservative coalition of Republicans and southern Democrats has been less effective.[68]

Congressional support for the president is built, then, primarily on fellow partisans and stems from the policy objectives they share and from their sense of party loyalty. Party affiliation is not by itself, however, a sufficient basis for the enactment of the president's legislative program. Constituency, regional, and ideological pressures reduce the number of partisan backers, and the president must try to attract support from members of the opposition party on the basis of their ideological orientations and their constituency and regional interests. Bond and Fleisher conclude that a president's legislative success "is mainly a function of the partisan and ideological makeup of Congress."[69]

Popular Support

According to Neustadt, the president's prestige, or popular support, affects congressional response to his policies. It has been widely observed that a popular president enjoys substantial leeway in dealing with Congress, and a president whose popularity is low or falling is likely to encounter considerable resistance. Bond and Fleisher argue that popular support is only marginally related to presidential success on congressional floor votes.[70] Similarly, Edwards finds that public approval is a background resource that provides presidents with leverage but not control over Congress.[71]

Although presidential popularity is clearly, if marginally, related to congressional support for the president's legislative program and can be used as a tool of influence, it cannot be easily manipulated. There are factors, such as the erosion of popular support over time and the condition of the economy, over which the president has no control.[72] What the president can do is to take advantage of his popularity when it is high to influence congressional opinion, as Lyndon Johnson did in 1964 and 1965 and Ronald Reagan did in 1981 and, to a lesser extent, in 1985 and 1986 until it plummeted because of the Iran-contra affair. The president can also appeal to the public beyond party lines for support.[73] To the extent that he succeeds in building popular support, he can strengthen his support in Congress, if his style in dealing with Congress enables him to exploit it.

Presidential Style and Legislative Skills

The president's style in dealing with Congress has long been considered an important determinant of his legislative success. Presidential style in congressional relations encompasses the degree to which the president is accessible to members of Congress, his interactions with and sensitivity to the members, and the extent of his involvement in the legislative process.[74]

Modern presidents have varied greatly in their accessibility to members of Congress. Johnson and Ford, for example, were usually available to members and leaders alike without great difficulty, whereas Nixon was remote and inaccessible most of the time. Kennedy and Reagan frequently sought contact through telephone calls. Bush maintained a wide range of congressional friends and acquaintances, but was criticized for not consulting enough with influential party and committee leaders. Although accessibility on demand is not feasible because of the pressures on the president's time, it enhances the president's congressional support if members know they can reach him on matters of great importance to them. Accessibility to congressional leaders of both parties is particularly important if the president is to work effectively with Congress.

The president's interactions with and sensitivity to members of Congress are related to his accessibility. Presidents who are relaxed and open with members of Congress and sensitive to their personal needs as well as to institutional prerogatives tend to be easily accessible. Kennedy, Johnson, Ford, Reagan, and Bush had relaxed and congenial relations with most members of Congress, whereas Eisenhower and Carter tended to be uncomfortable with many of them, and Nixon was ill at ease in most of his contacts with congressional members. Eisenhower and Carter regarded it as unseemly for the president to mingle with legislators as "one of the boys." It is not clear how much a president's interpersonal relations influence his congressional support, but they are a distinctive part of his style and affect the disposition of leaders and members toward him. If nothing else, presidential popularity with members of Congress can improve relations even when there are sharp differences over issues. If the president has strained personal relations with many representatives and senators, sustained congressional support will be difficult to achieve even when the president's party has a majority and many members share his goals.

The extent of presidential involvement in the legislative process is an important element of his style in congressional relations. Johnson, Ford, Kennedy, and Reagan all maintained a close interest in the course of legislation, and Johnson even actively directed its progress on occasion. In contrast, Nixon, Eisenhower, and Carter were more detached and had less interest in the building of congressional coalitions. Bush displayed a varied pattern of interest in the progress of legislation ranging from detachment to active engagement, as in the negotiations over the 1991 budget. Although it is not essential for the president to be a skilled legislative tactician, an open, highly involved approach to Congress serves a president better than a remote, detached posture.

As discussed earlier in this chapter, presidential legislative skills appear to be related to style. Johnson's engaged, interested style is associated with a high level of skill, which is to be expected. Presidents who care little for congressional involvement and for direct efforts to persuade Congress, such as Eisenhower or Nixon, are unlikely to exhibit much expertise. Conventional wisdom holds that a president's talent in this area is a major determinant of congressional support for his program. However, recent empirical analyses have provided little support for that argument.[75] According to Edwards and other scholars, presidential legislative skills are effective at the margins of congressional coalition building and not at the core.[76] Presenting a somewhat different argument, Mark Peterson states that presidents have some, but not unlimited, control over the timing, priorities, and size of their legislative programs. By clearly establishing their priorities and carefully adjusting their "ambitions to fit the opportunities of the day," he concludes, presidents can be perceived as successful leaders of Congress.[77] In partial agreement, Edwards maintains that "presidential legislative skills are more useful in exploiting discrete opportunities than in creating broad possibilities for change."[78] The conclusion that the president is weakly positioned to lead Congress is supported by careful analysis, but it runs counter to much of the conventional wisdom of scholars and journalists. If nothing else, these analyses should caution observers of the presidency against uncritical acceptance of personalized explanations of presidential success in Congress and encourage the search for other influences.

Contextual Factors

Most students of presidential-congressional relations agree that contextual factors over which the president has limited control—such as the structure of American political institutions and processes, public opinion, the alignment of political and social forces, economic and social conditions, and long-term trends in the political system—are more important than legislative skills as determinants of congressional decisions. For example, Edwards attaches considerable importance to the cultural context of American politics as a source of frustration for presidents attempting to influence Congress. He cites phenomena such as extremely high and often contradictory public expectations of presidential performance, individualism, and skepticism of authority as powerful constraints on presidential leadership.[79] Bond and Fleisher argue that Congress-centered variables, such as the partisan and ideological predispositions of members and leaders, which are determined by the outcome of the last election, are of greater importance than presidency-centered variables in explaining presidential influence in Congress.[80]

Taking a middle position between Edwards's presidency-centered analysis and the Congress-centered perspective of Bond and Fleisher, Peterson provides the most comprehensive and extensive analysis of contextual factors affecting presidential success in Congress. He identifies four contexts that shape congressional action on presidential programs: (1) the "pure context," which includes the "institutional properties" of Congress, political parties, and interest groups and over which the president has little influence and no control; (2) the "malleable context," which consists of "dynamic" political conditions resulting from electoral cycles and economic conditions and over which the president has "greater but unpredictable influence," but no control; (3) the "policy context," which the president can influence and to some extent control by making "strategic choices" in developing an agenda, including the consequence of various proposals for the political system, the relative importance of proposals for presidential policy goals, and the controversiality of proposals; and (4) the "individual context," which includes personal attributes, such as style and skills, and the choices the president makes concerning the organization of the presidency for the exercise of influence that distinguish the president and the administration.[81]

However one defines and classifies the contexts that affect the president's influence or success in Congress, it is important to recognize that they function to provide both constraints upon and opportunities for the exercise of presidential leadership. To a considerable extent, the president can do little to alter most of these contexts. What a president can do is take maximum advantage of the opportunities they present. In doing so the chief executive can act as a facilitator, but not a director who focuses change.

Cyclical Trends

Long-term cyclical fluctuations in presidential and congressional power also appear to affect the fate of specific presidential programs.[82] The inauguration of FDR in 1933 marked the beginning of a period of presidential ascendancy that lasted until Richard Nixon became enmeshed in the Watergate scandal. During that time Congress made extensive delegations of power to the president and to executive branch agencies; presidents assumed responsibility for legislative leadership; Congress acquiesced in presidential domination of foreign and military policy; and the public looked to the presidency more than to Congress to solve the nation's problems.[83] The president and Congress clashed often during that period, but the dominant trend was one of presidential aggrandizement. When conflict occurred, Congress usually took defensive stands against presidential assertiveness.

In 1973 a Congress jealous of what it perceived to be its constitutional prerogatives, angry over the protracted "presidential war" in Vietnam, and fed up with battling President Nixon over impoundment and executive privilege, moved to reassert itself. Seizing the opportunity afforded by Nixon's preoccupation with Watergate, Congress enacted the War Powers Resolution of 1973, the Budget and Impoundment Control Act of 1974, and the National Emergencies Act of 1976.[84] These statutes were the major elements in a congressional resurgence that restrained presidential power. In 1974 the House Judiciary Committee approved three impeachment charges against President Nixon, who resigned on August 9 before the House could act on them. Nixon's two immediate successors, Gerald Ford and Jimmy Carter, had to deal with a resurgent Congress intent on curbing the uses of presidential power and retaining the constitutional parity with the president that it regained, at least partially, in the 1970s. Increased skepticism of claims for presidential prerogative, careful scrutiny of presidential proposals, demands for more extensive consultation of congressional leaders by the White House, and more exacting senatorial confirmation hearings on presidential appointments were the hallmarks of this period of congressional resurgence.

During the Reagan presidency Congress was more willing to accept presidential policy leadership and less assertive in insisting on its institutional prerogatives. The presidential-congressional relationship did not, however, return to the conditions that prevailed under the "imperial presidency."[85] President Reagan had generally friendly relations with Congress despite sharp differences over policy, such as the budget deficit, and over presidential powers, such as impoundments and deferrals of appropriated funds. Reagan's relationship with Congress bent, but did not break, in 1987 following Democratic successes in the 1986 congressional elections and as a consequence of public disenchantment with his loose leadership, which was revealed by the Iran-contra affair.

President Bush enjoyed good relations with Congress until the fall of 1990 when he became embroiled in a protracted battle with leaders and members from both parties over the deficit in the 1991 budget. In October a coalition of Democratic and Republican House members defeated an agreement on a deficit reduction plan that the administration had negotiated with a bipartisan leadership group *(see Chapter 9)*. After several weeks of bitter wrangling, including charges and countercharges of bad faith, the administration and Congress agreed to a compromise. As the budget battle came to its unsatisfactory close, most congressional Democrats and some Republicans sharply questioned Bush's handling of the Persian Gulf crisis and pressed him to obtain the approval of Congress before initiating military action against Iraq. The administration insisted that it had such authority. Both sides cited the Constitution—Congress its power to declare war and the president his power as commander-in-chief—in defense of their positions. In early January 1991 Congress passed a resolution authorizing the use of U.S. forces to implement UN resolutions calling on Iraq to leave Kuwait or face economic sanctions and, if necessary, military action. The striking success of Operation Desert Storm boosted Bush's popular approval ratings and improved his relations with Congress. However, that relationship lacked durability. By the beginning of 1992 Bush's popular support had fallen to the lowest point of his presidency as the public blamed him for a protracted economic recession.

The President's Effect on Congress

What overall impact does the president have on Congress? How can one judge presidential effectiveness with Congress? Analysts have sought answers to these questions through examination of congressional roll call votes and of aggregate measures based on roll calls such as presidential support scores, discussed previously in this chapter, and presidential box scores, based on the number and percentage of presidential legislative requests that are enacted into law. (Both measures are calculated by Congressional Quarterly, but the box scores were discontinued in 1975.) To further refine the support scores, one can separate members by party and subdivide each group of partisans by region and faction.[86] Analysts also have refined the scores by classifying bills by domestic and foreign policy proposals, which has led to a protracted debate over whether there are "two presidencies," one for domestic policy, in which presidents have less success with Congress, and the other for foreign policy, in which they have more.[87] Such aggregate measures provide an overall picture of presidential effectiveness, but they leave a great many questions unanswered. For example, how controversial were a president's proposals? What potential effect did the proposals have on the economy and society? Did the president risk much or little by making them? Did the successful bills require a major effort at coalition building, and, if so, what was the partisan and regional composition of the coalitions?[88]

A comparison of congressional support for Presidents Johnson, Carter, and Reagan suggests the limitations of aggregate measures *(see Table 5-4)*. According to most assessments, Johnson's legislative accomplishments—mainly the social programs of the Great Society—outstripped those of all modern presidents since FDR in their significance. Carter's legislative record, in sharp contrast, is marked by frustration and limited achievement of major goals. Reagan, after a highly successful first year and difficulty thereafter, generally is regarded as standing close to Johnson in his ability to lead Congress.[89] Yet, data based on key votes on congressional roll calls indicate that differences among the three performances are not substantial.

The data also show that Carter enjoyed nearly the same level of support in the House as Johnson. They show that Carter actually did better among southern Democratic representatives and senators than Johnson and that

Table 5-4 Congressional Support on Key Votes for Presidents Johnson, Carter, and Reagan (Percent)

	Johnson	Carter	Reagan
House of Representatives			
Democrats	68%	59%	29%
Northern	81	64	21
Southern	40	45	50
Republicans	29	29	74
Senate			
Democrats	65	64	32
Northern	75	70	74
Southern	41	50	50
Republicans	49	33	75

Source: George C. Edwards III, *At the Margins: Presidential Leadership in Congress* (New Haven, Conn.: Yale University Press, 1989), 177, 178, 183, 184. Data for Reagan are for 1981–1986.

Reagan enjoyed more support from senators of his own party than either Carter or Johnson.

The data also suggest that measurement of presidential impact on Congress requires qualitative as well as quantitative assessments. For example, Randall Ripley reports that in 1977 President Carter made forty-three recommendations to Congress. At the end of the year Congress had approved twenty-one, rejected four, and left eighteen pending. Carter's first year was only moderately successful compared with the first-year performances of Wilson in 1913, FDR in 1933, and Reagan in 1981, or with Johnson in his second year, 1965.[90] Several of Carter's major proposals—a comprehensive energy program and welfare reform—were not enacted

Even though Congress subsequently passed several of Carter's principal requests, such as the Panama Canal Treaty and the establishment of the Departments of Energy and Education, the prevailing assessment of his legislative accomplishments is quite negative.[91] Why was this the case when, judged by standard quantitative measures of his achievements, he ranked well compared with most modern presidents? The answer seems to be that most assessments of presidential legislative records are based on qualitative evaluations of the substance of the measures that are enacted and the president's management of congressional relations. If the enacted statutes are thought to be of limited or moderate importance, if they fall short of the president's announced goals, or if they fail to provide satisfactory solutions to the problems they were designed to address, then the president is likely to be judged harshly. Procedurally, if the president appears to be inept or disinterested in handling congressional relations, critics will probably find fault with his legislative performance. Carter was found lacking on both substantive and procedural grounds; Johnson and Reagan were not.

Why was Carter unsuccessful with Congress, particularly in comparison with Reagan (assuming that one accepts that judgment)? A combination of the factors discussed in this chapter provides an explanation. First, the political context was more favorable to Reagan than to Carter. Reagan swept into office with a substantial election victory, in which Republicans won control of the Senate and substantially increased their strength in the House, whereas Carter won by a narrow margin. When Carter took office, Congress was in a period of cyclical assertiveness during which it closely examined and often challenged major presidential proposals. Four years later Congress, impressed by Ronald Reagan's electoral triumph, looked to him to provide it with leadership and direction. It appeared to recognize the limits of its institutional capacity to provide comprehensive alternatives to the president's program.

A second factor that helps to account for the disparity in Carter's and Reagan's legislative success is their contrasting agendas. (Agenda development is examined in Chapter 8.) Carter presented Congress with a lengthy agenda that included several comprehensive proposals. Moreover, he neglected to indicate to Congress which proposals had the highest priority. To have asked for so much, so soon, at a time when Congress was reasserting its prerogatives vis-à-vis the president almost guaranteed that little would be accomplished. In contrast, Reagan presented Congress with a limited agenda—the budget and economic policy—and assigned it the highest priority. As Charles Jones puts it, Reagan established "a new context for congressional choice," a "consolidative agenda" in which new social programs were not even proposed.[92] Even though Reagan encountered substantial resistance after 1981, Congress took no action outside the president's consolidative agenda.

Alternatively, it can be argued in Carter's defense that, although he may have attempted too much, he would not have been any more successful had he tried to accomplish less. There may be another reason for the differing evaluations: Carter's lengthy agenda raised numerous expectations, several of which were not met; as a result, he was judged ineffective. In contrast, Reagan's limited agenda raised fewer expectations, most of which were met; and he was perceived to be effective.

A third factor that distinguishes the Carter and Reagan legislative records is the leadership style and techniques used in dealing with Congress. Carter tended to cast proposals in moralistic tones that frequently alienated members of Congress. Also, he demonstrated little sensitivity to the institutional norms of Congress or to its members' sense of constitutional prerogatives. He expressed disdain for bargaining with congressional leaders and impatience with the preference of most members of Congress for incremental rather than comprehensive policies. Another stylistic aspect of Carter's leadership that proved disconcerting to his supporters in Congress was his tendency to shift positions quickly and without consultation. This difficulty was compounded by a legislative liaison operation that often lacked coordination of White House and departmental lobbying efforts.[93] Carter's initial strategic decision to invest much greater organizational effort in the domestic policy staff than in the congressional liaison office further limited his effectiveness with Congress.[94]

Carter's problems with Congress also stemmed from his definition of the roles of the president and Congress. He viewed the president as a trustee for the national interest and regarded Congress as an institution preoccupied with the parochial concerns of its members and beholden to special interests.[95] He saw little reason to cater to Congress or to bargain with it, but he expected it to respond promptly and positively to his proposals which, in his view embodied the whole public interest.

In contrast, Reagan approached Congress as a communicator president, a style Jones describes as "consistent with the classic separation of powers model of presidential-congressional relations."[96] Under this model the presidency is separate from but not independent of Congress. The president and his staff consult Congress regularly and extensively and engage willingly in direct negotiations; bargaining is the normal way business is conducted. Essential to this model is the maintenance of open channels of communication as a means of achieving political understanding between the two branches. Reagan was able to use the politics of communication to his advantage. He clearly defined his goals in terms of conservative ideology and consistently, but not inflexibly, pursued them. He manifested respect for the institutional prerogatives of Congress while articulating and advancing those of the presidency. And he established an effective working relationship with the Republican party organizations in Congress.[97]

The contrasting experiences of Carter and Reagan in their relations with Congress provide few new lessons. Both found, or at least should have found, that success is not automatic. It requires consultation before and during legislative consideration and a willingness to negotiate and bargain with Congress. Coordination of legislative proposals between the White House and the departments and agencies is essential. More important, cooperation between the president and congressional leaders and between the institutional presidency and Congress is mandatory. The constitutional separation of powers does not allow the two branches to operate independently of each other; rather, it requires that they exercise their shared powers jointly.[98]

Conclusion

The president's relationship with Congress takes place within the framework of the constitutional separation of powers. That framework requires cooperation but ensures conflict. This has been true during the more than 200 years that the Republic has operated under the Constitution. The Framers of the Constitution sought to prevent tyranny by establishing a balance between executive and legislative power. However, the concept of balance entails a static relationship, whereas the relationship that has existed between the president and Congress has been continually in flux. First one branch has expanded its authority; then the second branch has reasserted its prerogatives, recaptured lost powers, and acquired new ones. The cycle of institutional aggrandizement, decline, and resurgence reflects certain strengths and weaknesses in the presidency and Congress and their respective abilities to respond to social forces, economic conditions, and political change.

The need for presidential-congressional cooperation is clear, but there are few ways of obtaining it other than through consultation involving persuasion and bargaining. Presidents cannot command congressional approval of their proposals any more than Congress can direct them in the exercise of their constitutional powers. The threat of government stalemate is always present, and more often than not policy is an unsatisfactory compromise of presidential and various congressional viewpoints.

Clearly, the presidential-congressional relationship is a dynamic one. It varies according to contextual factors, cycles of presidential and congressional assertiveness, and the leadership skills and styles of individual presidents. Changes occur in the relationship, sometimes quickly and dramatically, as between the 1970s and 1980s and the presidencies of Jimmy Carter and Ronald Reagan. As the United States moves through its third century, the relationship between the president and Congress will be characterized—as it is today—by the stability provided by the Constitution as well as by adaptations to social, economic, and political change.

NOTES

1. "Background for Voting Analyses," *Congressional Quarterly Weekly Report*, Dec. 28, 1991, 3788.

2. Stephen J. Wayne, *The Legislative Presidency* (New York: Harper & Row, 1978), 8–12.

3. Theodore Roosevelt, *Autobiography* (New York: Macmillan, 1913), 292.

4. Woodrow Wilson, *Constitutional Government in the United States* (New York: Columbia University Press, 1908, 1961).

5. Richard E. Neustadt, "'The Presidency and Legislation: The Growth of Central Clearance," *American Political Science Review* (September 1954): 641–670.

6. Richard E. Neustadt, "The Presidency and Legislation: Planning the President's Program," *American Political Science Review* (December 1955): 980–1018; Wayne, *The Legislative Presidency;* Larry Berman, *The Office of Management and Budget and the Presidency* (Princeton, N.J.: Princeton University Press, 1979); Paul C. Light, *The President's Agenda: Domestic Policy Choice from Kennedy to Reagan,* rev. ed. (Baltimore: The Johns Hopkins University Press, 1991).

7. Samuel P. Huntington, "Congressional Responses to the Twentieth Century," in *The Congress and America's Future,* ed. David B. Truman (Englewood Cliffs, N.J.: Prentice Hall, 1965), 23.

8. Ronald C. Moe and Steven C. Teel, "Congress as Policy-Maker: A Necessary Reappraisal," *Political Science Quarterly* (Fall 1970): 443–470; John R. Johannes, *Policy Innovation in Congress* (Morristown, N.J.: General Learning Press, 1972); Gary Orfield, *Congressional Power: Congress and Social Change* (New York: Harcourt Brace Jovanovich, 1975).

9. In the Senate the Republicans had a 53–47 majority. In the House, the 192 Republicans, who voted together on the major elements of President Reagan's economic legislation in a remarkable display of cohesion, were joined by a sizable block of conservative southern Democrats called the "Boll Weevils." In both chambers, Republicans and conservatives maintained voting cohesion that provided the majorities to enact the Reagan program.

10. Bert A. Rockman, "Entrepreneur in the Political Marketplace: The Constitution and the Development of the Presidency" (Paper presented at the annual meeting of the American Political Science Association, San Francisco, Aug. 30–Sept. 2, 1990), 26–27.

11. Alexander Hamilton, John Jay, and James Madison, *The Federalist Papers* (New York: Modern Library, 1938), 335–337.

12. Lawrence C. Dodd, "Congress and the Quest for Power," in *Congress Recon-*

sidered, ed. Lawrence C. Dodd and Bruce I. Oppenheimer (New York: Praeger, 1977), 298–302.

13. James L. Sundquist, *The Decline and Resurgence of Congress* (Washington, D.C.: Brookings, 1981).

14. Thomas E. Mann, "Elections and Change in Congress," in *The New Congress,* ed. T. E. Mann (Washington, D.C.: American Enterprise Institute, 1981).

15. Roger H. Davidson and Walter J. Oleszek, *Congress and Its Members,* 3d ed. (Washington, D.C.: CQ Press, 1990), 60.

16. Among the leading critics of divided government are: James L. Sundquist, "Needed: A Political Theory for the New Era of Coalition Government in the United States," *Political Science Quarterly* (Winter 1988–1989): 613–635; Lloyd N. Cutler, "To Form a Government," *Foreign Affairs* 59 (Fall 1980): 126–143; Cutler, "Now Is the Time for All Good Men," *William and Mary Law Review* 30 (Fall 1989): 387–402; and Michael L. Mezey, *Congress, the President, & Public Policy* (Boulder, Colo.: Westview, 1989).

17. Gary W. Cox and Samuel Kernell, "Conclusion" in *The Politics of Divided Government,* ed. Cox and Kernell (Boulder, Colo.: Westview, 1991), 242–243. Also see Matthew D. McCubbins, "Government on Lay-Away: Federal Spending and Deficits Under Divided Party Control," in ibid., 113–153.

18. David R. Mayhew, *Divided We Govern: Party Control, Lawmaking, and Investigations 1946–1990* (New Haven, Conn.: Yale University Press, 1991), 198.

19. Morris Fiorina, *Divided Government* (New York: Macmillan, 1992), 107, 108.

20. Ibid., 111.

21. Ibid., chap. 6.

22. Davidson and Oleszek, *Congress and its Members,* chaps. 3–5; David R. Mayhew, *Congress: The Electoral Connection* (New Haven, Conn.: Yale University Press, 1974).

23. Joseph A. Califano, Jr., *A Presidential Nation* (New York: Norton, 1975), chap. 3.

24. Davidson and Oleszek, *Congress and Its Members,* chap. 1.

25. The main components of the Great Society were the Economic Opportunity Act of 1964, which launched a "war on poverty," the Civil Rights Act of 1964, the Voting Rights Act of 1965, the Elementary and Secondary Education Act of 1965, and the Medicare Act of 1965.

26. Joseph E. Kallenbach, *The American Chief Executive* (New York: Harper & Row, 1966), 327–328.

27. Sundquist, *The Decline and Resurgence of Congress,* 143.

28. Woodrow Wilson, *Congressional Government* (New York: Meridian, 1956), 53.

29. Charles L. Black, Jr., "Some Thoughts on the Veto," *Law and Contemporary Problems* (Spring 1976): 87, 90.

30. Louis Fisher, *Constitutional Conflicts Between Congress and the President,* 3d ed., rev. (Lawrence: University Press of Kansas, 1991), 118–119.

31. Hamilton, Jay, and Madison, *The Federalist Papers,* 476–477.

32. Fisher, *Constitutional Conflicts,* 117.

33. Kallenbach, *The American Chief Executive,* 354.

34. Robert J. Spitzer, *The Presidential Veto: Touchstone of the American Presidency* (Albany: State University of New York Press, 1988), 100–103.

35. Janet Hook, "Avalanche of Veto Threats Divides Bush, Congress," *Congressional Quarterly Weekly Report,* Sept. 22, 1990, 2991. Hook cites an OMB spokeswoman as stating that the Bush administration had issued 120 veto threats since January 1989.

36. Richard A. Watson, "Reasons Presidents Veto Legislation" (Paper presented at

the annual meeting of the American Political Science Association, Chicago, Sept. 3–6, 1987), 6, 7.

37. Albert C. Ringlestein, "Presidential Vetoes: Motivations and Classifications," *Congress and the Presidency* (Spring 1985): 52–53.

38. David W. Rhode and Dennis M. Simon, "Presidential Vetoes and Congressional Response: A Study of Institutional Conflict," *American Journal of Political Science* (August 1985): 307.

39. Ibid., 425.

40. Ibid.

41. Stephen J. Wayne, Richard L. Cole, and James F. C. Hyde, Jr., "Advising the President on Enrolled Legislation," *Political Science Quarterly* (Summer 1979): 303–318.

42. Ibid., 316.

43. Richard E. Neustadt, *Presidential Power: The Politics of Leadership* (New York: Wiley, 1960), 10.

44. Theodore J. Lowi, *The End of Liberalism*, 2d ed. (New York: St. Martin's Press, 1979); Randall B. Ripley and Grace A. Franklin, *Congress, the Bureaucracy, and Public Policy*, 5th ed. (Pacific Grove, Calif.: Brooks/Cole, 1991).

45. Joseph A. Pika, "White House Office of Congressional Relations: A Longitudinal Analysis" (Paper delivered at the annual meeting of the Midwest Political Science Association, Chicago, April 20–22, 1978).

46. Cary R. Covington, "Helping Friends or Wooing Enemies? How Presidents Use Favors to Build Coalitions in Congress" (Paper delivered at the annual meeting of the American Political Science Association, San Francisco, Aug. 30–Sept. 2, 1990), 5–7; Nelson W. Polsby, *Congress and the Presidency*, 4th ed. (Englewood Cliffs, N.J.: Prentice-Hall, 1986), 194–196.

47. Covington, "Helping Friends or Wooing Enemies?" 10.

48. Ibid., 23–25.

49. Ibid., 37, 38.

50. Lyndon B. Johnson, *Vantage Point* (New York: Holt, Rinehart & Winston, 1971), 448; Doris Kearns, *Lyndon Johnson and the American Dream* (New York: Harper & Row, 1976), 226.

51. George C. Edwards III, *Presidential Influence in Congress* (San Francisco: Freeman, 1980), 117–120.

52. Terry Sullivan, "Headcounts, Expectations, and Presidential Coalitions in Congress," *American Journal of Political Science* (August 1988): 567. Elsewhere, Sullivan demonstrates that head counts are a valuable presidential tool for signaling congressional supporters and for obtaining information from them. "Explaining Why Presidents Count: Signaling and Information," *Journal of Politics* (August 1990): 939–962.

53. Ibid., 582.

54. Jeffrey H. Birnbaum and Alan S. Murray, *Showdown at Gucci Gulch* (New York: Random House, 1987), 40–41, 94–95, 118, 169–171.

55. Chuck Alston, "Bush's High Public Standing Held Little Sway on Hill," *Congressional Quarterly Weekly Report*, Dec. 28, 1991, 3751.

56. Laurence L. Barrett, *Gambling With History* (Garden City, N.Y.: Doubleday, 1983), 334.

57. Edwards, *Presidential Influence in Congress*, 131.

58. Terry Sullivan, "Bargaining with the President: A Simple Game and New Evidence," *American Political Science Review* (December 1990): 1167–96.

59. Pika, "White House Office of Congressional Relations," 9.

60. Ibid., 10; Eric L. Davis, "Legislative Liaison in the Carter Administration," *Political Science Quarterly* (Summer 1979): 289.

61. George C. Edwards III, *At the Margins: Presidential Leadership of Congress* (New Haven, Conn.: Yale University Press, 1989), chap. 3.

62. Edwards developed four indexes, which are percentages of support for roll call votes on which the president has taken a stand: (1) overall support on all votes on which the president has taken a stand; (2) support that was not unanimous on votes on which the winning side fell below 80 percent; (3) support on the single most important vote on each bill; and (4) key votes selected by Congressional Quarterly as being highly significant. He found that the non-unanimous support index was the most broadly representative and that the key votes index revealed relationships hidden by the broader indexes. Ibid., chap. 2.

It should be noted that use of Congressional Quarterly's presidential support scores is controversial. See Anita Pritchard, "An Evaluation of CQ Presidential Support Scores: The Relationship between Presidential Election Results and Congressional Voting Decisions," *American Journal of Political Science* (May 1985): 493–494; Jon R. Bond and Richard Fleisher, *The President in the Legislative Arena* (Chicago: University of Chicago Press, 1990), 62–66; Mark A. Peterson, *Legislating Together: The White House and Capitol Hill from Eisenhower to Reagan* (Cambridge, Mass.: Harvard University Press, 1990), 303–305.

63. Edwards, *At the Margins*, 68–69; Bond and Fleisher, *The President in the Legislative Arena*, 171–175.

64. Gary C. Jacobson, *The Electoral Origins of Divided Government* (Boulder, Colo.: Westview, 1990), 80–81.

65. Gary C. Jacobson, *The Politics of Congressional Elections*, 3d ed. (New York: HarperCollins, 1992), 161–162.

66. Sullivan, "Headcounts, Expectations, and Presidential Coalitions in Congress," 573–582.

67. John W. Kingdon, *Congressmen's Voting Decisions* (New York: Harper & Row, 1981); Aage R. Clausen, *How Congressmen Decide* (New York: St. Martin's Press, 1973).

68. Kenneth A. Shepsle, "The Changing Textbook Congress," in *Can the Government Govern*, eds. John E. Chubb and Paul E. Peterson (Washington, D.C.: Brookings, 1989), 257–258.

69. Bond and Fleisher, *The President in the Legislative Arena*, 221.

70. Ibid., 182.

71. Edwards, *At the Margins*, 124–125.

72. John E. Mueller, *War, Presidents and Public Opinion* (New York: Wiley, 1973).

73. Samuel Kernell, *Going Public: New Strategies of Presidential Leadership* (Washington, D.C.: CQ Press, 1986), chap. 1.

74. Wayne, *The Legislative Presidency*, 166.

75. Edwards, *At the Margins*, chaps. 9, 10; Bond and Fleisher, *The President in the Legislative Arena*, chap. 8.

76. Edwards, *At the Margins*, 211. Also see Bond and Fleisher, *The President in the Legislative Arena*, 219; Bert A. Rockman, *The Leadership Question: The Presidency and the American Political System,* (New York: Praeger, 1984), 214; Anthony King, "A Mile and a Half Is a Long Way," in *Both Ends of the Avenue*, 254.

77. Peterson, *Legislating Together*, 267.

78. Edwards, *At the Margins*, 211.

79. Ibid., 8–15.

80. Bond and Fleisher, *The President in the Legislative Arena*, 220–234.

81. Peterson, *Legislating Together*, 92–94; chaps. 4 and 5.

82. Dodd, "Congress and the Quest for Power."

83. Arthur M. Schlesinger, Jr., *The Imperial Presidency* (Boston: Houghton Mifflin, 1973).

84. Sundquist, *The Decline and Resurgence of Congress;* Thomas E. Cronin, "A Resurgent Congress and the Imperial Presidency," *Political Science Quarterly* (Summer 1980): 209–238.

85. In the second edition of *The Imperial Presidency* (Boston: Houghton Mifflin, 1989), Schlesinger maintains that Reagan moved two-thirds of the way toward restoring the imperial presidency. He met two of Schlesinger's "tests"—extensive presidential war making and heavy reliance on secrecy—but Reagan did not direct his powers against administration critics, 451, 457.

86. Edwards distinguishes between northern and southern Democrats, chaps. 3, 5, and 9; Bond and Fleisher analyze factional support in both parties for and in opposition to the president, *The President in the Legislative Arena,* chap. 4.

87. Aaron Wildavsky, "The Two Presidencies," *Transaction,* vol. 4, 1966, 7–14; Lance T. LeLoup and Steven A. Shull, "Congress versus the Executive," *Social Science Quarterly* (March 1979): 704–719; Shull, ed., *The Two Presidencies: A Quarter-Century Assessment* (Chicago: Nelson-Hall, 1991); Edwards, *At the Margins,* chap. 4; and Bond and Fleisher, *The President in the Legislative Arena,* chap. 6.

88. Peterson provides an excellent discussion of the problems with aggregate measures and he offers useful suggestions for overcoming them. See *Legislating Together,* 209–315.

89. Charles O. Jones, "A New President, a Different Congress, a Maturing Agenda," in *The Reagan Presidency and the Governing of America,* ed. Lester M. Salamon and Michael S. Lund (Washington, D.C.: Urban Institute Press, 1984), 261–287.

90. Randall B. Ripley, "Carter and Congress," in *The Presidency: Studies in Policy Making,* ed. Steven A. Shull and Lance T. LeLoup (Brunswick, Ohio: King's Court Communications, 1979), 65–82.

91. Ripley, "Carter and Congress"; Davis, "Congressional Liaison."

92. Jones, "A New President," 285.

93. Joseph A. Califano's account of his service as secretary of the Health, Education, and Welfare Department in the Carter cabinet provides numerous examples of Carter's difficulties with Congress. *Governing America: An Insider's Report from the White House and the Cabinet* (New York: Simon & Schuster, 1981).

94. Sullivan, "Explaining Why Presidents Count," 957.

95. Charles O. Jones, *The Trusteeship Presidency: Jimmy Carter and the United States Congress* (Baton Rouge: Louisiana State University Press, 1988).

96. Jones, "A New President," 285.

97. Ibid., 286.

98. This is the central theme of Peterson's *Legislating Together,* in which he advocates a "tandem institutions" perspective on presidential-congressional relations.

READINGS

Bond, Jon R., and Richard Fleisher. *The President in the Legislative Arena.* Chicago: University of Chicago Press, 1990.

Cox, Gary W., and Samuel Kernell, eds. *The Politics of Divided Government.* Boulder, Colo.: Westview, 1991.

Edwards, George C., III. *At the Margins: Presidential Leadership of Congress.* New Haven, Conn.: Yale University Press, 1989.

Fiorina, Morris. *Divided Government.* New York: Macmillan, 1992.

Fisher, Louis. *Constitutional Conflicts between Congress and the President*, 3d ed. rev. Lawrence: University Press of Kansas, 1991.

King, Anthony, ed. *Both Ends of the Avenue*. Washington, D.C.: American Enterprise Institute, 1983.

Mayhew, David R. *Divided We Govern: Party Control, Lawmaking, and Investigations 1945–1990*. New Haven, Conn.: Yale University Press, 1991.

Peterson, Mark A. *Legislating Together: The White House and Capitol Hill from Eisenhower to Reagan*. Cambridge, Mass: Harvard University Press, 1990.

Shull, Steven A., ed. *The Two Presidencies: A Quarter-Century Assessment*. Chicago: Nelson-Hall, 1991.

Spitzer, Robert J. *The Presidential Veto: Touchstone of the American Presidency*. Albany: State University of New York Press, 1988.

Sundquist, James L. *The Decline and Resurgence of Congress*. Washington, D.C.: Brookings, 1981.

Thurber, James A., ed. *Divided Democracy: Cooperation and Conflict Between the President and Congress*. Washington, D.C.: CQ Press, 1991.

Wayne, Stephen J. *The Legislative Presidency*. New York: Harper & Row, 1978.

6 EXECUTIVE POLITICS

The White House—nerve center of the executive branch and home of its chief.

ONE OF THE COMMONEST SYNonyms for president is "chief executive." In U.S. political life the president is held responsible for the operation of the government, and, if government fails to meet popular expectations, the president takes the blame. Indeed, when President Jimmy Carter explained his administration's failure to fill some of its major campaign promises by saying that he had learned there were certain things that government cannot do, his critics suggested that it was time to replace him with someone who could make government work. But most modern presidents have encountered difficulties in their efforts to direct the executive branch. Franklin D. Roosevelt complained about the independence of the navy; John F. Kennedy lamented the inertia of the State Department; Richard Nixon railed against disloyal bureaucrats in various domestic program agencies; and Ronald Reagan made his campaign attack on an overgrown federal bureaucracy one of the enduring themes of his presidency. Richard Rose, who has studied the president as a manager, has remarked that the "president's title of chief executive is a misnomer; he can more accurately be described as a nonexecutive chief."[1] The essence of Rose's argument is that even within the executive branch the president's powers of command are limited and that his success as an administrator depends to a great extent on his ability to win the trust of others.

This chapter examines the president's responsibilities as chief executive and the factors that affect his administrative performance. It opens with a discussion of the president's executive role and an examination of that role's constitutional, legal, and administrative foundations. Then it explores the president's relationships with the executive branch and the cabinet. Having established that the president's powers of command over the units of the executive branch are limited, the chapter analyzes the formal powers and managerial tools that modern presidents have available to them in discharging their administrative duties.

The President as Executive

The president's executive role is grounded in Article II of the Constitution. In ambiguous language the Constitution vests "the executive power" in the president and directs him to "take care that the laws be faithfully executed." He may also "require the opinion, in writing, of the principal officer in each of the executive departments" and "grant reprieves and pardons." He derives substantial power from his designation as "commander-in- chief of the army and navy." Modern presidents have tended to interpret these constitutional provisions broadly and have derived from them substantial additional powers. In addition to their constitutionally based powers, presidents have received extensive delegations of statutory authority from Congress.

There is an apparent paradox in, on the one hand, the president's considerable formal legal powers and his position as head of a vast, complex military and civilian bureaucracy and, on the other hand, his limited ability to direct that bureaucracy toward the achievement of his policy objectives and program goals. One may better understand that paradox by considering the constitutional relationship of the presidency to the legislative and judicial branches of government and the nature of the federal bureaucracy and the president's relationship to it.

As discussed in Chapter 5, the Constitution not only created the executive branch, with the president as its head, but also established the legislative and judicial branches and prescribed a sharing of powers among those separate government institutions. The president is dependent on congressional cooperation to carry out the executive responsibilities of the office. Only Congress can authorize government programs, establish administrative agencies to implement the programs, and appropriate funds to finance them. However, presidents find that congressional cooperation may be difficult to obtain because presidents and members of Congress have different constituency and institutional perspectives.

There are also occasions when the exercise of presidential power must be approved by the judiciary. A notable instance of judicial disapproval of executive action involved President Harry S. Truman's seizure of U.S. steel mills in 1952 to forestall a strike during the Korean War.[2] The points to be made here are that presidential power is not self-executing and that it is subject to restraint. Presidents require the cooperation of Congress and the judiciary but frequently find themselves in conflict with these other branches of government.

Although the federal bureaucracy is the bulk of the executive branch, and the accomplishment of government objectives depends largely on its performance, it must be recognized legally as the creation of the legislative branch. In establishing federal departments and agencies, Congress is responding not only to presidential requests, but also to demands and pressures from constituency forces, interest groups, and the general public. The result is that the structure of the federal bureaucracy is not hierarchical; rather, it tends to reflect the political fragmentation and committee jurisdiction of Congress. The president does not look down upon subordinate administrative units from a position at the apex of a pyramid of authority. Instead, he confronts a complex and confusing array of departments and agencies with varying degrees of independence from him.

Arthur S. Miller argues that checks on presidential power come more from the "entrenched bureaucracy" than from Congress.[3] Bureaucratic units are staffed principally by career civil servants who constitute a permanent government. They respond to demands from interest groups and to direction from congressional committees as well as to presidential leadership. Most modern presidents have entered office believing, or soon became convinced, that they cannot take the support and loyalty of the bureaucracy for granted but must constantly strive to acquire them.[4]

Moreover, the vastness and scope of the federal bureaucracy, as measured by expenditures or numbers of employees, further contribute to the difficulty of the president's executive role. From 1933 through 1980, as the functions of the federal government expanded, the task of defining objectives and coordinating their achievement grew increasingly difficult for presidents. Attempting to do so while adhering to democratic procedures and without resort to authoritarian or extralegal methods provided an even greater challenge.

The president's task as the nation's chief executive (Rose's objections to the term notwithstanding) is much more, therefore, than issuing commands. Nor is the job mainly that of finding ways to bring a large complex bureaucracy under operational control. Rather, he must secure congressional cooperation while suppressing the executive branch's natural tendencies toward conflict with the legislative branch, and he must give direction to the bureaucracy so that it will work with him in accomplishing his administration's goals.

The President and the Executive Branch

Ideally, presidents should use the White House staff and other units of the Executive Office of the President to help them define their objectives, convert them into operating programs, allocate resources to the agencies that administer the programs, and coordinate the implementation of programs within the federal government and among federal, state, and local governments. Department managers should direct the work of the career civil servants, coordinate the operations of their component bureaus, and develop and maintain links with other federal departments and agencies and with state and local governments. Presidents quickly discover, however, that the reality of their relations with the federal bureaucracy bears little resemblance to the idealized vision just described. For example, Joseph Califano, a former presidential aide and cabinet officer, has observed that "smaller federal agencies and numerous bureaus within large departments respond to presidential leadership only in the minds of the most naive students of government administration."[5]

According to Thomas E. Cronin, there are "presidentialist" and "departmentalist" views of presidential-departmental relations.[6] The essence of the presidentialist view is that because presidents are held accountable for the performance of the bureaucracy, they must be given sufficient powers and management tools to control it. The departmentalist perspective holds that the president's objectives can best be achieved if the bureaucracy is granted a considerable degree of independence.

The tension between the White House and the bureaucracy that is reflected in these contrasting views has been present in every modern administration. It exists, at least in part, because of what Hugh Heclo has identified as the distinction between "political leadership in the bureaucracy" and "bureaucratic power."[7] The direction and effectiveness of the political leadership the president provides depend on the personality, leadership style, and values of the president as well as on external events and conditions. In contrast, bureaucratic power is relatively permanent and does not depend on personalities and transitory political and environmental factors. It is a power that belongs to the career civil servants who compose the permanent government. How the government performs, Heclo suggests, "can be thought of as the product of political leadership times bureaucratic power."[8]

At least five general factors contribute to bureaucratic power and shape the pattern of presidential-bureaucratic relations: the size, complexity, and dispersion of the executive branch; bureaucratic inertia and momentum; the personnel of the executive branch; the legal position of the executive branch; and the susceptibility of executive branch units to external political influence. Major consequences of the interaction of these factors are presidential frustration and a pattern of policy making that often is sharply at odds with the norm of democratic accountability.

Size, Complexity, and Dispersion of the Executive Branch

The enormous expansion in the scope of federal government activities since 1933 has tremendously increased the number of agencies and the programs they administer. The size of the budget and the number of federal employees indicate the magnitude of their operations. By early 1992 the proposed 1993 budget had grown to $1.5 trillion, and there were more than 2.9 million civilian and 2.5 million military employees. The domestic activities of the federal government reach into every community in the nation and touch the lives of individuals from birth to death. Considerations of national security extend U.S. military and foreign policy activities around the world. It is hardly surprising that providing leadership and direction to the federal bureaucracy is a difficult task. It would be so even if the president could command prompt and unquestioning obedience from subservient departments and agencies.

The multiplicity of agencies and programs creates an additional obstacle to effective political leadership in the executive branch. The complexity that results from overlapping jurisdictions leads to duplication of efforts and complicates the president's job. It places a premium on coordination by the presidency. When he defines his goals for a policy area, the president usually does not deal with individual administrative units but with many. In outdoor recreation, for example, the Forest Service (a unit of the Agriculture Department), the National Park Service (a unit of the Interior Department), and the Army Corps of Engineers all maintain facilities for public use. Or consider the use of land owned by the federal government. Policies of the Forest Service and the Interior Department's Bureau of Land Management are sometimes in sharp conflict. A legendary struggle within the bureaucracy is that waged between the Corps of Engineers and the Bureau of Reclamation of the Interior Department. Several presidents tried in vain to yoke the two agencies in common pursuit of a water resources development policy.[9]

Bureaucratic complexity also stems from the interdependence of many federal activities. It is apparent that policy goals in one area are affected by objectives in other areas. The difficult trade-off between energy and environmental policies, which was acutely experienced in the 1970s, illustrates policy interdependence. Efforts to conserve energy and reduce foreign oil imports often were at variance with attempts to reduce air and water pollution. At times the Department of Energy and the Environmental Protection Agency appeared to be working at cross purposes—for example, substituting coal for oil reduced dependence on imported oil but increased problems of maintaining air quality. Housing policy decisions also illustrate interdependence. Programs that may help to increase the stock of low- or middle-income housing may have undesirable consequences elsewhere. The impact of these decisions on inflation, unemployment, the environment, and racial segregation need to be considered.

The great size of the federal bureaucracy further frustrates presidential efforts at direction and control because its activities are so widely dispersed. Presidents, their aides, and their principal political appointees are at the center of government. The people who operate programs, deliver services to individuals, and regulate the conduct of businesses and other organizations are at the periphery. These people, almost all of whom are civil servants, were there when the president and his staff took office, and they will be there after the political executives have departed. They know their programs and the pitfalls involved in administering them. They control the resources, human and material, that are needed to implement programs successfully. Their position, at the point of delivery "where programs meet people," is the source of much of their power.[10]

Bureaucratic Inertia and Momentum

The executive branch, composed of multiple bureaucracies, is difficult to manage because of bureaucratic inertia. It is hard to get a new government activity started, and, once it is under way, it is even more difficult to stop or significantly change the activity. Francis Rourke cites a "celebrated law of bureaucratic inertia," which holds that "bureaucracies at rest tend to stay at rest and bureaucracies in motion tend to stay in motion."[11] Rourke attributes bureaucratic inertia to organizational routines—prescribed operating procedures that have worked successfully in the past. Another important factor contributing to bureaucratic inertia is the support of interest groups for programs that benefit them and in which they have material stake.

The aspect of bureaucratic inertia primarily responsible for presidential frustration is the momentum of ongoing programs. The degree of that momentum is revealed in the number of activities to which the government is committed by public laws, the amount of money allocated for those activities in annual appropriations, and the number of civil service and military employees who carry out the activities.[12] "Uncontrollable" expenditures that the government was obligated to make constituted about 75 percent of President George Bush's proposed 1993 budget. The principal uncontrollable items included interest on the national debt; entitlement programs such as Social Security, Medicare and Medicaid, federal retirement and veterans' benefits; and contractual obligations to pay for, among other things, weapons systems and public facilities. Even the "controllable" portion of the budget is highly resistant to cuts because of support from groups that benefit from those expenditures. Presidents can influence the shape of the federal budget, but major changes usually require several years to be implemented. From one year to the next, presidents tend to be limited to incremental changes.

Presidents, however, are often impatient to make changes. They have a fixed term of office in which to accomplish their objectives. The incremental adjustments that are possible through annual budgeting hardly seem adequate given the scope of their objectives and the time available to them. The time perspective of the bureaucracy is much different. Members of the permanent government can afford to be patient. In the budget process they fight to maintain their "base," which is their current appropriation, and to add as large an increment to it as possible.[13] Over time, successful pursuit of such a strategy results in sizable growth, as small annual increases are transformed into large permanent gains. Bureaucratic momentum thus works to the advantage of the permanent government and acts as a constraint on presidents who try to counter it. President Reagan tried to overcome the effects of incremental budgeting by means of a top-down process that restricts total government spending and forces agencies and their congressional and interest group supporters to accept cuts or limited growth. His efforts had only minimal success.[14] (The reasons are discussed in Chapter 9.)

The large number of career federal employees also commits the president to maintain ongoing programs. Major reductions in personnel or redirection of their activities are economically and politically costly. People will oppose actions that threaten to deprive them of their jobs or that require them to move, undergo additional training, or reduce their sense of security and importance. Most presidents can make only modest adjustments in the size and mission of the federal work force. Reagan was more successful in this regard than other modern presidents, but even his efforts brought about no large-scale changes.[15] During his eight years in office the number of civilian employees did not drop; but domestic social services agencies lost personnel, while the Department of Defense and other national security agencies gained.[16]

Bureaucratic Personnel

Presidents depend on political and career officials to operate the federal bureaucracy. The characteristics and roles of these political and career executives differ sharply, and the relationships between them have tended to hinder presidential direction of the implementation of policies. The political executives constitute what Hugh Heclo has called a "government of strangers."[17] Aside from cabinet officers, a few important subcabinet appointees, and the heads of major independent agencies, they are unknown to the president and to one another.

Selection of the cabinet, especially at the beginning of an administration, involves the president directly and traditionally in an attempt to build support for the administration by including representatives of various constituencies in the party and the country.[18] Cronin maintains that presidents sometimes appoint personal friends to inner cabinet departments because of the close counseling relationship involved.[19] In his study of cabinet appointments since 1861, Jeffrey Cohen found modest support for Cronin's thesis about pretenure ties between presidents and cabinet members.[20] Selection of other political executives is also affected by multiple and often conflicting pressures, such as loyalty to the president, party membership, technical competence, the wishes of the cabinet member under whom the appointee will serve, and the demands of congressional members, interest groups, and state and local party leaders.

The process through which presidents recruit people to serve in their administrations is significant as an instrument of control over policy, as a tool of administrative management, and as a major component of presidential relations with Congress, interest groups, and political parties. Consequently, it is a highly political process. Presidents since Eisenhower have used personnel staffs located in the White House to run the appointment process for them. The process has tended to be rather chaotic at the start of a new administration, because of the large number of positions to be filled and uncertainty about how to proceed, but it eventually becomes fairly systematic. Calvin Mackenzie, in a study of the process, concluded that presidential personnel staffs have served modern presidents well.[21]

According to Mackenzie, the essential ingredient for effective recruitment and selection of appointees is active presidential involvement in the process and sustained presidential support for the personnel staff. Ronald Reagan excelled in this regard, whereas Richard Nixon's lack of interest contributed to his inability to establish effective control over the executive branch. The Reagan administration succeeded in filling sensitive positions with individuals loyal to the president and committed to his ideology.[22] Its White House personnel staff, headed by E. Pendleton James, a professional executive recruiter with previous experience in the Nixon administration, exercised tight control over the recruitment of political executives.[23] Cabinet members were not permitted to conduct independent searches for subcabinet officials, and final approval of subordinate appointments was retained by the White House. Beginning work during the transition period, the personnel staff made ideological affinity the primary criterion for appointment. Prospective appointees were screened for policy views, political and personal backgrounds, and, if considered necessary, expertise. Although it took the Reagan administration a long time to get its political executives in place (it took the Bush administration even longer), the result was tighter control over the executive branch and greater cohesion within it than other modern presidents have been able to achieve.[24]

The political executives chosen by the presidential appointment process often are amateurs in the precarious world of Washington politics. They lack the political knowledge and substantive skills needed to provide effective leadership in their jobs. They quickly discover their dependence on career executives and other lower-ranking civil servants for the information and advice they need to serve the president effectively. That support is not obtained without a price, however—loyalty to the agency and support for its programs within the administration, before Congress, and with the public.[25]

By the time most political executives learn their jobs and strike a balance between the often conflicting claims of the White House and the permanent government, they will have left their positions. It is generally conceded that it takes from twelve to eighteen months for political executives to master their jobs, but their average tenure is only two years. The high rate of turnover makes it difficult to develop teamwork within departments and agencies. Cabinet secretaries are continually adapting to new subordinates, and people on the same administrative level barely get to know one another. One result is that expectations and roles are in flux, and there are problems of coordination and control.

Political executives in the bureaucracy are in a kind of twilight zone where they look upward to the president for support and direction and downward to the permanent government for support and services. In such a position they are imperfect instruments for presidential control of the bureaucracy. They can best serve the president by winning the trust of the careerists who make up the permanent government, but to do so they find it expedient to maintain a considerable degree of independence from the White House.

Career executives and other civil servants provide the institutional resources, such as political experience, substantive knowledge, and technical competence, required to accomplish an agency's mission. They are aware of political problems the agency faces and of its political resources. They have established links with its clientele and with the congressional committees that oversee it through legislative and appropriations powers. They also have a vested interest in their agencies and their programs. Their loyalties are based on norms of bureaucratic and occupational professionalism. They recognize the legitimacy of the president's position and of the claims of political executives for their support, but they will not hesitate to use their substantial capacity to resist the directives of their political superiors.

In most recent administrations, conflict has arisen between the White House and career executives. The reasons for this adversity lie in behavior patterns and perspectives that are fairly common among career executives. The relatively secure tenure of higher civil servants (as contrasted with the expendability and shorter tenure of political executives) allows them to take a more gradual approach to avoid direct confrontation and to pursue their objectives obliquely and by indirection, because such an approach is less likely to generate political opposition. In contrast, political executives tend to pursue their goals quite directly and to see virtue in conflict.

Careerists also try to avoid becoming identified with a political party or a political appointee. The civil servant must remain politically neutral to remain a civil servant; hence, he or she is cautious about political involvement. Political executives, many of whom are unfamiliar with the ways of the bureaucracy, often mistake such caution for opposition or disloyalty. This point of view is reinforced by the high value that career executives place on maintaining their relationships with clientele group representatives, congressional members and staff, and individuals outside the Washington community who are involved in or knowledgeable about their agency's programs.

Such relationships, or networks, provide information and support that help the bureaucrats be of service to their political superiors. Involvement in the networks, however, can place a strain on the career executives' relations with their superiors, who often regard civil servants' informal contacts outside the agency as evidence of disloyalty. This perspective, which is especially pronounced among members of the White House staff, is understandable, but it overlooks the importance of such relationships to the services that career executives provide.

To correct perceived deficiencies in the career service and to increase presidential control over the higher civil service, the Carter administration engineered the passage of the Civil Service Reform Act (CSRA) of 1978. The CSRA established the Senior Executive Service (SES), a professional managerial corps of career civil servants, whose members are eligible for financial bonuses. It also increased the ability of political executives to transfer career officials within and between agencies and to raise the number of noncareerists in SES and lower positions.[26] Another provision of the CSRA replaced the three-person bipartisan Civil Service Commission with the single-headed Office of Personnel Management (OPM), which gave the president more control of the career service. Reagan's first director of OPM, Donald J. Devine, aggressively implemented a partisan style of leadership.[27] So far Bush has not used politicization of the career service as extensively as Reagan did to direct the executive branch.

Legal Arrangements

The ambiguous legal position of the executive branch is the fourth factor that affects a president's control over the bureaucracy. All departments and agencies are established by Congress and derive their authority to operate from statutes. Moreover, "it is the agency heads, not the president, who have the men, money, material, and legal powers."[28] Presidents do not enter into contracts, initiate projects, or make grants. Their subordinates do so, but not in response to presidential directives. It is true that presidents act through subordinates, but they do so principally through persuasion because of the nature and source of their legal authority and that of their subordinates.

Although the Constitution charges the president with responsibility for executing the laws, his legal position as chief executive is somewhat unclear because Congress has—with presidential approval—delegated authority to and imposed duties directly on various administrative officials. In some cases, such as independent regulatory commissions and the Federal Reserve Board, the president has no formal power to direct agency actions or set agency policy. His influence upon these units is based on his budgetary and appointment powers and on his persuasive abilities. For cabinet members, heads of independent agencies, and other political executives with operating authority to whom Congress has directly delegated power, the situation is ambiguous. As chief executive the president, by virtue of the "take care" clause of the Constitution, can command the decisions of his subordinates. In doing so, however, he risks confrontation with Congress and with the clientele groups and individuals affected by the administrative units involved. Also, the Supreme Court long ago ruled that the president may not interfere with the performance of a "purely ministerial" duty that does not involve the exercise of discretion or judgment.[29] Nor may the president prevent the execution of the law by subordinates.

The growth of the public bureaucracy has been accompanied by broad delegations of discretionary authority to administrative officials. Such delegations have been necessary because Congress cannot legislate in sufficient detail to cover all contingencies that may arise. Congress also has made vague and general grants of power because it finds it politically advantageous to shift difficult and potentially unpopular decisions to the bureaucracy. The Supreme Court has approved the delegation of legislative authority to the executive branch with the proviso that the delegations be accompanied by clear statutory guidelines.[30] However, the Court's insistence on specific statutory standards has seldom been followed by Congress or by the judiciary.[31] The standards the Court uses have tended to be vague and unspecific, such as "just and reasonable rates," "excess profits," and "the public interest, convenience, and necessity." In spite of judicial review of the fairness of administrative procedures and judicial reference to the legislative history of statutes as found in congressional committee hearings and reports and floor debates in Congress, administrative officials retain substantial discretionary authority that complicates the president's task of controlling the bureaucracy.

Susceptibility to External Influence

It is often observed that the federal bureaucracy is susceptible to external influence and pressure. A primary reason for this susceptibility to forces outside of individual departments, agencies, and bureaus is the inability of American political parties to provide administrative units with political support and to link party programs with the pursuit of presidential policy goals.

In contrast to "the government" in parliamentary democracies such as the United Kingdom or Canada, American presidential administrations are not integrated by ties of party loyalty and commitment to a party program. Administrations lack internal policy cohesiveness and depend on the president's personal leadership to hold them together. In the face of external criticism and pressure, executive branch units are unable to find much support within the administration. Demands on the president are extensive, his energy and attention are not unlimited, and he tends to conserve his political resources for high-priority objectives.

If presidential support for an agency is lacking, the agency must look elsewhere for help in maintaining its authority, funding, and personnel. It looks to the public for support, especially among the individuals and groups who are affected by its programs, and it looks to Congress, particularly to the committees or subcommittees with jurisdiction over its legislative authorizations and its appropriations.

The regulations that agencies promulgate and enforce, or the benefits and services they deliver, provide the basis for the development of enduring ties between them and their clientele groups. An agency without a well-organized clientele is in a precarious position. Clientele groups can publicize an agency's accomplishments and defend it against attack. In exchange, the agency administers its programs with a manifest concern for the interests of the clientele. The agency consults with clientele group officials and with individual notables who are attentive to its activities. Such outsiders often are invited to participate in agency decision making. They do so by serving on advisory councils and panels and through informal personal contacts. Agencies seldom perform acts such as drafting guidelines and regulations or awarding grants without extensive external participation and consultation. There is also a two-way flow of personnel between agencies and their clientele organizations. These mutually beneficial relations between agencies and their clientele are characteristic of most domestic policy areas in the federal government.

Washington has countless examples of these relationships. The National Education Association (NEA) and several other education interest groups provide support and protection to the the Department of Education in exchange for access and information. The NEA led the congressional effort to elevate the former U.S. Office of Education to departmental status in 1979 and the battle to prevent the abolition of the fledgling department during the Reagan administration. Over the years several Department of Education political executives have found employment with the NEA and other education interest groups after leaving the government. On occasion, those lobbies have helped to recruit or have provided personnel to staff the agency.

Agencies also find it easy and convenient to develop strong ties to the congressional committees or subcommittees with which they deal. Committee members usually receive immediate attention and preferential treatment from agency personnel. Congressional requests for consideration on appointments and grants, suggestions concerning program administration, and inquiries on behalf of constituents are quickly acknowledged. Congressional influence with the agencies strengthens the committee members in their constituencies.[32] Bureaucrats use their connections with congressional committee members to affect changes in their statutory authority and gain favorable treatment during budget negotiations. Agencies may use their committee ties to obtain more funds than the president has recommended for them or to modify their activities in a way that is not fully in accord with presidential preferences.

If successful, the agencies' quest for support outside the executive branch results in the development of triangular relationships involving an agency, its clientele groups, and congressional committees. These "iron triangles"[33] or "policy subgovernments"[34] are semiautonomous centers of power. They abound in Washington and are a major obstacle to presidential control of the bureaucracy. They are not, however, totally resistant to presidential directives, nor is it in their interest to be so. Agencies frequently need presidential support and attention. Moreover, they often find that their interests coincide with those of the president. Agencies and the president need each other to accomplish their goals. If the true test of a president's power is his power to persuade, one of the best measures of an agency's strength is the degree to which a president must "bargain with it in order to secure its cooperation."[35]

The concept of policy subgovernments, although widely recognized as empirically accurate in some policy areas, is incomplete. The so-called iron triangles are complemented by myriad amorphous "issue networks" comprising individuals and groups with knowledge about and a desire to act on particular policy problems.[36] Issue networks differ from policy subgovernments in that they are unstructured and open. People move into and out of them freely and are more likely to be motivated by their positions on issues than by material interests.

Issue networks make policy making complicated and unpredictable. Also, they have differing implications for democratic politics and presidential control of the bureaucracy. On the one hand, they increase the potential involvement of a wide range of experts and policy specialists in government problem solving, provide a technocratic link between Congress and the executive branch, and give political executives increased room for maneuvering. On the other hand, issue networks make it more difficult for the president to control political executives by reducing his leverage over them, and they are not democratically accountable. In sum, although they may be good for policy making, they are "bad for democratic politics."[37]

The President and the Cabinet

Most modern presidents have come to office determined to make more extensive use of the cabinet as a collective decision-making body than the previous incumbent did. The public has tended to applaud candidates' pledges that the cabinet will play a major role in their administrations. Yet, with the exception of Dwight Eisenhower, presidents have not used their cabinets as vehicles of collective leadership. Moreover, they have experienced strained relationships with many individual cabinet members.

This gap between expectation and experience suggests that there is a widespread lack of understanding of the cabinet on the part of the public and most political leaders. According to Thomas Cronin, the cabinet "is simultaneously one of the best known and least understood aspects of our governmental system."[38] In point of fact, the Constitution places executive authority, ultimately, in the president alone. The notion of collective or collegial leadership is incompatible with constitutional reality and inconsistent with American practice. The president is not first among equals; he is explicitly "number one," the person in charge. Cabinet members are the president's appointees, and they serve at his pleasure. He has no obligation to consult them as a group or, when he does so, to act according to their wishes. The cabinet has no formal constitutional or legal standing. It exists by custom, and presidents are free to use it as little or as much as they see fit.

The fact that the cabinet has seldom been a high-level decision-making body does not mean that it lacks political significance. It has great symbolic value as a means of representing major social, economic, and political constituencies in the highest councils of the administration.[39] Newly elected presidents try to select cabinet members whose presence will unify those constituencies behind him and his administration.

Elevation of an agency to cabinet status signifies the importance the nation places on its activities. During the Carter administration, for example, the Federal Energy Agency became the nucleus of a new Department of Energy, and the Office of Education provided the core of the Department of Education. Opponents of these moves argued that the federal role in energy and education should be diminished rather than enhanced by the award of cabinet status. President Reagan proposed the abolition of the two new departments as part of his attempt to reduce the activities of the federal government. He later dropped the abolition effort, which had few supporters in Congress, among interest groups, or in the public. Despite his opposition to expanding the role of government or elevating its status, Reagan signed legislation giving cabinet status to the Veterans Administration as the Department of Veterans Affairs. Veterans organizations were among his most loyal supporters, and he was an advocate of strengthening national defense.

As noted previously, in selecting cabinet members, presidents have used criteria such as prior political experience, identification with politically significant groups, and technical expertise. There is no dominant criterion, but Nelson Polsby found in a study of the Nixon and Carter cabinets that presidents tend initially to select cabinets that are broadly representative and whose members can speak for clientele groups and party constituencies. This observation characterized George Bush's initial cabinet appointments (see Table 6-1). Over time they tend to choose people "of no independent public standing, with no constituencies of their own."[40]

Presidents face constraints in selecting cabinet members. Appointees to head some departments, such as Agriculture, generally must be acceptable to clientele groups. In choosing the secretaries of Defense and Treasury, presidents may give weight to their expertise and experience. Generalist administrators, however, often are named to head the departments of Commerce, Health and Human Services, Housing and Urban Development, and Transportation.

Presidents often try to use the cabinet as a decision-making body early in their administrations, but most of them eventually abandon the effort.[41] They find that most cabinet members are concerned primarily with issues that affect their departments and with their personal relationships

Table 6-1 Initial Bush Cabinet Appointments by Criteria of Appointment

	Political Experience	Clientele or Ethnic Group Identification	Technical Expertise	Pretenure Friendship
INNER CABINET				
Defense				
Richard Cheney	✔			
Justice				
Richard Thornburgh	✔			
State				
James A. Baker III	✔			✔
Treasury				
Nicholas Brady	✔			✔
OUTER CABINET				
Agriculture				
Clayton Yeutter	✔			
Commerce				
Robert Mosbacher		✔		✔
Education				
Lauro Cavazos		✔	✔	
Health and Human Services				
Louis Sullivan		✔	✔	
Housing and Urban Development				
Jack Kemp	✔			
Interior				
Manuel Lujan	✔	✔		
Labor				
Elizabeth Dole	✔			
Transportation				
Samuel Skinner	✔	✔		
Veterans Affairs				
Edward Derwinski	✔			

with the president. There is often competition between cabinet members for the president's attention, and personality clashes within the cabinet are not infrequent. Under these circumstances, cabinet meetings are unsatisfactory devices for focused, analytical discussion of major issues. At best they can serve as forums for informal discussion of issues and problems and for the exchange of information. Even President Eisenhower, who genuinely wanted his cabinet to function as a policy review and coordinating body, was unable to use it to formulate policy. The crucial factor limiting the role of the cabinet is the absence of any integrating force within the administration other than the president. The weakness of political parties in the governing process and the president's preeminent constitutional and political position combine to make him the only source of cohesion and policy coordination. Individual cabinet members feel loyal to the president *and* to the permanent governments within their departments. These conflicting loyalties inhibit the development of an informal sense of unity and purpose without which the cabinet cannot realize its potential as a formal advisory body and policy-making mechanism.[42]

Although it may be an overstatement to assert, as did Charles G. Dawes, the first director of the Bureau of the Budget, that departmental and clientele pressures make cabinet members "natural enemies" of the president, there is an unavoidable tension in their relationship that constitutes a great dilemma for him.[43] No president can function effectively if cabinet members regularly choose departmental over presidential interests. However, cabinet members who display unquestioning responsiveness to the president's desires and are insensitive to the needs and concerns of their departments jeopardize their capacity to implement his policies effectively. Furthermore, cabinet members are not fully in command of their departments. The strongest clientele pressures are applied to the bureaus that administer programs, not to the department heads. It is the operating bureaus, not the departments, that constitute the bureaucratic components of policy subgovernments and issue networks. Cabinet members deal with subgovernments mainly through persuasion, and the source of their strength is access to the president and presidential support. Presidents and presidential aides who fail to give cabinet members support and room to bargain with subgovernments and who expect quick and complete obedience to White House directives almost ensure the ineffectiveness of the cabinet members, as well as their own frustration.

Presidents frequently have developed strong, positive relationships with individual cabinet members and, through them, with their departments, but there is no guarantee that this will happen. A personality conflict between the president and a cabinet member or antipathy on the part of the White House staff can prevent such a development. There is a tendency in most administrations for one or two cabinet members to stand out and to develop close ties with the president. During Reagan's second term, Attorney General Edwin Meese III and Secretary of the Treasury James A. Baker III enjoyed considerable leeway to pursue their own agendas without aggressive interference from the White House staff, provided they did not conflict with the president's ideological precepts.[44] In the Bush administration James Baker (State), Robert A. Mosbacher (Commerce), and Nicholas F. Brady (Treasury), all old friends of the president, enjoyed high standing with him.[45] During the Persian Gulf crisis of 1990–1991, Secretary of Defense Richard Cheney also emerged as a major figure.

Whatever the variations in relations between individual presidents and their cabinet members, there has been a tendency for modern presidents to develop close ties with the heads of the departments of State, Defense, Treasury, and Justice. Cronin refers to these as the "inner cabinet" departments because their activities and responsibilities are of the highest priority—national security, the condition of the economy, civil rights, and the administration of justice—and because they cut across the concerns of the public and all members of Congress. These matters tend to dominate the president's time and attention.[46] Inner cabinet members, therefore, almost always have direct, frequent, and continuing contact with the president.

The heads of the other departments—Agriculture, Commerce, Education, Energy, Health and Human Services, Housing and Urban Development, Interior, Labor, Transportation, and Veterans Affairs—constitute the "outer cabinet."[47] Their departments have more sharply focused activities. Outer cabinet members, subjected to strong clientele and congressional pressures, find themselves acting as advocates for those interests within the administration.[48] Frequently, those pressures conflict with the president's broader priorities. Outer cabinet members may find themselves regarded with suspicion by White House aides, with whom they have frequent contact because the activities of their departments are not important enough to allow them to claim much of the president's time. Their necessary interaction with presidential staffers, who believe that these cabinet members have been captured by their departments' bureaucracies and clientele groups, and their relative lack of access to the president lead to a sense of isolation and frustration. The Bush White House ignored HUD secretary Jack Kemp's efforts to respond to urban problems until the Los Angeles riots in May 1992. Obviously, this pattern of operation does not work well for the president, the cabinet member, or the country.

Because of the diversity and scope of department activities and the particular orientations of some cabinet members, presidents generally have looked to sources other than the cabinet for advice on policy implementation. The inner cabinet reflects top policy priorities. Presidents have additional sources of advice in these areas in the Executive Office of the President. Since its creation in 1947, the National Security Council (NSC) and its staff have been used extensively by presidents to coordinate the making and execution of foreign and military policy *(see Chapter 10)*. In the important areas of economic policy, presidents work closely with the chair of the Council of Economic Advisers, the director of the Office of Management and Budget, the secretary of the Treasury, and the chair of the Federal Reserve Board *(Chapter 9)*. In the domestic policy areas, which involve primarily the outer cabinet departments, domestic policy staffs and OMB have provided assistance to the president in policy formulation *(Chapter 8)*, and cabinet committees, interagency committees, and policy councils have been employed to coordinate policy implementation.

Cabinet committees, which are usually appointed on an ad hoc basis to handle specific problems, can focus quickly on them and attempt to develop solutions. Their usefulness for long-term monitoring of policy implementation is limited, however, by other demands on their members and by the tendency of their operations to become routine and to lose flexibility. Interagency committees, which operate mostly at the agency and subcabinet levels, may achieve a measure of coordination, but their work is often hampered by competition between agencies and by their lack of status and visibility.

Presidents also have used policy councils to highlight particular problems. Before the Reagan administration, most policy councils, other than the NSC, had more symbolic value than operational utility to presidents in their management of the executive branch. In his first term Reagan invested heavily in the cabinet council approach. He established seven councils in addition to the NSC: commerce and trade, economic affairs, energy and natural resources, food and agriculture, human resources, legal policy, and management and administration. The theory behind the cabinet council system was that issues would move upward through the full cabinet to the president for decision. Over time, it became apparent that the system was unduly cumbersome, and for his second term Reagan reduced the number of cabinet councils to two. The remaining councils— the Economic Policy Council and the Domestic Policy Council—had more clearly defined jurisdictions and lines of authority. Baker and Meese chaired the two new councils. This system, which was designed to protect the president politically, allowed the more aggressive cabinet members, such as Baker, Meese, Secretary of State George Shultz, and Secretary of Defense Caspar Weinberger, to set the administration's policy tone within the framework of the president's broad ideologically defined agenda.

President Bush continued to utilize the Economic Policy Council and the Domestic Policy Council, but with apparently limited effectiveness. Early in 1992, amid reports of "squabbling over domestic policy and rivalries among policy makers," Secretary of Transportation Samuel Skinner replaced John Sununu as White House chief of staff and Secretary of Agriculture Clayton Yeutter was named to the new post of counselor for domestic policy and charged with "centralizing what had been a diffuse policy-making apparatus."[49]

Presidential Control of the Bureaucracy

George Edwards has identified four major factors that affect policy implementation: communication, resources, bureaucratic structure, and the dispositions of implementing officials.[50] The preceding analysis of presidential relations with the cabinet and the bureaucracy has revealed that presidents encounter obstacles to control of policy implementation in all four of these areas. Presidents are not, however, without resources for this effort. They have substantial powers granted by the Constitution, delegated by Congress, and derived from the nature of their office. The most important are the powers to appoint and remove subordinates, to issue executive orders, and to prepare the annual federal budget and regulate expenditures.

Appointment and Removal

The essential powers for presidential control of the bureaucracy are the powers to appoint and remove subordinate officials. As critical as these powers are to the president's executive responsibilities, however, they are subject to limitation by Congress.[51] The Constitution gives the president broad powers of appointment (Article II, Section 2, paragraph 2), but it makes high-ranking officials subject to senatorial confirmation, and it authorizes Congress to vest the appointment of lower officials in the president, in department heads, or in the courts. Congress determines whether an appointment to a position must be confirmed by the Senate. In addition, it can narrow the president's discretion in making appointments by establishing detailed qualifications for various offices. Congress cannot, however, give itself the power to appoint executive officials.[52] Neither can it force the president to make an appointment to a vacant position.[53] The president's appointive powers also are constrained by political considerations and practices such as senatorial courtesy whereby the president gives the senators of his own party a veto over certain administrative and judicial appointments in the states.

The Senate generally has given presidents considerable leeway in the appointment of top-level political executives, but confirmation is not automatic, and the Senate has used rejections to express disapproval of specific individuals or of particular practices.[54] Since the Watergate scandal of 1972–1974, the Senate has tended to be more careful and procedurally consistent in examining the backgrounds, qualifications, and relevant policy views of presidential nominees. However, the confirmation process has ''become more tedious, time-consuming, and intrusive for the nominees.''[55]

The Constitution also empowers the president to make appointments when the Senate is in recess. Such appointments must be confirmed by the end of the Senate's next session, but in the interim the appointee continues to serve. Senators often object to recess appointments to high-level positions because they feel inhibited from thoroughly examining people who have already begun their duties. Because Congress now remains in session most of the year, however, presidents have fewer opportunities to make recess appointments.

The removal power is the logical complement of the appointment power. The ability to remove subordinate officials on performance or policy grounds is fundamental to presidential control of the executive branch. Without the removal power, the president cannot be held fully responsible for the actions of his subordinates or for failure of departments and agencies to achieve his objectives. The Constitution is silent, however, concerning the removal of executive officials other than through impeachment, a cumbersome process that is limited to instances of ''bribery, treason, and other high crimes and misdemeanors.''

Presidents have clashed with Congress over the removal power. The post–Civil War conflict between President Andrew Johnson and Congress over reconstruction policy involved the removal power. In 1867 Congress brought impeachment proceedings against Johnson for violating the Tenure of Office Act, which it had passed over his veto. That statute authorized all persons appointed with the advice and consent of the Senate to continue to hold office until the president appointed and the Senate confirmed a successor. Although Johnson survived the impeachment trial by one vote, the issue of the removal power remained unresolved. (Congress repealed the Tenure of Office Act in 1887.)

The Supreme Court dealt directly with the removal power in a decision involving a challenge to President Woodrow Wilson's summary removal of a postmaster.[56] The Court invalidated an 1876 law that required senatorial consent for the removal of postmasters. It held that the Constitution gave the president the removal power and that Congress could not place restrictions on its exercise. Nine years later, however, the Court upheld the provisions of the Federal Trade Commission Act, which limited the grounds for removal of its members.[57] The Court ruled that the president's unqualified power of removal is limited to "purely executive offices" and that Congress may prescribe conditions for the removal of officials performing "quasi-legislative" and "quasi-judicial" functions. However, the Court has not clarified fully the meaning of these terms. One of the most dramatic instances of the removal power occurred in August 1981 when President Reagan fired 11,400 striking members of the Professional Air Traffic Controllers Organization. A U.S. court of appeals upheld the action, interpreting it as a discharge of the president's obligation to enforce a statute prohibiting strikes by federal employees.[58] In December 1990 President Bush dismissed Secretary of Education Lauro Cavazos for his "timidity" in supporting Bush's calls for educational reform.[59]

Although there are some statutory and judicial restrictions on the removal power, its precise limits remain somewhat undefined. Moreover, the president may be able through informal means to force officials from office for reasons other than statutory cause. The president can call publicly for an official's resignation, or he may revoke authority he has delegated to an official as a means of indicating displeasure and lack of confidence. In 1975 President Gerald Ford removed Robert Timm as chairman of the Civil Aeronautics Board on grounds of "incompetence," but allowed him to remain on the board. Timm resigned two months later.

Executive Orders

Under a strict interpretation of separation of powers, the president has no direct legislative authority. Established practice, however, based on liberal interpretations of the Constitution by presidents and the Supreme Court, has vested substantial authority in him to issue executive orders that have the force of law. From the beginnings of the Republic, presidents have issued orders and directives on the basis of Article II. Most modern presidents have followed Theodore Roosevelt's "stewardship" theory of executive power, which holds that Article II confers on them inherent power to take whatever actions they deem necessary in the national interest unless prohibited from doing so by the Constitution or by law. Executive orders have been a primary means of exercising this broad presidential prerogative power.

It is generally recognized that executive orders must find their authority in the Constitution or in an act of Congress. As noted, the Supreme Court has upheld delegations of legislative power to the executive branch provided Congress establishes "intelligible" standards to guide administrative officials in the exercise of their authority.[60] In reviewing challenges to statutory delegations, however, the Court has consistently adopted a presumption in favor of statutes authorizing executive action by order or rule.

Executive orders have played a major role in presidential policy making. Presidents have used them in crucial areas such as civil rights, economic stabilization, and national security. In the realm of civil rights Franklin Roosevelt established a Fair Employment Practices Commission in 1943 to prevent discriminatory hiring by government agencies and military suppliers. In 1948 Truman ended segregation in the armed forces by executive order. Shortly after taking office, John Kennedy in March 1961 issued a sweeping order creating the Equal Employment Opportunity Commission and giving it broad enforcement powers. Lyndon Johnson went even further, requiring by executive order preferential hiring of minorities by government contractors. Following passage of the Civil Rights Act of 1964, presidential orders involving civil rights declined, but before that landmark statute, presidents used executive orders to make policy in a sensitive area in which Congress was unable or unwilling to act.

Roosevelt established broad precedents for the use of executive orders to achieve economic stability. During World War II he issued executive orders to establish the Office of Price Administration (OPA) and the Office of Economic Stabilization and to give them extensive powers over prices, wages, and profits. The OPA also rationed scarce consumer goods such as meat, butter, sugar, shoes, automobile tires, and gasoline. As a basis for his actions Roosevelt cited his responsibility as president to respond to the "unlimited emergency" created by the war. The Emergency Price Control Act of 1942 provided retroactive statutory endorsement for the establishment of the emergency agencies and the measures implemented by them.

In 1970, in the face of persistent inflation, Congress passed the Economic Stabilization Act, which authorized the president to issue orders that would control wages and prices, but with few criteria to guide these actions. On August 15, 1971, President Nixon issued an executive order imposing a ninety-day freeze on nonagricultural wages and prices and establishing the Cost of Living Council to administer the controls. A subsequent order, issued October 15, extended the controls and established additional machinery to aid in administering them. A legal challenge to the statute, as an unconstitutional delegation of unbridled authority, failed before a U.S. district court.[61] The court found that Congress had considered the statute carefully and concluded that the president needed extensive discretion to deal with inflation. The court decided that the delegation was therefore reasonable, and it stated that experience in administering previous price control statutes, passed in 1942 and 1950, furnished implicit standards for guidance in implementing the 1970 law.

President Reagan used an executive order early in his first term to establish a comprehensive program to oversee the issuance of regulations by departments, agencies, and independent regulatory commissions. The order, which formally implemented Reagan's commitment to administrative deregulation, created the President's Task Force on Regulatory Relief, set up the Office of Information and Regulatory Affairs in OMB, and required that all regulations meet a uniform cost-benefit standard "to the extent permitted by law."[62] OMB used the cost-benefit standard and the paperwork review procedures of the order to substitute market forces for federal regulations, and on occasion it prevented the issuance of proposed regulations.

Presidents also have used executive orders in pursuit of national security. In 1942, for example, Roosevelt ordered the internment of all persons of Japanese ancestry living in the Pacific coastal states, 70,000 of whom were U.S. citizens. The Supreme Court upheld this massive deprivation of basic civil liberties on the basis of the commander-in-chief clause.[63] During the Korean War, however, the Supreme Court invalidated Truman's seizure of the steel industry on the grounds that he had not used the machinery established in the Taft-Hartley Act of 1947 to avert a strike.[64]

In another aspect of national security, presidents have used executive orders extensively to administer and structure federal intelligence agen-

cies. In 1973 Richard Nixon overhauled the system for classifying information, and in 1976 Gerald Ford reorganized the intelligence agencies,
imposed restrictions on their activities, and established procedures to
make them more directly accountable to the president.

From 1932 until 1983 Congress exerted a measure of control over
executive lawmaking through use of the legislative veto. Provisions added
to certain statutes gave Congress the power to review and reject executive
orders or administrative regulations authorized by the legislation. The
legislative veto took various forms. It allowed disapproval of regulations
by concurrent resolution, or by simple resolution of either house, or by
action of a committee of either house. In its most common form, the
legislative veto required that the proposed action lie before Congress for
a specified period—usually sixty or ninety days—during which either
chamber could disapprove it. The president's reorganization authority,
which Congress first authorized in 1939, carried such a procedure. Other
major statutes that contained a form of legislative veto include the War
Powers Resolution of 1973, the Budget and Impoundment Control Act of
1974, the Federal Elections Campaign Act of 1974, and the National
Emergencies Act of 1976. In all, more than 250 statutes provided for some
type of legislative veto before the Supreme Court invalidated it in 1983.[65]

The legislative veto sparked extensive controversy. Its supporters defended it as an effective means of controlling the exercise of delegated
legislative power by the executive branch. They contended that it was an
appropriate condition to attach to a delegation of power. Edward S. Corwin, one of the nation's most noted constitutional scholars, argued that
delegation can be kept from becoming abdication "only by rendering the
delegated powers recoverable without the consent of the delegate."[66]

Opponents of the legislative veto asserted that it unconstitutionally
violated the separation of powers because it interfered with the president's
authority to veto acts of Congress. They also maintained that in the case of
vetoes by one house or by a committee, the veto enabled a part of Congress to act for the whole institution.[67] Presidents from Truman through
Reagan regarded legislative veto provisions of statutes as unconstitutional, although before taking office Reagan had endorsed the idea of
granting to both houses of Congress and the president the authority to
veto administrative regulations. These presidents did not, however, refuse
to sign bills containing legislative veto provisions.

The Supreme Court did not confront the constitutionality of the legislative veto until June 1983 when it held, in *Immigration and Naturalization Service v. Chadha*, the one-house legislative veto provision of the Immigration and Nationality Act to be unconstitutional. The Court reasoned that the veto involved "the exercise of legislative power" without "bicameral passage followed by presentment to the President." Initial reaction to *Chadha* was that it was not a definitive ruling and that somehow Congress would find a way statutorily to control executive branch lawmaking.[68] The Court's ruling in *Chadha* appears to have invalidated the use of resolutions by one or both houses of Congress to disapprove an executive action on the basis of delegated power. Committee vetoes also are invalid, but since *Chadha* Congress has enacted more than 200 new legislative veto provisions, most of which require agencies to obtain approval from the Appropriations committees. In addition, it has made extensive use of informal nonstatutory agreements with agencies.[69] Arrangements between committees and agencies are not binding, but executive branch officials observe them because Congress can revoke the discretionary authority that it has delegated.

In addition to the persistence of de facto committee vetoes, Congress has employed a device, the joint resolution of approval, that accomplishes the purpose of the legislative veto and is compatible with the *Chadha* ruling. Instead of providing that an executive action will become effective unless Congress acts to disapprove it by joint resolution—in which case the president may exercise his veto—the resolution of approval requires passage of a joint resolution before an action can be taken.[70] For example, the Reorganization Act Amendments of 1984 provide that a presidentially prepared reorganization plan submitted to Congress cannot take effect unless approved by a joint resolution within ninety days.[71] This provision places the burden on the president rather than on Congress, and the president has only a specific number of days in which to act. In effect, the joint resolution of approval works like a one-house legislative veto: if either house refuses to approve an action, it cannot be taken. The major disadvantage of the device for Congress is that it requires much time, and extensive use of it would threaten the congressional agenda with legislative gridlock.

Presidents and Money

Presidents have substantial financial powers, delegated by Congress, which they use in their efforts to control the bureaucracy. The most important of these is the power to formulate the budget, which controls the amount of spending by federal departments and agencies. It also establishes the president's spending priorities, sets the timing of program initiatives, and distributes rewards to and imposes sanctions on executive branch units.[72] By controlling the total amount of the budget, the president can attempt to influence the performance of the economy *(see Chapter 9)*.

Presidential use of the executive budget is a twentieth century development. The enormous increase in expenditures during World War I, and the task of managing the sizable national debt that resulted, convinced Congress of the need for an executive budget. The Budget and Accounting Act of 1921 made the president responsible for compiling department and agency estimates and for submitting them annually to Congress in the form of a budget. The statute established the Bureau of the Budget (BOB), located in the Treasury Department, to assist the president in assembling and revising these estimates. The departments and agencies were prohibited from submitting their requests directly to Congress as they had done previously.

The initial emphasis in the development of the federal budget process was on the control of expenditures and the prevention of administrative abuses.[73] The focus of the budget was on objects of expenditure, that is, the personnel, supplies, and equipment needed to operate each agency. During the New Deal period, in the 1930s, the emphasis shifted from control to management. The budget was seen as a means of evaluating and improving administrative performance. The focus of the budget also shifted from objects of expenditure to the work and activities of departments and agencies. The transfer of BOB in 1939 from the Treasury Department to the new Executive Office of the President symbolized the management orientation. BOB was to become the president's management arm. A decade later, upon recommendation of the Hoover Commission, the government adopted a performance budget organized by functions and activities rather than by line items representing objects of expenditure.

The third stage in the development of budgeting is its orientation toward planning. This emphasis attempts to link annual budgeting, geared to the appropriations process in Congress, to long-range planning of government objectives. The focus is on the relationship of long-term policy goals to current and future spending decisions. The limited success of the planning orientation is reflected in the rapid arrival and departure of budgeting systems, such as the program planning budgeting system (PPBS) and zero base budgeting (ZBB).[74] The traditional budgeting process, as it had developed by the early 1970s, embodied all three orientations, but it was least effective as a planning device.

The limitations of the executive budget as an aid to presidential decision making stem from the incremental nature of the traditional budget process and from restrictions and conditions imposed by Congress. Budgeting is inherently incremental because it is done annually. The budget cycle forces the president and Congress to act according to a timetable that stretches from twenty-two months before the start of the fiscal year (October 1) through the ensuing year. Decision makers in Congress and the bureaucracy are concerned primarily with how large an increase or decrease will be made in a department's or agency's budget. Department and agency officials try to protect their current appropriation, which serves as a base, and add to it a portion of any increase in the total budget.

Congress makes its own budget decisions and is not bound to the president's requests. In the 1970s it quarreled bitterly with Nixon and Ford over spending for domestic programs, and, as already noted, in the 1980s it squared off with Reagan over the size of the deficits in his proposed budgets. In the 1990s it continued these battles with Bush. Congress limits total spending through resolutions proposed by the budget committees in each house. Although the Congress's budget total is usually fairly close to the president's, often there are sharp differences between their priorities.

Throughout the budget process the congressional and bureaucratic participants focus attention on spending for the forthcoming fiscal year. Pressures are intense, and the political stakes are high. There is little opportunity in such a setting for consideration of long-range objectives and costs or for examining the effects on other government programs of different spending levels for specific activities.

The fiscal stress that the government experienced beginning in the mid–1970s has led to adjustments in the budget process designed to reduce pressures for increased spending and to enhance restraint. Among the major adjustments are norms or targets imposed from the top down, baseline budgeting, and multiyear budgeting. The baseline assumes no changes in budget policy and extrapolates revenue and expenditure trends. Underlying the projections is the message that unless cutbacks are made, future spending deficits will be excessive.[75] Baseline budgeting reorients the process from increments to cutbacks. Multiyear budgets also have been redirected from plans for growth of programs and expenditures to devices for averting them.[76] These adaptations have not been overly successful, however, and pressures to protect and increase spending remain strong.

In addition to budgeting, presidents have certain discretionary spending powers that increase their leverage over the bureaucracy. They have substantial nonstatutory authority, based on understandings with congressional appropriations committees, to transfer funds within an appropriation and from one program to another. The committees expect to be kept informed of such "reprogramming" actions.[77] Fund transfer authority is essential to sound financial management, but it can be abused to circumvent congressional decisions. In 1970, for example, Nixon transferred funds to support an extensive unauthorized covert military operation in Cambodia. Nevertheless, Congress has given presidents and certain agencies the authority to spend substantial amounts of money on a confidential basis, the largest and most controversial of which are for intelligence activities.

Presidents also have exercised some measure of expenditure control through the practice of impounding or returning appropriated funds to the Treasury. Since George Washington, presidents have routinely impounded funds as a means of achieving savings when expenditures fall short of appropriations.[78] They also have withheld funds when authorized or directed to do so by Congress for purposes such as establishing contingency reserves or imposing a ceiling on total expenditures. Presidents from FDR through Lyndon Johnson also impounded some of the funds that Congress had added, over their objections, for various programs. Although such actions often drew congressional criticism, they did not lead to confrontation because they occurred infrequently and were generally focused on expenditures for specific programs or projects. Congress recognized that circumspect use of impoundments helped its members to resist strong pressures for increased spending.[79]

Impoundment became a major constitutional issue during the Nixon administration. Sweeping impoundments in domestic program areas, especially agriculture, housing, and water pollution control, led to charges that the president arbitrarily and illegally had substituted his spending priorities for those of Congress. What distinguished the Nixon impoundments from those of earlier administrations was their "magnitude, sever- ity, and belligerence."[80] Specifically, Nixon's impoundments differed from those of other presidents in several ways: they involved larger amounts; some were made in direct violation of explicit congressional instructions to spend the funds; some were designed to terminate entire programs rather than individual projects; and some were directed at ap- propriated funds that had not been included in the president's budget proposals. Moreover, Nixon claimed constitutional rather than statutory authority for impoundment.[81] He used impoundments as the primary weapon in a battle with Congress over domestic spending priorities. He did not bargain or negotiate over them but imposed his priorities by fiat.

Nixon's actions resulted in lawsuits to compel release of the funds, most of which were decided against the president on statutory grounds. Congress also passed the Budget and Impoundment Control Act of 1974. The Antideficiency Act of 1950 had limited the purposes of impound- ments to establishing contingency reserves and the saving of money that otherwise would be wasted. The 1974 statute established procedures for congressional review by requiring that the president report all impound- ments to Congress. Proposals to rescind appropriated funds, that is, to return them to the Treasury, must be approved by both houses within forty-five days. Proposals to defer spending to the next fiscal year could be disapproved by either house.

The Supreme Court's ruling invalidating the legislative veto affected congressional power to control deferrals. (Since the 1974 legislation called for approval of recisions by both houses, *Chadha* did not invalidate that procedure.) But the only way left for Congress to overturn a deferral is to pass a bill or joint resolution. Because such a measure is subject to presidential veto, the president's deferral power is strengthened. Con- gress's most effective way to circumvent a possible veto is to attach a rider canceling the deferral to an appropriation bill that the president feels compelled to sign in order to keep the involved agencies operating. But riders are a cumbersome device. When Reagan began to defer sizable amounts ($5.4 billion for fiscal 1986) in his second term as a means of reducing spending on programs he opposed, Congress found itself without a viable means of controlling the deferrals.[82]

Presidential Management of the Bureaucracy

In addition to their formal powers, modern presidents have relied on managerial tools in their ongoing efforts to coordinate and direct executive branch operations. Three major tools—staffing, reorganization, and planning—have been employed with mixed results. The limited success of presidential efforts to manage the federal bureaucracy more effectively stems primarily from the political character of the administration of the executive branch. This branch is not a tightly structured hierarchy in which the president is supreme and officials at all levels act in response to directives from above. As noted previously, the president must rely more on persuasion than command to achieve his objectives, and departments and agencies have substantial autonomy. This is not to argue that the public sector is inhospitable to modern management techniques, but to suggest that their use is significantly affected by political forces.[83]

Staffing

Unquestionably, staffing is crucial to presidential management of the bureaucracy. As discussed in Chapter 4, the institutionalized presidency has grown steadily as presidents have turned to staff support as a means of discharging their many roles and of directing the executive branch. The roles of presidential staff in program implementation and of the cabinet in advising the president have varied in recent administrations, but the tendency has been toward reliance on a strong, sizable, and centralized White House staff to protect the political interests of the president, to act as his principal policy advisers, and to direct (as opposed to monitor and coordinate) the implementation of his priorities by the bureaucracy.

Critics of this structure argue that it has undercut the advisory potential of the cabinet, narrowed the president's perspective on policy choices, and inhibited effective and responsive bureaucratic performance. Stephen Hess cautions that reliance on a centralized White House staff has been "self-defeating."[84] Experience under Nixon and Reagan supports this view. Yet, Ford and Carter both tried a decentralized model of White House staffing and abandoned it in favor of hierarchical arrangements.

President Bush adopted the hierarchical model of White House organization at the start of his administration. His chief of staff, former New Hampshire governor John Sununu, maintained tight control over White House operations, at times with a heavy hand. He functioned as the guardian of the president's political interests, serving as Bush's link to conservatives, and he often appeared to have set the administration's course on domestic social policy issues. In these roles, he was the target of considerable congressional and media criticism.[85] As that criticism extended to Sununu's ostentatious use of White House "perks," such as taking a White House car and chauffeur to attend a New York stamp auction, he became a political liability to the president. Bush replaced Sununu in late 1991. Samuel Skinner, the new chief of staff, brought in several new people and ran the office less despotically than his predecessor, but experienced difficulty in asserting and maintaining control.[86]

Since the Reagan administration, the presidency has become increasingly centralized and politicized. Terry Moe defends these developments as an inescapable consequence of the extensive expectations that impinge upon the presidency.[87] A similar conclusion emerged from a 1986 symposium featuring eight former White House chiefs of staff (or their functional equivalents) who served presidents from Eisenhower through Carter. In their view, "the demands for activism and the requirements of self-reliance encourage presidents to look favorably upon the kinds of services provided by a rationalized White House run by a strong chief."[88]

Reorganization

It has been almost an article of faith among political leaders and public administration theorists that executive reorganization can increase presidential power over the bureaucracy.[89] Johnson, Nixon, and especially Carter had strong convictions that the performance of the executive branch could be improved and the bureaucracy brought to heel through changes in administrative structure. Indeed, one of the main themes in Carter's 1976 campaign was the need for reorganization. In his 1979 State of the Union message Carter proclaimed that with congressional help his administration had "begun to reorganize and gain control of the bureaucracy." Yet by most accounts, the results of Carter's reorganization efforts were modest.[90]

Organizational structure and administrative arrangements are significant because they reflect values and priorities and because they affect access to decision makers. The location and status of an administrative unit—as a department, an independent agency, or a component of a department—symbolize the importance of its goals and the interests it serves. Administrative arrangements also can contribute to or frustrate the achievement of accountability to Congress and the public. Reorganizing, however, does not necessarily result in increased efficiency of operation, greater program effectiveness, or enhanced public accountability. This is true because there is no ideal form for a government agency or a consistent set of prescriptions for organizing the executive branch.

According to Herbert Kaufman, one set of standard prescriptions tends to centralize authority and another tends to disperse it. More important, Kaufman points out, the most profound consequences of organizational change are not in the "engineered realm of efficiency, simplicity, size, and cost of government"; rather, they lie in the areas of "political influence, policy emphasis, and communication of governmental intentions."[91] For example, the placement of the Occupational Safety and Health Administration in the Department of Labor rather than in the Department of Health, Education and Welfare led to an initial focus of regulations on mechanical rather than on biological hazards in the work place. Experience has shown that although the rationale for reorganization is couched in the rhetoric of economy and efficiency, the crucial factors in decisions to reorganize are power, policy, and symbolic significance.

In 1939 Congress authorized presidents to propose executive reorganization plans that take effect after sixty days unless disapproved by both houses. When extending that authority in 1949, Congress allowed either house to disapprove such plans. Congress continued to renew the reorganization authority with little change until 1973, when it was allowed to lapse in the conflict with Nixon over his efforts to centralize control of the executive branch. In 1977 Carter requested and received renewal of the authority with provision for veto by either house. Neither Reagan nor Bush displayed any interest in using the reorganization power to enhance presidential control of the executive branch. Congress extended the reorganization power in 1984, but in response to the Supreme Court's invalidation of the legislative veto, it required a joint resolution of approval for a plan to take effect.

Carter's reorganization achievements exceeded those of his immediate predecessors and of his successors but fell far short of the thorough restructuring of the executive branch and reduction in the number of agencies he had promised. Congress passed legislation that established new cabinet departments of Energy and of Education and allowed five reorganization plans to take effect.

In contrast to presidents who appointed special task forces or study commissions to advise them on executive branch organization, Carter established a special unit in the Office of Management and Budget, the President's Reorganization Board, to direct the effort. This approach enabled him to place his own emphasis on reorganization and to incorporate it as an ongoing aspect of his management of the executive branch. The approach lacked, however, the prestige and political support that could be obtained by a blue ribbon panel, and it tended to produce continuous incremental rather than breakthrough change. Also, it was susceptible to influence by individuals and groups with a stake in existing organizational arrangements.

There are both operational and conceptual explanations of the limited success of Carter's reorganization project. Operationally, observers assert, the president and his reorganization staff failed to comprehend the highly political nature of the task.[92] They were unprepared for the jurisdictional conflicts that accompanied congressional consideration of the proposals. Conceptually, the president lacked a well-conceived, comprehensive strategy that could be defended on political grounds. Most critically, Carter regarded reorganization as a "purpose in itself divorced from policy and program development."[93] For Carter the principal goal of reorganization was the fulfillment of campaign commitments. What was lacking was an understanding of reorganization as a means of redistributing influence and redirecting policy. The Carter experience indicates that reorganization has its uses, but they are more in the realm of policy and politics than of management improvement.

Planning

Aaron Wildavsky defines planning as "current action to secure future consequences."[94] Foresight in anticipating problems and developing solutions to them is the essence of effective planning. One of the hallmarks of successful corporate management has been long-range planning, but the federal government has not had a high degree of success in this area. Planning is applicable to all major activities of the government—national security, economic affairs, human resources, and natural resources—and the nation has "paid a heavy price" for the government's failure "to take adequate account of the future."[95] In the early 1950s, for example, experts were warning of the eventual depletion of domestic oil sources, yet only after the oil embargo of 1973–1974 did the government begin to develop an energy policy that looked to the future. When oil again became plentiful in the 1980s, the United States abandoned that policy because it was politically unpopular.

The reasons for the limited success of planning by the federal government lie in the nature of the planning process and its relationship to politics. Planning is a rational process. It operates on the assumption that objectives are known and accepted. The task is to select the best means appropriate to the achievement of the desired ends. Planning decisions are made comprehensively, that is, "as if a single mind were supporting a single set of preferences."[96] Conflict and disagreement do not interfere because the planners know what is desired. However, public planning, like all other planning, takes place in an uncertain world. Planners do not have adequate knowledge of the future, and their predictions often are fallible.

In addition to the intellectual limitations of all planning, public planning is limited by politics. Public planners do not have the power to command acceptance of their choices. Public choices are made on the basis of the preferences of individuals and groups through a process of bargaining and compromise. The agreements reached in the process of political decision making determine the objectives of public planners. There is no correct result because political preferences are continually changing. As a consequence, political planners make accommodations to social forces. They shorten their time frames (usually extending them no further into the future than the next election), thus reducing the need for prediction, and offer their plans as proposals or suggestions rather than as directives. The result is that political factors tend to dominate planning, and planning tends to blend with regular political decision making.

Presidents have engaged in long-range planning with only limited success. As noted, attempts to combine annual budgeting with comprehensive planning through the program planning budgeting system (PPBS) and zero base budgeting (ZBB) have not succeeded. Introduced throughout the government by President Johnson in 1965, PPBS used cost-benefit calculations to choose between alternative programs and formulate long-range objectives. ZBB, a project of President Carter, compared the effects of alternative funding levels on long-term objectives within a single program. Both approaches entailed comprehensive attempts to relate spending decisions to long-range consequences. Each required extensive amounts of information and analyses that were never integrated with budget decisions. Thus, bureau and agency officials did not find it worthwhile to take either process seriously. A fatal defect of both PPBS and ZBB was neglect of the hard political choices involved in the budget process. Nor was Congress supportive of either device.

President Nixon introduced a similar technique that focused on the goals of government, management by objectives (MBO), to strengthen presidential oversight of the executive branch. He directed twenty-one departments and agencies to prepare rank-order lists of their principal objectives. After the Office of Management and Budget reviewed the lists, the president approved objectives for each reporting unit. These presidential objectives then became the standard for monitoring the performance of the units. MBO differed from the planning process of PPBS and ZBB in that it focused first on immediate objectives, then on intermediate objectives that could be achieved in a fiscal year, and finally on long-term goals.[97] MBO was primarily useful within departments and agencies for routine oversight of agreed-on actions. It helped to spot problems and it facilitated communications between the departments and OMB. What it could not do was aid in the choice between objectives. In this respect it was outside the political process and the central concerns of the president.

MBO lapsed into desuetude under Carter. Aside from ZBB, Carter's major planning effort was to require agencies to use a multiyear framework in planning their budget requests. The objective was to integrate planning with the budget cycle. Other than to continue multiyear budgeting, Reagan demonstrated little interest in planning. He appeared to believe that domestic policy planning is socialistic and incompatible with a free-market economy. Bush, although neglecting domestic policy planning, was committed to and actively involved in foreign and defense policy planning. Generally, these areas have been more successful than domestic policy planning, and future presidents will always need to engage in national security planning. National security policy often is a matter of life or death, and the question of national survival makes planning imperative, whereas domestic policy issues are more diffuse and less compelling. Also, national security planning is not nearly as affected by government fragmentation and interest group demands as is domestic policy planning. Still, the large number of domestic programs and the intense pressures to restrict the growth of federal spending suggest that future presidents may of necessity turn to planning as a means of rationalizing and coordinating these programs.

Conclusion

Can the president lead the executive branch? Many of the studies discussed in the chapter raise doubts that he can.[98] It is apparent that although the president has substantial formal powers and managerial resources, he is by no means fully in control of his own branch of government. His capacity to direct its many departments and agencies in the implementation of his policies is limited by bureaucratic complexity and fragmentation, conflict between the presidency and the bureaucracy, external pressure and influence on the bureaucracy, and the extreme difficulty of establishing an effective management system within the government.

The continuing attempts of modern presidents to overcome such obstacles and to strengthen presidential leadership and management of the executive branch have involved three major areas: personnel administration, advice and assistance, and management. The most noteworthy examples include Roosevelt's creation of the Executive Office of the President in 1939, Johnson's enthusiastic endorsement of the program planning budgeting system in 1966, Nixon's centralization of executive authority in an administrative presidency, and Carter's reorganization program and endorsement of the Civil Service Reform Act of 1978. Reagan benefited from all these efforts and devised a strategy to accomplish policy change through administrative action.[99] The Reagan experience indicates that although presidents cannot achieve complete control of the executive branch, they can establish sustained direction of executive branch policy making.

Perhaps the most persistent theme in analyses and studies of the president's executive responsibilities is the need to improve the quality of his subordinates. Conventional wisdom holds that the key to presidential control of the bureaucracy is the appointment of top-level political executives who share his goals. In establishing control over the executive branch, President Reagan used to great advantage careful, centralized control of appointments, making ideological compatibility with his goals the principal criterion. (He rejected the recommendations of most experts that greater reliance should be placed on senior career officials who can provide continuity and institutional memory to an administration.) Reagan's controversial placement of loyal and ideologically sympathetic persons in sensitive positions and the downgrading of senior careerists appear to have served his purposes well.

The second element of Reagan's administrative strategy involved staffing and decision making. By initially selecting a model of White House organization that was compatible with his personal administrative style and his policy objectives—a modified spokes-in-a-wheel model—and using cabinet councils to coordinate policy, Reagan achieved a higher degree of policy consistency than other recent administrations. He also adapted staffing and decision-making arrangements to changes in personnel and in political and other conditions. However, his adoption of the chief-of-staff model in his second term failed to prevent the politically damaging Iranian arms scandal.

The major managerial feature of Reagan's administrative strategy was to use the budget to enforce presidential spending priorities on departments and agencies. In the face of strong pressures to reduce spending, Reagan reversed the traditional pattern of budget preparation from the bottom up, in which agencies attempt to protect their bases, and instituted top-down budgeting with presidential and OMB decisions being determinative.[100] Although the durability of centralized budgeting is questionable, it has enabled the president to gain leverage over Congress and the bureaucracy to control spending.

The final element in Reagan's administrative strategy was the attempt to accomplish policy change administratively wherever possible. This involved establishing procedures for review of regulations by OMB, diminution of the intensity of regulatory enforcement, and reinterpretation of agency functions and relations with clientele in accordance with the administration's ideology.[101]

The relatively successful administrative presidency of Ronald Reagan should not blind one to the substantial difficulties that the president faces in his role as chief executive.[102] Even a federal government that is no longer expanding its activities is still vast and complex. The triangular policy subgovernments, the issue networks, and the fragmented and parochial Congress present major external obstacles to presidential control and direction. Reagan overcame these to some extent by virtue of his temperament, leadership style, and perhaps most important, his limited, well-defined agenda, which tried to curtail rather than expand the role of government. Yet, his detached, "laid back" administrative style was a major factor leading to the most difficult event of his presidency, the Iran-contra scandal. Reagan's approach to his executive responsibilities should indicate to future presidents that leadership of the president's own branch is a difficult task at best and that there is no way to accomplish it that will ensure effectiveness and please everyone involved.

President Bush's experience indicates that a "hands on," engaged administrative style is no guarantee of success. Although the Bush administration was free of major scandals, it encountered difficulty dealing with problems such as controlling federal spending, managing the bailout of failed federal savings and loan institutions, and developing consistent domestic policies. While Bush's problems with the executive branch were less severe than Reagan's, his triumphs were less notable. He did not adopt Reagan's administrative presidency strategy, and he consciously sought to create a positive relationship with the career bureaucracy. He was skeptical of expanding the role of the state, but he clearly cared about its institutions, "including the bureaucracy."[103]

NOTES

1. Richard Rose, "Government Against Subgovernments: A European Perspective on Washington," in *Presidents and Prime Ministers*, ed. Richard Rose and Ezra N. Suleiman (Washington, D.C.: American Enterprise Institute, 1980), 339.

2. *Youngstown Sheet and Tube Co. v. Sawyer*, 343 U.S. 579 (1952).

3. Arthur S. Miller, *Presidential Power in a Nutshell* (St. Paul, Minn.: West Publishing, 1977), 24.

4. James P. Pfiffner challenges this viewpoint and maintains that presidents tend to overestimate the opposition they will get from the bureaucracy. See Pfiffner, "Political Appointees and Career Executives: The Democracy-Bureaucracy Nexus in the Third Century," *Public Administration Review* (January/February 1987): 57–65. Pfiffner cites evidence from a National Academy of Public Administration study that political appointees perceive career executives as responsive and competent. In addition, Francis E. Rourke argues that opposition to presidents is as likely to come from political appointees as from career executives. See Rourke, "Executive Responsiveness to Presidential Policies: The Reagan Presidency," *Congress and the Presidency* (Spring 1990):3–6.

5. Joseph A. Califano, Jr., *A Presidential Nation* (New York: Norton, 1975), 23.

6. Thomas E. Cronin, *The State of the Presidency*, 2d ed. (Boston: Little, Brown, 1980), 224–227.

7. Hugh Heclo, *A Government of Strangers* (Washington, D.C.: Brookings, 1977), 7.

8. Ibid.

9. Arthur Maas, *Muddy Waters: The Army Corps of Engineers and the Nation's Rivers* (Cambridge, Mass.: Harvard University Press, 1951).

10. Richard Rose, *Managing Presidential Objectives* (New York: Free Press, 1976), 160.

11. Francis E. Rourke, *Bureaucracy, Politics, and Public Policy*, 3d ed. (Boston: Little, Brown, 1984), 32.

12. Rose, *Managing Presidential Objectives*, 13–20.

13. Aaron Wildavsky, *The New Politics of the Budgetary Process*, 2d ed. (New York: HarperCollins, 1992), 87–88.

14. David A. Stockman, *The Triumph of Politics: Why the Reagan Revolution Failed* (New York: Harper & Row, 1986).

15. Ibid., 274–275, 313, 345–346.

16. Elizabeth Sanders, "The Presidency and the Bureaucratic State," in *The Presidency and the Political System*, 3d ed., ed. Michael Nelson (Washington, D.C.: CQ Press, 1990), 420.

17. Heclo, *Government of Strangers*.

18. Jeffrey C. Cohen, *The Politics of the U.S. Cabinet: Representation in the Executive Branch, 1789–1984* (Pittsburgh: University of Pittsburgh Press, 1988), chaps. 3, 4.

19. Cronin, *The State of the Presidency*, 282.

20. Cohen, *The Politics of the U.S. Cabinet*, 136–139.

21. G. Calvin Mackenzie, *The Politics of Presidential Appointments* (New York: Free Press, 1981). For a description of the development of the White House Personnel Office, see Dom Bonafede, "The White House Personnel Office from Roosevelt to Reagan," in *The In-and-Outers*, ed. G. C. Mackenzie (Baltimore: The Johns Hopkins University Press, 1987), 30–59.

22. Joseph A. Pika and Norman C. Thomas, "The President as Institution Builder: The Reagan Case," *Governance* (October 1990): 441.

23. James P. Pfiffner, *The Strategic Presidency* (Chicago: Dorsey, 1988), 74–76.

24. Richard P. Nathan, *The Administrative Presidency* (New York: Wiley, 1983), 74–76.

25. Paul C. Light, "When Worlds Collide: The Political-Career Nexus," in *The In-and-Outers*, 158–162.

26. Edie N. Goldenberg, "The Permanent Government in an Era of Retrenchment and Redirection," in *The Reagan Presidency and the Governing of America*, ed. Lester M. Salamon and Michael S. Lund (Washington, D.C.: Urban Institute Press, 1984), 381–404.

27. Chester A. Newland, "A Midterm Appraisal—The Reagan Presidency, Limited Government and Political Administration," *Public Administration Review* (January/February 1983): 15–16.

28. Harold Seidman and Robert Gilmour, *Politics, Position, and Power: From the Positive to the Regulatory State*, 4th ed. (New York: Norton, 1986), 85.

29. *Kendall v. United States*, 37 U.S. (12 Pet.) 524 (1838).

30. *Panama Refining Co. v. Ryan*, 293 U.S. 338 (1934); *Schechter Poultry Co. v. United States*, 295 U.S. 495 (1935).

31. Louis Fisher, *Constitutional Conflicts Between Congress and the President*, 3d. ed. (Lawrence: University Press of Kansas, 1991), 98; Theodore J. Lowi, *The End of Liberalism*, 2d ed. (New York: Norton, 1979), chap. 5.

32. Morris P. Fiorina, *Congress: Keystone of the Washington Establishment*, 2d ed. (New Haven, Conn.: Yale University Press, 1989).

33. Rose, *Managing Presidential Objectives*, 16.

34. Randall B. Ripley and Grace A. Franklin, *Congress, the Bureaucracy, and Public Policy*, 5th ed. (Pacific Grove, Calif.: Brooks/Cole 1991).

35. Rourke, *Bureaucracy, Politics, and Public Policy*, 74.

36. Hugh Heclo, "Issue Networks and the Executive Establishment," in *The New American Political System*, ed. Anthony King (Washington, D.C.: American Enterprise Institute, 1979), 102.

37. Ibid., 116–121.

38. Cronin, *The State of the Presidency*, 293.

39. Cohen, *The Politics of the U.S. Cabinet*, 173–176.

40. Nelson W. Polsby, "Presidential Cabinet-Making Lessons for the Political System," *Political Science Quarterly* (Spring 1978): 16.

41. Pfiffner, *The Strategic Presidency*, 41–42, 65–66; Stephen Hess, *Organizing the Presidency*, 2d ed. (Washington, D.C.: Brookings, 1988), 200.

42. Richard F. Fenno, Jr. *The President's Cabinet* (New York: Vintage Books, 1959), 132.

43. Cohen, *The Politics of the U.S. Cabinet*, 33.

44. Ronald Brownstein and Dick Kirschten, "Cabinet Power," *National Journal*, June 28, 1986, 1582–89.

45. Burt Solomon, "A Cabinet Member Gets the Boot . . . And More Turnover Seems Likely," *National Journal*, Dec. 22, 1990, 3098–99.

46. Cronin, *State of the Presidency*, 270–272.

47. Ibid., 282–285.

48. Cohen, in *The Politics of the U.S. Cabinet*, finds a distinction between the older and newer outer departments based on "the importance of interests in creating the department and on the complexity of its interest group environment," 144. The older departments—Agriculture, Commerce, Labor, and Interior—were created in response to demands from single interests that continue to provide them with some protection from presidential control. The newer departments tend to operate in "more complex interest group environments" that may result in "intradepartmental conflict among advocates of the competing interests," 138, 139.

49. Andrew Rosenthal, "Sununu's Out and Skinner Is In, But White House Troubles Persist," *New York Times*, Feb. 11, 1992, A1, A13. Also see Burt Solomon, "Bush's Renovated Inner Circle Has a Bit of a Reaganesque Look," *National Journal*, Feb. 8, 1992, 346–347.

50. George C. Edwards III, *Implementing Public Policy* (Washington, D.C.: CQ Press, 1980).

51. Fisher, *Constitutional Conflicts*, chaps. 2, 3.

52. *Buckley v. Valeo*, 421 U.S. 1 (1976).

53. In 1973 President Nixon named Howard J. Phillips acting director of the Office of Economic Opportunity (OEO), an agency that Nixon planned to dismantle. Phillips began to phase out its programs and withhold funds from it. Sen. Harrison A. Williams, D-N.J., took legal action to force Nixon either to submit Phillips's name to the Senate for confirmation or to stop dismantling the OEO. A U.S. court of appeals ruled that Phillips was illegally holding office and enjoined him from further actions. See James P. Pfiffner, *The President, the Budget and Congress: Impoundment and the 1974 Budget Act* (Boulder, Colo.: Westview, 1974), 116–117.

54. Perhaps the most notable examples are the Senate's rejection of former senator John Tower, R-Texas, to be secretary of defense in 1989 and of Admiral Lewis Strauss to be secretary of commerce in 1959, and its refusal to confirm the appointment of Leland Olds to serve a third five-year term as chairman of the Federal Power Commission in 1949. Tower had antagonized several of his former colleagues during his service in the chamber and was objectionable to many Democratic senators because of his hawkish views. Strauss had incurred the enmity of several senators during his prior service as chairman of the Atomic Energy Commission. Olds's rejection symbolized senatorial opposition to the oil and natural gas policies of the Truman administration.

55. Christopher J. Deering, "Damned If You Do and Damned If You Don't: The Senate's Role in the Appointment Process," in *The In-and-Outers*, 119.

56. *Myers v. United States*, 272 U.S. 52 (1926).

57. *Humphrey's Executor v. United States*, 295 U.S. 602 (1935).

58. Fisher, *Constitutional Conflicts*, 79.

59. Solomon, "A Cabinet Member Gets the Boot," 3098.

60. *J. W. Hampton and Co. v. United States*, 276 U.S. 394 (1928).

61. *Amalgamated Meat Cutters v. Connally*, 337 F. Supp. 737 (1971).

62. George C. Eads and Michael Fix, *Relief or Reform: Reagan's Regulatory Dilemma* (Washington, D.C.: Urban Institute Press, 1984).

63. *Hirabayashi v. United States*, 320 U.S. 581 (1943); *Korematsu v. United States*, 323 U.S. 214 (1944).

64. *Youngstown Sheet and Tube Co. v. Sawyer*, 343 U.S. 579 (1952).

65. *Immigration and Naturalization Service v. Chadha*, 462 U.S. 919 (1983).

66. Edward S. Corwin, *The President: Office and Powers*, 4th ed. (New York: New York University Press, 1957), 130.

67. Lee H. Watson, "Congress Steps Out: A Look at Congressional Control of the Executive," *California Law Review* (1975): 990.

68. Joseph Cooper, "Postscript on the Congressional Veto," *Political Science Quarterly* (Fall 1983): 427–430; Barbara Hinkson Craig, *The Legislative Veto: Congressional Control of Regulation* (Boulder, Colo.: Westview, 1983), 139–150; Fisher, *Constitutional Conflicts*, 152.

69. Fisher, *Constitutional Conflicts*, 150–152.

70. Louis Fisher, "Judicial Misjudgments about the Lawmaking Process: The Legislative Veto Case," *Public Administration Review* (November/December 1985): 709–710.

71. John Hart, *The Presidential Branch* (New York: Pergamon, 1987), 40.

72. Richard M. Pious, *The American Presidency* (New York: Basic Books, 1979), 256–257.

73. Allen Schick, "The Road to PPB: The States of Budget Reform," *Public Administration Review* (December 1966): 243–258.

74. Wildavsky, *The New Politics of the Budgetary Process*, 436–440.

75. Allen Schick, "Macro-Budgetary Adaptations to Fiscal Stress in Industrialized Democracies," *Public Administration Review* (March/April 1986): 129.

76. Ibid., 130.

77. Louis Fisher, *Presidential Spending Power* (Princeton, N.J.: Princeton University Press, 1979), chap. 4.

78. Ibid., 148.

79. Vivian Vale, "The Obligation to Spend: Presidential Impoundment of Congressional Appropriations," *Political Studies* (1977): 508–532.

80. Fisher, *Constitutional Conflicts*, 196.

81. Pfiffner, *President, Budget, and Congress*, 40–44.

82. Jonathan Rauch, "Power of the Purse," *National Journal*, May 24, 1986, 1261.

83. Peri Arnold concludes his authoritative study of "the managerial presidency" by observing that "no modern president has fully managed the executive branch." According to Arnold, the "dispersion of power in the executive branch" and congressional authority over administration limit the managerial effectiveness of presidents. He further argues that the "managerial conception of the presidency is untenable" because it "places impossible obligations on presidents" and creates unrealistic "public expectations of presidential performance." Peri E. Arnold, *Making the Managerial Presidency: Comprehensive Reorganization Planning 1905–1980* (Princeton, N.J.: Princeton University Press, 1986), 361–362.

84. Hess, *Organizing the Presidency*, 2d ed., 230–231.

85. Jack W. Germond and Jules Witcover, "Bush Left with Little Room for Error," *National Journal*, Dec. 22, 1990, 3104.

86. Rosenthal, "Sununu's Out and Skinner Is In."

87. Terry M. Moe, "The Politicized Presidency," in *The New Direction in American Politics*, ed. John E. Chubb and Paul E. Peterson (Washington, D.C.: Brookings, 1985), 235–271.

88. Samuel Kernell, "The Creed and Reality of Modern White House Management," in *Chief of Staff: Twenty-Five Years of Managing the Presidency*, ed. Samuel Kernell and Samuel L. Popkin (Berkeley: University of California Press, 1986), 228.

89. Arnold, *Making the Managerial Presidency*.

90. John R. Dempsey, "Carter Reorganization: A Midterm Appraisal," *Public Administration Review* (January/February 1979): 74–78; Seidman and Gilmour, *Politics, Position, and Power*, 48; Arnold, *Making the Managerial Presidency*, chap. 10.

91. Herbert Kaufman, "Reflections on Administrative Reorganization," in *Setting National Priorities: The 1978 Budget*, ed. Joseph A. Pechman (Washington, D.C.: Brookings, 1977), 403.

92. Dempsey, "Carter Reorganization," 75.

93. Seidman and Gilmour, *Politics, Position, and Power*, 116.

94. Aaron Wildavsky, *Speaking Truth to Power* (Boston: Little, Brown, 1979), 120.

95. Fred V. Malek, *Washington's Hidden Tragedy* (New York: Free Press, 1978), 129.

96. Wildavsky, *Speaking Truth to Power*, 129.

97. Rose, *Managing Presidential Objectives*, chap. 6.

98. See, for example, Arnold, *Making the Managerial Presidency*; Colin Campbell, *Managing the Presidency* (Pittsburgh: University of Pittsburgh Press, 1986); Hess, *Staffing the Presidency*; and Rose, *Managing Presidential Objectives*. Also see Walter Williams, *Mismanaging America: The Rise of the Anti-Analytic Presidency* (Lawrence: University Press of Kansas, 1990).

99. Richard P. Nathan, *The Administrative Presidency* (New York: Wiley, 1983).

100. Allen Schick, "The Budget as an Instrument of Presidential Policy," in *The Reagan Presidency and the Governing of America*, 113.

101. Lester M. Salamon and Alan J. Abramson, "Governance: The Politics of Retrenchment," in *The Reagan Record*, ed. John L. Palmer and Isabell V. Sawhill (Cambridge, Mass.: Ballinger, 1984), 97; Pika and Thomas, "The President as Institution Builder," 444–447.

102. For an analysis of the limitations of Reagan's administrative strategy with respect to the Environmental Protection Agency and the Nuclear Regulatory Agency, see Richard W. Waterman, *Presidential Influence and the Administrative State* (Knoxville: University of Tennessee Press, 1989), chaps. 5, 6.

103. Joel D. Aberbach, "The President and the Executive Branch," in *The Bush Presidency: First Appraisals*, Colin Campbell, S. J., and Bert A. Rockman, eds. (Chatham, N.J.: Chatham House, 1991), 243.

READINGS

Arnold, Peri E. *Making the Managerial Presidency*. Princeton, N.J.: Princeton University Press, 1986.

Berman, Larry. *The Office of Management and Budget and the Presidency, 1921–1979*. Princeton, N.J.: Princeton University Press, 1979.

Campbell, Colin. *Managing the Presidency: Carter, Reagan, and the Search for Executive Harmony*. Pittsburgh: University of Pittsburgh Press, 1986.

Cohen, Jeffrey E. *The Politics of the U.S. Cabinet: Representation in the Executive Branch, 1789–1984*. Pittsburgh: University of Pittsburgh Press, 1988.

Cronin, Thomas E. *The State of the Presidency*. 2d ed. Boston: Little, Brown, 1980.

Fisher, Louis. *Constitutional Conflicts Between Congress and the President*, 3d ed., rev. Lawrence: University Press of Kansas, 1991.

Hart, John. *The Presidential Branch*. New York: Pergamon, 1987.

Heclo, Hugh. *A Government of Strangers*. Washington, D.C.: Brookings, 1977.

Hess, Stephen. *Organizing the Presidency*. 2d ed. Washington, D.C.: Brookings, 1988.

Kernell, Samuel, and Samuel L. Popkin, eds. *Chief of Staff: Twenty-Five Years of Managing the Presidency*. Berkeley: University of California Press, 1986.

Mackenzie, G. Calvin. *The Politics of Presidential Appointments*. New York: Free Press, 1981.

Mackenzie, G. Calvin, ed. *The In–and–Outers*. Baltimore: Johns Hopkins University Press, 1987.

Nathan, Richard P. *The Administrative Presidency*. New York: Wiley, 1983.

Pfiffner, James P. *The Strategic Presidency*. Chicago: Dorsey, 1988.

Redford, Emmette S., and Richard T. McCulley. *White House Operations: The Johnson Presidency*. Austin: University of Texas Press, 1986.

Rourke, Francis E. *Bureaucracy, Politics, and Public Policy*. 3d ed. Boston: Little, Brown, 1984.

Salamon, Lester M., and Michael S. Lund, eds. *The Reagan Presidency and the Governing of America*. Washington, D.C.: Urban Institute Press, 1984.

Seidman, Harold, and Robert S. Gilmour. *Politics, Position, and Power: From the Positive to the Regulatory State*. New York: Oxford University Press, 1986.

Waterman, Richard W. *Presidential Influence and the Administrative State*. Knoxville: University of Tennessee Press, 1989.

President Truman's seizure of steel mills during the Korean War sparked a firestorm of public protest. The Supreme Court eventually ruled the action illegal.

IN OCTOBER 1991 HIGH DRA-ma gripped the nation as the Senate Judiciary Committee considered President George Bush's nomination of Clarence Thomas of Georgia to be an associate justice of the United States Supreme Court. If confirmed, the conservative Thomas would become the second African American to serve on the Court. He would replace the liberal Thurgood Marshall, the first African American justice.

During the hearings before the Judiciary Committee in September, Democratic senators had questioned Thomas about his views regarding a wide range of sensitive issues such as abortion and affirmative action. They also tried to ascertain his judicial philosophy, that is, how he believed the Supreme Court should interpret the Constitution and exercise its power of judicial review. Thomas resisted efforts to draw him out, saying that it would be inap-

281

propriate for him to respond as it would damage his ability to be impartial if such matters should come before the Court.[1] His critics questioned his qualifications for serving on the Court, pointing out that he had been a federal appeals court judge for only eighteen months, he had no other judicial experience, nor had he distinguished himself as a legal scholar. In addition, the hearings included appearances by representatives of interest groups supporting and opposing the nomination.

On September 27 the Judiciary Committee divided, 7–7, on recommending the nomination to the full Senate, then voted 13–1 to send it to the floor without a recommendation.[2] In spite of the protracted and stormy hearings, Thomas's confirmation appeared likely as thirteen Democratic senators announced their support. However, on October 5, two days before the Senate was scheduled to vote, news broke that Professor Anita Hill of the University of Oklahoma Law School had accused Thomas of sexually harassing her when she worked for him at the Equal Employment Opportunity Commission. It is thought that a Judiciary Committee staff person leaked the information, which was known to the committee for a month, to the press. When it became clear that the committee intended for the full Senate to vote on the confirmation without knowledge of the allegation, a firestorm of protest erupted. Women members of Congress, leaders of women's organizations, and women from across the nation complained that the all-male committee failed to understand the seriousness of the charge.

In response to angry bipartisan protests, the Senate's leaders postponed the vote and instructed the committee to reopen the hearings so that the charge could be investigated. The reopened hearings "marked one of the wildest spectacles in modern congressional history."[3] Televised nationwide during prime viewing hours over a weekend, the hearings produced poised and detailed testimony by Hill, who graphically described the alleged harassment, and Thomas's angry, categorical denial in which he accused the committee of a "high-tech lynching."[4] Their effect on the outcome was limited. Only three senators who had previously announced their position changed it. On October 19 the Senate confirmed Thomas, 52–48, with eleven Democrats supporting him and two Republicans opposing. It was the closest margin of approval for a Supreme Court justice in U.S. history.

The relationship between the president and the judiciary is highly visible when the Senate considers the confirmation of a Supreme Court justice. It is also apparent when the Court has had before it challenges to the constitutionality of a president's program, such as Franklin Roosevelt's New Deal, or actions, such as Harry Truman's seizure of the steel industry during the Korean War.

The Founders clearly expected the executive and legislative branches to be in perennial conflict with each other, and they deliberately constructed the U.S. constitutional system to accomplish that result. As James Madison explained in *Federalist* 51, "Ambition must be made to counteract ambition."[5] Their intentions toward the relationship between the executive and judicial arms of the government were, however, quite different. Neither John Locke nor Montesquieu, the two political philosophers from whom the Founders drew their ideas on the separation of powers, provided for a separate judicial branch of government. Rather, both considered the power to decide disputes and to enforce the law to be a function of the executive arm of the government. Although the Founders created a distinct judicial branch, they considered its principal function to be similar to that of the executive: both would expound and enforce the law once the legislature enacted it. In *Federalist* 78 Alexander Hamilton wrote that the major differences between judicial and executive powers were how they would be exercised: the former would depend on "judgment," the latter on "force" or "will."[6]

The Founders also based their expectations about the affinity of the executive and judicial branches on considerations other than the similarity of functions they were to perform. As Robert Scigliano points out, they deliberately increased the powers of both branches at the expense of Congress because they feared the legislature would dominate the political system as it had done under the Articles of Confederation.[7] Therefore, they granted broad authority to both the executive and the judiciary. Article II of the Constitution states, "The executive Power shall be vested in a President of the United States"; Article III says, "The judicial power of the United States shall be vested in one supreme Court, and in such inferior Courts as the Congress may from time to time ordain and establish." In contrast, Article I begins, "All legislative powers *herein granted* shall be vested in a Congress of the United States" (italics added). As a result, to undertake a particular activity, the first two branches need only claim that it is executive or judicial in nature and that it is not forbidden by the Constitution; however, to justify its passing a law, Congress must point to a specific power listed in Article I, Section 8, or show that such a law is, broadly speaking, "necessary and proper" for executing one or more of those specific powers.

There is some indication that the Founders wanted and expected the executive and judicial branches to represent social and economic interests different from those represented by members of the House. Unlike House members, who were elected directly by the people, the president was selected by the electoral college, and he, in turn, nominated the members of the Supreme Court, who were then to be approved by the Senate. Note that the Founders gave the House of Representatives no role in choosing judges. In addition, the longer term of the president (four years with the possibility of renewal) and of Supreme Court members (life) would make them less subject to public pressures than were members of the House of Representatives with their two-year terms. And because only a few would be chosen for the presidency and the Supreme Court, those positions would be far more prestigious than seats in the lower house of Congress.

These considerations lead Scigliano to conclude that the Founders intended that the presidency and the Supreme Court "act, for certain purposes, as an informal and limited alliance against Congress and that they have in fact done so."[8] At the same time, he suggests that the Founders left open another basic question that created a major source of potential conflict between the president and the Supreme Court: Who has the final power to interpret the Constitution? If, as Hamilton asserted in *Federalist* 78, the Supreme Court does, then it is in a position to nullify actions of the president that the judges consider to be unconstitutional. If each branch, however, is empowered to interpret the Constitution as far as its own duties are concerned—a position taken by Thomas Jefferson—then the president is the judge of the constitutionality of executive actions and will not be subject to judicial control in that respect.

This chapter examines the basic relationship between the president and the federal courts. The first section analyzes the most important influence the president exerts over these courts: the power, with the consent of the Senate, to appoint their members. The chapter next explores other means by which the chief executive affects the business of the courts, and, finally, it examines the reverse situation: how the federal courts, and the Supreme Court in particular, influence the actions of the president.

Presidential Appointment of Federal Judges

Perhaps the greatest impact the president can have on the courts is the selection of federal judges who share his policy goals. Certainly this impact has been apparent since 1981, as the conservatives appointed by Presidents Reagan and Bush have come to dominate all levels of the federal judiciary. Among modern presidents, only Franklin Roosevelt so fully realized this potential to control the courts.

Following its constitutional mandate, Congress has ordained and established two types of "inferior" federal courts: the district courts, the trial bodies in which federal cases are first heard, and the U.S. courts of appeals. The appeals courts are sometimes referred to as "circuit courts," which serve as major appellate tribunals, reviewing principally the civil and criminal decisions in cases initially heard in federal district courts, as well as the orders and decisions of federal administrative units, particularly the independent regulatory agencies.[9] As for the Supreme Court, the Constitution mentions only the method of appointment of its judges: they are to be chosen by the president with the advice and consent of the Senate. Congress has provided, however, for the same process to be used for staffing the lower federal courts, so the president and the Senate are partners in the appointment process for all federal judges.

Although the formal process for selecting all federal judges is the same—presidential nomination and ultimate appointment with the consent of the Senate—the president's role in federal judicial appointments varies considerably, depending upon the court involved. The following discussion analyzes first the appointments to the two lower federal courts and then the selection of justices to the nation's highest tribunal, the Supreme Court.

Selection of Lower Court Judges

Although the president makes the formal nomination of judges to the lower federal courts, in fact the responsibility usually is delegated to others. Harold Chase explains, "If a president takes seriously his legal responsibilities for nominating and appointing federal judges, the search for and screening of candidates requires more time than he can personally give to it."[10] The president typically assigns this task to the attorney general, who, in turn, often delegates it to the deputy attorney general with advice on how to proceed. In the Bush administration, however,

Attorney General Richard Thornburgh "decided that judicial selection should remain centered in his office."[11]

The executive branch recruitment and screening process for judicial candidates entails several considerations. Justice Department officials frequently turn to members of their department who may have special knowledge about lawyers in their own states. They also have the Federal Bureau of Investigation check into the professional standing and integrity of prospective candidates. As discussed later in this section, sitting federal judges often are asked for their opinion about candidates, and members of the Standing Committee on Federal Judiciary of the American Bar Association (ABA) usually are requested to investigate the qualifications of prospective nominees and to make recommendations regarding them.

Just as the attorney general plays a major role in choosing lower federal judges, so do senators of the president's party from the state in which the nominee is to serve (all states have at least one federal district court), or, for courts of appeals judges, the state of his or her residence. Joseph Harris notes that since the early days of George Washington's administration, an informal rule of "senatorial courtesy" has applied whereby members of the Senate generally refuse to confirm people to federal positions who do not have the support of the senator or senators of the president's party from the state in which the vacancy exists.[12] If there are no senators from the president's party in the state in which the vacancy occurs, the president usually consults the opposition senators.[13] This informal practice places the senators from the state in which a judge is to serve in a powerful position to influence judicial appointments.

Therefore, the attorney general and a particular senator determine who will be chosen. If these individuals differ, a stalemate may occur. The senator usually can block the president's nominee by invoking senatorial courtesy. The attorney general can advise the president not to fill the vacancy, thereby putting pressure on the senator to do something about the situation or face the problem of a backlog of federal cases in his or her home state. Or the president can wait until the end of the session and make a recess appointment, which does not require immediate Senate confirmation. Although Senate approval for the temporarily appointed judge is required in the next session of Congress, the president may benefit from the fact that in the meantime this person has been a sitting judge, and a good performance may deter the Senate from refusing the confirmation.

What typically occurs with lower federal court appointments is that one party is given the major role in initially recruiting candidates for the bench, but the other retains a veto power over those it finds unacceptable. On federal district court appointments, the attorney general (and thus the president) usually defers to the wishes of the senator from the state concerned. Few chief executives are willing to risk the loss of a senator's political support over a district court judgeship, since the work of such a tribunal is seldom crucial to the executive's political goals or programs.

The president is generally more interested and influential in the selection of judges to the U.S. courts of appeals, and there are two reasons why. First, the courts of appeals handle matters more important to the chief executive. Their review of actions of the independent regulatory commissions, for example, can affect his overall economic program. Second, courts of appeals judgeships are less numerous and more prestigious and therefore invite the interest of his major political supporters. Furthermore, senators are in a weaker bargaining position on appointments to the courts of appeals. Because these courts encompass several states, the Senate does not accord any senator the privilege to name an appointee. By political custom these judgeships are apportioned among the various states involved, but the president and his advisers determine how and in what sequence to do so. As a result, the president's advisers take the initiative in recruiting judges to the U.S. courts of appeals, and the senator from the state in which a candidate resides retains the right to veto the nomination, providing the lawmaker can persuade the rest of the Senate that the person truly is objectionable.

Although the attorney general and individual senators are chiefly responsible for appointments to the lower federal courts, many other people and groups are involved in the selection process. Ideally, the "post should seek the person," but in reality candidates who aspire to a federal judgeship must take actions to advance their own cause. As Joel Grossman states, "The candidate who does not make at least a minimum effort in his own behalf is likely to remain a private citizen."[14] Candidates must make it clear to those involved in the appointment process that they desire the position, either by actively seeking it or by having others campaign on their behalf. Candidates help their cause if they have been active in past political campaigns, especially those of the president or of the appropriate senator.

Party leaders also influence appointments to the lower federal courts.

Harold Chase reports that a Justice Department official in a Democratic administration was emphatic that in the making of judicial appointments to the district courts in Illinois the late mayor Richard J. Daley of Chicago "had to have a seat at the conference table."[15] Sitting federal judges can become involved in federal judicial appointments if they are asked their opinion about a prospective candidate by the attorney general or the ABA committee. At times, however, judges take the initiative either to advance a candidate of their own or to try to prevent the appointment of someone they feel will not make a good judge. Most often the judges involved are those who sit on a federal district court or court of appeals. Supreme Court justices also may interpose themselves into the process for choosing lower federal court judges. Most notorious in that respect was William Howard Taft, who took a keen interest in appointments to those courts while he served as chief justice.[16]

Another participant in the selection process for judges of lower federal courts is the Standing Committee on Federal Judiciary of the ABA. First established in 1946 with the goal of promoting professionally qualified people for the federal bench, the group had little success in influencing judicial appointments during the Truman administration. When Dwight D. Eisenhower came into office in 1953, however, his administration agreed to an arrangement whereby the Justice Department would ask the committee to evaluate nominees to the federal bench in return for the committee's agreement to stop recommending its own candidates for the federal courts. The committee was most influential during the last two years of the Eisenhower administration, when no one was nominated for a federal judgeship without committee approval. Grossman states, "It was during this period that the committee's right to be consulted on each prospective nomination grew into a virtual veto power."[17]

The committee has continued to be important in federal judicial selection, but it has never regained the virtual veto power it had from 1958 to 1961. Neither the administration of John F. Kennedy nor of Lyndon B. Johnson was as deferential to the committee as Eisenhower's had been. Initially, it was thought that Richard Nixon's Justice Department would restore the committee's veto power over nominations to the federal courts, but, as discussed in the following section, serious disagreements between the committee and the Nixon administration over the qualifications of some of his Supreme Court nominees damaged the relationship. Alan Neff's assessment of the influence of the committee at the end of the

Carter administration was that it was "somewhere below the level it reached during the later Eisenhower years and above that of the Nixon years."[18] The Reagan administration did not consult the ABA committee in the prenomination stage of judicial selection. However, the Bush administration, beginning in June 1989, provided it with the names of prospective nominees for rating purposes.[19] President Carter introduced changes in the selection of lower federal court judges that placed greater emphasis on professional competence and less on party loyalty. The effect of the changes was that individual senators became less influential while the president's role increased. However, most of the changes, including a new entity, the Circuit Judge Nominating Commission, did not survive his administration.

Major changes in the nomination of lower federal court judges also occurred during the Reagan administration. Sheldon Goldman notes that in Reagan's first term, responsibility in the Justice Department for suggesting prospective judges included not only the attorney general and deputy attorney general but also the assistant attorney general for legal policy and the special counsel for judicial selection.[20] An Office of Legal Policy was established in the Justice Department to screen candidates. Serious contenders came to Washington—at their own expense—for interviews by OLP staff. The President's Committee on Federal Judicial Selection, which was chaired by the counsel to the president and included the attorney general and the White House chief of staff, then evaluated the surviving candidates, paying close attention to ideology, judicial philosophy, and political factors. The committee also proposed candidates. The Reagan selection process subordinated traditional patronage and professional considerations to presidential policy priorities. Goldman concludes that when Edwin Meese III eventually became attorney general, "the cooptation of judicial selection by the Reagan White House" was "completed."[21]

As Goldman indicates, the Reagan administration introduced other changes in the nomination of lower federal court judges. His was the first Republican administration in thirty years in which the ABA's Standing Committee on Federal Judiciary was not actively used and consulted before judges were nominated. Reagan also abolished Carter's selection commission for appellate judges, and, as Goldman states, in the process abandoned "the most potentially effective mechanism for expanding the net of possible candidates to include women and racial minorities."[22] Lawrence Baum also suggests that the Carter administration sought to appoint liberals to the lower courts, but in the Reagan administration conservatism on issues such as abortion was an important criterion.[23]

According to David O'Brien, Reagan so extensively transformed the process of judicial selection "that future administrations, whether Democratic or Republican, are sure to follow Reagan's lead in vigorously pursuing their legal policy goals when picking judges."[24] The Bush administration appears to have validated this prediction. It continued the "systematic screening process emphasizing judicial philosophy and including extensive personal interview of the major candidates" and the President's Committee on Federal Judicial Selection.[25] However, it abolished the Office of Legal Policy, which played the central role in the Justice Department's judicial selection activities.

Despite the differences between Carter and Reagan/Bush in their appointments of lower federal court judges, all three presidents shared one great advantage: the opportunity to make a large number of appointments to the lower courts. In his four years in office, Carter named 258 judges. During his two terms, Reagan appointed 347 district and appeals court judges, constituting 47 percent of all sitting federal judges.[26] In addition, he appointed three associate justices of the Supreme Court, Sandra Day O'Connor, Antonin Scalia, and Anthony Kennedy, and raised Associate Justice William Rehnquist to chief justice. By the end of his third year in office, Bush had appointed 95 district court and 39 appeals court judges and two Supreme Court justices—David Souter and Clarence Thomas— or 17 percent of sitting federal judges on courts of general jurisdiction.[27] Goldman estimates that at the end of four years Bush will have filled more than 200 district and appeals court judgeships. Those judges, added to approximately 325 Reagan appointees still serving, constitute about two-thirds of the federal judiciary. They represent enormous potential for long-term impact on judicial policy making.

Characteristics of Lower Court Judges

All presidents tend to appoint to the lower federal courts people who have certain qualities in common. One is membership in the legal profession. Although this is not a legal requirement, it is an informal qualification: only lawyers have been appointed to federal judgeships. Moreover, in keeping with the contemporary preparation of lawyers, virtually every judge appointed to the federal bench since the end of World War II has been a graduate of a law school; in the past the typical method of studying law was to serve an apprenticeship in a law office. A second characteristic is that most have been active in political party affairs, which is how they get the attention of senators and attorneys general, and have held public office, most often an office associated with the courts, such as city, county, or state prosecutor, district attorney, or U.S. attorney. Another common trait is that many have held judicial positions: federal district judges quite often have been state judges, and those who sit on the courts of appeals frequently come to that bench from a federal district court.

The president, however, does make a difference in the types of lawyers who are appointed to the lower federal courts. Table 7-1, based upon information provided by Goldman, compares the individuals appointed to the federal district courts by Bush during his first two years in office with those chosen by Reagan, Carter, Ford, Nixon, and Johnson. The differences among Carter's appointees on the one hand and Reagan's and Bush's on the other, in addition to party affiliation, are particularly pronounced in their educational and racial backgrounds. Reagan's and Bush's appointees were more likely to have attended private rather than public undergraduate and law schools than were Carter's; about 14 percent of Carter's appointees were African Americans, whereas only 2 percent of Reagan's and Bush's were. Thus, as Goldman suggests, differences in the backgrounds of federal district judges mirror to some degree disparities in typical Republican and Democratic voters.[28]

In several respects, however, the Bush, Reagan, and Carter appointees had more in common with each other than they did with appointees of the three previous presidents, Democrat Johnson and Republicans Nixon and Ford. Judges appointed by Bush, Reagan, and Carter were more likely to have come from another judicial position to a federal district judgeship and to have had more judicial than prosecutory experience than were the Johnson, Nixon, and Ford appointees. Goldman suggests that a person's judicial position provides a record for determining his or her professional quality and judicial philosophy, matters in which the three most recent presidents have appeared to be particularly interested. Appointees of these presidents were more likely to have been active in their respective parties than were their predecessors. Bush, Reagan, and Carter also appointed more women than did their predecessors.

Table 7-2, also based on information provided by Goldman, shows similar comparisons of the appointees to the federal courts of appeals. The differences among the Bush, Reagan, and Carter judges are most pro-

Table 7-1 Characteristics of Appointees to District Courts of Presidents Bush,[a] Reagan, Carter, Ford, Nixon, and Johnson (Percent)

Characteristic	Appointees of					
	Bush	Reagan	Carter	Ford	Nixon	Johnson
Occupation						
Politics/govt	10.4	12.8	4.4	21.2	10.6	21.3
Judiciary	47.9	37.2	44.6	34.6	28.5	31.1
Large law firm	16.6	17.7	14.0	9.7	11.3	2.4
Moderate size firm	18.7	19.3	19.8	25.0	27.9	18.9
Solo or small law firm	4.2	10.4	13.9	9.6	19.0	23.0
Professor of Law	2.1	2.1	3.0	—	2.8	3.3
Other	—	0.7	0.5	—	—	—
Undergraduate education						
Public-supported	41.7	35.5	57.4	48.1	41.3	38.5
Private (not Ivy League)	50.0	50.3	32.7	34.6	38.5	31.1
Ivy League	8.3	14.1	9.9	17.3	19.6	16.4
None indicated	—	—	—	—	0.6	13.9
Law school education						
Public-supported	47.9	42.4	50.5	44.2	41.9	40.0
Private (not Ivy League)	39.6	45.5	32.2	38.5	36.9	36.9
Ivy League	12.5	12.1	17.3	17.3	21.2	21.3
Experience						
Judicial	50.0	46.6	54.5	42.3	35.2	34.4
Prosecutory	37.5	44.1	38.6	50.0	41.9	45.9
Neither one	27.1	28.3	28.2	30.8	36.3	33.6
Party						
Democratic	4.2	4.8	92.6	21.2	7.3	94.3
Republican	93.8	93.1	4.4	78.6	92.7	5.7
Independent	2.1	2.1	2.9	—	—	—
Past party activism	62.5	58.6	60.9	50.0	48.6	49.2
Religious origin or affiliation						
Protestant	64.6	60.3	60.4	73.1	73.2	58.2
Catholic	22.9	30.0	27.7	17.3	18.4	31.1
Jewish	12.5	9.3	11.9	9.6	8.4	10.7
Ethnicity or race						
White	95.8	92.4	78.7	88.5	95.5	93.4
Black	2.1	2.1	13.9	5.8	3.4	4.1
Hispanic	2.1	4.8	6.9	1.9	1.1	2.5
Asian	—	0.7	0.5	3.9	—	—
Sex						
Male	89.6	91.7	85.6	98.1	99.4	98.4
Female	10.4	8.3	14.4	1.9	0.6	1.6
ABA Ratings						
EWQ/WQ	58.3	54.1	50.9	46.1	45.3	48.4
Qualified	41.7	45.9	47.5	53.8	54.8	49.2

Table 7-1 (*Continued*)

Characteristic	Appointees of					
	Bush	Reagan	Carter	Ford	Nixon	Johnson
Not qualified	—	—	1.5	—	—	2.5
Total number of appointees	48	290	202	52	179	122
Average age at nomination	49.6	48.7	49.7	49.2	49.1	51.4

aBush appointees are for 1989–1990.
Source: Sheldon Goldman, "The Bush Imprint on the Judiciary: Carrying on a Tradition," *Judicature* (April/May 1991): 298–299.

nounced in their party and racial backgrounds. Bush and Reagan appointed only Republicans and a few independents to the appeals courts, whereas Carter chose primarily Democrats but some Republicans and independents as well. Bush and Reagan each named only one African American to the courts of appeals compared with Carter's appointment of nine African American judges. Moreover, unlike the situation for district judges, women fared far less well with Reagan than they did with Carter and Bush: Carter appointed nearly four times and Bush twice the percentage of women as Reagan. The financial backgrounds of the Bush and Reagan appointees to the courts of appeals were substantial: almost 39 percent of Bush's appointees and 18 percent of Reagan's were millionaires compared with 10 percent of Carter's.[29] A sizable majority of the Bush, Reagan, and Carter appeals court appointees went to private undergraduate institutions and law schools. Table 7-2 also reveals that Bush and Reagan named a greater percentage of Catholics to the federal appeals bench than did Carter. They may have been influenced by the fact that Catholic doctrine on abortion paralleled their own views on the subject. Finally, a substantially greater percentage of the appointees of the three most recent presidents lacked either judicial or prosecutory experience than did their predecessors, but they had more extensive records of party activism.

Effects of Lower Court Appointments

The appointment process and background characteristics of lower federal court judges reflect important political considerations. Presidents are in a position to reward people who have been active in their political campaigns or in those of important senators. Federal judgeships also give

Table 7-2 Characteristics of Appointees to Courts of Appeal of Presidents Bush,[a] Reagan, Carter, Ford, Nixon, and Johnson (Percent)

Characteristic	Appointees of					
	Bush	Reagan	Carter	Ford	Nixon	Johnson
Occupation						
Politics/govt	11.1	6.4	5.4	8.3	4.4	10.0
Judiciary	55.6	55.1	46.4	75.0	53.3	57.5
Large law firm	16.7	12.9	10.8	8.3	4.4	5.0
Moderate size firm	16.7	10.3	16.1	8.3	22.2	17.5
Solo or small law firm	—	1.3	5.4	—	6.7	7.5
Professor of Law	—	12.8	14.3	—	2.2	2.5
Other	—	1.3	1.8	—	6.7	—
Undergraduate education						
Public-supported	33.3	24.4	30.4	50.0	40.0	32.5
Private (not Ivy League)	50.0	51.3	50.0	41.7	35.6	40.0
Ivy League	16.7	24.4	19.6	8.3	20.0	17.5
None indicated	—	—	—	—	4.4	10.0
Law school education						
Public-supported	22.2	39.7	39.3	50.0	37.8	40.0
Private (not Ivy League)	44.4	37.2	19.6	25.0	26.7	32.5
Ivy League	33.3	23.1	41.1	25.0	35.6	27.5
Experience						
Judicial	55.6	60.3	53.6	75.0	57.8	65.0
Prosecutory	33.3	28.2	32.1	25.0	46.7	47.5
Neither one	38.9	34.6	37.5	25.0	17.8	20.0
Party						
Democratic	—	—	82.1	8.3	6.7	95.0
Republican	94.4	97.4	7.1	91.7	93.3	5.0
Independent	5.6	1.3	10.7	—	—	—
Other	—	1.3	—	—	—	—
Past party activism	66.7	69.2	73.2	58.3	60.0	57.5
Religious origin or affiliation						
Protestant	55.6	55.1	60.7	58.3	75.6	60.0
Catholic	38.9	30.8	23.2	33.3	15.6	25.0
Jewish	5.6	14.1	16.1	8.3	8.9	15.0
Ethnicity or race						
White	88.9	97.4	78.6	100	97.8	95.0
Black	5.6	1.3	16.1	—	—	5.0
Hispanic	5.6	1.3	3.6	—	—	—
Asian	—	—	1.8	—	2.2	—
Sex						
Male	88.9	94.9	80.4	100	100	97.5
Female	11.1	5.1	19.6	—	—	2.5
ABA Ratings						
EWQ/WQ	77.8	59.0	75.0	58.3	73.3	75.0

Table 7-2 (*Continued*)

Characteristic	Appointees of					
	Bush	Reagan	Carter	Ford	Nixon	Johnson
Qualified	22.2	41.0	25.0	33.3	26.7	20.0
Not qualified	—	—	—	8.3	—	2.5
Total number of appointees	18	78	56	12	45	40
Average age at nomination	48.5	50.0	51.9	52.1	53.8	52.2

aBush appointees are for 1989–1990.
Source: Sheldon Goldman, "The Bush Imprint on the Judiciary: Carrying on a Tradition," *Judicature* (April/May 1991): 302–303.

the president the opportunity to make appointments that have symbolic value for certain groups. These considerations may, in turn, help to win the loyalty of such groups to the president and his political party. Thus, judicial appointments, like those to executive posts, are an important form of political patronage.

The question remains, however, whether appointments to lower federal courts affect public issues that come before those courts, that is, whether there are consequences for *policy* as well as personnel in such appointments. A study by Jon Gottschall of voting by courts of appeals judges from July 1, 1983, to December 31, 1984, determined that judges appointed by Democratic presidents Carter, Johnson, and Kennedy were much more likely to vote on the liberal side of issues than were those chosen by Republican presidents Reagan, Ford, and Nixon.[30] Timothy Tomasi and Jess Veloma, in a study of decisions by Reagan's 1981–1986 appointees to the courts of appeals, found "a vast ideological gulf separating Republican from Democratic judges."[31]

It seems clear that presidential appointments to the lower federal courts do affect policy. Democratic presidents tend to take liberal positions on issues; Republican presidents, conservative positions. When presidents appoint judges from their own political party, the rulings of such judges usually are consistent with the president's philosophy. Therefore, it is logical to expect that Reagan's and Bush's appointees will "constitutionalize the Reagan-Bush social agenda, which means institutionalizing judicial restraint in matters of governmental civil liberties and civil rights policymaking."[32]

As the next section indicates, the politics of the appointment and confirmation of Supreme Court justices is quite different from that of lower federal court judges. Although the individuals and groups involved in choosing both kinds of judges are essentially the same, their relative influence in the two selection processes is not the same.

Selection of Supreme Court Justices

The president clearly dominates the process of selecting members of the Supreme Court. The decisions reached by the Court are of vital interest to the president because they affect his programs, the operation of the entire political system, and the functioning of U.S. society in general. Besides a keen interest in who sits on the Court, the chief executive has a relatively free hand in choosing its members.

As with lower federal court judges, the attorney general assists the president in identifying and screening potential candidates for the nation's highest court. Because vacancies for the Supreme Court occur so infrequently (one every two years, on average), the president can concentrate his efforts on the appointment in a way that simply is not possible for the numerous appointments made to the federal district and appeals courts. Scigliano estimates that as of mid–1970, presidents had known personally 60 percent of the 134 nominees for the High Court.[33] In some instances, presidents have had close personal relationships with their appointees. Frederick M. Vinson, an old friend of President Truman's, was serving as secretary of the Treasury at the time of his appointment as chief justice. Byron R. White had chaired a national citizens' committee for the election of John F. Kennedy in 1960. Thurgood Marshall had served as solicitor general for Lyndon Johnson before Johnson appointed him to the Court.

But not all presidents select personal acquaintances for the Court. Sometimes the attorney general plays the major role in an appointment, which is ultimately approved by the president. Attorney General Edward Levi, who served in the Ford administration, was the pivotal person in the selection of John Paul Stevens, who had been a colleague of Levi's on the faculty of the University of Chicago Law School, and William French Smith took the lead in recruiting Justice O'Connor, Reagan's first appointee to the Court. On occasion, close associates of the president may be influential. White House chief of staff John Sununu played an important role in President Bush's appointment of David Souter, a federal appeals court judge from Sununu's home state of New Hampshire.

Individual senators do not play as important a role in the selection of

Supreme Court justices as they do for judges appointed to the lower federal courts (especially the district courts). The principal reason for the distinction is that the High Court's geographical jurisdiction encompasses the entire nation, so no senator or group of senators can claim that the appointment is within his or her special province.[34] Presidents usually obtain the blessing of the senators of their own party from the state of residence of the nominee, as Reagan did from Barry Goldwater, R-Ariz., for the appointment of O'Connor, but senators generally are presented with a fait accompli rather than being involved in the recruitment process. A lawmaker would think long and hard about trying to prevent a constituent from having the honor of sitting on the nation's highest tribunal, especially knowing that in the face of opposition the president could then turn to a citizen of another state for the appointment. Both Democratic senators from Georgia, for example, voted to confirm Clarence Thomas in 1991.

Two other groups that play a much smaller role in the selection of Supreme Court justices than in the selection of members of the lower federal courts are the likely candidates and party leaders. The adage "the post should seek the person" is more applicable for positions on the nation's highest tribunal, so even those on the proverbial short list usually do not actively promote their own candidacy. Also, because appointments to the Supreme Court are considered to be above partisan politics, even the national party chairs do not influence appointments to the same extent as state party leaders influence appointments to the lower federal courts, especially at the district level.

Supreme Court justices themselves are more influential in selecting their colleagues than are their counterparts in lower federal courts. Henry Abraham and Bruce Murphy determined that no fewer than 48 of the 101 persons who had sat on the High Court as of 1976 attempted to exert influence in behalf of a candidate or a philosophy of judicial selection.[35] Leading the way were Taft with eighteen attempts (fourteen were successful) and Harlan F. Stone with nine (five were successful). This influence has been exerted both on behalf of proposed candidates (Chief Justice Warren E. Burger suggested the name of Harry A. Blackmun in 1970, and Rehnquist endorsed O'Connor in 1981) and against them.[36]

One group that is often consulted on lower federal court appointments, but rarely in those for the Supreme Court, is the ABA's Standing Committee on Federal Judiciary. Beginning with the appointment of Justice

William J. Brennan, Jr., by President Eisenhower in 1956 and continuing until 1970, the committee was asked to evaluate candidates for the Supreme Court but only *after* the appointment had been publicly announced and transmitted to the Senate Judiciary Committee for action. After the difficulties that led to the rejection of nominees Clement Haynsworth, Jr., and G. Harrold Carswell, the Nixon administration decided to allow the ABA committee to screen candidates before their names were submitted to the Senate Judiciary Committee. The arrangement was short-lived, however; one of the first actions of the ABA committee when two vacancies occurred in 1971 was to express serious doubts about the capabilities of President Nixon's two top choices, Mildred Lillie, a California appeals court judge, and Herschel Friday, an Arkansas lawyer. This led Attorney General John Mitchell to withdraw the screening privilege of the committee. Ford restored it, and the committee responded by giving his only nominee to the Court, John Paul Stevens, a high rating. The committee was not consulted, however, by Reagan or Bush prior to their nominations to the Court because of the opposition of conservative Republicans, who had long charged the committee with a liberal bias.

Thus, the process of recruiting justices to the Supreme Court is controlled by the president with the assistance of the attorney general and sitting Supreme Court justices. The president faces one other obstacle, however, that is far more formidable than obstacles to lower court appointments: the nominee must be confirmed by the *entire Senate*. Operating through the Judiciary Committee, which since 1955 has held hearings in which it questions nominees and receives testimony from interested groups, the Senate takes seriously its role of consenting to the appointment of a person to the nation's highest court. An indication of just how seriously the Senate takes this responsibility is that about 20 percent of the nominees to the Court have not been confirmed by the Senate, a much higher proportion than for any other federal office.[37]

Certain factors tend to be linked with the Senate's failure to confirm Supreme Court nominees. Rejections are most likely to occur when the Senate is controlled by the political party in opposition to the president.[38] Moreover, rejections are particularly evident in the last year of a president's term because opposition leaders in the Senate want to hold the position vacant in hopes that the new president will be from their party. The Senate refused to confirm Lyndon Johnson's nomination of Abe Fortas as chief justice when Earl Warren retired in 1968 in part to save the seat for the next president. When Richard Nixon became president in 1968 he appointed Republican Warren Burger as chief justice, and the Senate approved the choice.

Certain characteristics of the nominees also are associated with the Senate's failure to confirm.[39] One is involvement with controversial issues of public policy, a situation that often stimulates concerned interest groups to oppose the nomination. All five nominees who were rejected by the Senate in this century were opposed by interest groups. John P. Parker, a southern court of appeals judge nominated by Herbert Hoover in 1930, fell victim to the combined opposition of the American Federation of Labor and the National Association for the Advancement of Colored People, which considered his rulings as an appeals judge to be antilabor and racist. Two Nixon nominees, Haynsworth, a federal court of appeals judge from South Carolina, and Carswell, a federal court of appeals judge from Florida, were rejected within a few months of each other in late 1969 and early 1970. Both were opposed by African American and liberal interest groups for their rulings on civil rights cases. (Haynsworth was opposed by labor as well.) Fortas's nomination for chief justice was bitterly attacked by conservative groups because of his liberal decisions in obscenity cases and suits concerning the rights of the accused in criminal proceedings.[40] A major effort by civil rights, women's, and other liberal groups contributed to the defeat in 1987 of Reagan's nomination of Robert Bork, a controversial conservative federal appeals court judge.

Sometimes other problems are involved. Some considered Fortas's acceptance of a legal fee from a family foundation and his advising President Johnson on political matters to be unethical activities for a justice of the Supreme Court. Haynsworth was criticized for ruling on cases in which he had a personal financial interest. Much of the opposition to Carswell from members of the bar, particularly law professors, stemmed from his lack of professional qualifications, indicated by the mediocrity of his decisions.[41] The only presidential nominee to the Supreme Court since Carswell to be attacked on grounds of a lack of professional competence was Clarence Thomas. His critics also objected to his conservative ideology and his judicial philosophy. In the latter respect, the controversy over Thomas followed the pattern set in the Senate's challenges to Reagan's nominations of O'Connor, Rehnquist, Scalia, Bork, and Kennedy and Bush's nomination of Souter.[42]

Characteristics of Supreme Court Justices

The characteristics of Supreme Court justices reflect the informal qualifications that presidents take into account when appointing them. Scigliano places these qualifications into three categories: professional, representational, and doctrinal.[43]

The *professional* qualifications are similar to those described for lower court judges. Although not required to be lawyers, all of the justices who have served on the Supreme Court have been attorneys. Not only have they been trained as lawyers; their professional lives have been devoted primarily to the practice or teaching of law. Moreover, all but one justice previously held public office, many associated with the courts, such as prosecutor and district attorney. An analysis of the occupations of Supreme Court justices at the time of their appointment reveals that they have come principally from four types of positions: twenty-two held federal office in the executive branch; twenty-five were judges of a lower federal court; twenty-two were judges of a state court; and eighteen were attorneys in private practice. Elected officials also have served on the nation's highest bench, including one president, eight U.S. senators, four members of the House of Representatives, and three state governors.

Representational qualifications are the aspects of a nominee's background that are thought to make various groups feel that they have a representative on the Supreme Court. The representational qualification most often considered is the partisan affiliation of the justices, most of whom have been from the same political party as the president who appointed them.

Presidents are interested in other representational qualifications as well. Early in the nation's history, geography was a major consideration because various states, for example, Pennsylvania, New York, and Virginia, and sections of the country were thought to be entitled to representation on the Court. This factor has not been of consequence in this century, however, except when Nixon made clear early in his administration his intention to appoint a southerner. (His unsuccessful nominations of Haynsworth and Carswell failed to achieve that result, but he eventually appointed Lewis Powell, a Democrat from Virginia.) More salient in recent years are qualifications based on religion, race, and sex. At various times justices have been appointed to a "Catholic seat" (Justice Brennan) or a "Jewish seat" (Justice Fortas). In 1967 Johnson appointed Thurgood

Marshall, an African American, and in 1991 Bush appointed Clarence Thomas to Marshall's seat. Ronald Reagan pledged in his 1980 presidential campaign that, if elected, he would appoint a woman to one of his first vacancies on the Court, a promise he fulfilled by making Justice O'Connor his first appointee.[44]

Doctrinal qualifications refer to the perception by the president that a nominee shares his political philosophy and approach to public policy issues. For this reason, Reagan's choice of O'Connor had both representational and doctrinal qualifications. Meeting with her as a prospective nominee, Reagan discussed social and family issues and was reported to be pleased to hear that she regarded abortion as personally abhorrent; moreover, he found that her political views were generally conservative, like his own. As a state judge, O'Connor had been inclined to defer to the actions of legislative and executive officials and to favor shifting more responsibilities from the federal to the state courts, positions consistent with Reagan's judicial philosophy and advocacy of states' rights.

Reagan's choices of Rehnquist for chief justice, of Scalia, and Kennedy as associate justices, and the unsuccessful nomination of Robert Bork appear to have been motivated primarily by doctrinal considerations.[45] Rehnquist's fifteen-year record as an associate justice demonstrated that of all the justices, he came closest to Reagan's views in opposing abortion, busing, and affirmative action and in being generally disposed to defer to state and congressional legislation and to executive authority. Scalia's legal writings (he had served on the law school faculties of the University of Chicago and the University of Virginia) and his opinions written while he was a judge on the U.S. court of appeals in Washington reveal essentially the same conservative legal philosophy. Bork's extensive writings— he was also a former law professor at Yale and a sitting federal judge— gave clear indication of his conservative views. Senate and interest group opponents of his nomination focused on that written record, but it was Bork's coolly articulate performance in his confirmation hearings, which portrayed him as having an unacceptably narrow interpretation of the Constitution and of the Court's role in protecting constitutional rights, that led to his defeat. The 58–42 vote in the Senate ended one of "the most contentious [Supreme Court] confirmation battle[s] in American history."[46]

Bush's nomination of David Souter appears to have been based on doctrinal and professional qualifications. In contrast to Bork, Souter's views were not well known, and the opinions he had written as a state judge and a federal appeals court judge were not very revealing. This paucity of material frustrated liberal groups, who assumed that he was a conservative. They were unable to mount a successful campaign against his confirmation because he was professionally qualified and he had not left a "paper trail" that could be attacked.

The choice of Clarence Thomas reflected representational and doctrinal concerns. In naming an African American, Bush hoped to prevent the coalition that had defeated Bork from prevailing again. If the Senate rejected Thomas, there would be no African American on the Court. Although he had few published writings, Thomas's conservative views were widely known as a result of his service as head of the Equal Employment Opportunity Commission during the Reagan administration.

As Scigliano explains, however, doctrinal considerations are not always important to presidents, particularly in times of relative political and social calm, or when they feel that the general philosophy of the majority of the justices is similar to their own and is not likely to change in the near future. Moreover, as the following section indicates, even when presidents try to choose justices who will rule the way they want, they are not always successful.

Effects of Supreme Court Appointments

Do Supreme Court appointments have *policy* consequences? Are the actions presidents take while in office more likely to be supported by their appointees or by justices from their political party than by other members of the Court? An even broader question: Are presidents' values more likely to be protected in judicial rulings made by their appointees or by members of their party than by the other justices of the Court?

Stuart Nagel sought to answer the first question by examining the decisions in 100 Supreme Court cases involving the use of presidential power.[47] He found that when justices appointed by the president and those not appointed by him differed in their opinions (68 percent of the time), the president's appointees were more supportive of his actions. He also found that in 64 percent of comparable cases a greater proportion of justices from the president's own party upheld his use of power than did those from the opposing political party.

Scigliano examined the broader question of whether presidents get what they want and expect from the justices they appoint to the Court, that is, whether their appointees do in fact make decisions that reflect their values.[48] Taking into account presidents' direct and indirect statements about their appointees, as well as assumptions about whether decisions reached by such appointees reflected the views of the president, Scigliano concludes that approximately three-fourths of the justices conformed to the expectations of the chief executive who appointed them. The remaining one-fourth did not. The latter group includes some notable examples.

Shortly after Theodore Roosevelt appointed Oliver Wendell Holmes, Jr., to the Court, Holmes voted on the side of economic competition and against the administration in a famous antitrust case, *Northern Securities v. United States*, an action that provoked Roosevelt to say he could make "a judge with a stronger backbone out of a banana."[49] Upset by what he considered to be the extreme liberalism of rulings made by Chief Justice Warren and Associate Justice Brennan, President Eisenhower referred to them as two of the "mistakes" of his presidency.[50]

Scigliano suggests various reasons why one in four justices do not meet the expectations of the presidents who appoint them. One is that they simply do not have the values the president thinks they do, possibly because the president does not probe them sufficiently or thinks that because a prospective justice has a certain position on one issue, he or she will hold a comparable view on another. Also, people can and do change their views over time, and justices may do so after they go on the Court, especially if they are influenced by their peers.[51] Finally, justices have a sense of judicial obligation and may rule according to judicial precedents or their understanding of the Constitution rather than on the basis of their own value preferences. Whatever the reason for their actions, justices of the Supreme Court are virtually immune from pressures from the chief executive. There is no more prestigious office to which they can be appointed as a reward for pleasing the president; moreover, because they hold office for life (no Supreme Court justice has ever been removed from office), there is little chance to punish them.

Despite these limitations, if a president makes the effort to learn the values of prospective nominees, then appoints a person with values like his own, he usually is rewarded with decisions that reflect his views. Analyses by David Rohde and Harold Spaeth of Supreme Court cases decided from 1958 through 1973 reveal that the Court had a definite liberal cast when most of its members were appointees of Democratic presidents (and Eisenhower's two "mistakes"). However, with Nixon's appointment of Chief Justice Burger in 1969, the tide began to turn in a conservative direction.[52] That turn to conservatism accelerated with the five Reagan and Bush appointments to the Court.[53]

Other Presidential Influences on the Federal Courts

Although the appointment of federal judges is the most important method by which the president affects the courts, there are other ways to influence their activities. The first is his relationship with the solicitor general, an official Scigliano calls "the lawyer for the executive branch."[54] The second is the president's role in legislation that affects the operation of the Supreme Court. The third is the role the president plays in the enforcement of court decisions.

Role of the Solicitor General in the Appellate Courts

The solicitor general, an official appointed by the president with the consent of the Senate, is the most important individual in setting the agenda of the federal appellate courts. First, the solicitor general determines which cases of those the government loses in the federal district courts will be taken to the courts of appeals. Second, of the cases the government loses in the courts of appeals (or, in some instances, district court cases that are directly appealable to the Supreme Court), the solicitor general decides which to recommend that the High Court hear. Unlike the courts of appeals, which *must* take cases properly appealed to them, the Supreme Court chooses the cases it hears, and it is more likely to take those proposed by the solicitor general than by other parties, including those who lost to the federal government in the lower courts. The importance of this role of the solicitor general is reflected in the fact that the federal government has been a party in about 40 percent of the cases heard in the Supreme Court since 1979.[55]

The solicitor general's influence in determining the Supreme Court's agenda is not restricted, however, to cases in which the federal government itself is a party. He also decides whether the government will file an *amicus curiae* (friend of the court) brief supporting or opposing appeals by other parties to have their cases heard before the Court. In addition, he supervises the writing of briefs that present reasons why the Court should either accept or reject certain cases. Moreover, once the Court decides to accept a case involving the federal government, the "lawyer for the executive branch" decides the position the government should take and the arguments that should be made to support that position. The same applies when the government is not a direct party to the suit but an amicus supporting the position of one of the two immediate parties. Thus, as Scigliano points out, "the Solicitor General not only determines whether the executive branch goes to the Supreme Court but what it will say there."[56]

The federal government's amicus role has expanded greatly. Steven Puro, who analyzed the briefs filed from 1920 through 1973, found that 71 percent occurred in the last twenty years of that period.[57] He concluded that whether by its own initiative or as a result of an invitation from the Supreme Court, the federal government participated as amicus in almost every major domestic question presented before the Court since World War II. Particularly prominent is the government's entrance into the controversial issues of civil liberties, civil rights, and the jurisdiction and procedures of the courts.

When the federal government becomes involved in a case before the Supreme Court, it is usually successful. Scigliano's analysis of Court opinions chosen at ten-year intervals beginning in 1800 shows that the United States won 62 percent of its litigation there during the nineteenth century and 64 percent during this century.[58] Its record as amicus is even more impressive. Puro found that in the political cases he examined, the federal government supported the winning side in almost 74 percent of its appearances.[59] An analysis by Karen O'Connor of race discrimination employment cases from 1970 to 1981 showed that the government won 70 percent of the cases in which it was a direct party and 81.6 percent of those in which it filed amicus briefs.[60]

Scigliano suggests several reasons why the federal government is so successful in its appearances before the Supreme Court. One is that the solicitor general develops a great deal of expertise in dealing with the Court, since he or members of his staff argue far more cases there than any other party, including any law firm in the country.[61] Also, the solicitor general tends to build up credit with the Court because he helps its members manage their caseload by holding down the number of government appeals and provides the Court with high-quality briefs. Moreover, the executive and judicial branches share a common perspective based upon a similar concern with the execution or enforcement of the law. Finally, the justices tend to share the doctrinal attitudes of the presidents who appoint them. As Puro points out, amicus briefs filed by the solicitor general in the 1960s tended to take the liberal side in civil liberties cases; they defended the individual against state and local governments and corporations. That situation changed during the Nixon administration, however, when the federal government's amicus briefs took the conservative position on such issues, siding with state and local governments and corporations against the individual; and the Court began to adopt a more conservative position in its rulings.

With the Reagan administration came a concerted effort to use the solicitor general's office to help implement the president's conservative political agenda.[62] Termed by Elder Witt as Reagan's "other campaign" (separate from appointing conservatives to the federal bench), the campaign led by Solicitor General Rex Lee entailed efforts to persuade the Supreme Court to change previous "liberal" rulings on matters such as abortion, prayer in the public schools, busing, affirmative action, the rights of the accused in criminal cases, and federal-state relations.[63] Lee's successor, Charles Fried, continued that campaign.

Under Reagan, then, the solicitor general's function changed from a traditional posture of restraint to one of aggressively pushing the Court to take cases that advanced the administration's social policy agenda.[64] The result of this transformation, according to Lincoln Caplan, was a loss of the Supreme Court's trust in the solicitor general's presentation of facts and interpretation of the law.[65] There is, however, no evidence that President Bush continued Reagan's aggressive use of the solicitor general's office for policy purposes.

Although independent, the solicitor general is not immune from presidential influence. The appointment process parallels that for federal judges.[66] Sometimes the president makes the selection, as when Truman chose his friend J. Howard McGrath. In other instances, state political figures may influence the choice, as was true of McGrath's successor Philip Pearlman, who owed his appointment to the support of Maryland political leaders.

There is, however, a major distinction between the solicitor general and a federal judge: the solicitor general is an employee of the executive, not the judicial, branch and therefore is subject to direction from the attorney general and, on occasion, the president. Also, the solicitor general is considerably less politically insulated than a federal judge. The post does not entail life tenure; the average length of service of a solicitor general is two years. Not only can he be removed from office by the president but he can also be rewarded with a more prestigious position. For example, Stanley Reed and Robert Jackson, who served under Franklin Roosevelt, and Thurgood Marshall, who was solicitor general under Lyndon Johnson, all were appointed justices of the Supreme Court by the chief executive who had previously chosen them as solicitor general.

The President's Role in Legislation Affecting the Supreme Court

The president also can affect the actions of the Supreme Court through legislation. The president's authority to propose bills to Congress and to work for their adoption, as well as his power to oppose measures favored by members of Congress and, if necessary, to veto them, means that the president can influence legislation affecting the Court.

Over the years presidents have become involved in the power of Congress to establish the size of the Supreme Court. In the latter days of the John Adams administration, the lame-duck Congress, still controlled by the Federalists, passed the Judiciary Act of 1801, which reduced the number of justices from six to five, to prevent the incoming president, Democratic-Republican Thomas Jefferson, from appointing a replacement for an ailing justice, William Cushing. The following year, however, Congress—by then under control of the Democratic-Republicans—repealed the 1801 law and restored the number of justices to six. In 1807 the number of justices was increased to seven to accommodate population growth in Kentucky, Tennessee, and Ohio. This first attempt to thwart a president from making appointments to the Supreme Court, therefore, ended in failure: Jefferson went on to name three justices, including Thomas Todd to occupy the new seat. (Cushing recovered and lived until 1810; his successor was named by James Madison, not Jefferson.)

Manipulation of the size of the Court so as to affect presidential appointments also occurred in the 1860s. The 1863 Judiciary Act expanding the Court from nine to ten members enabled Abraham Lincoln to appoint Stephen J. Field, who subsequently supported the president on war issues. Shortly thereafter, the Radical Republicans, who controlled Congress, passed legislation reducing the number of justices to prevent Lincoln's successor, Andrew Johnson, from naming justices they feared would rule against the Reconstruction program. Soon after Ulysses S.

Grant was inaugurated in March 1869, the size of the Court was again expanded; this expansion, plus a retirement, enabled Grant to appoint Justices William Strong and Joseph P. Bradley. Both voted to reconsider a previous Supreme Court decision, *Hepburn v. Griswold*, that had declared unconstitutional the substitution of paper money for gold as legal tender for the payment of contracts.[67] The new decision validated the use of "greenbacks" as legal tender.[68] The three successive changes in the size of the Court within a six-year period brought the desired results.

In 1937 President Franklin Roosevelt attempted to increase the size of the Court once more. Frustrated by the invalidation of much of the early New Deal (between January 1935 and June 1936 the Court struck down eight separate statutes), Roosevelt asked Congress in early 1937, shortly after his landslide electoral victory in 1936, to pass legislation permitting him to appoint one justice, up to six in number, for each sitting member of the Court who failed to retire voluntarily at age seventy. The president contended that the additions were necessary to handle the Court's caseload, but his real purpose was to liberalize the Court. No one was deceived by the ploy, however, and the proposal stimulated violent opposition from members of the bar, the press, and many of Roosevelt's political supporters in Congress. At this point, Justice Owen J. Roberts, who had been aligned with four conservative colleagues in striking down New Deal legislation, began to vote with the other four justices to uphold the legislation. The unpopularity of Roosevelt's proposal, Justice Roberts's mitigating action—some observers dubbed this development "the switch in time that saved nine"—and the sudden death of Majority Leader Joseph Robinson of Arkansas, who was leading the president's effort in the Senate, resulted in Congress's failure to adopt the "court-packing plan." As Justice Robert Jackson described the outcome of the incident, "In politics the black-robed reactionary Justices had won over the master liberal politician of our day. In law the President defeated the recalcitrant Justices in their own Court."[69]

Presidents also can conceivably affect the operation of the Supreme Court by becoming involved in legislative actions of Congress that remove certain categories of cases from the appellate jurisdiction of the Supreme Court. The most notorious use of that congressional power occurred just after the Civil War. William McCardle, an editor of a Mississippi newspaper, was arrested and held for trial by a military tribunal for criticizing in his editorials the Reconstruction program imposed on the South by military government. He sought a writ of *habeas corpus* in the federal court of appeals, arguing that the Reconstruction Acts, which allowed his arrest and trial by a military tribunal, were unconstitutional. When the court denied the writ, he took advantage of an 1867 law expanding the appellate jurisdiction of the Supreme Court to review denials of such writs and brought his case to the High Court.[70] Concerned that the Supreme Court might use the *McCardle* case to declare the Reconstruction Acts unconstitutional, Congress passed a law repealing the 1867 statute and prohibiting the Court from acting on any appeals then pending. President Johnson, who opposed the Reconstruction program of the Radical Republicans, vetoed the law, but Congress overrode his veto. The Court then dismissed the *McCardle* case, on which it had heard arguments but not yet ruled. Although Congress prevailed over President Johnson in that particular instance by overriding his veto, the incident nonetheless illustrates the power of the president to affect the appellate jurisdiction of the Supreme Court through his sharing of the legislative power with Congress.

Presidents also have been involved in instances in which Congress has enacted legislation that had the effect of reversing specific rulings of the Supreme Court. The difference that individual presidents can make in such matters is illustrated by the tidelands oil dispute. In 1951, after the Supreme Court ruled first in 1947 and again in 1950 that the federal government, not the states, owned the three-mile strip of oil-rich, submerged lands off the ocean shores, Congress passed legislation granting ownership of these tidelands to the states. Democratic president Truman successfully vetoed the legislation, however, and the matter became an issue in the 1952 presidential campaign, in which the Republicans promised to restore the lands to the states. They kept their promise when Eisenhower won the election and subsequently approved new legislation passed in 1953 ceding the federal mineral rights in offshore lands to the states. More recently, Republican presidents Reagan and Bush have sought to overturn the Supreme Court's 1973 abortion decision by pressuring Congress to propose a constitutional amendment outlawing abortion.[71] Although unsuccessful in this effort, both presidents signed legislation that limited use of federal funds for abortions and made access to abortions more difficult.

These then are the major ways in which presidents can become involved with Congress in legislation affecting the Supreme Court. The next section analyzes the influence the president exercises through an important executive function—the enforcement of court decisions.

Enforcement of Court Decisions

Although the federal courts have the authority to hand down decisions on cases within their jurisdiction, in some instances they depend upon the president to enforce them. President Lincoln once refused to enforce a court order against a military officer under his direct command.[72] Lincoln's decision was, however, an exception to the rule, for chief executives usually have enforced court decisions, even when they would have preferred not to. Immediately after the Supreme Court held in 1952 that Truman's seizure of the steel mills was unconstitutional, he ordered them restored to private operation.[73] Nixon complied with the Court's 1974 ruling in *United States v. Nixon* that he turn over to a federal district court tapes of his conversations with executive aides.[74] That action produced evidence of the president's involvement in the Watergate affair and led to the House Judiciary Committee's impeachment charges against him.

Thus presidents, through their appointment of federal judges and solicitors general, their involvement in congressional legislation affecting the Supreme Court, and their authority to determine whether judicial decisions will be enforced, influence the operation of the federal courts. The following section analyzes the reverse situation: the extent to which federal courts affect the way presidents conduct the responsibilities of their office.

Judicial Checks of Presidential Action

The Founders left open the question of who had the final power to interpret the Constitution. If, as Jefferson contended, each branch has the authority to interpret the Constitution as far as its own duties are concerned, then the president, like Congress, is the judge of the constitutionality of executive actions. If, however, the Supreme Court has the right to make the final judgment on such matters through the power of judicial review, then the Court is in a position to check the actions of the president as well as those of Congress. Although the Court established its power of judicial review with respect to acts of Congress in 1803 in *Marbury v. Madison,*[75] it did not declare a presidential action unconstitutional until after the Civil War.

Major Cases Invalidating Presidential Actions

Of the forty people who have served as president over the course of the nation's history, only four have been objects of major court decisions invalidating their actions. The first, Abraham Lincoln, was a nineteenth century chief executive; the other three, Franklin Roosevelt, Harry Truman, and Richard Nixon, are products of the modern presidency.

Abraham Lincoln. Lincoln's battle with the judiciary stemmed from the conditions surrounding the Civil War. Early in that conflict Lincoln concluded that existing laws and judicial procedures were inadequate for dealing with spying, sabotage, and other acts of disloyalty, and he suspended the traditional writ of *habeas corpus* when he felt that the public safety required it. It is better, Lincoln argued, for the president to violate a single law to a limited extent than to have "the government itself go to pieces" because of a failure to suppress the rebellion. During the war many people, including civilians, who were engaged in activities thought to be dangerous to the public safety, were arrested and tried by military commissions.

In 1866, a year after Lincoln's death and the end of the war, the Supreme Court heard the case of L. P. Milligan, a civilian sentenced to death by a military commission for releasing and arming rebel prisoners for the purpose of invading Indiana. The Court held that the trial of a civilian by a military commission in an area remote from the theater of war violated the Constitution. In so ruling, the Court used language that seemed to reject the power claimed by Lincoln: "No doctrine, involving more pernicious consequences, was ever invented by the wit of man than that any of its [the Constitution's] provisions can be suspended during any of the great exigencies of government."[76] The majority opinion went on to state that martial law cannot arise from a *threatened* invasion but only an actual one that effectually closes the courts.

Franklin Roosevelt. President Roosevelt ran into major difficulties with the Supreme Court, which invalidated much of his early New Deal legislation for exceeding the powers of Congress. The Court also struck down an action entailing his administrative power. The case involved FDR's removal of Federal Trade Commissioner William Humphrey on policy grounds rather than statutory criteria for such removal.

Harry Truman. President Truman was the subject of a landmark case, *Youngstown Sheet and Tube Co. v. Sawyer,* invalidating one of his actions.[77] What became known as the "steel seizure case" grew out of an impending industrywide strike during the Korean War by the United Steel Workers of America when the Wage Stabilization Board failed to settle a dispute between the union and the owners. Truman ignored the provisions of the Taft-Hartley Act that permitted the president to obtain an injunction postponing for eighty days a strike that threatened the national safety and welfare. Instead, he issued an executive order seizing the steel mills, based on his authority under the Constitution and U.S. law and as commander in chief. The steel companies protested the seizure as unconstitutional, and the case went to the Supreme Court.

By a 6–3 vote the Court invalidated the president's action. Justice Hugo L. Black, who wrote the majority opinion (five other justices provided lengthy concurring opinions), summarily rejected Truman's claims of executive prerogative and based his decision on the fact that, in its deliberations over the Taft-Hartley Law, Congress had decided against authorizing the president to seize industrial property. Therefore, the chief executive had acted against the will of Congress, which amounted to an unconstitutional usurpation of legislative power. The dissenting opinion, written by Chief Justice Vinson, took the position that in times of a national crisis the president must exercise discretionary prerogative power.

Richard Nixon. When Nixon assumed the presidency, he vowed to appoint to the Supreme Court "strict constructionists" who would not read their own values into the Constitution so as to interfere with the right of public officials (especially police officers) to carry out their duties. During his first term the president appointed four new members to the Court: Chief Justice Burger and Associate Justices Blackmun, Powell, and Rehnquist. Ironically, Nixon himself became the object of no fewer than five adverse decisions of the Supreme Court, and in some of those decisions his own appointees voted against him.

The first case, *New York Times v. United States,* arose out of the publication by the *New York Times* and the *Washington Post* of the *Pentagon Papers,* an inside analysis of U.S. involvement in the war in Southeast Asia, prepared by the Department of Defense.[78] Acting under the president's direction, Attorney General John Mitchell sought a court injunction to prevent publication on the grounds that it would cause grave and irreparable damage to national security and that it violated a provision of the Espionage Act of 1917 forbidding the communication of defense information harmful to the nation's security. Six of the justices decided that such "prior restraint" was unconstitutional. Black and Douglas held that such restraint violates the First Amendment no matter how great the threat to national security; Brennan could find no threat to national security in this particular instance; and White, Marshall, and Stewart based their decision on the absence of statutory authority for federal courts' issuing prior restraint injunctions in national security cases. The three dissenters—Burger, Blackmun, and Harlan—felt that the courts should be more flexible in handling conflicts between First Amendment freedoms and issues of national security.

In 1972 Nixon lost another argument involving national security. In the Omnibus Crime Control and Safe Streets Act of 1968 Congress required that the federal government's use of wire taps and electronic surveillance be approved in advance by a judge, who would issue a search warrant authorizing the bugs. On the direction of the president, however, the attorney general's office, without obtaining a warrant, ordered surveillance of a person accused of bombing an office of the Central Intelligence Agency in Ann Arbor, Michigan. It claimed that such surveillance was a reasonable exercise of the president's power to protect the national security. The Court, in *United States v. United States District Court for the Eastern District of Michigan*, speaking through one of Nixon's own appointees, Justice Powell, held that warrantless surveillance in a domestic security matter is unconstitutional because it violates a "convergence of First and Fourth Amendment values."[79]

The most damaging decision for the president, *United States v. Nixon*, was handed down in July 1974 and led ultimately to his resignation.[80] The case grew out of the Watergate affair and involved Special Prosecutor Leon Jaworski's attempt to subpoena tapes of sixty-four conversations between the president and his assistants that Jaworski needed in criminal litigation against some of the leading figures in the Nixon administration. The president refused to surrender the tapes, claiming the existence of an executive privilege relating to private conversations between the chief executive and his advisers. In a unanimous opinion written by Chief Justice Burger, Nixon's first appointee to the Court, the Court recognized for the first time the principle of executive privilege as having "constitutional underpinnings." The opinion went on to say, however, that the

Court, not the president, is the final judge of the proper use of executive privilege. Moreover, in this instance, the general claim of the privilege, when unrelated to military, diplomatic, or national security issues, must give way to the more immediate need for evidence in a criminal case and to the fundamental principles of due process of law and the fair administration of justice.

After Nixon left office, he suffered two more judicial defeats. In *Train v. City of New York*, the Court held that the president's impoundment (refusal to make expenditures) of moneys appropriated by Congress under the Water Pollution Control Act of 1972 was unconstitutional because the statute gave him no authority to do so.[81] In so ruling, the Court rejected the president's argument that as chief executive he could impound funds when spending would result in either increased prices or taxes for the American people. In *Nixon v. Administrator, General Services Administration*, the Court upheld the Presidential Recordings and Materials Preservation Act of 1974, placing in federal custody tapes and papers of the Nixon administration.[82] In reaching its decision, the justices weighed the harm done to the individual rights of the former president against the public interest in preserving the Nixon materials and concluded that the latter interest should prevail.

Thus, the federal courts have been willing on some occasions to invalidate presidential actions that exceed constitutional authority. There are also, however, limitations on the willingness of justices to rule against the chief executive.

Limitations on Judicial Checks of Presidential Action

The fact that courts have struck down actions of the president as unconstitutional in only eleven major cases in almost 200 years indicates their reluctance to do so, especially in times of foreign and military crises. None of the major wartime presidents—Lincoln, Wilson, or Franklin Roosevelt—was seriously impeded by the courts in the prosecution of hostilities. During the Civil War the Court in the *Prize Cases* upheld the Union blockade of Southern ports on the grounds that Lincoln's action was necessary to deal with the rebellion.[83] As previously noted, it waited until after the war to decide the *Milligan* case.

During World War I the "hands-off" policy of the courts continued: convictions under the Espionage and Sedition Acts of persons charged with interfering with the war effort were upheld in cases decided after the war was over.[84] During World War II the Supreme Court upheld the government program relocating people of Japanese ancestry, including those who were American citizens, living on the West Coast to camps in the interior, as well as the trial of German saboteurs by a military commission.[85] Only after the relocation centers were being disbanded did the Supreme Court decide that it was unlawful to detain a loyal U.S. citizen of Japanese background.[86] Moreover, in a decision similar to that in the *Milligan* case, the Court ruled that it was unconstitutional for a civilian to be tried by a military commission in Hawaii, but that decision was handed down six months after the hostilities were over.[87] When the Court must rule on presidential actions, particularly in times of crisis, it tends to support the chief executive, or it delays making an adverse decision until the crisis is over.

The federal courts have devised another means of avoiding adverse decisions against the president: they simply declare that a particular issue is a "political question" and refuse to rule on the matter. As Elder Witt explains, "The doctrine rests on the separation of powers theory—that the Supreme Court exercises the judicial power and leaves political, or policy, questions to Congress and the president."[88] Differentiating between a judicial issue and a political or policy issue is not an easy matter, but the fact that the courts themselves make the distinction allows them to invoke the doctrine when for one reason or another they choose not to invalidate presidential or congressional action. The doctrine is invoked most often in the area of foreign policy. A federal court of appeals used it in 1973 to avoid ruling on the constitutionality of U.S. involvement in the civil war in Cambodia.[89] Finally, some presidential actions simply cannot be dealt with by the courts at all. The qualities Hamilton identified with the executive—"decision, activity, secrecy and despatch"—are such that the president can present the courts with a fait accompli, about which they can do little or nothing. The most momentous decisions that presidents make, such as those of President Truman to drop the atomic bomb and to send U.S. troops into Korea, do not lend themselves to adjudication and must be dealt with in the political, not the judicial, arena.

Conclusion

Although presidents do not have the day-to-day relationship with the federal courts that they have with Congress and other members of the executive branch, they possess two powers in particular through which they can significantly influence the activities of the courts. One is the power to appoint the members of all federal courts, especially U.S. district courts, U.S. courts of appeals, and the U.S. Supreme Court. The other is the power to help shape the agenda of the appellate courts through the actions of another appointee, the solicitor general of the United States. Moreover, both of these powers have long-term consequences: federal judges, unlike members of Congress and the political appointees of the executive branch, serve for life; and Supreme Court decisions that the solicitor general helps to determine usually are followed by future justices because of the principle of *stare decisis*.

There appears to be a trend towards greater presidential involvement in the selection of federal judges, even those who serve on the lower federal courts. The Carter, Reagan, and Bush administrations paid particularly close attention to the political philosophy of potential judges. The Carter administration also made a major effort to recruit women and members of minority groups to the lower federal bench, and the Reagan administration placed the first woman on the Supreme Court. Because Congress has recently created a large number of new lower court judgeships, Carter, Reagan, and Bush were able to choose an unusually large proportion of the members of those courts.

Recent presidents (especially Reagan) also made a greater effort to shape federal court opinions through the actions of the solicitor general. Increasingly, that official is chosen with the expectation that he or she will try to implement the president's political agenda, especially by filing *amicus curiae* briefs in a broad range of cases.

The Reagan administration was much more ambitious than other modern presidencies in its employment of a judicial strategy that attempted to use the federal courts to implement policy goals that it was unable to accomplish through the regular political process. It sought, for example, to outlaw abortion and to provide for voluntary prayer in the public schools. In addition to ideologically driven appointments, the elements of that strategy included an instrumental view of the law and politicization of the administration of justice. Although the Bush administration continued careful ideological screening of judicial appointees, it did not retain the other elements or Reagan's judicial strategy.

NOTES

1. Joan Biskupic, "Thomas Hearings Illustrate Politics of the Process," *Congressional Quarterly Weekly Report*, Sept. 21, 1991, 2688–89.

2. Joan Biskupic, "Thomas Picks Up Support as Senate Nears Vote," *Congressional Quarterly Weekly Report*, Oct. 5, 1991, 2867.

3. Joan Biskupic, "Thomas' Victory Puts Icing on Reagan-Bush Court," *Congressional Quarterly Weekly Report*, Oct. 19, 1991, 3026.

4. Ibid., 3030.

5. Alexander Hamilton, James Madison, and John Jay, *The Federalist Papers*, ed. Clinton Rossiter (New York: New American Library, 1961), 322.

6. Ibid., 465.

7. Robert Scigliano, *The Supreme Court and the Presidency* (New York: Free Press, 1971), chap. 1.

8. Ibid., vii.

9. In addition to the federal courts of general jurisdiction authorized by Article III, special courts handle disputes arising from particular functions of Congress under powers granted by Article I. Included are the U.S. Court of Appeals for the Federal Circuit, the U.S. Court of Military Appeals, the U.S. Court of Veterans Appeals, territorial courts, U.S. Claims Court, the U.S. Tax Court, and the U.S. Court of International Trade.

10. Harold Chase, *Federal Judges: The Appointing Process* (Minneapolis: University of Minnesota Press, 1972), 17.

11. Sheldon Goldman, "The Bush Imprint on the Judiciary: Carrying on a Tradition," *Judicature* (April/May 1991): 294–306.

12. Joseph Harris, *The Advice and Consent of the Senate* (Berkeley: University of California Press, 1953), 40.

13. Harold F. Bass, Jr., "Chief of Party," in *Guide to the Presidency*, ed. Michael Nelson (Washington, D.C.: Congressional Quarterly, 1989), 625.

14. Joel Grossman, *Lawyers and Judges: The ABA and the Politics of Judicial Selection* (New York: Wiley, 1965), 42.

15. Chase, *Federal Judges*, 29.

16. Walter Murphy, "Chief Justice Taft and the Lower Court Bureaucracy: A Study in Judicial Administration," *Journal of Politics* (August 1962): 453–476.

17. Grossman, *Lawyers and Judges*, 73.

18. Alan Neff, *The United States District Judge Nominating Commissions: Their Members, Procedures, and Candidates* (Chicago: American Judicature Society, 1981), 14.

19. Goldman, "The Bush Imprint on the Judiciary," 296.

20. Sheldon Goldman, "Reorganizing the Judiciary: The First Term Appointments," *Judicature* (April/May 1985): 315–317.

21. Ibid., 315–316.

22. Ibid., 316.

23. Lawrence Baum, *The Supreme Court*, 2d ed. (Washington, D.C.: CQ Press, 1985), 39.

24. David M. O'Brien, "The Reagan Judges: His Most Enduring Legacy?" in *The Reagan Legacy*, ed. Charles O. Jones (Chatham, N.J.: Chatham House, 1988), 63.

25. Goldman, "The Bush Imprint on the Judiciary," 296.

26. Goldman, "Reagan's Judicial Legacy: Completing the Puzzle and Summing Up," *Judicature* (April/May 1989): 319.

27. Denis Steven Rutkus, "President Bush's Judicial Nominations During the 101st and 102nd Congresses," *CRS Report for Congress* (Washington, D.C.: Congressional Research Service, Jan. 3, 1992).

28. Another difference not shown by the table is the disparity in the financial backgrounds of the appointees: more than 33 percent of Bush's appointees and 20 percent of the Reagan appointees had a net worth of over $1 million, but only 4 percent of Carter's did. Goldman, "The Bush Imprint on the Judiciary," 299.

29. Ibid., 303.

30. Jon Gottschall, "Reagan Appointments to the United States Court of Appeals: The Continuation of a Judicial Revolution," *Judicature* (June/July 1986): 48–54.

31. Timothy B. Tomasi and Jess A. Velona, "All the President's Men? A Study of Ronald Reagan's Appointments to the U.S. Courts of Appeals," *Columbia Law Review* 87 (May 1987): 792.

32. Goldman, "The Bush Imprint on the Judiciary," 306.

33. Scigliano, *The Supreme Court and the Presidency*, 95.

34. Earlier in the nation's history, an informal custom assigned certain states, such as New York, Pennsylvania, and Ohio, the right to have a seat on the Supreme Court, but that custom has not been followed in this century.

35. Henry Abraham and Bruce Murphy, "The Influence of Sitting and Retired Justices on Presidential Supreme Court Appointments," *Hastings Law Quarterly* (1975–1976): 37–63.

36. Lawrence Baum, *The Supreme Court*, 2d ed. (Washington, D.C.: CQ Press, 1985), 35.

37. Ibid., 46.

38. Scigliano, *The Supreme Court and the Presidency*, chap. 4.

39. Henry Abraham, *Justices and Presidents: A Political History of Appointments to the Supreme Court* (New York: Penguin Books, 1974), chap. 2.

40. It should be noted that Associate Justice William Rehnquist's nomination for chief justice in 1986 was attacked by liberal groups because of his alleged insensitivity to the rights of minorities and women. He was ultimately confirmed, but the thirty-three votes against him were the most ever cast against a confirmed justice up to that point.

41. One of Carswell's supporters, Republican senator Roman Hruska of Nebraska, tried to defend him on the grounds that there are many mediocre judges, lawyers, and other people who are entitled to representation on the Court. As Baum suggests, his statement seemed to support the charges of incompetence against Carswell (*The Supreme Court*, 50–51). In any event, the nomination was rejected by a 51–45 vote.

42. Walter Murphy notes that the ABA Standing Committee on the Federal Judiciary accorded "O'Connor, Rehnquist, Scalia, Bork, and Kennedy its highest ranking." (However, four members of the committee found Bork "not qualified" and one abstained.) Walter F. Murphy, "Reagan's Judicial Strategy," in *Looking Back on the Reagan Presidency*, ed. Larry Berman (Baltimore: The Johns Hopkins University Press, 1990), 217. Another Reagan nominee, federal appeals court judge Douglas Ginsburg withdrew before he could be rated following revelations that he had used marijuana while a faculty member at the Harvard Law School. The ABA committee also gave Souter its highest rating, but found Thomas only to be "qualified."

43. Scigliano, *The Supreme Court and the Presidency*, chap. 4.

44. Despite the recent concern with minority representation on the Supreme Court, as John Schmidhauser has pointed out, "The typical Supreme Court justice has generally been white, Protestant (with a penchant for a high social status), usually of ethnic stock originating in the British Isles, and born in comfortable circumstances in an urban

or small-town environment." See *Judges and Justices: The Federal Appellate Judiciary* (Boston: Little, Brown, 1979), 96. That description also fits the presidents who have appointed the justices.

45. Although Scalia is the first Italian-American to serve on the High Court, little was made of that fact at the time of his nomination and confirmation.

46. Herman Schwartz, *Packing the Courts: The Conservative Campaign to Rewrite the Constitution* (New York: Scribner's, 1988), 140.

47. Stuart Nagel, "Comparing Elected and Appointed Judicial Systems," *Sage Professional Papers, No. 64–001* (Beverly Hills, Calif.: Sage Publications, 1973), 25–26.

48. Scigliano, *The Supreme Court and the Presidency*, chap. 3.

49. *Northern Securities v. United States*, 193 U.S. 197 (1904); Stephen Wasby, *The Supreme Court in the Federal Judiciary System* (New York: Holt, Rinehart & Winston, 1978), 95.

50. Abraham, *Justices and Presidents*, 246.

51. A classic instance of justices changing their views was Thomas Jefferson's appointees to the Court, who came under the great influence of his political enemy, Chief Justice John Marshall. See Scigliano, *The Supreme Court and the Presidency*, 127.

52. David Rhode and Harold Spaeth, *Supreme Court Decision Making* (San Francisco: Freeman, 1976), 144.

53. Schwartz, *Packing the Courts*, 174–178; Linda Greenhouse, "Judicious Activism: Justice Thomas Hits the Ground Running," *New York Times*, March 1, 1992, E-1.

54. Scigliano, *The Supreme Court and the Presidency*, chap. 6.

55. *Annual Report of the Attorney General of the United States, 1984* (Washington, D.C.: Department of Justice, 1985), Table 1, page 7.

56. Scigliano, *The Supreme Court and the Presidency*, 172.

57. Steven Puro, "The United States as Amicus Curiae," in *Courts, Law, and Judicial Processes*, ed. S. Sidney Ulmer (New York: Free Press, 1981), 220–230.

58. Scigliano, *The Supreme Court and the Presidency*, chap. 6.

59. Puro, "The United States as Amicus Curiae."

60. Karen O'Connor, "The Amicus Curiae Role of the U.S. Solicitor General in Supreme Court Litigation," *Judicature* (December/January 1983): 261.

61. This situation is to be contrasted with the paucity of experience the attorney general has before the Court: traditionally, he argues only one case before his term is over. For an interesting account of Robert Kennedy's first appearance before the Court two years after he became attorney general, see Victor Navasky, *Kennedy Justice* (New York: Athenaeum, 1980), chap. 6.

62. Lincoln Caplan, *The Tenth Justice: The Solicitor General and the Rule of Law* (New York: Random House, 1987).

63. Elder Witt, *A Different Justice* (Washington, D.C.: Congressional Quarterly, 1986), chaps. 6, 7.

64. Caplan, *The Tenth Justice*, 79–80.

65. Ibid., 255–256.

66. Steven Puro, "Presidential Relationships with the Solicitor Generals of the United States: Political Science Research at Presidential Libraries" (Paper delivered at the 1978 annual meeting of the Missouri and Kansas Political Science Association).

67. *Hepburn v. Griswold (First Legal Tender Case)*, 8 Wall. 506 (1870).

68. *Knox v. Lee, Parker v. Davis (Second Legal Tender Case)*, 12 Wall. 457 (1871).

69. Robert Jackson, *The Struggle for Judicial Supremacy: A Study of a Crisis in American Power Politics* (New York: Knopf, 1941), 196.

70. *Ex Parte McCardle*, 7 Wall. 506 (1869).

71. *Roe v. Wade*, 410 U.S. 113 (1973).

72. *Ex Parte Merryman*, 17 Fed. Cases 144 (1861).

73. *Youngstown Sheet and Tube Co. v. Sawyer*, 343 U.S. 579 (1952).

74. *United States v. Nixon*, 418 U.S. 683 (1974).

75. *Marbury v. Madison*, 1 Cr. 137 (1803).

76. *Ex Parte Milligan*, 4 Wall. 2, 121 (1866).

77. *Youngstown Sheet and Tube Co. v. Sawyer*, 343 U.S. 579 (1952).

78. *New York Times v. United States*, 403 U.S. 713 (1971).

79. *United States v. United States District Court for the Eastern District of Michigan*, 407 U.S. 297 (1972).

80. *United States v. Nixon*, 403 U.S. 683 (1974).

81. *Train v. City of New York*, 420 U.S. 35 (1975).

82. *Nixon v. Administrator, General Services Administration*, 443 U.S. 425 (1977).

83. *Prize Cases*, 2 Black 635 (1863).

84. *Schenck v. United States*, 249 U.S. 47 (1919); *Abrams v. United States*, 250 U.S. 616 (1919); and *Pierce v. United States*, 252 U.S. 239 (1920).

85. *Korematsu v. United States*, 323 U.S. 214 (1944); *Ex Parte Quirin*, 317. U.S. 1 (1942).

86. *Ex Parte Endo*, 323 U.S. 283 (1944).

87. *Duncan v. Kahanamoku*, 327 U.S. 304 (1946).

88. Elder Witt, ed., *Guide to the U.S. Supreme Court*, 2d ed. (Washington, D.C.: Congressional Quarterly, 1990), 200.

89. *Holtzman v. Schlesinger*, 484 F. 2d 1307 (1973).

READINGS

Abraham, Henry. *Justices and Presidents: A Political History of Appointments to the Supreme Court*. 2d ed. New York: Oxford University Press, 1985.

Baum, Lawrence. *The Supreme Court*. 2d ed. Washington, D.C.: CQ Press, 1985.

Bonner, Ethan. *Battle for Justice: How the Bork Nomination Shook America*. New York: Norton, 1989.

Caplan, Lincoln. *The Tenth Justice: The Solicitor General and the Rule of Law*. New York: Random House, 1987.

Carp, Robert and Ronald Stidham. *The Federal Courts*. Washington, D.C.: CQ Press, 1985.

Chase, Harold. *Federal Judges: The Appointing Process*. Minneapolis: University of Minnesota Press, 1972.

Grossman, Joel. *Lawyers and Judges: The ABA and the Politics of Judicial Selection*. New York: Wiley, 1965.

Jackson, Robert. *The Struggle for Judicial Supremacy*. New York: Knopf, 1941.

Neff, Alan. *The United States District Judge Nominating Commissions: Their Members, Procedures, and Candidates*. Chicago: American Judicature Society, 1981.

Scigliano, Robert. *The Supreme Court and the Presidency*. New York: Free Press, 1971.

Schwartz, Herman. *Packing the Courts: The Conservative Campaign to Rewrite the Constitution*. New York: Scribner's, 1988.

Witt, Elder. *A Different Justice*. Washington, D.C.: Congressional Quarterly, 1986.

PART III
THE PRESIDENT AND PUBLIC POLICY

8 THE POLITICS OF DOMESTIC POLICY

President George Bush views visible evidence, after the 1992 Los Angeles riots, of the failure of urban policies.

DOMESTIC POLICY IS THE black hole of presidential politics. As soon as he takes the oath of office, the president confronts a vast array of problems, issues, and demands for government action. Already in operation are numerous complex and costly programs that compete for limited funds. Many of them enjoy the support of powerful interest groups and congressional leaders. Whatever the president does (or fails to do) in response to public demands is likely to cost him political support.

Presidents face a congested public policy agenda that results from the interrelatedness, overlapping, and layering of issues.[1] Many political scientists have classified public policy for analytical purposes, but the most widely used classification scheme, or typology, is Theodore Lowi's division of policies into distributive, regulatory, and redistributive categories.[2] He

323

based his categories on whom the policies affect, ranging from individuals to the entire society, and the likelihood that the government will have to exercise coercion to implement the policy.

Distributive policies have the most diffused impact. They affect specific groups of people and provide individualized benefits. They have low visibility, produce little conflict, and are not likely to require the application of coercion. Examples of distributive policies include agricultural price supports, public works projects, and research and development programs. *Regulatory* policies affect large segments of society and involve the application of coercion. Although regulatory issues tend to be highly technical, they often are quite visible and controversial. Examples include pollution control, antitrust, and occupational safety and health. *Redistributive* policies have the broadest impact on society. They involve the transfer of resources (wealth and income) from some groups to others. They require coercion, are highly visible, and usually are accompanied by social or class conflict. Examples of redistributive policies include Social Security and tax reform.

Lowi argued that the type of policy determines the focus and behavior of political actors. Distributive policy politics involve limited presidential and extensive congressional participation and decision making that relies heavily on logrolling—the mutual exchange of support for legislation. Regulatory policy politics produce moderate presidential and substantial congressional interest and involvement, with frequent conflict between the president and Congress. Redistributive policy politics often are fraught with ideological disputes and presidential-congressional conflict. Presidents tend to be most involved with redistributive policy issues. This is the case whether the government is seeking to expand or contract the scope of its activities.

Steven Shull has used Lowi's policy typology to examine presidential and congressional roles in domestic policy formation. He found that there were "some differences in presidential and congressional behavior . . . along lines anticipated by the 'theory,'"[3] and that "modest empirical distinctions" exist among the three policy categories.[4] The principal problem with Lowi's typology is the difficulty in making it operational for purposes of measurement. The problem arises because an issue may change its designation over time, starting out, for example, as a redistributive issue and becoming distributive. This is what happened to Title I of the Elementary and Secondary Education Act of 1965, a program of federal assistance to local school districts for economically disadvantaged children. As a new program, it sparked controversy because of its redistributive effects, but over time it became a routinized distribution of federal funds that was part of the established structure of school finance. In other words, Lowi's categories are not fixed in time. Shull concluded that Lowi's typology is not as useful as substantive classification based on policy content.

John Kessel has broken down domestic policy into areas involving social benefits, civil liberties, agriculture, and natural resources.[5] Each area entails a specific type of politics and its own temporal pattern, both of which have implications for presidential participation. The politics of social benefits, such as housing and Social Security retirement, are allocative: there is a strong similarity here to Lowi's distributive and redistributive categories. Presidents use the distribution of social benefits to build public support; therefore, they tend to pay most attention to social benefits as they approach reelection, after which, if they are successful, they are much less concerned. Civil rights involves a pattern of politics that is regulatory and highly sensitive because of differing conceptions of fairness. Presidents are most likely to act on civil rights issues immediately after their election, both because these issues are highly controversial and because campaign promises must be fulfilled. The politics of natural resources and environmental protection are primarily regulatory, and agriculture mostly involves allocation. The temporal patterns in natural resource and agricultural policy politics are a function of long-range developments and entail limited presidential participation.

Whether one approaches domestic policy using Lowi's analytical typology or Kessel's substantive classifications, it is clear that presidents can become fully involved with only a small number of problems and issues. The Lowi and Kessel approaches suggest that in domestic policy, presidents tend to focus on matters such as maintaining the financial integrity of the Social Security system, reforming welfare, and major civil rights proposals. They do not take up all major redistributive, social benefit, and civil rights issues and may consciously avoid some that may involve enormous financial costs. They are unlikely to become bogged down with routine distributive policies or with the technicalities of economic and social regulation. Jimmy Carter harmed himself politically when he tangled with Congress over eighteen water projects he regarded as unnecessary. Other presidents have been content to leave the distribution of "pork barrel" projects to Congress.

The range and complexity of domestic problems and issues produces a

policy congestion that makes coordination the essential presidential function in this area. Coordination has been complicated, however, by the
interrelatedness of domestic, economic, and national security policy. If
presidents attempt to coordinate policies through simplification, say, by
proposals to balance the budget or reorganize the bureaucracy, they encounter the opposition of powerful forces mobilized around policy issues,
programs, and administrative agencies. Ronald Reagan's 1982 proposals
to move toward a balanced budget by reducing Social Security cost-of-
living allowances provide an excellent example. Opposition from the
"gray lobby" and most members of Congress quickly stymied the idea.
George Bush's efforts to reduce the budget deficit by curtailing spending
on domestic programs met a similar fate. The proliferation and profes-
sionalization of interest groups and the expansion of their financial and
electoral power have been accompanied by a decline in the policy influence of political parties. Parties no longer play the role of broad-based
organizations with which presidents can bargain to bring coherence to
domestic policies and thus resolve policy congestion. Nor are parties a
centripetal counterweight to the centrifugal tendencies of organized group
interests.

The Domestic Policy Process

The domestic policy process has formal and informal dimensions, both
of which affect the presidency. The formal dimension consists of actions
that culminate in the development and presentation of legislative proposals to Congress, the issuance of executive orders, and the preparation
and submission of annual budgets. There is a cyclical regularity to much of
the formal policy process because annual events, such as the State of the
Union, budget, and economic messages, define the broad outlines of the
president's program.[6] (Although these events occur at approximately
the same time each year, the full cycles last longer than a year. The budget
for the fiscal year that began on October 1, 1992, for example, had its
origins in the budget review process conducted in the spring of 1990.) The
formal policy cycles are preceded by and merge with an informal process
that sets the president's agenda.

Policy Streams

The process of setting the president's domestic policy agenda can be
understood as the convergence in the White House of three tributary

streams: the first identifies problems and issues requiring attention; the second produces proposed solutions to the problems; and the third carries the political factors that establish the context for policy making.[7] According to John Kingdon, the three streams operate largely, but not absolutely, independently of one another. Problems and solutions develop separately and may or may not be joined, and political factors may change regardless of whether policy makers have recognized a problem or whether a potential solution is available. In Paul Light's model, the streams are brought together by two "filters"—resources and opportunities. In reality, he argues, presidents keep the flow of problems and solutions under control by having the White House staff, including the domestic policy apparatus, make the "filtering decisions." Successful policy leadership results from combining appropriate problems and solutions under favorable political circumstances.

Problems and Issues. Problems and issues move onto the president's domestic policy agenda either because their seriousness and high visibility make it impossible to avoid them or because of presidential discretion. Examples of unavoidable problems include the energy shortages of the 1970s, high rates of inflation and unemployment, the emergence of acquired immune deficiency syndrome (AIDS) as a major threat to public health, and the problems resulting from increased drug usage.

Problems and issues stand a good chance of gaining a place on the agenda when enough important people, inside and outside the government, begin to think that something should be done about them.[8] This may happen as a consequence of changes in economic and social indicators, such as rates of inflation, unemployment, infant mortality, and students' scores on various standardized tests. Influential decision makers in the presidency, the bureaucracy, Congress, the private sector, and state and local governments routinely monitor changes in a large array of indicators. Whether these changes add up to a problem is a matter of interpretation. That interpretation takes place in the context of the symbolic significance of the matter, the personal experiences of the president and the other decision makers with it, and the relationship of the subject to other problems and issues.

The president and other decision makers may be moved to recognize a condition as a compelling problem because of a "focusing event," such as a disaster or a crisis. For example, the near meltdown of a reactor at the

Three Mile Island power plant in March 1979 thrust the issue of nuclear safety to the forefront of the domestic agenda after its proponents had struggled for years with little success to gain recognition for it. Similarly, riots in Los Angeles in May 1992 rekindled interest in urban policy for the first time since the 1960s.

In addition, the president on occasion has no choice but to deal with a problem, even though he may prefer not to do so. In 1986, for instance, President Reagan had to confront demands from some U.S. industries and their workers for protection from foreign competition when the House of Representatives passed a bill restricting textile and apparel imports. Reagan announced his opposition to the bill and pledged to work against Senate passage. His commitment to free trade was stronger than his aversion to facing a difficult issue. The situation in Los Angeles prodded a reluctant President Bush to propose legislation to aid the damaged city.

Some problems and issues remain on the agenda through successive presidential administrations. Feasible solutions may not have been found, solutions may have been tried unsuccessfully, or the problem may have been "solved" only to reemerge in a different form. Education exemplifies such an issue. President Dwight D. Eisenhower turned to it reluctantly in 1958 as an appropriate response to the Soviet satellite *Sputnik*. The efforts of John F. Kennedy and Lyndon B. Johnson sparked the enactment of legislation establishing a wide range of federal programs that were expected to solve the problems of American education. Carter brought education back to the agenda to fulfill a campaign promise to establish a cabinet-level department for the various programs. Reagan took office publicly committed to abolish the new Department of Education. However, after several reports raised the issue of the falling quality of education, he called for improvement in the effectiveness of federal education programs (although with less funding) and dropped his proposal to abolish the department. Education remained on the domestic agenda even though Reagan would have liked to remove it. Ignoring it would have sent the wrong message. President Bush expressed a desire to be known as the "education president" and advocated measures such as giving parents greater choice of schools for their children and national examinations to monitor educational progress.[9]

Not all issues, however, can command a place on the president's agenda, and presidents have broad discretion to determine which they emphasize. Presidents choose to deal with certain problems because they see them as instrumental to the achievement of their goals. According to Paul Light, three goals affect presidents' selection of problems and issues for their agendas: reelection (for a first-term president); historical achievement; and a desire to shape public policy in accordance with their beliefs.[10] Presidents vary in the emphasis they place on these goals. Richard Nixon's willingness to propose innovative policies for welfare reform and revenue sharing, even at the expense of alienating some of his conservative supporters, reflected his concern with historical achievement.[11] Reagan consistently defined domestic policy in terms of his conservative ideology, even at the risk of electoral disadvantage. As he approached his reelection campaign, Carter shifted from making agenda decisions on the basis of his beliefs to making them on the basis of politics. Bush drew frequent criticism for his limited, largely reactive domestic agenda that "intrigued some in Washington less for what it contained . . . than for what it ignored."[12] Variations in presidential goals help one to understand why abortion was an important symbolic issue for Reagan and Bush but not for Gerald Ford and Jimmy Carter, who were strongly committed to ratification of the Equal Rights Amendment.

Solutions. Once a problem or an issue has been recognized, the availability of a solution becomes an important determinant of whether it will rise to a high position on the president's agenda.[13] Rarely do presidents attempt to find new solutions because the incentives to do so are few.[14] Solutions take several forms, ranging from direct actions, such as legislative proposals or executive orders, to symbolic actions, such as appointment of a study commission or a task force, to no action at all. Problems can have several solutions, and a solution can be applied to more than one problem. Solutions attach themselves to a problem, or they may be consciously selected from among competing alternatives. Most solutions that are coupled with problems on the president's agenda come from ideas generated outside the presidency, because the presidency is a small institution relative to its external environment, which contains an enormous number of potential sources of ideas. Also, there is not sufficient time for those assisting the president independently to analyze problems and issues and to evaluate alternative solutions to them. The principal external sources of ideas are Congress, the bureaucracy, interest groups, universities, research institutes, and state and local governments. Within the presidency, the president's campaign promises are a source of policy proposals and a benchmark for evaluating externally generated ideas.[15] Occasionally, the president's domestic policy staff may develop new ideas.

Many of the ideas that emerge as proposed solutions to problems on the president's agenda have been circulating among members of "issue networks" that develop around clusters of related problems and issues. (See the discussion in Chapter 6.) Individual policy entrepreneurs in Congress, government agencies, research organizations, universities, and state and local governments promote specific ideas and proposals, such as welfare reform and tax reform. These advocates are motivated by a desire to advance their personal and organizational interests and to influence public policy in accordance with their values. They study, analyze, and discuss problems and solutions among themselves, and they attempt to inform and influence the major decision makers in government, the most important of whom is the president.

The process by which ideas develop, advance, and either succeed or fail to gain acceptance in an issue network is often lengthy and generally diffused. John Kingdon describes it as a "policy primeval soup" in which ideas are continually bumping into one another, with some of them surviving, dying, combining, or emerging into new forms.[16] Those that manage to become incorporated into policy proposals that the president accepts are evaluated using three criteria: economic, political, and technical feasibility.

The cost of a potential solution is especially important, as demands for federal expenditures far outweigh the government's capacity to fund them. Few proposals for major new spending programs are likely to survive in an era of resource constraints. Proposals to restrain or reduce spending are more attractive to a president struggling to control the budget deficit. A proposal's political feasibility is determined initially by its compatibility with the values and interests of other important decision makers, particularly in Congress. Ultimately, a proposal must gain the acquiescence, if not the acceptance, of the public. The technical feasibility of a proposal—the question of its workability—does not receive as much attention as its economic and political costs. Some ideas—such as proposals for welfare reform that maintain reasonably high payments, reduce inequities between recipients in different states and between recipients and the working poor, and do not increase the cost to the government—are economically and politically very attractive but unworkable in practice. Presidents Nixon and Carter made this discovery, much to their dismay, after the failure of their major efforts to achieve welfare reform.[17] Such conflict among the three criteria is always present. Budget costs may rule out a proposal that is politically and technically feasible, such as rapid cleanup of toxic waste sites. Or political costs may prevent acceptance of a workable proposal that is compatible with a tight budget, such as freezing Social Security cost-of-living increases. Eventually, a short list of presidential proposals emerges from a multitude of potential solutions.

Political Factors. The third major component of the presidential policy stream is the tributary that carries political factors.[18] It flows independently of the problems and issues streams, but it affects the setting and implementation of the president's agenda. The principal political factors are the national mood, the balance of political forces, and events within the government.

The national mood is a somewhat amorphous phenomenon that is difficult to define. It is not identical with public opinion, nor can it be ascertained through survey research. It is perhaps best described as the perception among important decision makers that a consensus exists or is building in the country among various attentive publics and political activists for specific government policies. Politicians sense the national mood in suggestions, requests, and other communications from interest groups, state and local government officials, corporate executives, and politically active citizens; in news media coverage of events; and in editorial commentary. The national mood also reflects the influence of social movements such as civil rights, environmentalism, and consumerism. Without a favorable national mood, major new policies, such as the deregulation of air transportation in 1978 or the military buildup during the Reagan administration, are not likely to be adopted. The national mood is, then, a reflection of the politically relevant climate or temper of the times.

Considerably more concrete than the national mood is the extent of consensus and conflict among organized political forces. The prospects for adoption of a proposed policy change depend on the balance of organized interests and other forces, but assessing the balance on any issue is largely a matter of informed guesswork. The complex pattern of pluralistic political forces and the fragmentation of government authority combine to provide a strong advantage to the *opponents* of policy change. Often, heavy political costs are associated with even raising an issue for consideration, let alone obtaining adoption of a proposal. This is particularly the case with existing government programs, most of which have powerful clientele groups that stand ready to defend their programs. Clientele interests, in triangular subgovernment alliances with agencies that administer "their" programs and with congressional subcommittees with jurisdiction over those programs, engage in bargaining and logrolling to maintain and enhance the programs. To overcome the natural inertia of the government, a strong constituency for political change must be mobilized; otherwise, a proposal will encounter much difficulty. For example, the Carter administration's efforts to enact a national energy policy were unsuccessful despite widespread shortages of fuels, until compromises made the proposal acceptable to the oil industry and consumer interests.

Events in government are the third major political factor that shapes the president's policy agenda. Election outcomes that result in a change in personnel from the president down through the executive branch and in Congress can produce fundamental changes in the agenda. The 1980 election, which brought Ronald Reagan to the presidency and gave the Republicans control of the Senate for the first time in a quarter of a century, was such an event. An ideologically defined, conservative agenda replaced the liberal agenda that had been in effect since the New Deal. Even the appointment of one official, such as Donald Regan as White House chief of staff in February 1985, can have a substantial effect on the formulation and content of the agenda. Under Regan, the domestic issue agenda began to be determined by a few aggressive cabinet members—Attorney General Edwin Meese III and Treasury Secretary James A. Baker III—rather than by several cabinet committees, as in Reagan's first term.[19]

Jurisdictional matters are another intragovernmental development that may affect agenda setting. Disputes over bureaucratic and committee turf often delay or prevent action, although jurisdictional competition occasionally may accelerate consideration of a popular issue. Also, a proposal may be structured so that it will be handled by a committee or agency that is favorably disposed to it.

In sum, the most significant domestic policy action is likely to occur when the national mood and election outcomes combine to overcome the normal inertia produced by the balance of political forces and the fragmentation of government authority among numerous bureaucratic and congressional fiefdoms. Once items begin to rise on the agenda, however, organized political forces attempt to shape policy proposals to their advantage or to defeat them outright.

Resources and Opportunities

The convergence of specific problems and solutions under favorable circumstances creates a strong probability of a place on the president's agenda. Not all problems and solutions, however, can receive the president's attention and consideration. Because agenda space is limited, presidents must establish priorities.[20] This is accomplished through what Light calls a "filtering process" that maintains an orderly flow of problems and solutions to the president and merges them to produce policy proposals. The objectives of the process are to control the flow of items so that important problems, issues, and alternatives receive attention without overloading the president and to ensure that policy proposals have been formulated with due regard to relevant political factors. There are two filters through which problems and solutions pass as they are melded into presidential decisions: resources and opportunities.

Presidents cannot place all policy proposals they receive on their agenda. Some proposals are not compatible with their overall objectives and their ideologies, but many otherwise acceptable proposals never reach the agenda because limitations on their resources impose constraints on the choices open to presidents. When Reagan took office, a lengthy list of conservative policy goals awaited action. He decided to focus on reducing the scope of domestic programs, increasing military preparedness, and reducing taxes. He accomplished most of these goals during his first year in office. He disappointed many of his supporters, however, by not moving forward with equally strong support for proposals that would end abortion, restore prayer in public schools, and provide financial aid to parents of children enrolled in private schools. Reagan and his staff recognized that his resources, although substantial, were limited and that successful policy leadership requires the careful use of them.

"Political capital" is the reservoir of popular and congressional support with which newly elected presidents begin their terms. As they make controversial decisions, they "spend" some of their capital, which they seldom are able to replenish. They must decide which proposals merit the expenditure of political capital and in what amounts. Reagan, for example, was willing to spend his capital heavily on reducing the role of the federal government, cutting taxes, and reforming the income tax code, but not on anti-abortion or school prayer amendments to the Constitution. Material resources determine which proposals for new programs can be advanced and the emphasis to be placed on existing programs. Reagan's commitments to strengthen national defense and maintain Social Security meant that his costly proposal to provide income tax credits to parents of children attending private schools had little chance of being adopted. Bush began his presidency with limited political capital. His party had lost seats in both houses of Congress, and, although he won 54 percent of the vote, postelection commentary was unanimous in its judgment that he had not received a mandate.[21] Bush's limited domestic policy agenda and reactive stance appear to have been due at least partly to his lack of political capital.

Opportunities often are described metaphorically as windows: they open for a while and then close. They may be scheduled or unscheduled. Scheduled opportunities occur in conjunction with the annual cycle of presidential messages to Congress (State of the Union, budget, and economic report), the congressional calendar, and action-forcing deadlines, such as renewals of program authorizations. The president's greatest opportunity to set the agenda occurs during January and February, when Congress begins a new session and he delivers his messages, and in August and September, when Congress returns from recess and earlier proposals can be replaced or modified.[22] Unscheduled opportunities occur as the result of focusing events or changes in political conditions. Both scheduled and unscheduled windows of opportunity eventually close, some sooner than others. An opportunity is more likely to be seized and an issue given a high place on the president's agenda when problems, solutions, and political factors come together.[23] Without a viable solution and in the absence of favorable political conditions, a problem has a limited chance of moving up on the agenda. For instance, popular support for biomedical research is substantial, but the slow pace of development of treatments and cures for cancer limits presidential attention to the issue.

Opportunities also fluctuate as a presidential term progresses. In a president's first year in office, Congress and the public have high expectations of policy change based on campaign promises and the election mandate. Opportunities tend to be at their peak during the so-called honeymoon period. In the second and fourth years of a president's term, concern focuses increasingly on the forthcoming election campaign, and policy opportunities decline. The third year frequently is regarded as crucial, for the administration is by then experienced, mature, removed from immediate electoral pressures, and anxious to make its mark.[24] Opportunities are most likely to be exploited effectively then and in the first year of a president's second term, assuming he is reelected. Because a second-term president will not continue in office, his "lame-duck" status tends to restrict further his policy opportunities. The effects of lame-duck status on presidential initiatives are especially notable following the midterm congressional election in a president's second term.

There are conflicting patterns in the progression of a president's opportunities as he moves through his term. On the one hand, as presidents acquire experience and expertise, they become more effective and thus increase their policy opportunities. On the other hand, as their congressional and popular support declines through the term, they lose opportunities. Light describes these as cycles of increasing effectiveness and declining influence.[25] It is ironic that as presidents become more skilled at finding opportunities, they become less able to exploit them.

The Domestic Policy Environment

The most outstanding characteristic of the domestic policy environment is its complexity. Myriad actors—individuals, groups, and other government institutions and agencies—all pursue a seemingly incalculable range of objectives and protect countless interests. Although the president's power is limited, he is better situated than anyone else to give direction and bring some degree of coordination to the domestic policies of the U.S. government.

The fragmentation of political power and influence that is the hallmark of the U.S. political system is the product of a heterogeneous and pluralistic society and of constitutional arrangements designed to produce deliberate rather than expeditious government decision making. Nowhere is the fragmentation of power more apparent and more profound than in the domestic policy environment.

Outside the government, thousands of interest groups constantly seek to influence policy. They range from organizations that are concerned with the full range of the government's activities, such as Americans for Democratic Action, to those that focus on a single issue, such as the National Rifle Association (NRA), which is dedicated to preventing the adoption of strict gun control legislation. Interest groups are concerned not only with virtually every government program that distributes benefits to individuals and organizations and regulates their conduct but also with possibilities for new programs. Simply stated, the objectives of interest groups are to secure the adoption of policies that are beneficial to their members and to prevent the adoption of policies they view as harmful to them. Interest groups operate in all sectors of domestic policy—agriculture, civil rights, social welfare, and natural resources. They include organizations that represent business, labor, the professions, consumers, state and local governments and their subdivisions, public officials, social groupings based on age, sex, race, religion, shared attitudes and experiences, and groups that present themselves as protectors of the unorganized public interest.

Within the national government, interest groups attempt to exert influence directly on Congress, the bureaucracy, the courts, and the presidency. Beginning with Lyndon Johnson, presidents have responded by assigning individual White House aides the responsibility for maintaining liaison with interest groups in policy areas such as civil rights, education, and health. When a few individual aides were unable to manage the function of interest group liaison, as increasing numbers of groups sought access to the presidency, the White House established the Public Liaison Office as a counterpart to the Congressional Liaison Office. Interest groups have attempted to exert influence indirectly, principally by endorsing and making campaign contributions to presidential and congressional candidates and by urging their members to bring pressure to bear on the White House and on their representatives in Congress.

It is difficult to measure the effectiveness of interest group influence on public policy because there are multiple points of access to government decision makers; numerous groups usually seek to influence a particular policy or set of related policies; and powerful forces other than interest groups also are at work. Nonetheless, there is widespread belief that the growth in interest group activity since 1965 contributed substantially to the rise of federal spending on domestic programs and the expansion of federal regulation into noneconomic areas, such as consumer protection, product safety, and occupational safety and health.[26] Since 1965 previously unorganized groups—for example, consumer groups, public interest groups, and groups representing various minorities and the poor— have successfully demanded federal benefits and regulatory intervention in behalf of their members. These demands, often asserted as a matter of "right" and defended on grounds of fairness or improving the quality of life, strained the fiscal capacity of the federal government and created new conflicts in society.

Mancur Olson, an economist, has argued that societies with large numbers of powerful "distributional coalitions" (his term for interest groups) have experienced unsupportably high public spending and little or no economic growth as a consequence of the political influence of such groups. The groups press for public benefits for their members even though the result may be disadvantageous to the entire community. According to Olson, unless an interest group encompasses most of the population, there is "no constraint on the social cost such an organization will find it expedient to impose on the society in the cause of obtaining a larger share of the social output for itself."[27] To a substantial extent, domestic policy politics have become the pursuit of narrow group interests, even at the expense of the general public interest, which is usually unorganized, unarticulated, and difficult to identify or define. The president is better situated, in terms of political resources, than anyone else to define, enhance, and defend the public interest. That is his principal challenge in the domestic policy area. President Truman was fond of saying that his job was to act as a lobbyist for the American people, most of whom are not represented by lobbyists.

The pattern of interest group activity traditionally has been described as "policy subgovernments," mutually beneficial triangular relationships between interest groups, administrative agencies, and congressional subcommittees. Subgovernments, and the more open and amorphous "issue networks" that cut across and intersect with them, contribute to the fragmentation of power and influence in the domestic policy environment *(see Chapter 6)*. That fragmentation is enhanced by constitutional arrangements that divide power among the branches of government and between the national and state governments and also by the internal structures of Congress and the federal bureaucracy. The constitutional design was created to prevent the abuse of power through the establishment of a system of "separated institutions sharing power."[28]

The Framers invented federalism as a means of resolving the seemingly insoluble conflict between advocates of a consolidated system of government and the proponents of state sovereignty. Their ingenious compromise, which artfully avoided establishing a precise boundary between national and state powers, has been adapted to the needs of the times by successive generations of political leaders. The current system of centralized federalism still leaves primary responsibility for most basic government services in the hands of the states and their local subdivisions. These services include public education, public and mental health, public safety, and construction and maintenance of streets, roads, and highways. The federal government has programs that help finance state and local activities in these and other areas, and it exerts a substantial degree of influence on them by virtue of its grant and regulatory programs. Still, most of its domestic policy activity does not entail direct federal administration.

The president's leadership role in domestic policy requires that he persuade, bargain, and cooperate with Congress, federal administrators, and state and local officials. In these relationships he has limited power to command. Rather, he must rely on his skills as a political leader—principally persuasion and bargaining—to achieve his goals.

The structure of authority in Congress is highly decentralized, providing members with extensive opportunities to influence policy. Consequently, Congress finds it very difficult to give direction to public policy, and presidents encounter problems in their relations with Congress (see Chapter 5). In today's political environment, unlike that of the late 1950s and early 1960s, presidents cannot negotiate agreements with top party leaders and one or two influential committee chairs in each house and be confident that those agreements will prevail in floor voting. Rather, contemporary presidents must deal separately, in each house, with several committee chairs, subcommittee chairs, and party leaders. In addition, they must remain attentive to the positions of party caucuses and sub-caucuses. Agreements reached at one stage in the legislative process often come undone later on; such reverses happened frequently during the 1980s and early 1990s as Presidents Reagan and Bush struggled with Congress to reduce budget deficits. There is also increasing conflict within Congress between committees, which results from the practice of referring bills to more than one committee and from the establishment of the congressional budget process in 1974. The functions of the budget committees established in the Budget Act of 1974 encroached upon the powers of the appropriations and authorization (legislative) committees.

The effects of Congress's extensive fragmentation on the president's involvement in domestic policy are mixed. On the one hand, Congress is unable to counterbalance the presidency by providing alternative policy

leadership. On the other hand, presidents have found it increasingly difficult to lead Congress. Congressional influence is extensive because of its
inertia and its ability to resist presidential direction.

Fragmentation of a different sort characterizes the federal bureaucracy.
As noted in Chapter 6, an independent power exists in the bureaucracy
that is based in career civil servants who constitute a permanent government. The members of the permanent government have professional and
agency loyalties and close ties to the interest groups who constitute their
clientele and to the congressional subcommittees with jurisdiction over
their appropriations and the legislation that authorizes their programs.
Subgovernments and issue networks comprise members of the permanent
government and complicate presidential control of policy development
and implementation in the bureaucracy. Also, the fragmentation resulting
from the size and complexity of the federal bureaucracy creates enormous
problems of management and policy coordination for the president.

The Domestic Policy Apparatus

The need for presidential coordination in domestic policy has been
recognized for some time. The principal effort to enable presidents to
provide the necessary coordination was the development of a domestic
policy staff apparatus in the Executive Office of the President. The domestic policy staff evolved slowly, in conjunction with the development of the
president's legislative role *(see Chapter 5)*. This was an evolutionary process that relied initially on the Bureau of the Budget (BOB) and later saw
the establishment of a separate staff to formulate and implement domestic
policy.

BOB: Central Clearance and Legislative Program Planning

From the early nineteenth century until the creation of the Bureau of
the Budget in 1921, the president's role in domestic policy formulation
was ad hoc and unorganized.[29] In its first year of operation, BOB required
that all agency legislative proposals for the expenditure of federal funds be
submitted to it before being sent to Congress. Those proposals that BOB
determined were not in accord with the president's financial program
were not sent forward, and agencies were to inform Congress if pending
legislation had been found not in accord. This procedure, known as "central clearance," was expanded during Franklin D. Roosevelt's administra-

tion to cover the substantive content of proposed legislation. Its original function was to ensure that legislative proposals of various departments and agencies were compatible with the president's overall program goals.[30] Over time, central clearance acquired additional functions, including supervising and coordinating executive branch legislative initiatives, providing a clear indication to congressional committees of the president's position on proposed legislation, and making various administrative units aware of one another's goals and activities.

Beginning in 1947, BOB's domestic policy role expanded to include participation in developing the president's legislative program.[31] Its Legislative Reference Division worked directly with Truman's White House staff in reviewing agency recommendations and integrating them in a comprehensive legislative program. The addition of responsibilities to formulate policy involved BOB personnel in the pursuit of the president's political goals, a development that may later have resulted in questions about its ability to provide professional staff services to the president. Moreover, in the 1960s, as BOB became deeply involved in program planning, White House staff played a larger role in the clearance process, and the line between clearance and legislative planning became more and more blurred.[32]

When Eisenhower came into office, he was initially unprepared to submit a legislative program to Congress, but quickly recognized that he was expected to do so. The centralized clearance and planning processes lodged in BOB were quite compatible with Eisenhower's penchant for systematic staff operations, and he continued to employ them throughout his administration. The principal distinction between him and his predecessor in this regard was that Eisenhower attached a lower priority to new domestic policy proposals. Central to the process of legislative programming as it had developed by 1960 were annual submissions of legislative proposals by departments and agencies. Items that were not enacted in one year were introduced in the next. The result was a highly routinized process that was nearly impervious to new ideas. This system was quite suitable for Eisenhower's limited domestic policy initiatives.

Task Forces and Study Commissions

The activist Democratic presidents of the 1960s, John Kennedy and Lyndon Johnson, overcame the rigidities and bureaucratic domination of the BOB-based program planning process by obtaining ideas and suggestions from nongovernment sources.[33] The mechanism used for this purpose was the task force. Before his inauguration, Kennedy appointed several study groups, or task forces, of experts from inside and outside the government to advise him on the major issues and problems facing the new administration. The reports of these task forces, and of a number of others appointed after Kennedy took office, provided the basis for much of his New Frontier program.[34]

Although Kennedy remained eager for new ideas and suggestions, he did not rely heavily on outside sources of advice after the initial round of task forces. Instead, he turned primarily to his cabinet for suggestions. Johnson appointed a set of task forces in the spring of 1964 with the specific mission of developing a distinctive program for his administration. Johnson's task forces were made up of outsiders, and they operated in secret. He was so pleased with their reports, which furnished much of the form and substance of his Great Society program, that he made task forces a regular part of his program development process. The White House staff coordinated the task force operations, and BOB integrated the proposals into the annual legislative program.

Johnson favored the task force process because it largely avoided the tortuous task of bargaining with departments and agencies and because it was not adulterated by bureaucratic, congressional, and interest group pressures.[35] He used the task force device so extensively, however—in 1967 alone at least fifty task forces were preparing reports—that it became routinized and lost the informality and flexibility that had made it so valuable for developing new proposals. Moreover, later in his presidency, Johnson's emphasis shifted from domestic to foreign and military policy as the nation became embroiled in the Vietnam War.

The presidents who followed Johnson made little use of task forces. (Nixon appointed fourteen task forces during his campaign, but their suggestions did not figure prominently in his initial legislative proposals.) Instead, they relied on more formal advisory bodies, such as commissions and White House conferences, to study issues and problems and to gather outside recommendations. Presidential commissions are broadly representative bodies that often are appointed to defuse highly sensitive issues. In September 1981, for example, President Reagan appointed the National Commission on Social Security Reform to develop a solution to a crisis in Social Security funding. Although the commission did not solve the crisis, it provided "cover" under which the principals, Reagan and House Speaker Thomas P. O'Neill, worked out a compromise solution.[36]

Because of the representative character of presidential commissions, their reports often blur critical issues. This occurs in consequence of their efforts to obtain consensus. Or, commissions may make findings and suggestions that embarrass the president, as did the 1970 report of the Scranton commission, which blamed campus disorders on President Nixon.

White House conferences bring together groups of experts and distinguished citizens for public forums held under presidential auspices. Their principal function is to build support among experts, political leaders, and relevant interests for presidential leadership to deal with the problems at issue. Neither White House conferences nor presidential commissions have served as the basis for major legislative proposals, but they have given legitimacy to certain presidential undertakings.

Domestic Policy Staffs

Since Johnson, presidents have not regularly employed task forces in developing their legislative programs, nor have they relied almost entirely on agency submissions, as did Truman and Eisenhower. Instead, they have used domestic policy staffs in the Executive Office of the President and a more politicized Office of Management and Budget (OMB).

Nixon established the Domestic Council in 1970 as part of a reorganization of the presidency, in which the Bureau of the Budget was renamed the Office of Management and Budget.[37] The Domestic Council comprised the president, the vice president, the attorney general, and the secretaries of agriculture, commerce, housing and urban development, interior, labor, transportation, Treasury, and health, education and welfare, as well as the director and deputy director of OMB. The Domestic Council was to be a top-level forum for discussion, debate, and determination of policy analogous to the National Security Council (NSC). (See Chapter 10.) Like the NSC, the Domestic Council had a staff of professionals and support personnel. Headed by John Ehrlichman, the presidential assistant for domestic policy, the staff dominated Nixon's domestic policy-making process during the last two years of his first term, 1971–1972.[38]

The Domestic Council conducted its activity through work groups headed by one of six assistant directors. These groups prepared working papers for the president, evaluated departmental proposals for legislation, and participated in drafting presidential messages to Congress and preparing supportive materials for specific legislative proposals. In addition to assisting the president in formulating policy proposals, the Domestic Council also advocated, monitored, and evaluated policy.[39] This arrangement, in effect, made Ehrlichman the president's general agent for domestic policy. Under him the Domestic Council centralized control over domestic policy in the White House. The president's interests, as defined and expressed by Ehrlichman, took precedence over the interests of departments and agencies, as conveyed by cabinet members and agency heads.

The council's domination of domestic policy did not survive Ehrlichman's departure from the White House in April 1973.[40] The influence of the staff was clearly a function of Ehrlichman's status with the president. Under Ehrlichman's successor, Kenneth Cole, the Domestic Council became more of a service unit, and OMB resumed many of the functions of planning legislative programs.

In addition to the development of a presidential staff for domestic policy, Nixon also effected a major transformation in OMB by using it for political purposes. The OMB director became indistinguishable from other high-level presidential assistants, and a layer of political appointees, called "program assistant directors," was placed above OMB's career staff. Nixon's politicization of OMB reduced its ability to serve the institutional needs of the presidency as an impartial professional staff agency.[41]

President Ford used OMB to facilitate the unusual transfer of power from Nixon to himself, and he relied on it to help plan and coordinate programs in a more traditional and less partisan manner than Nixon had. Initially, Ford intended to give the Domestic Council a major planning role by making Vice President Nelson Rockefeller its chair. However, Rockefeller never became Ford's general agent for domestic policy. The long delay in congressional confirmation of Rockefeller's appointment and his conflict with White House chief of staff Donald Rumsfeld appear to have prevented such a development.[42] The council's staff director, James Cannon, a Rockefeller appointee, never gained influence with Ford, who sought advice from a wide range of sources including OMB, several cabinet members, and the Economic Policy Board, which was established in 1974 as a result of Ford's concern with economic policy problems (see Chapter 9). That emphasis partly explains why Ford seldom used the Domestic Council for policy planning. Indeed, Stephen Wayne reports that by the fall of 1976 the council no longer participated in legislative programming, and the staff was engaged in diverse activities such as answering presidential mail, preparing policy option memoranda, drafting presidential statements on legislation, and helping to explain the president's program to Congress.[43]

President Carter abolished the Domestic Council shortly after taking office, but he retained a domestic policy staff headed by one of his top aides, Stuart Eizenstat. In some respects Eizenstat and his staff acquired a policy-making role that resembled that of Ehrlichman and the Domestic Council in the Nixon administration. Margaret Wyszomirski concludes, however, that Eizenstat and the domestic policy staff did not dominate the domestic policy process and that they functioned more in the role of "effective administrator and of contributing advisor."[44] Lester Salamon believes that Ford and Carter brought about a "significant de-institutionalization" of the White House domestic policy role through the use of interagency policy task forces chaired by department or agency heads.[45] He further maintains that during the Carter administration these task forces produced undesirable effects, including interagency rivalry, lack of timeliness and coherence in decisions, and a disorderly process that bypassed career personnel in the Executive Office of the President.

Ronald Reagan, who came to office with a set, ideologically defined policy agenda and a strong commitment to cabinet government, created a new policy apparatus. The principal units were OMB, the Office of Policy Development (OPD), and seven cabinet councils. OMB's domestic policy involvement was especially crucial during Reagan's first year in office (1981) when the prime objective of drastically reducing the role of the federal government was linked to a budget reduction strategy that was implemented through use of the congressional budget process (see Chapter 9). OMB director David Stockman was the principal architect of the first substantial rollback of the government's domestic programs since the New Deal.

The OPD was the Reagan administration's equivalent of Carter's domestic policy staff. Headed by a presidential assistant for policy development, the OPD worked through cabinet councils, which had jurisdiction over economic affairs, commerce and trade, human resources, natural resources and environment, food and agriculture, legal policy, and management and administration.[46] The councils' members included appropriate cabinet and subcabinet officers and personnel from OMB and the

White House staff. Each council had a secretariat composed of department and agency representatives and used working groups to provide expertise and to analyze issues.

The OPD/cabinet council system did not, however, become the directing force for domestic policy. Other factors, particularly the president's long-range objectives and budget pressures, determined the agenda from the beginning of the administration. According to Chester Newland, Reagan's domestic policy apparatus worked out "details secondary to the president's fixed view of government."[47] In other words, it performed an administrative rather than an advisory role.

Developments in the first year of Reagan's second term resulted in a further diminution of the OPD/cabinet council system. The newly appointed White House chief of staff, former Treasury secretary Donald Regan, moved quickly to bring the three major policy areas—economics, national security, and domestic policy—under his control. The number of cabinet councils was reduced from seven to two, Economic Affairs and Domestic Policy. (The National Security Council, a statutory body, remained as it was.) Secretary of the Treasury Baker and Attorney General Meese chaired the economic and domestic policy councils, respectively. OPD was reduced in size, and its director reported to Regan. In addition to simplifying and reducing the size of the OPD/cabinet council system, Regan centralized authority over domestic policy in his office. However, the two remaining cabinet council chairs, Meese and Baker, enjoyed substantial autonomy to pursue policy projects of their own choosing. By early 1986 Regan had gained control of all access to the president with respect to domestic policy not under the purview of the two cabinet councils.

The diminished domestic policy apparatus of Reagan's second term reflected a shift in the administration's orientation from changing policies to defending them. Having accomplished most of his initial domestic agenda, principally curtailment of the growth of federal agencies and a reduction in spending on them, Reagan concentrated his energies on national security and economic policy objectives. The domestic policy apparatus under Reagan was at least partially deinstitutionalized.

The same condition continued in President Bush's first term.[48] The assistant to the president for economic and domestic affairs, former Harvard professor Roger Porter, directed the Office of Policy Development. The OPD and the White House Office of Cabinet Affairs provided staff support for the Domestic Policy Council and the Economic Policy Council.

However, major issues usually bypassed the cabinet council system and were resolved by Chief of Staff John Sununu or budget director Richard Darman. Sununu's self-defined role was to protect the conservative integrity of the administration against the incursions of pragmatism, while Darman functioned as a nonideological guardian of the budget and advocate of economic growth. Both intervened frequently on low-level issues. However, some cabinet members, such as Secretary of Housing and Urban Development Jack Kemp and Secretary of Transportation Samuel Skinner, took the lead in developing major domestic legislative proposals and pushing them in Congress.[49]

Modern Presidents and Domestic Policy

Modern presidents have varied greatly in the extent of their interest and involvement in domestic policy. Franklin Roosevelt was preoccupied with domestic policy during his first two terms (1933–1941) as he orchestrated the development, enactment, and implementation of the New Deal, which encompassed the most extensive set of social and economic reforms in U.S. history. Its immediate stimulus was the Great Depression, but it was also a response to the effects of urbanization and industrialization.

Roosevelt's approach to domestic policy was pragmatic. He tried a wide range of policies. Those that did not work were quickly discarded. Those that were successful were incorporated in a greatly expanded role for the federal government, which assumed positive responsibilities for individual, corporate, and general welfare that went far beyond the traditional negative functions of safeguarding public health, safety, and morals. Among the most prominent legacies of the New Deal are the Social Security system, unemployment compensation, support of agricultural prices, insurance of bank deposits, extensive public works projects such as the Grand Coulee Dam, the Tennessee Valley Authority, and federal regulation of securities exchanges, communications, and energy. During his final years in office (1941–1945), FDR devoted himself almost exclusively to national security policy, as "Dr. Win-the-War" took over from "Dr. New Deal."

Roosevelt's successor, Harry Truman, was deeply involved with national security from the start of his presidency, even though his interests and experience lay in the area of domestic policy. In his first term (1945–

1949) Truman offered few domestic policy initiatives, for he was occupied with the transition from war to peace and with difficulties in dealing with America's wartime ally, the Soviet Union. Following his upset reelection victory in 1948, Truman proposed a comprehensive set of domestic policy reforms called the Fair Deal. The Fair Deal agenda included national health insurance, federal aid to education, and expanded agricultural price supports. Little of the Fair Deal was implemented, however, as the cold war intensified and the United States became involved in the Korean War (1950–1953).

Truman's successor, General Dwight Eisenhower, a World War II hero, was a conservative who had no desire to expand the federal government's role in the life of the nation. He did not, however, attempt to repeal any of the New Deal reforms. His administration (1953–1961) was marked by economic expansion, punctuated by recessions in 1954 and 1958, and by stabilization in international affairs. Among Eisenhower's major domestic policy accomplishments were the passage of legislation authorizing construction of the Interstate Highway System; the National Defense Education Act in 1958, a direct response to the Soviet success in launching the first earth satellite; and limited civil rights bills in 1957 and 1960.

Domestic policy innovation and expansion of federal programs were a central objective of John Kennedy (1961–1963) and Lyndon Johnson (1963–1969). Kennedy developed and submitted to Congress an extensive domestic policy agenda labeled the New Frontier. It included most of the unfinished agenda of the Fair Deal plus proposals for expanded civil rights legislation.

At the time of Kennedy's assassination, in November 1963, Congress was considering several pieces of New Frontier legislation. Johnson moved quickly and effectively in 1964 to secure passage of much of the Kennedy agenda, for example, the Vocational Education Act, the Higher Education Act, and the Civil Rights Act of 1964. In addition, Johnson launched the War on Poverty, featuring the Economic Opportunity Act of 1964, which established the Office of Economic Opportunity. In his 1964 election campaign, Johnson proposed additional domestic reforms under the rubric the Great Society. The year 1965 witnessed the largest outpouring of new domestic policy legislation since the New Deal. Congress passed the Elementary and Secondary Education Act, the Voting Rights Act, and legislation authorizing Medicare, Medicaid, and the model cities program. The departments of Housing and Urban Development and

Transportation were established. Hundreds of new federal grant-in-aid programs for state and local governments were implemented. Johnson's zealous pursuit of domestic policy goals gave way, however, to international concerns. His attention in his last two years in office (1967 and 1968) was taken up by the Vietnam War. Funds for Great Society programs were restricted before many of them could be fully implemented as the costs of the war consumed an increasing portion of the federal budget. Opposition to the war in the United States and from abroad led Johnson to retire from public life rather than seek reelection.

Although Richard Nixon, who succeeded Johnson in 1969, was primarily interested in national security policy, he offered an innovative proposal to reform the welfare system, which Congress ultimately rejected. He also considered a variety of suggestions for reforming the financing of public education. Perhaps his principal domestic policy accomplishment was the establishment of federal revenue-sharing with state and local governments. Nixon's major achievements, however, were in the realm of national security policy.

Nixon's successor, Gerald Ford, was a conservative who had no strong commitments to domestic policy innovation. Despite his substantial background in domestic policy, Ford was essentially a passive president in this area.

Jimmy Carter, a moderate in a largely liberal party, presented a wide range of domestic policy proposals during his administration. He struggled with Congress over a national energy policy; the legislation that eventually passed was a watered-down compromise. He was unable to obtain passage of his proposal for welfare reform, and he temporized at length before proposing a national health insurance plan. Carter was an active president in domestic policy, but he achieved few of his major objectives.

Reagan campaigned successfully for the presidency in 1980 with the most radically conservative proposals for domestic policy since the New Deal. Reagan's stated purpose was no less than to institute a "new American Revolution." The essentials of that revolution in domestic policy were defined in terms of Reagan's conservative ideology. Except for the armed forces and support for law enforcement, the role of the federal government would be drastically curtailed. There would be a massive devolution of federal programs to state and local governments. The reduction in federal spending for domestic programs would provide the resources for an overdue military buildup, made necessary by the threat posed by the

Soviet Union, and for a substantial cut in income taxes. Reagan further believed that the tax cut would stimulate an economic expansion that would generate enough revenue to bring the federal budget into balance. Finally, he was committed to drastic reductions of federal regulation of the economy, the environment, and the work place.

The foundation of Reagan's domestic policy goals was an unswerving belief in the viability of a free market as the means of rationally and efficiently allocating resources and maximizing productivity. Allowing the free market to operate would increase material well-being and enhance individual freedom. Reagan's domestic policy objectives were long-range. He was not interested in the details of specific programs. What was done in domestic policy had to be compatible with the long-term goals that flowed from his ideological frame of reference. Pragmatic adjustments and compromises with individuals and interests who did not share his ideology were to be avoided at all costs. In this respect Reagan stood in sharp contrast to his predecessors from FDR to Carter.

George Bush's domestic policy agenda was characterized by its limited scope and the absence of a clear vision of American society.[50] A major theme for domestic policy—"empowerment" of individuals by means such as allowing public housing residents to buy their homes and giving parents greater freedom in choosing schools for their children—did not emerge until late in the second year of his administration.[51] Taking office at a time "ripe for inaction"[52] (the public supported neither further reductions in the size of government nor major new domestic programs), the nonideological Bush devoted most of his energy to national security issues.[53] Moreover, budget constraints created by the massive deficits of the Reagan years permitted very little opportunity for policy initiatives.

In spite of the lack of a comprehensive domestic policy agenda, the Bush administration was not without several major legislative achievements.[54] During the first three years (1989–1991) these included a bailout for the financially devastated savings and loan industry, the first major revision of the Clean Air Act in a decade, a bill establishing rights for the disabled, a sweeping child care bill, and revision and reauthorization of federal housing programs. One close observer remarked that "in many domestic policy fields, Bush has done better than his Administration's phlegmatic reputation suggests."[55]

The relationship of the modern presidents to domestic policy can be understood in terms of a cyclical theory of politics and policy developed by Erwin Hargrove and Michael Nelson. They argue that domestic political change in the twentieth century has taken place in "recurring cycles of electoral political competition and public policy making" that focus on the presidency. At the center of each cycle is a "presidency of achievement," marked by major legislation that alters "the role of government in society."[56] Three conditions are necessary for a presidency of achievement to occur: first, a campaign that promises significant reform; second, a landslide election victory; and third, substantial gains for the president's party in both houses of Congress.[57] Each presidency of achievement usually has been preceded by one or more presidencies of "preparation" and followed by one or more presidencies of "consolidation," in which the reforms are rationalized and legitimized. Hargrove and Nelson take care to point out that although the cycle of preparation, achievement, and consolidation is recurring it is not inevitable.[58]

In terms of this theory, Roosevelt was a president of achievement, even though a presidency of preparation did not precede him because the system-threatening crisis of the Great Depression disrupted the cycle. Truman's was a "presidency of stalemate" in which he sought to "set off a new round of achievement in the face of a strong public disposition for consolidation."[59] Eisenhower was "the quintessential president of consolidation" who brought stability and order to the changes initiated under Roosevelt's New Deal.[60] Kennedy served to prepare the way for Johnson's presidency of achievement—the Great Society—which was consolidated under Nixon. Ford fell outside the cycle with a "presidency of stasis," characterized by confusion regarding policy problems and solutions.[61] Carter's was a presidency of preparation for Reagan's achievements. His rhetoric and some of his actions involving deregulation, scaling back the size and scope of domestic programs, and strengthening the military foreshadowed the achievements of Reagan's conservative "revolution."[62] Bush has consolidated the changes implemented under Reagan and thus fits nicely into the cycle.

Conclusion

Presidents approach the task of making domestic policy with varying amounts of resources and differing policy opportunities. Their domestic policy leadership depends to a large extent on their effectiveness in using the available resources to exploit existing opportunities and create new ones. They are most apt to do this effectively when the three components of the policy stream—problems, solutions, and politics—converge. A president's ability to bring these three tributary streams together is one indication of effective policy leadership.

Successful policy leadership requires careful expenditure of presidential resources and skillful exploitation of opportunities. To do so further requires that presidents pay particular attention to four strategic factors: goals, priorities, timing, and costs and benefits.

Modest, flexible goals usually are easier to achieve than those that are extensive and ideologically derived. So too, are goals that enjoy substantial support among the public and policy-making elites. In establishing their goals, presidents take such considerations into account along with their values and beliefs. A primarily pragmatic set of objectives tends to be easier to accomplish than one that is ideologically derived. It is less likely, however, to have an impact on society than a more visionary and comprehensive set of objectives. In some circumstances ideological goals may be highly appropriate. For example, Ronald Reagan initially struck a responsive note in Congress and the public with his unabashedly conservative domestic program. Presidents are free to be as pragmatic or as ideological as they wish in establishing their goals. However they decide, the mix they choose affects their policy leadership.

Closely related to goals, priorities also affect policy leadership. Presidents who clearly define their priorities generally have been more successful than those who have not done so, because the policy process can handle only a few major issues at a time, even though many contend for attention. If a president does not indicate his preferences, other participants will pursue their own objectives, possibly to the detriment of the president's. Nor is it realistic for presidents to expect that all of their goals will receive consideration to the exclusion of those of other participants. In this respect a comparison between Carter and Reagan is instructive. Carter developed a lengthy domestic agenda and insisted that all of his goals were vitally important to the nation and deserving of enactment. Congress responded by taking its time in dealing with Carter's program and by pursuing many of its own objectives. Some of Carter's goals, such as welfare reform and national health insurance, were never adopted; others, such as a national energy policy, were passed in greatly modified form after extensive delay and bargaining. Many congressional Democrats complained that Carter failed to provide them with direction and guidance for his domestic proposals. In contrast, Reagan made his priorities clear at the beginning of his administration, and he continued to do so. Congress had little doubt about which goals Reagan considered vital and on which he would spend political capital and those that were less important to him. Cutting domestic spending, strengthening national defense, and reducing and reforming taxes took precedence over balancing the federal budget, ending legalized abortion, and restoring school prayer.

Timing, the third strategic consideration in successful policy leadership, is crucial to effective exploitation of opportunities. If opportunities are missed, they may be lost indefinitely. Good timing also involves taking advantage of the regular policy and electoral cycles. Proposals submitted at appropriate times in those cycles have greater likelihood of adoption. Proposals also can be withheld until conditions are ripe for their submission. A proposal that has limited support can be moved to the top of the agenda and pushed successfully as the result of a disaster, crisis, or other focusing event. Presidents who are able to time the presentation of proposals to coincide with favorable events and conditions are more likely to be effective policy leaders than those who lack such a sense of timing. Two presidents whose timing of domestic proposals was effective were Franklin Roosevelt during the first 100 days of the New Deal, when the Great Depression provided the rationale for a comprehensive set of economic recovery and reform laws, and Lyndon Johnson, who in early 1964 used the shock of the Kennedy assassination to secure passage of the Civil Rights Act.

Finally, successful policy leadership requires that presidents be attentive to the costs and benefits of raising problems for consideration and posing solutions to them. As presidents decide which problems and issues to emphasize, they focus on political benefits. They select agenda items according to the prospective electoral, historical, and programmatic benefits of the times.[63] When presidents select solutions for problems they are addressing, their emphasis is on costs.[64] Political costs, assessed in terms of congressional, electoral, bureaucratic, and interest group support, enter their calculations at each stage of the process. Increasingly, presidents and other actors have tended to view political costs in terms of avoiding blame and claiming credit for the outcomes.[65]

Economic costs have sharply limited the alternatives in recent years as budget pressures have mounted. They force presidents to make hard choices, such as whether to support new programs and which existing programs to emphasize, maintain, or reduce. Technical costs and questions of workability also enter the selection of policy alternatives.

No prescription or formula can guarantee that a president will provide successful domestic policy leadership, in part because some problems, such as the high unemployment rate among African American men, are very difficult to solve, or solutions do not exist for them. Another reason for the absence of a workable formula is that conditions constantly change. Some problems may be solved only to reemerge in a new form; others may decline in importance. Solutions that are viable today may not be so a few years hence, or solutions may have unanticipated consequences or side effects that become problems in their own right. Political conditions, such as the popular mood or control of Congress, are in flux, so strategies may have to be modified frequently. Because many of the requirements of successful policy leadership are not fixed, what worked well for one president may be only partially useful to those who come later.

Even presidents who take office committed to concentrating their energies on domestic policy encounter extensive frustrations. They may enjoy some initial successes, as did Reagan; but the difficulties of accomplishing additional objectives eventually increase, and the sharing of power with Congress, the bureaucracy, and organized interests becomes ever more burdensome. The natural tendency is for presidents to turn their attention to national security or economic policy. In these policy areas, the challenges are more immediately threatening to the general welfare; the constraints on their ability to act, although very real, are not as frustrating; and successful policy leadership appears less elusive.

NOTES

1. The concept of "issue congestion" was developed by Hugh Heclo, "One Executive Branch or Many?" in *Both Ends of the Avenue*, ed. Anthony King (Washington, D.C.: American Enterprise Institute, 1983), 26–58.

2. Theodore J. Lowi, "American Business, Public Policy, Case Studies, and Political Theory," *World Politics* (July 1964): 677–715.

3. Steven A. Shull, *Domestic Policy Formation: Presidential-Congressional Partnership?* (Westport, Conn.: Greenwood Press, 1983), 155.

4. Steven A. Shull, "Change in Presidential Policy Initiatives," *Western Political Quarterly* (September 1983): 497.

5. John H. Kessel, *Presidential Parties* (Homewood, Ill.: Dorsey, 1984), 112–115.

6. Ibid., 68–69.

7. The policy stream metaphor borrows from Paul Light, "The Presidential Policy Stream," in *The Presidency and the Political System*, ed. Michael Nelson (Washington,

D.C.: CQ Press, 1984), 423–448; and John W. Kingdon, *Agendas, Alternatives, and Public Policies* (Boston: Little, Brown, 1984), 92–94.

8. This discussion follows Kingdon, *Agendas*, chap. 5.

9. Burt Solomon, "Politically Punctual President Launches His Education Crusade," *National Journal*, April 20, 1991, 948–949.

10. Paul Light, *The President's Agenda: Domestic Policy Choice from Kennedy to Reagan*, 2d rev. ed (Baltimore: The Johns Hopkins University Press, 1991), chap. 3; and Light, "Presidential Policy Stream," 427–428.

11. Ironically, Nixon's preoccupation with the judgment of history helped to cut short his presidency. He has consistently explained the installation of the secret taping system in the Oval Office as motivated by his desire to have a complete and accurate record for use by historians. That taped record provided the "smoking gun," that led the House Judiciary Committee to vote the impeachment charges that prompted his resignation in August 1974.

12. Burt Solomon, "Bush Plays Down Domestic Policy in Coasting Toward Reelection," *National Journal*, March 30, 1991, 752–753.

13. Kingdon, *Agendas*, 150.

14. Light, *The President's Agenda*, 149.

15. Jeff Fishel, *Presidents and Promises: From Campaign Pledge to Presidential Performance* (Washington, D.C.: CQ Press, 1984).

16. Kingdon, *Agendas*, 138.

17. Vincent J. Burke and Vee Burke, *Nixon's Good Deed: Welfare Reform* (New York: Columbia University Press, 1974); Laurence E. Lynn, Jr., and David deF. Whitman, *The President as Policymaker: Jimmy Carter and Welfare Reform* (Philadelphia: Temple University Press, 1981).

18. This discussion is based on Kingdon, *Agendas*, chap. 7.

19. Ronald Brownstein and Dick Kirschten, "Cabinet Power," *National Journal*, June 28, 1986, 1589.

20. This discussion follows Light, "Presidential Policy Stream," 440–446.

21. Charles O. Jones, "Meeting Low Expectations: Strategy and Prospects of the Bush Presidency," in *The Bush Presidency: First Appraisals*, ed. Colin Campbell, S.J., and Bert A. Rockman (Chatham, N.J.: Chatham House, 1991), 50–52; and Barbara Sinclair, "Governing Unheroically (and Sometimes Unappetizingly): Bush and the 101st Congress," in *The Bush Presidency*, 157–159.

22. Light, "Presidential Policy Stream," 444–445.

23. Kingdon, *Agendas*, 204.

24. Kessel, *Presidential Parties*, 60.

25. Light, *The President's Agenda*, 36–38.

26. Harold Wolman and Fred Tietlebaum, "Interest Groups and the Reagan Presidency," in *The Reagan Presidency and the Governing of America*, ed. Lester M. Salamon and Michael S. Lund (Washington, D.C.: Urban Institute Press, 1985), 299–301.

27. Mancur Olson, *The Rise and Decline of Nations* (New Haven, Conn.: Yale University Press, 1982), 44.

28. Richard E. Neustadt, *Presidential Power and the Modern Presidents: The Politics of Leadership From Roosevelt To Reagan* (New York: Free Press, 1990), 29.

29. Lester M. Salamon, "The Presidency and Domestic Policy Formulation," in *The Illusion of Presidential Government*, ed. Hugh Heclo and Lester M. Salamon (Boulder, Colo.: Westview, 1981), 179.

30. Richard E. Neustadt, "The Presidency and Legislation: The Growth of Central Clearance," *American Political Science Review* (September 1954): 641–670; Robert S. Gilmour, "Central Clearance: A Revised Perspective," *Public Administration Review* (March/April 1971): 150–158.

31. Richard E. Neustadt, "The Presidency and Legislation: Planning the President's Program," *American Political Science Review* (December 1955): 980–1018; Larry Berman, *The Office of Management and Budget and the Presidency* (Princeton, N.J.: Princeton University Press, 1979), 42–43; Stephen J. Wayne, *The Legislative Presidency* (New York: Harper & Row, 1978), 103–105.

32. Gilmour, "Central Clearance"; Berman, *Office of Management and Budget*.

33. Norman C. Thomas and Harold L. Wolman, "The Presidency and Policy Formation: The Task Force Device," *Public Administration Review* (September/October 1969): 459–471.

34. Texts of the reports were published in *New Frontiers of the Kennedy Administration* (Washington, D.C.: Public Affairs Press, 1961).

35. Lyndon B. Johnson, *The Vantage Point* (New York: Holt, Rinehart & Winston, 1971), 326.

36. Paul Light, *Artful Work: The Politics of Social Security Reform* (New York: Random House, 1985), 232.

37. Berman, *Office of Management and Budget*, 106–113.

38. Raymond J. Waldman, "The Domestic Council: Innovation in Presidential Government," *Public Administration Review* (May/June 1976).

39. Margaret Jane Wyszomirski, "The Roles of a Presidential Office for Domestic Policy: Three Models and Four Cases," in *The Presidency and Policy Making*, ed. George C. Edwards, Steven A. Shull, and Norman C. Thomas (Pittsburgh: University of Pittsburgh Press, 1985), 134.

40. John Helmer and Louis Maisel, "Analytical Problems in the Study of Presidential Advice: The Domestic Council Staff in Flux," *Presidential Studies Quarterly* (Winter 1978), 52–53.

41. A sharp debate rages over politicization of OMB and the institutionalized presidency generally. Berman, in *The Office of Management and Budget and the Presidency*, argues that politicization has damaged, if not destroyed, the capacity of OMB to serve the institutional needs of the presidency in a professional manner. In contrast, Terry Moe in a seminal essay, views politicization as a logical (indeed necessary) institutional development resulting from the extensive and steady growth of "expectations surrounding presidential performance." See "The Politicized Presidency," in *The New Direction in American Politics*, ed. John E. Chubb and Paul E. Peterson (Washington, D.C.: Brookings, 1985), 269.

42. Wyszomirski, "Roles of a Presidential Office," 136–137.

43. Stephen J. Wayne, *The Legislative Presidency* (New York: Harper & Row, 1978), 123.

44. Wyszomirski, "Roles of a Presidential Office," 140.

45. Salamon, "The Presidency and Domestic Policy Formulation," 184.

46. For an extended description of the OPD/cabinet council system, see Chester A. Newland, "Executive Office Policy Apparatus: Enforcing the Reagan Agenda," in *The Reagan Presidency*, 153–159. Martin Anderson, who was Reagan's first director of the OPD, provides a participant's perspective on the cabinet councils in *Revolution* (New York: Harcourt Brace Jovanovich, 1988), chap. 19.

47. Ibid., 160.

48. This discussion follows Colin Campbell, S.J., "The White House and the Presidency under the 'Let's Deal' President," in *The Bush Presidency*, 210–212.

49. Julie Rovner, "On Policy Front, Home Is Not Where Bush's Heart Is," *Congressional Quarterly Weekly Report*, Feb. 2, 1991, 292.

50. Paul J. Quirk, "Domestic Policy: Divided Government and Cooperative Presidential Leadership," in *The Bush Presidency*, 73–76.

51. Burt Solomon, "'Empowerment,' Whatever It Is Powers Ahead in Policy Cir-

cles," *National Journal,* Dec. 12, 1990, 3046–47; Solomon, "Power to the People?" *National Journal,* Jan. 26, 1991, 204–209.

52. Quirk, "Domestic Policy," 73.

53. Kenneth T. Walsh, "George Bush's Idea-free Zone," *U.S. News & World Report,* Jan. 14, 1991, 34–35.

54. Rovner, "Home Is Not Where Bush's Heart Is," 292–293; Burt Solomon, "Grading Bush," *National Journal,* June 8, 1991, 1331–35.

55. Solomon, "Grading Bush," 1331.

56. Erwin C. Hargrove and Michael Nelson, *Presidents, Politics, and Policy* (New York: Knopf, 1984), 67.

57. Ibid., 76.

58. Ibid., 68.

59. Ibid.

60. Ibid., 72.

61. Ibid., 68.

62. Ibid., 81–83.

63. Light, *The President's Agenda,* 71.

64. Ibid., 134–136.

65. R. Kent Weaver, *Automatic Government: The Politics of Indexation* (Washington, D.C.: Brookings, 1988), chap. 2.

READINGS

Anderson, Martin. *Revolution.* New York: Harcourt Brace Jovanovich, 1988.

Boaz, David, ed. *Assessing the Reagan Years.* Washington, D.C.: Cato Institute, 1988.

Derthick, Martha. *Agency Under Stress: The Social Security Administration in American Government.* Washington, D.C.: Brookings, 1990.

Fishel, Jeff. *Presidents and Promises: From Campaign Pledge to Presidential Performance.* Washington, D.C.: CQ Press, 1984.

Hargrove, Erwin C., and Michael Nelson. *Presidents, Politics, and Policy.* New York: Knopf, 1984.

Kessel, John H. *Presidential Parties.* Homewood, Ill.: Dorsey, 1984.

Kingdon, John W. *Agendas, Alternatives, and Public Policies.* Boston: Little, Brown, 1984.

Light, Paul C. *The President's Agenda: Domestic Policy Choice from Kennedy to Reagan,* 2d rev. ed. Baltimore: The Johns Hopkins University Press, 1991.

———. *Artful Work: The Politics of Social Security Reform.* New York: Random House, 1985.

Lynn, Laurence E., Jr., and David deF. Whitman. *The President As Policymaker: Jimmy Carter and Welfare Reform.* Philadelphia: Temple University Press, 1981.

Palmer, John L., and Isabel V. Sawhill, eds. *The Reagan Record.* Washington, D.C.: Urban Institute Press, 1984.

Shull, Steven A. *Domestic Policy Formation: Presidential-Congressional Partnership.* Westport, Conn.: Greenwood Press, 1983.

———. *The President and Civil Rights Policy: Leadership and Change.* Westport, Conn.: Greenwood Press, 1989.

Sundquist, James L. *Politics and Policy: The Eisenhower, Kennedy, and Johnson Years.* Washington, D.C.: Brookings, 1968.

Weaver, R. Kent. *Automatic Government: The Politics of Indexation.* Washington, D.C.: Brookings, 1988.

9 THE POLITICS OF ECONOMIC POLICY

During the Great Depression, Franklin Roosevelt used radio broadcasts from the White House, known as "fireside chats," to persuade the public to support his unprecedented economic policies

THE FIRST HALF OF 1992 WAS not propitious for President George Bush. As his campaign for a second term got under way, the U.S. economy was struggling to emerge from its first recession in nine years. Bush's reelection prospects, which six months earlier were seldom questioned even by Democrats, appeared shaky. His approval ratings had fallen from record highs of nearly 90 percent after the successful conclusion of the Persian Gulf War to less than 35 percent. An angry public placed much of the blame for the recession on the president, who kept insisting that the economy was fundamentally sound and that recovery from the recession had begun. In the early presidential primaries, many disgruntled voters, including conservative Republicans, supported right-wing journalist Patrick Buchanan's challenge to the president's renomination. Buchanan's criticism, that Bush had shown little concern for the health of the economy and what he had done had harmed it, echoed the experience of some past presidents.

Presidents have been concerned about the condition of the economy since the early years of the Republic. Some who confronted serious economic adversity, such as Martin Van Buren in 1837, Ulysses S. Grant in 1873, Grover Cleveland in 1893, Theodore Roosevelt in 1907, and Warren G. Harding in 1921, did little more than ride out the storm. The electorate, however, reacted by denying reelection to Van Buren and inflicting sizable losses on the president's party in the midterm congressional elections of 1838, 1874, and 1894. In fact, the existence of a relationship between business cycles and election results was known long before Edward Tufte's precise empirical analysis of the phenomenon.[1] Only since the 1930s, however, have presidents attempted to control business cycles through public policy, and the public has come to expect them to do so.

This chapter examines the president's economic policy responsibilities and activities. It begins by distinguishing between actions designed to manage the entire economy (macroeconomic policy) and to control specific aspects of the economy (microeconomic policy). The primary focus of the chapter is on macroeconomic policy. It reviews presidential efforts to manage the economy from 1933 to 1992 and then describes the politics of macroeconomic policy making. Next, the chapter analyzes how the presidency functions in making economic policy and the ways in which presidents since Dwight D. Eisenhower have handled the problem of coordinating economic policy. The chapter concludes with an assessment of the congressional role in macroeconomic policy making.

Macroeconomic Policy

Management of the entire economy by the government is known as macroeconomic policy, and the government has two principal tools to use: fiscal policy and monetary policy. Fiscal policy refers to the government's efforts to regulate the level of the nation's economic activity by varying taxes and public expenditures. Fiscal policy seeks to expand the economy by increasing spending and reducing taxes or to contract it by decreasing spending and increasing taxes. A budget deficit, therefore, is expansionary whereas a budget surplus is deflationary. The president and Congress jointly make fiscal policy. They determine expenditures through budgeting and appropriations, and they establish taxes through legislation. Monetary policy refers to a government's efforts, through its central bank (in the United States, the Federal Reserve System), to regulate economic activity by controlling the supply of money. An independent agency, the Board of Governors of the Federal Reserve System, makes monetary policy.

The goals of macroeconomic policy have remained constant since the Great Depression of the 1930s: to hold down the rate of inflation, to establish and maintain full employment, and to achieve a steady rate of economic growth. There are, however, alternative theories that have guided policy makers in their pursuit of these goals: classical conservative economics, Keynesianism, monetarism, and supply-side economics.

Conservative economic theory lost credibility during the Great Depression when the budget-balancing efforts of the administrations of Herbert Hoover and, early on, of Franklin D. Roosevelt failed to restore confidence to the economy and produce the desired upturn. FDR quickly discovered that emergency spending and loan programs provided relief and produced a measure of recovery. The ideas of John Maynard Kcynes, a British economist whom Roosevelt met in 1934, offered an explanation of the phenomenon of economic response to fiscal stimulus and eventually provided a rationale for deficit spending. Keynes argued that the cause of an economic decline was a drop in private demand for goods and services. Government could stimulate demand by increasing its expenditures or by reducing taxes. The temporary deficits created by fiscal stimulation would be financed by government borrowing and repaid during periods of hyperactivity in the economy. FDR did not fully accept Keyneslan Ideas until a sharp recession followed his attempt to return to a balanced budget in 1937. Eventually, the recovery of the economy as a result of mobilization during World War II provided most economists with empirical validation of Keynes's basic theories. Conservative economics, however, retained its hold on many political leaders, such as Eisenhower, who made balanced budgets their goal and regarded fiscal stimulation of lagging demand as an emergency measure.

While Keynesianism was establishing itself as the new orthodoxy, another theory emerged to challenge it. The monetarists, under the leadership of economist Milton Friedman, held that the key to maintaining economic stability lay, not in the stimulation of demand, but in limiting the growth rate of the money supply to no more than the actual growth rate of the economy. Inflation occurs, monetarists claim, when the money supply expands too rapidly. The only remedy for inflation is a painful contraction in the money supply. Fiscal policy and the size of budget deficits are held to be subordinate to the basic means of managing the economy.

Monetarism gained adherents as the limitations of Keynesianism became apparent during the 1970s. A primary defect of Keynesian theory as the basis for macroeconomic policy was its inflationary bias. Decisions on taxing and spending are made by the president and members of Congress—politicians concerned with reelection— and not by professional economists. Consequently, it has proved easier in practice to increase spending and cut taxes, the Keynesian prescription for expansion, than to cut spending and increase taxes, the remedy for inflation. In the 1970s, when inflation became the nation's leading economic problem, the Keynesian solution was ineffective because political decision makers were unwilling to impose it. They feared the electoral consequences of reducing government spending and raising taxes when their constituents were struggling to make ends meet. Although the inflationary bias of Keynesianism is a political defect rather than a weakness in the theory itself, the effect has been its reduced attractiveness as a guide to policy.

Monetarism, whatever its theoretical merits and limitations, offered the prospect of controlling inflation in a politically less painful manner by having the autonomous Federal Reserve Board, known as "the Fed," contract the money supply. Political officeholders can blame the consequences of monetary contractions, such as high interest rates and rising unemployment, on the Fed and its amorphous supporters: "Wall Street" and the banks. The attempt to compensate for the lack of fiscal discipline by monetary contraction during the 1970s eventually proved so painful that monetarism also became politically unattractive. By the early 1980s a new theoretical approach, supply-side economics, had emerged and was embraced by President Ronald Reagan.

Essentially, supply-side economics is an amalgam of Keynesianism and monetarism.[2] Supply-siders endorse strict monetary restraint as the means to control inflation, but they reject the monetarist reluctance to use fiscal policy to achieve macroeconomic policy objectives. The supply-siders maintain, however, that the Keynesian focus on stimulating demand is misdirected. Instead, they advocate tax cuts designed to provide incentives that encourage investments and productivity, which in turn increase the supply of goods and services. Increasing the *supply* of goods and services stimulates the demand for them. Supply-siders are not disturbed by budget deficits resulting from tax-cut incentives. They argue that the stimulative effect of the tax cuts will create enough additional savings to finance the added deficits without an inflationary expansion of the money supply, and an expanded economy eventually will generate enough revenues at lower rates of taxation to balance the budget.

Supply-side economics draws sharp criticism, on the one hand, from liberals who charge that it is but another version of the discredited "trickle down" approach to economic policy under which tax advantages for the affluent are justified on the grounds that they eventually lead to prosperity for all. On the other hand, conservatives fear that supply-side tolerance of budget deficits will lead to excessive rates of inflation and erosion of confidence in the monetary system. Conservatives and Keynesian liberals alike doubt the validity of the assumptions on which supply-side economics rests. Although they would like it to work, they do not believe that it can. Experience since 1981 with a massive cut in federal income taxes, based on supply-side reasoning, supports their pessimism. The economy expanded during the 1980s, but revenues did not rise sufficiently to reduce, let alone balance, the federal budget. *(See the discussion of the budget deficit under ''The Congressional Role in Macroeconomic Policy.'')*

Microeconomic Policy

Microeconomic policy is a term used to describe government regulation of specific economic activities; it also encompasses antitrust policy. Microeconomic policies focus on specific industries or on economic practices in several industries. They are designed to affect directly the infrastructure of the economy and only indirectly its performance. Modern presidents generally have paid less attention to microeconomic than to macroeconomic policy, largely because its impact is so much more narrowly focused. Most presidents, however, have on occasion endorsed specific microeconomic policies or used microeconomic policy tools to achieve macroeconomic or other policy goals. President Reagan, for example, strongly supported deregulation and privatization as a means of reducing the role of government and strengthening the free market. Greater reliance on the market, he believed, would lead to a more productive economy.

Earlier in the nation's history, presidents were involved only with microeconomic policy and did not regard overall management of the economy as a primary policy responsibility. To preserve competition in the market, Theodore Roosevelt and William Howard Taft vigorously enforced the Sherman Anti-Trust Act of 1890—Roosevelt with great fanfare and Taft with quiet effectiveness. Woodrow Wilson persuaded Congress to establish an independent regulatory agency, the Federal Trade Commission, with extensive authority to regulate anticompetitive and unfair business practices. Roosevelt, Taft, and Wilson believed that the federal government should act to correct imperfections in the operations of the free market economy.

During the New Deal, Franklin Roosevelt endorsed legislation that established or strengthened independent regulatory agencies: the Securities and Exchange Commission (SEC), the Federal Power Commission (FPC), the Federal Communications Commission (FCC), the Civil Aeronautics Board (CAB), and the National Labor Relations Board (NLRB). These agencies received broad grants of authority to regulate the interstate aspects of specific industries, such as trade in stocks and bonds, electric power and natural gas, broadcasting and wire communications, and air transportation, as well as economywide activities such as labor-management relations. In addition, Roosevelt experimented with a form of government-sponsored industrial self-government in the National Industrial Recovery Act as a means of mitigating the effects of destructive competition. In 1937 he ordered an intensified enforcement of the antitrust laws, charging that anticompetitive practices were responsible for the continuation of the Great Depression. FDR's use of microeconomic policy was characterized by a pragmatic search for techniques of government intervention that would improve the operation of certain economic sectors or lead to an improvement in the overall health of the economy. Policies that worked were retained; those that failed were abandoned.

FDR's successors varied in their use of microeconomic policies. Presidents Harry S. Truman, Dwight D. Eisenhower, John F. Kennedy, and Lyndon B. Johnson appeared to accept the legitimacy of the pattern of government regulation of economic activity that had been established by 1940, including antitrust policy. They differed mainly in the intensity of enforcement and their willingness to use certain microeconomic policy tools.

Beginning in the late 1960s and continuing into the 1970s, Congress passed a new set of statutes expanding federal regulation of economic activity as a means of achieving noneconomic goals, such as a cleaner physical environment, safer automobiles and other consumer products, and a higher degree of safety and health in the work place. Presidents initially approved the new regulatory activities, but as their economic costs became apparent, Richard Nixon and Gerald R. Ford raised questions about the appropriateness of federal regulation in general. A deregulatory movement gained support, endorsed by Ford and Jimmy Carter. Ford assigned overall responsibility for deregulation to a member of the Council of Economic Advisers (CEA) and issued an order that required agencies to analyze the impact of their actions on inflation. Carter established the Regulatory Analysis Review Group, chaired by a CEA member, with responsibility for reviewing new rules and regulations with potential economic costs of $100 million or more. There is little evidence, however, that these actions reduced the volume of new regulations or the economic impact of regulation on industry.[3] Carter also gave his support to legislation that provided for deregulation of the airline and trucking industries. (The CAB ceased to function at the end of 1984, but the Interstate Commerce Commission continued to regulate railroads.)

Ronald Reagan promised in his 1980 election campaign to reduce substantially the amount of federal regulation; he argued that regulation was a primary cause of the decline of productivity in the economy. Reagan established the Task Force on Regulatory Relief, headed by Vice President George Bush, to analyze the economic effects of existing and proposed regulations. The task force prepared the way for the establishment, in the Office of Management and Budget (OMB), of the Office of Information and Regulatory Affairs to review proposed agency regulations. Reagan also issued two executive orders, numbers 12291 and 12498, that mandated that all major regulations be subjected to cost-benefit analysis, authorized the OMB director to delay the implementation of regulations, and required agencies to prepare annual regulatory programs. These changes ensured "continued presidential influence over the regulatory process."[4] The Reagan administration employed a three-pronged administrative strategy that substantially reduced the effectiveness of regulation.[5] First, OMB review procedures were used to kill or to slow the issuance of regulations. Second, the intensity of regulatory enforcement was reduced. Third, Reagan appointees changed their agencies' orientation from confrontation to cooperation as a means of achieving compliance.

President Bush did not change the regulatory review process that Reagan established with his two executive orders. Like Reagan, he involved his vice president in an antiregulation effort. Dan Quayle chaired the Council on Competitiveness, which had broad authority to intervene in drafting federal regulations. However, Bush's regulatory policy differed markedly from that of his predecessor. Whereas Reagan implemented a regulatory reform agenda based on his conservative ideology, Bush had no holistic vision for regulatory reform. His regulatory strategy was passive and fragmentary. With respect to policy content, Bush did not continue Reagan's opposition to social regulation—especially occupational safety and environmental protection—and he gave stronger support to economic regulatory policy. His appointments of moderates to regulatory positions contrasted sharply with Reagan's, who were primarily ideologues opposed to regulation.[6]

In all modern presidential administrations, microeconomic policies have been secondary to macroeconomic policy. Microeconomic policies, such as vigorous antitrust enforcement or support for deregulation, can be used to achieve macroeconomic policy goals and to highlight the theoretical rationale for administration policy, but microeconomic policies cannot replace fiscal and monetary policies as the primary means by which presidents discharge their responsibility for the health of the nation's economy.

Presidents and the Economy: 1933–1992

The modern era of macroeconomic policy and the president's role as manager of the economy date from FDR's New Deal. One of the hallmarks of the New Deal was its commitment to make positive use of the federal government's power to bring about recovery from the Great Depression. The most significant theoretical achievement of the New Deal for economic policy was not the adoption of a comprehensive ideology for the development of a welfare state but the discovery of Keynesian economics and its prescription of increased government spending to compensate for inadequate private spending for investment and consumption.

Ultimately, it was not the New Deal reforms and recovery programs that ended the depression but the huge increase in government spending during World War II. All of the nation's unused productive capacity—

capital facilities and human resources—were mobilized to achieve victory, and government borrowing financed much of that mobilization.

After the war Congress passed the Employment Act of 1946, a statute that committed the U.S. government to maintain "maximum employment, production, and purchasing power." The act translated into law the widespread expectation that had developed during the Roosevelt administration that the government would guarantee to the fullest extent possible a prosperous economy. It also made the president primarily responsible for providing economic policy leadership, although it furnished him with few new tools for the task. It created a Council of Economic Advisers and an accompanying staff, and it required the president to report annually to Congress on the condition of the economy and to offer proposals for improving or maintaining its health. Ultimate power over the president's economic proposals, however, remains with Congress.

From the end of World War II until the late 1960s, presidents and Congress fought with each other over economic policy. Truman struggled unsuccessfully with Congress over its desire to reduce wartime taxes. He was somewhat more effective in controlling the inflation that resulted from spending for the Korean War. Eisenhower's conservative policies tended to prevail over the plans of a Democratic Congress to increase domestic spending. The Eisenhower administration was marked by two recessions, in 1954 and 1958, interspersed by a period of expansion. The Kennedy-Johnson administration fully embraced Keynesian theory, and a 1964 income tax cut had the desired effect of expanding the economy and increasing revenues. It was thought that economic forecasting and management of the economy had developed to the point where fine-tuning of unemployment and the inflation rate was possible.[7]

In 1966, however, economic conditions began to change. Vietnam War expenditures rose rapidly, the deficit increased, and President Johnson shifted his focus from economic expansion to economic restraint. Congress resisted Johnson's requests for higher excise taxes, and for political reasons he refrained from asking for income tax increases. He feared that Congress would refuse the request and that in the course of congressional debate embarrassing questions would be raised about the war and its cost. With a congressional election scheduled in 1966, he was unwilling to risk debate and defeat. By the time Johnson requested additional income taxes and Congress responded by approving a temporary 10 percent income surtax, the economy had begun a prolonged inflationary period in which the conditions that had been relatively stable since 1946 began to change drastically. (An inflation rate of approximately 3 percent a year, an unemployment variance between 4 percent and 8 percent, and sustained growth in the gross national product had characterized the first twenty-five years of the post–World War II period.)

Presidents since Johnson have had to contend with a changing and increasingly less manageable economy. Inflation rates crept upward into double digits in the late 1970s before declining; unemployment has remained high by postwar standards; and the federal budget has run a deficit in every year since 1970 *(see Table 9-1)*. Underlying these developments have been systemic factors beyond the control of the government: the increased dependence of the economy on foreign sources of raw materials, especially oil; the growing interdependence of the U.S. economy with those of other industrial democracies; the declining productivity of the U.S. economy relative to foreign competition; the growth and maturation of domestic social welfare programs based on statutory entitlements; and a commitment to improve the quality of the physical environment even at substantial cost to economic growth and productivity.

Richard Nixon was the first president to encounter the changing economic environment of the United States. His response was two-pronged. He consistently pursued the classical conservative course of attempting to counter inflation by pushing Congress for reductions in federal spending in order to balance the budget. In addition, Nixon took the extraordinary step, for a conservative Republican, of freezing prices and wages in August 1971. The imposition of wage and price controls is an extreme measure, for through it the president suspends the normal operation of market forces. Although Roosevelt and Truman imposed controls during World War II and the Korean War, Nixon is the only president to do so in peacetime. He acted under authority that Congress delegated to the president in the Economic Stabilization Act of 1970, which it passed over his strong objections. The 1971–1973 experience suggests that peacetime wage and price controls are at best a temporary means of curbing inflation and that they can quickly become a political liability unless their impact is moderated.

Upon taking office in August 1974, President Ford assumed that the principal economic problem confronting the United States was inflation, and he pushed to cut federal spending. Almost before his anti-inflation campaign was launched, however, economic conditions changed, and

Table 9-1 Inflation, Unemployment, and Federal Budget Deficits, 1970–1991

	Inflation[a]	Unemployment[b]	Deficit[c]
1970	5.7%	4.9%	$ 2.8
1971	4.4	5.9	23.0
1972	3.2	5.6	23.4
1973	6.2	4.9	14.9
1974	11.0	5.6	6.1
1975	9.1	8.5	53.2
1976	5.6	7.7	73.7
1977	6.5	7.0	53.6
1978	7.6	6.6	59.2
1979	11.3	5.8	40.2
1980	13.5	7.1	73.8
1981	10.3	7.5	78.9
1982	6.2	9.5	127.9
1983	3.2	9.6	207.8
1984	4.3	7.5	185.3
1985	3.6	7.2	212.3
1986	1.9	7.0	221.2
1987	3.6	6.2	149.7
1988	4.1	5.5	155.1
1989	4.8	5.3	153.4
1990	5.4	5.5	220.4
1991	NA	6.7	268.7

[a] Percent increase in the consumer price index.
[b] Percent of the civilian noninstitutional population 16 years of age or over.
[c] In billions of dollars.
Source: Statistical Abstract of the United States.

Ford spent his last year as president combating a recession that contributed to his electoral defeat in 1976. Ford's successor, Jimmy Carter, fared little better. Carter initiated an antirecession program of increased federal spending and tax cuts to stimulate business investment. The economy responded almost too quickly, and Carter was confronted with surging inflation rates that reached double digits during his last year in office.

Perhaps Carter's most important decision affecting the economy was his naming of Paul Volcker as chairman of the Federal Reserve Board in 1979. Volcker's appointment reflected Carter's disenchantment with the ability of Keynesian theory to provide solutions to the problem of stagflation, a combination of a stagnant economy and rising prices. Essentially a monetarist, Volcker moved quickly to curb inflation by restraining the growth of the money supply. Although Carter did not fully abandon Keynesianism, he gave monetarism a prominent role in macroeconomic policy making for the first time.

The rate of inflation did not respond quickly to Volcker's efforts to tighten the money supply, but interest rates rose sharply. These developments undoubtedly contributed to Carter's defeat by Ronald Reagan in the 1980 election. One of Reagan's campaign pledges was to restore vitality to the economy through a revolutionary program of major reductions in taxing and spending. Congress responded positively to Reagan's initiatives in 1981 by enacting the largest income tax cut in U.S. history and by reducing domestic spending in nonentitlement programs. Congress also supported Reagan's proposals for a major defense buildup, projected over five years from 1981 through 1986.

The results of the Reagan administration's macroeconomic policies were mixed. The major accomplishment—credit for which must also be given to the Fed—was the curtailment of inflation, which fluctuated between annual rates of 1.9 to 4.3 percent from 1983 through 1988. Also, in 1983 the economy began a sustained period of growth that lasted through 1990. Before that growth spurt, however, the United States experienced the most severe recession since World War II, with unemployment rising to 10.75 percent in the fourth quarter of 1982. In spite of the prosperity achieved since 1982, unemployment did not drop below 5 percent.

Without question, the major problem resulting from the Reagan administration's macroeconomic policies has been massive federal budget deficits *(see Table 9-1)*. The deficits grew rapidly as a result of the recession of 1982, when revenues fell, automatic countercyclical spending (such as unemployment compensation) rose, and the tax cuts and increased defense spending authorized in 1981 became effective. The latter created a large structural, or permanent, deficit as the increases in federal revenues promised by supply-side advocates failed to materialize, and sizable additional cuts in nondefense spending could not be obtained from Congress.

In addition, the large annual deficits resulted in a rapid growth in the national debt and in interest payments on the debt. From $990 billion in 1980, the debt rose to $3.1 trillion ten years later.[8] Net interest payments have become one of the fastest growing items in the federal budget. Interest has become a major obstacle to reducing the deficit and a constraint on spending for other purposes.

The deficits proved embarrassing to President Reagan because they are contradictory to traditional conservative values of fiscal restraint. But the deficits also brought political advantage to the Reagan administration. They served as the basis for the sustained recovery from the 1981–1982 recession. That recovery was crucial to Reagan's 1984 reelection victory, for voters concluded that his economic policies had worked quite well. That Reagan had become a practitioner of Keynesian demand management on a grand scale was immaterial to him and his supporters. The deficits also provided Reagan with an effective short-term rationale for restraining the growth of nondefense spending.

George Bush's victory in the 1988 presidential election was an endorsement of the status quo. The country was prosperous and not at war. The only economic policy mandate Bush received derived from his pledge that there would be "no new taxes." Like Reagan, Bush promised to eliminate the budget deficit by reducing spending. He held to his promise not to raise taxes until October 1990 when his administration negotiated a budget deal with Congress that would balance the budget by 1996. However, the reductions in the deficits for 1991 and 1992 were overcome by unanticipated expenditures for the Persian Gulf War and bailing out failed savings and loan institutions insured by the federal government, shortfalls in revenues arising from "technical re-estimates," and higher projected spending for Medicaid.[9] The deficits for fiscal 1991 ($268.7 billion) and 1992 (estimated by OMB at $399 billion) were the highest ever. In 1991 interest on the debt amounted to $214.3 billion and was estimated to rise to $224.2 billion in 1992.[10] The recession that began in late 1990 and continued into 1992 increased spending pressures and constrained any moves to raise taxes, thus impeding administration and congressional efforts to curb the deficit.

The Politics of Macroeconomic Policy Making

Presidents do not make macroeconomic policy in a vacuum solely according to economic theories. Their decisions in this crucial area are intensely political and are affected by consideration of other policy goals (including microeconomic policy), electoral politics, interest group politics, and bureaucratic politics among institutional participants in the policy-making process. In a very real sense the United States has a political economy, and it is an economic polity. The president is the focal point of the relationships involved in both of these entities.

Policy Politics

The achievement of macroeconomic policy goals is affected by, and has an effect on, other policy goals. National security policy objectives, for example, often have a profound impact on economic policy. In the 1980s

the widely held consensus that U.S. military strength had declined compared with that of the Soviet Union resulted in substantial increases in
defense spending beginning in fiscal year 1982. These increases, however,
were a major obstacle to efforts to balance the budget. The added deficit
resulting from increased military expenditures contributed to upward
pressure on interest rates, which in turn impeded the ability of tax-cut
incentives to stimulate productivity.

Budget-balancing efforts in domestic program areas conflicted with
commitments made to Social Security beneficiaries, welfare recipients,
retired federal employees, and numerous other groups served by federal
programs. In addition, the macroeconomic goals of economic growth,
increased productivity, and full employment often are at odds with regulatory policies designed to improve environmental quality, enhance occupational safety and health, increase the safety of automobiles and other
consumer products, and protect consumers against a variety of unfair
business practices.

Foreign policy also intrudes on macroeconomic policy. For example,
foreign military and economic assistance and the stationing of U.S. forces
overseas contribute to the nation's balance-of-payments deficit, which in
turn undercuts confidence in the dollar and reduces economic stability.
The end of the cold war between the United States and the Soviet Union
in late 1991 precipitated a budget struggle over the disposition of the
"peace dividend" that congressional Democrats believed should result
from the reduction of tensions. An October 1990 budget agreement between President Bush and Congress required that for the next three years
any reductions in either defense or discretionary domestic spending be
devoted to reducing the deficit. Democratic leaders in Congress sought to
reopen the agreement so as to use some defense cuts for domestic programs. President Bush opposed their plans to slash defense spending as
premature and argued that in any event the agreement should remain in
place. These examples illustrate the interrelationship of macroeconomic
policy goals with those of other policies.

Electoral Politics

A second dimension of the politics of macroeconomic policy is its relationship to electoral politics. It has long been recognized that presidential
administrations and congressional majorities have manipulated economic
policy to produce short-term improvements in economic conditions to

enhance their party's election prospects. The timing and location of benefits may be adjusted to achieve this end.

Presidents do not, however, attempt to change the underlying structure of the economy for short-term political advantage. Rather, they seek to make marginal adjustments in the rates of inflation and unemployment or in disposable income. Because of electoral politics, however, what is economically optimal is not always done or may be substantially modified as a result of the pressures. Political influence on economic policy can have substantial costs, including "a lurching, stop-and-go economy," a preference for policies that contain "highly visible benefits and deferred hidden costs," and responsiveness of "coalition-building politicians" to special interests.[11] In such a politically sensitive environment, long-range economic planning is most difficult.

Few presidents can resist the pressures of party and special constituencies to seek short-term political gain even at the expense of future economic stability and efficiency.[12] Ronald Reagan, however, remained firm throughout his presidency in his commitment to the income tax cut of supply-side theory, even though it meant proposing and defending budget deficits that fluctuated around $200 billion. President Bush adhered to his 1988 campaign pledge not to raise taxes until the budget agreement with Congress in October 1990. He reluctantly agreed to tax increases of $146 billion over five years as part of a $496 billion deficit reduction package.[13]

Interest Group Politics

Presidents also are subjected to pressures from several important groupings of interests, including business, labor, agriculture, the financial community, state and local governments, and foreign governments. Their effect on policy varies according to the issues and to current economic conditions in the United States and elsewhere.

Business interests include the full array of private corporations engaged in producing goods and services (except those involved in financial affairs, which will be considered separately). Businesses attempt to exert influence collectively through umbrella organizations, such as the Chamber of Commerce of the United States and the National Association of Manufacturers, and through industry-based trade associations like the Automobile Manufacturers Association and the American Gas Association. Individual companies, especially large corporations, also try to shape policy to their liking. Businesses usually concentrate their lobbying on microeconomic policies that specifically affect their operations. To the extent that business influences macroeconomic policy, it does so by expressing support for balanced budgets, tax-cut incentives, and monetary restraint to control inflation. Presidents know that conservative fiscal and monetary policies normally will receive strong business support.

Labor encompasses the giant AFL-CIO and a host of independent unions. Its position on macroeconomic policy issues is usually in sharp contrast to that of business. Labor supports fiscal stimulation of the economy in periods of recession and opposes the use of monetary restraints to curb inflation. It is not unduly disturbed by budget deficits. As a rule, labor is much more worried by unemployment than by inflation. Labor takes great interest in microeconomic policy, including regulation of labor-management relations and regulations in behalf of occupational safety and health.

Agricultural interests groups are not monolithic. The American Farm Bureau Federation and the National Grange support conservative policies, while the National Farmers Union and the National Farmers Organization take a much more liberal stance. Regardless of their ideology, farm organizations tend to oppose monetary policies that result in high interest rates, because the use of credit is an essential feature of farm management.

The financial community consists of two principal components, the securities exchanges, or Wall Street, and banks and other financial institutions. Wall Street and financial institutions buy and sell "paper," which are government and private financial obligations, and bonds, the longer-term securities. The reaction of Wall Street to monetary and fiscal policies is registered in the price of corporate stocks traded on the major stock exchanges. Movements of stock market indicators, such as the Dow Jones Index of thirty leading industrial stocks, often reflect the degree of investor confidence in administration policies. Bond prices move upward or downward inversely with interest rates and thus reflect monetary policy shifts. The interest paid on short-term government and commercial paper varies directly with monetary policy.

An administration's main interest in the financial community is that its policies be favorably received by Wall Street. It also seeks the approval of major banks and other leading financial institutions. A vote of "no confidence" by the financial community in the government's economic policies makes the administration vulnerable to criticism by political opponents and weakens its popular support. As in the broader business world, members of the financial community tend to support conservative fiscal policies and monetary restraint to control inflation. They fear large deficits, whether due to high spending levels or sizable tax cuts.

With the advent of the Great Society domestic programs in the mid–1960s, state and local governments became vitally interested in macroeconomic policy. The federal government is a source of funding for a wide range of state and local programs in areas such as education, welfare and social services, housing and urban development, transportation, and health care. In addition, states and their local subdivisions received unrestricted federal revenue-sharing funds from 1972 through 1987. Consequently, many state and local governments, both through national associations, such as the U.S. Conference of Mayors, and individually through the efforts of members of Congress, have exerted pressure to maintain the flow of federal funds, even though this could be accomplished only at the expense of larger and potentially inflationary budget deficits.

President Reagan's successful effort in 1981 to reduce federal funding for many state and local activities and his subsequent proposals for further reductions were an essential part of his long-term objective of balancing the budget. Although some state and local officials backed Reagan, the responses of most such officials ranged from cautious skepticism to strong opposition. His objective of a major reordering of federal fiscal functions was not accomplished.[14] Perhaps the most important aspect of Reagan's approach to intergovernmental financial relations was that he seized the initiative. Instead of responding to the requests of state and local officials for ever-increasing support, he sought to direct state and local governments into a posture of reduced dependence on federal funding. This innovative attempt to restructure fiscal federalism in a way that served macroeconomic policy objectives appears to have provided a model for President Bush.

Foreign governments are another important constituency with an interest in macroeconomic policy. Friendly governments—the European Community, Japan, and Saudi Arabia—are especially significant. They favor a dollar that is neither overvalued nor undervalued and a healthy U.S. economy with full employment and a low inflation rate. If the dollar is weak, the value of much of their international currency reserves declines, and their goods are less competitive in U.S. markets. If the dollar is too strong, their investment capital migrates to the United States, and the

high competitiveness of their products in U.S. markets threatens to pro-
voke trade restrictions. If unemployment in the United States rises, the
major market for their goods declines. If interest rates are higher in the
United States than in Europe or Japan, investment capital moves to
the United States. Consequently, foreign governments press U.S. administrations to keep the exchange value of the dollar from fluctuating widely
and to hold down interest rates. Foreign governments feel less free to
influence fiscal policies designed to stimulate the economy because these
entail essentially domestic decisions. Presidents and their administrations
are constrained to some degree, however, by the effect of economic policy
decisions on the economies of other countries.

Presidents do not respond to all interest group constituencies, and the
constituencies whose support they do seek vary in importance to them. In
no case, however, do presidents make macroeconomic policy decisions
without regard to some of the interest groups, which are a major feature in
the politics of economic policy making.

Bureaucratic Politics

The president's economic policies also reflect the organizational interests of the institutions involved in the policy-making process—the Council of Economic Advisers, the Office of Management and Budget, the
Treasury Department, and the Federal Reserve Board—and the beliefs of
the officials whom he has appointed to manage them. The next section
describes the functions and organizational perspectives of those agencies
and the nature of their relationship with the president.

The Economic Subpresidency

The president's macroeconomic policy-making role entails discharging
statutory duties and responsibilities and meeting popular and elite expectations that his actions will result in a prosperous economy. In his role as
economic manager, the president must develop and implement policies
and build support for those policies in the public and within the Washington community. To accomplish this complex and demanding task, he
needs information, advice, and administrative assistance to focus energy
on major issues, integrate the policies of his administration, take account
of all important interests, and maintain the cohesion of his administration. This advice and assistance is provided by certain organizations and

processes, located in the presidency and within the executive branch, which James Anderson and Jared Hazleton call "the economic subpresidency." The use of the economic subpresidency varies among presidents and with economic conditions, but it is central to policy making and presidential management of the economy.

According to Anderson and Hazleton, the economic subpresidency comprises all those who are engaged in making, defining, communicating, and implementing economic policy decisions, "whether they act personally or as part of an institution."[15] Activities of the economic subpresidency include direct advisory relationships with the president and interaction between other advisers with respect to economic policy. The economic subpresidency consists of four major administrative units—the CEA, OMB, the Treasury Department, and the Fed—and various intragovernmental committees and councils, presidential assistants, and other advisers.

The Council of Economic Advisers

The Council of Economic Advisers has three members who are appointed by the president and subject to Senate confirmation, plus a small staff of approximately thirty-five divided evenly between professional economists and support personnel. Traditionally, most CEA members and professional staffers have had extensive experience in business or government. The CEA's chair is responsible for administration of the council, hiring staff, representing it on other government councils and committees, and reporting to the president. He or she establishes the council's orientation according to the president's overall objectives. The chair's relationship with the president largely determines the CEA's influence in shaping economic policy.

The CEA has no operational responsibility but serves entirely in a staff capacity. Its principal functions are to gather information, make economic forecasts, analyze economic issues, and prepare the president's annual economic report to Congress. Its primary role has been to provide the president with expert economic advice. On occasion CEA members have acted as public spokespersons for the president. The council usually has not performed coordinating or brokerage functions, although its members tend to reflect the theories and policy views of professional economists who share the president's perspectives. In general, Democratic presidents have had Keynesian CEA members, and Republicans have selected classical conservative and monetarist economists. Reagan, for example, appointed a conservative economist to chair the CEA at the start of his presidency and added a monetarist and a supply-sider. All three were committed to free trade, reduced government spending, a balanced federal budget, and limited federal intervention in the economy. In his second term, Reagan selected a monetarist to chair the CEA.

The CEA's relationship with the president is a function of how he perceives the need for economic expertise. If he feels such a need—and most presidents have when confronted with the seriousness and complexity of economic issues—and if he and the CEA members share basic interests and values, then the council plays an important role in economic policy making. Its expertise enhances presidential policies, and its analyses and forecasts acquire political significance through association with the presidency. However, the council can do only what the president asks and allows it to do.

Carter's and Reagan's relationship to the CEA illustrates the range of uses that can be made of the council and of its influence on policy. The chairman of Carter's CEA was Charles Schultze, who had served as director of the budget under President Johnson. Schultze played a major role in shaping the Carter administration's economic policies, and the CEA was very much at the center of the economic subpresidency. In contrast, the two CEA chairmen in Reagan's first term, Murray Weidenbaum and Martin Feldstein, were overshadowed by budget director David Stockman and Secretary of the Treasury Donald Regan, neither of whom were economists. Weidenbaum's influence was primarily in regulatory policy. Feldstein, a distinguished academician, quickly fell out of favor with the president and the White House because of his dire predictions of the probable consequences of administration policies. The CEA was at the periphery of the economic subpresidency during Reagan's first term. Indeed, when Feldstein returned to Harvard in July 1984, the president delayed appointing a successor for almost a year. The council's professional staff shrank in size, and rumors circulated in Washington that Reagan wanted to abolish the unit. He finally named Beryl Sprinkel as chairman in April 1985. Sprinkel was an economist who had served for four years as undersecretary of the Treasury for monetary affairs and was well known to Reagan and Regan, who by then was the White House chief of staff. Sprinkel rebuilt the council's staff and moved it back into the mainstream of the economic subpresidency.[16] Under President Bush the CEA has played a more significant role with respect to the deficit than it did under Reagan. Its chairman, monetarist economist Michael Boskin, has enjoyed the president's confidence and often acted as a spokesman for the administration.

The council's forecasts help to set the boundaries of the president's legislative program and budget proposals. It is to the president's advantage for the council to approach its advisory task deductively, fitting program pieces together within the framework of his overall objectives. As former CEA chairman Paul McCracken has observed, "An economic adviser does his most effective work when he is positioned to look at the general interest."[17] The council's contribution to policy making is, then, primarily conceptual and not in the realm of implementation or coordination. The council is most influential in the early stages of policy formulation, where its expertise is "the dominant body of relevant knowledge," many alternatives are under consideration, institutional positions are not fixed, and decisions reflect "general objectives and plans" rather than "operating commitments."[18]

The Office of Management and Budget

Presidents receive economic advice of a different sort from the Office of Management and Budget. While the CEA's primary concern is with controlling the business cycle and achieving sustained economic growth, OMB's major focus is the allocation of resources to administrative agencies and their programs through the annual preparation of the president's budget. Its institutional bias is toward holding down spending. It is the principal instrument through which the president fashions the expenditure component of fiscal policy. In addition, OMB provides economic forecasts to the president and acts as a "legislative and regulatory gatekeeper" by conducting detailed policy analysis of proposed bills and agency rules.[19]

The Office of Management and Budget was originally a presidential staff agency comprising an elite group of government careerists devoted to serving the presidency and the president. Since President Nixon reorganized it in 1970, OMB has been more actively involved in serving the political needs of the president. Beginning in the Nixon administration, OMB directors have actively participated in developing presidential policies and in building support for them. The budget has become as much a political weapon as a managerial tool or an instrument of fiscal policy.

The politicization of OMB and the political utilization of the budget were never more apparent than during the Reagan administration and David Stockman's tenure as budget director (1981–1985). Stockman dominated federal budgeting in a manner unknown before him. He centralized the executive budget process in OMB and involved himself extensively in the congressional budget process through direct negotiations and bargaining with congressional committees.

Hugh Heclo has identified four major characteristics of Stockman's system of budget management.[20] First, he dealt with the total budget rather than with incremental choices at the margins. Subjecting every budget item to scrutiny forced political decisions on all factors affecting spending with the terms of debate framed by the White House. Second, Stockman imposed a top-down approach to budgeting by continually readdressing the deficit. Successive searches for spending cuts went to the core of domestic programs, the previously sacrosanct budgetary base. This part of the plan led to the third element of Stockman's approach to managing the budget, which was to "move the debate from program particulars to general politico-economic justifications."[21] The fourth aspect of Stockman's system was the adoption of a single budgetary strategy of cutting back domestic spending wherever politically possible. That strategy was continually strengthened by the pressure of ever-increasing deficits. Stockman also made less extensive use of OMB's career staff than his predecessors did.

Stockman not only politicized OMB, he also personalized it. Heclo concludes that although OMB's political power increased, the agency was weakened institutionally. The Stockman experience suggests that neither OMB, the presidency, nor the incumbent president are well served by a budget director who, with the president's blessing, becomes a master sales agent for presidential decisions.

Under Stockman's successor, economist James C. Miller III, OMB continued to serve Reagan's political interests, but much less visibly. The budget remained the primary instrument for the achievement of the president's goals, and Miller continued Stockman's role as a spokesperson to Congress. Miller, however, was not as intimately involved in shaping economic strategy and in direct negotiations with Congress as Stockman had been. During the Bush presidency OMB was a major player in the economic subpresidency. Its director, Richard Darman, and White House chief of staff John Sununu were the major negotiators with Congress concerning fiscal policy. (Darman dealt primarily with spending and Sununu with taxes.) OMB also became the dominant agency for economic forecasting.

The Treasury Department

The third institutional participant in the economic subpresidency is the Treasury Department, which is responsible for collecting taxes, managing the national debt, controlling the currency, collecting customs, and handling international monetary affairs, including management of the balance of payments and the value of the dollar relative to other currencies. It is the primary government source of information on revenues, the tax system, and financial markets. It also takes the lead in developing tax bills and steering them through Congress.[22]

The primary concerns of the Treasury Department traditionally have been the adequacy of revenues, the soundness of the dollar, and the cost of financing the debt. To finance the debt, the department has advocated either low interest rates or a balanced budget. Since 1951, however, it has opposed easy credit and usually has acted as a restraint on expansionary fiscal policies. Before the Reagan administration, a situation in which high interest rates accompanied a large deficit was anathema to the institutional interests of the Treasury. Its position altered substantially under President Reagan and Donald Regan, secretary of the Treasury during Reagan's first term. An avowed believer in supply-side economics, Regan argued that temporary deficits resulting from tax-cut incentives would lead ultimately to economic growth, expanded revenues, and balanced budgets. He opposed efforts to reduce the deficit by raising taxes. His concern was much more with the supply of money in the domestic economy than with the exchange value of the dollar. Regan's successor at Treasury, James A. Baker III, concentrated heavily on exchange rate problems.

The Treasury and Secretary Nicholas Brady played a rather marginal role in the economic subpresidency under President Bush. As noted, Darman and Sununu dominated administration negotiations over the deficit. One veteran White House observer and analyst suggests that the "patrician" Brady was no match for the "pit bull approach of his two economic policy colleagues."[23]

Organizationally, the Treasury Department is divided between large units with major line responsibilities, such as the Internal Revenue Service, and policy-related units, such as the office of the undersecretary for monetary affairs. The policy-related units, located in the office of the secretary, never have provided coordination of economic policy for an administration, although the potential to do so exists.[24]

Federal Reserve Board

The Federal Reserve Board is an independent agency charged with responsibility for regulating the money supply and the banking system. Its seven members are appointed by the president to fourteen-year terms with the consent of the Senate. The president designates one member of the board to act as its chair for a four-year term. The Fed has three means by which it controls the money supply: the rediscount rate, reserve requirements, and open-market operations.

The rediscount rate is the interest rate charged commercial banks to borrow from the Federal Reserve. An increase in the rediscount rate tightens the availability of credit because it forces banks to charge more to their borrowers.

Reserves are balances that commercial banks belonging to the Federal Reserve System must maintain with it. Reserve requirements are expressed as percentages of a commercial bank's deposits, usually 10 to 20 percent. A reduction in reserve requirements increases the availability of credit.

Open-market operations are the major instrument through which the Fed manages the money supply, through the purchase and sale of U.S. government securities by regional Federal Reserve Banks. When the Fed wants to expand the supply of money, it orders its regional banks to buy government securities on the money market. The regional Reserve Banks pay for the securities by drawing checks on themselves. The checks are cashed by the Treasury at commercial banks, and as a result the Treasury's account balances are increased. The commercial banks present the checks to regional Reserve Banks on which they were drawn for redemption. The regional Reserve Banks credit the checks to the commercial banks' reserve accounts with the Federal Reserve. The commercial banks may then lend money at the reserve requirement ratio. If the ratio is, say, 10 percent, the banks can lend to private borrowers ten times the original amount of the securities purchased. Conversely, sale of government securities by the Federal Reserve in the open market contracts the money supply in a similar manner.[25]

Although neither the president nor Congress can tell the Fed how to conduct monetary policy, the board traditionally has been responsive to political pressures. According to Robert Shapiro, the Fed has shown far greater responsiveness to political timing than to cyclical fluctuations in the economy.[26] He maintains that the formal independence of the Fed is a myth and that its policies are designed primarily to maintain its internal cohesion and reduce its external vulnerability.

In some respects the independence of the Fed has political value to the president and Congress because it can serve as a convenient scapegoat for adverse economic conditions. Traditionally, expansionary monetary policy has been attacked as a major cause of inflation, and restrictive policy has drawn fire for contributing to economic stagnation and unemployment. In 1981–1982 presidential and congressional frustration over efforts to improve the economy resulted in criticism from the White House and Capitol Hill that ultra-high interest rates were causing unemployment, pushing up prices, and increasing the size of the budget deficit. After 1982 the sharp drop in inflation and the prolonged recovery from the 1981–1982 recession enabled the Fed to reduce interest rates. Political attacks on the Fed largely ceased as it gauged the money supply to the needs of an expanding economy not plagued by inflation. Also, as Reagan appointees began to serve on the board (by 1986 they were a majority), the White House criticized the Fed less often. President Bush pushed the Fed to reduce rates during the recession that began in 1990. The Fed responded slowly, after assuring itself that to do so would not stimulate inflation.

Presidents and Economic Policy Coordination

The independence of the Fed, the operational needs and organizational interests of the Treasury, and the institutional perspectives of other departments and agencies have led presidents to seek various ways of coordinating economic policy. For reasons explained in Chapter 6, the cabinet has not been a satisfactory vehicle for collective leadership. Instead, presidents have developed a variety of intragovernmental councils and committees designed to provide a cohesive macroeconomic policy and to integrate it with other policy objectives. Most of these entities failed to survive the administrations of their creators, for subsequent presidents sought mechanisms more compatible with their own operating styles.

However, a brief review of these undertakings reveals common patterns in their approaches and indicates the essential requirements for a minimal amount of coordination.

Eisenhower displayed a preference for sharply focused groups, which, although they met often, were too numerous to bring about effective coordination. In keeping with his preference for a less formal structure in policy-making processes, Kennedy abolished most of the groups his predecessor had established and worked primarily with groups created to address specific problems, such as housing credit and labor-management relations. The most significant development for macroeconomic policy making during the Kennedy administration was the creation of the "troika," an informal committee consisting of the chair of the CEA, the secretary of the Treasury, and the director of the budget. The troika's original purpose was to coordinate economic forecasting, but it quickly became a mechanism for developing cooperation within the economic subpresidency in formulating fiscal policy and, when joined by the chair of the Fed, for coordinating monetary policy. (When the group included the chair of the Fed, it was known a the "quadriad.")

Working with staff support from the CEA, the Treasury, OMB, and occasionally the Fed, the troika/quadriad has helped many presidents formulate macroeconomic policy in a rapid, adaptive manner with some measure of protection from political and bureaucratic pressures. Not all presidents have made extensive use of the troika, but it is a natural institutional grouping that continues to operate, with the Treasury assuming responsibility for revenue estimates, OMB generating estimates of federal expenditures, the CEA forecasting economic trends, and the Fed (when involved) projecting money supply requirements.

Under Lyndon Johnson, the troika operation became regularized, and it emerged as the principal mechanism for the development of fiscal policy advice and alternatives.[27] The troika's proposals, arrived at through discussion and debate, usually resulted in a consensus, which Johnson accepted. He had other sources of advice, but most of them were informal. He listened to other cabinet members and a wide variety of outsiders. The loosely structured informality of the troika operation and the use of informal channels of advice were characteristic of Johnson's ad hoc approach to policy formulation generally.

Nixon was uncomfortable with attempts to make policy by cabinet-level committees. In early 1971 he designated Secretary of the Treasury

John Connally as his economic "czar" with the responsibility for making major decisions. Connally worked through the troika, which he dominated. His successor as Treasury secretary, George Shultz, inherited Connally's title but operated in a more collegial manner. At the start of his second term, in January 1973, Nixon made Shultz assistant to the president for economic affairs and named him to chair a new cabinet-level coordinating body, the Council on Economic Policy. Shultz soon became the dominant figure in making and expounding economic policy for the Nixon administration. He worked primarily through interdepartmental committees focused on specific problems rather than through the council.

Gerald Ford moved quickly to replace the Nixon machinery with a more formal and structured process that would operate openly and comprehensively and reflect Ford's intense interest in economic affairs. In September 1974 Ford established the Economic Policy Board (EPB) and assigned it responsibility for coordinating domestic and foreign economic policy. The secretary of the Treasury chaired the EPB, which also included the secretaries of labor, commerce, and state, the chair of the CEA, the director of OMB, and the assistant to the president for economic affairs, who also directed the small EPB staff, which was housed in the Executive Office of the President. Departments and agencies provided information, analysis, and expertise. Roger Porter, who served as executive secretary to the EPB throughout its existence, has described it as providing systematic advice to the president by exposing him to competing arguments "in a group discussion that permitted exchange and argument among the advocates before the president."[28]

President Carter replaced the EPB with the Economic Policy Group (EPG), cochaired by the secretary of the Treasury and the chair of the CEA. The EPG was a large unwieldy body. It had no staff, was accessible to a wide range of interested officials, and was not organized as a formal advisory body to the president. Attempts to focus its work led to the creation of a steering committee, chaired by the secretary of the Treasury and including the chair of the CEA, the director of the budget, and the presidential assistants for domestic affairs and for national security affairs. However, its operations remained so unstructured that it was unable to coordinate even major policy initiatives.[29]

Perhaps the most significant influence on economic policy within the economic subpresidency belonged to domestic policy assistant Stuart Eizenstat, CEA chairman Charles Schultze, and special trade representative Robert Strauss. According to Colin Campbell, Eizenstat effectively defended domestic program interests in EPG steering committee deliberations, Schultze dominated policies designed to protect the exchange value of the dollar, and Strauss played the lead role in trade policy, a major concern of Carter's.[30] Carter did not appoint an assistant for economic affairs, nor did he rely on any one person to make policy recommendations. Throughout his administration he made the major decisions and was very much in charge of economic policy. Aside from the activities of the troika in coordinating economic forecasting, Carter managed macroeconomic policy with limited staff assistance. Although the results—the performance of the economy—were not especially salutary, they were not appreciably worse (or better) than those achieved by Ford.

Reagan replaced the Economic Policy Group with the Cabinet Council on Economic Affairs (CCEA). Like its predecessor in the Nixon administration, the CCEA was a forum for discussion of issues and alternatives. Roger Porter was its secretary and informally coordinated its operations. The council served to establish consensus within the administration. In addition to the council, the troika met regularly to coordinate economic forecasting.

Against the backdrop of the relatively smooth operation of the CCEA, economic policy making during Reagan's first term involved a struggle for influence within the economic subpresidency. The major participants were Donald Regan, David Stockman, and presidential assistants James Baker and Edwin Meese. The administration had clearly defined macroeconomic policy goals: to reduce the role of the federal government in the U.S. economy, thus reducing taxes and spending, and to increase productivity, savings, and investment, thus ensuring vigorous and sustained economic growth and full employment. There was, however, sharp disagreement over the means to that end. That conflict reflected competition among classical conservative, monetarist, and supply-side theories and focused on the significance of federal budget deficits. According to Stockman's memoir, the winners in the conflict were Regan and Meese. He (Stockman) was the principal loser. The reasons for that outcome, as seen by Stockman, were his own political naiveté, Regan's Iago-like cultivation of the president, Meese's political expediency, and Reagan's stubborn refusal to abandon the ideological principles that he brought with him when he took office (for example, a commitment to supply-side economics and opposition to taxes).[31]

During Reagan's second term, the content of macroeconomic policy changed very little. This absence of change suggests that a carefully managed economic policy process, designed along the lines of Ford's Economic Policy Board, would not have made much difference in Reagan's economic policy decisions, which were based more on an unyielding commitment to a theory (supply-side economics) than on carefully reasoned analysis or on accurate economic forecasts.

President Bush continued the Economic Policy Council. Its activities were managed by Roger Porter, as assistant to the president for economic and domestic affairs, with the help of his staff in the Office of Policy Development.[32] However, the council met irregularly and did not established an effective round-table process for preparing issues for presidential decision. Nor did the troika, which fell into disuse during Reagan's second term, acquire its former importance.

In addition, the Bush White House tended to bypass both the cabinet council system and the interagency process.[33] The major players in shaping economic policy in the Bush administration were OMB director Darman and chief of staff Sununu. The former was the principal opponent of increases in spending, and the latter assumed the role of spokesman for conservative interests. They functioned in these capacities during the October 1990 budget agreement negotiations. But no single individual or group had responsibility for defining for the economic subpresidency how policies were to be integrated. This apparently was due, at least in part, to the lack of any change in the basic direction of policy as set in the Reagan administration. Although not ideologically committed to the policy, President Bush refused to deviate substantially from it. He opposed new taxes (except for those approved as part of the 1990 budget agreement with Congress), proposed no new major spending programs, and advocated reductions in discretionary nondefense spending.

As in other areas of policy, the nation is heavily dependent on presidents' attitudes, values, and operating styles for economic leadership. Congressionally established advisory mechanisms, such as the CEA, are helpful, and presidents can take other measures to assist them in identifying issues and achieving policy coordination; but there is no guarantee that the president will adopt effective policies or achieve his objectives. There is, moreover, an important check on presidential economic policy making—the powers of Congress over taxing, spending, and the monetary system.

The Congressional Role in Macroeconomic Policy

Most of the executive branch agencies and processes that involve macroeconomic policy and the president's economic role were established by statute: the Federal Reserve Act of 1914, the Budget and Accounting Act of 1921, and the Employment Act of 1946. Traditionally, Congress has dealt with economic policy through separate consideration of tax legislation and annual appropriations. Tax bills have entailed redistributive issues—that is, questions of who bears the burdens, and efforts of special interests to secure favorable provisions, or "loopholes." The congressional tax-writing committees (House Ways and Means and Senate Finance) have jealously guarded their powers and been unwilling to propose new tax legislation that did not accommodate special interests. The 1986 tax reform act departed substantially from traditional revenue legislation that contains numerous advantages and benefits for a wide range of interests. The two tax-writing committees, under the strong-willed leadership of their chairmen, Sen. Bob Packwood, R-Ore., and Rep. Dan Rostenkowski, D-Ill., responded positively to Reagan's call for simplification and reform of the federal tax code.[34]

Appropriations decision making, centered in the House and Senate Appropriations committees, traditionally focused on incremental changes in budget requests of departments and agencies. The politics of the budget process were a highly stylized game in which the institutional participants played specific roles. The primary consideration in Congress was the amount of increase or decrease in each agency's base, which was the previous year's appropriation. The total level of expenditures was the sum of the thirteen major appropriations bills.

Neither through its taxing nor its spending legislation did Congress attempt consciously to shape fiscal policy. Rather, its money decisions were the product of its fragmented structure of authority, as reflected in the multiplicity of powerful committees and subcommittees, the weakness of its party organizations, and the strong constituency orientation of its members because of their constant concern with reelection.

Although the Budget and Accounting Act of 1921 required the president to prepare an annual budget, a comprehensive plan for spending, and the Employment Act of 1946 required an annual economic report that projected revenues and expenditures in light of economic forecasts, Congress imposed no such requirements on itself. Fiscal policy was whatever remained of the president's program after it emerged from "a piece-meal and haphazard legislative process."[35] Consequently, presidents and their economic advisers lacked the capacity to predict accurately the economic impact of the federal government. The inability of Congress to participate rationally on an equal basis with the presidency in shaping fiscal policy led to conflict during the Nixon administration when federal spending became a politically significant issue. Spending grew rapidly in response to previously enacted statutory "entitlements" that could not be disregarded without revising the original authorizing legislation. Entitlements include Social Security benefits, federal retirement payments, farm price support payments, welfare payments, and food stamps. Most entitlement payments to individuals increase automatically with the cost of living.[36] Presidents struggled to control spending as Congress continued to commit the government to future outlays through the passage of legislation. The problem was compounded by "off-budget" spending through loan guarantees and tax credits.

Nixon challenged Congress to act responsibly on fiscal issues by curbing spending; when it did not do so, he frequently vetoed spending bills and made extensive use of impoundment. The primary response of Congress to this controversy with Nixon and to frustration over its inability to shape policy was the Budget and Impoundment Control Act of 1974, which created a procedure for handling impoundments. More important, that statute established a congressional budget process, created House and Senate Budget committees, and provided Congress with independent staff support for macroeconomic forecasting and budget analysis in the form of the Congressional Budget Office.

Central to the congressional budget process, in its original form,[37] were the two budget resolutions that Congress had to pass each year. The first resolution, which had a May 15 deadline, set targets for revenues, total spending, and the thirteen appropriations bills for the forthcoming fiscal year beginning on October 1. These targets could be exceeded only by revising them upward in the second budget resolution, which Congress had to adopt by September 15. In contrast to the first resolution, which served as a guide, the second was binding. (Because of time constraints, Congress failed to pass second resolutions from 1984 through 1987, which made the first resolutions binding.)

The House and Senate budget committees played a major role in the process as authors of the resolutions, which embodied congressionally determined fiscal policy. Their principal, and most difficult, task was to persuade the revenue and appropriations committees to consider the effects of their actions on the fiscal goals in the binding budget resolution.

The creation of the congressional budget process did not, however, "significantly alter the established process in Congress for raising and spending money."[38] Nor did it enable Congress to solve the problem of uncontrollable spending arising from the automatic growth of entitlement programs and statutory obligations. The budget process did contain a technique, the "reconciliation" procedure, for maintaining fiscal discipline. Reconciliation entails incorporating in the binding budget resolution instructions to specific committees to recommend statutory changes that will achieve the spending or revenue levels set in the resolution. The committees' recommendations are subsequently enacted in a reconciliation bill. Congress used reconciliation to accomplish massive expenditure cutbacks ($35.2 billion) proposed by President Reagan in 1981.

The sweeping scope of the reductions, which carried over through fiscal year 1984 and were made without extensive committee hearings or detailed floor debate, prompted complaints that Congress had abandoned its independent control of spending and created a process whereby the president can obtain approval of his entire package in a single vote. Allen Schick observed that "overreaching in 1981 poisoned the well for expansive use of the reconciliation process in subsequent years."[39] Since then, savings achieved through reconciliation have been small by comparison, but the process remains available for use by a congressional majority determined to make major cutbacks.

The principal effect of the congressional budget process, at least until passage of the Budget Enforcement Act of 1990 *(see the discussion below)*, was a change in executive-legislative budget relationships.[40] The increased centralization of budgetary decision making in Congress enhanced its ability to influence presidential budget policies while providing the president with greater leverage over congressional budget decisions. Congress and the president became, as Schick put it, "more interdependent: each [was] more vulnerable than before to having its budget preferences blocked or modified by the other."[41]

But the budget process did not make Congress more fiscally responsible. Nor did it prevail over the political and economic forces that, after 1982, produced record deficits. The deficit increased, as a percentage of gross national product, from 1.6 percent in fiscal 1979 to nearly 6 percent in 1992.[42] The primary causes of the growth in the deficit were the tax cuts enacted in 1981, increases in defense spending begun in 1981, increased interest charges on the expanding national debt, and automatic increases in entitlement programs through indexation.[43]

Concern over the record deficits and frustration over its inability to control their growth led Congress, in December 1985, to pass the Balanced Budget and Emergency Deficit Control Act, known as the Gramm-Rudman-Hollings Act (GRH I) after the senators who sponsored it—Phil Gramm, R-Texas, Warren B. Rudman, R-N.H., and Ernest F. Hollings, D-S.C. GRH I established an automatic deficit reduction process designed to bring the budget into balance by 1991.[44] GRH I established specific annual deficit targets and created the automatic spending reduction device, the mandatory sequestering order. The rationale behind Gramm-Rudman-Hollings was that the cuts would be so unacceptable that the president and Congress would compromise their budget differences to avoid them.

Before the process could be used, however, the Supreme Court ruled unconstitutional the provision authorizing the comptroller general to determine the need for a sequestering order and its amount. The Court said that it violated the separation of powers between the legislative and executive branches.[45] For the Court, the fatal flaw was the granting of executive-type powers to the comptroller general, an agent of Congress, who can be removed only by Congress.

Although GRH I contained a fallback procedure for imposing sequestration—a joint resolution—it was "politically too difficult to implement."[46] Consequently, in 1987 Congress amended the legislation by vesting authority over the sequestration process in the director of OMB, who is a member of the executive branch. The process still operated automatically, and the primary objective was still deficit reduction. However, in GRH II Congress also adjusted upward the annual deficit targets and advanced the date for achieving a balanced budget to 1993.[47]

Through the use of optimistic economic forecasts, baseline budgeting,[48] and various accounting techniques (known in Washington as "blue smoke and mirrors"), Congress and the president managed to avoid the imposition of a sequestration order through fiscal 1990. However, during 1990, as Congress considered President Bush's 1991 proposed budget, it became apparent that the GRH II target could not be met without increasing revenues or imposing draconian spending cuts. In May the president invited congressional leaders of both parties to participate in high level "summit" discussions to break the deadlock over the deficit. Significantly, the invitation contained no preconditions regarding taxes or spending, although OMB director Darman suggested in a television interview that the administration would be willing to exchange reforms in the budget process for a tax increase.[49]

Following protracted negotiations, the summit negotiators reached an agreement on October 27, after the House had rejected an initial deal.[50] The agreement consisted of two parts, the Omnibus Budget Reconciliation Act (OBRA) and the Budget Enforcement Act (BEA). OBRA provided for a deficit reduction package covering fiscal years 1991 through 1995 and amounting to $496.2 billion.[51] BEA made major changes in the congressional budget process by altering the Gramm-Rudman-Hollings Act.[52] Under the new rules, Congress and the president are relieved of responsibility for any increases in the deficit due to events beyond their control. In 1991 these factors included Operation Desert Storm, increased costs of the savings and loan bailout, slower than anticipated economic growth, and lower than expected revenues due to recession.

The changes implemented by OBRA and BEA shifted the focus of the budget process, as established in GRH I and GRH II, from deficit reduction to "limiting spending and guaranteeing that the baseline level of revenues is collected."[53] However, as Wildavsky observes, "The deadlock over the budgetary base—the levels of revenue and expenditure and, within them, different proportions for different programs and taxpayers—remains and may eventually undermine all hopes."[54]

Since 1981 Congress has been locked in protracted conflict with first President Reagan and then President Bush over fiscal policy and the deficit. The taming of inflation through monetary policy has undermined the traditional belief that large budget deficits cause inflation. Insofar as the business cycle is the outcome of monetary policy, it is possible for politicians to ignore the short-term effects of deficits. Politicians continue to make ritualistic denunciations of deficits, but few of them are willing to cut popular or strongly supported programs, such as Social Security, or to raise taxes to reduce or eliminate them. As Reagan's and Bush's experiences have demonstrated, there is little payoff, in support from public opinion or the voters, for efforts to curtail popular programs or to raise taxes. The budget deficit is not a winning political issue.

Only in the long run do policy makers and economists regard deficits as dangerous because they eventually reduce private investment by diverting capital into public sector spending.[55] This development will slow the rate of growth in economic output and productivity. There is little evidence, however, that the public has yet come to accept the need for tax increases and program reductions to curtail deficits and to begin reducing the national debt.

Conclusion

Can the president bring order and cohesion to macroeconomic policy? Can the presidency serve as the instrument for effective management of the economy? Such questions have become increasingly important since 1970 as the U.S. economy has matured, interdependence with other economies has increased, and the ability to increase productivity, sustain economic growth, and keep inflation and unemployment at acceptably low levels has faltered from time to time. Clearly, the challenge to presidents posed by macroeconomic policy is of continuing importance. Presidents face formidable obstacles and problems as they respond to that challenge.

Three major obstacles confront presidents in the performance of their economic policy role: expectations are inordinately and unrealistically high; they have limited authority to meet those expectations; and the base of knowledge on which they act is often limited and unreliable. The problem of unrealistic expectations is not peculiar to macroeconomic policy. Modern presidents have tended to make sweeping promises to be elected, and the American people have developed a deep faith that a strong, capable president can provide solutions to their most pressing problems.

As presidents attempt to develop policies that will produce outcomes to meet popular expectations, they encounter problems. Bush discovered as the recession of 1991 dragged on into 1992 that the public is impatient for tangible results, and the pressure for actions that can provide a "quick fix" is great. Approaching elections heighten the search for measures that will produce immediate results. Also, fulfillment of one set of expectations, such as curbing inflation, may lead to consequences, such as increased unemployment and high interest rates, that dampen others. Pressure for action is usually strong, and the popular bias against inaction runs deep; yet inaction may be the most prudent course to follow. In short, exaggerated popular expectations that the president will manage the economy effectively may limit his capacity to do so.

In striving to meet the unrealistic expectations of a public eager to place its trust in executive leadership, presidents discover that their authority to act is quite limited. In the area of macroeconomic policy three factors restrict presidential ability to act: congressional prerogatives, the independence of the Federal Reserve Board, and the absence of coordinating power within the executive branch. Presidents must collaborate with Congress in making fiscal policy. Their success depends on congressional responsiveness to their leadership, to their effectiveness as communicators and persuaders. They do not have independent authority to increase or reduce taxes or spending.

Although fiscal policy leadership is a difficult task under the best of circumstances because of congressional prerogatives, monetary policy is equally confining because of the independence of the Fed. The only resources the president has available to influence the Fed are persuasion and the periodic opportunity to appoint new members to the board and to designate its chair. Although presidents have regularly exerted pressure on the Fed, and it has taken political factors into consideration, there is no assurance that monetary policy will be compatible with fiscal policy or that it will not impede the achievement of other policy objectives. Presidents lack the authority to coordinate fiscal and monetary policy. They must rely instead on persuasion and on ad hoc committees to coordinate their economic policies and to integrate economic policy goals with those of other policies.

Presidents also discover that economics provides a rather shaky foundation for recommending policies that directly affect the operation of the entire economy. Economic forecasting is an inexact science and is subject to considerable margins of error. The validity of the projections of the Council of Economic Advisers, the Office of Management and Budget, the Treasury, and the Federal Reserve Board depends on the assumptions that underlie them and on the quality and quantity of information available. The assumptions vary with the institutional orientation of the agency making the forecast, the theories of the economists on the agency's staff, and political pressures on the agency. The Fed's assumptions, for example, reflect the influence of monetarism; OMB's, a traditional concern with budget balancing. As Stockman's account of his tenure as OMB director indicates, there is also pressure on forecasters to resolve budget problems by adopting best-case or "rosy" scenarios of economic perfor-mance.[56] If the assumptions underlying a forecast prove wrong, then policies based on the forecast may lead to unanticipated outcomes. For example, the record deficits incurred during his administration initially caught President Reagan by surprise because he enthusiastically accepted OMB's rosy scenario.

The nation has moved from a conservative consensus on economic policy in the 1920s and early 1930s to a Keynesian consensus in the 1950s and 1960s to a lack of consensus in the 1980s and 1990s. Policies have shifted from Nixon's imposition of wage and price controls to Reagan's embrace of supply-side theory and Bush's pragmatism. Despite all these changes, presidents still lack the capacity to control the economy even though rapidly changing economic conditions, in the United States and elsewhere, would seem to require a maximum amount of adaptiveness. The president's ability to respond to new situations, such as a sudden, large increase in the price of oil, is very limited. Institutional arrange-ments, both statutory and constitutional, restrict the president's actions and dictate that he rely primarily on persuasion to accomplish his objec-tives. Moreover, experience with different processes for economic policy making and coordination suggests that the internal structure of the presi-dency has little effect on policy outcomes in this area. Beyond economic conditions, over which the president has little control, the factors that appear to affect economic policy making and outcomes most substantially are the president's ideology and leadership.

NOTES

1. Edward R. Tufte, *Political Control of the Economy* (Princeton, N.J.: Princeton University Press, 1978).

2. A. James Reichley, "A Change in Direction," in *Setting National Priorities: The 1982 Budget,* ed. Joseph A. Pechman (Washington, D.C.: Brookings, 1981), 236–240.

3. Alan Stone, *Regulation and Its Alternatives* (Washington, D.C.: CQ Press, 1982), 262.

4. Joseph A. Pika and Norman C. Thomas, "The President as Institution Builder: The Reagan Case," *Governance* 3 (October 1990): 444.

5. Lester M. Salamon and Alan J. Abramson, "Governance: The Politics of Re-trenchment," in *The Reagan Record,* ed. John L. Palmer and Isabel V. Sawhill (Wash-ington, D.C.: Urban Institute Press, 1984), 47.

6. Marshall R. Goodman, "A Kinder and Gentler Regulatory Reform: The Bush Regulatory Strategy and Its Impact" (Paper presented at the annual meeting of the Midwest Political Science Association, Chicago, April 1991).

7. Walter W. Heller, *New Dimensions in Political Economy* (New York: Norton, 1966).

8. Jackie Calmes, "The Voracious National Debt," *Congressional Quarterly Weekly Report,* March 24, 1990, 896.

9. George Hager, "Deficit Shows No Gain From Pain of Spending Rules," *Congressional Quarterly Weekly Report,* July 20, 1991, 1963.

10. "Fiscal 1993 Budget by Function," *Congressional Quarterly Weekly Report,* Feb. 1, 1992, 245.

11. Tufte, *Political Control of the Economy,* 143.

12. In contrast, Paul E. Peterson and Mark Rom argue that there is little incentive for presidents to "manipulate the economy for either electoral or partisan reasons." In their view, presidents can best achieve their diverse objectives through economic policies that maintain a balance between steady economic growth with minimal rates of unemployment and inflation. "Macroeconomic Policymaking: Who Is In Control?" in *Can the Government Govern?* ed. John E. Chubb and Paul E. Peterson (Washington, D.C.: Brookings, 1989), 149.

13. George Hager, "One Outcome of Budget Package: Higher Deficits on the Way," *Congressional Quarterly Weekly Report,* Nov. 3, 1990, 3710–13.

14. David R. Beam, "New Federalism, Old Realities: The Reagan Administration and Intergovernmental Reform," in *The Reagan Presidency and the Governing of America,* ed. Lester M. Salamon and Michael S. Lund (Washington, D.C.: Urban Institute Press, 1984), 440.

15. James E. Anderson and Jared E. Hazleton, *Managing Macroeconomic Policy: The Johnson Presidency* (Austin: University of Texas Press, 1986), 14.

16. Dick Kirschten, "Sprinkel Finds a Better Market for Advice in Second Reagan Term," *National Journal,* March 22, 1986, 714–715. According to Reagan CEA member William Niskanen, Feldstein's assumption of a public role destroyed his effectiveness. His successor, who had no ties to academia, was "comfortable with a short leash" and thus more effective. W.A. Niskanen, *Reaganomics* (New York: Oxford University Press, 1988), 295, 296.

17. Paul W. McCracken, "Reflections on Economic Advising" (Paper delivered at the Princeton University Conference on Advising the President, Princeton, N.J., Oct. 31, 1975), 4.

18. Edward S. Flash, "Macro-Economics for Macro-Policy," *The Annals of the American Academy of Political and Social Science* (March 1971): 51.

19. Joseph A. Davis, "Policy and Regulatory Review: Growth in Legislative Role Sparks Concern in Congress," *Congressional Quarterly Weekly Report,* Sept. 14, 1985, 1809.

20. Hugh Heclo, "Executive Budget Making," in *Federal Budget Policy in the 1980s,* ed. Gregory B. Mills and John L. Palmer (Washington, D.C.: Urban Institute Press, 1984), 266–267.

21. Ibid., 291.

22. Anderson and Hazleton, *Managing Macroeconomic Policy,* 27.

23. Colin Campbell, "The White House and the Cabinet under the 'Let's Deal' President," in *The Bush Presidency: First Appraisals,* ed. Colin Campbell, S.J., and Bert A. Rockman (Chatham, N.J.: Chatham House, 1991), 211.

24. Colin Campbell, *Managing the Presidency: Carter, Reagan and the Search for Executive Harmony* (Pittsburgh: University of Pittsburgh Press, 1986), 123–135.

25. Robert J. Shapiro, "Politics and the Federal Reserve," *The Public Interest* 66 (Winter 1982): 122.

26. Ibid., 120.

27. Anderson and Hazleton, *Managing Macroeconomic Policy*, 83.

28. Roger B. Porter, *Presidential Decision Making: The Economic Policy Board* (New York: Cambridge University Press, 1980), 176.

29. Campbell, *Managing the Presidency*, 138.

30. Ibid., 139.

31. David A. Stockman, *The Triumph of Politics: Why the Reagan Revolution Failed* (New York: Harper & Row), 1986.

32. Colin Campbell, "The 'Let's Deal' President," 210.

33. Ibid., 211.

34. Jeffrey H. Birnbaum and Alan S. Murray, *Showdown at Gucci Gulch: Lawmakers, Lobbyists, and the Unlikely Triumph of Tax Reform* (New York: Random House, 1987).

35. James L. Sundquist, *The Decline and Resurgence of Congress* (Washington, D.C.: Brookings, 1981), 199.

36. R. Kent Weaver, *Automatic Government: The Politics of Indexation* (Washington, D.C.: Brookings, 1988).

37. Congress has modified the budget process three times: in the Balanced Budget and Emergency Deficit Control Act of 1985, popularly known as the Gramm-Rudman-Hollings Act (GRH I); in the Balanced Budget and Emergency Deficit Control Reaffirmation Act of 1987 (GRH II); and in the Budget Enforcement Act of 1990 (BEA).

38. Allen Schick, "The Evolution of Congressional Budgeting," in *Crisis in the Budget Process: Exercising Political Choice*, ed. Allen Schick (Washington, D.C.: American Enterprise Institute, 1986), 8.

39. Ibid., 29.

40. Ibid., 15.

41. Ibid.

42. "The Deficit: Trouble Ahead," *Congressional Quarterly Weekly Report*, Feb. 1, 1992, 226.

43. For example, increases in Social Security retirement are based on rises in the U.S. Bureau of Labor Statistics' consumer price index. More than one-third of programs in the federal budget contain indexing provisions, and since 1985 federal income tax brackets have been indexed. According to Weaver, indexing has deprived the government of flexibility in making fiscal policy by placing upward pressure on spending and downward pressure on revenues. See *Automatic Government*, 257.

44. The statute set annual targets, beginning in fiscal 1986, that would reduce the deficit to zero by 1991. Each year, in August, the Congressional Budget Office and the Office of Management and Budget were to estimate the amount by which spending had to be reduced to meet the target. Using these estimates, the General Accounting Office (GAO) was to develop its estimate of the deficit. If GAO predicted that the deficit would exceed the target by more than $10 billion, and if it saw no recession in prospect, it then determined the percentage that programs would have to be cut to meet the target. Half of the cuts were to come from defense and half from eligible domestic programs. (Exemptions were granted for interest on the debt, Social Security, Medicaid, and partially for Medicare.) On September 1 the president was required to issue a "sequestering" order making the cuts determined by the comptroller general, who is the head of GAO. The sequestration would become effective on October 15 unless, in the interim, Congress and the president were to enact other spending cuts or tax increases sufficient to hit the target.

The cuts did not apply across the board and did not distinguish between expenditures for equipment, personnel, or services to beneficiaries. Neither the president nor Congress could alter or modify the percentages determined by GAO; the process was automatic.

45. *Bowsher v. Synar*, 478 U.S. 714 (1986).

46. Stanley E. Collender, *The Guide to the Federal Budget: Fiscal 1990* (Washington, D.C.: Urban Institute Press, 1989), 55.

47. Ibid., 17.

48. According to Allen Schick, baseline budgeting "assumes that programs will continue without policy change. It adjusts projected expenditures for inflation and mandated workload changes." For example, if a program now spending $100 million is expected to experience a 5 percent increase in participants in the next year and the inflation rate is expected to be 5 percent, the program would have a $110 million baseline. An expenditure in the next year of, say $105 million, would be counted as a "savings" of $5 million even though an increase occurred. Schick, *The Capacity to Budget* (Washington, D.C.: Urban Institute, 1990), 96.

49. Burt Solomon, "Bush's Altered Stance on Taxes Was No Political Ploy," *National Journal*, May 19, 1990, 1240–41.

50. For an insightful analysis of the 1990 budget negotiations, see Aaron Wildavsky, *The New Politics of the Budgetary Process*, 2d ed. (New York: HarperCollins, 1992), chap. 12.

51. George Hager, "One Outcome of Budget Package." The major sources of savings included: revenue increases of $146.3 billion; discretionary spending cuts of $182.4 billion; cuts in entitlements and user fee increases totaling $99.0 billion; and $68.4 billion in lower interest payments on the national debt resulting from the other savings.

52. For a detailed analysis of the changes that BEA made in the congressional budget process, see Stanley E. Collender, *The Guide to the Federal Budget: Fiscal 1992* (Washington, D.C.: Urban Institute Press, 1992), chap. 1. The following summary is based on Collender, 20–26, and George Hager, "New Rules on Taxes, Spending May Mean Budget Standoff," *Congressional Quarterly Weekly Report*, Jan. 26, 1991, 232–237.

The major changes involved the following: revised deficit maximums; the establishment of caps on discretionary spending (which must be appropriated) and a new sequestration process to ensure that those limits are not exceeded; and the imposition of pay-as-you-go restrictions on revenues and mandatory spending programs, such as entitlements.

BEA set the deficit maximums above GRH I and GRH II targets and removed the Social Security Trust Fund, which has been running a surplus, from the calculations. However, the maximums are not fixed, as was the case under GRH, but may be revised to reflect the economic forecast in the president's budget submittal to Congress, technical changes, and any changes in discretionary spending caps. These changes will relieve Congress and the president from having to deal with a situation in which a fixed deficit maximum and a growing baseline deficit require ever larger deficit reductions to avoid sequestration.

BEA divides discretionary spending into separate categories—defense, domestic, and international—for fiscal 1991–1993 and places it under a single cap for 1994–1995. In the first period, Congress must observe the caps or there will be a sequester in any category that exceeds its cap. Spending may not be reduced in one category to pay for an increase in another, nor can revenue increases be used to fund increased spending in any category.

The pay-as-you-go feature requires that increases in entitlements be funded by revenue increases or reductions in other entitlements and that tax cuts be offset by corresponding tax increases or by reductions in entitlements.

53. Collender, *The Guide to the Federal Budget: Fiscal 1992*, 19.

54. Wildavsky, *The New Politics of the Budgetary Process*, 483.

55. Herbert Stein, *Presidential Economics: The Making of Economic Policy from Roosevelt to Reagan and Beyond* (New York: Simon & Schuster, 1984), 347.

56. Stockman, *The Triumph of Politics*, 97–98, 329–332.

READINGS

Anderson, James E., and Jared E. Hazleton. *Managing Macroeconomic Policy: The Johnson Presidency*. Austin: University of Texas Press, 1986.

Anderson, Martin. *Revolution*. New York: Harcourt Brace Jovanovich, 1988.

Collender, Stanley E. *Guide to the Federal Budget: Fiscal 1992*. Washington, D.C.: Urban Institute Press, 1991. Published annually.

Fisher, Louis. *Presidential Spending Power*. Princeton, N.J.: Princeton University Press, 1975.

Greider, William. *Secrets of the Temple: How the Federal Reserve Runs the Country*. New York: Simon & Schuster, 1987.

Kettl, Donald F. *Leadership at the Fed*. New Haven, Conn.: Yale University Press, 1986.

Mills, Gregory B., and John L. Palmer, eds. *Federal Budget Policy in the 1980s*. Washington, D.C.: Urban Institute Press, 1984.

Niskanen, William A. *Reaganomics*. New York: Oxford University Press, 1988.

Pfiffner, James P., ed. *The President and Economic Policy*. Philadelphia: Institute for the Study of Human Issues, 1986.

Porter, Roger B. *Presidential Decision Making: The Economic Policy Board*. New York: Cambridge University Press, 1980.

Schick, Allen, ed. *Crisis in the Budget Process: Exercising Political Choice*. Washington, D.C.: American Enterprise Institute, 1986.

Schick, Allen. *The Capacity to Budget*. Washington, D.C.: Urban Institute Press, 1990.

Stein, Herbert. *Presidential Economics: The Making of Economic Policy from Roosevelt to Reagan and Beyond*. 2d rev. ed. Washington, D.C.: American Enterprise Institute, 1988.

Stockman, David A. *The Triumph of Politics: Why the Reagan Revolution Failed*. New York: Harper & Row, 1986.

Tufte, Edward R. *Political Control of the Economy*. Princeton, N.J.: Princeton University Press, 1978.

Wildavsky, Aaron. *The New Politics of the Budgetary Process*. 2d ed. New York: HarperCollins, 1992.

10 THE POLITICS OF NATIONAL SECURITY POLICY

FOLLOWING WORLD WAR II the United States and the Soviet Union were the dominant countries in world affairs. Cast in the role of adversaries, they led two armed camps of nations—one democratically governed, the other ruled by Communist party dictatorships. The industrial democracies and the communist bloc coexisted in an uneasy peace, maintained in part by the threat of mutual nuclear annihilation. At the same time, each power grouping actively courted the support of the "uncommitted" nations of the so-called Third World. These countries, most of which faced enormous economic and social problems, varied in their orientations toward Washington and Moscow.

Superimposed on the basic pattern of U.S.-Soviet competition was the twentieth century technological revolution in communications, transporta-

President Richard Nixon's visit to the Great Wall of China was an important milestone in diplomatic history, symbolizing the end of twenty-three years of hostility between the United States and China.

tion, and weaponry, which had the effect of shrinking the world and making the risks of military confrontation greater than ever. In addition, the United States grew more economically dependent on other countries, especially suppliers of basic raw materials, such as oil. In an environment characterized by military precariousness and economic interdependence, national security policy—that is, foreign affairs and military policy— necessarily claimed the lion's share of the president's attention. No chief executive, however much he may have wished to do so, could focus primarily and indefinitely on domestic policy. Sooner or later, presidents found themselves caught up with national security issues.

Modern presidents since Franklin D. Roosevelt have been drawn almost irresistibly to concentrate on national security policy rather than domestic policy. Even those who were not strongly oriented toward national security issues when they took office, such as Ronald Reagan and Jimmy Carter, devoted much of their energy and resources to foreign and military affairs. The reasons for the domination of national security in presidential policy-making politics are at least twofold: first, the crucial importance of the United States in the international community; second, the political advantages that presidents normally derive from devoting much of their energy to national security.[1]

Reagan came into office in 1981 committed to bringing about a conservative revolution in domestic and economic policy, but found himself drawn toward national security policy issues. His successor, George Bush, was preoccupied with foreign and military policy from the start of his administration and only reluctantly turned his attention home when the economy faltered and his reelection campaign approached. Contrary to first impressions, the end of the cold war may mean that presidents must spend more time on foreign policy as alliances shift and new conflicts emerge.

This chapter examines the president's role as the dominant figure in making and directing national security policy. It reviews the major concepts and issues that have dominated national security policy since World War II. It then defines the national security policy-making problem as one in which the president is both the solution and the problem. It explains this situation by analyzing (1) the relationship between the president and Congress with respect to national security and (2) the problem of organizing an effective policy-making system for national security.

Issues and Conflicts in National Security Policy

From the end of World War II until March 1968, when the North Vietnamese Tet offensive precipitated Lyndon Johnson's decision to end the escalation of American involvement in the Vietnam War, U.S. national security policy rested on a single overarching concept or doctrine, which was supported by a broad consensus: the necessity for military *containment* of communism. That goal was pursued consistently, and differences of opinion within the policy-making elite and in the mass public were accommodated by compromises. Bipartisan support for the consensus in Congress gave presidents a free hand in formulating and implementing foreign and military policies. The only effective constraints imposed on presidential actions were the boundaries of the consensus, which began to break up in 1968 when it became apparent that containment could be preserved only through an indefinite, limited war in Vietnam or greatly expanded U.S. involvement that carried risks of conflict with the Soviet Union.

In a systematic study of U.S. involvement in Vietnam, Leslie Gelb concluded that presidents would do well to avoid the temptation to cast national security policy in the framework of an overall doctrine supported by consensus.[2] The problem with policy doctrines such as containment, Gelb argues, is that they create a "framework of necessity" in which "anything that becomes necessary to do in the first place becomes virtually impossible to undo thereafter."[3] Overarching policy concepts or doctrines also stifle dissent and lead to operational rigidity.

Nevertheless, even after the United States failed to "contain" communism in Vietnam, presidents continued to employ single, overarching concepts to build domestic political support for their national security policies. They found, as James Chace put it, that "selling programs to Congress and the American people in the postwar era was always made easier if they could be clothed in one garment."[4] In 1972 and 1973 President Nixon told the American people that a policy of détente would ease, if not end, the precarious Soviet-American tensions of the cold war. Détente was to be implemented through actions such as cultural exchanges, increased trade between the two countries, and negotiations to limit strategic nuclear weapons. Established attitudes and behavior patterns are not easy to change, however, and Nixon and his successor, Gerald Ford, found it convenient to seek support for their policies by citing threatening Soviet actions in various parts of the world, such as Africa, Latin America, and the Middle East.

Jimmy Carter effectively campaigned on the pledge, which he reaffirmed at the outset of his administration, that morality, manifested in universal commitment to the defense of human rights, could be the cornerstone of U.S. foreign policy. However, Carter's human rights focus failed to provide the basis for a new consensus because it would not be consistently applied. The United States found it easier to protest and threaten to take action against human rights violations in countries not vital to its interests, like the Soviet Union and its allies, than in those that were vital, like South Korea and South Africa. Indeed, misguided application of the human rights doctrine hastened the downfall of the shah's friendly but authoritarian government in Iran and contributed to the establishment of the equally oppressive, but virulently anti–American, Islamic republic of Ayatollah Ruhollah Khomeini. Nor did the United States have the capacity to enforce the doctrine against powerful violators.

Carter's inability to establish a new foreign policy consensus based on human rights illustrates the contradictions that have become inherent in the international environment of the United States. From an American perspective, that environment has become more and more unmanageable because of the decline in the relative economic power of the United States, which stems from continued dependence on imported oil and from economic interdependence with other industrial democracies. In addition to the contradiction between the commitment to human rights and the need for stable allies, serious dilemmas for the United States are embodied in many issues: devotion to Israel versus the need for Arab oil; the desire for military strength sufficient to protect vital U.S. interests versus domestic political pressures (for example, the drive, following the collapse of communism and the end of the cold war, to use part of the defense budget to fund domestic programs); and the preference for imported goods, such as Japanese automobiles and electronics equipment, versus the demand to preserve the health of domestic industries. The intermingling of new international issues, predominantly economic, with domestic social and macroeconomic policy issues further complicates the president's efforts to present national security policy in terms of an overarching framework. These new issues include the leverage exerted on the United States by foreign producers of oil and other natural resources, the management of the international monetary system, international sales of U.S. agricultural products, and international trade policy. These issues have immediate and powerful effects on important domestic constituencies and must be dealt with through negotiations. In addressing such issues presidents do not enjoy the discretion or broad support that traditionally has been accorded them in foreign and military policy.

The Reagan administration's handling of national security policy exemplifies the issues and conflicts presidents face in this area of policy making. Reagan took office proclaiming belligerently that his administration's framework for national security policy was continued opposition to and competition with the Soviet Union,[5] which he once called "the evil empire." In practice, his anti-Soviet stance was less than doctrinaire. In November 1981, for example, facing a growing peace movement in Western Europe, Reagan offered to cancel plans to place additional land-based intermediate-range missiles in West Germany and in several other North Atlantic Treaty Organization (NATO) countries in exchange for the withdrawal of comparable Soviet SS-20 missiles from Eastern Europe and the western part of Russia.

The pattern of strong anti-Soviet rhetoric and restrained conduct continued through the Reagan administration. The president, however, who throughout his political career had steadfastly proclaimed opposition to accommodating the Soviet Union, found it difficult to build a successful national security policy on that position. For example, negotiations to limit nuclear weapons and curtail the arms race, although initially unsuccessful, eventually produced the Intermediate Range Nuclear Forces Treaty, the first arms *reduction* agreement of the cold war.

Throughout the Reagan administration, journalists and political critics questioned its interpretation and explanation of its actions. The critics also raised questions about the president's knowledge of the details of events and the role of the State Department, the Central Intelligence Agency (CIA), and the National Security Council and its staff in handling them.

The Reagan administration's foreign policy surged out of control late in its sixth year with the disclosure of the Iran-contra affair.[6] In November 1986 the administration acknowledged that it had sent arms to Iran, but stated that only a small number of obsolete weapons had been involved. It maintained that the shipments were designed to establish contact with and encourage moderate elements in Iran. Reagan refused to acknowledge that selling arms to Iran had been an error, and he vigorously denied that there had been any explicit exchange of arms for hostages, although each hostage's release had been preceded by an arms shipment. The seriousness and complexity of the affair snowballed in late November 1986 when the president acknowledged, through Attorney General Edwin Meese, that profits from the arms sales ($10 million-$30 million) had been diverted to the Nicaraguan contras through a numbered Swiss bank account.

The Iran-contra affair raised questions about the content of the policies involved, the appropriateness and even legality of certain actions by the president and members of his staff, and the president's credibility and competence. The selling of arms to Iran in apparent exchange for American hostages called into question the commitment of the United States to resisting terrorism and isolating countries, such as Iran, that support terrorism. It also undermined the U.S. position of neutrality in the seven-year war between Iran and Iraq and damaged its relations with moderate Arab states such as Saudi Arabia. Several members of Congress charged that the arms sales apparently violated laws requiring "the administration to report on covert operations and other diplomatic and military operations overseas."[7] (The president exempted himself from the legislation and the embargo against arms sales to Iran that had been in effect since the 1979–1980 hostage crisis by formally making a finding, on January 17, 1986, that the sales were necessary to national security.)

The diversion of profits from the arms sales to the contras was in direct conflict with the Boland Amendment of 1984, which prohibited use of government funds to support covert operations against the government of Nicaragua, and the decision of Congress not to authorize military aid to the contras in 1986. To the surprise of many, when Reagan disclosed that funds had secretly been diverted to the contras, he stated that he had not been fully informed about the matter. His biographer, Lou Cannon, observes that Reagan had "a difficult time keeping his story straight" because of mental confusion and his desire to "claim credit for helping the contras even while distancing himself from the diversion."[8]

Questions about Reagan's competence in managing foreign policy focused on his detached administrative style, which entailed extensive delegation and a disdain for factual details. His supporters explained that he took care of "the big picture" and left the rest to subordinates. Until late 1986 this approach seemed to serve him quite effectively. The Iran-contra affair emboldened critics to point out that regardless of how little Reagan may have known, he was accountable for the actions of his administration. Journalist Elizabeth Drew charged Reagan with intellectual laziness and remarked that "he did not understand the nature of the trouble he was in."[9] The operation of the foreign policy process, especially the NSC staff, contributed a great deal to Reagan's political difficulties and did little to protect him from foreign policy mistakes. Iran-contra nearly destroyed the Reagan presidency, but he was able to control the damage "because the contra diversion could not be pinned on him."[10] He staged a partial recovery through improved relations with the Soviet Union and its leader, Mikhail Gorbachev. The economic difficulties experienced by the communist giant facilitated the easing of cold war tensions.

In contrast to Reagan, President George Bush was a hands-on president deeply engaged in the formulation and implementation of national security policy. He concerned himself with its details and participated actively in negotiations with foreign leaders. In addition, Bush approached foreign policy with a pragmatic, as opposed to Reagan's ideological, orientation. All of this resulted, however, in the criticism that his administration's foreign policy was purely tactical and lacked a strategic design.[11]

In general, the Bush administration's national security policies met with popular approval, although its refusal to retaliate against the government of China for the June 1989 Tiananmen Square massacre of students pressing for democratic reforms drew sharp criticism. Many members of Congress questioned the administration's conduct of relations with Panama and Iraq, but the public remained supportive. For the most part, Bush continued the policies of the late Reagan years, but with greater flexibility and adaptiveness.[12] As Terry Deibel put it, "Bush has provided just what the American people seemed to want when they elected him: a kind of competent Reaganism." He "restore[d] professionalism to the conduct of foreign policy."[13] In the Persian Gulf War, for example, Bush skillfully mobilized domestic and world opinion behind the most effective international coalition since World War II. He demonstrated the ability of the United States to project its power far from its home base. However, by not removing Iraqi president Saddam Hussein from power and bringing peace and stability to the Middle East, Bush failed to realize fully the fruits of victory.

Despite its success, the Bush foreign policy was essentially reactive. Even its major initiatives—the invasion of Panama and the gulf war—were responses to crises. The absence of a strategic framework led to an emphasis on individual problems and to policies that lacked cohesion.

While Bush spoke grandly of a "new world order," he gave little indication of its shape and dimensions. His administration was unable to develop a strategic design for the post-cold-war world or a replacement for
the Soviet threat as the unifying force that held the NATO countries and
Japan together.[14] Moreover, the absence of a strategic focus for national
security may have left the Bush administration with little sense of how to
counter growing domestic pressures for reduced international involvement or to cope with the increasing impact of international factors on the
domestic economy.

The National Security Policy–Making Problem

When the Soviet Union collapsed in 1991, and with it the threat posed
by international communism, isolationist forces long dormant in the
United States reawoke to challenge the dominant internationalism of the
post–World War II era. This development made any prospect of a national
security policy built on a broad consensus beyond reach in the foreseeable
future. Isolationism and the end of bipartisan congressional support for
administration policies, which resulted from the Vietnam War, have made
the need for effective international leadership in the United States all the
more critical. The governmental structure established in the Constitution—separate institutions sharing powers—creates continuing tension
between the president and Congress over the control of national security
policy. Edward S. Corwin observed that the Constitution "is an invitation
to struggle" between the two branches "for the privilege of directing
American foreign policy."[15] Although the struggle continues, and power
over foreign policy is divided, the president has played the dominant role
in shaping national security policy through most of the nation's history.
As I. M. Destler noted, "Americans are unavoidably dependent on their
presidents for foreign and defense policy leadership."[16]

Dependence on presidential leadership carries risks, however. The idio-
syncrasies of individual presidents' operating styles and personalities can
be sources of uncertainty and lack of cohesiveness in policy and can
reinforce the institutional tensions between Congress and the president.
(To some extent this happened in consequence of the Iran-contra affair.)
The nation needs in its national security policy "institutions that provide
continuity" and "structures and processes that promote coherence."[17]
The problem is that if institutions, structures, and procedures respond to

the short-term needs and whims of individual presidents, discontinuity in policy is likely to multiply. National security policy making presents the United States with a circular and seemingly inescapable problem: the country's dependence on the president for central policy leadership, born of constitutional arrangements and operational imperatives, leads to discontinuity in policy and a lack of cohesiveness that result from a policy-making system geared to presidential domination. The president is, then, "both solution and problem."[18]

The President, Congress, and National Security

The powers of the United States in international affairs are "inherent, plenary, and exclusive."[19] They are not granted expressly by the Constitution; rather they derive from the nation's existence as a sovereign entity in the international community. To say that the national power over international affairs is inherent means that it does not depend on an affirmative grant of power in the Constitution. The exclusive and plenary character of that power means that it cannot be exercised by the states or anyone else and that its exercise is not limited by the reserved powers of the states.

The Constitution, however, is ambiguous in its assignment of the power to control foreign relations. That both the president and Congress have formal constitutional powers in that sphere indicates that the Founders intended control to be shared. In a 1793 debate with James Madison in the *Gazette of the United States,* Alexander Hamilton argued that direction of the nation's foreign policy is inherently an executive function.[20] Madison's position—that since the power to declare war is vested in Congress, presidential powers in this regard are merely instrumental—has not been borne out by subsequent events. Longstanding usages and the practical aspects of the conduct of foreign relations have combined to make the president the sole organ of the United States in the conduct of its external affairs. Negotiations and communications with other governments have been from the early years of the Republic a presidential monopoly.

Congress, however, has retained considerable ability to influence the substantive content of the foreign and defense policies that the president implements. Policies formulated by the president cannot remain viable for long without congressional support in the form of implementing legislation and appropriations. Nevertheless, throughout most of U.S. history the president has been and is today the "most important single factor in the determination of American foreign policy."[21] The reasons can be understood, at least in part, through examination of the powers of the president and Congress in national security matters.

The Powers of the President

In addition to the inherent powers of the executive derived from the involvement of the United States in the international community, the president's powers over national security stem from two sources: formal powers granted by or implied from specific constitutional provisions and powers delegated to the executive branch by Congress. The specific constitutional provisions on which the president's dominant national security policy role is based include the power to receive ambassadors and ministers, the power to negotiate treaties, the clause designating him as commander in chief of the armed forces, the general grant of executive power, and the clause enjoining him to "take care that the laws be faithfully executed." Operationally, these provisions result in four major areas of presidential authority over national security: recognition and nonrecognition of other governments; making, implementing, and terminating international agreements; the appointment of personnel to conduct foreign and military policy; and the use of military force as a means of achieving policy goals.

Recognition and Nonrecognition of Foreign Governments. The president's power, granted in Article II, Section 3, of the Constitution, to "receive Ambassadors and other public Ministers" is the source of the power of recognition and nonrecognition of foreign governments. Because foreign diplomats are accredited to the president, the decision whether to receive them and thus recognize their governments is exclusively the president's. Congress may formally pressure the president to grant or refuse recognition, but it has no direct involvement in the decision. Because the president can grant recognition, by implication he can also refuse to grant it or withdraw it.

Traditionally, under international law, governments grant recognition to other governments provided they are stable, have effectively established their authority, and are meeting their international obligations. The United States has expressed its approval or disapproval of foreign regimes through recognition and nonrecognition. This weapon is particularly effective when exercised by a nation as powerful and influential as the United States. Nonrecognition by the United States connotes a lack of respectability, if not a lack of legitimacy, in the international community. The prospect of U.S. recognition and the threat of its withdrawal can be used to influence the conduct of another nation. Although the leverage gained through use of the recognition power is limited, its considerable symbolic significance makes it an important presidential instrument in international politics. But recognition or nonrecognition is not a casual decision. Once recognition is granted or relations are broken, much of the leverage that the power provides is lost.

Some well-known instances involving use of the recognition power illustrate its value as well as its limitations. After the Russian Revolution in 1917–1918, the United States refused to recognize the communist government of the Soviet Union on the grounds that it had obtained power illegally, expropriated foreign-owned property without compensation, and oppressed its citizens. Although the disapproval of the Soviet regime implied through nonrecognition did not end, FDR established diplomatic relations with the Soviet Union in 1933; he believed that practical considerations made recognition advantageous to the United States. In contrast, immediately following the proclamation of the new state of Israel in 1948, President Harry Truman granted it recognition, making the United States the first nation to do so. The support of the United States has been vital to the survival of Israel under precarious conditions.

When a communist regime took power in China in 1949 after a revolutionary struggle, the United States refused to recognize it and persisted in regarding the nationalist government on the island of Taiwan as the legitimate government of China. Not until 1979 did the United States establish diplomatic relations with the People's Republic of China. Recognition of the PRC symbolized a resumption of the historic friendship between the two countries. It was made possible by a relaxation of ideological rigidity by the Chinese regime, U.S. acceptance of the regime as the legitimate government of China, and mutual awareness of the policy and economic advantages that would accrue to each nation. At the same time, however, the United States did not recognize PRC sovereignty over Taiwan.

The United States broke diplomatic relations with the Islamic Republic of Iran in December 1979 because of that government's support of the seizure of the U.S. embassy by radicals a month earlier. The damage to U.S.-Iranian relations resulting from the hostage crisis that ensued and the continued anti-Americanism of the Islamic regime have prevented resumption of diplomatic relations. President Reagan's approval of limited arms sales as a way to improve the climate between the two countries failed to provide the basis for renewed diplomatic ties. The release in late 1991 of the last three American hostages held by Iranian-dominated radicals in Lebanon indicated that conditions in Iran had changed enough to permit some improvement in relations with the United States. But U.S. recognition remained dependent on further evidence of moderation, such as official renunciation of support for international terrorism.

In 1991 the United States granted recognition to the three Baltic republics of Estonia, Latvia, and Lithuania, which had declared their independence from the Soviet Union in 1990. Although sympathetic to the Baltics, the Bush administration had delayed recognition because it did not wish to upset the precarious position of Soviet president Gorbachev in his efforts to reform that country. Following the failure of a coup against Gorbachev in August 1991, the United States moved cautiously by delaying recognition of several more Soviet republics that had declared their independence. Its major concern was that the collapse of the Soviet Union would leave control of its vast arsenal of 27,000 nuclear weapons in the hands of local political leaders and military commanders. In December 1991, as several republics led by Russia and Ukraine dissolved the Soviet Union and formed the Commonwealth of Independent States, a new union with limited powers, the Bush administration voiced support. However, it did not recognize the CIS and delayed recognition of all but one of the component republics until early 1992 when their viability and popular support were established.

In these instances, and in other cases involving the recognition power, presidents are legally free to act without regard to Congress. However, congressional views and public opinion effectively limit the range of presidential discretion. Nonrecognition of communist China, for example, had outlived its usefulness for some time before the first tentative steps were taken in 1971 to normalize relations. Still, it was not until China had broken with the Soviet Union and the excesses of the Chinese regime began to moderate that President Nixon, whose credentials as an unrelenting opponent of communism were impeccable, felt free to initiate the informal contacts that led to recognition.

International Agreements. The Constitution provides a second influential presidential power in foreign affairs: the authority to conduct negotiations with other nations that result in treaties or binding executive agreements. The constitutional basis for the treaty-making power is found in Article II, Section 2, which declares that the president "shall have Power, by and with the Advice and Consent of the Senate, to make Treaties, provided two thirds of the Senators present concur." The authority to make executive agreements is not mentioned explicitly, but its constitutionality is "universally conceded."[22] That authority may be implied from the president's function as the nation's official organ for the conduct of foreign relations or as a convenient means of implementing a recognized executive power, such as the commander-in-chief power and the "take care" clause of the Constitution.[23] In addition, executive agreements may be concluded pursuant to provisions of valid treaties and of existing legislation.

The principal distinction between treaties and executive agreements is that Senate approval is required for treaties. The Senate's role in the treaty-making process has been limited by a precedent established in 1789, when the Senate refused George Washington's request to advise him on provisions of a treaty under negotiation. The Senate may, however, amend or attach reservations to treaties submitted for its approval. Amendments change the content of a treaty and thus require additional negotiations; reservations merely clarify the Senate's understanding of the treaty's provisions. The requirement of a two-thirds vote for approval gives the Senate substantial leverage over the executive in the treaty-making process.[24]

As an alternative to the formal treaty process, modern presidents have relied on executive agreements to conclude understandings with other governments. The distinction between treaties and executive agreements is unclear because the latter are not specifically mentioned in the Constitution. In practice, any international agreement the president submits to the Senate for approval as a treaty is a treaty. All other agreements are executive agreements. Congress repeatedly has expressed its disapproval of the use of executive agreements in lieu of treaties, but the only limitation it has imposed, in the Case-Zablocki Act of 1972, is to require that it be notified of all such agreements. Although Congress is free to take action against executive agreements to which it objects, it has been unable to impose effective limits on the president's power to make them.[25]

Presidents have continued to submit international agreements for Senate approval as treaties because of domestic political considerations. Approval by the Senate gives an international agreement a degree of legitimacy that otherwise would be lacking. For instance, President Carter chose to submit to the Senate as a treaty the agreement providing for gradual termination of U.S. control of the Panama Canal. Carter apparently knew that such action would be difficult to defend publicly in any case, and avoidance of Senate approval could impose unacceptable political costs on his administration. For similar reasons, Carter submitted the second Strategic Arms Limitation Talks agreement to the Senate as a treaty even though approval was doubtful.

On several occasions, however, modern presidents have taken important action through executive agreements: in 1940 Franklin Roosevelt exchanged fifty "over-age" destroyers for ninety-nine-year leases on bases in British possessions in the Western hemisphere; toward the end of World War II, Roosevelt, British prime minister Winston Churchill, and Soviet leader Joseph Stalin entered into extensive agreements on the occupation of Germany and the restoration of civil government in Eastern Europe; in 1973 the United States and North Vietnam ended hostilities and exchanged prisoners of war through an executive agreement; and in 1981 the United States and Israel negotiated an agreement for strategic cooperation in the Middle East.

The decision to designate an international agreement as a treaty is the president's.[26] Such a decision is political rather than legal. But Congress is not without influence, especially if the agreement is not self-executing. In other words, if a treaty or an executive agreement requires legislation or an appropriation for its implementation, Congress can require the executive to take note of its views. Congress has no constitutional duty to implement a treaty or an executive agreement. Moreover, even though treaties and executive agreements have the force of law, they cannot contravene specific provisions of the Constitution.

Although the president's power to negotiate international agreements is subject to political and constitutional limitations, the power to terminate such agreements is not. Clearly, the president can cancel an agreement that did not receive Senate approval. The Constitution is silent, however, about whether approval of the Senate is required to terminate a treaty. The Supreme Court ruled in 1979 that the president could unilaterally abrogate a defense treaty with Taiwan that was part of the agreements establishing diplomatic relations between the United States and the People's Republic of China.[27] Although the Court based its decision on the recognition of foreign governments, it has been interpreted as authorizing unilateral presidential breaking of treaties in accordance with their terms. President Reagan, for example, terminated without congressional approval U.S. acceptance of the jurisdiction of the International Court of Justice, a bilateral commercial treaty with Nicaragua, and U.S. membership in the United Nations Educational, Scientific, and Cultural Organization.[28] Since the Vietnam War, presidents also have expanded their power in the treaty area through reinterpretation. The Reagan administration provides the best example: in 1985 it broadened the terms of the 1972 Anti-Ballistic Missile Treaty, over the objections of the Senate and the Soviet Union, to accommodate development of the strategic defense initiative.[29]

The power to negotiate international agreements is an important aspect of the president's role in foreign affairs. It has a firm constitutional basis and as a practical matter is almost solely an executive function. However, the constitutional role of the Senate in the treaty approval process and the necessity for congressional action to implement most international agreements ensure that congressional influence will be felt in making and implementing such agreements.

Appointments. As noted in Chapter 6, the power to appoint subordinates is an important part of presidential control over policy. It is a power that the president shares with the Senate, however, in naming high-ranking officials. Although the general considerations affecting presidential appointments also apply to national security policy makers, specific concerns in this sphere warrant attention here.

The most important appointments affecting national security are the positions of secretary of state, secretary of defense, the director of central intelligence, and the president's assistant for national security affairs. With these appointments, the president indicates the direction and orientation of the foreign and military policy of his administration. The appointment of the secretary of state is significant for procedural and substantive reasons. The choice of a well-known figure with definite policy views, such as the selection of Gen. George C. Marshall by President Truman, John Foster Dulles by President Eisenhower, or Gen. Alexander Haig by President Reagan, reflects the intention to rely heavily on the secretary for advice and guidance. The choice of a relatively unknown individual, such as President Kennedy's designation of Dean Rusk or President Nixon's selection of William P. Rogers, indicates that the president intends to play the dominant role in foreign policy formulation and to relegate to the secretary the management of the foreign affairs bureaucracy. The president may change his procedural role, however, as Nixon did at the start of his second term when he replaced Rogers with Henry Kissinger. By selecting a secretary with strong policy views, such as Dulles or Kissinger, the president indicates his own policy preferences.

The appointment of the secretary of defense also can indicate the president's plans for the department. Kennedy's choice of Ford Motor Company president Robert S. McNamara signified his determination to make the armed forces more efficient through application of modern management techniques. Nixon's selection of Rep. Melvin Laird of Wisconsin, a powerful Republican leader, symbolized his intention to give greater weight to congressional views in the operation of the department. In contrast, Reagan's appointment of Caspar Weinberger, who had earned a reputation through service in the Nixon administration as a budget cutter (he was called "Cap the Knife"), created confusion because Reagan was publicly committed to increases in defense spending. President Bush's first nominee for the defense portfolio, former Republican senator John Tower of Texas, failed to win confirmation. Democratic senators opposed Tower on the grounds that he drank excessively and that he was a notorious womanizer. It seems more likely that they were retaliating for Tower's often abrasive, offensive, and highly partisan conduct during his four terms in the Senate. Bush's next nominee, Rep. Richard Cheney, R-Wyo., who had served as President Ford's chief of staff, received quick, enthusiastic approval. Cheney was highly respected and well liked in both houses of Congress.

The position of director of central intelligence involves managing the CIA and coordinating the activities of the intelligence community.[30] The directorship was often politically controversial during the cold war because of charges that the CIA and other intelligence agencies had engaged in covert activities designed to assassinate foreign political leaders and overthrow foreign governments. Critics also charged the CIA with ineffective intelligence work, such as the failure to anticipate the Iranian revolution of 1978–1979 or Iraq's invasion of Kuwait in 1990. CIA directors have tended to be either intelligence professionals such as William Colby and Robert Gates, or experienced politicians such as George Bush and William Casey. The latter, Reagan's first CIA director, apparently played a major role in the Iran-contra affair. His involvement could not be proved, however, because he became ill with terminal cancer and died before the congressional investigation into the affair.[31] Casey's successor was FBI director William Webster, a former federal judge. Reagan appointed him to remove the aura of illegality and scandal that Casey's freewheeling activities had cast upon the agency. President Bush's first nominee to head the CIA was Robert Gates, whose nomination drew substantial opposition in the Senate because of his connection with the Iran-contra affair. After lengthy hearings and floor debate, the Senate confirmed Gates, 64–31, in November 1991.[32] The appointment was significant because Gates would have the task of reshaping the role of the CIA and the rest of the intelligence community in the post-cold war era.

In making high-level executive and diplomatic appointments, the president must be attentive to senatorial attitudes and concerns, although the Senate normally defers to presidential choices even in the face of doubts about the competence of the nominee. Reagan's nomination of a longtime political associate, California Supreme Court justice William P. Clark, as deputy secretary of state brought strong criticism from the press and several senators when Clark revealed a dreadful lack of knowledge of foreign affairs during his confirmation hearing before the Foreign Relations Committee. Nevertheless, the committee recommended his approval and the Senate complied.[33]

One of the most important national security appointments, that of the national security assistant, is not subject to Senate approval. The president also is free to designate personal representatives to conduct negotiations or perform specific missions without the requirement of confirmation. President Carter used distinguished career diplomats Ellsworth Bunker and Sol Linowitz to negotiate with the governments of Panama and several Middle East countries, respectively. W. Averell Harriman, a prominent Democratic statesman, served as a roving ambassador without portfolio under several presidents beginning with FDR.

The appointment power is essential to presidential control of direction and implementation of foreign and military policy. It is a means whereby the president can shape both the conduct and the content of policy. He enjoys wide latitude in exercising the power, but he must be sensitive to the limits imposed by international and domestic politics and by the Senate.

The Use of Military Force. The Constitution states, "The President shall be Commander in Chief of the Army and Navy of the United States" and of the state militia when they are called into federal service (Article II, Section 2). It does not, however, define the nature of the president's powers and duties as commander in chief. In fact, extensive powers pertaining to the use of military force are found in Article I, the legislative article. Most important, Congress is empowered to declare war. Constitutionally, then, the power to use military force is shared between Congress and the president. Historical practice, however, has resulted in a vast expansion of presidential authority to use force at the expense of the powers of Congress. The dominance of the president in this regard has been almost total in wartime; in times of peace Congress has partially reclaimed the ground it lost. Nonetheless, the result has been the continual aggrandizement of presidential power.[34]

The war powers of the president are sweeping and have their basis in the Constitution, in statutory delegations of authority by Congress, and in judicial interpretations. The constitutional foundation of the president's war powers was laid early in the Civil War when Abraham Lincoln married the commander in chief clause to the "take care" clause.[35] He used the resulting war powers to justify a wide range of actions to suppress the rebellion. These included activation of state militias, expenditure of appropriated funds for unauthorized purposes, suspension of the writ of habeas corpus in militarily insecure areas, and the imposition of a naval blockade of Confederate ports. The Supreme Court upheld the legality of the blockade in the *Prize Cases,* in which it declared that the president had a duty to defend the nation by appropriate means, including military action.[36] The refusal of the Court to overturn any of Lincoln's actions until after the war set a precedent of judicial deference that would be followed in future wars.

Lincoln's actions demonstrated that the war powers of the president extend far beyond mere military command. During World War II the president's powers as commander in chief expanded exponentially under FDR. Among other things, Roosevelt ordered the internment of all persons of Japanese ancestry, including both naturalized and native-born U.S. citizens, who were residing in the Pacific Coast states. The Supreme

Court acquiesced in this deprivation of basic civil liberties.[37] Roosevelt also created by executive order emergency agencies, such as the War Labor Board, and endowed them with sweeping regulatory powers and accompanying sanctions. In his most dramatic assertion of the war power, FDR demanded of Congress on September 7, 1942, that it repeal certain sections of the Emergency Price Control Act. If Congress did not act by October 1, he threatened to act on his own authority. Congress responded as the president wished, thus avoiding a constitutional showdown.

Congress has further contributed to the development of the president's war powers through extensive delegations by statute. During World War I Congress enacted laws that authorized the president to regulate, requisition, and purchase a wide range of materials and products, to prohibit exports, to license trade, to censor international communications, to regulate enemy aliens in the United States, and to seize and operate the railroads. These powers were expanded during World War II through passage of legislation such as the Lend-Lease Act, which authorized the procurement and leasing of war materials to countries regarded as vital to the defense of the United States; the Emergency Price Control Act, which established the Office of Price Administration and authorized it to fix prices and ration a wide range of goods and services; and a host of other statutes. Many congressional delegations of authority to the president were open-ended and not revised or withdrawn until passage of the National Emergencies Act of 1976.

In short, once war is declared, presidential powers are vast. To ensure national survival, whatever the president says must be done is done without regard to constitutional considerations and with the acquiescence, if not full approval, of the Supreme Court and Congress. Some leading constitutional scholars have charged that the Constitution is suspended in wartime and the president becomes a de facto dictator.[38]

The president's power to use military force in peacetime, or even in periods of undeclared war, is less clear-cut. Although the Supreme Court has been reluctant to resolve questions in this area, Congress has been more assertive of its prerogatives. However, the president still has substantial responsibilities and concomitant powers to protect American lives and property abroad, discharge international obligations, and preserve national security. Constitutional language is vague, and statutory enactments are an incomplete guide to the exercise of this authority.

Between the two world wars Congress circumscribed the president's military powers through enactment of the Neutrality Acts. However, the failure of Congress to declare and implement a foreign policy of isolation from world conflicts became manifest in the 1930s when Germany, Italy, and Japan aggressively expanded their territorial holdings and began a war into which the United States inevitably was drawn. Following World War II successive presidents fashioned an internationalist foreign policy, with bipartisan congressional support, based on the military containment of communism. Presidents were expected to take the initiative, and Congress reviewed their actions through the passage of necessary legislation and appropriations.[39]

The most sensitive issue during this period, which ended in 1968 with the failure of U.S. military involvement in Vietnam, was the authority of the president to commit U.S. troops to fight abroad. On several occasions between 1945 and 1965, presidents sent U.S. forces into combat or placed them in situations that could easily result in combat.[40] These included the Korean War, the dispatch of four divisions to Western Europe as a permanent commitment to NATO, Eisenhower's responses to Chinese pressures on Taiwan and to increased tensions in the Middle East, the 1965 intervention in the Dominican Republic, as well as the Vietnam War.

Vietnam produced the most extensive and controversial instances of presidential war making in the post–World War II era. Beginning with Truman, presidents made commitments of military aid and provided military advisers to the government of South Vietnam. By the end of 1963, more than 16,000 military advisers were in that country, many of them actively participating in combat although not formally authorized to do so. In August 1964 the Johnson administration reported a confrontation in the Gulf of Tonkin between a North Vietnamese gunboat and a U.S. destroyer. At Johnson's request Congress passed the Gulf of Tonkin Resolution, which authorized the president to "take all necessary steps including use of armed force" to assist nations belonging to the Southeast Asia Treaty Organization (to which the United States was a signatory) in defense of their freedom. Only two negative votes were cast against the resolution, both in the Senate. The resolution did not distinguish between powers the president already possessed and newly delegated authority. On the authority of the Constitution, the Southeast Asia Treaty, and the Gulf of Tonkin Resolution, Johnson ordered a vast increase in the strength of U.S. forces in Vietnam, so that by late 1967 they exceeded 500,000. He also authorized military commanders to conduct air raids against military targets in North Vietnam.[41] President Nixon extended the scope of military operations even while trying to negotiate an end to U.S. involvement in the war. In 1970 he ordered a covert invasion of Cambodia to destroy enemy supply and staging areas, and in December 1972 he authorized the bombing of the North Vietnamese capital city of Hanoi and the major port city of Haiphong. These actions were taken without consulting Congress.

Initially, Congress backed administration efforts to contain communism in Southeast Asia through the use of military force. As the war dragged on, however, popular support began to wane, a widespread domestic protest movement began to take shape, and opposition to U.S. policy developed abroad from its allies and from Third World nations. Many members of Congress questioned the wisdom and the legality of placing the decision to use military force entirely in the president's hands. As long as presidential use of force appeared to be successful, congressional opposition was minimal; but when the use of force appeared to be failing, or the risks increased and the costs in popular support became too great, Congress reasserted its constitutional authority to participate as an equal partner with the president in determining where and under what conditions the United States would wage war.

The Assertion of Congressional Powers

Congress has substantial constitutional powers that enable it to claim parity with the president in shaping national security policy. As noted in the discussion of the president's powers, the Senate is directly involved in the treaty approval process and the confirmation of appointments; congressional action in the form of authorizations and appropriations is necessary to implement all presidential decisions that are not self-executing; and the power to declare war rests solely with Congress and implies a congressional prerogative over the use of military force. However, operational realities and a bipartisan foreign policy consensus led to presidential domination of national security policy during the cold war.

The failure of the Vietnam War—essentially a presidential war—ended, at least temporarily, Congress's deference to White House domination of national security policy. During the 1970s Congress limited presidents' ability to wage undeclared war, reduced unrestrained use of executive agreements, restored the treaty as the principal means of making international agreements, reassessed its sweeping delegations of authority to presidents in past wars and emergencies, and curbed secrecy and covert activities in the conduct of foreign and military affairs.

The most important congressional attempt to reclaim powers lost or given to the executive was the War Powers Resolution of 1973. Passed over Nixon's veto, House Joint Resolution 542 provided that the president may commit the armed forces to combat only in the event of a declaration of war, specific statutory authorization, or a national emergency created by an attack on the United States or its armed forces. The resolution urged the president to consult with Congress in "every possible instance" before committing forces to combat abroad, and it required consultation after such commitment. Specifically, it required a written report to Congress within forty-eight hours of a commitment and required ending the commitment within sixty days unless authorized by Congress. The commitment could be extended for thirty additional days if the president certified to Congress that military conditions required continued use of the forces to ensure their safety. Finally, it stated that, through use of a concurrent resolution that would not be subject to presidential veto, Congress may order the disengagement of U.S. forces before the end of the first sixty days.[42]

The effectiveness of the War Powers Resolution as a congressional means of controlling presidentially initiated military action is unclear. Presidents Ford, Carter, Reagan, and Bush had filed twenty-four reports of military actions with Congress as of the end of 1991.[43] In only one of these, the rescue of the *Mayaguez,* a merchant ship that had been seized by Cambodian gunboats in 1975, did the president activate the sixty-day clock. Since its passage, all presidents have regarded the War Powers Resolution as an unconstitutional encroachment on their powers, and their reports have carefully avoided any acknowledgment of its constitutionality. In addition, they have been able to circumvent the intent of the resolution by not activating the sixty-day clock, by stating that they were reporting "consistent with the War Powers Resolution," and by holding that merely informing Congress meets the resolution's requirement of consultation. The position of the executive has been consistent across administrations, while Congress has been unable to formulate a "unitary position or statement of institutional interest."[44] Nor has Congress challenged the president by starting the sixty-day clock. In the 1983 legislation authorizing U.S. participation in a multinational force in Lebanon, Congress actually extended the time to eighteen months.

President Bush's actions in the invasion of Panama in December 1989 are typical of how presidents deal with the War Powers Resolution.[45] He informed congressional leaders of the pending action a few hours before it began. Three days later he reported the action in a letter to Thomas Foley, Speaker of the House, and Robert Byrd, president pro tem of the Senate. In that letter, which avoided triggering the clock, he gave reasons for the action, which he maintained was consistent with the War Powers Resolution.

Bush operated in similar fashion during the Persian Gulf War of 1990–1991.[46] Before sending U.S. armed forces to the gulf in response to Iraq's August 2, 1990, invasion of Kuwait, he notified congressional leaders of the planned deployment on August 8. The next day he sent the Speaker and the president pro tem a letter in which he stated that the report was "consistent with" the War Powers Resolution. During the next six months there was a massive buildup of U.S. forces in the gulf area, the U.S. and Iraq exchanged bellicose threats, and the United Nations adopted a resolution imposing a deadline for Iraq to withdraw from Kuwait. At no point, however, did either the president or Congress begin the sixty-day countdown. Rather, the president argued that he had the authority to force Iraq to leave Kuwait without congressional approval. Nevertheless, on January 8, 1991, one week prior to the UN deadline, Bush asked Congress to approve a joint resolution authorizing the use of force. Congress did so four days later by votes of 52–47 in the Senate and 250–183 in the House.[47] When Bush signed the resolution, he reasserted his position that the War Powers Resolution is unconstitutional. The January 12, 1991, resolution has been recognized as the functional equivalent of a declaration of war. Whether Bush weakened his position, that he already had the authority to initiate hostilities, is an unanswered question.

The effect of the War Powers Resolution on the constitutional roles of the president and Congress in making decisions about war and peace is unclear. At the very least, the legislation was a symbolic victory for Congress, serving notice that sustained military commitments outside the country could no longer be made by presidential fiat but required congressional approval and, by implication, popular support. Destler observed, "It is hard to conceive of a formula better crafted to balance the need for presidential capacity to respond quickly to foreign emergencies and the need—as a matter of right *and* effective policy—for democratic judgment on the deployment of troops in combat."[48]

However, most commentary on the War Powers Resolution has been negative. There is "growing consensus" that it "has not worked as Congress envisioned."[49] Presidents have neither consulted Congress in "any meaningful manner" nor have they sought to make the law work by invoking its provisions.[50] Instead, they have sought to circumvent it. For its part, Congress has been unwilling to challenge presidential nonresponsiveness to the War Powers Resolution. According to Michael Glennon, "Whatever congressional intent underlay the War Powers Resolution, any expectation that its procedures would actually lead to collective Legislative-Executive judgment in the war-making process was mistaken."[51]

However, it must be noted that, although Congress is quite aware of the deficiencies of the War Powers Resolution, it has not acted to repeal or revise it. The reason may be that the resolution suits congressional purposes. It "allows Congress the luxury of being politically comfortable with its decisions regarding a military action while providing a convenient forum for criticizing the President."[52] Congress can use the War Powers Resolution to force the president to end an unpopular military operation, or it can criticize presidential failure to comply with the procedural requirements of the resolution when public opinion is supportive or divided. Either way, Congress cannot lose.[53] From this perspective, the War Powers Resolution constrains presidential war making by forcing presidents to take it into account and to recognize the possibility, albeit distant, of congressional action. The resolution reminds the president that, under the Constitution, he shares with Congress the crucial decision to lead the nation into war. That Congress has not vigorously applied the War Powers Resolution or buttressed it by denying funding for military action does not mean it is of little consequence.

The ambiguities surrounding the resolution could be clarified by tightening its language and subjecting it to Supreme Court interpretation, but neither Congress nor the president has so far been willing to take such action, perhaps because the outcome is uncertain. Citing as precedent the history of presidential war making, the Court could sustain the resolution. Or, noting that since it was forced on the presidency at a time of institutional weakness, it "undercuts the legitimacy of the executive branch," the Court might choose to overturn it.[54]

Increased congressional participation in national security decision making may not be constitutionally mandatory, but it has become necessary on political grounds. The impact of international issues on domestic politics and the entry of domestic political interests, such as the Israel lobby, into the policy-making process force presidents to seek congressional support to protect their own political positions.

It is somewhat ironic, however, that Congress's desire to share in making national security policy and increased knowledge and competence on the part of individual members and expanded committee staffs have not been accompanied by congressional capability to assume the added responsibility.[55] Congressional reforms during the 1970s, especially in the House, and additional changes in the 1980s further fragmented power and made it more difficult for Congress to speak authoritatively with one voice. The proliferation of subcommittees and the growing interdependence of domestic and foreign policy issues have added to the number of congressional participants in national security policy matters. Congressional staffs have grown in size and influence so that they, too, are drawn into negotiations between the branches. These developments, along with expanded pressures from interest groups and other domestic constituencies, make more elusive the achievement of interbranch consensus.

The difficulty that Congress currently faces in assuming a more active and constructive role in national security policy should not obscure its positive contributions. Among other things, it has curbed unrestrained presidential war making; it has forced reconsideration of extensive if not excessive overseas commitments and imposed caution on assuming new obligations; it has broadened the popular base of U.S. foreign policy; and it has instituted more careful scrutiny of agencies involved in national security. Following the exposure of the Iran-contra affair, Congress moved through its relevant committees to find the facts so that responsibility could be affixed and recommendations made for changes in procedures. In sum, Congress has expanded the base of legitimacy for foreign and military policy.

The constitutional "invitation to struggle" is still present. Congress has open to it alternative approaches for developing its national security policy role in the complex international environment of the 1990s. At times it will be tempted to revert to the pattern of acquiescence in presidential domination that prevailed from World War II until 1973. On other occasions Congress may be tempted to take matters into its own hands, because of popular pressures or distrust of the president's policies and capabilities. A third path is that of collaboration tempered by a sense of constitutional and political responsibility to be constructively critical. Although the president must provide leadership, and only the executive branch can conduct and implement national security policy, Congress has a vital role to play in refining, legitimating, and reviewing all policies.

Organizing and Managing National Security

Beyond dealing with the constitutional issues and political considerations involved in national security policy, the president also confronts a formidable administrative task: organizing the presidency and the executive branch for the formulation and implementation of policy and managing the processes that have been established. The organizational task entails establishing and changing structures and processes. As the Iran-contra investigation revealed, a lax approach to these tasks can be costly.

One of the soundest observations on these problems came from the Commission on the Organization of the Government for the Conduct of Foreign Policy (the Murphy Commission). It opened its 1975 report with the observation that "good organization does not insure successful policy, nor does poor organization preclude it."[56] The commission went on to assert, however, that organizational arrangements have a continuing and powerful impact on the content of public policy and the effectiveness with which it is implemented.[57] Organization determines the level of government (national, state, or local) and the agency that will deal with a problem. Government organization performs three primary functions: it "creates capabilities" for performing tasks that are beyond the reach of individuals; it "vests and weighs particular interests and perspectives" by increasing or reducing the probability of their inclusion in decision making; and it "legitimates decisions" by ensuring that relevant parties are consulted and that decisions are made by proper authorities.[58]

Although there is no specific model to which national security organization must conform, two considerations are paramount: it must be capable of adapting to changing events and conditions, and it must be able to accommodate the operating style of the president whose constitutional roles make him the focal point of the policy-making process. Congress has enacted legislation, such as the National Security Act of 1947, establishing organizational units to aid the president in the conduct of national security policy. The principal units are the National Security Council and its staff, the Departments of State and Defense, the joint chiefs of staff, and the Central Intelligence Agency. Congress cannot, however, effectively prescribe how the president uses those units or the processes by which the president develops broad policy goals and strategies for carrying them out; nor can it prescribe how he manages and coordinates the complex and far-reaching activities of the military establishment, the foreign policy bureaucracy, and the intelligence community. The president needs help to discharge these responsibilities, and he has the authority to obtain it. Specifically, he needs staff assistance, mechanisms and procedures for the discharge of his responsibilities, and support and effective performance by cabinet departments and independent agencies. How he obtains that assistance is the essence of his management of national security.

Although the National Security Council, which is the basic structure for the management of national security affairs, has remained substantially unchanged since its creation in 1947, presidents have used it in various ways. Congress established the council in response to the pressures of the cold war and in reaction, at least in part, to the administrative confusion that often characterized Franklin Roosevelt's freewheeling approach to management.

The experience of presidents from Truman through Bush substantiates Alexander George's observation that every chief executive, upon taking office, must define his role in the national security policy-making system before he can design and manage the roles and relationships of other major participants in it.[59] According to conventional wisdom, the basic choice the president must make is whether to manage the system through the secretary of state and the State Department, as Truman did, or to centralize it in the White House, as Nixon did, with the national security assistant playing the major role. Failure to decide on either approach is likely to result in confusion over policy goals and lack of cohesion in policy implementation, as was the case with Reagan.

Crabb and Mulcahy have developed a typology for analyzing presidential management of national security that is based on responsibility for policy making and for implementation of policy.[60] They identify four presidential management styles—department-centered, formalized, collegial, and palace guard—with accompanying roles for the national security assistant—administrator, coordinator, counselor, and agent *(see Figure 10–1)*. A president, such as Truman, who has limited interest in the formation and implementation of foreign policy, deputizes the secretary of state to act and speak for him (while making final decisions himself), and relies primarily on the State Department for analysis and implementation has a *department-centered* style. The national security assistant, in the corresponding role of administrator, acts primarily as a high-level staff aide who supervises the advisory process and facilitates the presentation of views to the president. He or she does not act independently or function

**Figure 10.1 Presidential Management Styles and National Security
Assistant's Roles**

Implementation Responsibility

		Low	High
Policy-Making Responsibility	Low	Department-centered administrator	Formalized coordinator
	High	Collegial counselor	Palace guard agent

Source: Cecil V. Crabb, Jr. and Kevin V. Mulcahy, *American National Security: A Presidential Perspective* (Pacific Grove, Calif.: Brooks/Cole, 1991), 189.

as a primary policy adviser. Adm. Sidney Souers, Truman's executive secretary for the National Security Council, functioned in this capacity.

Dwight Eisenhower looked to the national security bureaucracy—the departments of State and Defense and the intelligence community—for policy recommendations, carefully examined a wide range of proposals and plans, and retained control over policy making and implementation. He exemplifies the *formalized* management style. His national security assistant, Robert Cutler, functioned as a coordinator. The coordinator acts in a staff role, but may have considerable influence. His principal task is to facilitate the making of national security policy by defining options and managing the flow of ideas and information. He also reviews policy, but the president and the secretary of state make the final decisions.

The *collegial* management style, typified by Kennedy and Johnson, involves an informal national security process. In this model, the president operates with ad hoc working groups, tends to distrust the national security bureaucracy, and seeks to centralize decision making in the White House with the NSC staff performing independent analysis and policy review functions. The counselor role of the national security assistant, exemplified by McGeorge Bundy under Kennedy and Walt Rostow in the Johnson administration, entails a close personal relationship with the president in which the assistant is a major policy adviser and acts to safeguard the president's interests.

In the *palace guard* management style, associated with Richard Nixon, the president centralizes policy making in the White House and maintains a tight rein on implementation. The State Department and other units of the national security bureaucracy are "virtually excluded" from an active policy-making role and "relegated" to implementing the decisions of the president and the national security assistant.[61] Nixon's national security assistant, Henry Kissinger, acted as the president's agent. In that capacity he directed the policy-making process, served as the president's closest policy adviser, and on occasion actively implemented policy—in Kissinger's case by conducting negotiations with foreign governments.

Crabb and Mulcahy argue that experience since 1947 reveals that neither the administrator nor the agent roles for the national security assistant are to be recommended. By implication, they suggest that the president adopt either the formalized or collegial management style for national security. The administrator role is likely to be ineffective unless the president and the secretary of state are capable, hands-on administrators. The agent role carries the risk that the national security assistant may go into business for himself, acting without presidential knowledge or approval as Reagan claimed was the case with Adm. John Poindexter and his assistant, Lt. Col. Oliver North in the Iran-contra affair. Whether the president chooses the coordinator or counselor role for his national security assistant should be determined by his management style. According to Crabb and Mulcahy, the president also must exercise care to select a national security assistant whose personality is compatible with the designated role.[62] Jimmy Carter encountered considerable difficulty in managing national security because of conflict and competition between Secretary of State Cyrus Vance and Zbigniew Brzezinski, the national security assistant. At least part of the problem stemmed from Carter's apparent failure to recognize that Brzezinski was an ambitious, assertive individual more suited to the role of agent than that of administrator, which Carter apparently wished him to play.

A president, such as Reagan, who vacillates in establishing a preferred management style and defining the national security assistant's role is almost certain to experience trouble formulating a coherent foreign policy and implementing it effectively. That six individuals served as national security assistant during the Reagan administration highlights the instability in the president's management of national security. In the first term, Secretary of State Alexander Haig battled with White House staff aides over primacy in foreign policy, and the first national security assistant,

Richard Allen, lacked direct access to Reagan. Their successors, George Shultz at the State Department and William Clark as national security assistant, had an uneasy relationship with each other but avoided public conflict. Except for ideological rhetoric castigating the Soviet Union, the president demonstrated little interest in foreign policy and was notably detached from the national security process.

By Reagan's second term, the administration had developed a national security policy system characterized by turmoil in the relationship between the State Department and the White House. Secretary Shultz was the principal foreign policy spokesperson, but he was not privy to some of the covert operations conducted by North and other members of the NSC staff, and his views on the arms sales to Iran were rejected. One national security assistant, Robert McFarlane, acted as a policy advocate rather than as an honest broker coordinating policy making by departments and agencies, and he even carried out special missions for the president. Mulcahy describes the system as a "collegial arrangement for the management of foreign affairs with the White House acting as umpire."[63] It may well have been, but it could not keep the president from the major blunder that was the Iran-contra affair. An unanswered question is whether any conceivable system for managing foreign policy could have overcome Reagan's deliberate disengagement from policy making and his lack of interest in and concern with policy implementation.

In marked contrast to Reagan, George Bush has been a hands-on president deeply engaged in the formulation and implementation of national security policy. He has concerned himself with its details and been actively involved in negotiations with foreign leaders. Bush has adopted a collegial management style and prescribed a counselor's role for Brent Scowcroft, his national security assistant. He has organized the national security process in a manner that most resembles Lyndon Johnson's.[64] He makes little use of a formal process to identify and analyze options and relies instead on a small group of intimate advisers. There has been little evidence of conflict within Bush's national security inner circle, and it has received high marks for its cohesiveness and competence.[65]

Major decisions, however, involving events such as the 1989 invasion of Panama and the Persian Gulf War, have tended to be made in secret. Formal NSC meetings have been infrequent. Experts in the State and Defense departments have been kept at a distance and consultation with Congress has been minimal. There is no evidence of a multiple advocacy decision-making process along the lines recommended by Alexander George and Roger Porter, and the risks of Irving Janis's "groupthink" phenomenon, in which disagreement and consideration of options are repressed, are real.[66]

Conclusion

National security is the president's most important substantive policy responsibility; it presents him with major and complex problems of leadership and management. For the nation, the effectiveness of foreign and military policy in preserving and protecting its sovereignty and independence is the paramount interest. That interest stands or falls to a large extent on the president's performance. He must interpret and exercise his powers within constitutional and statutory limits. He finds it imperative to consult with Congress, and to be effective he must have congressional cooperation. Yet, operational realities require that he be accorded ample latitude to act independently and often secretly. Tensions inevitably arise between Congress and the president over national security policy. The tasks involved are predominantly executive in nature, but the Constitution provides a major role for Congress. It and political prudence require, as Koh states, "shared power and balanced institutional participation" as norms in national security decision making.[67]

Perhaps the most important lesson in this regard is that since 1945 most of the nation's successful foreign policies—the Truman Doctrine, the Marshall Plan, NATO, the Panama Canal treaty, arms control, and the Persian Gulf War—"have been adopted by Congress and the people after meaningful debate."[68] For the most part, the major failures—FDR's Yalta agreements with Stalin, the Bay of Pigs invasion, the Vietnam War, and the Iran-contra affair—have been initiated and implemented unilaterally by presidents.

Presidents also discover that resolution of national security issues must be coordinated with the handling of domestic and economic concerns because major issues tend to overlap and solutions cannot be compartmentalized. Presidents no longer can fashion national security policies without regard to domestic political and economic pressures. Such pressures in turn lead presidents to seek ways of managing national security policy that provide them with flexibility in action and protect their personal political stakes.

The principal institutional means that modern presidents have used to manage national security—a White House-centered national security system directed by a national security assistant heading a professional NSC staff—has served this purpose, but often at the expense of long-range continuity and cohesion in policy. The alternative organizational strategy—a State Department-centered system with the secretary of state playing a dominant policy-making and advisory role—has attracted support from some students of national security policy and from political outsiders as a means of obtaining the desired degree of continuity and integration. Presidents since Eisenhower, however, have found such an arrangement unsuitable to their style of operation.

Neither Reagan's nor Bush's approaches to managing national security provide an answer to the question of the extent to which organizational arrangements can contribute to making those efforts effective. Reagan's approach was eclectic. At first, he enhanced the role of the secretary without strengthening the State Department, and he downgraded the position of the national security assistant and the NSC staff. When that arrangement resulted in conflict within the administration, criticism from outside, and confusion everywhere, Reagan then adopted a more collegial system centered neither in the State Department nor in the White House and dominated by neither the secretary of state nor the national security assistant. That system served him fairly well until the Iran-contra affair erupted. But it is not clear whether Reagan would have avoided that fiasco had he made the organizational choice that analysts assumed was inescapable. Bush's informal but more professional approach has had several successes and avoided failures but left a sense of unfilled potential and the absence of direction. Victory in the cold war came during Bush's first term but not as a consequence of his management of the foreign and military policy of the United States. When it happened, his administration was singularly unprepared for it.

What is clear is that in the emerging international system the United States is the world's major power. Its people and the rest of the world are deeply affected by the policy preferences, personality, and operating style of its presidents. The statecraft they employ and how they view and exercise national power will critically affect the shape of that system.

NOTES

1. The "two presidencies" thesis holds that presidents enjoy relatively greater success with Congress in foreign than in domestic policy. According to Terry Sullivan, modern Republican and Democratic presidents have had approximately equal success with foreign policy proposals, but Democratic administrations have done better with domestic policy because of their party's domination of Congress. See Sullivan, "A Matter of Fact: The 'Two Presidencies' Thesis Revitalized," in *The Two Presidencies: A Quarter Century Assessment*, ed. Steven A. Shull (Chicago: Nelson Hall, 1991), 143–157.

2. Leslie H. Gelb, with Richard K. Betts, *The Irony of Vietnam: The System Worked* (Washington, D.C.: Brookings, 1979).

3. Ibid., 362–363.

4. James Chace, "Is a Foreign Policy Consensus Possible?" *Foreign Affairs* 57 (Fall 1978): 3.

5. Strobe Talbot, *The Russians and Reagan* (New York: Vintage Books, 1984).

6. The most comprehensive and informative account of the Iran-contra affair is by Theodore Draper, *A Very Thin Line: The Iran-Contra Affairs* (New York: Hill & Wang, 1991). For the perspective of two participants in the congressional hearings, see William S. Cohen and George J. Mitchell, *Men of Zeal* (New York: Viking, 1988). The role of the CIA and its director William Casey receive careful attention by Bob Woodward in *Veil: The Secret Wars of the CIA, 1981–1978* (New York: Simon & Shuster, 1987). Also essential to a full understanding of Iran-contra is the report of the Tower Commission (John Tower, Edmund Muskie, and Brent Scowcroft). President's Special Review Board, *Report of the President's Special Review Board* (Washington, D.C.: Government Printing Office, 1987).

7. John Felton, "Secret Weapons Sale Stirs Up Legal Questions," *Congressional Quarterly Weekly Report*, Nov. 22, 1986, 2929.

8. Lou Cannon, *President Reagan: The Role of a Lifetime* (New York: Simon & Shuster, 1991), 717.

9. Elizabeth Drew, "Letter from Washington," *New Yorker*, Dec. 19, 1986, 86.

10. Cannon, *President Reagan*, 718.

11. Terry L. Deibel, "Bush's Foreign Policy: Mastery and Inaction," *Foreign Policy* 84 (Fall 1991): 20–22; Steven V. Roberts, "The Second Sin of George Bush," *New Leader*, March 11–15, 1991, 3.

12. Daniel P. Franklin and Robert Shepard, "Analyzing the Bush Foreign Policy" (Paper presented at the annual meeting of the American Political Science Association, Washington, D.C., Aug. 29-Sept. 1, 1991), 2–3.

13. Deibel, "Bush's Foreign Policy," 3–4.

14. Christopher Madison, "Sounding Retreat," *National Journal*, Nov. 16, 1991, 2784–88.

15. Edward S. Corwin, *The President: Office and Powers*, 4th ed. (New York: New York University Press, 1957), 171.

16. I. M. Destler, "National Security Management: What Presidents Have Wrought," *Political Science Quarterly* 95 (Winter 1980–81): 574.

17. Ibid.

18. Ibid., 588.

19. Joseph E. Kallenbach, *The American Chief Executive* (New York: Harper & Row, 1966), 485.

20. Corwin, *The President*, 179.

21. Ibid., 185.

22. Ibid., 213.

23. Ibid.; Kallenbach, *The American Chief Executive*, 502.

24. The treaty-making process entails three distinct stages: negotiation, Senate approval, and ratification by the president. Contrary to popular understanding, the Senate does not ratify a treaty, it approves the treaty negotiated by the president. The president may refuse to sign, that is, to ratify, a treaty approved by the Senate, either because of amendments or reservations or because it was negotiated by a previous administration.

25. Cecil V. Crabb, Jr., and Pat M. Holt, *Invitation to Struggle: Congress, the President, and Foreign Policy*, 4th ed. (Washington, D.C.: CQ Press, 1992), 6.

26. Harold Hongju Koh argues, however, that Congress should create by statute its own procedures for determining when international agreements should be submitted to the Senate for approval. See Koh, *The National Security Constitution* (New Haven, Conn.: Yale University Press, 1990), 195.

27. *Goldwater v. Carter*, 444 U.S. 996 (1979).

28. Koh, *The National Security Constitution*, 44.

29. Ibid., 43.

30. The intelligence community consists of the Central Intelligence Agency; the National Security Agency; the Bureau of Intelligence and Research in the Department of State; the Defense Intelligence Agency and the intelligence offices of the army, navy, air force, and marine corps; and intelligence offices in the departments of Energy and Treasury. Crabb and Holt, *Invitation to Struggle*, 25.

31. Woodward, *Veil*, chap. 25.

32. Pamela Fessler, "Gates Confirmed to Lead CIA Into Post–Soviet Era," *Congressional Quarterly Weekly Report*, Nov. 9, 1991, 3291–92.

33. Clark subsequently proved to be a quick learner and a person of great administrative ability. In less than a year he was receiving praise from many of his former critics.

34. Corwin, *The President*, chap. 6; Arthur M. Schlesinger, Jr., *The Imperial Presidency* (Boston: Houghton Mifflin, 1989), chaps 1–7.

35. Corwin, *The President*, 229.

36. *Prize Cases*, 67 U.S. (2 Black) 635 (1863).

37. *Korematsu v. United States*, 323 U.S. 214 (1944).

38. Clinton Rossiter, *Constitutional Dictatorship: Crisis Government in Modern Democracies* (New York: Harcourt, Brace & World, 1963).

39. James L. Sundquist, *The Decline and Resurgence of Congress* (Washington, D.C.: Brookings, 1981), 107.

40. Such actions have numerous precedents, including Jefferson's dispatch of the Navy to stop the Barbary pirates from seizing U.S. merchant ships and holding their crews for ransom, and Theodore Roosevelt's contribution of U.S. Marines to the international expeditionary force that put down the Boxer Rebellion in China in 1904.

41. Larry Berman, *Planning a Tragedy: The Americanization of the War in Vietnam* (New York: Norton, 1982). For a comparative analysis of how Eisenhower and Johnson dealt with pressures to intervene militarily in Vietnam, see John R. Burke and Fred I. Greenstein, *How Presidents Test Reality: Decisions on Vietnam, 1954 and 1965* (New York: Russell Sage Foundation, 1989).

42. The Supreme Court's decision in *Immigration and Naturalization Service v. Chadha*, 462 U.S. 919 (1983), which held that the legislative veto was unconstitutional, made this provision inoperative. Congress subsequently substituted a joint reso-

lution for the concurrent resolution; however, the former is subject to a presidential veto.

43. Ellen C. Collier, *War Powers Resolution: Presidential Compliance,* Congressional Research Service Issue Brief IB81050 (Washington, D.C.: Congressional Research Service, 1991). Ford submitted four reports; Carter, one; Reagan, fourteen; and Bush, five. The following discussion is adapted from Norman C. Thomas, "Presidential Accountability after Reagan" (Paper presented at the annual meeting of the American Political Science Association, Washington, D.C., Aug. 29-Sept. 1, 1991).

44. Robert A. Katzman, "War Powers: Toward a New Accommodation," in *A Question of Balance: The President, Congress and Foreign Policy,* ed. Thomas E. Mann (Washington, D.C.: Brookings, 1990), 55.

45. Richard E. Cohen, "Marching Through the War Powers Act," *National Journal,* Dec. 30, 1989, 3120.

46. Joshua Lee Prober, "Congress, the War Powers Resolution, and the Secret Political Life of 'a Dead Letter,'" *Journal of Law and Politics* 7 (1990): 177–229.

47. Carroll J. Doherty, "Bush Is Given Authorization to Use Force Against Iraq," *Congressional Quarterly Weekly Report,* Jan. 12, 1991, 65–70.

48. I. M. Destler, "The Constitution and Foreign Affairs," *News for Teachers of Political Science* (Spring 1985): 16.

49. Katzman, "War Powers," 35; Thomas M. Franck, "Rethinking War Powers: By Law or by 'Thaumaturgic Invocation'?" *American Journal of International Law* 83 (1989): 768.

50. John M. Hillebrecht, "Ensuring Affirmative Congressional Control Over the Use of Force: Two Proposals for Collective Decision Making," *Stanford Journal of International Law* 26 (1990): 511.

51. Michael J. Glennon, *Constitutional Diplomacy* (Princeton, N.J.: Princeton University Press, 1990), 102–103.

52. Prober, "Congress, the War Powers Resolution," 229.

53. Ibid., 223–226, 229.

54. Destler, "The Constitution and Foreign Affairs," 15.

55. Sundquist, *The Decline and Resurgence of Congress,* 270.

56. *Report of the U.S. Commission on the Organization of the Government for the Conduct of Foreign Policy* (Washington, D.C.: Government Printing Office, 1975), 1.

57. Also see Burke and Greenstein, *How Presidents Test Reality,* esp. chap. 13.

58. Graham T. Allison and Peter Szanton, "Organizing for the Decade Ahead," in *Setting National Priorities: The Next Ten Years,* ed. Henry Owen and Charles Schultze (Washington, D.C.: Brookings, 1976), 232–233.

59. Alexander L. George, *Presidential Decisionmaking in Foreign Policy: The Effective Use of Information and Advice* (Boulder, Colo.: Westview, 1980), 146.

60. Cecil V. Crabb, Jr., and Kevin V. Mulcahy, *American National Security: A Presidential Perspective* (Pacific Grove, Calif.: Brooks/Cole, 1991), chap. 9. The discussion relies on Crabb and Mulcahy.

61. Ibid., 189–190.

62. Ibid.

63. Kevin V. Mulcahy, "The Secretary of State: Foreign Policymaking in the Carter and Reagan Administrations," *Presidential Studies Quarterly* (Spring 1986): 296.

64. Burt Solomon, "Making Foreign Policy in Secret May Be Easy, But It Carries Risks," *National Journal,* Jan. 12, 1991, 90–91.

65. Larry Berman and Bruce W. Jentelson, "Bush and the Post-Cold-War World: New Challenges for American Leadership," in *The Bush Presidency: First Appraisals,* ed.

Colin Campbell and Bert A. Rockman (Chatham, N.J.: Chatham House, 1991), 99–103.

66. George, *Presidential Decisionmaking;* Roger Porter, *Presidential Decision Making* (New York: Cambridge University Press, 1980); and Irving L. Janis, *Groupthink: Psychological Studies of Policy Decisions and Fiascoes,* 2d ed. (Boston: Houghton Mifflin, 1982).

67. Koh, *The National Security Constitution,* 207.

68. Stephen E. Ambrose, "The Presidency and Foreign Policy," *Foreign Affairs* (Winter 1991–1992): 136.

READINGS

Berman, Larry. *Planning a Tragedy: The Americanization of the War in Vietnam.* New York: Norton, 1982.

Burke, John P., and Fred I. Greenstein. *How Presidents Test Reality: Decisions on Vietnam, 1954 and 1965.* New York: Russell Sage Foundation, 1989.

Crabb, Cecil V., Jr., and Pat M. Holt. *Invitation to Struggle: Congress, the President, and Foreign Policy.* 4th ed. Washington, D.C.: CQ Press, 1991.

Crabb, Cecil V., Jr., and Kevin V. Mulcahy. *American National Security: A Presidential Perspective.* Pacific Grove, Calif.: Brooks/Cole, 1991.

Destler, I. M. *Presidents, Bureaucrats, and Foreign Policy: The Politics of Organizational Reform.* Princeton, N.J.: Princeton University Press, 1974.

Draper, Theodore. *A Very Thin Line: The Iran–Contra Affairs.* New York: Hill & Wang, 1991.

Gelb, Leslie H. *The Irony of Vietnam: The System Worked.* Washington, D.C.: Brookings, 1979.

George, Alexander L. *Presidential Decisionmaking in Foreign Policy: The Effective Use of Information and Advice.* Boulder, Colo.: Westview, 1980.

Glennon, Michael J. *Constitutional Diplomacy.* Princeton, N.J.: Princeton University Press, 1990.

Halperin, Morton M. *Bureaucratic Politics and Foreign Policy.* Washington, D.C.: Brookings, 1974.

Henderson, Philip G. *Managing the Presidency: The Eisenhower Legacy–From Kennedy to Reagan.* Boulder, Colo.: Westview, 1988.

Henkin, Louis. *Democracy and Foreign Affairs.* New York: Columbia University Press, 1990.

Janis, Irving. *Groupthink.* 2d ed. Boston: Houghton Mifflin, 1982.

Koh, Harold Hongju. *The National Security Constitution: Sharing Power after the Iran–Contra Affair.* New Haven, Conn.: Yale University Press, 1990.

Mann, Thomas E., ed. *A Question of Balance: The President, the Congress, and Foreign Policy.* Washington, D.C.: Brookings, 1990.

President's Special Review Board (Tower Commission). *Report of the President's Special Review Board.* Washington, D.C.: Government Printing Office, 1987.

Schlesinger, Arthur M., Jr. *The Imperial Presidency.* Rev. ed. Boston: Houghton Mifflin, 1989.

Spanier, John. *American Foreign Policy Since World War II.* rev. 12th ed. Washington, D.C.: CQ Press, 1992.

11 THE PRESIDENCY AT
CENTURY'S END

AS THE TWENTIETH CENTURY draws to a close, students of the presidency are reflecting on how the institution and its context have changed in the past as a way to understand what to expect in the future. It is particularly critical to examine the two features identified at the beginning of this book as central to the modern presidency: politics and change. How have the political conditions confronting the presidency changed? What changes in the institution and its environment will shape presidential conduct as the nation enters the twenty-first century? This chapter is different from the others in the book. It is a brief interpretive essay that integrates many observations and arguments touched upon previously.[1] Ultimately, we return to the central problem that has perplexed the nation since its creation—how to empower the president without endangering the system.

Rutherford B. Hayes was the first president to use an eagle as the official presidential seal. In 1903 Theodore Roosevelt added the circle bearing the words around it. Harry Truman turned the eagle's head from one side to the other in 1945.

The Presidency Since Midcentury

The twentieth century could well be termed the "presidential century." Throughout the nineteenth century, the federal government was dominated by Congress and its closely associated political parties whose power was based on the distribution of jobs and local benefits. Bold presidential leadership, as evidenced by Thomas Jefferson, Andrew Jackson, and Abraham Lincoln, stands out precisely because it was so rare. During the present century, particularly since World War II, the presidency went through a sweeping transformation: national politics now hinge on assertive presidential leadership that draws its strength from direct links with the public.

Changes in the presidency and its role in the larger political system accompanied several long-term developments, including a shift in responsibility for public action from state governments to the federal government, the political mobilization of citizens, and the emergence of the United States as a world power. Franklin D. Roosevelt is credited most often with ushering in a "modern presidency" that contrasts with the "traditional presidency."[2] One group of scholars has challenged this analytic convention by reexamining the presidency's historical roots and suggesting that nineteenth century presidents were not as passive or peripheral to public affairs as they are sometimes depicted. Still other observers suggest that the presidency has moved into a new, "postmodern" era consistent with changes in the domestic and international environments. We remain convinced that traditional presidents played a far less critical role in the life of the nation than even the least active twentieth century presidents. Later in this chapter we examine the claims for a postmodern presidency.

In an essay that was later expanded into his influential book, *Presidential Power*, Richard Neustadt described "The President at Mid-Century." Neustadt was principally concerned with the imbalance between the "demands and expectations pressing in upon the President" and his limited capacity to respond to them.[3] By midcentury the presidency had become the focal point for initiative in government with responsibility for action routinized and institutionalized in units and processes within the Executive Office of the President. But the president lacked the authority to implement his initiatives; the Constitution forced him to share powers with other institutions—Congress, the judiciary, and the states. In terms of formal powers the presidency was a weak institution hindered by constitutional, and consequently political, restraints. The presidency had become a "clerkship" whose services were needed by others, but whose influence over them was limited because none of them shared his obligations or outlook.[4] The major problem confronting the American political system at midcentury was that presidents would fail because of restraints imposed by other participants in the political system.

Presidents could overcome the weakness of their office through the exercise of leadership skills, primarily the power to persuade. In the American system of fragmented power, presidents had to function as the preeminent bargainer. Governing rested on acts of persuasion, not commands. Presidents could help themselves by consciously making choices that maximized their power to persuade.[5]

From the "Mid-century" essay and *Presidential Power* emerged a prescriptive model for presidential leadership. This model was persuasive because of its accurate portrayal of how the American political system had become dependent on a single leader. Power (defined as influence) is at the core of Neustadt's model. Presidents should understand its nature and guard their power prospects at all times. In making choices they must recognize the power stakes involved in those choices. Others cannot do it for them; they must be their own power experts, and they must be sensitive to the power stakes of others, the targets of their persuasive efforts. Persuasion, which is where real presidential power lies, entails bargaining. The president has three resources for bargaining: vantage points, which are the formal powers of the office; his reputation among Washington insiders; and popular prestige, which is based on public approval of his performance. Presidents should be professional politicians who understand power and know how to bargain. This is no job for an amateur.

Two Decades of Reappraisal and Reform

Neustadt's model reflected and shaped the dominant themes in the scholarship and textbooks of the 1950s and early 1960s, which stressed that only the president truly represented the American people and that heroic presidential leadership was a necessary and sufficient means to deal with the domestic and international problems confronting the nation.[6] With few exceptions, weakness was regarded as the principal problem with the presidency, not its potential for the abuse of power.

Vietnam and Watergate drastically altered the public and elite perspective. Fewer people believed that an omnipotent president would benevolently lead the nation to a resolution of its problems. The major concern of scholars and politicians shifted from the weakness of presidential power to its abuse. Historian Arthur M. Schlesinger, Jr., a biographer of heroic presidents, led the way by renouncing his earlier advocacy of aggressive presidential leadership and by charging that the presidency was out of control.[7] Congress acted to reestablish constitutional parity with the presidency, asserting legislative prerogatives in the areas of war powers, spending, budget control, executive agreements, national emergencies, and confirmation of presidential aides.[8]

Congress, however, lacked the ability to provide an effective substitute for presidential leadership. It could block presidential initiatives but could not establish broad policy goals and provide policy coordination and integration on its own. By 1980 James Sundquist predicted that because of the "crisis of competence" in the national government "the same fundamental forces that brought about the modern strong presidency in the first place will again reassert their influence."[9]

Much of the concern with competence was prompted by the difficulty Gerald Ford and Jimmy Carter experienced in adjusting to major changes in the larger political environment. Even before the publication of *Presidential Power,* the House Democratic Study Group, a caucus of northern liberal Democrats founded in 1958, set in motion a push for internal reform that thoroughly revamped the U.S. Congress.[10] Some of the congressional reforms adopted during the 1970s responded to presidential aggrandizement, but others reflected dissatisfaction with internal legislative conditions. What developed was a legislature where power was far more broadly distributed among members than in the past and where traditional norms, such as the seniority rule, were rejected or made less stringent. Leadership, it has been argued, was the principal casualty as individualism ran rampant in the halls of Congress.

Congress was not, however, the only part of the president's environment to undergo change. The early 1960s witnessed the beginning of substantial changes in the media that carried through into the following decade. These included the expansion of the television evening news to its current half-hour format, a dramatic rise in public reliance on television as the major source of news, a startling proliferation of Washington correspondents, and a shift in professional norms toward aggressive investigative reporting. Political parties underwent massive change. The Democrats' national convention of 1968 served as the launch pad for a wide-ranging series of internal reforms that transformed the presidential nominating process; they also have been blamed for accelerating party decline. Simultaneous changes in the electorate made citizens candidate-centered rather than party-centered. Finally, social movements that arose during the 1960s and 1970s—civil rights, women's rights, consumer protection, the elderly, gay rights, and environmental protection—began to transform American politics. They were joined by a new surge of organizational representatives in Washington as lobbying efforts multiplied, became more sophisticated, and were supplemented by the creation of political action committees.[11]

The reforms of Congress and political parties, industry trends in the media, and changes in interest representation contributed to an unsettled environment, which gave rise to discussion of how these new conditions would affect the presidency. Fred Greenstein termed it an "intractable environment"; Neustadt characterized it as "atomization"; Samuel Kernell considered the cumulative changes tantamount to a restructuring of American politics from "institutionalized" to "individualized" pluralism, necessitating that presidents shift from bargaining to going public.[12] Ronald Reagan's entry on stage seemed to offer a test of the new imperatives.

The Reagan–Bush Era

The Reagan presidency brought to an end the intentional reduction of presidential power that followed Vietnam and Watergate, and the reluctance to impinge on presidential power extended into George Bush's term. Although these presidents reclaimed a number of powers lost by their predecessors, the Reagan and Bush years have by no means restored the imperial presidencies of Johnson and Nixon.[13] Congress remained, for the most part, assertive and jealous of the prerogatives and independence it had acquired during the 1970s and was determined not to surrender them to a popular president.

Elsewhere in this book, we review the important institutional and policy changes brought about during the Reagan presidency. Centralized control of executive and judicial appointments provided Reagan and Bush with substantial power over policy. Reagan was the first president to implement broad administrative and judicial strategies for pursuing domestic policy objectives outside legislative action. His principal policy legacy was a large structural budget deficit that has curtailed the growth of existing federal domestic programs and discouraged the creation of new programs during the Bush administration, a trend that promises to continue for years to come. Although the largest peacetime military expansion in the nation's history, initiated under Reagan, came to a halt under Bush, both administrations demonstrated a willingness to use their enhanced power in Grenada (1983), Libya (1986), Panama (1989), and the Persian Gulf (1990–1991). More important, Reagan abandoned his confrontational rhetoric toward the Soviet Union during his second term, moved toward major arms reduction agreements, and substantially improved relations prior to the unexpected demise of the Soviet system that occurred under Bush.

Neustadt has offered four major reflections on Reagan's conduct of the presidency. First, his presidency "restored the public image of the office . . . [as] a place of popularity, influence, and initiative, a source of programmatic and symbolic leadership." Second, Reagan used his professional skills as an actor and television spokesman to "exploit fresh opportunities for influence," which were "effectively used" to help compensate for the weakness of his party in Congress. Third, in contrast with other modern presidents, Reagan combined a lack of intellectual curiosity, a disinterest in detail, and a penchant for delegation to subordinates with intense, sustained convictions and commitments. Fourth, that "peculiar combination exaggerated every risk to which a President is heir by virtue of imperfect information." Reagan's failure, in the Iran-contra affair, "both of method and policy was so resounding as to cast enduring doubt on the utility of combining ignorance with insistence."[14] According to Neustadt, Iran-contra demonstrated anew his 1960 precepts that the president can protect his prospects for future influence only through present choices and that he can rely only on himself to gauge those prospects.

Bush succeeded in avoiding any single misstep as grand as the Iran-contra incident, but he was criticized for lacking vision and a sense of direction. Exhibiting a far more engaged approach to the office than his predecessor, Bush garnered broad praise for an exemplary performance during the Persian Gulf War, which came on the heels of democracy's triumph in Eastern Europe and the former Soviet Union. But in struggling to overcome the budget deficit, Bush was far less adept in projecting the kind of optimistic symbolic leadership at which Reagan excelled. Moreover, the economic recession of 1991–1992, although far milder than that of 1981–1982, came at the end of Bush's term, whereas Reagan's bout with recession was well behind him before his campaign for reelection began. A political malaise seemed to grip the Bush administration, particularly on domestic issues. Some commentators saw this development not as a reflection of Bush's personal limitations, but as the inevitable problem of an administration whose ideological and programmatic agenda was exhausted after twelve years in office.

The Reagan presidency (and one might safely assume the Bush presidency) did not cause Neustadt to abandon or substantially revise his model of leadership. Although Neustadt recognizes that there have been substantial changes in the political and institutional setting since midcentury, he contends that the president's "power problem" remains "roughly what it was then, if not more so," something he would not have expected in 1960.[15] But Neustadt may assign insufficient importance to changes in the presidential environment that have overtaken the ability of one individual to achieve government effectiveness through personal action. If so, Neustadt's advice on presidential leadership could prove disastrous for the nation. Moreover, continued adherence to the "personal solution"— finding a president whose skills and temperament are commensurate with the demands of the position—may inhibit the pursuit of alternative avenues for achieving effectiveness, what Theodore Lowi terms the "institutionalist approach."[16]

The Presidency at Century's End

Three aspects in particular of the presidency's contemporary condition have attracted scholarly attention: presidents' relationships with the public; changes in the international position of the United States; and divided party control of the presidency and Congress. In each case, scholars have evaluated the significance of recent changes and their implications for the future. We examine each of these areas, with reminders of themes raised earlier in the book.

The People's Tribune

Central to the contemporary presidency is its unique relationship with the public. Today's president serves as the tribune of the people—their champion. Presidents have come to personify the federal government for millions of citizens, and the public's support for presidential initiatives has become the principal weapon in a chief executive's political arsenal. To assess this development and its significance for the future, we explore its origins as well as its importance for the Reagan–Bush era.

Far from viewing the change in the president's relationship with the public as a new development, Jeffrey Tulis in *The Rhetorical Presidency* stresses doctrines of governance and constitutional understandings that emerged early in the twentieth century. Before entering public office, Woodrow Wilson offered a constitutional reinterpretation that called for presidents to expand their use of public rhetoric as a way to provide the kind of inspirational leadership pioneered by Theodore Roosevelt. Wilson, in essence, designed and implemented a de facto "second Constitution" that rested on "active and continuous presidential leadership of public opinion" as a means to provide the political system with the energy it requires.[17] In his role as "leader-interpreter," a Wilsonian president would interact directly with the people, shaping as well as responding to their desires. With Wilson's example and justification, subsequent presidents have sought to exercise personal leadership over an otherwise balky institutional system, although Tulis suggests that such efforts are likely to succeed only under limited conditions. Nonetheless, presidents, other political elites, and the public have accepted the new doctrine, thereby encouraging efforts at inspirational leadership even when conditions are not right.

Barbara Hinckley also regards the Constitution as lying at the heart of the symbolic presidency, but with markedly different effects: because the presidency is an undefined office, "presidents become what people want them to be"; "the office is open to become what people say it is and expect it to be."[18] As a result, the presidency has become shrouded in symbolism reflecting the traits projected onto it by American culture. By portraying themselves as one with the people, presidents claim to serve as true representatives of the nation as well as champion of the people's cause, precisely what the people want.

Theodore Lowi offers yet another long-term view of the special relationship that has developed between the presidency and the people, but his view rests on more tangible foundations. The public, Lowi suggests, is engaged in a collective exchange relationship with its leader: the citizenry will invest the presidency with power and accept presidents as the embodiment of their hopes and fears so long as they receive tangible benefits in return. When presidents fail to provide peace and prosperity, the public withdraws its support. Because it is not always possible to deliver economic and international security, successive presidents, regardless of partisan and personality differences, have engaged in similar "pathological" behaviors: seeking to maintain initiative by centralizing power, using illusions of success or outright deception as a means to cover their shortcomings, and relying on charisma and "plebiscitary aspects" of the office to "mobilize the electorate in order to unify the elite."[19] The "personal presidency," which Lowi dates from 1961, is "an office of tremendous personal power drawn from the people" and resting "on the new democratic theory that the presidency with all powers is the necessary condition for governing a large, democratic nation."[20] With the impossibility of meeting such daunting expectations, each president is doomed to failure.

Of these three scholars, only Lowi locates the beginning of the new public-presidency relationship in the midcentury period.[21] All three, far from viewing Reagan's presidency as a turning point, see it as wholly consistent with the trends they identify. From the perspective of these authors, Reagan illustrates the maturing of long-term trends that are not especially welcome. Far from endorsing "the people's tribune" as a solution to the system's search for effective leadership, each regards the development as unhealthy for the larger political system and concludes by calling for the public to become educated on the presidency's limitations as well as its potential for leadership.[22]

Some scholars, however, have been more positive about the modern president's public prominence. Bert Rockman suggests that a more plebiscitary office—one deriving power from public support—might strengthen political accountability; and Samuel Kernell concludes that "as one looks to the future, the prospect for the continued use of going public as presidential strategy shines bright."[23] Kernell seems to endorse going public as a necessity, driven partly by technological innovation and partly by the disappearance of alternatives. With power broadly dispersed in the public and Congress, bargaining provides an insufficient answer to the problem of leadership. But in the long run, Kernell recognizes that presidents encounter problems in going public. Not only is it difficult to control public opinion, but also presidents discover that the advantages they once enjoyed are likely to evaporate as other elites, particularly in Congress and the media, adopt the same techniques.

A Postmodern Presidency

Evaporation of American advantages in the international system is the starting point for Richard Rose's discussion of the postmodern president. Far from rejecting Neustadt's model, Rose takes it a step further: bargaining is now necessary abroad as well as at home. Victory in World War II meant that the United States emerged as the sole economic *and* military superpower. Operating from a dominant position, presidents found international bargaining largely unnecessary. The disappearance of American hegemony removes an advantage that citizens and presidents have taken for granted.

In the future, Americans must contend with interdependence, the effect that other nations can have on domestic policies, and a decline in national influence. The imbalance between responsibility and capability afflicting the modern presidency will become even greater for postmodern presidents. "International responsibilities remain great, but the United States can no longer be sure that other nations will fall into line once decisions are taken in Washington."[24] Moreover, external shocks ranging from oil embargoes to currency adjustments will have a direct impact on domestic policies.

The transition to interdependence will be especially painful for the United States because the nation is so ill-prepared for the shift. "While the traditional President did not participate in the international system and the modern President could dominate it, the postmodern President has no choice but to cooperate and compete."[25] Under these conditions, the president has a new imperative: "going international" (foreign bargaining) is now more critical and more difficult, whereas "going Washington" (domestic bargaining) and going public used to be sufficient.[26]

The international hegemony that the United States enjoyed after World War II began to erode during the Johnson administration and the Vietnam War. Carter was the first president forced to contend fully with the new forces, and Reagan followed suit. During the Persian Gulf crisis, George Bush demonstrated that he was the first postmodern president to meet Rose's criteria of "world leader," exerting influence on policy and having other major nations reinforce his actions by their own.[27] Rose makes a convincing case for how altered conditions in the international environment now impinge on presidential calculations, but he identifies no particular changes in the presidency, as an office, that would distinguish it from the modern presidency of the last half century.[28]

Leadership of Divided Government

For the the past twenty-four years, from January 1969 to January 1993, the presidency and both houses of Congress have been controlled by the same political party only during the four years of the Carter administration. Unified party government has prevailed during only 17 percent of the last quarter century, while "same-party control existed 79 percent of the time from 1900 to 1968."[29] The four earlier instances of divided government in the twentieth century occurred for periods of only two years when Taft, Wilson, Hoover, and Truman lost majorities in the second half of a term.[30] The modern cases are strikingly different. Nixon and Bush assumed office with partisan majorities in neither house of Congress, a situation confronted by Eisenhower during his second term, and by Ford, as well. Reagan enjoyed a Republican majority in the Senate for six years, but the House remained solidly Democratic.

This partisan division of power has been persistent rather than brief. Going into the 1992 election, Republicans had won five of the last six presidential elections and seven of the last ten, and the Democrats had become congressional fixtures, serving as the majority party in the House of Representatives since 1954 and in the Senate for all but six years over the same period.

What has divided party control of government meant for the presidency? Does it constitute a permanent feature of the presidency that will carry over into the next century? Divided government has raised serious problems for customary models of presidential leadership. James Sundquist notes that "the dominant school of the midcentury" believed "in party government and presidential leadership," holding "that in the long run a government that is able to act, even if it makes mistakes, is less dangerous than one that is rendered impotent by deadlock and division."[31] Since 1969, however, party government has been replaced by a system of "forced coalition government" in order to contend with the accidents of the electoral process.[32] The results of this experiment have not been heartening, Sundquist argues. Rather, divided government has produced stalemate over domestic issues under Eisenhower, deadlock on both foreign and domestic fronts during the Nixon–Ford era, and immobility for seven of the eight years under Reagan, even when a consensus existed on the need to address the burgeoning national debt. The same inertia on the budget afflicted Bush. Sundquist therefore issues an urgent call for political scientists to address the problem and either develop a new theory to replace the party responsiblity model or seriously confront the need for constitutional reform.

Charles O. Jones finds that "separated presidents" have adopted distinctive styles in seeking to provide leadership within this constrained setting. Even Carter, the sole case of unified party government since 1968, adopted a "trusteeship" style that separated him from members of his own congressional party, just as he had pursued and won the presidency as an outsider. But Jones believes that presidents are locked into a new dynamic in Washington. As described by Neustadt in 1960, the Constitution's separation of powers was better understood as "separated institutions sharing powers," but for the contemporary period Jones suggests that the formulation should be "separated institutions competing for shared power," with "each institution protecting and promoting itself through a broad interpretation of its constitutional and political status, even usurping the other's power when the opportunity presents itself."[33] To further complicate matters, the separation based on divided electoral outcomes has coincided with the new assertiveness of a Congress that reformed itself to regain power lost to the executive.

The persistence of divided government represents a fundamental alteration in the strategic conditions confronted by presidents since midcentury. Eisenhower experienced six years of "separation," just as Truman was tested for two. Sundquist suggests that these episodes of divided government were regarded as exceptions, and observers expected that presidential leadership would be restored through traditional party structures. The situation has proved anything but temporary. The weakening of party organization, degeneration of partisanship in the electorate, and growth of split-ticket voting contributed to a split-level realignment characterized by persistent Republican control of the presidency and Democratic control of Congress.

Can presidents cope with the consequences? Only marginally, says George C. Edwards III, and the constraints on presidents imposed by the decline of political parties and divided government should force us to reconsider broadly held models of presidential leadership. Edwards concludes that none of the president's three sources of influence—party leadership, public leadership, and personal legislative skills—enables him to do anything more than influence congressional actions at the margins. The first two constitute the "principal underpinnings" of presidential influence but are subject to only limited presidential control.[34] The most important skill presidents can have is to recognize and exploit opportunities for leadership offered by the conditions they confront. In the game of politics, presidents' strategic and tactical decisions may be more or less astute, but they can play only with the hand they are dealt. Edwards agrees with Lowi and Tulis that going public is not a cure-all: while "the public relations skills of Reagan's administration were impressive . . . they could not by themselves create or sustain goodwill."[35] Reagan's greatest resource flowed from the 1980 election when his victory changed the terms of policy debate. In sum, Edwards's principal advice to presidents would be simple: seek an electoral mandate. But what if, as is often the case, presidential elections do not produce a mandate but are uncertain? And, because even a clear mandate has a limited life, how is the president to govern in its absence?

Presidents, argues Edwards, are better thought of as facilitators who "help others go where they want to go anyway" than as directors "leading others where they otherwise would not go."[36] A facilitator operating at the margins sounds very much like Neustadt's model of the president as bargainer, a prospect that observers concerned with policy effectiveness, like Sundquist, are likely to view with dismay. Short of an electoral solution, there appears to be little likelihood of overcoming the institutional competition that has characterized end-of-the-century governance.

Not all analysts take a negative view of divided government. Morris Fiorina views it as an American form of coalition government flowing from the absence of third party options at the polls. Ticket-splitting resembles voting for a third party and produces similar patterns of governance.[37] Jones offers a "diffused responsibility perspective" to supplant the more familiar party responsibility model articulated in the early 1950s.[38] Under this view, the president certifies the nation's policy agenda by triggering proposals and helping Congress to set priorities, but each party attempts to preserve and protect its existing strengths—the Republicans in the White House and the Democrats in Congress. This perspective does not offer a solution to the impasse, but provides a realistic basis for evaluating the current political agenda.

The Presidency at Century's End: An Assessment

What, then, is the condition of the presidency as the twentieth century comes to a close? In most respects, contemporary presidents are more isolated than ever. If the world seemed lonely from the perspective of Neustadt's executive at midcentury, it must seem even more so now that party and congressional reforms have further weakened leadership in both these institutions. As Washington folklore has it, Eisenhower could conduct business with Sam Rayburn and Lyndon Johnson while they sat around sipping bourbon and branch water. Today's president would need a state banquet to entertain the significant leadership of a reformed Congress. Hinckley's research demonstrates that contemporary presidents go to great lengths to portray themselves as above party, and, when Congress is mentioned, it is largely to criticize its abilities as a governing institution. Presidents project themselves as governing alone, thereby reflecting the image of heroic leadership that the public has come to expect. Problems arise when the solitary hero cannot fill the bill.

At the same time, modern presidents desperately need to mobilize support and now do so through presidency-centered techniques rather than traditional party structures. White House aides construct "presidential parties" to serve as electoral and governing coalitions, but the new structures are less stable and less useful than traditional party coalitions.[39] Public relations, a high presidential priority, is made necessary by the need to generate "mass" support through direct and mediated appeals. Ironically, the media, on which presidents now depend for reaching the public, are far more independent and critical than the political parties they partially replaced. While they help presidents broadcast appeals to general audiences, the media have reduced the latitude within which presidents must operate.

Finally, presidents have less control than ever over policy outcomes, both domestic and international. Leadership of domestic policy was difficult enough in conjunction with the unreformed Congress, but the legislative reforms adopted over the past twenty-five years have exacerbated the stresses produced by divided government. The proliferation of interest groups and the mobilization of new population groups into politics have made the already fragmented policy-making process even more difficult. In the past, it was sometimes suggested that modern presidents turned to the international system, perhaps out of frustration, as an area where policy making was more likely to succeed. But Richard Rose predicts that foreign policy will no longer offer relief; international problems will prove less easy to resolve than in the past, and they will assume new urgency and new forms as interdependence makes itself felt into the next century. Therefore, the policy area over which presidents traditionally have held the greatest constitutional authority has become more complex and less subject to executive influence.

Despite these changes, Americans seem more firmly rooted in their conception of heroic leadership than ever before. For more than two decades, political scientists have labored long and hard to revise their own textbook version of the presidency, but the readers of this revised standard version were unconvinced. Moreover, the scholarly consensus may be disintegrating. New justifications have emerged for presidents' use of politicized and centralized decision making as a means to pursue "responsive competence" rather than "neutral competence."[40] And in his reflections on presidents since Nixon, Arthur Schlesinger seems to have returned to a search for heroic qualities.[41] We are left, then, with the traditional quandary of presidential leadership: Can presidents find sufficient power to fulfill their responsibilities without endangering the system? End-of-the-century presidents, it might be argued, confront an even greater gap between demands and capabilities; certainly, the gap has widened since midcentury. Recent presidents' reliance upon appeals to the public as an answer to their power problem lends new vibrancy to concerns expressed at the Constitutional Convention about the danger of executive demagoguery. But at the same time, the need for strong executive leadership seems greater than ever. Fears of executive power renewed by the Vietnam and Watergate experiences have since been replaced by concern about presidential effectiveness. Reform proposals search for ways to enhance presidential power or reduce public expectations.

Institutional stalemate and deadlock have not yet become the permanent state of affairs, but they occur with sufficient frequency to encourage efforts to help presidents by reforming the system. Proposals have been made to limit congressional terms and do away with PACs, actions that are likely to reduce the power of incumbents and the institutional power of Congress. There have also been suggestions to link presidential and congressional elections by making their terms coincide. Such reform proposals, however, will produce heated legislative battles (because Democratic incumbents are more likely to be adversely affected) and are un-likely to be successful.

Scholars are especially attracted to proposals for reeducating the public and enhancing civic consciousness and responsibility as ways to make public expectations of presidential performance more realistic. However, it is probably more reasonable to expect either the Democrats, the Republicans, or a new party to emerge as a majority party between now and the beginning of a new century than to expect a massive transformation in deeply ingrained and widely reinforced public expectations of government and politics. A party realignment would not make it any easier for presidents to meet performance expectations, but it would probably ease the institutional gridlock that has become increasingly commonplace.

In the absence of realignment, political analysts and practitioners should give serious consideration to their continued adherence to the party responsibility model. If divided government has become the normal state of political affairs during this final decade of the twentieth century and is a condition resulting from free electoral choice, then a new conceptual basis for establishing political accountability is needed. Jones's diffused responsibility perspective accepts a diminished presidential role and suggests a new way to evaluate presidential, congressional, and party performance in coping with the policy agenda. It will not remove policy deadlocks or institutional conflict, but it promises to make them more understandable. Prospects for such understanding through acceptance of a diffused responsibility perspective are limited. Dissatisfaction with government performance and presidential leadership seems likely to remain high so long as public expectations of the national government remain unrealistic, analysts continue to think in terms of the party responsibility model, and presidents are regarded as the principal agents of collective action.

This, then, is the condition of the presidency at the conclusion of the twentieth century. It remains at least as weak an office as Neustadt described at midcentury. Increased capacity to generate popular support and expanded institutional resources have not been sufficient for presidents to overcome the combined effects of party decay, a more highly fragmented and independent Congress, greater international interdependence, and persistently unrealistic public expectations of presidential performance. Constitutional reform proposals abound, but serve only as a basis for discussion and analysis of the deficiencies of the present system. There is virtually no likelihood of their adoption any time soon. Bargaining remains necessary even if no longer sufficient for success; power stakes are ignored only at enormous risk. In some respects, Neustadt's model may actually have gained relevance as constitutional relations became more strained and political conditions more fragmented since the mid-1950s. In this regard, it remains a helpful guide for making governance viable.

At midcentury, Neustadt reflected a scholarly consensus on the kind of leadership the nation required, but at century's end, the confidence derived from that agreement has vanished. End-of-the-century presidents find themselves in an ambiguous position, and scholarly opinion is appropriately ambivalent. The conditions that gave rise to Neustadt's classic interpretation remain no less a limitation on presidential leadership than they were more than three decades ago and probably impose even greater constraints on executive initiative than they did earlier. But Neustadt's answers to the president's power problem as well as those provided by his critics have proved unable to close the gap between performance and expectations. Until the conditions confronted by presidents change further, as eventually we believe they will, the end-of-the-century presidency can best be described as still functioning but unable to govern single-handedly, precisely what the Framers of the Constitution intended.

NOTES

1. The argument in this chapter follows closely that found in our article "The Presidency Since Mid–Century," *Congress and the Presidency* 19 (Spring 1992): 29–46. We wish to thank the editors of *Congress and the Presidency* for allowing us to use portions of the article.

2. Fred I. Greenstein, "Change and Continuity in the Modern Presidency," in *The New American Political System*, ed. Anthony King (Washington, D.C.: American Enterprise Institute, 1979), 45–46.

3. Richard E. Neustadt, "The Presidency at Mid-Century," *Law and Contemporary Problems* 21 (1956): 613.

4. Richard E. Neustadt, *Presidential Power* (New York: Wiley, 1960), 6–8.

5. Neustadt, "The Presidency at Mid-Century," 617–619.

6. Thomas E. Cronin, "The Textbook Presidency," in *Perspectives on the Presidency: A Collection*, ed. Stanley Bach and George T. Sulzner (Lexington, Mass.: D. C. Heath, 1974), 54–74.

7. Arthur M. Schlesinger, Jr., *The Imperial Presidency* (Boston: Houghton Mifflin, 1973).

8. James L. Sundquist, *The Decline and Resurgence of Congress* (Washington, D.C.: Brookings, 1981).

9. James L. Sundquist, "The Crisis of Competence in the National Government," *Political Science Quarterly* 95 (1980): 205.

10. A comprehensive list of reform efforts can be found in Charles O. Jones's essay, "Congress and the Constitutional Balance of Power," in *Congressional Politics*, ed. Christopher J. Deering (Chicago: Dorsey, 1989), 335.

11. For discussions of these developments, see Samuel Kernell, *Going Public: New Strategies of Presidential Leadership* (Washington, D.C.: CQ Press, 1986); Nelson W. Polsby *Consequences of Party Reform* (Oxford: Oxford University Press, 1983); Martin P. Wattenberg, "From a Partisan to a Candidate-Centered Electorate," in *The New American Political System*, 3d ed., ed. Anthony King (Washington, D.C.: American Enterprise Institute, 1990); Jack L. Walker, "The Origins and Maintenance of Interest Groups in America," *American Political Science Review* 77 (June 1983); and Robert H. Salisbury, "The Paradox of Interest Groups in Washington—More Groups, Less Clout," in *The New American Political System*, 3d ed.

12. Greenstein, "Change and Continuity in the Modern Presidency," 70–75; Richard E. Neustadt, *Presidential Power: The Politics of Leadership from F.D.R. to Carter* (New York: Wiley, 1980), 217; Kernell, *Going Public*, 9–26.

13. In the second edition of *The Imperial Presidency* (1989), however, Arthur M. Schlesinger, Jr., suggests that Reagan moved two-thirds of the way toward restoring an imperial presidency. Reagan meets two of the three "tests" posited by Schlesinger (page 441)—assertion of presidential warmaking powers and heavy reliance on secrecy—but unlike Nixon, Reagan did not direct his powers against administration critics (page 457).

14. Richard E. Neustadt, *Presidential Power: The Politics of Leadership From Roosevelt to Reagan* (New York: Free Press, 1990), 269–270.

15. Ibid., xiv.

16. Theodore J. Lowi, *The Personal President: Power Invested and Promise Unfulfilled* (Ithaca, N.Y.: Cornell University Press, 1985), 137.

17. Jeffrey K. Tulis, *The Rhetorical Presidency: The Pursuit of Popular Support* (Princeton, N.J.: Princeton University Press, 1987), 18.

18. Barbara Hinckley, *The Symbolic Presidency: How Presidents Portray Themselves* (New York: Routledge, 1990), 8, 148.

19. Lowi, *The Personal President*, 165.

20. Ibid., 20.

21. This seems largely an artifact of Lowi's desire to present Neustadt's *Presidential Power* as the work that redefined the presidency's role within the constitutional order. See Lowi, *The Personal President*, 9–10. The incidence of presidential failures, one might argue, are the truly defining indicators of Lowi's analysis, and here he includes Truman while recognizing that Eisenhower was the only "clear exception" to his dynamic of failure (page 10).

22. Tulis, *The Rhetorical Presidency* (page 9), explicitly rejects the fascination with effectiveness found in the presidency literature. He distinguishes his own concerns from those of most analysts who adopt the stance of "institutional partisanship," taking "the side of the presidency in the executive's contests with other institutions." Understanding the political order is the explicit purpose of his work rather than contributing to presidential effectiveness, although he recognizes the potential for integrating skillful rhetoric into a bargaining perspective (pages 11–12). The discussions on public education can be found in Tulis, *The Rhetorical Presidency*, 204; Hinckley, *The Symbolic Presidency*, 148; and Lowi, *The Personal President*, 212.

23. Bert A. Rockman, "The Modern Presidency and Theories of Accountability: Old

Wine and Old Bottles," *Congress and the Presidency* 13 (Autumn 1986): 135–156; Kernell, *Going Public*, 227.

24. Richard Rose, *The Postmodern President: The White House Meets the World*, 2d ed. (Chatham, N.J.: Chatham House, 1991), 73.

25. Ibid., 28.

26. Ibid., 40.

27. Ibid., 57, 332–336.

28. Michael Nelson makes a similar point in his review of Rose's book. "Is There a Postmodern Presidency?" *Congress and the Presidency* 16 (Autumn 1989): 155–162.

29. Michael Nelson, "Constitutional Aspects of the Elections," in *The Elections of 1988*, ed. Michael Nelson (Washington, D.C.: CQ Press, 1989), 196.

30. James L. Sundquist, "Needed: A Political Theory for the New Era of Coalition Government in the United States," *Political Science Quarterly* 103 (Winter 1988): 625.

31. Ibid., 632, 633.

32. Ibid., 626.

33. Charles O. Jones, "The Separated Presidency—Making It Work in Contemporary Politics," in *The New American Political System*, 4. Jones also sets forth eight different combinations of party control ranging from Republican control of all three institutions to Democrats enjoying threefold control. Since World War II the system has experienced five of the eight combinations.

34. George C. Edwards III, *At the Margins: Presidential Leadership of Congress* (New Haven, Conn.: Yale University Press, 1989), 217.

35. Ibid., 215–216.

36. Ibid., 5, 4.

37. Morris P. Fiorina, "Coalition Governments, Divided Governments and Electoral Theory" (Unpublished paper presented at the annual meeting of the American Political Science Association, San Francisco, Aug. 30-Sept. 2, 1990).

38. Charles O. Jones, "The Diffusion of Responsibility: An Alternative Perspective for National Policy Politics in the U.S.," *Governance* 4 (April 1991); American Political Science Association, Committee on Political Parties, "Toward a More Responsible Two-Party System," *American Political Science Review* 44 (1950).

39. Lester G. Seligman and Cary R. Covington, *The Coalitional Presidency* (Chicago: Dorsey, 1986).

40. Terry Moe, "The Politicized Presidency," in *The New Directions in American Politics*, ed. John E. Chubb and Paul E. Peterson (Washington, D.C.: Brookings, 1985).

41. This is most evident in Schlesinger's discussion of Ford and Carter, *The Imperial Presidency*, 2d ed., 437–438.

READINGS

Hinckley, Barbara. *The Symbolic Presidency: How Presidents Portray Themselves*. New York: Routledge, 1990.

Jones, Charles O. "The Diffusion of Responsibility: An Alternative Perspective for National Policy Politics in the U.S." *Governance* 4 (April 1991).

Kernell, Samuel. *Going Public: New Strategies of Presidential Leadership*. Washington, D.C.: CQ Press, 1986.

Lowi, Theodore. *The Personal President: Power Invested and Promise Unfulfilled*. Ithaca, N.Y.: Cornell University Press, 1985.

Moe, Terry. "The Politicized Presidency," in *The New Directions in American Politics*. Ed. John E. Chubb and Paul E. Peterson. Washington, D.C.: Brookings, 1985.

Neustadt, Richard E. "The Presidency at Mid-Century." *Law and Contemporary Problems* 21 (1956).

———. *Presidential Power*. New York. Wiley, 1960.

———. *Presidential Power: The Politics of Leadership From Roosevelt to Reagan*. New York: Free Press, 1990.

Rose, Richard. *The Postmodern President: The White House Meets the World*. 2d ed. Chatham, N.J.: Chatham House, 1991.

Schlesinger, Arthur M., Jr. *The Imperial Presidency*. Boston: Houghton Mifflin, 1989.

Sundquist, James L. *The Decline and Resurgence of Congress*. Washington, D.C.: Brookings, 1981.

———. "Needed: A Political Theory for the New Era of Coalition Government in the United States." *Political Science Quarterly* 103 (Winter 1988): 625.

Tulis, Jeffrey K. *The Rhetorical Presidency: The Pursuit of Popular Support*. Princeton, N.J.: Princeton University Press, 1987.

EPILOGUE: THE CLINTON
PRESIDENCY BEGINS

ON ELECTION NIGHT, NOVEM-
ber 4, 1992, president-elect Bill Clinton and his wife, Hillary Rodham Clinton, celebrated his victory to the strains
of Fleetwood Mac. Clinton and the
crowd that joined him in Little Rock—
running mate Al Gore, campaign
staffers, and party loyalists—were enthusiastic about the next four years.
But there was to be little time for relaxation as political and economic realities quickly tempered their jubilation.

Although Clinton won by a decisive
electoral college majority (370–168
electoral votes) and enjoyed a comfortable plurality of popular votes (43 percent to 38 percent for George Bush and
19 percent for Ross Perot), his election
was not a sweeping mandate for
change. As Senate minority leader Bob
Dole, R-Kan., commented to a television interviewer on the morning after
the election, 57 percent of the voters
opposed Clinton. The Democrats man-

*William Jefferson Clinton, the forty-
second president of the United
States, meets the press accompanied
by Vice President Albert Gore, Jr.*

aged only to retain their 57–43 margin in the Senate and lost 10 House seats, leaving them a 258–176 margin (there is one independent). These results ended divided party control of the government, but provided no assurance that the eleven-year policy stalemate between the presidency and Congress would end.

In addition to political limitations, the economic context imposed powerful constraints on what Clinton might be able to accomplish. In fiscal 1992 the United States had a budget deficit of $290 billion, a $4 trillion national debt, and annual interest payments of $200 billion. Reduction of the deficit and any policy initiatives would have to be financed through additional taxes and/or spending cuts, unpopular and politically difficult actions. Moreover, recovery from the 1990–1991 economic recession was sluggish at best.

The 1992 election not only ended twelve years of Republican control of the presidency and the executive branch, but also it marked a generational shift in the nation's highest office from a man who came of age during World War II to a baby boomer born after that war. Led by the first boomer president, the Democratic party—particularly members of Congress and interest group supporters—looked forward to pursuing an active policy agenda that had received little attention during the conservative administrations of Ronald Reagan and George Bush. Even though Clinton's electoral mandate was ambiguous, the meaning of the election was clear. It sharply delineated the "basic philosophical and policy differences between the major parties."[1] The Republicans distrust government and prefer to rely primarily on market forces to provide a healthy economy and solve social problems. In contrast, the Democrats regard government positively as a means, along with the private sector, to achieve prosperity and a good society. Ross Perot's startling electoral success as an independent candidate demonstrated the "voters' willingness to abandon partisan loyalties and receptivity to new appeals."[2]

Clinton campaigned as the candidate of change, especially with respect to economic policy. He promised to cut the huge federal budget deficit in half by 1997, create new jobs, restore economic growth and competitiveness, and provide the beleaguered middle class with tax relief. He would finance these goals by reducing defense spending and increasing taxes on the wealthy and foreign corporations. Other major campaign promises included solving the twin health care problems of runaway costs and the lack of health insurance for more than 35 million people; reform of the welfare system; a quick end to administrative rules prohibiting abortion counseling in federally funded clinics, fetal tissue research, and homosexuals serving in the armed forces; and measures to curb the influence of special interests, for example, campaign finance reform. Clinton's ability to meet the expectations generated by his election and to fill his campaign promises would depend substantially on his actions during the transition period between the election and when he "establishes his control over the government"—in this case, mid-April.[3]

Presidential Transitions

The 1993 transition, from Bush to Clinton, marked the ninth time in the twentieth century that control of the presidency passed between political parties.[4] Party turnovers entail substantial changes in policy, priorities, and style, and they require more time to complete than intraparty transitions. Consequently, they involve more uncertainty, ambiguity, and potential for mistakes and the disruption of government activity. However, they also provide the best opportunity for policy innovation.

According to James Pfiffner, a leading authority on presidential transitions, the power of the presidency does not automatically pass to the president-elect; it must be seized. "Only the authority of the president is transferred on January 20; the power of the presidency—in terms of effective control of the policy agenda—must be consciously developed."[5]

Pfiffner advises newly elected presidents to adopt a self-conscious strategic approach to planning "the assumption of governmental control" so that the new administration can "hit the ground running."[6] Presidents Carter and Reagan adopted such a strategic approach to their transitions. In June 1976 Jimmy Carter established a transition planning group of about fifty people who concentrated on policy and personnel. Reagan began in April 1980 to create an elaborate bureaucracy, which eventually swelled to more than 550, to plan for and manage the transition. Presidents need to hit the ground running to take full advantage of the brief period known as the "honeymoon," the popular and congressional support that accompanies their election victory. The influence derived from that support starts to decline soon after they take office and begin to make difficult choices that invariably alienate some voters and members of Congress.[7]

If the transition is a time of opportunity, it is also fraught with danger for presidents-elect. They must shift the style and focus of their leadership from campaigning to governing, which requires them to temper their rhetoric so as to reduce expectations lest they disappoint the public too soon and too severely. They must develop a new relationship with the press, which is always attentive to leaks and missteps. In responding to the imperative to move quickly, they may act on the basis of inadequate or inaccurate information and thereby run the risk of making serious mistakes. In the euphoria of partisan triumph, they may categorically reject the policies and advice of the outgoing administration and later find themselves having to "reinvent the wheel." In staffing the White House and the executive branch, presidents must strike a new balance between loyalty and competence that differs from that employed in the campaign. Pfiffner neatly summarizes the challenge facing new presidents: "Blunders in the early days of an administration may haunt it, while early victories may establish the momentum necessary to accomplish presidential goals."[8] Acknowledging one of the greatest modern-day blunders, the Bay of Pigs invasion of 1961, Richard Neustadt refers to these early errors as "pigs" and "piglets."[9]

During the transition presidents-elect must perform simultaneously several critical tasks: transform their approach to the public and their relations with the press from a campaigning to a governing mode; organize the White House; staff the administration; take over the budget; establish a process for congressional liaison; set the policy agenda; and establish priorities for the policies. Once in office, presidents also must be prepared to confront any crises that arise or that are inherited from the previous administration. As with all newly installed presidents, the media is especially attentive during an administration's initial days, looking for signs of things to come. Clinton's performance of these tasks provides early evidence of the nature of his presidency.

The Clinton Transition

Clinton and the Public

During the campaign Bill Clinton established a direct relationship with the public as a candidate who understood and cared about individual citizens and the problems they faced. His wide-ranging promises raised the hopes and expectations of the public and various groups whose support he sought. His television appearances, in which he answered questions from young people on MTV and wore "shades" while playing the saxophone on the Arsenio Hall show, and his frequent visits to McDonald's symbolized his identity with the public. Early in the campaign, Clinton enjoyed cordial relations with the media, but, as coverage increased and intensified, his accessibility declined.[10] His staff excelled at quick responses to questions, which enabled it to retain control over the flow of news. After the election, Clinton's tone in public appearances changed "from a candidate's ingratiating eagerness to a presidential restraint."[11] His rhetoric, which got him labeled a policy wonk during the campaign, became more direct and conversational. He presented himself as decisive and vigorous while remaining relaxed and at ease.

Shortly after the election Clinton began to bring the expectations generated by his grandiloquent campaign promises "into line with the grimly difficult realities of governance."[12] The task was difficult: maintain popular hopes at a high enough level to pressure Congress, the bureaucracy, and interest groups to approve his policies while increasing public awareness of what the new administration could realistically achieve. In contrast to the campaign's urgent message of change, Clinton and his staff cautioned the public to be patient and not to expect any immediate solutions to longstanding problems.[13] Clinton also shifted from the aggressively open style of campaign decision making to the consciously deliberate, advice-seeking approach that he employed as governor of Arkansas.[14] This approach is typified by the televised economic conference he held in Little Rock December 14 and 15, with more than 300 participants, including corporate executives, small business owners, and economists. In addition to listening to these experts, Clinton took telephone calls from viewers and lectured the audience about the seriousness of the nation's economic and health care problems and the obstacles to solving them.[15] Clinton received rave reviews; the breadth and depth of his knowledge and his thoughtfulness were impressive.[16]

Not all of Clinton's actions during the transition enhanced his public image. The first policy decision he announced, in a Veterans Day speech on November 11, 1992, was his plan to remove the ban on homosexuals in the military. The proposal was met with widespread opposition, receiving support primarily from gay rights organizations. Opponents of his action included Gen. Colin Powell, chairman of the joint chiefs of staff; several other high ranking military officers; Sen. Sam Nunn, D-Ga., powerful chairman of the Armed Services Committee; many congressional conservatives; and the American Legion and the Veterans of Foreign Wars, two influential veterans organizations. Critics complained that Clinton had failed to consult with Powell or Nunn prior to announcing his plan, an oversight that threatened the president with an embarrassing defeat. In the absence of other news early in the transition period, media coverage was intense. To limit the damage, Clinton sought broader consultation, but, by moving hastily to keep this campaign promise, Clinton placed himself in a lose-lose situation.

Clinton also attracted criticism during the transition for *backing away* from several major campaign promises and for the slow pace of organizing the White House and staffing his administration. Staffing the upper levels of the new administration proceeded slowly; Clinton's pace was deliberate and his commitment to gender and racial diversity in his appointments proved difficult to keep. Media reports created the impression that he is easily swayed.[17] He retreated from several prominent campaign pledges: the middle class tax cut, a 50 percent reduction of the budget deficit by 1997, submission of his economic plan to Congress by January 21, a 25 percent reduction in the White House staff, a high priority for welfare reform, and reversal of the Bush administration's policy of returning refugees to Haiti.[18]

Clinton's response to critics of his "bent" (if not broken) promises was that circumstances had changed since the campaign and he had acquired new information. Although Clinton's flexibility and adaptiveness drew praise, new life was breathed into the old "slick Willie" image and damaged his presidency before it began. He also discovered before the inauguration that everything a president says is carefully scrutinized and analyzed for nuances and hidden messages. For example, following President Bush's mid-January order to bomb Iraqi missile sites, an informal comment to reporters resulted in trouble. Clinton suggested that if Saddam Hussein "wants a different relationship with the United States, all he has to do is change his behavior," a statement interpreted in Baghdad and Washington to mean that he intended to normalize relations with Iraq. *New York Times* reporter R. W. Apple, Jr., remarked that Clinton would "have to learn when and how to be precise, when to send a message that cannot possibly be misinterpreted, and when a little studied ambiguity would better serve him."[19]

Clinton's style of communication with the public and his approach to the media became apparent during the administration's first three months. He sought a direct and unmediated relationship with the public.[20] His rhetoric is simple, conversational, and it conveys a grasp of substance that is continually upbeat. He prefers focused communication with the public through appearances on talk shows, such as "Larry King Live," and interviews with local reporters as opposed to nationally televised speeches and formal press conferences. According to Sidney Blumenthal, Clinton finds the national press "too blunt, too unfocused, too superficial. [N]ot only is it unable to provide intense immediacy to specific groups and places but its compulsive reduction of reality to sound-bite dimensions makes it incapable of carrying broad, sustained explanation."[21] Clinton has adopted a cable television marketing strategy for his presidency, with appearances before smaller audiences on morning news shows, C-SPAN, local television and town meetings, talk radio, and MTV, which served him well during the campaign. He exposes himself, says Blumenthal, "as no President before him has, and he does so in the service of his policies."[22] Restructuring presidential communications has displeased the White House press corps and the national news media, whose role in interpreting presidential actions and statements has been diminished. That tension emerged in the intense concern of the White House with leaks and the press corps' complaints about their lack of access to Clinton's first communications director, George Stephanopolous, and his "persistently vague" responses to their questions.[23]

The Clinton White House

President Clinton proceeded slowly with the crucial task of organizing and staffing the White House. Consistent with the prevailing professional consensus, he adopted a modified version of the centralized chief-of-staff model of White House organization rather than the decentralized spokes-of-a-wheel model preferred by previous Democratic presidents. In mid-December he named his lifelong friend, Arkansas natural gas executive Thomas ("Mac") McLarty, chief of staff. McLarty's lack of Washington experience raised concerns among Democratic party insiders that there would be no one able to guide Clinton through Washington's political labyrinth the way James A. Baker III did for Reagan.[24] (Both Reagan and Clinton took office as newcomers to Washington).

Early indications were that McLarty would adopt a low profile, acting as a broker and facilitator, not as an enforcer and gatekeeper in the manner of John Sununu, George Bush's first top aide. McLarty's appointment appeared to validate predictions that Clinton would control the White House policy process himself.[25] McLarty would manage the flow of information while leaving decisions on policy and personnel to the president. He would act as an administration spokesman and give policy advice only upon Clinton's orders. Other important White House staff appointments went to former campaign staffers (most of whom were in their thirties), various individuals with Washington experience, people whom Clinton had known as a student, others who had advised him in Arkansas, and a miscellaneous group that included friends of the Clintons and individuals recommended to the president-elect.[26] Most of the people in a highly cohesive inner circle, such as Clinton's, owe their primary loyalty to the president and not to powerful external constituencies. The results are likely to be mixed. On the one hand, there will be little public outcry when an insider loses a policy battle or is dismissed. On the other hand, few people have the power to check the president's actions.

As with all modern presidencies, the structure and processes of the Clinton White House reflect the leadership style of the incumbent. Journalist David Gergen, a veteran of the Reagan White House, described the new president's personal style as "all-consuming" and "hands-on."[27] That style is manifested in Clinton's insistence on immersing himself in the daily details of governing, undertaking time-consuming tasks that most presidents assign to others, and reviewing all major decisions.[28] Formally, policy decisions were to be thoroughly debated through the National Economic Council, the Domestic Policy Council, and the National Security Council, with the council chairpersons coordinating the discussions. However, the president planned to resolve disagreements and make the final decisions.

The policy process that developed during the first months of the administration was even less formal. It involved extensive use of task forces, ad hoc study committees, and "loosely defined clusters of friends and advisers." It appeared to be designed to circumvent the established channels for policy making, especially those that involve the bureaucracy. Several cabinet members found themselves excluded from the power loop in favor of "Friends of Bill."[29] Health policy, for example, was led by presidential adviser Ira Magaziner and Hillary Rodham Clinton with Health and Human Services Secretary Donna Shalala relegated to a secondary role. The principal adviser on the all-important policy toward Russia was

neither Secretary of State Warren Christopher nor national security adviser Anthony Lake, but roving ambassador Strobe Talbot, a classmate
from Oxford. Energy Secretary Hazel O'Leary had little impact on the
inclusion of the proposed energy tax in the president's economic plan.
One new executive office unit, the National Economic Council, acquired
influence over policy at the expense of the Office of Management and
Budget (OMB) and the Office of the Special Trade Representative.[30]

The structure of the Clinton White House also reflects the major policy
changes planned by the administration. After several early missteps, outside political advisers James Carville and Paul Begala, top strategists in the
1992 campaign, assumed a major role that includes assessing the risks of
various policy alternatives and helping to sell the administration's proposals.[31] The public liaison office shares in that role, working to build
coalitions of interest groups in support of policy proposals and to maintain
the focus of interest groups on the overall benefits of the proposals rather
than on the specific costs they will impose.[32]

Although the loose structure and informal, free-flowing policy process
of the Clinton White House produced a high sense of camaraderie and
teamwork, its long-term durability and value are uncertain. According to
political scientist Fred Greenstein, "It is a severely under-organized presidency; there is almost a kind of contempt for the routine [which] is what
gave us the Bay of Pigs with Kennedy."[33]

Clinton's Appointments

President-elect Clinton approached the task of staffing his administration guided by three values to which he had committed himself in his
campaign: diversity, competence, and ethical propriety. He was determined that his cabinet and other top-level appointees would reflect the
gender, racial, and ethnic composition of American society. Like all new
presidents, he wanted the best and the brightest people from those committed to his policies and goals. He also sought to field an administration
team whose members were free from any suggestion of conflict of interest
or ethical transgressions.

Clinton's pursuit of diversity, competence, and ethical rectitude forced
him to proceed deliberately in filling high-level positions. The initial cabinet appointments were not completed until Christmas. The first announced nominees were members of the economic policy team, followed
by the domestic policy departments, and concluding with the national

security policy team. This schedule was intended to signify the high priority to be accorded to economic and domestic policy. Although the pace of Clinton's appointments during his first month in office matched George Bush's, it was about half that set during the Carter and Reagan transitions. Through February 24, 1993, the president had submitted nominations to fill only 30 of the 290 positions that require Senate confirmation.[34] Some of the delay stemmed from the thoroughness with which prospective appointees were investigated; some of it was due to the push for diversity; and some of it resulted from the extensive involvement of the president and his wife in deciding on appointees. Clinton established a time-consuming and systematic process for "vetting" (conducting background checks) prospective appointees to cabinet and sub-cabinet positions. Search teams, consisting of campaign workers, Democratic politicians, and professional "headhunters," were created for every federal department and agency. The teams identified prospects for positions and then winnowed them down. Those who remained were then questioned and investigated by teams of "vetters" who explored every aspect of their past lives that could conceivably affect their job performance or embarrass the administration. The vetters contacted people in networks of "friends and foes" of the prospects as far back as possible.[35] The vetting was intended to find negative, not positive, information. Clinton's effectiveness in balancing the three values in his appointments is a matter of judgment, but the quest for diversity produced several embarrassments. At a press conference on December 20, 1992, for example, in response to questions about complaints from women's organizations that too many of his appointees were white males, Clinton lashed out at his critics as "bean counters" who placed more emphasis on quotas than competence.[36] A few days later, however, he named several women and minorities to important positions.

The push for diversity left some high-profile office seekers disappointed and others confused.[37] Sen. Tim Wirth, D-Colo., expected to become secretary of energy only to discover a few days prior to the announcement of his appointment that the post was going to O'Leary, an African-American utility company executive. Wirth later rejected a compensatory offer to become under-secretary of state. In spite of his denials, Clinton's actions drew charges that he was yielding to pressure from special interests for sexual and racial balance.

If Wirth was upset, former Arizona governor Bruce Babbitt was puzzled when he became secretary of the interior rather than U.S. trade representative, as he had been led to expect. Apparently, Rep. Bill Richardson, D-N.M., a Hispanic, was slated for the Interior Department until opposition arose from environmental groups. Their objections resulted in the shift of Babbitt, a westerner with a good environmental record, to interior. At the same time, in response to pressure from the Hispanic caucus in the House, former Denver mayor Fredrico Peña was named secretary of transportation. However, that position had previously been offered to William Daley, brother of Chicago mayor Richard M. Daley, a powerful Democratic figure.

Clinton's encounter with "the whirling centrifugal force of identity politics" and the consequent exposure of the inconsistency of his commitments did not derail the transition.[38] But these events indicated the political difficulties he could expect to encounter from his own supporters and provided evidence to his adversaries that reinforced his reputation as "slick Willie."

Clinton did succeed in appointing a diverse team *(Table 1)*. His initial cabinet of fourteen members included three women, four African-Americans, two Hispanics, and six white males. To the four other cabinet-level positions he appointed two women and two white males. The eighteen appointees ranged in age from thirty-six (Browner) to seventy-one (Bentsen), and all but four of them were in their forties and fifties. Occupational diversity was lacking: two-thirds of them trained as lawyers.

Ethical concerns also affected Clinton's appointments. His initial intention to appoint transition director Vernon Jordan, a prominent Washington lawyer and former head of the Urban League, as attorney general had to be dropped because of Jordan's membership on several corporate boards of directors. The appointment of Democratic National Chairman Ron Brown, a high-profile Washington lawyer and lobbyist, as secretary of commerce drew criticism because his clients had included foreign governments and several corporations, including Japanese electronics firms and the authoritarian government of Haiti under "Papa Doc" Duvalier.[39]

In spite of Clinton's emphasis on ethics, his and the transition team's inability to recognize and grasp the significance of past ethical impropriety on the part of Zoë Baird, his original nominee for attorney general, resulted in the first major blunder of his term.[40] Baird had to ask Clinton to withdraw her nomination because she and her husband, a Yale Law School professor, had knowingly violated immigration laws by employing

Table 1 Clinton's Initial Appointees

THE CABINET

Department	Secretary	Age	Sex	Race	Previous Position
State	Warren Christopher	67	M	W	Law practice
Treasury	Lloyd Bentsen	71	M	W	U.S. Senate
Defense	Les Aspin	54	M	W	U.S. House
Justice	Janet Reno	54	F	W	Prosecuting attorney
Interior	Bruce Babbitt	55	M	W	Governor/law practice
Agriculture	Mike Espy	39	M	AA	U.S. House
Commerce	Ron Brown	51	M	AA	Chairman, DNC
Labor	Robert Reich	48	M	W	Professor
HHS	Donna Shalala	51	F	W	University administrator
HUD	Henry Cisneros	45	M	H	Business
Transportation	Fredrico Peña	45	M	H	Business
Energy	Hazel O'Leary	55	F	AA	Business
Education	Richard Riley	60	M	W	Law practice
Vet's Aff.	Jesse Brown	48	M	AA	Lobbyist

CABINET LEVEL POSITIONS

OMB Director	Leon Panetta	54	M	W	U.S. House
U.S. Trade Rep.	Mickey Kantor	53	M	W	Law practice
UN Ambassador	Madeleine Albright	55	F	W	Professor
EPA Admin.	Carol Browner	36	F	W	State govt. administrator

two illegal aliens from Peru as domestic workers. They also failed to pay Social Security taxes for the couple. At first, transition officials and several members of the Senate Judiciary Committee, which would conduct hearings on the nomination, discounted the issue as an honest mistake involving no more than a technical violation of the law. Seldom in recent history had supposedly sensitive politicians so badly misjudged the mood of the public. Soon after the televised hearings began on January 19, a wave of angry telephone calls flooded the Senate and radio and cable television talk shows across the nation. Two days later, following another grueling day of testimony before the committee, a distraught Baird and her lawyers threw in the towel. In withdrawing Baird's nomination, Clinton criticized himself for not appreciating the issue's significance before nominating her.[41] At no point during Baird's ordeal did support develop among women's groups or civil rights organizations. The public appeared to associate her cool, detached professionalism with her corporate clients rather than with parents struggling to solve their child care problems. The incident demonstrated, however, that Clinton knew when to cut his losses and drop a lost cause.

Clinton's second attempt to find a female attorney general also faltered on the hiring of an illegal alien for child care.[42] However, this prospective nominee, federal judge Kimba Wood of New York, had hired the undocumented alien before it was illegal to do so and had paid all required taxes. Shortly after the president and his counsel interviewed Wood, on January 29, the White House announced that she would be nominated following completion of background checks. When, however, White House vetters learned of the matter the president accepted the recommendation of personnel director Bruce Lindsey and counsel Bernard Nussbaum that Wood be dropped on the ground that it would be impossible to explain to the public the distinctions between her case and Baird's. The Wood incident left the White House feeling more frustrated than embarrassed. The search for an attorney general finally ended satisfactorily in late February when Dade County, Florida, prosecuting attorney Janet Reno, who was single, survived the vetting process and sailed through senatorial confirmation without incident. It was Reno's later misfortune, however, to be blamed for FBI actions that may have triggered the deaths of David Koresh and more than eighty members of his religious cult in Waco, Texas.

The appointment of subcabinet officials moved even more slowly than the selection of the cabinet team, although the administration dropped the use of outside vetters at the end of February and the process became less thorough.[43] Early in the transition Clinton decided to follow Reagan's practice of having the White House manage subcabinet appointments rather than delegating their selection to the cabinet members. He felt that Carter lost control of the bureaucracy by delegating this job, while Reagan retained it by keeping a tight rein on the process. White House control of subcabinet appointments carries a price; the administration is not ready to move ahead shortly after the president takes office. Positions are either vacant or remain filled by appointees of the previous administration. The new administration proceeds haltingly and then it must depend on career civil servants, who in the United States have limited capacity to act as political agents of the president. This situation was the case in the Clinton administration with most departments and agencies.

Clinton and Congress

Soon after the election it became apparent that President Clinton would employ a hands-on, engaged approach to Congress similar to his successful style with the Arkansas legislature. He was determined to demonstrate that cooperation rather than gridlock would characterize presidential-congressional relations during his administration. He wanted to avoid the conflicts and mistakes that had plagued Carter's legislative relations, when the Democrats last controlled the executive and legislative branches.[44] Among the faults Congress attributed to Carter were his disdain for the institution and most of its members, lack of accessibility, failure to appreciate and acknowledge congressional support, and his presentation of a massive legislative agenda with no indication of his priorities.

Clinton almost immediately courted the Democratic congressional leadership by inviting House Speaker Tom Foley, House majority leader Richard Gephardt, and Senate majority leader George Mitchell to Little Rock for an "intimate dinner meeting" on November 15.[45] During the remainder of the transition he twice visited Capitol Hill, where he met with committee chairs in both houses, House and Senate Democrats, Democratic House freshmen, and Republican leaders. In the first six weeks after the inauguration he made three more trips to the Hill, held several meetings with Democratic and Republican leaders, and entertained numerous smaller groups of legislators at the White House.[46] He excelled at stroking congressional egos and made clear his accessibility to members of both parties.

Clinton's staffing of the White House Office of Legislative Affairs also reflected his desire for congenial and cooperative relations with Congress. As its director he picked Howard Paster, an Washington veteran with long service as a congressional staff member and lobbyist. Paster's principal deputies also had extensive experience on the Hill.

Clinton had hoped to present Congress with legislative proposals for his top priority items—stimulating the economy and reducing the deficit—a day after the inauguration and to follow with his plan for health care reform within 100 days. He did not reveal his economic plan until February 17 and delayed submitting his 1994 budget until April 8. He also postponed unveiling the health care proposal beyond its original May 1 target. These slowdowns resulted in uneasiness among congressional Democrats, while Republicans complained that the White House had not been forthcoming with the details of how the president intended to reach his goals.

Clinton's early relations with the House were considerably smoother than those with the Senate. House Democrats and their leaders were strongly united in their support of initial administration bills, which they passed over the opposition of Republicans and a few conservative Democrats. On March 19, exhibiting "remarkable" party discipline, 96 percent of the House Democrats supported the budget resolution that embodied the essentials of the president's economic plan.[47] Clinton also established excellent rapport with the chairman of the crucial Ways and Means Committee, Dan Rostenkowski, D-Ill., whose support was essential for passage of the economic plan.

In the Senate an early April filibuster of the president's economic stimulus bill, which the House had passed previously, demonstrated the power of the forty-three Republican members. Acting together, they could demand concessions and compromises on major administration bills. Nor were Senate Republicans the only legislators with whom it was necessary to compromise. In late March, under pressure from western Democrats, Clinton scaled back Interior Department proposals to regulate destructive land use practices by ranchers, loggers, and miners by sharply raising fees.[48] The westerners had threatened to oppose the president's budget package, and their votes were crucial. Clinton's tiffs with two powerful Senate committee chairmen, Sam Nunn of armed services (over gays in the military) and Pat Moynihan, D-N.Y., of finance, who complained that he had not been consulted over the taxes in the president's economic plan, also proved vexing.

After four months in office, it was apparent that Clinton had effectively organized and staffed his White House for dealing with Congress. His personal style, respect for its institutional prerogatives, and willingness to give and take in shaping legislation produced, at least temporarily, the cooperative relationship that he desired. However, members of Congress have their own constituencies, and each is, in his or her own way, an independent political entrepreneur. Members will support the president as long as it is in their political interest to do so. When, for example, his relatively high public approval ratings inevitably fell (initially Clinton's were in the low to mid–60s and by late May they had dropped to the low 40s), congressional support began to erode. Moreover, when members (even in his own party) confront administrative initiatives that threaten economic interests in their constituencies, the president has to choose between compromise and their opposition. Clinton quickly grasped the reality that confronts any president in his relations with Congress: that his power is limited; he can do only so much to create and maintain majorities; and many of the factors that determine legislative outcomes are beyond his control.

Clinton's Agenda

President-elect Clinton was well aware of the lessons to be drawn from the Carter and Reagan first-year experiences: there is a critical linkage among the tasks of taking over the budget, setting the legislative agenda, and establishing priorities among the new administration's goals. There was no question that Clinton's top priority would be the issue that got him elected, economic policy. Two objectives dominated the formulation of economic policy: immediate stimulation of a lagging economy and promotion of sustained economic growth. The federal budget deficit imposed major obstacles to the achievement of both the short- and long-term goals and, therefore, would have to be addressed at once.[49]

Clinton also accorded a high priority to reforming health care, another issue to which the public had responded positively in the campaign.[50] However, health care reform would be costly and would have an impact on and be affected by efforts to reduce the budget deficit. Health care costs had been increasing at double-digit rates for several years, especially in the large federally funded entitlement programs, Medicare and Medicaid. There would be substantial additional costs if coverage was to be extended to the uninsured. Although public support for health care was strong, the political costs of health care reform would be steep as they would entail either reduced services or higher taxes, if not both. To develop the administration's health care proposals, Clinton established the National Task Force on Health Care Reform, chaired by his wife. The use of outside experts temporarily removed the new president and the White House from the potentially explosive issues surrounding health care, but eventually he would have to decide how much political capital to invest in the reform effort.

The remainder of the agenda broke down into two groups of actions: goals that could be accomplished quickly by executive order or the passage of relatively noncontroversial legislation and less important long-term objectives. Among the measures implemented soon after the inauguration were executive orders removing the bans on fetal tissue research and abortion counseling, and enactment of a family leave bill similar to the one that President Bush had vetoed in 1992. Early efforts to end the ban on gays in the military and to reform campaign finance laws encountered substantial congressional opposition, which shifted them to the back burner. Long-term goals with lower priority included welfare reform and the establishment of a National Service Corps. Despite Clinton's emphasis on the primacy of his economic plan, his frequent references to a wide range of other policy goals resulted in criticism that his agenda lacked focus.

Economic Policy

Although economic policy planning began soon after the election, President Clinton did not present his economic plan to Congress until February 17. The issue of whether to concentrate initially on a short-term economic stimulus package that would create jobs or on long-term actions that would balance the goals of growth and deficit reduction dominated postelection planning.[51] Despite pressures from Congress, local officials, and groups lobbying for public works spending to quickly pump money into the economy, two developments shifted Clinton's focus toward deficit reduction.[52] First, reports of improved economic performance eased pressures to jump start the economy and refocused concerns on the deficit. Second, OMB disclosed (in President's Bush's January 6 budget proposal for fiscal 1994) that the 1992 deficit would be $290 billion rather than the $268 billion projected in July 1992. Revised OMB projections for fiscal 1994 through 1997 showed an additional $189 billion in deficits and gave further impetus for deficit reduction.[53] Thus, Clinton's delay in fashioning his economic plan resulted from the need to balance short- and long-term objectives as well as cope with larger deficit projections than he had anticipated during the campaign.

Also contributing to the delay were other difficult choices and conflicting imperatives. It was apparent that taxes would be required to help finance new spending and make deficit reduction credible, but the question of who would pay them was most painful. Not only would the middle class not receive the promised tax cut, but also it would have to pay more taxes. Among the several alternatives considered were a sharp increase in the gasoline tax as proposed by Ross Perot in the campaign, a new tax on all forms of energy, a broad-based consumption tax similar to the value added tax found in Western Europe or Canada's goods and services tax, increased taxation of Social Security benefits, taxation of employer-provided health insurance as income, and increases in federal income taxes paid by individuals and corporations. Spending cuts also were difficult to determine. Defense was to be a prime target, but how much could national security be risked in the uncertain environment of the post–cold war era? Where could meaningful cuts be made among the discretionary social spending programs traditionally supported by Democrats and the distributive pork barrel projects favored by almost all members of Congress? The biggest, most costly, and most rapidly growing spending programs are entitlements—Social Security, Medicare, Medicaid, federal employee pensions, farm subsidies, and food stamps—but they are almost sacrosanct. How much could members of Congress cut entitlements without committing political suicide? Even if savings could be wrung out of Medicare and Medicaid, should they be used to reduce the deficit or extend health care coverage?

Clinton made his first economic policy decision a day after taking office when he announced that he would retain the flexible deficit targets authorized in President Bush's 1990 budget deal with Congress.[54] The 1990 budget legislation required the president to decide on January 21, 1993, whether to stick with the flexible targets or revert to the fixed targets of the Gramm-Rudman-Hollings Act and across-the-board spending cuts— mandatory sequesters—to enforce them. A return to fixed targets would present the threat of a $22.4 billion sequester in October 1993.[55] Congressional Republicans charged that Clinton's decision demonstrated that he was not serious about reducing the deficit.

The economic plan emerged on February 17 after a lengthy process that involved extensive pre-inauguration discussions with advisers, the mid-December economic conference, post-inauguration meetings between Clinton and the members of his economic team and Federal Reserve chairman Alan Greenspan, and fine-tuning sessions with congressional leaders and Democratic House members.[56] Clinton unveiled the plan in his first speech to a joint session of Congress where reaction followed predictable party lines. Most Democrats endorsed it enthusiastically, while Republicans and a few conservative Democrats criticized it for basing deficit reduction too heavily on tax increases and not enough on spending cuts. Public response to the overall plan was strongly positive, with the *Time*/CNN poll showing 62 percent approval and 27 percent disapproval.[57] However, the polls also revealed that the public's acceptance of higher taxes was conditioned on greater cuts in spending than were proposed in the plan.

The plan contained three major parts: a two-year stimulus package; a four-year program to end an "investment deficit" in spending for infrastructure, education, child care, job training, and health care; and a plan to reduce the deficit by $493 billion over four years.[58] The centerpiece of the stimulus package was $16.3 billion in spending, primarily for highway construction, summer jobs, extended unemployment benefits, and community development grants. The investment proposal included $100 billion in spending increases for more than seventy programs in technology, transportation, housing, education and job training, child nutrition, and crime control.[59] The politically sensitive plan to reduce the deficit would obtain $247 billion from spending cuts and $246 from tax increases; however, a proposed $21 billion increase in Social Security taxes was treated as a spending cut. Moreover, "the plan would produce net, cumulative four-year spending cuts of $117 billion and tax increases of $207 billion."[60]

The plan's proposed tax changes would produce $357 billion in additional revenues in the period 1993–1998.[61] The increases would be provided mainly by higher taxes on the incomes of affluent individuals ($126 billion), increased taxes on the Social Security benefits of higher-income recipients ($29 billion), removal of the cap on the Medicare payroll tax ($29.2 billion), higher corporate income taxes ($30.6 billion), a comprehensive energy tax ($71.4 billion), and making permanent a 2.5 cents per gallon tax on gasoline slated to expire in 1995. The plan contained two major tax expenditures: expansion of the earned income tax credit, which benefits poor families (at a cost of $26.8 billion), and a 7 percent investment tax credit for businesses, effective during 1993 and 1994 (at a cost of $28.8 billion).

Clinton's proposed use of taxes to cut the deficit and provide funding for new programs to stimulate and strengthen the economy reverses the approach of the Reagan and Bush administrations. According to *The Economist*, a conservative British magazine, "Mr. Clinton is instigating . . . a counter-revolution, designed to overthrow 12 years of pro-defence, anti-tax Republican ideology. In its stead he offers an idea of government that . . . is decidedly liberal, activist and, in many ways, profoundly traditional." Reagan used the deficit strategically to prevent congressional Democrats from increasing nondefense spending. Likewise, Clinton is employing it to "pursue two hoary Democratic objectives: cutting military spending and soaking the rich."[62]

The president's economic plan depended on passage of three pieces of legislation: the 1994 budget resolution, which is required by the congressional budget process; the economic stimulus package; and a reconciliation bill containing actions recommended by authorizing and tax-writing committees to meet the spending and revenue targets in the budget resolution. In addition, Congress has the opportunity to react to the president's recommendations for reductions and increases in discretionary spending when it considers the thirteen regular appropriations bills for 1994. Initially, the White House and congressional leaders decided to bring the stimulus package to the floor before the budget resolution. However, criticism from Republicans and public concern that the schedule showed that the Democrats were not serious about cutting spending resulted in an adjustment that provided for the first vote to be on the budget resolution.[63] The revised schedule, which entailed voting on all of the proposed spending cuts and tax increases prior to authorizing the specific spending in the stimulus bill, calmed apprehensive congressional Democrats and placed the Republicans on the defensive by pressuring them to come up with an alternative to Clinton's proposals. The Republican goal of exceeding Clinton's deficit reduction figure without increasing taxes could be achieved only by draconian new spending cuts, many of which would alienate their supporters.[64]

Although it has no statutory authority, the budget resolution establishes targets that bind Congress for fiscal 1994. These guidelines include caps on appropriations and the gross amount of increases in taxes and cuts in spending on entitlement programs. The appropriating and authorizing committees have discretion to determine how they will meet those broad limits. The House passed the budget resolution March 18, 243–183, a vote in which only eleven Democrats joined all 172 Republicans.[65] The resolution contained Clinton's entire economic plan, but it did not provide detailed instructions for reducing spending and increasing taxes. The next day the House passed the administration's stimulus proposal by a 235–190 vote in which three Republicans and twenty-two Democrats crossed party lines.[66] The measure provided for $16.3 billion in supplemental appropriations for fiscal 1993 and $3.2 billion in trust fund spending. Although its rules limit debate on budget resolutions, the Senate spent six days on the budget resolution before passing it March 25, in a 54–45 party-line vote on which the forty-three Republicans were united.[67] The two chambers differed mainly over how to obtain an additional $22 billion for deficit reduction. The Senate proposed to get the money from tax increases, and the House from spending cuts. A House-Senate conference committee resolved the differences between the two versions with the Senate abandoning the new taxes it had added to the president's plan and the House yielding half of its extra spending cuts. Although Congress preserved most of the Clinton plan's proposed tax increases, spending cuts, "investment" spending, and the $496 billion deficit reduction target, it added $50 billion in spending cuts to the original package.[68] This addition suggests that Clinton may have underestimated congressional support for deficit reduction.

The early passage of the budget resolution was a triumph for Clinton's economic plan and marked the high point in his honeymoon with congressional Democrats.[69] The stimulus package, which sailed easily through the House, "sank into a partisan Senate quagmire" the week of March 29, with Republicans united in demanding major reductions in it.[70] The Republican leaders hoped to force concessions through delaying amendments and a filibuster. The Democrats were unable to find the sixty votes required to invoke cloture prior to shelving the bill on April 5, until the end of the spring recess two weeks later.[71] During that hiatus, the White House and Senate Democratic leaders modified the bill so as to attract Republican votes to end debate. The $19.5 billion package was trimmed to $15.4 billion, and the president pressured moderate Republicans by publicly pointing out their unwillingness to even allow a vote on creating new jobs. But these efforts proved unsuccessful: after the fourth effort at cloture failed on April 21, the Senate merely approved $4 billion for extended unemployment benefits, and the outcome was presented as a major legislative defeat for the administration. Clinton seems to have miscalculated the Republicans' ability to offer unified opposition, and he learned a painful lesson on the need for consultation, even with a minority.

The outcome assumed unexpected political significance as a test of Clinton's deftness at mustering popular support for his legislation and the Republican senators' power to force compromises through use of the filibuster. Clinton faced a danger in the situation: the more he had to compromise with the Republicans to pass his legislation the more he would appear to the public as a practitioner of old-style, wheeler-dealer politics.[72] But the public, despite Clinton's best efforts, appeared unconcerned about the stalemate over the stimulus bill, perhaps because they believed that the president had already won whereas he was actually defeated on the secondary issue. By failing to clarify the public's confusion about the purpose and importance of the stimulus package, Clinton had committed a "public relations blunder."[73] As the dust settled, it remained unclear what lessons administration policy makers would draw from this episode. Would they learn the importance of negotiating more fully with the opposition, particularly when such highly controversial matters as health care and campaign finance reform were still to be considered? Or would they conclude that hardball tactics, such as branding Senate Republicans "the guardians of gridlock," would work?[74] The administration appeared chastened by the experience, and the fate of Clinton's remaining legislative program appeared far more problematic.

The $1.52 trillion budget for fiscal 1994 that Clinton submitted to Congress on April 8 (it had been due February 1) contained detailed proposals for spending and tax changes. Many of those recommendations would be the focus of conflict—much of it partisan—in Congress.[75] The budget's spending priorities gave clear indication of the policy direction of the new administration. Clinton would tilt government away from defense and consumption (both private and public) toward investment in physical infrastructure, education and training, and research and development. Because of the end of divided government, Clinton's budget reached Capitol Hill "alive and kicking" with a realistic chance of passing, rather than "dead on arrival" like the Reagan and Bush budgets of the previous ten years.[76] The budget made no major changes in the president's economic plan, nor did it mention the administration's goal of health care reform and its probable costs, two subjects bound to be highly controversial.

Foreign Policy

Since 1940 presidents have had to devote much of their own time and energy, as well as the nation's resources to foreign and military policy. The external threats to national security—fascism during World War II and international communism afterward—defined and clarified U.S. policy. George Kennan's strategy of containment provided the conceptual framework for cold war foreign policy.

Bill Clinton entered office as the first president of the post–cold war era. For the first time since 1936 foreign policy issues played no part in the presidential election campaign. He won on the basis of economic and domestic issues and limited his statements on international problems. Generally, Clinton supported the Bush administration's policies, except its handling of the civil war in Bosnia and its refusal to allow the immigration of Haitian refugees. Given his domestic policy emphasis, Clinton's inclination was to incorporate economic and environmental goals into his international agenda.

Upon taking office Clinton faced immediate political crises involving Bosnia, Somalia, Iraq, Haiti, and Russia. Also awaiting him were pressing international economic issues such as whether to approve the North American Free Trade Agreement (NAFTA), how to move stalled talks affecting the future of the General Agreement on Tariffs and Trade (GATT), and sharp fluctuations in foreign exchange markets. He avoided making a major foreign policy blunder by retreating from campaign commitments on Bosnia and Haiti that could have had unforeseen consequences and damaged his image as an effective leader.[77] He also deftly managed his first meeting with Russia's imperiled president, Boris Yeltsin. Clinton promised a $1.5 billion package of economic assistance that was large enough to help the faltering Russian economy, thus shoring up Yeltsin's precarious government, but sufficiently small that it did not elicit much criticism from the public and Congress.

Clinton's initial international forays demonstrated the extent to which the international environment and U.S. foreign policy have changed since the collapse of the Soviet Union in late 1991. Whereas previous presidents dealt with well-defined conflicts between nation-states, Clinton must address "the international spillover of conflicts within states."[78] Although the United States stands as the world's single superpower, its ability to influence conditions within other countries is limited. Managing intranational conflicts and adapting to the "broad transnational forces" that are shaping contemporary international events require a different approach from that used in conventional diplomacy and international relations.[79]

The nature of such a new approach is not yet apparent, but some of its elements and the choices that must be made in shaping it can be perceived. To begin, there must be a redefinition of success in foreign policy.[80] The United States no longer seeks to prevail over military adversaries but is still vitally concerned with its security. That security will be enhanced through the achievement of objectives such as the spread of democracy and prosperous market economies, effective control of environmental degradation, and an end to proliferation of weapons of mass destruction. These goals are, to be sure, highly idealistic, but they cannot be achieved without a realistic assessment of the nation's capabilities and limitations. The challenge to Clinton and his advisers is to develop or acquire an approach that provides conceptual clarity to foreign policy. Otherwise, policy will emerge through a series of ad hoc responses to crises and recurring issues. When and if that approach is in hand, the president needs to make certain that Congress, the public, and other countries understand it. He should explain his decisions in terms of the approach and use it to implement them. After four months in office, Clinton and the new administration had just embarked on this daunting assignment.

Conclusion: Clinton's Prospects

By April 21, 1993, President Clinton had completed the essential tasks of his transition. He had organized and staffed the White House, picked his cabinet and begun filling other important positions in the administration, taken over the budget, geared up for dealing with Congress, set and prioritized his agenda, won and lost his first battles on Capitol Hill over central features of his economic plan, and begun meeting other world leaders. Overall, the transition went smoothly in spite of some embarrassing mistakes. Arguably, Clinton was off to a better start than Carter, the last Democratic president, and in certain respects his transition measured up to the efficacious model provided by Reagan.

Based on these early signs, what kind of president is Clinton likely to be? What are the prospects for his presidency? There are a number of possible answers. The transformation of the international system resulting from the end of the cold war and the revolutionary changes in presidential communications led journalist Steven Stark to characterize Clinton's as "the first postmodern presidency," a term he borrowed from political scientist Richard Rose.[81] The distinguishing feature of Rose's postmodern president is "the gap between the international responsibilities of the White House and its resources."[82] Certainly Clinton's success depends to a considerable extent on international events and conditions and on his ability to persuade and cooperate with foreign leaders. Clinton also has developed a distinctive direct approach to presidential communications with the public and a new relationship with the media. These developments were made possible by the changing technology of telecommunications.

Television is central to the new style of politics that political analyst

William Schneider views Clinton as having introduced.[83] It is a politics in which pragmatism displaces ideology, populism prevails over the elitist Establishment, and personalism replaces political parties. The policies the president pursues are determined by the pragmatic test of what works and not by ideological principles. The president depends for support on his mass personal following and not on his political party. His power is personal and derives from the people and not from bureaucrats, lobbyists, and legislators. After four months, Clinton appears to be learning, as did George Bush, that new populist politics is highly volatile as the public is fickle and can quickly withdraw its support.

The prospects for significant policy change under Clinton become less clear under such changing and uncertain conditions. Political scientist Michael Nelson and historian Arthur Schlesinger, Jr., employ cyclical theories to reach somewhat different assessments of Clinton's prospects. Nelson and his colleague Erwin Hargrove have argued that twentieth century American electoral politics and domestic policy making manifest a cyclical pattern focused on the presidency. At the heart of the cycle is a "presidency of achievement," "during which great bursts of presidentially inspired legislation are enacted that significantly alter the role of the federal government in American society."[84] Presidents of achievement are preceded by presidents of preparation and followed by presidents of consolidation. The cycle has made four complete turns with Woodrow Wilson, Franklin D. Roosevelt, Lyndon B. Johnson, and Ronald Reagan. Nelson maintains that Clinton's will be a presidency of preparation that follows Bush's presidency of consolidation. He argues that the conditions required for a presidency of achievement—an empowering election, presidential leadership skills, and ideas—are not present in the Clinton presidency.[85] The election did not produce a clear mandate. Clinton's skills are primarily tactical, and his strong desire to please may be his undoing. Although brimming over with ideas, Clinton will discover that "the same economic problems that made possible his election also promise to constrain the expansiveness of his policy ideas."[86] Nelson concludes with the observation that Clinton's prospects for becoming a president of achievement rest mainly on a landslide reelection victory in 1996.

Schlesinger uses a theory, originally propounded by his father, that "American politics alternate at roughly thirty-year intervals between conservative and liberal periods."[87] During conservative times, the public regards private action, private interests, and an unregulated market as the best means of solving problems and advancing society. In liberal eras, the public turns to public action, the public interest, and regulation. Previous periods of twentieth century liberalism began in 1901 with Theodore Roosevelt, 1933 with Franklin Roosevelt, and 1961 with John Kennedy. Generational change drives the cycle. People tend to acquire the ideas that are dominant when they become politically conscious. Persons who grew up, for example, during the New Deal embodied its progressive ideals in the Great Society. If the cycle continues, the 1990s should be a period of liberal activism. Schlesinger cautions against regarding his theory as deterministic. They are "cycles of opportunity" that present possibilities for achievement to leaders. What happens depends on the skills, ideas, and vision of those leaders.[88] In a piece written near the end of the transition period, Schlesinger expressed his belief that Clinton will be a leader in the pattern of FDR and Kennedy. If so, and the cycle holds, "the 1996 election should do for Mr. Clinton what the 1936 election did for Roosevelt and the 1964 election did for Johnson . . . confirm the course and give a reform program the unmistakable stamp of popular approval."[89] Both Nelson and Schlesinger believe that Clinton's major policy achievements probably will have to wait until his second term (assuming there is one).

One area in which Clinton can have an enduring effect on the future is through his judicial appointments. In March Justice Byron White announced his plans to retire from the Supreme Court at the end of the term. Another senior justice, Harry Blackmun, reportedly has retirement plans, and John Paul Stevens, Sandra Day O'Connor, and Chief Justice William Rehnquist are believed to have health problems. Should Clinton make even two appointments in his first term, the potential impact on the Court is enormous. In addition, he can expect to fill approximately 40 percent of the seats on the U.S. district courts and courts of appeal during his first four years. His appointees would substantially counter the conservative bent of the lower courts imposed by Reagan's and Bush's judges.

As Clinton approached the 100-day mark in office, the media's traditional time for issuing evaluations of performance, there were reasons for optimism but also grounds for concern. In the single week of April 18–24, the administration was rocked by the cult deaths in Texas, which produced a call for congressional investigations; sustained the Senate defeat of Clinton's stimulus package; and struggled to define a viable policy in Bosnia while awaiting the outcome of a critical referendum on Boris Yeltsin's future in Russia. The president dramatically reversed his predecessor's position on two international agreements on the environment and provided support to gay rights activists. Final touches were being put on a controversial proposal for campaign finance reform, but the much anticipated plan for health care reform seemed a distant promise.

By late May the Clinton presidency appeared to be in serious trouble. Approval of the president's performance had sunk to about 40 percent. Contributing to the decline in popular support were an apparent lack of focus in his agenda; defeat of his economic stimulus package in the Senate; his inability to develop a policy to end the civil war in Bosnia that would meet the approval of the American people, Congress, the European Community, Russia, and the combatants; and mistakes that damaged his image as an effective and sensitive leader. Two major blunders occurred in May. One involved the dismissal of the White House travel staff for questionable reasons and a clumsy attempt to use the FBI to justify the action. The other was a $200 haircut from a Hollywood stylist that the president received aboard Air Force One while the plane was on the tarmac at Los Angeles International Airport. The media reported that the haircut held up air traffic for an hour.

Clinton moved quickly to correct his problems. At the end of May he hired Republican journalist David Gergen, a personal friend who had served as counselor to the president in the Nixon and Reagan administrations. Paramount among Gergen's responsibilities was communications. (Clinton reassigned his first communications director, George Stephanopolous, to policy development activities.) After the House narrowly passed the bulk of his economic program by a 219–213 margin, Clinton expressed his willingness to compromise with the Senate, where conservative Democrats and moderate Republicans were demanding more spending cuts and fewer tax increases.

These actions reflected the adaptability that had characterized Clinton's presidential campaign. He could still look forward to a significant term— one fraught with difficult issues likely to engage his and the nation's attention—provided he could regain the policy focus and image of effective leadership that he projected early in the transition. But after four months it remained highly uncertain how Congress and the American people would receive Clinton's many proposals on a wide range of domestic problems and whether he could reach a compromise with Congress on his economic plan that would improve the economy. Nor was it clear whether Clinton and his foreign policy team would devise an overarching conceptual framework with which to approach world problems. Ironically, uncertainty about the future, one of Clinton's principal assets in the unseating of George Bush, had returned to haunt the new administration.

NOTES

1. Gerald M. Pomper, "The Presidential Election," in *The Election of 1992*, ed. Pomper (Chatham, N.J.: Chatham House, 1993), 150.

2. Ibid.

3. James P. Pfiffner, *The Strategic Presidency: Hitting the Ground Running* (Chicago: Dorsey Press, 1988), 3. Pfiffner emphasizes that the transition does not end with the inauguration but continues for some time afterward.

4. In the twentieth century party turnovers have occurred in the following years: 1913 from Taft (R) to Wilson (D); 1921 from Wilson (D) to Harding (R); 1933 from Hoover (R) to F. D. Roosevelt (D); 1953 from Truman (D) to Eisenhower (R); 1961 from Eisenhower (R) to Kennedy (D); 1969 from Johnson (D) to Nixon (R); 1977 from Ford (R) to Carter (D); 1981 from Carter (D) to Reagan (R); and 1993 from Bush (R) to Clinton (D).

5. Pfiffner, *The Strategic Presidency*, 4.

6. Ibid.

7. Paul C. Light, *The President's Agenda: Domestic Policy Choice from Kennedy to Reagan* (Baltimore: The Johns Hopkins University Press, 1991), 36.

8. Pfiffner, *The Strategic Presidency*, 19.

9. Richard E. Neustadt, *Presidential Power and the Modern Presidency: The Politics of Leadership from Roosevelt to Reagan* (New York: The Free Press, 1990) 249, 254.

10. Burt Solomon, "How A Leak-Loathing White House Is Putting the Press in Its Place," *National Journal*, Feb. 13, 1993, 416–417.

11. Burt Solomon, "Clinton May Have to Pay Later for Transition's Prudent Pace," *National Journal*, Dec. 12, 1992, 2852.

12. Michael Kelly, "Clinton, After Raising Hopes, Tries to Lower Expectations," *New York Times* Nov. 9, 1992, A–1.

13. Michael Kelly, "Clinton, Sketching Plan for Economy, Counsels Patience," *New York Times*, Nov. 13, 1992, A–1.

14. Thomas L. Friedman, "Change of Tone for Clinton: High Energy to Low Profile," *New York Times*, Nov. 12, 1992, A–1.

15. Thomas L. Friedman, "Clinton as U.S. Teacher: More Than a Talk Show," *New York Times*, Dec. 15, 1992, A–15.

16. "A Valuable Economics Seminar," Editorial, *New York Times*, Dec. 16, 1992, A–14.

17. John P. Sears, "Clinton Too Easily Pressured," *Cincinnati Enquirer*, Jan. 5, 1993, A–4; Michael Duffy, "Ready or Not: As Clinton Takes Office, a Slow Start and a String of Broken Promises Signal a Rough Ride Ahead," *Time*, Jan. 25, 1993, 29.

18. "Bent Promises," *Time*, Jan. 25, 1993, 17.

19. R. W. Apple, Jr., "Surprise! When You Talk as President, People Listen," *New York Times*, Jan. 17, 1993, E–1, E–3.

20. Sidney Blumenthal, "The Syndicated Presidency," *New Yorker*, April 5, 1993, 47; Burt Solomon, "Clinton's Rhetoric May Not Be Pretty But So Far, Anyway, It's

Working," *National Journal*, March 27, 1993, 775; Gwen Ifill, "Clinton Takes Case Directly to Public," *New York Times*, Feb. 7, 1993, A–17.

21. Blumenthal, "The Syndicated Presidency," 43.

22. Ibid., 47.

23. Solomon, "How a Leak-Loathing White House," 416.

24. Burt Solomon, "Sizing Up the Company Clinton Keeps," *National Journal*, Jan. 23, 1993, 210.

25. Burt Solomon, "Playing Majordomo in a Minor Key," *National Journal*, Dec. 19, 1992, 2909.

26. In the first group were persons such as communications director George Stephanopolous, press secretary Dee Dee Myers, deputy domestic policy adviser Bruce Reed, and environmental adviser Bob Hattoy. "Never before," observed journalist Matthew Cooper, "has an administration assigned so many young people to such visible—and powerful—roles." "Clinton's 'Brady Kids': How a Staff Full of Thirtysomethings Will Run His Government," *U.S. News & World Report*, Jan. 18, 1993.

The second category included national security adviser Anthony Lake and his deputy, Samuel Berger; former Democratic representative Leon Panetta, director of the Office of Management and Budget; deputy OMB director Alice Rivlin, an economist who formerly headed the Congressional Budget Office; and legislative affairs director Howard Paster. Health policy adviser Ira Magaziner and ambassador-at-large Strobe Talbot were student friends of Clinton at Georgetown and Oxford, respectively. Former Arkansas advisers Bruce Lindsey and Carol Rasco were named personnel director and domestic policy adviser. Advisers recommended by others included investment banker Robert Rubin to be chairman of the National Economic Council and Stanford professor Laura D'Andrea Tyson, chair of the Council of Economic Advisers.

The most trusted member of Clinton's inner circle is his wife, Hillary Rodham Clinton. They have common values, and he has always shared his major decisions with her. Her role was going to be quite different from that of any previous first lady.

27. David Gergen, "He Keeps Going and Going and Going," *U.S. News & World Report*, Jan. 18, 1993, 38.

28. Ibid. Gergen worried that Clinton would "eventually wear himself out" or that he "could become his own bottleneck, slowing down important decisions."

29. Michael K. Frisby, "At the White House, Titles Offer Few Clues About Real Influence," *Wall Street Journal*, March 26, 1993, A–1.

30. Ibid, A–12. In an op-ed piece, two distinguished economists, former members of the Council of Economic Advisers, warned that it would be a "great mistake" for Clinton to interpose the new National Economic Council between himself and "officials charged by statute and presidential appointment with roles in making economic and fiscal policies." They expressed particular concern that the CEA would become a "sideshow" and the goals and mechanisms of the Employment Act of 1946 a "dead letter." James Tobin and Robert M. Solow, "Clintonomics Doesn't Need a Czar," *New York Times*, Dec. 10, 1992.

31. James A. Barnes, "They Can Sell, But Can They Close?" *National Journal*, March 20, 1993, 712.

32. Burt Solomon, "Clinton Tries a Reagan-Style Pitch But with Just a Bush-Sized Bench," *National Journal*, Feb. 27, 1993, 532.

33. Quoted in ibid.

34. Douglas Jehl, "High-Level Grumbling Over the Pace of Appointments," *New York Times*, Jan. 28, 1993, A–8.

35. Ibid.

36. Gwen Ifill, "Clinton Chooses 2 and Deplores Idea of Cabinet Quotas," *New*

York Times, Dec. 22, 1992, A–1. Clinton was especially piqued because some women's advocates downgraded the importance of two of his appointees, CEA chair Laura Tyson and EPA administrator Carol Browner. He charged that had he appointed white males to those positions, "those same people . . . would have been counting those positions against our Administration."

37. Sidney Blumenthal, "Waiting for the Call," *New Yorker*, Jan. 25, 1993, 48–53.

38. Ibid., 52–53.

39. Pamela Fessler, "Clinton Steps Closer to Wishes of Full Cabinet by Christmas," *Congressional Quarterly Weekly Report*, Dec. 19, 1992, 3876.

40. Kenneth T. Walsh et al, "Mr. President: Bill Clinton Ushers in His Regime with Pomp, Ceremony—and a Big Snafu," *U.S. News and World Report*, Feb. 1, 1993, 26; Nancy Gibbs, "Thumbs Down," *Time*, Feb. 1, 1993, 27–29; Jill Smolowe, "How It Happened," *Time*, Feb. 1, 1993, 31–35. Holly Idelson, "Baird's Wrenching Withdrawal Mars the Inaugural Week," *Congressional Quarterly Weekly Report*, Jan. 23, 1993, 179.

41. Idelson, "Baird's Wrenching Withdrawal," 179.

42. Robert D. McFadden, "Backers Say Wood Gave Full Account of Employing Alien," *New York Times*, Feb. 7, 1993, A–1. The White House and a close associate of the nominee, Judge Kimba Wood, disagreed sharply over the timing of the information she provided regarding the issue.

According to Wood's associate, she disclosed the problem in detail in interviews with the president and his counsel Bernard Nussbaum on January 29. Communications Director George Stephanopolous claimed that no one in the White House knew of the problem until they received her financial records on February 4, the day before Wood announced her withdrawal from consideration. He also asserted that prior to her interview with the president, "She was asked if she had a problem related to illegal aliens and she said no."

43. Solomon, "The True Secrets of Clintonites," 645.

44. Adam Clymer, "Clinton Discusses Legislative Moves with Congressmen," *New York Times*, Nov. 16, 1992, A–1.

45. Graeme Browning, "Teaming Up," *National Journal*, Dec. 5, 1992, 2772.

46. Richard E. Cohen, "Leadership Test," *National Journal*, March 13, 1993, 608.

47. Adam Clymer, "Clinton's Plan Gets Moving," March 21, 1993, E–1.

48. Keith Schneider, "Clinton the Conservationist Thinks Twice," *New York Times*, April 4, 1993, E–1.

49. In a mid-December interview, shortly after the conference to discuss economic policy, Clinton emphasized his concern about the long-term effects of the deficit and indicated that his economic plan would emphasize deficit reduction. Jeffrey H. Birnbaum and Michael K. Frisby, "Clinton Puts Emphasis on Deficit Goals as He Maps Economic Plan," *Wall Street Journal*, Dec. 18, 1992, A–1.

50. In remarks December 7 at Wilbur Wright Community College in Chicago, Clinton expressed his desire to "bring health costs in line with inflation and provide a basic [insurance] package for everybody." Richard L. Berke, "Clinton Warns That Economy May Still Be Bad," *New York Times*, Dec. 8, 1992, A–13.

51. Mike Mills, "Public Works: A Quick Boost Becomes a Tough Call," *Congressional Quarterly Weekly Report*, Dec. 19, 1992, 3884.

52. Steven Greenhouse, "Better Times May Lead Clinton to Focus on Deficit," *New York Times*, Dec. 7, 1992, A–1.

53. George Hager, "Time Bombs for Clinton Seen In Bush's Final Budget," *Congressional Quarterly Weekly Report*, Jan. 9, 1993, 68. The revised projections gave Clinton maneuvering room to back away from his campaign pledge to cut the deficit in half by 1997.

54. George Hager, "GOP Ready to Fight Clinton Over Economic Policy," *Congressional Quarterly Weekly Report*, Jan. 23, 1993, 170.

55. Hager, "Time Bombs for Clinton," 72.

56. Gwen Ifill, "Economic Plan Grew Slowly Out of Marathon of Debate," *New York Times*, Feb. 21, 1993, A–14.

57. Nancy Gibbs, "Working the Crowd," *Time*, March 1, 1993, 20. The U.S. News poll reported "nearly 80 percent approval." Kenneth T. Walsh, Gloria Borger, and Matthew Cooper, "Public Fever for New Budget Cuts," *U.S. News and World Report*, March 1, 1993, 30.

58. George Hager, "President Throws Down the Gauntlet," *Congressional Quarterly Weekly Report*, Feb. 20, 1993, 358.

59. "The Presidential Investment Plan," *Congressional Quarterly Weekly Report*, Feb. 20, 1993, 369.

60. Hager, "President Throws Down the Gauntlet," 358.

61. "A Look at the Highlights of Clinton's Tax Proposals," *Congressional Quarterly Weekly Report*, Feb. 20, 1993, 362.

62. "Scenes from the Counter-Revolution," *The Economist*, Feb. 27, 1993, 29.

63. George Hager, "Clinton Program Sails Ahead Despite Turmoil on Hill," *Congressional Quarterly Weekly Report*, Feb. 27, 1993, 442.

64. George Hager, "Both Parties Struggle for Unity as First Votes Draw Near," *Congressional Quarterly Weekly Report*, March 6, 1993, 504.

65. George Hager, "House Democrats Easily Back Clinton Budget Blueprint," *Congressional Quarterly Weekly Report*, March 20, 1993, 653.

66. Jon Healey and Chuck Alston, "Stimulus Bill Prevails in House, But Senate Battle Awaits," *Congressional Quarterly Weekly Report*, March 20, 1993, 649.

67. George Hager, "Senate Democrats Close Ranks, Endorse Clinton Budget," *Congressional Quarterly Weekly Report*, March 27, 1993, 731.

68. George Hager, "Democrats Hail Quick Passage Of Clinton's Budget Plan," *Congressional Quarterly Weekly Report*, April 3, 1993, 823.

69. David E. Rosenbaum, "Voting on the Budget: The Easy Part's Over," *New York Times*, April 4, 1993, E–3.

70. Jon Healey, "Republicans Slam the Brakes on Economic Stimulus Plan," *Congressional Quarterly Weekly Report*, April 3, 1993, 817.

71. Jon Healey, "Clinton Must Now Sell Urgency of Stimulus Bill's Jobs," *Congressional Quarterly Weekly Report*, April 10, 1993, 907.

72. Comments of Kevin Phillips in Thomas L. Friedman, "Clinton's Jobs Plan Rallies the Republicans," *New York Times*, April 11, 1993, E–3.

73. Comments of Thomas E. Mann, reported in Friedman, ibid., E–3.

74. Sen. Robert Byrd, D-W.Va., who had managed the stimulus package on the floor described the Republicans in this way. Adam Clymer, "G.O.P. Senators Prevail, Sinking Clinton's Economic Stimulus Bill," *New York Times*, April 22, 1993, 18.

75. Robert Pear, "Clinton Outlines Spending Package of $1.52 Trillion," *New York Times*, April 9, 1993, A–1; George Hager, "$1.5 Trillion Clinton Plan: Getting Down to Details," *Congressional Quarterly Weekly Report*, April 10, 1993, 885.

76. David E. Rosenbaum, "Alive and Kicking," *New York Times*, April 9, 1993, A–1.

77. Burt Solomon, "Clinton Ventures into Diplomacy with the Touch of a Politician," *National Journal*, April 3, 1993, 834.

78. Thomas L. Friedman, "Friends Like Russia Make Diplomacy a Mess," *New York Times*, March 28, 1993, E–5.

79. Paul Kennedy, "True Leadership for the Next Millennium," *New York Times*, Jan. 3, 1993, E–11. Kennedy also notes that increasingly "what happens in the world

outside affects America's prospects, simply because we have become so much more integrated economically, strategically, and politically.''

80. Friedman, ''Friends Like Russia.''

81. Steven Stark, ''The First Postmodern Presidency,'' *Atlantic,* April 1993, 26.

82. Richard Rose, *The Postmodern President: George Bush Meets the World,* 2d ed. (Chatham, N.J.: Chatham House, 1992), 305.

83. William Schneider, ''Surviving the New Era of Populism'' *National Journal,* April 10, 1993, 902.

84. Michael Nelson, ''The Presidency: Clinton and the Cycle of Politics and Policy,'' in *The Elections of 1992,* ed Michael Nelson (Washington, D.C.: CQ Press, 1993), 126.

85. Ibid., 145–149.

86. Ibid., 149.

87. Arthur M. Schlesinger, Jr., ''The Turn of the Cycle,'' *New Yorker,* Nov. 16, 1992, 53.

88. Ibid., 54.

89. Arthur M. Schlesinger, Jr., ''A Clinton Report Card, So Far,'' *New York Times,* April 11, 1993, E–13.

APPENDIX A

RESULTS OF PRESIDENTIAL CONTESTS, 1912–1992

Year	Republican nominee (in *italics*) and other major candidates	Democratic nominee (in *italics) and* other major candidates	Election winner	Division of popular vote[a] (percent)	Division of electoral vote[b]
1912	*William Howard Taft* (incumbent president)	*Woodrow Wilson* (governor of New Jersey)	Wilson (D)	42–23	435–8
	Theodore Roosevelt[c] (former president)	James Champ Clark (representative from Missouri and Speaker of the House)			
1916	*Charles Evans Hughes* (justice, U.S. Supreme Court)	*Woodrow Wilson* (incumbent president)	Wilson (D)	49–46	277–254
	Elihu Root (former secretary of state)	None			
1920	*Warren G. Harding* (senator from Ohio)	*James Cox* (governor of Ohio)	Harding (R)	60–34	404–127
	Leonard Wood (general)	William McAdoo (former secretary of the Treasury)			
	Frank Lowden (governor of Illinois)	A. Mitchell Palmer (attorney general)			
	Hiram Johnson (senator from California)				
1924	*Calvin Coolidge* (incumbent president)	*John W. Davis* (former solicitor general)	Coolidge (R)	54–29	382–136
	Hiram Johnson (senator from California)	Alfred Smith (governor of New York)			
		William McAdoo (former secretary of the Treasury)			
1928	*Herbert Hoover* (former secretary of commerce)	*Alfred Smith* (governor of New York)	Hoover (R)	58–41	444–87
	Frank Lowden (governor of Illinois)	James Reed (senator from Missouri)			
		Cordell Hull (representative from Tennessee)			

487

Results of Presidential Contests, 1912–1992 *(Continued)*

Year	Republican nominee (in *italics*) and other major candidates	Democratic nominee (in *italics*) and other major candidates	Election winner	Division of popular vote[a] (percent)	Division of electoral vote[b]
1932	*Herbert Hoover* (incumbent president)	*Franklin D. Roosevelt* (governor of New York)	Roosevelt (D)	57–40	472–59
	Joseph France (former senator from Missouri)	Alfred Smith (former governor of New York)			
		John Garner (representative from Texas and Speaker of the House)			
1936	*Alfred Landon* (governor of Kansas)	*Franklin D. Roosevelt* (incumbent president)	Roosevelt (D)	61–37	523–8
	William Borah (senator from Idaho)	None			
1940	*Wendell Willkie* (Indiana lawyer and public utility executive)	*Franklin D. Roosevelt* (incumbent president)	Roosevelt (D)	55–45	449–82
	Thomas E. Dewey (U.S. district attorney for New York)	None			
	Robert Taft (senator from Ohio)				
1944	*Thomas E. Dewey* (governor of New York)	*Franklin D. Roosevelt* (incumbent president)	Roosevelt (D)	53–46	432–99
	Wendell Willkie (previous Republican presidential nominee)	Harry Byrd (senator from Virginia)			
1948	*Thomas E. Dewey* (governor of New York)	*Harry S. Truman* (incumbent president)	Truman (D)	50–45	303–189
	Harold Stassen (former governor of Minnesota)	Richard Russell (senator from Georgia)			
	Robert Taft (senator from Ohio)				
1952	*Dwight D. Eisenhower* (general)	*Adlai Stevenson* (governor of Illinois)	Eisenhower (R)	55–44	442-89
	Robert Taft (senator from Ohio)	Estes Kefauver (senator from Tennessee)			
		Richard Russell (senator from Georgia)			
1956	*Dwight D. Eisenhower* (incumbent president)	*Adlai Stevenson* (previous Democratic presidential nominee)	Eisenhower (R)	57–42	457–73
	None	Averell Harriman (governor of New York)			
1960	*Richard Nixon* (vice president)	*John F. Kennedy* (senator from Massachusetts)	Kennedy (D)	49.7–49.5	303–219
	None	Hubert Humphrey (senator from Minnesota)			
		Lyndon B. Johnson (senator from Texas)			

Results of Presidential Contests, 1912–1992 (Continued)

Year	Republican nominee (in *italics*) and other major candidates	Democratic nominee (in *italics*) and other major candidates	Election winner	Division of popular vote[a] (percent)	Division of electoral vote[b]
1964	*Barry Goldwater* (senator from Arizona) Nelson Rockefeller (governor of New York)	*Lyndon B. Johnson* (incumbent president) None	Johnson (D)	61–39	486–52
1968	*Richard Nixon* (former Republican presidential nominee) Ronald Reagan (governor of California)	*Hubert Humphrey* (incumbent vice president) Robert F. Kennedy (senator from New York) Eugene McCarthy (senator from Minnesota)	Nixon (R)	43.4–42.7	301–191
1972	*Richard Nixon* (incumbent president) None	*George McGovern* (senator from South Dakota) Hubert Humphrey (senator from Minnesota) George Wallace (governor of Alabama)	Nixon (R)	61–38	520–17
1976	*Gerald R. Ford* (incumbent president) Ronald Reagan (former governor of California)	*Jimmy Carter* (former governor of Georgia) Edmund Brown, Jr. (governor of California) George Wallace (governor of Alabama)	Carter (D)	50–48	297–240
1980	*Ronald Reagan* (former governor of California) George Bush (former director of Central Intelligence Agency) John Anderson (representative from Illinois)	*Jimmy Carter* (incumbent president) Edward M. Kennedy (senator from Massachusetts)	Reagan (R)	51–41	489–49
1984	*Ronald Reagan* (incumbent president) None	*Walter F. Mondale* (former vice president) Gary Hart (senator from Colorado)	Reagan (R)	59–41	525–13
1988	*George Bush* (vice president) Robert Dole (senator from Kansas)	*Michael Dukakis* (governor of Massachusetts) Jesse Jackson (civil rights activist)	Bush (R)	53–46	426–111
1992	*George Bush* (incumbent president) Patrick Buchanan (journalist)	*William Clinton* (governor of Arkansas) Paul Tsongas (former senator)	Clinton (D)	43–37	357–168

Note: The table begins with the year 1912 because presidential primaries were first held that year.

a Division of popular vote is between the Republican and Democratic nominees.

b Division of electoral votes is between the Republican and Democratic nominees.

c When the Republican convention failed to choose him as its nominee (selecting instead the incumbent president, William Howard Taft), former president Theodore Roosevelt withdrew from the party and created the Progressive party. As the Progressive party nominee, Roosevelt received 27 percent of the popular vote and 88 electoral votes.

APPENDIX B

PERSONAL BACKGROUNDS
OF U.S. PRESIDENTS

President	Age at first political office	First political office Last political office[a]	Age at becoming president	State of residence[b]	Father's occupation	Higher education[c]	Occupation
1. Washington (1789–1792)	17	County surveyor Commander in chief	57	Va.	Farmer	None	Farmer, surveyor
2. Adams, J. (1797–1801)	39	Surveyor of highways Vice president	61	Mass.	Farmer	Harvard	Farmer, lawyer
3. Jefferson (1801–1809)	26	State legislator Vice president	58	Va.	Farmer	William and Mary	Farmer, lawyer
4. Madison (1809–1817)	25	State legislator Secretary of state	58	Va.	Farmer	Princeton	Farmer
5. Monroe (1817–1825)	24	State legislator Secretary of state	59	Va.	Farmer	William and Mary	Lawyer, farmer
6. Adams, J. Q. (1825–1829)	27	Minister to Netherlands Secretary of state	58	Mass.	Farmer, lawyer	Harvard	Lawyer
7. Jackson (1829–1837)	21	Prosecuting attorney U.S. Senate	62	Tenn.	Farmer	None	Lawyer
8. Van Buren (1837–1841)	30	Surrogate of county Vice president	55	N.Y.	Tavern keeper	None	Lawyer
9. Harrison, W. H. (1841)	26	Territorial delegate to Congress Minister to Colombia	68	Ind.	Farmer	Hampden-Sydney	Military
10. Tyler (1841–1845)	21	State legislator Vice president	51	Va.	Planter, lawyer	William and Mary	Lawyer
11. Polk (1845–1849)	28	State legislator Governor	50	Tenn.	Surveyor	U. of North Carolina	Lawyer
12. Taylor (1849–1850)	None	None [a]	65	Ky.	Collector of internal revenue	None	Military
13. Fillmore (1850–1853)	28	State legislator Vice president	50	N.Y.	Farmer	None	Lawyer
14. Pierce (1853–1857)	25	State legislator U.S. district attorney	48	N.H.	General	Bowdoin	Lawyer
15. Buchanan (1857–1861)	22	Assistant county prosecutor Minister to Great Britain	65	Pa.	Farmer	Dickinson	Lawyer

Personal Backgrounds of U.S. Presidents (*Continued*)

President	Age at first political office	First political office / Last political office[a]	Age at becoming president	State of residence[b]	Father's occupation	Higher education[c]	Occupation
16. Lincoln (1861–1865)	25	State legislator / U.S. House of Representatives	52	Ill.	Farmer, carpenter	None	Lawyer
17. Johnson, A. (1865–1869)	20	City alderman / Vice president	57	Tenn.	Janitor-porter	None	Tailor
18. Grant (1869–1877)	None	None / a	47	Ohio	Tanner	West Point	Military
19. Hayes (1877–1881)	36	City solicitor / Governor	55	Ohio	Farmer	Kenyon	Lawyer
20. Garfield (1881)	28	State legislator / U.S. Senate	50	Ohio	Canal worker	Williams	Educator, lawyer
21. Arthur (1881–1885)	31	State engineer / Vice president	51	N.Y.	Minister	Union	Lawyer
22. Cleveland (1885–1889) 24. (1893–1897)	26	Assistant district attorney / Governor	48	N.Y.	Minister	None	Lawyer
23. Harrison, B. (1889–1893)	24	City attorney / U.S. Senate	56	Ind.	Military	Miami of Ohio	Lawyer
25. McKinley (1897–1901)	26	Prosecuting attorney / Governor	54	Ohio	Ironmonger	Allegheny	Lawyer
26. Roosevelt, T. (1901–1909)	24	State legislator / Vice president	43	N.Y.	Business-man	Harvard	Lawyer, author
27. Taft (1909–1913)	24	Assistant prosecuting attorney / Secretary of war	52	Ohio	Lawyer	Yale	Lawyer
28. Wilson (1913–1921)	54	Governor / Governor	56	N.J.	Minister	Princeton	Educator
29. Harding (1921–1923)	35	State legislator / U.S. Senate	56	Ohio	Physician, editor	Ohio Central	Newspaper editor
30. Coolidge (1923–1929)	26	City councilman / Vice president	51	Mass.	Storekeeper	Amherst	Lawyer
31. Hoover (1929–1933)	43	Relief and food administrator / Secretary of commerce	55	Calif.	Blacksmith	Stanford	Mining engineer
32. Roosevelt, F. (1933–1945)	28	State legislator / Governor	49	N.Y.	Business-man, landowner	Harvard	Lawyer
33. Truman (1945–1953)	38	County judge (commissioner) / Vice president	61	Mo.	Farmer, livestock	None	Clerk, store owner
34. Eisenhower (1953–1961)	None	None / a	63	Kan.	Mechanic	West Point	Military

Personal Backgrounds of U.S. Presidents (*Continued*)

President	Age at first political office	First political office / Last political office[a]	Age at becoming president	State of residence[b]	Father's occupation	Higher education[c]	Occupation
35. Kennedy (1961–1963)	29	U.S. House of Representatives / U.S. Senate	43	Mass.	Businessman	Harvard	Newspaper reporter
36. Johnson, L. (1963–1969)	28	U.S. House of Representatives / Vice president	55	Texas	Farmer, real estate	Southwest Texas State Teacher's College	Educator
37. Nixon (1969–1974)	34	U.S. House of Representatives / Vice president	56	Calif.	Streetcar conductor	Whittier	Lawyer
38. Ford (1974–1977)	36	U.S. House of Representatives / Vice president	61	Mich.	Businessman	U. of Michigan	Lawyer
39. Carter (1977–1981)	38	County Board of Education / Governor	52	Ga.	Farmer, businessman	U.S. Naval Academy	Farmer, business
40. Reagan (1981–1989)	55	Governor / Governor	69	Calif.	Shoe salesman	Eureka	Entertainer
41. Bush (1989–1993)	42	U.S. House of Representatives / Vice president	64	Texas	Businessman, U.S. senator	Yale	Businessman
42. Clinton (1993–)	30	State attorney general / Governor	46	Ark.	Car dealer	Georgetown	Lawyer

a This category refers to the last civilian office held before the presidency. Taylor, Grant and Eisenhower had served as generals before becoming president.
b The state is where the president spent his important adult years, not necessarily where he was born.
c Refers to undergraduate education.

Section 3. . . . The Vice President of the United States shall be President of the Senate, but shall have no Vote, unless they be equally divided.

The Senate shall chuse their other Officers, and also a President pro tempore, in the Absence of the Vice President, or when he shall exercise the Office of President of the United States.

The Senate shall have the sole Power to try all Impeachments. When sitting for that Purpose, they shall be on Oath or Affirmation. When the President of the United States is tried the Chief Justice shall preside: And no Person shall be convicted without the Concurrence of two thirds of the Members present.

Judgment in Cases of Impeachment shall not extend further than to removal from Office, and disqualification to hold and enjoy any Office of honor, Trust or Profit under the United States: but the Party convicted shall nevertheless be liable and subject to Indictment, Trial, Judgment and Punishment, according to Law.

Section 7. . . . Every Bill which shall have passed the House of Representatives and the Senate, shall, before it become a Law, be presented to the President of the United States; If he approve he shall sign it, but if not he shall return it, with his Objections to that House in which it shall have originated, who shall enter the Objections at large on their Journal, and proceed to reconsider it. If after such Reconsideration two thirds of that House shall agree to pass the Bill, it shall be sent, together with the Objections, to the other House, by which it shall likewise be reconsidered, and if approved by two thirds of that House, it shall become a Law. But in all such Cases the Votes of both Houses shall be determined by yeas and Nays, and the Names of the Persons voting for and against the Bill shall be entered on the Journal of each House respectively. If any Bill shall not be returned by the President within ten Days (Sundays excepted) after it shall have been presented to him, the Same shall be a Law, in like Manner as if he had signed it, unless the Congress by their Adjournment prevent its Return, in which Case it shall not be a Law.

Every Order, Resolution, or Vote to which the Concurrence of the Senate and House of Representatives may be necessary (except on a question of Adjournment) shall be presented to the President of the United States; and before the Same shall take Effect, shall be approved by him, or being disapproved by him, shall be repassed by two thirds of the Senate and House of Representatives, according to the Rules and Limitations prescribed in the Case of a Bill.

ARTICLE II

Section 1.   The executive Power shall be vested in a President of the United States of America. He shall hold his Office during the Term of four Years, and, together with the Vice President, chosen for the same Term, be elected, as follows.

Each State shall appoint, in such Manner as the Legislature thereof may direct, a Number of Electors, equal to the whole Number of Senators and Representatives to which the State may be entitled in the Congress: but no Senator or Representative, or Person holding an Office of Trust or Profit under the United States, shall be appointed an Elector.

[The Electors shall meet in their respective States, and vote by Ballot for two Persons, of whom one at least shall not be an Inhabitant of the same State with themselves. And they shall make a List of all the Persons voted for, and of the Number of Votes for each; which List they shall sign and certify, and transmit sealed to the Seat of the Government of the United States, directed to the President of the Senate. The President of the Senate shall, in the Presence of the Senate and House of Representatives, open all the Certificates, and the Votes shall then be counted. The Person having the greatest Number of Votes shall be the President, if such Number be a Majority of the whole Number of Electors appointed; and if there be more than one who have such Majority, and have an equal Number of Votes, then the House of Representatives shall immediately chuse by Ballot one of them for President; and if no Person have a Majority, then from the five highest on the list the said House shall in like Manner chuse the President. But in chusing the President, the Votes shall be taken by States, the Representation from each State having one Vote; a quorum for this Purpose shall consist of a Member or Members from two thirds of the States, and a Majority of all the States shall be necessary to a Choice. In every Case, after the Choice of the President, the Person having the greatest Number of Votes of the Electors shall be the Vice President. But if there should remain two or more who have equal Votes, the Senate shall chuse from them by Ballot the Vice President.][1]

The Congress may determine the Time of chusing the Electors, and the Day on which they shall give their Votes; which Day shall be the same throughout the United States.

No Person except a natural born Citizen, or a Citizen of the United States, at the time of the Adoption of this Constitution, shall be eligible to the Office of President; neither shall any Person be eligible to that Office who shall not have attained to the Age of thirty five Years, and been fourteen Years a Resident within the United States.

In Case of the Removal of the President from Office, or of his Death, Resignation, or Inability to discharge the Powers and Duties of the said Office,[2] the Same shall devolve on the Vice President, and the Congress may by Law provide for the Case of Removal, Death, Resignation or Inability, both of the President and Vice

President, declaring what Officer shall then act as President, and such Officer shall act accordingly, until the Disability be removed, or a President shall be elected.

The President shall, at stated Times, receive for his Services, a Compensation, which shall neither be encreased nor diminished during the Period for which he shall have been elected, and he shall not receive within that Period any other Emolument from the United States, or any of them.

Before he enter on the Execution of his Office, he shall take the following Oath or Affirmation: — "I do solemnly swear (or affirm) that I will faithfully execute the Office of President of the United States, and will to the best of my Ability, preserve, protect and defend the Constitution of the United States."

Section 2.   The President shall be Commander in Chief of the Army and Navy of the United States, and of the Militia of the several States, when called into the actual Service of the United States; he may require the Opinion, in writing, of the principal Officer in each of the executive Departments, upon any Subject relating to the Duties of their respective Offices, and he shall have Power to grant Reprieves and Pardons for Offenses against the United States, except in Cases of Impeachment.

He shall have Power, by and with the Advice and Consent of the Senate, to make Treaties, provided two thirds of the Senators present concur; and he shall nominate, and by and with the Advice and Consent of the Senate, shall appoint Ambassadors, other public Ministers and Consuls, Judges of the supreme Court, and all other Officers of the United States, whose Appointments are not herein otherwise provided for, and which shall be established by Law: but the Congress may by Law vest the Appointment of such inferior Officers, as they think proper, in the President alone, in the Courts of Law, or in the Heads of Departments.

The President shall have Power to fill up all Vacancies that may happen during the Recess of the Senate, by granting Commissions which shall expire at the End of their next Session.

Section 3.   He shall from time to time give to the Congress Information of the State of the Union, and recommend to their Consideration such Measures as he shall judge necessary and expedient; he may, on extraordinary Occasions, convene both Houses, or either of them, and in Case of Disagreement between them, with Respect to the Time of Adjournment, he may adjourn them to such Time as he shall think proper; he shall receive Ambassadors and other public Ministers; he shall take Care that the Laws be faithfully executed, and shall Commission all the Officers of the United States.

Section 4.   The President, Vice President and all Civil Officers of the United States, shall be removed from office on Impeachment for, and Conviction of, Treason, Bribery, or other high Crimes and Misdemeanors.

ARTICLE VI

. . . This Constitution, and the Laws of the United States which shall be made in Pursuance thereof; and all Treaties made, or which shall be made, under the Authority of the United States, shall be the supreme Law of the Land; and the

Judges in every State shall be bound thereby, any Thing in the Constitution or Laws of any State to the Contrary notwithstanding.

The Senators and Representatives before mentioned, and the Members of the several State Legislatures, and all executive and judicial Officers, both of the United States and of the several States, shall be bound by Oath or Affirmation, to support this Constitution; but no religious Test shall ever be required as a Qualification to any Office or public Trust under the United States.

AMENDMENT XII (*Ratified June 15, 1804*)

The Electors shall meet in their respective states and vote by ballot for President and Vice-President, one of whom, at least, shall not be an inhabitant of the same state with themselves; they shall name in their ballots the person voted for as President, and in distinct ballots the person voted for as Vice-President, and they shall make distinct lists of all persons voted for as President, and of all persons voted for as Vice-President, and of the number of votes for each, which lists they shall sign and certify, and transmit sealed to the seat of the government of the United States, directed to the President of the Senate; — The President of the Senate shall, in the presence of the Senate and House of Representatives, open all the certificates and the votes shall then be counted; — The person having the greatest number of votes for President, shall be the President, if such number be a majority of the whole number of Electors appointed; and if no person have such majority, then from the persons having the highest numbers not exceeding three on the list of those voted for as President, the House of Representatives shall choose immediately, by ballot, the President. But in choosing the President, the votes shall be taken by states, the representation from each state having one vote; a quorum for this purpose shall consist of a member or members from two-thirds of the states, and a majority of all the states shall be necessary to a choice. [And if the House of Representatives shall not choose a President whenever the right of choice shall devolve upon them, before the fourth day of March next following, then the Vice-President shall act as President, as in the case of the death or other constitutional disability of the President—][3] The person having the greatest number of votes as Vice-President, shall be the Vice-President, if such number be a majority of the whole number of Electors appointed, and if no person have a majority, then from the two highest numbers on the list, the Senate shall choose the Vice-President; a quorum for the purpose shall consist of two-thirds of the whole number of Senators, and a majority of the whole number shall be necessary to a choice. But no person constitutionally ineligible to the office of President shall be eligible to that of Vice-President of the United States.

AMENDMENT XX (*Ratified Jan. 23, 1933*)

Section 1. The terms of the President and Vice President shall end at noon on the 20th day of January, and the terms of Senators and Representatives at noon on the 3d day of January, of the years in which such terms would have ended if this article had not been ratified; and the terms of their successors shall then begin.

Section 2. The Congress shall assemble at least once in every year, and such meeting shall begin at noon on the 3d day of January, unless they shall by law appoint a different day.

Section 3.[4] If, at the time fixed for the beginning of the term of the President, the President elect shall have died, the Vice President elect shall become President. If a President shall not have been chosen before the time fixed for the beginning of his term, or if the President elect shall have failed to qualify, then the Vice President elect shall act as President until a President shall have qualified; and the Congress may by law provide for the case wherein neither a President elect nor a Vice President elect shall have qualified, declaring who shall then act as President, or the manner in which one who is to act shall be selected, and such person shall act accordingly until a President or Vice President shall have qualified.

Section 4. The Congress may by law provide for the case of the death of any of the persons from whom the House of Representatives may choose a President whenever the right of choice shall have devolved upon them, and for the case of the death of any of the persons from whom the Senate may choose a Vice President whenever the right of choice shall have devolved upon them.

Section 5. Sections 1 and 2 shall take effect on the 15th day of October following the ratification of this article.

Section 6. This article shall be inoperative unless it shall have been ratified as an amendment to the Constitution by the legislatures of three-fourths of the several States within seven years from the date of its submission.

AMENDMENT XXII (*Ratified Feb. 27, 1951*)

Section 1. No person shall be elected to the office of the President more than twice, and no person who has held the office of President, or acted as President, for more than two years of a term to which some other person was elected President shall be elected to the office of the President more than once. But this Article shall not apply to any person holding the office of President when this Article was proposed by the Congress, and shall not prevent any person who may be holding the office of President, or acting as President, during the term within which this Article become operative from holding the office of President or acting as President during the remainder of such term.

Section 2. This Article shall be inoperative unless it shall have been ratified as an amendment to the Constitution by the legislatures of three-fourths of the several States within seven years from the date of its submission to the States by the Congress.

AMENDMENT XXIII (*Ratified March 29, 1961*)

Section 1. The District constituting the seat of Government of the United States shall appoint in such manner as the Congress may direct:

A number of electors of President and Vice President equal to the whole number of Senators and Representatives in Congress to which the District would be entitled if it were a State, but in no event more than the least populous State; they shall be in addition to those appointed by the States, but they shall be considered, for the purposes of the election of President and Vice President, to be electors appointed by a State; and they shall meet in the District and perform such duties as provided by the twelfth article of amendment.

Section 2.   The Congress shall have power to enforce this article by appropriate legislation.

A M E N D M E N T   X X V (*Ratified Feb. 10, 1967*)

Section 1.   In case of the removal of the President from office or of his death or resignation, the Vice President shall become President.

Section 2.   Whenever there is a vacancy in the office of the Vice President, the President shall nominate a Vice President who shall take office upon confirmation by a majority vote of both Houses of Congress.

Section 3.   Whenever the President transmits to the President pro tempore of the Senate and the Speaker of the House of Representatives his written declaration that he is unable to discharge the powers and duties of his office, and until he transmits to them a written declaration to the contrary, such powers and duties shall be discharged by the Vice President as Acting President.

Section 4.   Whenever the Vice President and a majority of either the principal officers of the executive departments or of such other body as Congress may by law provide, transmit to the President pro tempore of the Senate and the Speaker of the House of Representatives their written declaration that the President is unable to discharge the powers and duties of his office, the Vice President shall immediately assume the powers and duties of the office as Acting President.

Thereafter, when the President transmits to the President pro tempore of the Senate and the Speaker of the House of Representatives his written declaration that no inability exists, he shall resume the powers and duties of his office unless the Vice President and a majority of either the principal officers of the executive department or of such other body as Congress may by law provide, transmit within four days to the President pro tempore of the Senate and the Speaker of the House of Representatives their written declaration that the President is unable to discharge the powers and duties of his office. Thereupon Congress shall decide the issue, assembling within forty-eight hours for that purpose if not in session. If the Congress, within twenty-one days after receipt of the latter written declaration, or, if Congress is not in session, within twenty-one days after Congress is required to assemble, determines by two-thirds vote of both houses that the President is unable to discharge the powers and duties of his office, the Vice President shall continue to discharge the same as Acting President; otherwise, the President shall resume the powers and duties of his office.

NOTES

1. The material in brackets has been superseded by the Twelfth Amendment.

2. This provision has been affected by the Twenty-fifth Amendment.

3. The part in brackets has been superseded by Section 3 of the Twentieth Amendment.

4. See the Twenty-fifth Amendment.

Index

ACKNOWLEDGMENTS

78 *Gallup Report*, November 1988, pp. 6–7. © 1988 by The Gallup Reports; *The Gallup Poll Monthly*, November 1992, page 9. Used by permission. **106** Harold W. Stanley and Richard G. Niemi, *Vital Statistics on American Politics*, 3d ed., p. 280. © 1992 by CQ Press, Washington, D.C. Used by permission of the publisher. **120** Harold W. Stanley and Richard G. Niemi, *Vital Statistics on American Politics*, 3d ed., p. 59. © 1992 by CQ Press, Washington, D.C. Used by permission of the publisher. **143** Reprinted by permission of Greenwood Publishing Group, Inc. Westport, Conn., from *The Leadership Question*, by Bert A. Rockman. © by Praeger Publishers, 1984. Fred I. Greenstein, *Personality and Politics*, p. 27. © 1975 by W. W. Norton. Used by permission of the author. **145** Henry J. Abraham, *Justices and Presidents: Appointments to the Supreme Court*, 2d ed., pp. 380–383. © Henry J. Abraham, 1974, 1985. Reprinted by permission of Oxford University Press, Inc. Harold W. Stanley and Richard G. Niemi, *Vital Statistics on American Politics*, 3d ed., pp. 258–259. ©1992 by CQ Press, Washington, D.C. Used by permission of the publisher. **148** Edward Pessen, *The Log Cabin Myth: The Social Backgrounds of the Presidents*, p. 68. © 1984 by Yale University Press, New Haven, Conn. Used by permission of the publisher. **204** Michael Nelson, ed., *Guide to the Presidency*, p. 451. © 1989 by Congressional Quarterly Inc. Reprinted by permission of the publisher. **206** Stephen J. Wayne, Richard L. Cole, James F. C. Hyde, "Advising the President on Enrolled Legislation," *Political Science Quarterly* 94 (Summer 1979): 310. © 1979 by Political Science Quarterly. Used by permission of the publisher. **225** George C. Edwards III, *At the Margins: Political Leadership in Congress*, pp. 177, 178, 183, 184. © 1989 by Yale University Press, New Haven, Conn. Used by permission of the publisher. **292, 294** Sheldon Goldman, "The Bush Imprint on the Judiciary: Carrying on a Tradition," *Judicature* (April/May 1991): 298–299; 302–303. © 1991 by Sheldon Goldman. Used by permission of the author. **Chap. 10** A small portion of this material was originally written for a chapter in LEADERSHIP AND THE BUSH PRESIDENCY, Ryan J. Barilleaux and Mary Stuckey, eds. (Praeger Publishers, an imprint of Greenwood Publishing Group, Inc, Westport, Conn., forthcoming October 1992). © 1992 by Ryan J. Barilleaux and Mary Stuckey. Reprinted with permission of the publisher. **425** Cecil V. Crabb, Jr., and Kevin V. Mulcahy, *American National Security: A Presidential Perspective*, p. 189. © 1991 by Wadsworth Publishing, Belmont, Calif. Used by permission of the publisher.

PHOTOGRAPHS

3, 94, 189, 281 Library of Congress. **43** General Dynamics. **141, 357** National Archives. **235, 323, 434** White House. **398** Nixon Project, National Archives. **454** Reuters/Bettmann.